Lecture Notes in Artificial Intelligence 7057

Subseries of Lecture Notes in Computer Science

Nirmit Desai Alan Liu Michael Winikoff (Eds.)

Principles and Practice of Multi-Agent Systems

13th International Conference, PRIMA 2010
Kolkata, India, November 12-15, 2010
Revised Selected Papers

Springer

Volume Editors

Nirmit Desai
IBM Research – India, Manyata Embassy Business Park
Outer Ring Road, Block D4, 2nd Floor, Nagawara
Bangalore 560045, India
E-mail: nirmit.desai@in.ibm.com

Alan Liu
National Chung Cheng University, Department of Electrical Engineering
168 University Road, Min-Hsiung Chia-Yi, Taiwan
E-mail: aliu@ee.ccu.edu.tw

Michael Winikoff
University of Otago, Department of Information Science
60 Clyde Street, Dunedin, New Zealand
E-mail: mwinikoff@infoscience.otago.ac.nz

ISSN 0302-9743 e-ISSN 1611-3349
ISBN 978-3-642-25919-7 e-ISBN 978-3-642-25920-3
DOI 10.1007/978-3-642-25920-3
Springer Heidelberg Dordrecht London New York

Library of Congress Control Number: 2011944655

CR Subject Classification (1998): I.2.11, I.2.9, I.2, C.2.4, K.4, D.2, H.3-5

LNCS Sublibrary: SL 7 – Artificial Intelligence

Typesetting: Camera-ready by author, data conversion by Scientific Publishing Services, Chennai, India

Printed on acid-free paper

Springer is part of Springer Science+Business Media (www.springer.com)

Preface

Agent computing and technology is an exciting emerging paradigm expected to play a key role in many society-changing practices from disaster response to manufacturing, and from energy management to healthcare. Agent and multi-agent researchers are focused on building working systems that bring together a broad range of technical areas from market theory to software engineering to user interfaces. Agent systems are expected to operate in real-world environments, with all the challenges that such environments present.

This volume contains the papers presented at PRIMA 2010: the 13th International Conference on Principles and Practice of Multi-Agent Systems held during November 12–15, 2010 in Kolkata, India.

PRIMA is a leading scientific conference for research on intelligent agent and multi-agent systems, attracting high-quality, state-of-the-art research from all over the world. The conference endeavors to bring together researchers, developers, and academic and industry leaders who are active and interested in agents and multi-agent systems, their practices and related areas. The conference has a strong focus on practice, and is focused on becoming the premier forum for prototype and deployed agent systems.

PRIMA 2010 continued to build on the success of its predecessor workshops and conferences held in Nagoya, Hanoi, Bangkok, Guilin, Kuala Lumpur, Auckland, Seoul, Tokyo, Taipei, Melbourne, Kyoto, and Singapore. Since 2007, due to the need for an additional high-quality forum for international researchers and practitioners to meet and share their work, the meeting has been expanded from a workshop to a full-fledged conference.

A key theme for PRIMA 2010 was agents and services, where the intent was to explore the connections between agent technology and services (both in the sense of service science and service-oriented computing).

PRIMA 2010 received 63 submissions, each of which was assigned to four Program Committee (PC) members, who were overseen by a Senior PC (SPC) member. Each paper received at least three reviews, which was followed by an author response phase, and discussion amongst the PC, led by the SPC member assigned to the paper. Of the 63 submissions, PRIMA 2010 accepted 18 full papers (acceptance rate: 29%), and 15 Early Innovation papers. The Early Innovation papers are papers that were seen as being promising, but that were not yet well enough developed to be full papers.

In addition to the accepted papers, the conference included a well-received panel discussion ("What can agent-based computing offer service-oriented architectures, and vice versa?"), three keynote speeches (by Frank Dignum, Henry Prakken, and Makoto Yokoo), and three workshops:

- The First International Workshop on Services and Agents (ServAgents 2010)
- The First International Workshop on Intelligent Agents in Health Care (IAHC 2010)
- The First Pacific Rim Workshop on Agent-Based Modeling and Simulation of Complex Systems (PRACSYS 2010)

This book serves as a scientific record of the PRIMA 2010 conference. It contains the papers presented at the conference and at the workshops. The book has four sections, the first being the panel discussion, the second the full papers, the third the early innovation papers, and the last the workshop papers.

As Program Chairs, we sincerely thank the organizers, SPC and PC members, and all contributors for this great event. In addition, we acknowledge the organizers of these workshops and especially thank Hoa Khanh Dam for his effort in overseeing the completion of the workshop papers. A special thanks goes to Aditya Ghose and Abdul Sattar for their coordination, Natalie Dunstan for her organization, Sankalp Khanna for managing registrations, Nabendu Chaki with his colleagues at University of Calcutta for local arrangements, and the Smart Services CRC for sponsorship. We especially acknowledge Jadavpur University and the Institute for Integrated and Intelligent Systems at Griffith University for providing a venue for workshops and substantial support. Finally, we acknowledge the support from EasyChair in organizing the reviews and preparing the proceedings.

Nirmit Desai
Alan Liu
Michael Winikoff

Organization

General Chairs

B.P. Sinha	Indian Statistical Institute, India
Chandan Mazumdar	Jadavpur University, India
Abdul Sattar	Griffith University, Australia

ServAgents 2010

Hoa Khanh Dam	University of Wollongong, Australia
Aditya Ghose	University of Wollongong, Australia
Nirmit V. Desai	IBM India Research Lab, India
Srinivas Narasimhamurthy	Infosys Technologies, India

IACH 2010

Andrew Miller	University of Wollongong, Australia
Chee Fon Chang	University of Wollongong, Australia
Graham Billiau	University of Wollongong, Australia
Konstantin Hoesch-Klohe	University of Wollongong, Australia
Evan Morrison	University of Wollongong, Australia

PRACSYS 2010

Alexis Drogoul	UMI 209 UMMISCO, IRD, UPMC, MSI-IFI, Vietnam
Benoit Gaudou	UMI 209 UMMISCO, IRD, MSI-IFI, Vietnam
Patrick Taillandier	UMI 209 UMMISCO, IRD, MSI-IFI, Vietnam
Jean Daniel Zucker	UMI 209 UMMISCO, IRD, France

Advisory Board

Jane Hsu	National Taiwan University, Taiwan
Toru Ishida	Kyoto University, Japan
Hideyuki Nakashima	Future University Hakodate, Japan
Sung Joo Park	Korea Advanced Institute of Science and Technology, Korea
Munindar P. Singh	North Carolina State University, USA
Zhongzhi Shi	Chinese Academy of Sciences, China
Von-Wun Soo	National Tsing Hua University, Taiwan
Jung-Jin Yang	The Catholic University of Korea, Korea

Senior Program Committee

Victor Lesser	University of Massachusetts Amherst, USA
Michael Luck	King's College London, UK
John-Jules Meyer	Utrecht University, The Netherlands
Paul Scerri	Carnegie Mellon University, USA
Sandip Sen	University of Tulsa, USA
Carles Sierra	IIA-CSIC, Spain
Munindar P. Singh	North Carolina State University, USA
Wiebe Van Der Hoek	University of Liverpool, UK
Makoto Yokoo	Kyushu University, Japan

Program Committee

Salem Benferhat	CRIL UMR CNRS, France
Frances Brazier	TU Delft, The Netherlands
Longbing Cao	University of Technology Sydney, Australia
Brahim Chaib-Draa	Laval University, Canada
Nilanjan Chakraborty	Carnegie Mellon University, USA
Sanjay Chaudhary	DA-IICT, India
Shih-Fen Cheng	Singapore Management University, Singapore
Mohan Chhetri	Swinburne University of Technology, Australia
Sung-Bae Cho	Yonsei University, Korea
Amit Chopra	University of Trento, Italy
Khanh Hoa Dam	University of Wollongong, Australia
Mehdi Dastani	Utrecht University, The Netherlands
Frank Dignum	Utrecht University, The Netherlands
Patrick Doherty	Linkoping University, Sweden
Thomas Eiter	Vienna University of Technology, Austria
Edith Elkind	Nanyang Technological University, Singapore
Marc Esteva	IIIA-CSIC, Spain
Joseph Giampapa	Carnegie Mellon University, USA
Robin Glinton	Carnegie Mellon University, USA
Eduardo Gomes	Swinburne University of Technology, Australia
Guido Governatori	National ICT Australia Ltd., Australia
Nathan Griffiths	University of Warwick, UK
Chung-Wei Hang	North Carolina State University, USA
Hiromitsu Hattori	Kyoto University, Japan
Christopher Hazard	North Carolina State University, USA
Koen Hindriks	Delft University of Technology, The Netherlands
Michal Jakob	FEE Czech Technical University in Prague, Czech Republic

Yichuan Jiang	Southeast University, China
Wan-Rong Jih	National Taiwan University, Taiwan
Zhi Jin	Peking University, China
Benjamin Johnston	University of Sydney, Australia
Kamalakar Karlapalem	CDE, IIIT Hyderabad, India
Kee-Eung Kim	Korea Advanced Institute of Science and Technology, Korea
Yasuhiko Kitamura	Kwansei Gakuin University, Japan
Kazuhiro Kuwabara	Ritsumeikan University, Japan
Jérôme Lang	LAMSADE, France
Habin Lee	Brunel University, UK
Jaeho Lee	The University of Seoul, Korea
Ho-Fung Leung	The Chinese University of Hong Kong
Minyi Li	Swinburne University of Technology, Australia
Lin Liu	Tsinghua University, China
Wei Liu	The University of Western Australia, Australia
Beatriz López	University of Girona, Spain
Graham Low	University of New South Wales, Australia
Xinjun Mao	National University of Defense Technology, China
Shigeo Matsubara	Kyoto University, Japan
Felipe Meneguzzi	Carnegie Mellon University, USA
Simon Miles	King's College London, UK
Yohei Murakami	NICT, Japan
Hideyuki Nakanishi	Osaka University, Japan
Mariusz Nowostawski	University of Otago, New Zealand
Nir Oren	King's College London, UK
Juan Pavón	Universidad Complutense Madrid, Spain
Henry Prakken	Utrecht University and University of Groningen, The Netherlands
Martin Purvis	University of Otago, New Zealand
Maryam Purvis	University of Otago, New Zealand
Jan Richter	Swinburne University of Technology, Australia
Michael Rovatsos	The University of Edinburgh, UK
Ji Ruan	St. Francis Xavier University, Canada
Yuko Sakurai	Yahoo Japan Corporation, Japan
Bastin Tony Roy Savarimuthu	University of Otago, New Zealand
Tino Schlegel	Swinburne University of Technology, Australia
Murat Sensoy	University of Aberdeen, UK
Kiam Tian Seow	Nanyang Technological University, Singapore
Von-Wun Soo	National Tsing Hua University, Taiwan
Biplav Srivastava	IBM India Research Labs, India
Eugen Staab	University of Luxembourg, Luxembourg

Bas Steunebrink	Universiteit Utrecht, The Netherlands
Toshiharu Sugawara	Waseda University, Japan
John Thangarajah	RMIT University, Australia
Nicolas Troquard	University of Liverpool, UK
Leon Van Der Torre	University of Luxembourg, Luxembourg
M. Birna Van Riemsdijk	TU Delft, The Netherlands
Pradeep Varakantham	Singapore Management University, Singapore
Gerard Vreeswijk	Utrecht University, The Netherlands
Yonghong Wang	North Carolina State University, USA
Glenn Wightwick	IBM Research and Development, Australia
Brendon J. Woodford	University of Otago, New Zealand
Yang Xu	University of Science and Technology of China, China
Yifeng Zeng	Aalborg University, Denmark

Table of Contents

Panel Discussion

Conference Papers

Agent Communication

Agent Cooperation and Negotiation

Agent Reasoning

Agent-Based Simulation

Mobile and Semantic Agents

Early Innovation Papers

Agent Cooperation and Negotiation

Agent Reasoning

Agent Technologies for Service Computing

Agent-Based Simulation

Agent-Based System Development

ServAgents Workshop

IAHC Workshop

PRACSYS Workshop

What Can Agent-Based Computing Offer Service-Oriented Architectures, and Vice Versa?

Wayne Wobcke[1], Nirmit Desai[2], Frank Dignum[3], Aditya Ghose[4], Srinivas Padmanabhuni[5], and Biplav Srivastava[6]

[1] School of Comp. Sci. and Eng., University of New South Wales, Sydney NSW 2052, Australia
wobcke@cse.unsw.edu.au

[2] IBM India Research Lab, Embassy Golf Links Business Park
Bangalore 560071, India
nirmit.desai@in.ibm.com

[3] Dept of Information and Comp. Sciences, Utrecht University, 3508 TB Utrecht, The Netherlands
dignum@cs.uu.nl

[4] School of Comp. Sci. and Software Eng., University of Wollongong, Wollongong NSW 2522, Australia
aditya@uow.edu.au

[5] Software Engineering and Tech. Labs, Infosys Technologies Ltd, Bangalore 560100 India
srinivas_p@infosys.com

[6] IBM India Research Lab, Block 1, IIT Campus, Hauz Khas, New Delhi 110016, India
sbiplav@in.ibm.com

Abstract. This article serves as a record of a panel discussion held at PRIMA in November, 2010. The panel consisted of two academic and three industry representatives, and thus provided a rare opportunity to discuss the relationship between agent-based computing and service-oriented architectures from both points of view. The basic question for the panel was to identify the key research and industry issues that arise in the deployment of systems based on service-oriented architectures, and in particular to address whether the agent-based computing paradigm offers any resolution of those issues. The question was also posed whether applications based on service-oriented architectures provide a suitable platform for implementing agent-based systems, which are presently limited in application by comparison. This summary is presented with the aim of stimulating further academic and industry collaborative research in this fast growing area which potentially has wide-ranging practical application.

1 Introduction: Wayne Wobcke (University of New South Wales)

By now it is hardly news that there is a close relationship between service-oriented architectures [8] and agent-based computing. It was noticed quite early that, at a technical level, service-oriented computing platforms would require mechanisms for service discovery (of the sort used in agent-based platforms such as KQML [6]), service aggregation or composition (analogous to planning complex series of actions) [13], coordination of multiple services (similar to multi-agent plan coordination [7]), execution monitoring (as agent systems monitor plan execution), and quality assurance (involving mechanisms for selection of appropriate actions in dynamic environments, a central concern of rational agent architectures [11]).

N. Desai, A. Liu, and M. Winikoff (Eds.): PRIMA 2010, LNAI 7057, pp. 1–10, 2012.

The purpose of this panel discussion is to reconsider this connection in the light of nearly a decade of industry experience during which service-oriented architectures (SOA) have become mainstream in the software industry. The basic question is whether the close technical relationship to agent-based computing still exists, and if so, whether this connection is of purely theoretical interest or has genuine practical implications, and, further, whether there are more fundamental obstacles to the deployment of SOA-based systems in industry contexts that are not covered by the narrow technical view outlined above. The implicit objective is to formulate a research agenda for the short-to-medium term that would enable agent researchers to contribute to the fast growing area of service-oriented computing, and (this is the "vice versa" part) to consider whether service-oriented architectures offer suitable platformis for the implementation and ultimately commercialization of agent-based systems. A concern here is whether there is currently the degree of flexibility and interoperability in commercial service-oriented computing platforms required to support agent-based applications. To this end, we are grateful for the participation on the panel of representatives from Infosys Technologies and IBM Research India who are able to provide an industry perspective on these issues.

The topic of the panel is deliberately framed towards technical aspects to encourage concrete discussion, in doing so presupposing that this close underlying technical connection exists, and this partly to provoke panellists into possibly rejecting this assumption (none of them did). Of course it is also recognized that "services" are far broader than just SOA-based systems, and so the panellists are also invited to comment on wider-ranging issues. Though not specifically the topic of the panel, the question of the role of standardization generally and of standard ontologies and their associated reasoning frameworks is one that naturally arises during discussion.

In keeping with the open ended nature of panel discussions, there is no formal conclusion given here. Readers must draw their own conclusions based on the panellist statements that follow.

2 Frank Dignum (Utrecht University)

2.1 ALIVE: The Role of Agents in Adaptive Service-Oriented Architectures

Web services [5] and service-oriented architectures [9] have the potential to increase significantly the utilization, compatibility and interoperability of information and communication systems. This progress has, for the first time, raised the realistic possibility of deploying large numbers of services in companies' and public organizations' intranets and extranets, and in the public Internet, in order to create communities of services which are always connected, always changing, open or semi-open, and form the baseline environment for software applications. However, this shift brought about not only potential benefits, but also serious challenges about how such systems and applications should be designed, managed and deployed. Existing approaches in some important areas (such as security, transactions and federation) tend to only cover technology issues such as, for example, how to secure a protocol or connect federated directories, without considering the paradigm change that occurs when large numbers of services are deployed and managed over time. In particular, existing approaches do not offer satisfactory solutions to the following issues:

– How to dynamically compose services into workflows that serve a specific purpose and adhere to some overall requirements (like efficiency, security, etc.).
– How to align the configurations and settings, needed by a service to operate, to the operational environment.
– How service execution is affected by issues of trust, rights, obligations and permission.
– What if critical applications simply cease to function if services provisioned from third parties disappear or malfunction?
– How to deal with knowledge representation, when connecting or binding together two or more actual entities or services using different ontologies.

All these issues point to the need for a "social layer" as part of the service interaction context. From an engineering perspective, new approaches are needed which take a holistic view of service environments, and take into account not only the properties of individual applications, but also the objectives, structure and dynamics of the system as a whole. In the ALIVE project[1] [4,15], we have combined existing work in coordination and organizational models with the state-of-the-art in service-oriented computing. The project extends current trends in service-oriented engineering by adding three extra layers [3]:

– The *organization layer* provides context for the other levels, specifying the organizational roles, objectives and rules that govern interaction and using developments in organization dynamics to allow structural adaptation of distributed systems over time.
– The *coordination layer* provides the means to specify, at a high level, the patterns of interactions between services, using a variety of coordination techniques. At this level agent technology is used.
– The *service layer* augments the existing service models with semantic descriptions to make components aware of their social context and rules of engagement with other services.

In practical terms, agent solutions combined with organization structures facilitate the implementation of purpose-oriented workflow mechanisms. The organization model defines the purpose of the content composition – e.g. metrics for quality of information, interaction patterns, acceptable processing time, etc. The workflow actors inherit the goals and plan rules to implement these characteristics from the organization structure. Using the three layers we are able to divide the knowledge and abilities that are necessary to dynamically create and maintain the complex workflows of services in a natural way.

At the service layer we concentrate on the knowledge necessary to see which service is best suited for a certain purpose. For example, there might be many weather prediction services; some predict weather for only one day, others for a week. If we want to plan a holiday, we want to check the weather for a whole period but it does not have to be very accurate, whereas for a farmer accuracy might be very important.

[1] ALIVE Project: http://www.ist-alive.eu/

At the coordination layer we use typical agent methods to create plans of service invocations to reach certain goals. Agents can interact to combine their plans in order to profit from each other's services. Especially useful is the fact that agents can recover from failures of their plans and replan for a goal. This is very difficult to do in current service-oriented tools.

At the organization level the overall objectives of the system can be specified such that the autonomy of the agents is only used in order to reach those objectives. This is also the level where service level agreements can be specified that should be fulfilled by the service(-compositions) and the agents.

In the ALIVE project we have tested the above sketched framework in several use cases. Although we can conclude that the framework indeed is useful, it also needs some perseverance to get things working. Compared to a more traditional service-oriented approach a lot more constructs have to be specified and implemented. We need to specify semantics for the services, tasks and plan rules for the agents, interaction patterns for the agents to create workflows, organizational structures in which the agents have to function, etc. These structures only start paying off with complex systems, especially when services change, fail or are aborted. In these cases the ALIVE framework provides a very high level of robustness.

A second lesson learnt is that it is far easier to construct the whole framework for a specific application than to generate a software engineering tool set that can create the framework for many different applications. We used a model driven approach to connect the elements of the different layers. This does help to keep consistency throughout the framework. However, it also means that meta-models have to be available for every module in the framework. This is not trivial if existing (and especially third party) components are used, e.g. one needs a meta-model for the agents (including their plan structures).

Also in the ALIVE framework we had to device a general way for agents to find the most suitable service to execute a (part of a) plan. Because the steps in a plan are usually not all instantiated before executing the plan (in order to allow for flexibility in planning) the queries for services also contain variables which have to be dealt with on the service level and possibly passed back up. These mechanisms are not part of traditional service-oriented methods and take much work and care to construct. This is not just the case for the way we implemented the ALIVE framework, but is inherent in any agent driven service-oriented system. Once agents are used to flexibly use and compose the services, one needs this type of query mechanism that can deal with requests for services that are not (fully) instantiated. Thus there is a seemingly inherent tradeoff between efficiency of implementing (note: not efficiency of the implementation) an application and the flexibility of the system. The need of the flexibility of the system should warrant the extra effort in the specification and design of the system. In our use cases, flexibility was needed because services could fail and be changed on the fly. An extreme case is that of our crisis management use case [10] where services might fail at any moment due to the crisis, but you need your system to handle the crisis properly nonetheless.

3 Biplav Srivastava (IBM Research – India)

3.1 The Problem Context

Changes are continuously happening in enterprises and they impact the Information Technology (IT) landscape. This leads to widespread needs like quickly delivering new applications and integrating existing applications. However, application development is often done in an ad-hoc manner resulting in poor reuse of software assets and longer time-to-delivery. Service-oriented architectures like web services have received much interest due to their potential in facilitating seamless business-to-business or enterprise application integration. A web service composition system can help automate the process, from specifying business process functionalities, to developing executable workflows that capture non-functional (e.g. QoS) requirements, to deploying them on a runtime infrastructure. Intuitively, web services can be viewed as software components and the process of web service composition similar to software synthesis. In addition, service composition needs to address the buildtime and runtime issues of the integrated application, thereby making it a more challenging and practical problem than software synthesis.

3.2 The Case for Service-Oriented Architecture and Issues Learnt in the Field

There are many approaches for composing and executing web services (see the survey [2]) and open problems [13]. Synthy is an example of one of the approaches which has been tried in the enterprise setting [1]. It is based on a novel two-staged composition approach that addresses the information modelling aspects of web services, provides support for contextual information while composing services, employs efficient decoupling of functional and non-functional requirements, and leads to improved scalability and failure handling. Synthy is a technology for semi-automatically composing SOA-compliant components such that the new component meets the desired functional and non-functional requirements and the resultant component can be flexibly executed.

The experience from the field has been that SOA can indeed help with application integration [14]. But there are many issues in practice:

- Domain modelling is hard.
    - SOA needs modelling of services, and if Business Process Management (BPM) is being followed, the business services. But this is not easy. A common problem is which domain expert to believe.
    - Companies in monopolistic situations (e.g. Microsoft, SAP) have an easier time.
    - Domain experts are expensive and there is an open question on the quality of models built by typical IT professionals.
    - An open research issue is to determine the right level of abstraction.
- Managing runtime is hard.
    - How to prove a composition of services is correct at runtime? There is a human-in-the-loop requirement for many applications.
    - Graceful degradation during runtime is often required.
- Interoperable tooling is unavailable.

3.3 The Case for Agent-Oriented Computing in SOA

Agent-oriented computing has delved extensively in modelling and coordination issues for autonomous agents. Moreover, the community has experience in designing, simulating and executing agent-based solutions to long-running, mission-critical defence problems. These are exactly the areas where SOA needs help.

The agent community needs help in standardization and wider adoption by mainstream business. SOA has lessons on how to make a technology widely usable. After all, WSDL, UDDI and BEPL4WS are the mainstay of modern SOA IT platforms, and very widely supported by major IT vendors.

4 Srinivas Padmanabhuni (Infosys Technologies)

4.1 Agent Orientation: Complementing Process and Service Orientation for Ultimate Flexibility

With the increase in the complexity of IT systems, it has become difficult for administrators to manually maintain and tune IT systems to meet the requirements of individual consumers. To meet the increasing complexity of IT systems, there is a requirement for the systems to become more human independent and self-managing. We firmly believe agent technologies are a potent technology to address the issue of IT complexity, especially when viewed from the lens of flexible business processes.

As already well established, a service-oriented foundation, forming the bridge between IT implementations and business processes, is at the centre of the future proof enterprise process architectures. Hence, service-oriented architecture (SOA) is considered an inherent foundational base for today's Business Process Management (BPM) implementations, wherein individual services form the crucial business activities, and orchestration of the services forms the basis of executable business processes.

However, flexibility at process level is incomplete without a thorough understanding of the different variations possible in the manifestations of an individual service as part of a dynamic business process. In this context of dynamic reconfigurability of individual services, we envisage a crucial role agent-based systems can play. The issue of dynamic reconfigurability of individual service implementations in dynamic processes is an important problem. Their need is to reconfigure themselves and coordinate with participating components automatically (without human interaction) to cater to the changing consumer requirements. We have researched the role of an agent-based approach to endow service variations, with the ability to dynamically reconfigure services automatically to meet the needs of their users. The role of agent-based architectures lies in dynamically sensing in an autonomic mode the external environmental variables, and thereupon dynamically evolve the corresponding service implementation by embodying the right variation, to evolve the right service interface, which will be the final true face of the service, in the ongoing dynamic business process. Our ongoing research is looking at a systematic exploration of several combinations of multi-agent system tools and protocols in conjunction with dynamic services-based business processes.

Yet another area where agents are relevant is in the problem of policy reconciliation of multiple actors interacting via service interfaces. We have researched approaches using soft constraints to provide an extensible and flexible mechanism for reconciliation of policies between multiple interacting actors. In the context of multiple actors needing to collaborate together to carry on shared activity, or a sequential activity with dependence upon one another, the policy constraints need to be mutually consistent in order to carry on a transaction. Especially in context of business-to-business (B2B) business processes, where two heterogeneous actors work together as part of a B2B process, this kind of policy reconciliation is a must. We are researching the role agent systems can play in effective and dynamic policy reconciliation for B2B processes. The framework is applicable to any heterogeneous environment in need of reconciling policies, and is illustrated in the real business use case of a demand driven supply chain framework. For details of the preliminary work in this area, please see [12].

Overall, we see promise for multi-agent systems technology working to enable a truly autonomic and dynamic environment for flexible service-based executable business processes.

5 Nirmit Desai (IBM Research – India)

5.1 Services Industry is the Application Area "Agents" Have Been Waiting For!

The agent research community can benefit immensely by demonstrating what their research can do for the services industry. Before I get into backing that statement up, let me say what "services" are and what they are not.

- Services cannot be supported by SOA as it is. When services are proclaimed as having major economic significance, we are not referring to services as in SOA. We are referring to business services. SOA is too low-level a concept to support services.
- Services are not invoked, they are engaged. When was the last time you "invoked" your domestic help? How about the health care service? If you were to believe SOA, these services would have a WSDL description. They would take input from you, go off somewhere, and come back with a cleaned house or a mended tooth.
- Services are hardly automated. Would you go to a robot to have your disease diagnosed? It is good if the robot can serve you but we are far from it. As a result, services involve people. There are specialized skills and deep domain knowledge in almost any services industry. There is an aspect of face-to-face interaction.
- Services are measured by satisfaction. The customer needs vary greatly and they evolve with time. Nonetheless they need to be satisfied to "buy" a service again. However, "satisfaction" is not well understood. Can the customer be satisfied if the provider meets the service level agreements (SLAs)? Can the customer be satisfied even though some SLAs have been violated?

Most importantly, services comprise a major part of the world's economy. Unfortunately, most of the work by computer scientists that is branded as "services" research does not meet these criteria. We need to meet these criteria because they characterize services in a true sense. Fortunately, the multi-agent systems community has worked on the principles underlying services for decades. So why worry about services now? And why should we as an agent research community care?

Distributed AI as an area has for long taken on this apparently difficult mission. We have theories that explain how agents ought to communicate in a business environment and how they can fulfil the needs of their principal. We have agents who are smart enough to interact with humans. We draw ideas from philosophy, social sciences, and cognitive psychology. We study automated negotiation and argumentation. We study trust and commitments. We study rationality and decision making. All of these belong to the heart of the service science.

So what is missing? Game changing applications. The Distributed AI community cannot boast of scientific impact that several other fields of Computer Science can do. For example, communication networks have revolutionized how we communicate, relational databases have revolutionized business transactions. There is a need to justify our programs of research. So far, services have not been a favourite application area of scientists for three main reasons: (1) it is a low-margin and cost-based business – to the service providers, immediate solutions have infinitely more "perceived" value than a long-term scientific effort, (2) the fundamental issues in this area are too hard to make an impact on, and (3) services did not command major economic significance.

However, there are two encouraging trends: (1) services have grown to be the largest chunk of the world's economy, and (2) we are starting to see a certain degree of success in attacking these difficult problems. For example, we have *Watson* that can play Jeopardy and beat the best players ever to play that game. While *Deep Blue* was 14 years ago, chess is not exactly an area of difficulty to computers. Still, what *Watson* and *Deep Blue* have accomplished is far short of the holistic vision of multi-agent research. This is why we need to care for applying our research to the services industry.

6 Aditya Ghose (University of Wollongong)

6.1 An Agent-Based Response to the Climate Change Challenge[2]

The climate change crisis presents both a challenge and an opportunity of unprecedented proportions to the agent community. Current thinking on climate change responses emphasizes the development of alternative energy sources, the development of smart automotive technology and the introduction of macro-economic levers (e.g. carbon taxes, emission trading schemes etc.) to alter energy consumption behaviour at the level of both enterprises and individuals. Fundamental to any solution to the problem is *efficient planning and optimization* (in particular, ensuring that energy use is optimized) – yet this has been largely ignored in the current discourse.

Reducing energy consumption requires that we seek to make all behaviour efficient, *everywhere, all the time*. This requires *pervasive, distributed, continual, reactive* and *autonomous* decision support. The agent community prides itself on its ability to deliver systems with precisely these attributes.

The *Optimizing Web* project at the University of Wollongong offers an example of what can be achieved. The project is based on the following observations. First, optimization is fundamental to carbon mitigation – optimization enables efficient resource

[2] This response was prompted by a question on the "grand challenges" in a future "services science".

utilization, thus lowering energy consumption and the carbon footprint. Second, the global industrial/technological infrastructure, including transportation systems, manufacturing plants, human habitat and so on, is typically operated in an ad-hoc and significantly sub-optimal fashion. This remains the case despite the availability of sophisticated optimization technology for almost the past seven decades (present day operations research techniques trace their roots to the work of George Dantzig in the early 1940s that resulted in the original optimization algorithm – linear programming). Third, locally optimal behaviour does not guarantee "globally" optimal behaviour (i.e. if all agents in a multi-agent system adopt locally efficient behaviours, that does not guarantee that the behaviour of the system as a whole is efficient). Conversely, an optimal solution for a multi-agent problem might not necessarily be optimal for each of its constituent sub-problems. This suggests that more widespread uptake of "piecemeal" optimization alone will not work what is needed is a network of local optimizers that collaborate (and potentially negotiate) to obtain system-wide solutions that improve efficiency despite the competing pulls of local objectives.

The Optimizing Web leverages the global (near-)consensus (without being too pessimistic!) on a carbon-footprint minimization objective. It achieves large-scale *collaborative optimization*, where large numbers of agents collaborate to obtain an optimal value for a shared objective function. The vision is to provide ubiquitous collaborative optimization services, at the level of individual devices, vehicles within transportation systems, units within organizations or manufacturing plants – as well aggregations of all of these. The optimizing web provides a set of protocols for local optimizing agents to interoperate to improve the value of a global carbon footprint minimization objective, while making appropriate trade-offs in relation to their local objectives.

The Optimizing Web leverages and integrates two aspects of agent technology: (1) distributed constraint optimization (DCOP) and (2) distributed reactive planning. While we know that planning problems can be formulated as optimization problems, it is also well understood that some problems are more naturally modelled as planning problems, while others as optimization problems. The project therefore leverages DCOP insights for distributed optimal reactive planning.

Ultimately, the agent community needs to do much more along similar lines. The climate change crisis is real, and the agent community has real solutions to offer. This is therefore a call to arms.

Acknowledgements. We would like to thank Smart Services Cooperative Research Centre for its support of PRIMA 2010 which provided the impetus for this panel discussion.

References

1. Agarwal, V., Chafle, G., Dasgupta, K., Karnik, N., Kumar, A., Mittal, S., Srivastava, B.: Synthy: A System for End to End Composition of Web Services. Journal of Web Semantics 3, 311–339 (2005)
2. Agarwal, V., Chafle, G., Mittal, S., Srivastava, B.: Understanding Approaches for Web Service Composition and Execution. In: Proceedings of the 1st Bangalore Annual Compute Conference (2008)

3. Aldewereld, H., Penserini, L., Dignum, F., Dignum, V.: Regulating Organizations: The ALIVE Approach. In: Proceedings of the International Workshop on Regulations Modelling and Deployment (ReMoD 2008) Held in Conjunction with the CAiSE 2008 Conference, pp. 37–48 (2008)
4. Álvarez-Napagao, S., Cliffe, O., Vázquez-Salceda, J., Padget, J.: Norms, Organisations and Semantic Web Services: The ALIVE Approach. In: Proceedings of the Workshop on Coordination, Organization, Institutions and Norms in Agent Systems in Online Communities at MALLOW 2009 (2009)
5. Booth, D., Haas, H., McCabe, F., Newcomer, E., Champion, M., Ferris, C., Orchad, D.: Web Services Architecture. W3C Working Group Note 11, The World Wide Web Consortium (W3C) (February 2004)
6. Finin, T., Fritzson, R., McKay, D., McEntire, R.: KQML as an Agent Communication Language. In: Proceedings of the Third International Conference on Information and Knowledge Management (CIKM 1994), pp. 456–463 (1994)
7. Jennings, N.R.: Controlling Cooperative Problem Solving in Industrial Multi-Agent Systems Using Joint Intentions. Artificial Intelligence 75, 195–240 (1995)
8. Papazoglou, M.P., Georgakopoulos, D.: Service-Oriented Computing. Communications of the ACM 40, 25–28 (2003)
9. Papazoglou, M.P., van den Heuvel, W.-J.: Service Oriented Architectures: Approaches, Technologies and Research Issues. The VLDB Journal 16, 389–415 (2007)
10. Quillinan, T., Brazier, F., Aldewereld, H., Dignum, F., Dignum, M.V., Penserini, L., Wijngaards, N.: Developing Agent-Based Organizational Models for Crisis Management. In: Proceedings of the Industry Track of the 8th International Joint Conference on Autonomous Agents and Multi-Agent Systems (2009)
11. Rao, A.S., Georgeff, M.P.: BDI Agents: From Theory to Practice. In: Proceedings of the First International Conference on Multi-Agent Systems (ICMAS 1995), pp. 312–319 (1995)
12. Schmid, A., Padmanabhuni, S., Schroeder, A.: A Soft Constraints-Based Approach for Reconciliation of Non-Functional Requirements in Web Services-Based Multi-Agent Systems. In: Proceedings of the 2007 IEEE International Conference on Web Services, pp. 711–718 (2007)
13. Srivastava, B., Koehler, J.: Web Service Composition - Current Solutions and Open Problems. In: Proceedings of the ICAPS 2003 Workshop on Planning and Scheduling for Web Services (2003)
14. Srivastava, B., Mazzoleni, P.: Business Driven Consolidation of SOA Implementations. In: Proceedings of the 2010 IEEE International Conference on Services Computing, pp. 49–56 (2010)
15. Vázquez-Salceda, J., Dignum, F., Vasconcelos, W., Padget, J., Clarke, S., Ceccaroni, L., Nieuwenhuis, K., Sergean, P.: ALIVE: Combining Organizational and Coordination Theory with Model Driven Approaches to Develop Dynamic, Flexible Distributed Business Systems. In: Telesca, L., Stanoevska-Slabeva, K., Rakocevic, V. (eds.) Digital Business. Springer, Berlin (2009)

SBDO: A New Robust Approach to Dynamic Distributed Constraint Optimisation

Graham Billiau, Chee Fon Chang, and Aditya Ghose

Decision Systems Lab
School of Computer Science and Software Engg
University of Wollongong, NSW, Australia
{gdb339,c03,aditya}@uow.edu.au

Abstract. Dynamic distributed constraint optimisation problems are a very effective tool for solving multi-agent problems. However they require protocols for agents to collaborate in optimising shared objectives in a decentralised manner without necessarily revealing all of their private constraints. In this paper, we present the details of the Support-Based Distributed Optimisation (SBDO) algorithm for solving dynamic distributed constraint optimisation problems. This algorithm is complete wrt hard constraints but not wrt objectives. Furthermore, we show that SBDO is completely asynchronous, sound and fault tolerant. Finally, we evaluate the performance of SDBO with respect to DynCOAA for Dyn-DCOP and ADOPT, DPOP for DCOP. The results highlight that in general, SBDO out performs these algorithms on criteria such as time, solution quality, number of messages, non-concurrent constraint checks and memory usage.

1 Introduction

Dynamic Distributed Constraint Optimisation Problems (DynDCOP) are a problem domain that has not been well explored. DynDCOPs allow us to model problems that can not be assumed to be static, that is they change so frequently that by the time a DCOP solver has found a solution it is already obsolete. DynDCOPs are very useful for modelling and solving multi-agent coordination and planning problems. These problems appear in many areas such as scheduling patient treatment in a hospital or managing the airspace above an airport. As DynDCOP is an extension of the well explored Distributed Constraint Optimisation Problem (DCOP), techniques utilised to solve DCOP present a good foundation.

Very few of the DCOP algorithms consider what happens when agents fail. The max-sum algorithms [11] have been shown to be robust even when 90% of messages are not delivered. While none of the others consider what happens when agents fail. There are many reasons, such as hardware failures or malicious attack that may cause an agent to fail. It is particularly important to be able to continue solving even when agents fail in dynamic solvers, as they are often expected to run continuously for a long duration.

N. Desai, A. Liu, and M. Winikoff (Eds.): PRIMA 2010, LNAI 7057, pp. 11–26, 2012.

1.1 Related Work

At this time there are only two other algorithms that can solve DynDCOPs, Dynamic Constraint Optimisation Ant Algorithm (DynCOAA)[6] and Self-Stabilising Distributed Psuedo-tree Optimisation Procedure (S-DPOP)[8]. Of these two DynCOAA is incomplete and S-DPOP is complete. Neither of these two algorithms consider the possibility of agent failure, so are unable to recover from failures.

As DynDCOP is an extension of the well explored Distributed Constraint Optimisation Problem (DCOP), techniques utilised to solve DCOP present a good foundation. There are a large number of DCOP algorithms, such as ADOPT [7], NCBB [1], DALO [3] and Divide-and-Coordinate [12]. As none of these algorithms are currently capable of solving dynamic problems we do not consider them further.

In section 2, we will present the Support Based Distributed Optimisation algorithm (SBDO) which improves on the existing DynDCOP solvers by being completely asynchronous, fault tolerant and having no hierarchy among agents. Section 3 describes the performance results comparison from the dynamic problems, the fault tolerance and static problem dimension. In section 4, we present the conclusions.

2 Support Based Distributed Optimisation

SBDO is an extension of the SBDS algorithm[2]. SBDS is a complete Distributed Constraint Satisfaction Problem solver. SBDO extends it by adding a local search mechanism for optimising the solution found while maintaining the completeness wrt hard constraints. SBDO also adds support for solving dynamic problems.

We define DynDCOPs as follows. Our definitions differ to that in the literature as we treat hard constraints and soft constraints/objectives differently.

Definition 1. *A Constraint Optimisation Problem (COP) is a tuple* $\langle \mathcal{X}, \mathcal{D}, \mathcal{C}, \mathcal{R} \rangle$ *where* $\mathcal{X}$ *is a set* $\{x_1, \ldots, x_n\}$ *of variables,* $\mathcal{D}$ *is a set* $\{d_1, \ldots, d_n\}$ *of variable domains,* $\mathcal{C}$ *is a set* $\{c_1, \ldots, c_m\}$ *of constraints defined over* $\mathcal{X}$ *and* $\mathcal{R}$ *is a set* $\{r_1, \ldots, r_o\}$ *of utility functions defined over* $\mathcal{X}$*.*

Definition 2. *A Distributed Constraint Optimisation Problem (DCOP) is a tuple* $\langle \mathcal{A}, COP, \mathcal{C}, \mathcal{R} \rangle$ *where* $\mathcal{A}$ *is a set* $\{a_1, \ldots, a_p\}$ *of agents,* COP *is a set* $\{COP_1, \ldots, COP_p\}$ *of disjoint COPs,* $\mathcal{C}$ *is a set* $\{c_1, \ldots, c_m\}$ *of shared constraints and* $\mathcal{R}$ *is a set* $\{r_1, \ldots, r_q\}$ *of shared utility functions.*

The shared constraints and utility functions are defined over variables from several different COPs.

Definition 3. *A Dynamic Distributed Constraint Optimisation Problem (DynDCOP) is a sequence* $\langle DCOP_1, \ldots, DCOP_n \rangle$ *where each DCOP differs from the previous one by an added or removed constraint/objective/agent. The goal is to find and maintain a solution where all the constraints are satisfied and the objective function optimised.*

We assume the existence of a global objective function that the collection of agents seeks to optimise, but we require that it must be possible to decompose this function into agent-specific objective functions such that the optimal assignment of variables for the decomposed set of objective functions corresponds to the optimal assignment for the global objective.

Note that to maintain generality of this discussion, we leave the details for the decomposition up to the designer. However, each objective function must return a value proportionate to how good the partial solution is, a utility value, such that a better solution returns a higher utility value. The utility values returned by all of the objective functions must be comparable and can be aggregated.

To further increase the generality of the algorithm, shared objectives can be used as well as local objectives. Shared objectives are used when a (sub)objective can not be decomposed to include only the variables of one agent. In this case the objective can be shared between the agents that together control the variables used in the objective. The objective is evaluated by any of the agents that share it as soon as that agent knows an assignment to all the variables in the objective. The utility returned by the shared objective is added to the utility of the agent's local objective. If the agent does not have enough information to evaluate the objective it is ignored and only the agent's local objective is used.

2.1 Communication

The physical communication channels that agents must use to communicate are never perfect, so it is desirable for algorithms to be able to tolerate messages arriving in random order. That is the messages sent between two agents may not arrive in the same order they were sent, or they may never arrive at all. The proposed algorithm is robust against messages arriving in random order but not robust against message loss.

The most common message used for communication in SBDO is an 'isgood', which is very similar to a partial assignment and is in part inspired by techniques used in formal argumentation, where the notion of an argument is used to encode alternate points of view.

Definition 4. *The neighbour graph is an undirected graph $\langle N, E\rangle$. N is the set of agents and $E \subseteq N \times N$ such that there is an edge $\{A_i, A_j\}$ iff there exists a shared constraint or a shared objective defined over both A_i and A_j.*

Definition 5. *Given a $DCOP = \langle \mathcal{A}, COP, \mathcal{C}, \mathcal{R}\rangle$. An isgood is a sequence $\langle A_1, \ldots, A_n\rangle$ of assignments such that the sequence is a simple path through the neighbour graph. Each assignment is a triple $\langle a, \{\langle x_1, \mathcal{D}_{1i}\rangle, \ldots, \langle x_n, \mathcal{D}_{nj}\rangle\}, utility\rangle$ such that none of the constraints in the DCOP are violated. The total utility of an isgood is the aggregation of the utilities of all the assignments within it. As such an isgood encodes a partial solution to the problem as well as the relative utility of the partial solution.*

An isgood can be considered as an argument, in which case the first $n-1$ assignments form the justification and the last assignment is the conclusion. As in formal argumentation theories, an argument may attack/defeat other arguments and the agent receiving these potentially competing arguments must pick the winning argument. Because of this, each agent attempts to send stronger arguments over time to influence their neighbours.

Definition 6. *The ordering over isgoods is: First the total utility of the isgoods is compared, with higher being better. If they are equal then the number of assignments in each isgood is compared, with more being better. Finally if they are equal then one is picked randomly but consistently.*[1] *That is, if an agent picks isgood A over isgood B then in all future comparisons it will choose A over B.*

Instead of using an ordering over the variables, which causes problems in dynamic environments, we use a total ordering over the partial solutions, or isgoods. This ordering is needed so that the solution can be optimised as well as to prevent cyclic behaviour. Whenever we refer to one isgood being better than another in this paper it is with respect to this ordering

To avoid cycles of oscillating values which might occur because there is no variable ordering we increase the length of successive isgoods that are sent. This is achieved by recording the last isgood sent and attempting to send a longer one. As any cycle must be finite eventually the isgoods being sent will contain the cycle itself. If the cycle is made up of inconsistent values then a nogood will be generated, breaking the cycle. Else the cycle breaking mechanism of `update_view()` (alg. 2) will break the cycle. The proofs of soundness and termination from SBDS[10] still hold. Due to space limitation, readers are directed to [2] for details.

Rather than using all the information contained in all the isgoods that an agent has received, which is often inconsistent. Each agent picks a single isgood to use as the justification for the assignments to its own variables. The agent who has sent the best isgood is chosen as the support for the agent. The isgood that agent sent is used as the basis for the agents view.

Definition 7. *Given a DCOP* $\langle \mathcal{A}, COP, \mathcal{C}, \mathcal{R} \rangle$. *A nogood is a pair* $\langle P, C \rangle$ *where* P *is a set of variable value pairs* $\{\langle x_1, \mathcal{D}_{1i} \rangle, \ldots, \langle x_n, \mathcal{D}_{nj} \rangle\}$ *forming a partial assignment and* $C \subset \mathcal{C}$, *is the justification such that* P *violates at least one constraint in* C. *As such a nogood represents a partial solution that is proven to not be part of any global solution.*

Hard constraints are handled differently to objectives in order to guarantee that any solution found will satisfy all of the hard constraints. Nogoods with justifications [10] are used as these allow us to guarantee that all the hard constraints are satisfied (as shown in [2]) as well as allowing obsolete nogoods to be identified after hard constraints are removed from the problem.

Due to the dynamic nature of the input problem the algorithm never terminates (detecting that the network of agents has reached a quiescent state, or detecting that the problem is over-constrained are in themselves insufficient as terminating criteria, since new inputs from the environment, in the form of added or deleted variables/constraints/objectives might invalidate them).

[1] Cryptographic hash functions can provide a suitable comparison.

2.2 Dynamic Problems

Unlike other dynamic algorithms we do not explicitly model the concept of solution stability. Instead we assume that if there is a cost associated with changing the value of a variable the agent takes it into account in its local objective function(s).

Most of the changes to the problem that can occur in a dynamic system are straightforward to implement, except for removing hard constraints (which we discuss later). Several messages are required to communicate any changes to the problem to the agents: add constraint, pre-remove constraint, post-remove constraint, add objective, remove objective, add domain and remove domain. These messages all reflect changes to the environment and as such are referred to as environment messages. With the exception of post-remove constraint they are assumed to be sent by the environment. Only the agents that control the variables involved in the objective or hard constraint that is added or removed must be notified.

A change to the agents involved is handled implicitly by the other messages. When an agent no longer has any links to one of its neighbours, that agent is no longer a neighbour. Once an agent has no links to any other agents it is effectively removed from the problem. Agents are added to the problem by creating a link between them and another agent. In the process they are then also a neighbour of that agent.

When a hard constraint is removed in an update to the underlying COP all of the nogoods that were generated because of the removed constraint must also be removed. They can be identified via the nogoods justification. If the justification contains the deleted constraint then the nogood might be obsolete and must be deleted. This does mean that a nogood which violates two or more constraints, and so is still valid, may be deleted. If this occurs the nogood will be re-posted later. As it is possible for a nogood to arrive after the message that renders it obsolete, `pre-remove constraint(C)` (alg. 3) and `post-remove constraint()` (alg. 5) are required to ensure correctness.

To catch any nogoods that arrive after the constraint removed message that makes them obsolete, the agent must also check the removed constraints it knows of when it receives a new nogood. If the nogood is obsolete then it is discarded and the associated counter decremented.

2.3 Fault Tolerance

Due to the nature of the algorithm, when an agent fails it has a minimal impact on the other agents. Unlike algorithms that impose a hierarchy, agents do not require a message from the failed agent(s) before they can continue processing. Instead all agents just continue oblivious to the fact that an agent has failed. The only limitation is that the value assigned to affected variables can not change, other agents must continue using the last known value for the variables.

When an agent fails all its knowledge regarding sent and received isgoods is lost. This effectively means that messages have been lost, which this algorithm can not account for. So when the failed agent restarts it must request that its neighbours send it the last isgood and all nogoods that they sent to this agent, as well as the last isgood and all nogoods they have received from this agent. This prevents most knowledge loss and allows the failed agent to resume solving faster. But if two neighbouring agents both fail at the same time then some information is irretrievably lost.There is a simple extension to the algorithm that will ensure that will ensure it functions correctly wrt agent failure and random message order. Unfortunately there is not enough space to present it here. Only accounting for agent failure is affected by this issue.

Theorem 1. *Given that messages always arrive in the order they are sent, SBDO is correct when agents in the network fail.*

Proof. When a single agent A fails all of the information required for correctness is preserved by its neighbours. Each of its neighbours records the set of nogood messages that it sent to A. Similarly they record all the nogood messages that they received from A. When A restarts it requests this information from its neighbours.

When two or more neighbouring agents A and B fail simultaneously, the messages that A sent to and received from agents other than B will be preserved by those other agents and vice versa. So only the messages exchanged between A and B are lost. Between A and B, A forgets that it sent message M to B and B forgets that it received message M from A. Because of this each agents set of sent and received messages are still consistent. Therefore the procedure for removing obsolete nogoods is still correct.

Theorem 2. *SBDO can continue solving when one or more agents fail.*

Proof. Because of the flat communication model no agent is ever waiting for a message from a specific agent before they can continue solving (they may be waiting for a message from any agent, but if this is the case they currently have no work to do). Because of this the other agents can always continue to solve the problem, using the last known value for the agents variables. When the agent restarts it is immediately informed of the current state of the problem so that it can resume solving.

2.4 Algorithm

Each agent must store the following information:

- view. This is an isgood consisting of the isgood received from support + an assignment to all this agents variables.
- recv(A). This is a mapping from an agent A to the last isgood received from that agent.
- nogoods. This is an unbounded store of all nogoods received.
- sent(A). This is a mapping from an agent A to the last isgood sent to that agent.

Algorithm 1. main()

```
begin
  while Not Terminated do
    for All received nogoods N do
      if this nogood is obsolete then
        decrement counter on the removed-constraint message
        if counter = zero then
          delete constraint-removed message
      else
        Add N to nogoods
        for All neighbours A do
          if There is no valid assignment to myself wrt recv(A) then
            send_nogood(A)
    for All received environment messages do
      Process message
    for All received isgoods I do
      Let A be the agent who sent I
      set recv(A) to I
      if There is no valid assignment to myself wrt I then
        send_nogood(A)
    update_view()
    Let I be the best isgood in recv(A)
    if I is better than view then
      Set support to the agent that sent I
      Let view be recv(support) extended by a valid assignment to all local,
      public variables, chosen greedily
    for All neighbours A do
      if self and A are the first two variables in view then
        if view ≮ sent(A) or sent(A) is not consistent then
          Send view to A
          Set sent(A) to view
      else
        Let length be the longest sub-isgood that can be sent to A
        Let preferred be 0
        if sent(A) is ⟨⟩ or sent(A) ⋢ view then
          Set preferred to |sent(A)| + 1
        if sent(A) < recv(A) and view is inconsistent with recv(A) then
          Set preferred to max(preferred, |recv(A)| + 1)
        if preferred > 0 then
          Let I be an isgood such that I ⊑ view and |I| =
          min(length, preferred)
          Let U be the utility of I as returned by the local objective function
          + any shared objectives
          Set the utility of the assignment to self in I to U
          Send I to A
          Set sent(A) to I
    Wait until at least one message has been received
end
```

Algorithm 2. update_view()

```
begin
    Let view' be recv(support) extended by a valid assignment to all local, public
    variables, chosen greedily
    Let V be the first variable assigned in view'
    if scope(view') = scope(view) or view is better than view' or the assignment
    to V is the same in view' and recv(A) or the assignment to V is unequal in
    view and recv(A) then
        Set view to view'
end
```

Algorithm 3. pre-remove_constraint (M)

```
begin
    Let C be the removed constraint
    for Each neighbour A do
        Let counter be 0
        for Each nogood N sent to A do
            if N contains C as part of its justification then
                Increment counter by 1
                Delete N from sent nogoods
        if counter > 0 then
            Let M be a new constraint removed message with C and counter
            Send M to A
end
```

- support. The agent that this agent is using as its support.
- sent-nogoods. This is an unbounded store of all nogoods sent.
- removed-constraints. An unbounded store of received remove constraint messages.

We use the notation $A \sqsubseteq B$ to say that A is a sub-isgood of B. By sub-isgood we mean that A is the tail (or entirety) of B, $|A|$ to denote the number of assignments in A and scope(A) is the set of variables that are assigned in A.

Each agent greedily chooses what agent to use as its support and the values to assign to its own variables. As each agent may control many variables, each agent requires its own centralised Dynamic COP solver. Because of the way the support is selected a collection of agents can combine to cause an agent that has chosen sub-optimal assignments to change its assignments.

The basic steps each agent takes are quite simple. First it processes all the messages in its message queue. Then it decides what values to assign to its own variables. Last it sends all of its neighbours a message telling them what values it has chosen for its variables.

Processing messages starts with all of the nogoods received. Nogoods are processed first in case they are later rendered obsolete by a message from the

Algorithm 4. send_nogood(A)

```
begin
    Let N be a nogood derived from recv(A)
    Send N to A
    Set recv(A) to none
    if support = A then
        Set support to self
end
```

Algorithm 5. post-remove_constraint(M)

```
begin
    Let C be the constraint referenced
    if removed-constraints already contains a message regarding C then
        Increment the counter of that message by the counter in M
    else
        for Each received nogood N do
            if N is justified by C then
                Delete N
                Decrement the counter by 1
        if counter ≠ 0 then
            Add M to removed-constraints
        pre-remove constraint(C)
end
```

environment and because one of them might invalidate one of the isgoods in the message queue. When a nogood is received it is added to the set of all known nogoods. Once all nogoods are processed the received isgoods must be rechecked to see if they are now inconsistent with this agent's assignment. If so, the isgood's sender must be informed by sending a nogood. This will force the sender to change their value in the next iteration. Next all environment messages are processed. The order within this group doesn't matter, but they may affect how the isgoods are processed. Finally, the received isgoods are processed. First, recv(A) is updated with this most recent isgood, then it checks if there is a valid assignment to its own variable. If there isn't, a nogood is created and sent back to the agent that sent the isgood. This will force the sender to change their value in the next iteration.

While the processing of most environment messages is straightforward, removing constraints requires special mention. When a constraint is removed from the problem all of the nogoods that were generated because of that constraint must also be removed. This is made more difficult because it is possible for the nogood message to arrive after the pre-remove constraint message that makes it obsolete. In order to ensure they are all deleted each agent must also maintain a store of all the nogoods it has sent and who it sent them to. When a pre-remove constraint message is received by an agent it checks its sent nogood store to see if any of its neighbours must be notified. If any of the nogoods have the removed constraint as part of their justification, they are now obsolete and the agents neighbour must be notified. To notify the neighbour, this agent sends a post-remove constraint message with the constraint that has been removed and the total number of nogoods sent to that agent that are made obsolete.

Whenever an agent receives a post-remove constraint message it must go through its store of received nogoods and delete any that have this constraint as part of their justification. For each one that is deleted, the counter of total obsolete nogoods in the post-remove constraint message is decremented. When the counter reaches zero, all of the obsolete nogoods have been deleted and the post-remove constraint message can be deleted. The agent must also check its own store of sent nogoods to see if any of its neighbours must be notified of the change. This is exactly as above. If an agent receives two or more post-remove constraint messages for the same constraint, the counters are simply added together.

Now that the agent has the most recent information about its environment, it can choose the best assignments for its own variables. This will normally require a centralised COP solver.

After the agent has updated its view it then checks to see if one of the other agents would make a better support than the current one. To do so, it picks the best isgood out of all of the isgoods it has received, then compares it with its view. If the isgood is better then it changes its support to the agent which sent the best isgood and then has to call `update_view()` (alg. 2) again to update its view. If its view is better then it keeps its current support.

Finally the agent must communicate changes to its local state to its neighbours. If it detects that it is part of a cycle with the agent it is currently sending an isgood to then it must send its entire view to that agent. Unless its view is worse than the last isgood sent to that agent. In which case it postpones sending a message to prevent cyclic behaviour. If it does not detect a cycle then it must decide how long an isgood to send. If the agent is updating obsolete information that it sent earlier then it attempts to send a longer isgood than sent previously. If the agent is in conflict with the agent than it also attempts to send a longer isgood than was received from the agent. However obviously it can't send an isgood longer than its view, but it also can not send an isgood that is self supporting i.e. if view is $\langle\langle B, \langle b, 1\rangle, 4\rangle, \langle C, \langle c, 5\rangle, 20\rangle, \langle A, \langle a, 1\rangle, 3\rangle, \langle D, \langle d, 3\rangle, 15\rangle\rangle$ and sending an isgood to A then the maximum length is 3.

2.5 Example

Example 1. Consider the following constraint optimisation problem with three variables, δ, θ and γ, each controlled by one agent Δ, Θ and Γ respectively. Their respective domains are $\{0, 1, 2\}, \{-1, 0, 1\}$ and $\{-1, 0, 1\}$. The objectives are $\min(\delta \times \theta), \min(\theta), \min(\gamma)$ and there is one hard constraint, $\theta < \gamma$. The utility of the best assignment is 2, and the worst is 0.

In this problem agents δ and θ are neighbours as they share an objective, and agents θ and γ are neighbours as they share a constraint.

Initially no agents have any information from their neighbours so in alg. 2 they chose their assignments based on only local information, in this case, $\theta = -1$ and $\gamma = -1$ from their local objectives, while $\delta = 1$ is chosen randomly. All agents then inform their neighbours of their decision by sending isgoods. Δ sends the isgood $\langle\langle \Delta, \{\langle \delta, 1\rangle\}, 0\rangle\rangle$ to Θ, Θ sends the isgood $\langle\langle \Theta, \{\langle \theta, -1\rangle\}, 2\rangle\rangle$ to Δ and Γ and Γ sends the isgood $\langle\langle \Gamma, \{\langle \gamma, -1\rangle\}, 2\rangle\rangle$ to Θ.

When Θ receives the isgood from Γ, it notices that the isgood is inconsistent with its knowledge, as there is no value in its domain less then -1. So Θ sends the nogood $\langle \{\langle \gamma, -1\rangle\}, \{\theta < \gamma\}\rangle$. After receiving the isgoods all the agents decide which agent to use as their support. Θ has to chose between itself and Δ. The utility of Θ's current view is 2, which is better than or equal to all the others so it keeps itself as its support. Similarly Δ and Γ change their support to Θ. When Δ chooses Θ as its support, its view now includes the assignment to Θ, therefore it now has enough information to evaluate the shared objective and so picks $\delta = 2$. Θ and Γ view's have not changed, so they don't send new isgoods, while Δ sends the isgood $\langle\langle \Delta, \{\langle \delta, 2\rangle\}, 2\rangle\rangle$ to Θ. Normally it would include the assignment to θ as well, but that would create a circular argument, so the assignment to Θ is trimmed. Next, Γ receives the nogood from Θ and so is forced to change its assignment to $\gamma = 0$ and sends another isgood to Θ with its new assignment. Simultaneously Θ receives the new isgood from Δ, but does not make any changes because of it, so does not send a new isgood.

Then the problem changes. The constraint $\theta < \gamma$ is removed from the problem. So the environment sends messages to Θ and Γ. Γ has not sent any nogoods so has nothing to do, while Θ has sent a nogood to Γ which is now obsolete, so it sends the constraint removed message $((\theta < \gamma), 1)$ to Γ. Also as there is no longer a link between Θ and Γ they are no longer neighbours. Meanwhile Δ has not received any messages so is still waiting.

Finally γ receives the constraint removed message, deletes the obsolete nogood and so is again able to adopt the assignment $\gamma = -1$, however it has no neighbours to send an isgood to. As no agents have any messages to send the network has reached quiescence.

3 Results

To evaluate SBDO, we implemented it using Python and compared it with the two other DynDCOP algorithms, S-DPOP and DynCOAA. We used the reference implementation of S-DPOP[4], written in Java and we implemented DynCOAA and SBDO in python. We used the parameters for DynCOAA that are recommended by its authors [6], with 15 ants in each swarm. The different implementation languages mean that the memory and time used by each algorithm can't be compared directly. The Quality, Non-Concurrent Constraint Checks (NCCCs)[5], and messages required are independent of the implementation and so still directly comparable.

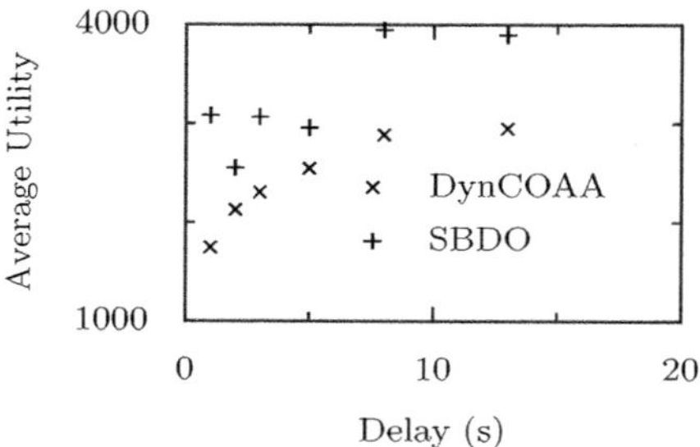

Fig. 1. Average solution quality per time step

The test platform was an AMD Athlon X2 6000+ processor with 4GB of RAM running OpenSolaris 10 release 06/09. Memory usage was measured by using DTrace to count all anonymous memory allocations and deallocations.

We used three sets of test problems: easy, moderate and hard. The easy set consists of the 120 handcrafted meeting scheduling problems provided in [9]. These problems have between 8 and 12 variables with a constraint density (number of constraints divided by number of variables) of between 1.333 and 1.875. The moderate set consists of 12 randomly generated meeting scheduling problems. These problems have between 9 and 24 variables with a constraint density between 1.000 and 1.860. The hard set consists of 16 randomly generated meeting scheduling problems. These problems have between 12 and 48 variables with a constraint density between 1.750 and 4.000. We ran each problem ten times to ensure the results represent the average performance of each algorithm.

3.1 Dynamic Problems

To evaluate SBDO's performance on dynamic problems we compared it against DynCOAA on the moderate and hard sets of problems. Both algorithms were allowed to run for a set amount of time (1, 2, 3, 5, 8 and 13 seconds), after which they were paused, the utility of the current solution calculated, then two of the hard constraints were randomly replaced then the algorithm resumed. The problems objective function was left unchanged. This was repeated 25 times for each problem. By using the same random seed we guarantee that the dynamic problems are the same for all trials. We could not compare against S-DPOP as the provided implementation does not support terminating the current solving process after a period of time.

As fig 3.1 shows, SBDO always outperforms DynCOAA, however it is obvious that the solutions found by SBDO are not monotonically non-decreasing. This is because it does not have a global communication mechanism to coordinate value changes like DynCOAA does.

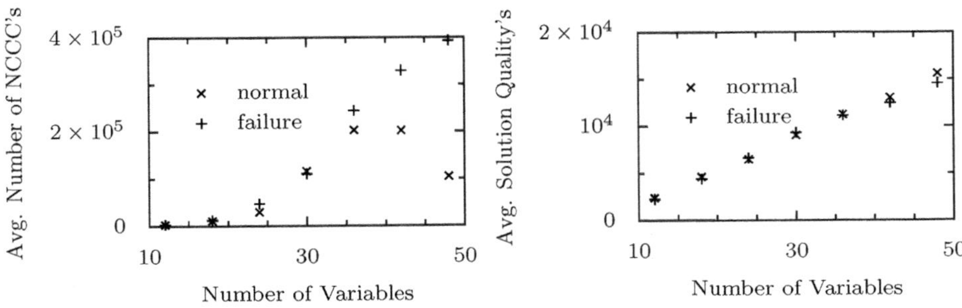

Fig. 2. Performance with unreliable agents

3.2 Fault Tolerance

To demonstrate the fault tolerance of SBDO it was run on the set of hard problems. Every 3 seconds a random agent was killed, then restarted between 1 and 3 seconds later. So at most one of the 12 to 48 agents was not operating at any time. We tried with other failure rates and got similar results. We choose to restart failed agents as our test problems are from the meeting scheduling domain. Where it is reasonable to expect that agents will be restarted when their failure is detected. As shown in figure 1 the algorithm requires more NCCCs, so therefore more time and messages to reach quiescence. Though as shown in figure 1 when it does terminate the solution is only slightly worse than when no agents fail.

3.3 Static Problems

To evaluate how SBDO performs on static problems we tested it against S-DPOP and DynCOAA. Table 1 describes the average and standard deviation for each of the metrics. Separated by easy, moderate and hard problems respectively. We were unable to measure NCCCs for DynCOAA, so they have not been reported. It also represents the average and standard deviation of the ratio of the 'utility' (or objective function value) computed over the optimal utility (represented as a percentage) for each of these algorithms. We note that SBDO generates near optimal, but not optimal, solutions in general. The SBDO algorithm performs very well, requiring slightly more messages and NCCCs, but less memory than S-DPOP. While producing slightly worse solutions that DynCOAA, but with much less time and messages.

3.4 Scalability

To evaluate how SBDO scales with different problem sizes we compared it against DPOP and DynCOAA on the moderate and hard sets of problems. Each instance was terminated after 10 minutes or if it used more than 3.5GB of memory. SBDO completed 98.6% of the moderate problems and 61.8% of the hard problems.

Table 1. Performance on static problems

Algorithm	Quality		Messages		NCCCs		Memory (MB)		Time (s)	
	avg	SD	avg	SD	avg	SD	avg	SD	avg	SD
SBDO	99.80%	0.87	70.48	25.87	643.45	451.73	0.49	0.04	0.16	0.06
DynCOAA	99.95%	2.4E-4	8715.35	2745.23	–	–	0.34	0.02	14.22	5.58
S-DPOP	100%	0.00	19.73	3.24	591.75	155.54	46.08	4.34	0.16	0.06

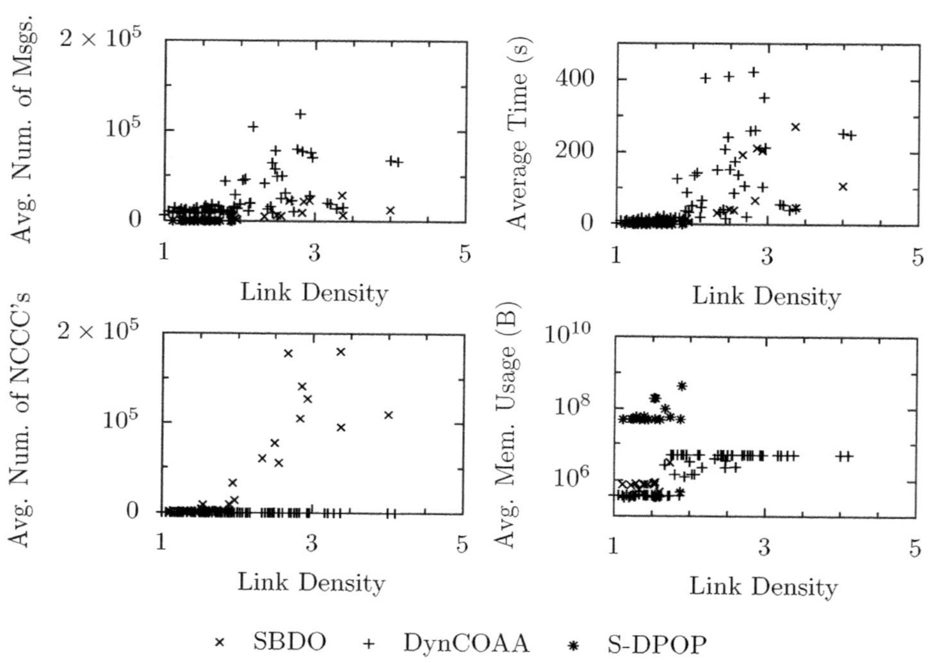

Fig. 3. Scalability of SBDO, DynCOAA and DPOP

DPOP completed all of the moderate problems and 17.5% of the hard problems. DynCOAA completed all of the moderate problems and 61.75% of the hard problems.

The plots in figure 3 have been created by averaging the data collected from all the instances the algorithms were tested on. The plots show that SBDO scales well, though it does not scale as well as DPOP on most metrics, it scales much better on memory usage.

4 Conclusion

We have presented the Support Based Distributed Optimisation algorithm that can solve Dynamic Distributed Constraint Optimisation problems using a novel approach inspired by argumentation. In this approach there is no hierarchy among the different agents, instead each agent is able to send 'isgoods', which can be viewed as arguments. An isgood contains the assignment to the variables of an agent as well as the utility of the assignment and the context in which the decision was made. Each agent can choose one of the other agents as its support and in turn uses that agent's assignment and context as the context for its own decision. By constantly creating and communicating stronger and stronger arguments each agent is able to influence the assignment to other agents. In this way the agents are able to arrive at a good solution using few resources, as shown in table 1. Also figure 3 shows that the resources required scale well with the size of the problem.

The lack of hierarchy makes this approach very flexible regarding change in the environment. So it is highly suited for solving dynamic problems, as shown in figure 1. This flexibility, coupled with the knowledge redundancy in the network makes it fault tolerant. Other agents are able to continue solving unimpeded when one or even many agents fail. Error recovery is hastened by allowing an agent that has just restarted to recreate its previous state, as shown in figure 2.

The resulting algorithm is completely asynchronous, fault tolerant, complete with respect to hard constraints but incomplete with respect to soft constraints.

In future we plan to extend the concept of objectives to allow stability constraints to be expressed. We also intend to identify how to make the algorithm complete, or at least provide theoretical guarantees on solution quality.

References

1. Chechetka, A., Sycara, K.: No-commitment branch and bound search for distributed constraint optimization. In: AAMAS 2006, pp. 1427–1429. ACM (2006)
2. Harvey, P., Chang, C.F., Ghose, A.: Support-based distributed search: a new approach for multiagent constraint processing. In: AAMAS 2006, pp. 377–383. ACM (2006)
3. Kiekintveld, C., Yin, Z., Kumar, A., Tambe, M.: Asynchronous algorithms for approximate distributed constraint optimization with quality bounds. In: AAMAS, pp. 133–140 (2010)
4. Léauté, T., Ottens, B., Szymanek, R.: FRODO 2.0: An open-source framework for distributed constraint optimization. In: Proceedings of the IJCAI 2009 Distributed Constraint Reasoning Workshop (DCR 2009), Pasadena, California, USA, pp. 160–164 (July 13, 2009), `http://liawww.epfl.ch/frodo/`
5. Meisels, A., Kaplansky, E., Razgon, I., Zivan, R.: Comparing performance of distributed constraints processing algorithms. In: Proceedings of DCR Workshop, AAMAS 2002 (2002)
6. Mertens, K.: An Ant-Based Approach for Solving Dynamic Constraint Optimization Problems. PhD thesis, Katholieke Universiteit Leuven (December 2006)
7. Modi, P.J., Shen, W.-M., Tambe, M., Yokoo, M.: Adopt: asynchronous distributed constraint optimization with quality guarantees. Artificial Intelligence 161, 149–180 (2005)
8. Petcu, A., Faltings, B.: S-dpop: Superstabilizing, fault-containing multiagent combinatorial optimization. In: Proceedings of the National Conference on Artificial Intelligence, AAAI-2005, pp. 449–454. AAAI, Pittsburgh (July 2005)

9. Portway, C.P.: USC dcop repository (2008), http://teamcore.usc.edu/dcop
10. Schiex, T., Verfaillie, G.: Nogood recording for static and dynamic constraint satisfaction problems. In: TAI 1993, pp. 48–55 (1993)
11. Stranders, R., Farinelli, A., Rogers, A., Jennings, N.R.: Decentralised coordination of continuously valued control parameters using the max-sum algorithm. In: AAMAS, vol. (1), pp. 601–608 (2009)
12. Vinyals, M., Pujol, M., Rodríguez-Aguilar, J.A., Cerquides, J.: Divide-and-coordinate: Dcops by agreement. In: AAMAS, pp. 149–156 (2010)

Solving Distributed CSPs Using Dynamic, Partial Centralization without Explicit Constraint Passing

Roger Mailler and Jacob Graves

Computational Neuroscience and Adaptive Systems Lab
University of Tulsa, USA
roger-mailler@utulsa.edu
http://www.cnas.utulsa.edu

Abstract. Dynamic, partial centralization has received a considerable amount of attention in the distributed problem solving community. As the name implies, this technique works by dynamically identifying portions of a shared problem to centralize in order to speed the problem solving process. Currently, a number of algorithms have been created which employ this simple, yet powerful technique to solve problems such as distributed constraint satisfaction (DCSP), distributed constraint optimization (DCOP), and distributed resource allocation.

In fact, one such algorithm, Asynchronous Partial Overlay (APO), was shown to outperform the Asynchronous Weak Commitment (AWC) protocol, which is one of the best known methods for solving DCSPs. One of the key differences between these algorithms is that APO uses explicit constraint passing. AWC, on the other hand, passed *nogoods* because it tries to provide security and privacy. Because of these differences in underlying assumptions, a number of researchers have criticized the comparison between these two protocols.

This paper attempts to resolve this disparity by introducing a new hybrid algorithm called Nogood-APO. Like AWC, this new algorithm uses nogood passing to provide security and privacy, but like APO uses dynamic partial centralization to speed the problem solving process. Like its parent algorithms, this new protocol is sound and complete and performs nearly as well as APO, while still outperforming AWC, on distributed 3-coloring problems. In addition, this paper shows that Nogood-APO provides more privacy to the agents than both APO and AWC on all but the sparsest problems. These findings demonstrate that a dynamic, partial centralization-based protocol can provide privacy and that even when operating with the same assumptions as AWC still solves problems in fewer cycles using less computation and communication.

1 Introduction

Over the years, distributed problem solving has received a great deal of attention for a number of reasons. The most compelling reasons are that some problems are naturally distributed, multiple processor can compute solution faster, and privacy

N. Desai, A. Liu, and M. Winikoff (Eds.): PRIMA 2010, LNAI 7057, pp. 27–41, 2012.

and security can be maintained. These reasons can often be quite contradictory because, for example, the more information an agent is willing to reveal upfront as part of the problem solving process, the faster a solution can be computed.

One methodology for solving distributed problems, called dynamic, partial centralization tries to solve naturally distributed problems in the fastest manner possible by performing focused, incremental and asynchronous centralization of portions of a shared problem. Several protocols have already been created that use this hybrid centralized/distributed search technique and have been shown to outperform existing protocols on a large number of distributed problems.

One of the key characteristics of each of these algorithms, however, is that the agents have to be willing to directly reveal a great deal of information to each other. For example, in Asynchronous Partial Overlay (APO) [8], agents willingly reveal their variable's constraints and domain whenever requested. The Asynchronous Weak Commitment (AWC) protocol [15], on the other hand, only reveals information about a variable's constraints and domain, using a *nogood*, when it reaches a *deadend* in the problem solving process. The willingness to reveal information is one reason, although not the only one, that APO outperforms AWC across a wide spectrum of problem sizes and difficulties.

The purpose of this paper is to present a new hybrid AWC/APO algorithm, called Nogood-APO. Like APO, this new algorithm uses dynamic, partial centralization and like AWC only reveals information, in the form of a nogood, when necessary during the problem solving process. The two main goals in creating this algorithm are to show that although partial centralization involves revealing knowledge in order to solve a shared problem, the knowledge that is exposed can be minimized, obscured, or revealed in an incremental manner. The second goal is to demonstrate that even when constraints are not explicitly revealed, that dynamic, partial centralization still outperforms the AWC-like trial-and-error approach to solving distributed problems.

The rest of this paper is organized as follows. In the next section, we will introduce the distributed constraint satisfaction problem. We will go on to describe the Nogood-APO algorithm, give an example of its execution on a simple problem, and mention the issues of soundness and completeness. We will then present the setup for our experimental evaluation followed by the results. Finally, we will present our conclusions and future work.

2 Distributed Constraint Satisfaction

A Distributed Constraint Satisfaction Problem (DCSP), $P = \langle V, A, D, R \rangle$, consists of the following [16]:

- A set of n variables $V = \{x_1, \ldots, x_n\}$.
- A set of g agents $A = \{a_1, \ldots, a_g\}$
- discrete, finite domains for each of the variables $D = \{D_1, \ldots, D_n\}$.
- a set of constraints $R = \{R_1, \ldots, R_m\}$ where each $R_i(d_{i1}, \ldots, d_{ij})$ is a predicate on the Cartesian product $D_{i1} \times \cdots \times D_{ij}$ that returns true iff the value assignments of the variables satisfies the constraint.

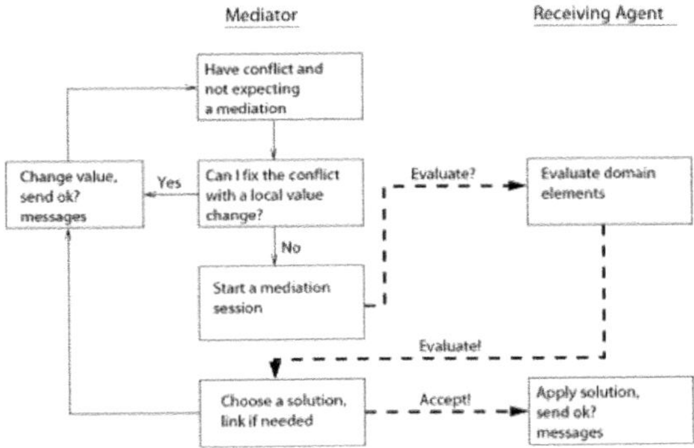

Fig. 1. The basic APO protocol

The problem is to find an assignment $S = \{d_1, \ldots, d_n | d_i \in D_i\}$ such that each of the constraints in R is satisfied. DCSP, like its centralized counterpart CSP, has been shown to be NP-complete, making some form of search a necessity.

In this work, we focus on the case where each agent is assigned a single variable and the constraints are binary. Since each agent is assigned a single variable, we will refer to the agent by the name of the variable it manages. Because the constraints are binary, we can refer to the graph created by representing variables as vertices and constraints as edges as the *constraint graph*. In addition, two variables are considered to be *neighbors* if they share a constraint.

3 The Protocols

3.1 Asynchronous Weak Commitment (AWC)

The Asynchronous Weak Commitment (AWC) protocol is heavily based on its predecessor the Asynchronous Backtracking (ABT) protocol [17]. ABT works by assigning each agent a priority value. These priority values establish an absolute ordering amongst the agents that is used to control the search process. Agents perform the search by sending *value* messages to lower priority agents they are linked with. Value messages inform these lower priority agents about the variable values of higher priority agents. The agents use these values to determine if any of their domain values can satisfy their constraints with higher priority agents. Whenever the values of the higher priority prevent them from assigning their variable a conflict free value, the agent generates a *nogood* message.

Nogoods are composed of a set variable/value pairs that indicate that the combination of the variable assignments cannot be part of a satisfying solution. A nogood can be thought of as an implied constraint. After generating a nogood, it is sent to all the agent that are contained within it. Upon receiving a nogood, agents perform a linking step with any agent that is listed in the nogood and was previously unknown. This step is necessary to ensure the completeness of the search. Initially, the linking structure mirrors the constraint graph, but because of linking as a result of nogoods, can quickly grow causing higher priority agents to send value messages to a large number of agents.

Like centralized backtracking algorithms, the ordering of the agents (variables) in ABT strongly affects the speed of the search. To overcome this problem, Yokoo created the AWC protocol [15]. The AWC algorithm is a variant of the ABT algorithm that allows the agents to re-prioritize themselves using the weak-commitment search heuristic [14]. This heuristic strategy basically says that whenever a backtrack occurs, that variable that triggered the backtrack should be moved up in the search tree. The principle idea behind this technique is to identify variables that are at the center of complex or critical constraints and assign them values first. Their values can then act as constraints on less critical variables instead of the other way around. In practice, this techniques has been shown to be quite effective in reducing the overall runtime of DCSP searches.

A later addition to the AWC protocol was the use of resolvent-based nogood learning [6]. This technique works by selecting, for each of the variable's possible values, one nogood that prohibits that value. These nogood are then merged together to form a new nogood. If the nogoods are selected wisely, they can actually generate smaller, more powerful nogoods.

3.2 Asynchronous Partial Overlay (APO)

Conceptually, APO is based on the *cooperative mediation* paradigm [8]. Cooperative mediation entails three main principles. The first is that agents use local, centralized search to solve portions of the overall problem. Second, agents should use experience to dynamically increase their understanding of their role in the overall problem. Third, agents should overlap the knowledge that they have to promote coherence. Together these three ideas create a powerful paradigm which has been applied to several distributed problems [10,11].

The basic APO algorithm is presented in Figure 1. The APO algorithm works by constructing two main data structures; the *good_list* and the *agent_view*. The *agent_view* holds the names, values, domains, and constraints of variables to which an agent is linked. The *good_list* holds the names of the variables that are known to be connected to the owner by a path in the constraint graph.

As the problem solving unfolds, the agents try to solve the subproblem they have centralized within their *good_list* or determine that this subproblem is unsolvable (indicating that the entire problem is overconstrained). To do this, whenever an agent recognizes a constraint violation involving its variable, it takes the role of the mediator and attempts to change the values of the variables within the mediation session to achieve a satisfied subsystem. When this cannot be achieved without causing a violation for agents outside of the session, the mediator links with those agents assuming that they are somehow related to the mediator's variable. This step increases the size of the *good_list*. This process continues until one of the agents finds an unsatisfiable subsystem, or all of the conflicts have been removed.

Like AWC, agents that use APO have a dynamic priority value that is used to determine which agent mediates when a conflict is detected. Currently, the heuristic for setting this priority value is to use the size of the subproblem that the agent knows. Although one could conceive of a number of other heuristics which optimize different metrics, this particular heuristic was chosen to minimize the number of parallel cycles needed to compute a solution. Benisch and Sadeh, for instance, developed an inverted mediator selection strategy that improves the parallelism of the protocol at the expense of requiring additional communication cycles [1].

When an agent links in APO, the agents exchange the domain values, D_i, and constraints, $\forall R_i\ x_i \in R_i$, on the their variable. In many environments, particular in ones where every agent is trusted and cooperative, the open exchange of this knowledge is quite acceptable and leads to significant improvements in the runtime of the algorithm. However, there are times when directly exchanging this information is impossible due to privacy or security.

3.3 Nogood-APO

The Nogood-APO (NAPO) algorithm is very similar in nature to the APO algorithm. The key difference is that instead of directly exchanging constraints, the agents exchange *nogoods* as part of the problem solving process.

By exchanging nogoods, the agents gain two things. First, because the agents incrementally reveal information, they may not have to reveal all of the details about their constraints in order to solve a problem. This is particular important in domains where the variables have very large domains. The second is that agents can obscure their constraints by padding the most minimal nogood with additional variable/value pairs. By padding them in this way, it is harder for another agent to actually know the details of the constraints, but it slows the execution of the algorithm because it is harder to identify when the problem is unsolvable.

There are several secondary effects of changing the algorithm in this way. The most important is that the agents need to maintain a *nogood list*. Like AWC, the size of the nogood list can grow quite large (exponential in the worst case), especially if agents try to hide their direct constraints by padding their nogoods. However, if the agents are willing to exchange nogoods that are directly derived from their constraints, the size of the nogood list becomes quite manageable being directly related to the number and complexity of the constraints as opposed to the number of possible assignments to the variables.

Initialization. Like APO, on startup, the agents are provided with the value (they pick it randomly if one isn't assigned) and the constraints on their variable. Using these constraints, the agents derived their direct nogoods and place them in their nogood lists. Unlike APO however, initialization proceeds by having each of the agents send out an "ok?" message to its neighbors. The content of this message is considerably different from the "ok?" messages in APO. In NAPO, the agents send their current priority, the value of their variable, their variable's current domain, and the current set of violated nogoods from their nogood list that involve their variable.

Agents send their domain values as part of the "ok?" message because it ensures that the mediator always has the current set of allowable values for the variables in its good_list. This is particularly important if an agent calculates that one of its values is not arc-consistent. This can be thought of as the agent deriving a unary nogood which disallows one of its variable's values.

The "ok?" message also includes the set of currently violated nogoods that include the agent's variable. There are two reasons for including this information. First, when this set is empty, it indicates that the agent does not wish to mediate. Second, as will be illustrated later, this information is used to ensure that mediators are informed of inadvertent nogood violations that result from changing the values of multiple variables in a session without knowing that they are related to one another.

When an agent receives an "ok?" message (either during the initialization, through a later link request, or as a state update), it records the information in its agent_view and adds the variable to the good_list if it can. A variable is only added to the good_list if it shares a nogood with a variable that is already in the list. This restriction ensures that the graph created by the variables in the good_list always remains connected.

Checking the agent view. Whenever the agent receives a message that indicates a possible change to the status of its variable, it checks the current agent_view (which contains the assigned, known variable values) to identify violated nogoods. If, during this check, an agent finds a violation and has not been told by a higher priority agent that they want to mediate, it assumes the role of the mediator.

As the mediator, an agent first attempts to rectify the violation(s) by changing its own variable. This simple, but effective technique prevents sessions from occurring unnecessarily, which stabilizes the system and saves messages and time. If the mediator finds a value that removes the violations, it makes the change and sends out an "ok?" message to the agents in its agent_view. If it cannot find a non-conflicting value (it's at a deadend), it starts a mediation session.

Mediation. The most complex and certainly most interesting part of the protocol is the mediation. The mediation starts with the mediator sending out "evaluate?" messages to each of the agents in its good_list. The purpose of this message is two-fold. First, it informs the receiving agent that a mediation is about to begin and tries to obtain a lock from that agent. This lock prevents the agent from engaging in two sessions simultaneously or from doing a local value change during the course of a session. The second purpose of the message is to obtain information from the agent about the effects of making them change their local value. This is a key point.

When an agent receives a mediation request, it will respond with either a "wait!" or "evaluate!" message. The "wait" message indicates to the requester that the agent is currently involved in a session with a higher priority agent or is expecting a request from an higher priority agent. If the agent is available, it

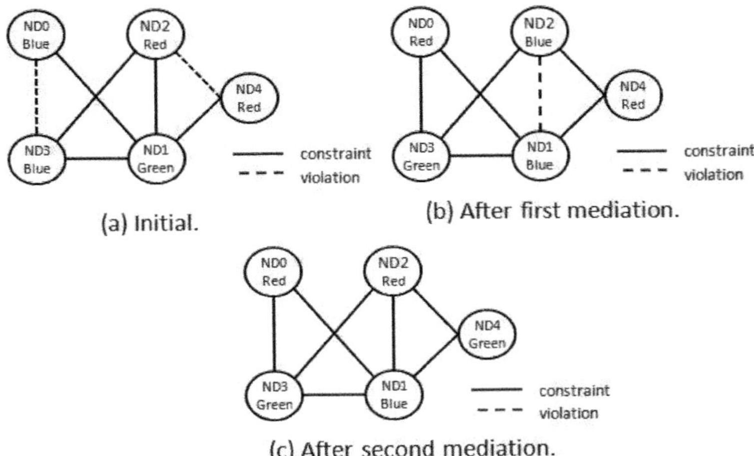

Fig. 2. Example 3-coloring problem with 5 variables and 7 not-equals constraints

labels each of its domain elements with the nogoods that would be violated if it were asked to take that value which is returned in an "evaluate!" message.

When the mediator has received either a "wait!" or "evaluate!" message from all of the agents that it has sent a request to, it computes a solution using a Branch and Bound search [3]. The goal of the search is to find a conflict-free solution for the variables in the session and to minimize the number of conflicts for variables outside the session (like the min-conflict heuristic [13]). During this search, new nogoods can be derived using nogood learning [4]. These nogoods are recorded in the nogood list and can be used during subsequent searches to prune the search space.

If no satisfying assignments are found, the agent announces that the problem is unsatisfiable and the algorithm terminates. If a solution is found, "accept!" messages are sent to the agents in the session and "ok?" messages are sent to the agents that are in its agent_view, but, for whatever reason, were not in the session, and to any agent that is not in its agent_view, but it caused conflict for as a result of selecting its solution.

3.4 Example Execution

Consider the 3-coloring problem in Figure 2a. In this problem there are 5 variables, each assigned to an agent and 7 constraints which represent the "not equals" predicate. Being a 3-coloring problem, the variables can only take the value red, green, or blue. There are currently two constraint violations, between ND2 and ND4 and between ND0 and ND3.

On initialization, each of the agents adds nogoods to their nogood lists for the constraints that they have on their variable. They then send "ok?" messages to the agents with whom they share constraints (their neighbors).

Once the initialization has completed, each of the agents checks its *agent_view* to determine if its variable is involved in a violation. In this case, ND0, ND2, ND3, and ND4 determine that have a conflict. Because of the priority ordering, ND4 (priority 3) waits for ND2 (priority 4) to mediate. ND0 (priority 3) and ND2 wait for ND3 (priority 3 tie broken by name). ND3, knowing it is higher priority than ND0 and ND2, first checks to see if it can resolve its conflicts by changing its value, which it can't. It then starts a mediation session and sends "evaluate?" messages to ND0, ND1, and ND2.

Upon receiving the "evaluate?" messages, ND0, ND1, and ND2 evaluate their domain elements to identify the nogoods that would be violated by each of them. This information is then returned to ND3 in an "evaluate!" message. The following are the labeled domains for the agents in the session with ND3:

- ND0
  Green violates (ND0=G,ND1=G)
  Blue violates (ND0=B,ND3=B)
  Red causes no violations
- ND1
  Green cause no violations
  Blue violates (ND1=B,ND0=B) and (ND1=B,ND3=B)
  Red violates (ND1=R,ND2=R) and (ND1=R,ND4=R)
- ND2
  Green violates (ND2=G,ND1=G)
  Blue violates (ND2=B,ND3=B)
  Red violates (ND2=R,ND4=R)

ND3 computes a solution that changes the values of all of the variables in the session (see Figure 2b). Based on the information that ND3 obtained from the "evaluate!" messages, it believes that this solution solves its subproblem and causes no conflicts for agents outside of the session. ND3 sends "accept!" message to the agents in the session.

After receiving the "accept" messages, each agent changes its value and checks its agent_view. This time, ND1 and ND2 are in conflict. This happened because ND3 changing their values to blue, inadvertently causing the violation. To prevent this from happening again, the "ok?" messages that are sent by ND1 and ND2 include their current conflict set. This allows ND3 to learn of the relationship between ND2 and ND1 so it doesn't repeat the same error.

ND1, the higher priority (priority 5) agent, cannot solve the conflict by making a local value change, so it starts a mediation session. Below are the responses to the "evaluate?" messages sent by ND1:

- ND0
  Green violates (ND0=G,ND3=G)
  Blue violates (ND0=B,ND1=B)
  Red causes no violations
- ND2
  Green violates (ND2=G,ND3=G)
  Blue violates (ND2=B,ND1=B)
  Red violates (ND2=R,ND4=R)

- ND3
  Green causes no violations
  Blue violates (ND3=B,ND1=B)and (ND3=B,ND2=B);
  Red violates (ND3=R,ND0=R)
- ND4
  Green causes no violations
  Blue violates (ND4=B,ND2=B)and (ND4=B,ND1=B)
  Red causes no violations

ND1 computes a solution which changes its value to green and ND2's to red and sends "accept!" messages. All of the agent's check their agent_view and find no conflicts so the problem is solved (Figure 2c).

3.5 Soundness and Completeness

The soundness and completeness of the NAPO algorithm are derived directly from the soundness and completeness of APO. We refer the reader to [9] and [5] for the complete details of the proofs for APO. Here is a basic outline of the proof for NAPO:

- If at anytime an agent identifies a constraint subgraph that is not satisfiable, it announces that the problem cannot be solved. Half of the soundness.
- If a nogood is violated, someone will try to fix it. The protocol is dead-lock and live-lock free. The other half of the soundness proof.
- Eventually, in the worst case, one or more of the agents will centralize the entire problem and will derive a solution, or report that no solution exists. This is done by collecting nogoods from both "evaluate!" messages and "ok?" messages. This ensures completeness.

4 Empirical Evaluation

4.1 Experimental Setup

To test the NAPO algorithm, we implemented the AWC, APO, and NAPO algorithms and conducted experiments in the distributed 3-coloring domain. The particular AWC algorithm we implemented can be found in [18] which includes the resolvent *nogood* learning mechanism described in [6]. We conducted two sets of experiments.

In the first set of experiments we compared the algorithms using 30 variable, randomly generated graph coloring problems while varying the edge densities across the known phase transition for 3-coloring problems [2]. In the second set of experiments, we tested the scalability of the algorithms by varying the size of the problems from 15 to 60 variables in the three major regions of the phase transition. Each data point represents an average over 30 randomly generated problems. Each algorithm was given the same problems with the same initial

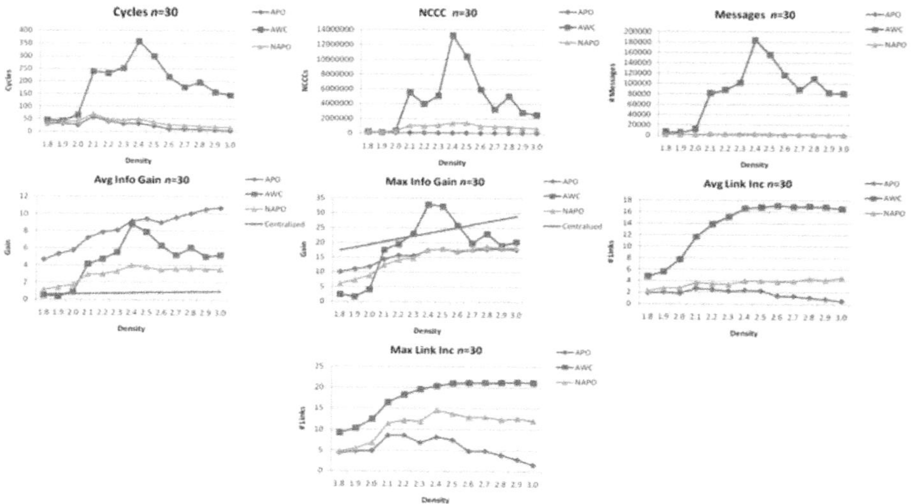

Fig. 3. Phase transition results for 30 node graphs of various density

variable assignments to minimize variance. The algorithms were allowed to run for up to 1,000 cycles. This upper limit only affected the AWC protocol, which frequently could not finish on larger, higher density problems. A total of 2,250 test runs were conducted.

During these tests we measured the number of messages, cycles, and non-concurrent constraint checks (NCCCs) [12] used by the algorithms. During a cycle, incoming messages are delivered, the agent is allowed to process the information, and any messages that were created during the processing are added to the outgoing queue to be delivered at the beginning of the next cycle. The actual execution time given to one agent during a cycle varies according to the amount of work needed to process all of the incoming messages. We also instrumented the algorithms to measure the number of non-concurrent constraint checks used during each cycle. This measure has gained popularity in the DCSP community because it provides an implementation independent view of the parallel computation usage of a protocol.

In addition to these standard measures of computation and communication cost, we also gathered data to quantify the information that the agents revealed to one another during the problem solving process. One measure we used was to count the number of links that the protocols created during execution. This metric provides insight into "who" the agents send information to in order to solve the problem. We also wanted to measure "what" and how much information was being sent. To do this we used the following measure of information gain:

$$gain(a_i) = \sum_{ng \in nogoods-rcvd_i} \frac{1}{|D_i|^{|ng|}} \tag{1}$$

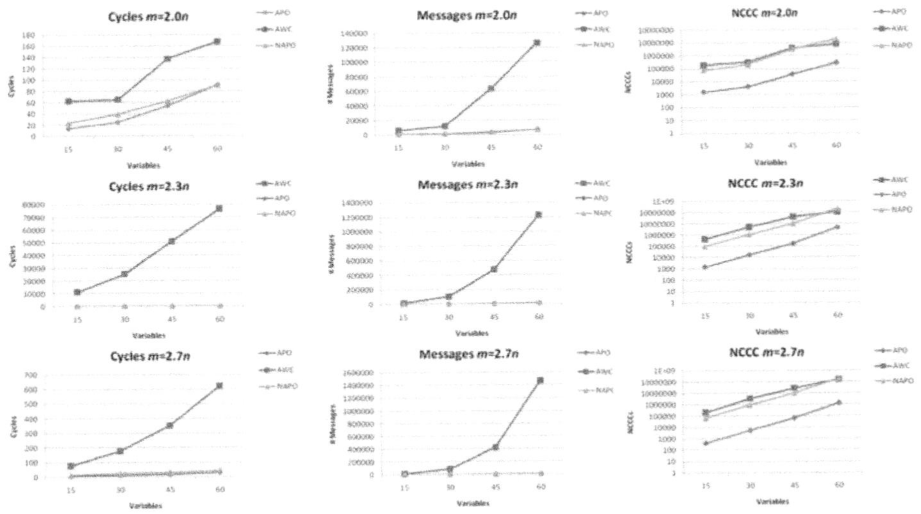

Fig. 4. Scalability cost results for AWC, APO, and NAPO

where a_i is an agent, $nogoods - rcvd_i$ is the set of unique nogoods that have been received from other agents by a_i, $|D_i|$, is the size of the domain, and $|ng|$ is the size of an individual nogood based on the number of variable/value pairs it contains. The logic behind this equation is that the power of a nogood can be measured based on the number of potential solutions that it invalidates in the search space. Shorter nogoods are more powerful because they are more general and eliminate a larger number of value combinations. This metric is similar to the Value of Possible States (VPS) metric developed by Meheswaran et al. [7]. For both of these metrics we determined the average across the agents, measuring the distribution of information gain, as well as the maximum value for any single agent, measuring the amount of centralization.

To provide a frame of reference, we also included data for the average and maximum information gain had the agents elected a leader and centralized the problem. The centralized maximum and average information gain can easily be computed as:

$$max\_gain(a) = \frac{m(n-1)}{n * |D_i|} \tag{2}$$

$$avg\_gain(a) = \frac{max\_gain(a)}{n} \tag{3}$$

4.2 Results

The result of the phase transition experiments can be seen in Figure 3. These graphs show that AWC outperforms both APO and NAPO on very sparse

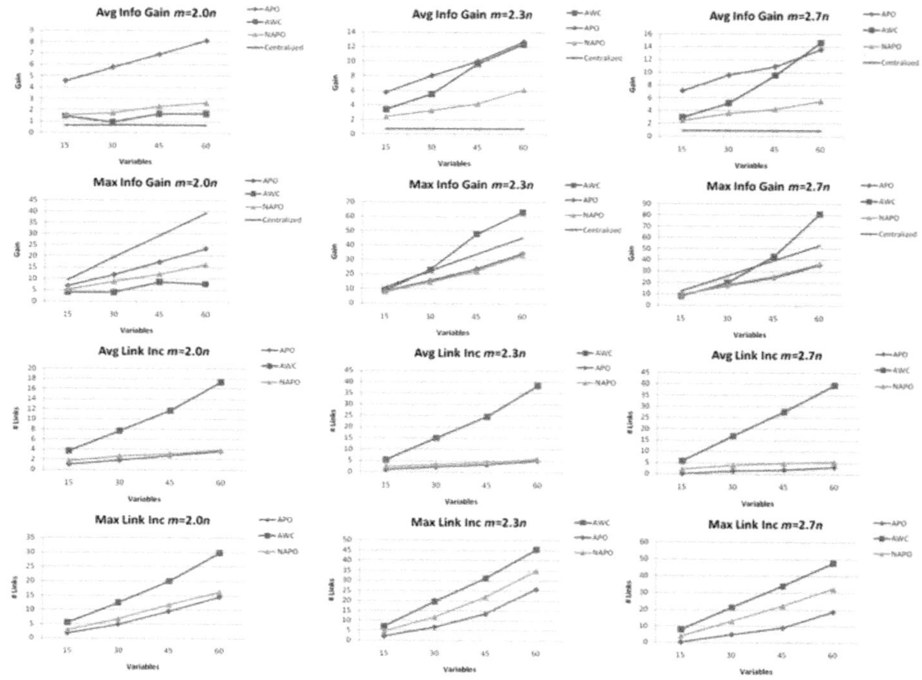

Fig. 5. Scalability information results for AWC, APO, and NAPO

problems, but on problems at or above the phase transition, the story is quite different. APO uses the least number of NCCCs, cycles, and messages with NAPO using slightly more. These results seem to contradict the findings of presented by Grinshpoun and Meisels [5] who reported that APO used more NCCCs on medium density problems across various levels of constraint tightness. The discrepancy between these results can likely be explained by the difference in the experiments that were conducted. Grinshpoun and Meisels used general CSP instances where the variables have large domains ($|D_i| = 10$) as opposed to the small domain of the variables ($|D_i| = 3$) and fixed tightness of the constraints ($p_2 = 0.33$) in 3-coloring. The large domains create equally large branching factors that severely impact the branch and bound solver used at the core of APO.

When looking at the results for information exchange, the nature of the protocols becomes apparent. APO, which uses explicit constraint passing, has the worse average information exchange across the entire transition, centralizes about 50% of the problem within a single agent, but creates the least number of new links. NAPO has the lowest average information gain, is equivalent to APO in the amount of information centralized in a single agent, and produces more links than APO. This can be interpreted as meaning that NAPO centralizes as much as APO, but does it in a more intelligent manner. AWC has the least average information gain on very sparse problems, but within the phase transition performs worse than NAPO and actually approaches APO. AWC has very minimal centralization on sparse problems, but as the density increases, the agent with the maximum information gain actually gets more information than if the problem had just been completely centralized. At first, this doesn't appear to make sense, but AWC agents not only send original constraints, they also send implied constraints. So the agent with the maximum information gain is not only being told the other agents' constraints, it is being told about constraints that are learned by the other agents as well. AWC also creates more links meaning that agents are exchanging information with more of their peers than APO and NAPO

The results of the scalability experiments can be seen in Figures 4 and 5. The results for the cost metrics are as expected with APO using the least cycles, communication, and NCCCs of the three protocols. The protocol cost for NAPO is somewhere between APO and AWC. In the NCCCs category it appears that AWC and NAPO are competitive. However, one should keep in mind that many of the AWC runs did not actually complete on the 60 node test cases because they did not find a solution within 1,000 cycles. So the results for AWC in these graphs are skewed toward being lower than they actually are.

The results for scalability of information gain also present some interesting findings. They show that on sparse problem, both AWC and NAPO have less average information gain than APO. However, on denser problems, AWC becomes less scalable having a rapid increase in average information gain that exceeds even APO. The same trend holds true when looking at maximum information gain. AWC is dominate on sparse problems, but on dense examples has poor scalability. APO performs best overall in the number of new links it creates, with NAPO in the middle and AWC creating the most links.

The take-home message from these experiments are not directly straightforward, but can be summarized as follows:

- On sparse 3-coloring problems, the AWC protocol exchanges the least amount of information in order to compute a solution, but takes more cycles, uses more messages, creates more links, and performs more NCCCs than APO.
- On dense 3-coloring problems, AWC exchanges more information, to more agents, uses more cycles, more messages, and more NCCCs than either NAPO or APO.
- If you are solely concerned about speed then APO is your best choice.
- If you are willing to trade speed for privacy than NAPO is the best choice on everything except very sparse problems.
- The speedups associated with partial centralization cannot be directly attributed to explicit constraint passing alone. Even when nogoods are exchanged, the algorithm performs as well or better than the distributed backtracking-based search.

5 Conclusions and Future Work

In this paper, we presented a new hybrid AWC/APO algorithm called Nogood-APO. As was shown in experimentation, this algorithm, like APO, outperform

AWC on all but the simplest 3-coloring problems across various size and density on several metrics. By creating this algorithm, we showed that constraint passing is not necessary in an algorithm that is based on dynamic, partial centralization and that the likely reason why algorithms like APO outperform AWC is the combination of distributed/centralized search techniques they use.

A number of questions are raised as a result of this work. First, and foremost, it revives the competition between DCSP algorithms that are based on partial centralization and distributed backtracking because for the first time, we have examples that are designed using the same basic assumptions. It also identifies another dimension for doing scalability experiments, namely the size of the variable's domains. As these results indicate, on problems that have variables with small domains, the performance characteristics AWC and APO are quite different then they are on domains with larger domains. This may point to areas for improvement in both of these protocols.

Acknowledgement. The authors gratefully acknowledge support of the Defense Advanced Research Projects Agency under DARPA grants HR0011-07-C-0060. Views and conclusions contained in this document are those of the authors and do not necessarily represent the official opinion or policies, either expressed or implied of the US government or of DARPA.

References

1. Benisch, M., Sadeh, N.: Examining distributed constraint satisfaction problem (dcsp) coordination tradeoffs. In: International Conference on Automated Agents and Multi-Agent Systems, AAMAS (2006)
2. Culberson, J., Gent, I.: Frozen development in graph coloring. Theoretical Computer Science 265(1-2), 227–264 (2001)
3. Freuder, E.C., Wallace, R.J.: Partial constraint satisfaction. Artificial Intelligence 58(1-3), 21–70 (1992)
4. Frost, D., Dechter, R.: Dead-end driven learning. In: Proceedings of the Twelfth Natioanl Conference on Artificial Intelligence, pp. 294–300 (1994)
5. Grinshpoun, T., Meisels, A.: Completeness and performance of the apo algorithm. Journal of Artificial Intelligence Research 33, 223–258 (2008)
6. Hirayama, K., Yokoo, M.: The effect of nogood learning in distributed constraint satisfaction. In: The 20th International Conference on Distributed Computing Systems (ICDCS), pp. 169–177 (2000)
7. Maheswaran, R.T., Pearce, J.P., Varakantham, P., Bowring, E., Tambe, M.: Valuations of possible states (vps):a quantitative framework for analysis of privacy loss among collaborative personal assistant agents. In: Proceeding of Autonomous Agents and Multi-Agents Systems (2005)
8. Mailler, Lesser: Asynchronous partial overlay: A new algorithm for solving distributed constraint satisfaction problems. Journal of Artificial Intelligence Research 25, 529–576 (2006)
9. Mailler, R.: A Mediation-Based Approach to Cooperative, Distributed Problem Solving. PhD thesis, University of Massachusetts (2004)
10. Mailler, R., Lesser, V.: Solving distributed constraint optimization problems using cooperative mediation. In: Proceeding of AAMAS-2004, pp. 438–445 (2004)

11. Mailler, R., Lesser, V.: A cooperative mediation-based protocol for dynamic, distributed resource allocation. IEEE Transaction on Systems, Man, and Cybernetics, Part C, Special Issue on Game-theoretic Analysis and Stochastic Simulation of Negotiation Agents (2006)
12. Meisels, A., Razgon, I., Kaplansky, E., Zivan, R.: Comparing performance of distributed constraints processing algorithms. In: Proc. AAMAS-2002 Workshop on Distributed Constraint Reasoning DCR, pp. 86–93 (2002)
13. Minton, S., Johnston, M.D., Philips, A.B., Laird, P.: Minimizing conflicts: A heuristic repair method for constraint satisfaction and scheduling problems. Artificial Intelligence 58(1-3), 161–205 (1992)
14. Yokoo, M.: Weak-commitment search for solving constraint satisfaction problems. In: Proceedings of the 12th National Conference on Artificial Intelligence (AAAI-1994), Seattle, WA, USA, vol, July 31-August 4, vol. 1, pp. 313–318. AAAI Press (1994)
15. Yokoo, M.: Asynchronous weak-commitment search for solving distributed constraint satisfaction problems. In: Int'l Conf. on Principles and Practice of Constraint Programming, pp. 88–102 (1995)
16. Yokoo, M., Durfee, E.H.: Distributed constraint optimization as a formal model of partially adversarial cooperation. Technical Report CSE-TR-101-91, University of Michigan, Ann Arbor, MI 48109 (1991)
17. Yokoo, M., Durfee, E.H., Ishida, T., Kuwabara, K.: Distributed constraint satisfaction for formalizing distributed problem solving. In: Proceedings of the 12th Int'l Conf. on Distributed Computing Systems, pp. 614–621 (1992)
18. Yokoo, M., Hirayama, K.: Algorithms for distributed constraint satisfaction: A review. Autonomous Agents and Multi-Agent Systems 3(2), 198–212 (2000)

A Distributed Task Specification Language for Mixed-Initiative Delegation*

Patrick Doherty, Fredrik Heintz, and David Landén

Dept. of Computer and Information Science, Linköping University, Sweden
{patrick.doherty,fredrik.heintz,david.landen}@liu.se

Abstract. In the next decades, practically viable robotic/agent systems are going to be mixed-initiative in nature. Humans will request help from such systems and such systems will request help from humans in achieving the complex mission tasks required. Pragmatically, one requires a distributed task specification language to define tasks and a suitable data structure which satisfies the specification and can be used flexibly by collaborative multi-agent/robotic systems. This paper defines such a task specification language and an abstract data structure called Task Specification Trees which has many of the requisite properties required for mixed-initiative problem solving and adjustable autonomy in a distributed context. A prototype system has been implemented for this delegation framework and has been used practically with collaborative unmanned aircraft systems.

1 Introduction

In the past decade, the Unmanned Aircraft Systems Technologies Lab[1] at the Department of Computer and Information Science, Linköping University, has been involved in the development of autonomous unmanned aircraft systems (UAS's) and associated hardware and software technologies (7). The size of our research platforms range from the RMAX helicopter system (100kg) (4, 8, 23) developed by Yamaha Motor Company, to smaller micro-size rotor based systems such as the LinkQuad[2] (1kg) and LinkMAV (10, 20) (500g) in addition to a fixed wing platform, the PingWing (5) (500g). These UAS platforms are shown in Figure 1. The latter three have been designed and developed by the Unmanned Aircraft Systems Technologies Lab. All four platforms are fully autonomous and have been deployed.

Previous work has focused on the development of robust autonomous systems for UAS's which seamlessly integrate control, reactive and deliberative capabilities that meet the requirements of hard and soft real-time constraints (8, 18). More recently, our research efforts have begun to focus on applications where UAS's with heterogeneous

* This work is partially supported by grants from the Swedish Foundation for Strategic Research (SSF) Strategic Research Center MOVIII, the Swedish Research Council (VR), the VR Linnaeus Center CADICS, the ELLIIT Excellence Center at Linköping-Lund for Information Technology, and the Center for Industrial Information Technology CENIIT.

[1] www.ida.liu.se/divisions/aiics

[2] www.uastech.com

N. Desai, A. Liu, and M. Winikoff (Eds.): PRIMA 2010, LNAI 7057, pp. 42–57, 2012.

Fig. 1. The UASTech RMAX (upper left), PingWing (upper right), LinkQuad (lower left) and LinkMAV (lower right)

unmanned aircraft are required to collaborate not only with each other but also with diverse human resources (9).

As UAS's become more autonomous, mixed-initiative interaction between human operators and such systems will be central in mission planning and tasking. In the near future, the practical use and acceptance of UAS's will have to be based on a verifiable, principled and well-defined interaction foundation between one or more human operators and one or more autonomous systems. In developing a principled framework for such complex interaction between UAS's and humans in complex scenarios, a great many interdependent conceptual and pragmatic issues arise and need clarification both theoretically, but also pragmatically in the form of demonstrators.

In our current research, we have targeted a triad of fundamental, interdependent conceptual issues: delegation, mixed-initiative interaction and adjustable autonomy. The triad of concepts is being used as a basis for developing a principled and well-defined framework for interaction that can be used to clarify, validate and verify different types of interaction between human operators and UAS's both theoretically and practically in experimentation with our deployed platforms. The concept of delegation is particularly important and in some sense provides a bridge between mixed-initiative interaction and adjustable autonomy.

Delegation – In any mixed-initiative interaction, humans may request help from robotic systems and robotic systems may request help from humans. One can abstract and concisely model such requests as a form of delegation, $Delegate(A, B, task, constraints)$, where A is the delegating agent, B is the contractor, $task$ is the task being delegated and consists of a goal and possibly a plan to achieve the goal, and $constraints$ represents a context in which the request is made and the task should be carried out. In our framework, delegation is formalized as a speech act and the delegation process invoked can be recursive.

Adjustable Autonomy – In solving tasks in a mixed-initiative setting, the robotic system involved will have a potentially wide spectrum of autonomy, yet should only use as much autonomy as is required for a task and should not violate the degree of autonomy mandated by a human operator unless agreement is made. One can begin to develop a principled means of adjusting autonomy through the use of the $task$ and $constraint$ parameters in $Delegate(A, B, task, constraints)$. A task delegated with only a goal and no plan, with few constraints, allows the robot to use much of its autonomy in solving the task, whereas a task specified as a sequence of actions and many constraints allows only limited autonomy. It may even be the case that the delegator does not allow the contractor to recursively delegate.

Mixed-Initiative Interaction – By mixed-initiative, we mean that interaction and negotiation between a robotic system, such as an unmanned aerial vehicle (UAV) and a human, will take advantage of each of their skills, capacities and knowledge in developing a mission plan, executing the plan and adapting to contingencies during the execution of the plan. Mixed-initiative interaction involves a very broad set of issues, both theoretical and pragmatic. One central part of such interaction is the ability of a ground operator (GOP) to be able to delegate tasks to a UAV, $Delegate(GOP, UAV, task, constraints)$ and in a symmetric manner, the ability of a UAV to be able to delegate tasks to a GOP, $Delegate(UAV, GOP, task, constraints)$. Issues pertaining to safety, security, trust, etc., have to be dealt with in the interaction process and can be formalized as particular types of constraints associated with a delegated task.

An important conceptual and pragmatic issue which is central to the three concepts and their theoretical and pragmatic integration is that of a task and its representation and semantics in practical systems. The task representation must be highly flexible, distributed and dynamic. Tasks need to be delegated at varying levels of abstraction and also expanded and modified as parts of tasks are recursively delegated to different UAS agents. Consequently, the structure must also be distributable. Additionally, a task structure is a form of compromise between a compiled plan at one end of the spectrum and a plan generated through an automated planner (14, 15) at the other end of the spectrum. The task representation and semantics must seamlessly accommodate plan representations and their compilation into the task structure. Finally, the task representation should support the adjustment of autonomy through the addition of constraints or parameters by agents and human resources.

Paper Structure: The first part of the paper sets the broader context by providing a short summary in Section 2 of a formal delegation framework based on the use of speech acts in addition to a short summary about the pragmatics of implementing such a system in a UAS in Section 3. The second part of the paper described in Section 4 is specifically about task specification and provides details about task representation and semantics through the use of Task Specification Trees. This section also provides an example. The paper then concludes with related work and conclusions.

2 Semantic Perspective

In (1, 12), Falcone & Castelfranchi provide an illuminating, but informal discussion about delegation as a concept from a social perspective. Their approach to delegation builds on a BDI model of agents, that is, agents having beliefs, goals, intentions, and plans (2), but the specification lacks a formal semantics for the operators used. Based on intuitions from their work, we have previously provided a formal characterization of their concept of strong delegation using a communicative speech act with pre- and post-conditions which update the belief states associated with the delegator and contractor, respectively (9). In order to formally characterize the operators used in the definition of the speech act, we use KARO (13) to provide a formal semantics. The KARO formalism is an amalgam of dynamic logic and epistemic / doxastic logic, augmented with several additional (modal) operators in order to deal with the motivational aspects of agents.

First, we define the notion of a task as a pair consisting of a goal and a plan for that goal, or rather, a plan and the goal associated with that plan. Paraphrasing Falcone & Castelfranchi into KARO terms, we consider a notion of strong delegation represented by a speech act $S\text{-}Delegate(A, B, \tau)$ of A delegating a task $\tau = (\alpha, \phi)$ to B, where α is a possible plan and ϕ is a goal.

Preconditions:

(1) $Goal_A(\phi)$
(2) $Bel_A Can_B(\tau)$ (Note that this implies $Bel_A Bel_B(Can_B(\tau))$)
(3) $Bel_A(Dependent(A, B, \tau))$
(4) $Bel_B Can_B(\tau)$

Postconditions:

(1) $Goal_B(\phi)$ and $Bel_B Goal_B(\phi)$
(2) $Committed_B(\alpha)$ (also written $Committed_B(\tau)$)
(3) $Bel_B Goal_A(\phi)$
(4) $Can_B(\tau)$ (and hence $Bel_B Can_B(\tau)$, and by (1) also $Intend_B(\tau)$)
(5) $Intend_A(do_B(\alpha))$
(6) $MutualBel_{AB}$("the statements above" $\wedge$ $SociallyCommitted(B, A, \tau)$)[3]

Informally speaking this expresses the following: the preconditions of the delegate act of A delegating task τ to B are that (1) ϕ is a goal of delegator A (2) A believes that B can (is able to) perform the task τ (which implies that A believes that B itself believes that it can do the task) (3) A believes that with respect to the task τ it is dependent on B. The speech act S-Delegate is a communication command and can be viewed as a request for a synchronization (a "handshake") between sender and receiver. Of course, this can only be successful if the receiver also believes it can do the task, which is expressed by (4).

The postconditions of the strong delegation act mean: (1) B has ϕ as its goal and is aware of this (2) it is committed to the task τ (3) B believes that A has the goal ϕ (4) B can do the task τ (and hence believes it can do it, and furthermore it holds that B intends to do the task, which was a separate condition in Falcone & Castelfranchi's formalization), (5) A intends that B performs α (so we have formalized the notion of a goal to have an acheivement in Falcone & Castelfranchi's informal theory to an intention to perform a task) and (6) there is a mutual belief between A and B that all preconditions and other postconditions mentioned hold, as well as that there is a contract between A

[3] A discussion pertaining to the semantics of non-KARO modal operators may be found in (9).

and B, i.e. B is socially committed to A to achieve τ for A. In this situation we will call agent A the *delegator* and B the *contractor*.

Typically a social commitment (contract) between two agents induces obligations to the partners involved, depending on how the task is specified in the delegation action. This dimension has to be added in order to consider how the contract affects the autonomy of the agents, in particular the contractor's autonomy. Falcone & Castelfranchi discuss the following variants:

- Closed delegation: the task is completely specified and both the goal and the plan should be adhered to.
- Open delegation: the task is not completely specified, either only the goal has to be adhered to while the plan may be chosen by the contractor, or the specified plan contains abstract actions that need further elaboration (a sub-plan) to be dealt with by the contractor.

In open delegation the contractor may have some freedom in how to perform the delegated task, and thus it provides a large degree of flexibility in multi-agent planning and allows for truly distributed planning.

The specification of the delegation act above is based on closed delegation. In case of open delegation, α in the postconditions can be replaced by an α', and τ by $\tau' = (\alpha', \phi)$. Note that the fourth clause, $Can_B(\tau')$, now implies that α' is indeed believed to be an alternative for achieving ϕ, since it implies that $Bel_B[\alpha']\phi$ (B believes that ϕ is true after α' is executed). Of course, in the delegation process, A must agree that α' is indeed viable. This would depend on what degree of autonomy is allowed.

This particular specification of delegation follows Falcone & Castelfranchi closely. One can easily foresee other constraints one might add or relax in respect to the basic specification resulting in other variants of delegation (3, 6). In (9), we also provide an instantiation of the framework using 2APL, a popular agent programming language.

3 Pragmatic Perspective

From a semantic perspective, delegation as a speech act provides us with conceptual insight and an abstract specification which can be used as a basis for a more pragmatic implementation on actual UAS platforms. There is a large gap between semantics and pragmatics which one would like to reduce in a principled manner. To do this, we have chosen to also work from a bottom-up perspective and have developed a prototype software system that implements the delegation framework using a JADE-based architecture specified in the next section. This system has been tested using a number of complex collaborative scenarios described in (15, 19).

One particularly interesting result of approaching the complex characterization of delegation from a top-down abstract semantic perspective and a bottom-up implementation perspective is that one can ground the semantic insights into the implementation in a very direct manner. A central component in the speech-act based characterization of delegation is the use of $Can()$ in the pre-conditions to the speech act. It turns out that verifying the truth of the $Can()$ pre-conditions becomes equivalent to checking the satisfiability of a distributed constraint network generated through recursive calls to the delegation operator in the implementation. This will be shown in Section 4.

3.1 An Agent-Based UAS Architecture

Our RMAX UAV's use a CORBA-based distributed architecture (8). For our experimentation with collaborative UAS's, we view this as a legacy system and extend it with what is conceptually an additional outer layer in order to leverage the functionality of JADE (11). "JADE (Java Agent Development Framework) is a software environment to build agent systems for the management of networked information resources in compliance with the FIPA specifications for interoperable multi-agent systems." (11). The reason for using JADE is pragmatic. Our formal characterization of the *Delegate()* operator is as a speech act. We also use speech acts for agent communication and JADE provides a straightforward means for integrating the FIPA ACL language which supports speech acts with our existing systems. The outer layer may be viewed as a collection of JADE agents that interface to the legacy system. We are currently using four agents in the outer layer:

1. **Interface agent** - This agent is the clearinghouse for communication. All requests for delegation and other types of communication pass through this agent. Externally, it provides the interface to a specific robotic system or ground control station.
2. **Delegation agent**- The delegation agent coordinates delegation requests to and from other robotic systems and ground control stations, with the Execution, Resource and Interface agents. It does this essentially by verifying that the pre-conditions to a $Delegate()$ request are satisfied.
3. **Execution agent** - After a task is contracted to a particular robotic system or ground station operator, it must eventually execute that task relative to the constraints associated with it. The Execution agent coordinates this execution process.
4. **Resource agent** - The Resource agent determines whether the robotic system or ground station of which it is part has the resources and ability to actually do a task as a potential contractor. Such a determination may include the invocation of schedulers, planners and constraint solvers in order to determine this.

A prototype implementation of this system has been tested both in the field with RMAX UAV's and in-the-loop simulation.

4 Task Specification Trees

Both the declarative and procedural representation and semantics of tasks are central to the delegation process. The relation between the two representations is also essential if one has the goal of formally grounding the delegation process in the system implementation. A task was previously defined abstractly as a pair (α, ϕ) consisting of a composite action α and a goal ϕ. In this section, we introduce a formal task specification language which allows us to represent tasks as *Task Specification Trees* (TST's). The task specification trees map directly to procedural representations in our proposed system implementation.

For our purposes, the task representation must be highly flexible, sharable, dynamically extendible, and distributed in nature. Tasks need to be delegated at varying levels of abstraction and also expanded and modified because parts of complex tasks can be recursively delegated to different robotic agents which are in turn expanded or modified. Consequently, the structure must also be distributable. Additionally, a task structure is a form of compromise between an explicit plan in a plan library at one end of the spectrum and a plan generated through an automated planner (14, 15) at the other end of the spectrum. The task representation and semantics must seamlessly accommodate plan representations and their compilation into the task structure. Finally, the task representation should support the adjustment of autonomy through the addition of constraints or parameters by agents and human resources.

The flexibility allows for the use of both central and distributed planning, and also to move along the scale between these two extremes. At one extreme, the operator plans everything, creating a central plan, while at the other extreme the agents are delegated goals and generate parts of the distributed plan themselves. Sometimes neither completely centralized nor completely distributed planning is appropriate. In those cases the operator would like to retain some control of how the work is done while leaving the details to the agents. Task Specification Trees provide a formalism that captures the scale from one extreme to the next. This allows the operator to specify the task at the point which fits the current mission and environment.

The task specification formalism should allow for the specification of various types of task compositions, including sequential and concurrent, in addition to more general constructs such as loops and conditionals. The task specification should also provide a clear separation between tasks and platform specific details for handling the tasks. The specification should focus on what should be done and hide the details about how it could be done by different platforms.

In the general case, A TST is a declarative representation of a complex multi-agent task. In the architecture realizing the delegation framework a TST is also a distributed data structure. Each node in a TST corresponds to a task that should be performed. There are six types of nodes: sequence, concurrent, loop, select, goal, and elementary action. All nodes are directly executable except goal nodes which require some form of expansion or planning to generate a plan for achieving the goal.

Each node has a *node interface* containing a set of parameters, called *node parameters*, that can be specified for the node. The node interface always contains a platform assignment parameter and parameters for the start and end times of the task, usually denoted P, T_S and T_E, respectively. These parameters can be part of the constraints associated with the node called *node constraints*. A TST also has *tree constraints*, expressing precedence and organizational relations between the nodes in the TST. Together the constraints form a constraint network covering the TST. In fact, the node parameters function as constraint variables in a constraint network, and setting the value of a node parameter constrains not only the network, but implicitly, the degree of autonomy of an agent.

4.1 TST Syntax

The syntax of a TST specification has the following BNF:

TST ::= NAME ('(' VARS ')')? '=' (**with** VARS)? TASK (**where** CONS)?
TSTS ::= TST | TST ';' TSTS

TASK ::= <elementary action> | <goal> | **sequence** TSTS | **concurrent** TSTS
| **while** <cond> TST | **if** <cond> **then** TST **else** TST
VAR ::= <var name> | <var name> '.' <var name>
VARS ::= VAR | VAR ',' VARS
CONSTRAINT ::= <constraint>
CONS ::= CONSTRAINT | CONSTRAINT **and** CONS
ARG ::= VAR | <value>
ARGS ::= ARG | ARG ',' ARGS
NAME ::= <node name>

Where <elementary action> is an elementary action $name(p_0, ..., p_N)$, <goal> is a goal $name(p_0, ..., p_N)$, $p_0, ..., p_N$ are parameters, and <cond> is a FIPA ACL query message requesting the value of a boolean expression..

The TST clause introduces the main recursive pattern. The right hand side of the equality provides the general pattern of providing a variable context for a task (using **with**) and a set of constraints (using **where**) over the variables previously introduced.

Example. Consider a small scenario where the mission is to first scan $\mathsf{Area_A}$ and $\mathsf{Area_B}$, and then fly to $\mathsf{Dest_4}$. A TST describing this mission is shown in Figure 2. Nodes N_0 and N_1 are composite action nodes, sequential and concurrent, respectively. Nodes N_2, N_3 and N_4 are elementary action nodes. Each node specifies a task and has a node interface containing node parameters and a platform assignment variable. In this case only temporal parameters are shown representing the respective intervals a task should be completed in. The nodes N_0 to N_4 have the task names τ_0 to τ_4 associated with them respectively. The resulting TST specification is:

$\tau_0(T_{S_0}, T_{E_0}) =$
  with $T_{S_1}, T_{E_1}, T_{S_4}, T_{E_4}$ **sequence**
    $\tau_1(T_{S_1}, T_{E_1}) =$
      with $T_{S_2}, T_{E_2}, T_{S_3}, T_{E_3}$ **concurrent**
        $\tau_2(T_{S_2}, T_{E_2}) = \text{scan}(T_{S_2}, T_{E_2}, Speed_2, Area_A);$
        $\tau_3(T_{S_3}, T_{E_3}) = \text{scan}(T_{S_3}, T_{E_3}, Speed_3, Area_B)$
      where $cons_{\tau_1}$;
    $\tau_4(T_{S_4}, T_{E_4}) = \text{flyto}(T_{S_4}, T_{E_4}, Speed_4, Dest_4)$
  where $cons_{\tau_0}$

$$cons_{\tau_0} = T_{S_0} \leq T_{S_1} \wedge T_{S_1} < T_{E_1} \wedge T_{E_1} \leq T_{S_4} \wedge T_{S_4} < T_{E_4} \wedge T_{E_4} \leq T_{E_0}$$
$$cons_{\tau_1} = T_{S_1} \leq T_{S_2} \wedge T_{S_2} < T_{E_2} \wedge T_{E_2} \leq T_{E_1} \wedge T_{S_1} \leq T_{S_3} \wedge T_{S_3} < T_{E_3} \wedge T_{E_3} \leq T_{E_1}$$

4.2 TST Semantics

A TST specifies a complex task (composite action) under a set of tree-specific and node-specific constraints which together are intended to represent the context in which a task should be executed in order to meet the task's intrinsic requirements, in addition to contingent requirements demanded by a particular mission. The leaf nodes of a TST represent elementary actions used in the definition of the composite action the TST represents and the non-leaf nodes essentially represent control structures for the ordering and execution of the elementary actions. The semantic meaning of non-leaf nodes is

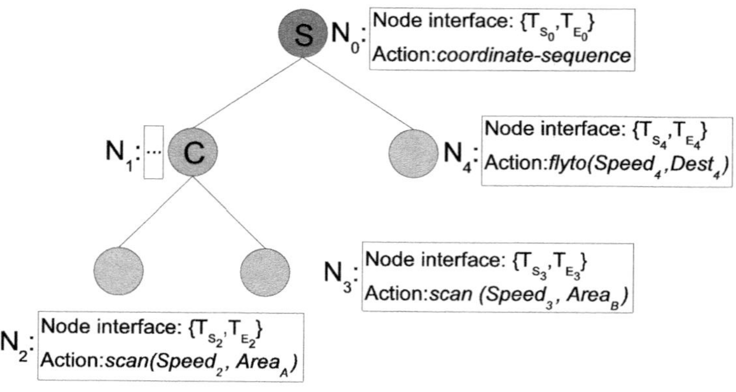

Fig. 2. A TST for the example mission

essentially application independent, whereas the semantic meaning of the leaf nodes are highly domain dependent. They represent the specific actions or processes that an agent will in fact execute. The procedural correlate of a TST is a program.

During the delegation process, a TST is either provided or generated to achieve a specific set of goals, and if the delegation process is successful, each node is associated with an agent responsible for the execution of that node.

Informally, the semantics of a TST node will be characterized in terms of whether an agent believes it *can* successfully execute the task associated with the node in a given context represented by constraints, given its capabilities and resources. This can only be a belief because the task will be executed in the future and even under the best of conditions, real-world contingencies may arise which prevent the agent from successfully completing the task. The formal semantics for TST nodes will be given in terms of the logical predicate $Can()$ which we have used previously in the formal definition of the S-Delegate speech act, although in this case, we will add additional arguments. This is not a coincidence since our goal is to ground the formal specification of the S-Delegate speech act into the implementation in a very direct manner.

Recall that in the formal semantics for the speech act S-Delegate (described in Section 2), the logical predicate $Can_X(\tau)$ is used to state that an agent X has the capabilities and resources to achieve task τ. An important precondition for the successful application of the speech act is that the delegator (A)believes in the contractor's (B) ability to achieve the task τ, (2): $Bel_A Can_B(\tau)$. Additionally, an important result of the successful application of the speech act is that the contractor actually has the capabilities and resources to achieve the task τ, (4): $Can_B(\tau)$. In order to directly couple the semantic characterization of the S-Delegate speech act to the semantic characterization of TST's, we will assume that a task $\tau = (\alpha, \phi)$ in the speech act characterization corresponds to a TST. Additionally, the TST semantics will be characterized in terms of a Can predicate with additional parameters to incorporate constraints.

In this case, the Can predicate is extended to include as arguments a list $[p_1, \ldots, p_k]$ denoting all node parameters in the node interface together with other parameters provided in the (**with** VARS) construct[4] and an argument for an additional constraint set $cons$ provided in the (**where** CONS) construct.[5] Observe that $cons$ can be formed incrementally and may in fact contain constraints inherited or passed to it through a recursive delegation process. The formula $Can(B, \tau, [t_s, t_e, \ldots], cons)$ then asserts that an agent B has the capabilities and resources for achieving task τ if $cons$, which also contains node constraints for τ, is consistent. The temporal variables t_s and t_e associated with the task τ are part of the node interface which may also contain other variables which are often related to the constraints in $cons$.

Determining whether a fully instantiated TST satisfies its specification, will now be equivalent to the successful solution of a constraint problem in the formal logical sense. The constraint problem in fact provides the formal semantics for a TST. Constraints associated with a TST are derived from a reduction process associated with the $Can()$ predicate for each node in the TST. The generation and solution of constraints will occur on-line during the delegation process. Let us provide some more specific details. In particular, we will show the very tight coupling between the TST's and their logical semantics.

The basic structure of a Task Specification Tree is:

TST ::= NAME ('(' VARS$_1$ ')')? '=' (**with** VARS$_2$)? TASK (**where** CONS)?

where VARS$_1$ denotes node parameters, VARS$_2$ denotes additional variables used in the constraint context for a TST node, and CONS denotes the constraints associated with a TST node. Additionally, TASK denotes the specific type of TST node. In specifying a logical semantics for a TST node, we would like to map these arguments directly over to arguments of the predicate $Can()$. Informally, an abstraction of the mapping is

$$Can(agent_1, TASK, VARS_1 \cup VARS_2, CONS) \tag{1}$$

The idea is that for any fully allocated TST, the meaning of each allocated TST node in the tree is the meaning of the associated $Can()$ predicate instantiated with the TST specific parameters and constraints. The meaning of the instantiated $Can()$ predicate can then be associated with an equivalent Constraint Satisfaction Problem (CSP) which turns out to be true or false dependent upon whether that CSP can be satisfied or not. The meaning of the fully allocated TST is then the aggregation of the meanings of each individual TST node associated with the TST, in other words, a conjunction of CSP's.

One would also like to capture the meaning of partial TST's. The idea is that as the delegation process unfolds, a TST is incrementally expanded with additional TST nodes. At each step, a partial TST may contain a number of fully expanded and allocated nodes in addition to other nodes which remain to be delegated. In order to capture this process semantically, one extends the semantics by providing meaning for an unallocated TST node in terms of both a $Can()$ predicate and a $Delegate()$ predicate:

$$\exists agent_2\ Delegate(agent_1, agent_2, TASK, VARS_1 \cup VARS_2, CONS) \tag{2}$$

[4] For reasons of clarity, we only list the node parameters for the start and end times for a task, $[t_s, t_e, \ldots]$, in this article.

[5] For pedagogical expediency, we can assume that there is a constraint language which is reified in the logic and is used in the CONS constructs.

Either $agent_1$ can achieve a task, or (exclusively) it can find an agent, $agent_2$, to which the task can be delegated. In fact, it may need to find one or more agents if the task to be delegated is a composite action.

Given the $S\text{-}Delegate(agent_1, agent_2, TASK)$ speech act semantics, we know that if delegation is successful then as one of the postconditions of the speech act, $agent_2$ can in fact achieve $TASK$ (assuming no additional contingencies):

$$\begin{aligned} &Delegate(agent_1, agent_2, TASK, VARS_1 \cup VARS_2, CONS) \\ &\quad \to Can(agent_2, TASK, VARS_1 \cup VARS_2, CONS) \end{aligned} \tag{3}$$

Consequently, during the computational process associated with delegation, as the TST expands through delegation where previously unallocated nodes become allocated, each instance of the $Delegate()$ predicate associated with an unallocated node is replaced with an instance of the $Can()$ predicate. This recursive process preserves the meaning of a TST as a conjunction of instances of the $Can()$ predicate which in turn are compiled into a (interdependent) set of CSPs and which are checked for satisfaction using distributed constraint solving algorithms.

Sequence Node. For a *sequence node*, the child nodes should be executed in sequence, from left to right, during the execution time of the sequence node.

$Can(B, S(\alpha_1, ..., \alpha_n), [t_s, t_e, \ldots], cons) \leftrightarrow$
$\exists t_1, \ldots, t_{2n}, \ldots \bigwedge_{k=1}^{n} (Can(B, \alpha_k, [t_{2k-1}, t_{2k}, \ldots], cons_k)$
$\qquad \vee \exists a_k Delegate(B, a_k, \alpha_k, [t_{2k-1}, t_{2k}, \ldots], cons_k))$
$\wedge\, consistent(cons)$[6]
where $cons = \{t_s \le t_1 \wedge (\bigwedge_{i=1}^{n} t_{2i-1} < t_{2i}) \wedge (\bigwedge_{i=1}^{n-1} t_{2i} \le t_{2i+1}) \wedge t_{2n} \le t_e\} \cup cons'$

Concurrent Node. For a *concurrent node*, the child nodes should be executed during the time interval of the concurrent node.

$Can(B, C(\alpha_1, ..., \alpha_n), [t_s, t_e, \ldots], cons) \leftrightarrow$
$\exists t_1, \ldots, t_{2n}, \ldots \bigwedge_{k=1}^{n} (Can(B, \alpha_k, [t_{2k-1}, t_{2k}, \ldots], cons_k)$
$\qquad \vee \exists a_k Delegate(B, a_k, \alpha_k, [t_{2k-1}, t_{2k}, \ldots], cons_k))$
$\wedge\, consistent(cons)$
where $cons = \{\bigwedge_{i=1}^{n} t_s \le t_{2i-1} < t_{2i} \le t_e\} \cup cons'$.

Observe that the constraint sets $cons_k$ in the semantics for the concurrent and sequential nodes are simply the constraint sets defined in the (**where** CONS) constructs for the child nodes included with the sequential or concurrent nodes, respectively. Additionally, the definition of the constraint set $cons$ in the semantics for the concurrent and sequential nodes contains the structural temporal constraints which define sequence and concurrency, respectively, together with possibly additional constraints, denoted by $cons'$ that one may want to include in the constraint set. Note also, that we are assuming that scoping and overloading issues for variables in embedded TST structures are dealt with appropriately in the recursive expansion of the $Can()$ predicates in the definitions.

Selector Node. Compared to a sequence or concurrent node, only one of the *selector node*'s children will be executed, which one is determined by a test condition in the selector node. The child node should be executed during the time interval of the selector

[6] The predicate $consistent()$ has the standard logical meaning and checking for consistency would be done through a call to a constraint solver which is part of the architecture.

node. A selector node is used to postpone a choice which can not be known when the TST is specified. When expanded at runtime, the net result can be any of the node types.

Loop Node. A *loop node* will add a child node for each iteration the loop condition allows. In this way the loop node works as a sequence node but with an increasing number of child nodes which are dynamically added. Loop nodes are similar to selector nodes, they describe additions to the TST that can not be known when the TST is specified. When expanded at runtime, the net result is a sequence node.

Goal. A *goal node* is a leaf node which can not be directly executed. Instead it has to be expanded by using an automated planner or related planning functionality. After expansion, a TST branch representing the generated plan is added to the original TST.

$Can(B, Goal(\phi), [t_s, t_e, \ldots], cons) \leftrightarrow$
$\exists \alpha\, (GeneratePlan(B, \alpha, \phi, [t_s, t_e, \ldots], cons) \wedge Can(B, \alpha, [t_s, t_e, \ldots], cons))$
$\wedge\ consistent(cons)$

Observe that the agent B can generate a partial or complete plan α and then further delegate execution or completion of the plan recursively via the $Can()$ statement in the second conjunct.

Elementary Action. An *elementary action node* is a leaf node that specifies a domain-dependent action. The semantics of Can for an elementary action is platform dependent.

$Can(B, \tau, [t_s, t_e, \ldots], cons, \ldots) \leftrightarrow$
$Capabilities(B, \tau, [t_s, t_e, \ldots], cons) \wedge Resources(B, \tau, [t_s, t_e, \ldots], cons)$
$\wedge\ consistent(cons)$

There are two parts to the definition of Can for an elementary action node. These are defined in terms of a *platform specification* which is assumed to exist for each agent potentially involved in a collaborative mission. The platform specification has two components.

The first, specified by the predicate $Capabilities(B, \tau, [t_s, t_e, \ldots], cons)$ is intended to characterize all static capabilities associated with platform B that are required as capabilities for the successful execution of τ. If platform B has the necessary static capabilities for executing task τ in the interval $[t_s, t_e]$ with constraints $cons$, then this predicate will be true.

The second, specified by the predicate $Resources(B, \tau, [t_s, t_e, \ldots], cons)$ is intended to characterize dynamic resources such as fuel and battery power, which are consumable, or cameras and other sensors which are borrowable. Since resources generally vary through time, the semantic meaning of the predicate is temporally dependent.

Resources for an agent are represented as a set of parameterized resource constraint predicates, one per task. The parameters to the predicate are the task's parameters, in addition to the start time and the end time for the task. For example, assume there is a task $flyto(dest, speed)$. The resource constraint predicate for this task would be $flyto(t_s, t_e, dest, speed)$. The resource constraint predicate is defined as a conjunction of constraints, in the logical sense. As an example, consider the task $flyto(dest, speed)$ with the corresponding resource constraint predicate $flyto(t_s, t_e, dest, speed)$. The constraint model associated with the task for a particular platform P_1 might be:

$t_e = t_s + \frac{distance(pos(t_s, P_1), dest)}{speed} \wedge (Speed_{Min} \leq speed \leq Speed_{Max})$

4.3 Example

The constraint problem for a TST is derived by recursively reducing the Can predicate statements associated with each task node with formally equivalent expressions, beginning with the top-node τ_0 until the logical statements reduce to a constraint network. Below, we show the reduction of the TST from Figure 2 when there are three platforms, P_0, P_1 and P_2, with the appropriate capabilities. P_0 has been delegated the composite actions τ_0 and τ_1. P_0 has recursively delegated parts of these tasks to P_1 (τ_2 and τ_4) and P_2 (τ_3).

$$
\begin{aligned}
&Can(P_0, \alpha_0, [t_{s0}, t_{e0}], cons) = Can(P_0, S(\alpha_1, \alpha_4), [t_{s0}, t_{e0}], cons) \leftrightarrow \\
&\exists t_{s_1}, t_{e_1}, t_{s_4}, t_{e_4} (Can(P_0, \alpha_1, [t_{s_1}, t_{e_1}], cons_{P_0}) \vee \exists a_1 Delegate(P_0, a_1, \alpha_1, [t_{s_1}, t_{e_1}], cons_{P_0})) \\
&\qquad \wedge (Can(P_0, \alpha_4, [t_{s_4}, t_{e_4}], cons_{P_0}) \vee \exists a_2 Delegate(P_0, a_2, \alpha_4, [t_{s_4}, t_{e_4}], cons_{P_0}))
\end{aligned}
$$

Let's continue with a reduction of the 1st element in the sequence α_1 (the 1st conjunct in the previous formula on the right-hand side of the biconditional):

$$Can(P_0, \alpha_1, [t_{s_1}, t_{e_1}], cons_{P_0}) \vee \exists a_1(Delegate(P_0, a_1, \alpha_1, [t_{s_1}, t_{e_1}], cons_{P_0}))$$

Since P_0 has been allocated α_1, the 2nd disjunct is false.

$$
\begin{aligned}
&Can(P_0, \alpha_1, [t_{s_1}, t_{e_1}], cons_{P_0}) = Can(P_0, C(\alpha_2, \alpha_3), [t_{s_1}, t_{e_1}], cons_{P_0}) \leftrightarrow \\
&\exists t_{s_2}, t_{e_2}, t_{s_3}, t_{e_3} (Can(P_0, \alpha_2, [t_{s_2}, t_{e_2}], cons_{P_0}) \vee \exists a_1 Delegate(P_0, a_1, \alpha_2, [t_{s_2}, t_{e_2}], cons_{P_0})) \\
&\qquad \wedge (Can(P_0, \alpha_3, [t_{s_3}, t_{e_3}], cons_{P_0}) \vee \exists a_2 Delegate(P_0, a_2, \alpha_3, [t_{s_3}, t_{e_3}], cons_{P_0}))
\end{aligned}
$$

The node constraints for τ_0 and τ_1 are then added to P_0's constraint store. What remains to be done is a reduction of tasks τ_2 and τ_4 associated with P_1 and τ_3 associated with P_2. We can assume that P_1 has been delegated α_2 and P_2 has been delegated α_3 as specified. Consequently, we can reduce to

$$
\begin{aligned}
&Can(P_0, \alpha_1, [t_{s_1}, t_{e_1}], cons_{P_0}) = Can(P_0, C(\alpha_2, \alpha_3), [t_{s_1}, t_{e_1}], cons_{P_0}) \leftrightarrow \\
&\exists t_{s_2}, t_{e_2}, t_{s_3}, t_{e_3} Can(P_1, \alpha_2, [t_{s_2}, t_{e_2}], cons_{P_1}) \wedge Can(P_2, \alpha_3, [t_{s_3}, t_{e_3}], cons_{P_2})
\end{aligned}
$$

Since P_0 has recursively delegated α_4 to P_1 (the 2nd conjunct in the original formula on the right-hand side of the biconditional) we can complete the reduction and end up with the following:

$$
\begin{aligned}
&Can(P_0, \alpha_0, [t_{s0}, t_{e0}], cons) = Can(P_0, S(C(\alpha_2, \alpha_3), \alpha_4), [t_{s0}, t_{e0}], cons) \leftrightarrow \\
&\exists t_{s_1}, t_{e_1}, t_{s_4}, t_{e_4} \\
&\qquad \exists t_{s_2}, t_{e_2}, t_{s_3}, t_{e_3} Can(P_1, \alpha_2, [t_{s_2}, t_{e_2}], cons_{P_1}) \wedge Can(P_2, \alpha_3, [t_{s_3}, t_{e_3}], cons_{P_2}) \\
&\quad \wedge Can(P_1, \alpha_4, [t_{s_4}, t_{e_4}], cons_{P_1})
\end{aligned}
$$

These remaining tasks are elementary actions and consequently the definitions of Can for these action nodes are platform dependent. When a platform is assigned to an elementary action node a local constraint problem is created on the platform and then connected to the global constraint problem through the node parameters of the assigned node's node interface. In this case, the node parameters only include temporal constraints and these are coupled to the internal constraint variables associated with the elementary actions. The completely allocated and reduced TST is shown in Figure 3. The reduction of Can for an elementary action node contains no further Can predicates, since an elementary action only depends on the platform itself. All remaining Can predicates in the recursion are replaced with constraint sub-networks associated

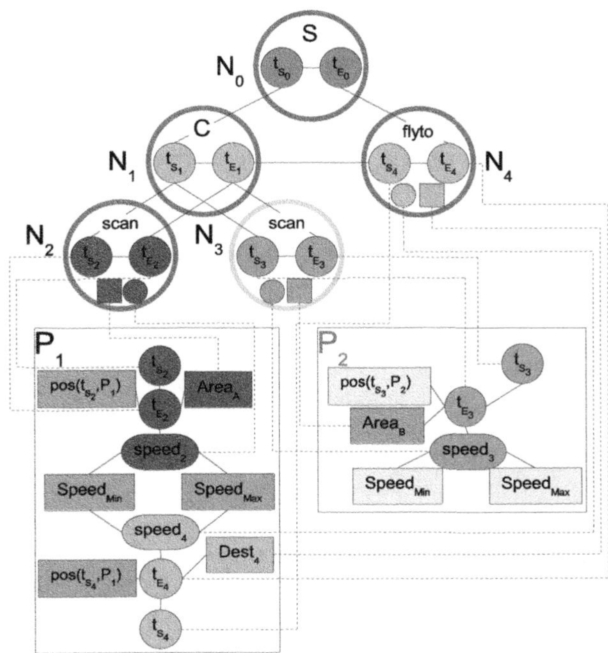

Fig. 3. The completely allocated and reduced TST showing the interaction between the TST constraints and the platform dependent constraints

with specific platforms as shown in Figure 3. To check that distributed constraint problem is consistent we use local CSP solvers together with a DCSP solver (16).

In summary, the delegation process, if successful, provides a TST that is both valid and completely allocated. During this process, a network of distributed constraints is generated which if solved, guarantees the validity of the multi-agent solution to the original problem, provided that additional contingencies do not arise when the TST is actually executed in a distributed manner by the different agents involved in the collaborative solution. This approach is intended to ground the original formal specification of the S-Delegate speech act with the actual processes of delegation used in the implementation. Although the process is pragmatic in the sense that it is a computational process, it in effect strongly grounds this process formally, due to the reduction of the collaboration to a distributed constraint network which is in effect a formal representation. This results in real-world grounding of the semantics of the Delegation speech act via the Can predicate.

5 Related Work

Two related task specification languages which are representative of state of the art in this area are the Configuration Description Language (17), used in *MissionLab* and the task description language (TDL) (21).

CDL has a recursive composition of configurations, similar to our TST task structure. In CDL a behavior and a set of parameters creates an agent. Agents can be composed into larger entities, called assemblages, that function as macro-agents. Assemblages can in turn be part of larger assemblages. CDL has been used as the basis for MissionLab, a tool for mission specification using case based reasoning. Task-allocation is done using a market-based paradigm with contract-nets. Task allocation can be done together with mission specification, or at run time (22).

With TDL it is possible to specify task decomposition, synchronization, execution monitoring, and exception handling. TDL is an extension to C++, meaning the specification is compiled and executed on the robots. Task are in the form of task-trees. A task has parameters and is either a goal or a command, where a command is similar to an action node in a TST. Goal nodes can have both goal and command nodes as children, but commands nodes have no goal children. An action can perform computations dynamically and add child nodes or perform some physical action in the world. An action can contain conditional, iterative and recursive code.

Both CDL and TDL are similar to TST, but with the difference that the specification of a TST is not precompiled and therefore allow more dynamic handling of tasks in the case of changing circumstances. The specification remains through the stages of task-allocation (delegation) and execution. Each node in a TST has parameter values which are restricted by constraints. Each node has an executor object (for each platform) that can be instantiated with the parameter values determined in the task allocation stage. Since we have this separation between specification and execution of a task, connected as a constraint problem of the node parameters and platform assignments, we can go back and forth from the task-allocation and execution stage, which must be done when monitoring formulas fails and an error is detected, or when the mission is changed with mixed-initiative input. The loose coupling between specification and execution is needed for combining the adjustable autonomy and mixed-initiative features.

6 Conclusions

The complexity of developing deployed architectures for realistic collaborative activities among agents that operate in the real world and under time and space constraints is extreme when compared to much existing formal work which tackles parts of the larger problem at very high levels of abstraction. We have tried to show the benefits of using both strategies, working abstractly at a formal logical level and also concretely at a system building level. More importantly, we have shown how one might relate the two approaches to each other by *grounding* the formal abstractions into actual software implementations. This of course guarantees the fidelity of the actual system to the formal specification.

We proposed TST's as a vehicle for representing tasks and showed how they relate to the formal delegation abstraction, how its semantics can be described as a constraint model and how that model is used in an actual implemented system to give meaning to the ability of an agent to be able to do or execute a task. There is much future work to be done in this complex research area, but work in this direction can continue based on the foundations provided in this work.

References

1. Castelfranchi, C., Falcone, R.: Toward a theory of delegation for agent-based systems. In: Robotics and Autonomous Systems, vol. 24, pp. 141–157 (1998)
2. Cohen, P., Levesque, H.: Intention is choice with commitment. AI 42(3), 213–261 (1990)
3. Cohen, P., Levesque, H.: Teamwork. Nous 25(4), 487–512 (1991)
4. Conte, G., Doherty, P.: Vision-based unmanned aerial vehicle navigation using geo-referenced information. EURASIP Journal of Advances in Signal Processing (2009)
5. Conte, G., Hempel, M., Rudol, P., Lundström, D., Duranti, S., Wzorek, M., Doherty, P.: High accuracy ground target geo-location using autonomous micro aerial vehicle platforms. In: Proceedings of the AIAA-2008 Guidance, Navigation, and Control Conference (2008)
6. Davis, E., Morgenstern, L.: A first-order theory of communication and multi-agent plans. Journal Logic and Computation 15(5), 701–749 (2005)
7. Doherty, P., Granlund, G., Kuchcinski, K., Sandewall, E., Nordberg, K., Skarman, E., Wiklund, J.: The WITAS unmanned aerial vehicle project. In: Proc. ECAI (2000)
8. Doherty, P., Haslum, P., Heintz, F., Merz, T., Persson, T., Wingman, B.: A distributed architecture for intelligent unmanned aerial vehicle experimentation. In: Proc. DARS (2004)
9. Doherty, P., Meyer, J.-J.C.: Towards a Delegation Framework for Aerial Robotic Mission Scenarios. In: Klusch, M., Hindriks, K.V., Papazoglou, M.P., Sterling, L. (eds.) CIA 2007. LNCS (LNAI), vol. 4676, pp. 5–26. Springer, Heidelberg (2007)
10. Duranti, S., Conte, G., Lundström, D., Rudol, P., Wzorek, M., Doherty, P.: LinkMAV, a prototype rotary wing micro aerial vehicle. In: Proc. IFAC Symposium on Automatic Control in Aerospace (2007)
11. Bellifemine, F., Bergenti, F., Caire, G., Poggi, A.: JADE – a Java agent development framework. In: Multi-Agent Programming - Languages, Platforms and Applications (2005)
12. Falcone, R., Castelfranchi, C.: The human in the loop of a delegated agent: The theory of adjustable social autonomy. IEEE Transactions on Systems, Man and Cybernetics–Part A: Systems and Humans 31(5), 406–418 (2001)
13. van der Hoek, W., van Linder, B., Meyer, J.J.C.: An integrated modal approach to rational agents. In: Wooldridge, M., Rao, A. (eds.) Foundations of Rational Agency (1998)
14. Kvarnström, J.: Planning for loosely coupled agents using patrial order forward-chaining. In: Proc. ICAPS (2011)
15. Kvarnström, J., Doherty, P.: Automated planning for collaborative systems. In: Proceedings of the International Conference on Control, Automation, Robotics and Vision (2010)
16. Landén, D., Heintz, F., Doherty, P.: Complex Task Allocation in Mixed-Initiative Delegation: A UAV Case Study (Early Innovation). In: Desai, N., Liu, A., Winikoff, M. (eds.) PRIMA 2010. LNCS(LNAI), vol. 7057, pp. 288–303. Springer, Heidelberg (2011)
17. MacKenzie, D.C., Arkin, R., Cameron, J.M.: Multiagent mission specification and execution. Auton. Robots 4(1), 29–52 (1997)
18. Merz, T., Rudol, P., Wzorek, M.: Control System Framework for Autonomous Robots Based on Extended State Machines. In: Int. Conf. on Autonomic and Autonomous Systems (2006)
19. Olsson, P.M., Kvarnström, J., Doherty, P., Burdakov, O., Holmberg, K.: Generating UAV communication networks for monitoring and surveillance. In: ICARCV (2010)
20. Rudol, P., Wzorek, M., Conte, G., Doherty, P.: Micro unmanned aerial vehicle visual servoing for cooperative indoor exploration. In: Proc. of the IEEE Aerospace Conference (2008)
21. Simmons, R., Apfelbaum, D.: A task description language for robot control. In: IROS (1998)
22. Ulam, P., Endo, Y., Wagner, A., Arkin, R.C.: Integrated mission specification and task allocation for robot teams - design and implementation. In: ICRA (2007)
23. Wzorek, M., Conte, G., Rudol, P., Merz, T., Duranti, S., Doherty, P.: From motion planning to control – a navigation framework for an unmanned aerial vehicle. In: Proceedings of the 21st Bristol International Conference on UAV Systems (2006)

Adaptive and Non-adaptive Distribution Functions for DSA

Melanie Smith, Sandip Sen, and Roger Mailler

Computational Neuroscience and Adaptive Systems Lab
University of Tulsa, USA
roger-mailler@utulsa.edu
http://www.cnas.utulsa.edu

Abstract. Distributed hill-climbing algorithms are a powerful, practical technique for solving large Distributed Constraint Satisfaction Problems (DSCPs) such as distributed scheduling, resource allocation, and distributed optimization. Although incomplete, an ideal hill-climbing algorithm finds a solution that is very close to optimal while also minimizing the cost (i.e. the required bandwidth, processing cycles, etc.) of finding the solution. The Distributed Stochastic Algorithm (DSA) is a hill-climbing technique that works by having agents change their value with probability p when making that change will reduce the number of constraint violations. Traditionally, the value of p is constant, chosen by a developer at design time to be a value that works for the general case, meaning the algorithm does not change or learn over the time taken to find a solution. In this paper, we replace the constant value of p with different probability distribution functions in the context of solving graph-coloring problems to determine if DSA can be optimized when the probability values are agent-specific. We experiment with non-adaptive and adaptive distribution functions and evaluate our results based on the number of violations remaining in a solution and the total number of messages that were exchanged.

1 Introduction

Distributed hill-climbing algorithms are very powerful tools for solving numerous real-world problems including distributed scheduling, resource allocation, and distributed optimization. These problems can be easily mapped to distributed constraint satisfaction, and like DSCPs, they must be solved using algorithms that can make decisions about how to best improve the global state of the problem from an agent's limited, local perspective. The ultimate goal of distributed constraint satisfaction is to find a solution, if one exists, while also minimizing the cost (i.e. the required bandwidth, processing cycles, etc.) [3,7]. Complete algorithms, such as Asynchronous Weak Commitment (AWC) [13], Asynchronous Backtracking (ABT) [14], and Asynchronous Partial Overlay (APO) [6], are guaranteed to find a solution if one exists, but tend not to be very scalable. In practice, however, one must accept a close-enough solution, especially if the

N. Desai, A. Liu, and M. Winikoff (Eds.): PRIMA 2010, LNAI 7057, pp. 58–73, 2012.

problem is large or the solution needs to be derived quickly. Hill-climbing algorithms tend to work very quickly even on large problems, but do not guarantee that they will find a solution if there is one. One of the most powerful algorithms from this class is the Distributed Stochastic Algorithm (DSA) [4,?].

DSA is a hill-climbing technique that works by having agents change their value with probability p when making that change will reduce the number of constraint violations. DSA requires the user to specify p. Traditionally, the value of p is constant, chosen by a developer at design time to be a value that works for the general case, meaning the algorithm does not adapt its behavior based on the problem's characteristics. In fact, the setting of p can have dramatic effects on the behavior of the protocol and can be quite problem specific. For instance, on very dense problems, having high values of p can cause the protocol to converge more quickly, but the same setting on a sparse problem will cause it to oscillate unnecessarily. Because p's value is so crucial to the success of finding a good solution, we believe choosing p to be more agent- and problem-specific will improve the solution and the process by which the solution is found.

In this paper, we investigate different probability functions for the Distributed Stochastic Algorithm in the context of solving graph-coloring problems. First, we examine four non-adaptive techniques that define p as a function of how much improvement an agent can have. The second set of techniques involves adaptation, where the function used to compute p is modified over time based on the agent's experiences.

Section 2 presents a formalization of the distributed constraint satisfaction problem that is used as the basis for this paper. Section 3 gives a detailed description of DSA. Sections 4 and 5 discuss our non-adaptive and adaptive approaches, and Section 6 discusses both the setup and results of empirical testing that has been done to compare these adaptations to DSA. Finally, the paper closes with some concluding remarks and some future directions for this work.

2 Distributed Constraint Satisfaction

A Distributed Constraint Satisfaction Problem (DCSP) consists of the following [14]:

- a set of n variables $V = \{x_1, \ldots, x_n\}$
- a set of k Agents $A = \{a_1, \ldots, a_k\}$
- discrete, finite domains for each of the variables $D = \{D_1, \ldots, D_n\}$
- a set of m constraints $R = \{R_1, \ldots, R_m\}$ where each $R_i(d_{i1}, \ldots, d_{ij})$ is a predicate on the Cartesian product $D_{i1} \times \cdots \times D_{ij}$ that returns true iff the value assignments of the variables satisfy the constraint

The problem is to find an assignment, $S = \{d_1, \ldots, d_n \mid d_i \in D_i\}$, such that each of the constraints in R is satisfied. DCSP, like its centralized counterpart, has been shown to be NP-complete, making some form of search a necessity [2].

In DCSP, each agent is assigned one or more variables along with constraints on those variables. The goal of each agent, from a local perspective, is to ensure that each of the constraints on its variables is satisfied. For each of the agents, achieving this goal is not independent of the goals of the other agents in the system. In fact, in all but the simplest cases, the goals of the agents are strongly interrelated. For example, in order for one agent to satisfy its local constraints, another agent, potentially not directly related through a constraint, may have to change the value of its variable.

In this paper, for the sake of clarity, each agent is assigned a single variable and is given knowledge of the constraints on that variable. Since each agent is assigned a single variable, the agent is referred to by the name of the variable it manages. Also, this paper considers only binary constraints that are of the form $R_i(x_{i1}, x_{i2})$. It is fairly easy to extend all the algorithms presented in this paper to handle more general problems where these restrictions are removed, either by changing the algorithm or by changing the problem as done in [1].

Definition 1. *A binary CSP is a CSP where all of the constraints in R are of the form $R_i(x_{i1}, x_{i2})$.*

Definition 2. *The constraint graph of a binary CSP is a graph $G = < V, E >$ where V is the set of variables in the CSP and E is the set of edges representing the set of constraints in R (i.e. $R_i(x_{i1}, x_{i2}) \in R \Rightarrow (x_{i1}, x_{i2}) \in E$).*

Additionally, throughout this paper the word *neighbor* is used to refer to agents that share constraints. In other words, if an agent A has a constraint R_i that contains a variable owned by some other agent B, then agent A and agent B are considered neighbors.

3 Related Work

3.1 Distributed Stochastic Algorithm

The Distributed Stochastic Algorithm (DSA) is one of a class of algorithms based on the idea that at each step, each variable should change to its best value with some probability $p \in [0, 1]$. Because each variable changes with p probability, the likelihood of two neighbors changing at the same time is p^2. As long as p is selected correctly, the protocol will hill climb to a better state.

The DSA algorithm has a number of implementation variants. Figure 1 details DSA-B, which follows the basic rule of DSA by changing values with probability p when it reduces the number of constraint violations. However, it also changes the value with p probability when the number of constraint violations remains the same (i.e. its improve value is 0). In this way, the DSA-B variant is able to escape certain types of local minima in the search space by making *lateral moves*.

The DSA protocol is quite popular because it is by far the easiest protocol to implement. However, it is also one of the hardest to tune because it requires the user to specify p. The process of choosing this value can require a great

```
procedure main
  while (not terminated) do
    update agent_view with incoming
      ok? (x_j, d_j) messages;
    new_value ← choose_value;
    if new_value ≠ d_i do
      d_i ← new_value;
      send ((ok?, (x_i, d_i)) to all x_j ∈ neighbors;
    end if;
  end do;
end main;

procedure choose_value
  if d_i has no conflicts do
    return d_i;
  v ← the value with the least conflict (v ≠ d_i);
  if v has the same or fewer conflicts than d_i
      and random < p do
    return v;
  else
    return d_i;
end choose_value;
```

Fig. 1. The procedures of the DSA-B algorithm

deal of empirical testing because it is problem specific. Higher values of p cause the protocol to exhibit a rapid decrease in the number of constraint violations, which can level off far from an optimal solution depending on the problem. Lower values of p tend to correct violations more slowly, but often end up with a better solution in the end.

One of the greatest benefits of the DSA protocol is that it uses considerably fewer messages than other protocols like the Distributed Breakout Algorithm [15] because agents communicate only when they change their values. As the protocol executes and the number of violations decrease, so do the number of messages. However, while DSA converges on a solution in a reasonable amount of time, finding a better solution in less time while using even fewer messages is important.

Manipulating DSA's probability variable allows the algorithm to vary its results. Some studies suggest that the most general value is about $p = 0.3$ [16]. However, these values are simple constants and do not change based on the state of the problem.

3.2 Distributed Breakout Algorithm

The Distributed Breakout Algorithm (DBA) [15] is a distributed adaptation of the Centralized Breakout Algorithm [9]. DBA works by alternating between two modes. The first mode (see figure 2) is called the *wait_ok?* mode where the agent collects *ok?* messages from each of its neighbors. Once this has happened, the agent calculates the best new value for its variable along with the improvement in its local evaluation. The agent then sends out an *improve?* message to each of its neighbors and changes to the *wait_improve?* mode.

In the *wait_improve* mode (see figure 2), the agent collects *improve?* messages from each of its neighbors. Once all of the messages have been received, the agent checks to see if its improvement is the best among its neighbors. If it is, it changes its value to the new improved value. If the agent believes it is in a quasi-local-minimum (QLM), it increase the weights on all its of violated constraints. Finally, the agent sends *ok?* messages to each of its neighbors and changes back to the *wait_ok?* mode. The algorithm starts up with each agent sending *ok?* messages and going into the *wait_ok?* mode.

Because of the strict locking mechanism employed in the algorithm, the overall behavior of the agents is to simultaneously switch back and forth between the two modes. So, if one or more of the agents reacts slowly or messages are delayed, the neighboring agents wait for the correct message to arrive. This makes the protocol's communication usage very predictable because in each mode, each agent sends exactly one message to each of its neighbors. Thus, if there are m constraints, exactly $2m$ messages are transmitted during each step.

Conversely, the locking mechanism in DBA can be very beneficial because it does not allow neighboring agents to change their values at the same time, which prevents oscillations. However, it can also prevent opportunities for additional parallelism because it limits the number of variables that can change at each *wait_improve* step to at most half when they are in a fully connected problem. These limitations effectively allow at most $1/4$ of the variables to change during any individual step of the protocol's execution.

Two variants of the DBA protocol have been created to improve its overall parallelism and prevent pathological behavior by introducing randomness [17]. The weak-probabilistic DBA protocol (DBA-WP) uses randomness to break ties when two neighboring agents have the same improve value. The result is that either one agent, both, or neither of the agents change values when this situation occurs. The strong-probabilistic DBA protocol (DBA-SP) attempts to improve parallelism by allowing agents to change their value with some probability when they can improve, but don't have the best improve among their neighbors. This technique helps to improve parallelism because in many situations, the agent's neighbor with the best improve doesn't have the the best improve among its neighbors. This causes agents to wait unnecessarily for their neighbor to change when their neighbor has no intention of actually doing so.

3.3 Distributed Probabilistic Protocol

Conceptually, the Distributed Probabilistic Protocol (DPP) is a hybrid of the DSA and DBA protocols that aims to merge the benefits of both algorithms while correcting their weakness. The DPP protocol uses a dynamic mixture of randomness and direct control that changes based on the structure and current state of the problem to mitigate the effects of asynchrony. The key insight that inspired the creation of the protocol is that an agent doesn't necessarily need receive improve messages from all of its neighbors in order for it to determine that it is or is not the best agent to make a value change.

DPP works by having agents exchange probability distributions (PDF) that describe the likelihood they are going to have a particular improve value given the configuration of the constraints on their variable(s). This allows the agents to estimate the likelihood that it has the best improve value among its neighbors without communicating at all. Using this likelihood as a basis for randomly

```
when received (ok?, x_j, d_j) do
  if mode == wait_improve
    add message to queue;
    return;
  else
    add (x_j, d_j) to agent_view;
    when received all ok? messages do
      send_improve;
      mode ← wait_improve;
    end do;
  end if;
end do;

procedure send_improve
  current_eval ← evaluation value of current_value;
  improve_i ← possible maximum improvement;
  new_value ← the best value ;
  send (improve, x_i, improve_i, current_eval);
end send_improve;
```

```
when received (improve, x_j, improve_j, eval) do
  if mode == wait_ok
    add message to queue;
    return;
  else
    record message;
    when received all improve messages do
      send_ok;
      clear agent_view;
      mode ← wait_ok;
    end do;
  end if;
end do;

procedure send_ok
  if improve_i is better than all of my neighbors
    current_value ← new_value;
  end if;
  when in a quasi-local-minimum do
    increase the weights on all violated constraints;
  end do;
  send (ok?, x_i, current_value) to neighbors;
end send_ok;
```

Fig. 2. The procedures of the *wait_ok?* and *wait_improve* modes in Distributed Breakout

determining when to change an agent's value, we end up with a DSA-like protocol where each agent's probability p_i is dictated by the improve distributions of its neighbors and its current improve value.

This process is further enhanced by considering the use of explicit improve messages like those used in DBA. Unlike DBA, DPP sends out improve messages with a probability that is associated with its estimate of a neighbor having a prediction error of its improve value. This means that if agent X knows agent Y's improve PDF and agent Y behaves according to the protocol, agent X can even predict the probability that Y will have an improve value less than its own, even when Y has not sent X an improve message for a long period of time.

As a result of these modifications, DPP uses considerably fewer messages than both DSA and DBA, does not require a user to define p values as in DSA, and more quickly converges onto good solutions. The drawback to DPP is that calculating the initial PDF function can be very difficult because it often does not have a closed-form solution. Because of this, improve PDFs are created by exhaustive enumeration or by employing some form of statistical sampling over the possible configuration space of the constraints on an agent's variable, both of which cause a steep overhead when starting up the algorithm.

4 Non-adaptive DSA

DPP's inspiration was that the probability of an agent changing its value should be associated with how much improvement it expects to have. Similarly motivated, we decided to investigate versions of the DSA protocol that determine the value of p as a function of the current improve value for an agent. In the non-adaptive version of the protocol, we altered the DSA-B algorithm to update p based on a function, as shown in Figure 3. The algorithm uses the same

```
procedure choose_value
  if d_i has no conflicts do
    return d_i;
  v ← the value with the least conflict (v ≠ d_i);
  improve ← d_i − v;
  maxImprove ← number of neighbors for agent;
  p ← P(improve, maxImprove);  (see text)
  if improve ≥ 0 and random < p do
    return v;
  else
    return d_i;
end choose_value;
```

Fig. 3. The choose_value procedure of the Non-Adaptive DSA-B algorithm

main procedure as DSA, but changes the **choose_value** procedure to calculate an *improve* value and uses that value to determine p. Like DBA and DPP, the improve value for a variable is simply the difference between the current number of conflicts and the number of conflicts for the best possible value. The $maxImprove$ value, which is used to normalize the functions that calculate p, is the maximum total cost of all of the variable's constraints. This assumes that the maximum improvement occurs when all constraints are in conflict and changing the variable's value causes all the conflicts to be resolved. The value of p gets returned by the $P(improve,\ maxImprove)$ function, and depending on whether an improvement can be made, the agent's value is changed with probability p.

For our tests, we tried four non-adaptive functions to compute p: linear, sub-linear, super-linear, and Weibull. Figure 4 shows a graph of these non-adaptive P functions. We initially chose the linear function on the basis that there should be a higher probability of changing values if there is a higher improve value associated with that move. The other three functions were chosen to examine whether variations on the linear function would be better suited than using the simple linear function.

4.1 Distribution Functions

For our first function, we looked at a simple linear function on the amount of improve. Basically, when the linear function has a positive slope and a node has a high improve value (i.e. changing colors would allow a large number of conflicts to be abated), there is a good chance that the color will change. Using a normalized linear distribution instead of a constant value for p allows the change probability to be higher the more an agent can improve. We set $p_0 = 0.1$ to give some probability of change for the case where lateral movement occurs. As a reminder, lateral movements occur when multiple values have an improve of 0 and the agent can switch between the values without violating any constraints. The linear technique forms the basis of all the other functions we evaluate in this paper. The normalized linear function is as follows:

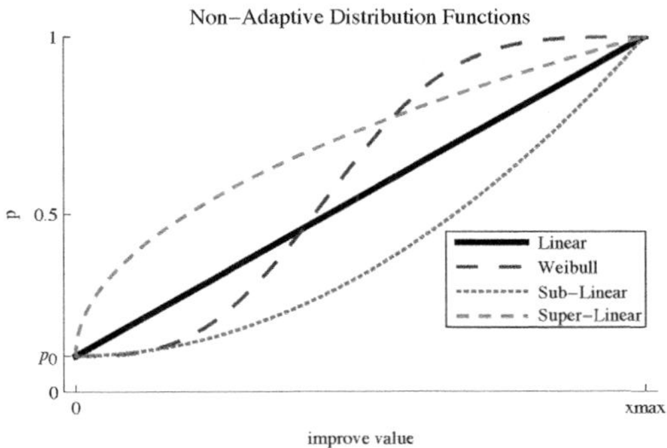

Fig. 4. Non-Adaptive Distribution Functions: Linear, Sub-Linear, Super-Linear, and Weibull Distributions

$$P(imp, maxImp) = (1 - p_0)\left(\frac{imp}{maxImp}\right) + p_0 \quad (1)$$

A sub-linear function is similar to a linear one, but keeps the probably of the agent changing its value low until a sufficiently large improvement value is likely. Below is the sub-linear function that we used in this paper:

$$P(imp, maxImp) = (1 - p_0)\left(\frac{imp}{maxImp}\right)^2 + p_0 \quad (2)$$

The opposite of sub-linear is super-linear. This function has the characteristic that the agents have a higher-than-linear likelihood of changing their value, except in the cases where they expect 0 or maximum improve. The following is the super-linear function we use:

$$P(imp, maxImp) = (1 - p_0)\sqrt{\frac{imp}{maxImp}} + p_0 \quad (3)$$

The Weibull distribution, part of the family of Sigmoid functions, is a combination of the sub- and super-linear cases, acting sub-linear until the amount of improvement is approximately half of the maximum possible improvement and then switching into a super-linear function. This means for small improvements, the likelihood of an agent changing its value is slim, but for large improvements, the likelihood is quite high. Below is the function used for our tests:

$$P(imp, maxImp) = (1 - p_0)\left(1 - e^{-\left(\frac{imp}{0.5 \times maxImp}\right)^{maxImp}}\right) + p_0 \quad (4)$$

4.2 Example

Consider the 3-coloring problem presented in Figure 5. In this problem, there are six agents, each with a variable and nine constraints between them. Because

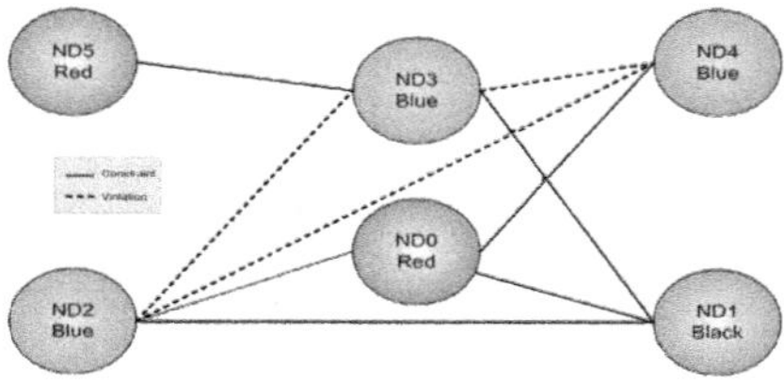

Fig. 5. Example 3-coloring problem with six variables and nine constraints.

this is a 3-coloring problem, each variable can be assigned only one of the three available colors {Black, Red, or Blue}. The goal is to find an assignment of colors to the variables such that no two variables, connected by a constraint, have the same color.

In this example, three constraints are in violation: (ND2, ND3), (ND2, ND4), and (ND3, ND4). Following the protocol, at startup, each of the agents sends its current value to all its neighbors in an *ok*? message. After receiving all the messages, each agent determines their *improve*, *maxImprove*, and p values. In this example, p is calculated using equation 1.

- ND0 has improve = 0, maxImprove = 3, and p = 0.1
- ND1 has improve = 0, maxImprove = 3, and p = 0.1
- ND2 has improve = 1, maxImprove = 4, and p = 0.325
- ND3 has improve = 1, maxImprove = 4, and p = 0.325
- ND4 has improve = 2, maxImprove = 3, and p = 0.7
- ND5 has improve = 0, maxImprove = 1, and p = 0.1

After finding the probability of change, a random number is generated such that if the random number is less than p, the value for the node actually changes. Every node that changes sends a message to all its neighbors and the process starts over again until execution ends.

5 Adaptive DSA

In addition to looking at non-constant, although static functions for determining the value of p, we also investigated two methods that allow the function to adapt based on experience. The learning problem that the agents encounter in this algorithm is to learn a mapping from their improve value at a time t to a probability that determines whether they should be the one that changes their value at t. In situations where this leads to an action being produced, the agent is rewarded based on the relative goodness of the action (i.e. how much improvement is actually made).

Like most learning methods, including Temporal difference (TD) learning [10], the general form of the update we use in this paper can be seen in equation 5. Basically there is an error term calculated at each time step that is used to move the probability by some small amount, α, toward the correct value.

5.1 Algorithm

The modifications needed to support the ability to adapt the function used to determine p are fairly simple. First, we introduce two global variables, a probability array, *prob*, of size *maxImprove* that holds the function values for each improve value and an integer *predImprove* that holds the predicted improvement value of the agent from the previous cycle. While still operating like the DSA algorithm, we alter the **main** procedure to initialize *maxImprove*, *prob*, and *lastPred*. Each time the main loop cycles, we save the predicted improve from the previous cycle so that we can compare the actual change to what was predicted. To find the actual change (*actualImprove*), we count the number of conflicts before and after the messages are processed and take the difference. The probability array is updated if the last predicted value is greater than 0, meaning we made a change to our variable's value on the last cycle. Each of our approaches introduces a new **update_prob** method that does the probability array updating.

The **choose_value** procedure is also changed in the adaptive algorithm, although minimally. We initialize *predImprove* to -1 every time the method is called to indicate that no change is made. If a change is made, *predImprove* is set to the *improve* value. This value is what is saved to compare in the next iteration to the actual improve of the agent and trigger the **update_prob** procedure call.

5.2 Update Methods

The *discrete update* function limits the impact that the error value has to only correct the probablity assocated with the agent's last predication. To initialize the *prob* array, we calculate the linear value for each unit using equation 1. As the problem is solved, the probabilities are changed to reflect whether the decision made by the agent was a good decision.

After each cycle, the probability array is updated by taking into account the current value of p and adding a fraction of the difference between the actual and predicted improve values. The **update_prob** procedure for the discrete algorithm takes as input the actual improve value, the last predicted improvement, and the maximum improvement possible for the particular agent. The procedure changes the global *prob* array by changing the $prob_{pred}$ to increase (or decrease) by a constant, α, times the normalized difference in the predicted value and the actual value at time t. None of the other values in the *prob* array are affected, and if no change is made to the agent's value, the $prob_{pred}$ value will not change. In our evaluation, we set $\alpha = 0.3$.

$$prob^{t}_{pred} \leftarrow prob^{t-1}_{pred} + \alpha \left(\frac{actual - pred}{max} \right) \tag{5}$$

The *exponential decay update* technique updates to the *prob* array just like in the discrete method, but also updates other values in the array based on an exponential decay. Again, the array is initialized using the linear function (equation 1) to initialize the probability array.

The **update_prob** procedure for the exponential decay update algorithm contains a loop that iterates through the *prob* array, adjusting each value a slight amount based on how far from the *pred* position it is. For example, if the *pred* is 4, and i is 2, then the value for $prob_i$ will be adjusted by a factor of α^3, as will the value of $prob_6$ because it is the same distance from the center at 4. The further away from one another i and *pred* are, the smaller the factor, and the smaller the change in the probability. One could easily think of this updating technique as being similar in nature to a radial basis function [8] with each function centered at an individual improve value. As you adjust one of the kernels, it affects the probabilities in an exponentially decaying manner based on its distance from the prediction.

$$prob_i^t \leftarrow prob_i^{t-1} + \alpha^{(|pred-i|+1)} \left(\frac{actual - pred}{max} \right) \quad (6)$$

6 Evaluation

To test our DSA variants, we implemented each in a distributed 3-coloring domain. The DSA algorithm was the DSA-B variant and the test series consisted of randomly generated graphs with $n = \{100, 200, 300, 400, 500\}$ variables and $m = \{2.0n, 2.3n, 2.7n\}$ constraint densities to cover under-constrained, normally constrained, and over-constrained environments. For each setting of n and m, 30 problems were created and each of the probability distributions were used, both adaptive and non-adaptive. Each run was given 500 cycles of execution time. During a cycle, each agent was given the opportunity to process its incoming messages, change its value, and queue up messages for delivery during the next cycle. The actual amount of execution time per cycle varied depending on the cycle, the problem, and the distribution function.

The test cases were compared on two main factors. During each cycle, the number of current violations and the number of messages transmitted were measured. These values were used to plot the graphs shown in Figures 6 and 7. Although not shown here, for the adaptive cases, we kept track of the probability array values for each cycle to see how the probability functions were affected over time. As expected, the exponential decay update technique changes more often and to a greater degree because more values in *prob* change during each cycle. One thing we noticed is that even though the values changed more, they still didn't change very much from their initial values. In future work, we plan to use the resulting function from one run and using it as the input to the next run so that each successive run would be improving the final function instead of starting over with the linear values. This would make it work much more like classical reinforcement learning because the agents would get multiple trials in addition to multiple updates.

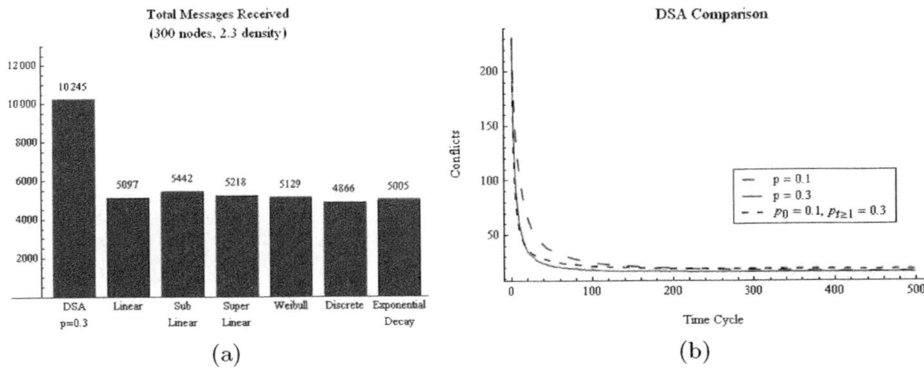

Fig. 6. (a) Number of messages sent for all algorithms at 500 nodes and 2.3 edge density, and (b) Conflicts over time for DSA with $p = 0.1, 0.3$ and DBH with $p_0 = 0.1$ and $p_{1...i} = 0.3$

6.1 Total Messages Received

In terms of total messages sent/received, all of our algorithms used less than half of the number of messages that traditional DSA (see Figure 6) uses for all combinations of nodes and edge densities. This seems to indicate that adapting the p values to be more situation specific facilitated significantly more effective communication between agents. Thus, it is our conjecture that it will require half the transmission bandwidth and allow for a more scalable solution.

In comparison to DPP, based on the results presented in [5], the amount of messaging is about the same. However, using any of our distribution functions alleviates the need to calculate the initial PDF function. We plan to do a more empirical comparison between DPP and our DSA variant in the future.

6.2 Total Conflicts

Even though our approach dramatically improves the communication cost, none of our alterations to DSA showed consistent improvement to the solution found by normal DSA as far as the total conflicts are concerned. Table 1 shows the conflicts remaining for 2.3 density and all nodes after 500 cycles. Out of our six probability functions, a clear leader did not emerge, although they were within a standard deviation of one another and DSA.

One possible reason for finding a slightly worse solution is that when traditional DSA has an agent with only a small or no improvement possible, the probability of having it change values is still fairly high at $p = 0.3$, whereas with our experiments, we set $p_0 = 0.1$, which is significantly lower than traditional DSA. The probability of an agent having only a small or no amount of improve for any particular time cycle is also fairly high, meaning that the 0.2 difference in initial probability values is likely a significant factor. In many cases, a probability function that has a high probability of change in the early part of the run

Table 1. Remaining Conflicts after 500 cycles for 2.3 density

Algorithm	100 nodes	200 nodes	300 nodes	400 nodes	500 nodes
DSA	6.1	12	15.9	22.5	28.6
Linear	6.0	12.8	18.4	24.8	30.7
Sub-Linear	7.1	12.5	20.1	24.9	30.2
Super-Linear	6.6	12.8	19.1	24.7	29.4
Weibull	6.9	12	18.6	23.6	30.8
Discrete	5.9	11.9	17.5	24	29.5
Contextual Discrete	6.2	12.4	17.9	24.3	31.0

is more likely to do well overall because the agent has the chance to hill-climb to a better state. In the cases where the starting value is too low, the agent may not have had the opportunity to find a better solution because it has already hill climbed into such a bad state that there is no escape.

6.3 Further Analysis and Experimentation

To determine if the difference in p_0 is the cause of our solutions coming out with slightly more constraint violations, we ran traditional DSA again with $p = 0.1$ instead of $p = 0.3$. In this case, the solutions ended up consistently worse with the lower value of p because there is a smaller likelihood that an agent will change its value no matter how much it can improve. Our probability functions result in conflict curves over time that fall between the traditional DSA curves for $p = 0.1$ and $p = 0.3$. This implies that there are two separate components at play in finding good solutions with DSA-B: lateral movement and hill-climbing.

To test this hypothesis, we augmented the traditional DSA algorithm to give $p_0 = 0.1$ and $p_{improve \geq 1} = 0.3$ to segregate the approach into lateral movement and hill-climbing portions. Figure 6 shows all three traditional DSA algorithms with different static values for p at 300 nodes and 2.3 density. The higher the value for p_0, the faster the number of remaining conflicts falls due to the higher probability of lateral motion. We also notice that the higher the number of nodes, the more of an impact the lateral motion has. In Figure 8, we show the average distribution of the *improve* value for an agent with 4 neighbors. Because $improve = 0$ occurs more frequently than larger improve values, we know that lateral movement plays a large part in finding a good solution. This isn't entirely surprising as it has been reported numerous times that randomness in centralized hill-climbing searches has a fairly significant impact on the overall solution quality [11].

Examining the hill-climbing portion of the runs, we look at the slope of the conflict lines in Figure 7. The thicker line is DSA with $p = 0.3$, and the other lines are our non-adaptive and adaptive results. The slope of each line indicates the effectiveness of the hill-climbing part of the algorithm. Traditional DSA flattens out as time goes on with little to no slope while our algorithms have a more defined slope as time progresses. We believe that this indicates that our

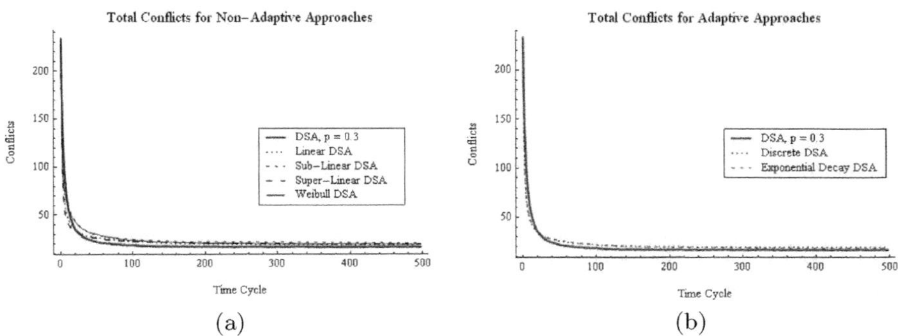

Fig. 7. Conflicts Remaining Over Time: (a) Non-Adaptive and (b) Adaptive

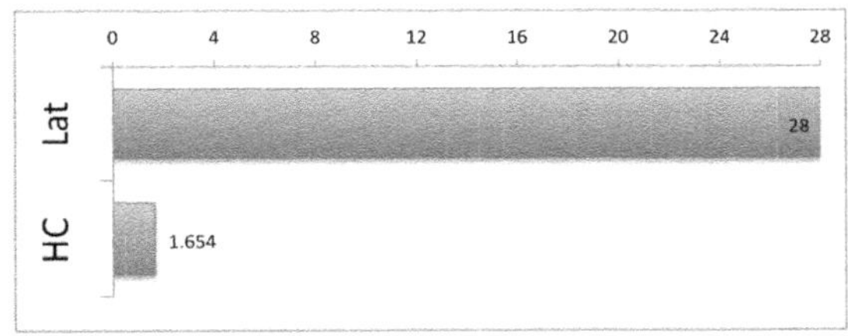

Fig. 8. Average number of Lateral Moves (Lat) vs. Hill-Climbing Moves (HC) for graph-coloring agents with four neighbors

hill-climbing methods are more effective than normal DSA, but that our choice of p for the lateral movement case was sub-optimal. Our adaptive algorithms have a steeper slope than our non-adaptive algorithms, indicating that having the values for p evolve as the problem is solved improves the hill-climbing method over finding p based on a static function. In addition, using static functions results in a more defined slope than having p defined as a static constant. In future work, we will explore this discovery and experiment with different p_0 values over each of our distribution functions.

7 Conclusion

This paper presents different adaptive and non-adaptive alterations to the Distributed Stochastic Algorithm (DSA), which turns the traditional constant p into an situation-specific function for p based on the predicted improvement of the agent during a time cycle. By allowing p to change and adapt, we reduce the number of messages needed to communicate between agents by more than half. In discovering the heavy influence of lateral movement, we believe that given a more optimal p_0 value, our DSA variants should improve even further. Other work we have done includes experimenting with fine-tuning the lateral movement probability [12].

As agent systems become more complex and start to evolve more autonomously, and as this extends into complex software systems, cutting communication costs (i.e. bandwidth and throughput needs) may become more desirable than finding a more optimal solution if the difference is within a tolerable range. In cases like these, using any of our techniques would make a dramatic impact on the networking footprint required by traditional DSA, even without an optimal p_0 probability for lateral movement.

Because of the significant reduction in messaging, we believe fine-tuning the lateral movement probability in our distribution functions can find more optimal solutions. Running more tests in a variety of domains would help determine how the algorithms adapt to more than just graph-coloring problems. Also testing the adaptive approaches using different initialization vectors may result in finding a more optimal probability function. We are also planning on incorporating more complex machine learning, where each successive run takes the probability function from previous runs as the initial value, allowing the simulation to improve upon a function that starts off in a more optimal state than the static functions we used in this paper.

Acknowledgments. The authors gratefully acknowledge support of the Defense Advanced Research Projects Agency under DARPA grants HR0011-07-C-0060. Views and conclusions contained in this document are those of the authors and do not necessarily represent the official opinion or policies, either expressed or implied of the US government or of DARPA.

References

1. Bacchus, F., van Beek, P.: On the conversion between non-binary constraint satisfaction problems. In: AAAI 1998/IAAI 1998: Proceedings of the Fifteenth National/Tenth Conference on Artificial Intelligence/Innovative Applications of Artificial Intelligence, pp. 311–318. American Association for Artificial Intelligence, Menlo Park (1998)
2. Bulatov, A., Krokhin, A., Jeavons, P.: The complexity of maximal constraint languages. In: STOC 2001: Proceedings of the Thirty-Third Annual ACM Symposium on Theory of Computing, pp. 667–674. ACM, New York (2001)
3. Faltings, B.: Distributed constraint programming. In: van Beek, P., Rossi, F., Walsh, T. (eds.) Handbook of Constraint Programming. Foundations of Artificial Intelligence, ch. 20, vol. 2, pp. 699–729. Elsevier (2006)
4. Fitzpatrick, S., Meertens, L.: Distributed Coordination Through Anarchic Optimization. In: Distributed Sensor Networks: A Multiagent Perspective, pp. 257–294. Kluwer Academic Publishers (2003)
5. Mailler, R.: Using prior knowledge to improve distributed hill climbing. In: Proceedings of the 2006 International Conference on Intelligent Agent Technology (IAT 2006) (2006)
6. Mailler, R., Lesser, V.: Using Cooperative Mediation to Solve Distributed Constraint Satisfaction Problems. In: Proceedings of Third International Joint Conference on Autonomous Agents and MultiAgent Systems (AAMAS 2004) (2004)
7. Meisels, A.: Distributed search by constrained agents: algorithms, performance, communication. Springer, Heidelberg (2008)

8. Moody, J., Darken, C.J.: Fast learning in networks of locally-tuned processing units. Neural Comput. 1(2), 281–294 (1989)
9. Morris, P.: The breakout method for escaping local minima. In: Proceedings of the Eleventh National Conference on Artificial Intelligence, pp. 40–45 (1993)
10. Richard, A.G.B., Sutton, S.: Reinforcement Learning: An Introduction. MIT Press, Cambridge (1999)
11. Selman, B., Kautz, H., Cohen, B.: Noise strategies for improving local search. In: Proceedings of the Twelfth National Conference on Artificial Intelligence (AAAI 1994), pp. 337–343 (1994)
12. Smith, M., Mailler, R.: Getting What You Pay For: Is Exploration in Distributed Hill Climbing Really Worth It?. In: Int'l Conference on Web Intelligence and Intelligent Agent Technology, WI-IAT (2010)
13. Yokoo, M.: Asynchronous Weak-Commitment Search for Solving Distributed Constraint Satisfaction Problems. In: Montanari, U., Rossi, F. (eds.) CP 1995. LNCS, vol. 976, pp. 88–102. Springer, Heidelberg (1995)
14. Yokoo, M., Durfee, E.H., Ishida, T., Kuwabara, K.: Distributed constraint satisfaction for formalizing distributed problem solving. In: International Conference on Distributed Computing Systems, pp. 614–621 (1992)
15. Yokoo, M., Hirayama, K.: Distributed breakout algorithm for solving distributed constraint satisfaction problems. In: International Conference on Multi-Agent Systems, ICMAS (1996)
16. Zhang, W., Wang, G., Wittenburg, L.: Distributed stochastic search for constraint satisfaction and optimization: Parallelism, phase transitions and performance. In: Proceedings of the AAAI Workshop on Probabilistic Approaches in Search, pp. 53–59 (2002)
17. Zhang, W., Wittenburg, L.: Distributed breakout revisited. In: Proceedings of the Eighteenth National Conference on Artificial Intelligence (AAAI-2002), pp. 352–357 (2002)

Multiagent Based Scheduling of Elective Surgery

Sankalp Khanna[1,2], Timothy Cleaver[1], Abdul Sattar[1], David Hansen[2], and Bela Stantic[1]

[1] Institute for Integrated and Intelligent Systems, Griffith University, QLD 4111, Australia
{S.Khanna,T.Cleaver,A.Sattar,B.Stantic}@griffith.edu.au
[2] The Australian e-Health Research Centre, 71/918,RBWH, Herston, QLD 4029, Australia
David.Hansen@csiro.au

Abstract. Scheduling of patients, staff, and resources for elective surgery in an under-resourced and overburdened public health system represents an inherently distributed class of problems. The complexity and dynamics of interacting factors demand a flexible, reactive and timely solution, in order to achieve a high level of utilization. In this paper, we present an Automated Scheduler for Elective Surgery (ASES) wherein we model the problem using the multiagent systems paradigm. ASES is designed to reflect and complement the existing manual methods of elective surgery scheduling, while offering efficient mechanisms for negotiation and optimization. Inter-agent negotiation in ASES is powered by a distributed constraint optimization algorithm. This strategy provides hospital departments with control over their individual schedules while ensuring conflict free optimal scheduling. We evaluate ASES to demonstrate the feasibility of our approach and demonstrate the effect of fluctuation in staffing levels on theatre utilization. We also discuss ongoing development of the system, mapping key challenges in the journey towards deployment.

Keywords: Multiagent Systems, Distributed Constraint Optimization.

1 Introduction

" *The performance of Australia's public hospital system continues to deteriorate...... Waiting times for elective surgery have been getting longer. [1]* "

Scheduling in a complex, dynamic environment remains an open research problem. The problem is made particularly difficult when scheduling needs to occur in a distributed manner across several departments. While each department is working at optimizing its own resources, optimal utilization requires several departmental schedules to be optimized horizontally. The problem is further compounded in the case of under-resourced and overburdened systems, and even slight improvements in scheduling here can lead to much needed gains. Faced with the challenge of an encumbered public health system, the Elective Surgery Scheduling Problem (ESSP) presents an excellent real-world example of

N. Desai, A. Liu, and M. Winikoff (Eds.): PRIMA 2010, LNAI 7057, pp. 74–89, 2012.

this class of problems. A collaboration between leading national research facilities in ICT for healthcare innovations and Artificial Intelligence, and a leading public hospital, this research is focused on tackling problems of this nature.

Our research into public elective surgery wait times in Queensland, Australia, found that a significant number of patients were subjected to longer than desirable wait times. This was despite recent initiatives including increased budget allocation, treatment of long-wait patients in private hospitals, and increased clinical staffing. As of 1 April 2010, 33,620 patients were waiting for elective surgery, of whom almost 18% had waited longer than a clinically desirable time [22]. Any improvement in scheduling processes would not only result in improved staff and resource utilization, but also lead to reduced patient in-waiting and in-care times, increased patient and staff satisfaction, and increased hospital revenue.

We have developed ASES, an Automated Scheduler for Elective Surgery, in an attempt to address this class of problems. ASES is a multiagent system designed to reflect and complement existing manual methods of elective surgery scheduling, while offering efficient mechanisms for negotiation and optimization. The use of the multiagent paradigm is a natural fit given the distributed nature of the problem. It also captures the autonomy of hospital departments in constructing and managing their individual schedules. In order to ensure optimality and compatibility of departmental schedules, we employ distributed constraint optimization to guide coordination and resolution of schedule conflicts. This marriage of rational agency and distributed constraint optimization, wherein the optimization algorithm forms the core of the agent negotiation protocol and guides interaction between agents working on related but departmentally autonomous problems, is novel and necessitated by the problem domain.

The rest of this paper is organized as follows. In Section 2, we motivate our research with a discussion of the processes involved in scheduling elective surgery at a large public hospital in Queensland. We then discuss state-of-the-art solutions to the problem. This is followed by a brief introduction to multiagent systems and distributed constraint optimization. In Section 3, we present the intelligent agent architecture of the ASES system and justify our choice of distributed optimization algorithm. We then map the elective surgery scheduling problem to a distributed constraint optimization problem and present particulars of the ASES implementation. In Section 4, we discuss the feasibility and benefits of our approach and demonstrate the effect of fluctuation in staffing levels on theatre utilization. We conclude with a description of ongoing and future work, mapping key challenges in the journey towards deployment.

2 Background

2.1 Elective Surgery Scheduling - A Case Study

Elective surgery is a planned, non-emergency surgical procedure, which can be scheduled at the patient's and surgeon's convenience. The escalating demand for elective surgery is however compounded by a shortage of trained surgeons,

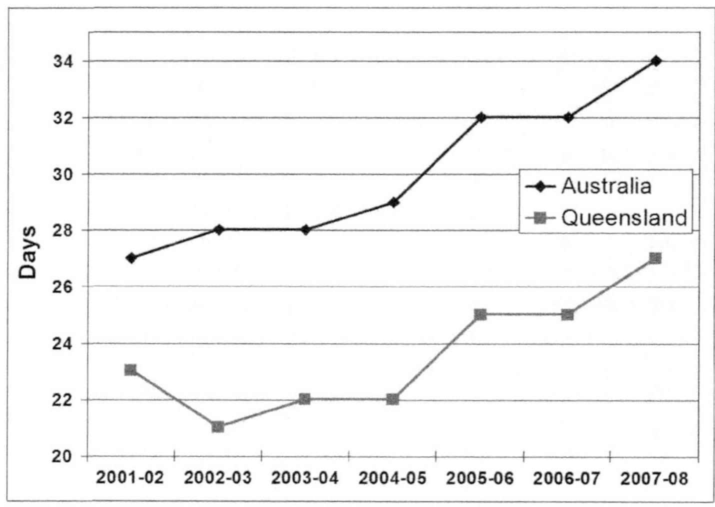

Fig. 1. Median Waiting Time for Elective Surgery

anaesthetists and nurses. Recent statistics [1] show that despite repeated government intervention, elective surgery wait times continue to grow in Australia (Fig. 1). Though slightly better, Queensland statistics follow similar trends. We discuss scheduling processes at a leading public hospital in Queensland to help establish a better understanding of the intricacies involved.

21 operating theatres are available. The theatre schedule is divided into 3.5 hour slots. Two slots are allocated per day, one in the morning and one in the afternoon. Elective procedures are generally rescheduled in case of emergency.

Each department connected (i.e. allocating staff or other resources) to the surgery carries out their individual scheduling activity. The bookings department assigns patients to slots in consultation with the relevant surgical teams. The bookings are recorded into the *Operating Room Management Information System* (ORMIS). The different departments can access this information by looking into ORMIS or by accessing the latest *Bookings Schedule* on the shared drive, where it is updated everyday at 3PM.

Every Thursday the managers of the different departments meet and review bookings for the week ahead (Fig. 2). Each session is discussed and existing schedule conflicts are resolved. However, events like unexpected emergencies, variation in patients' health state, and sudden perturbations in staffing, often lead to schedule changes. All changes made subsequent to the meeting are conducted on a case-by-case basis by individual departments. Coordinating these changes requires ad-hoc conventional communication. In keeping with the dynamics of the domain, the schedule needs to be updated quickly and efficiently. This is often not possible because of delays in inter-departmental communication. Changes made under such circumstances can often result in inefficient or compromised schedules. For example, if a procedure is canceled at the last minute, the bookings

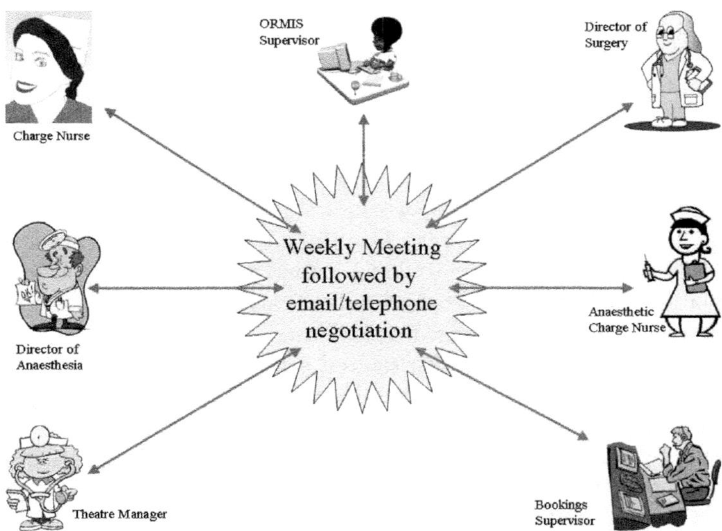

Fig. 2. Current Model for Scheduling Elective Surgery at the Princess Alexandra Hospital

department may want to offer the slot to another patient. However, due to the reliance on ad-hoc inter-departmental coordination, the involved parties may be unreachable. As a consequence, the slot would then go unused.

2.2 Current State-of-the-Art

Historically, a number of solutions to the scheduling problem in the area of intelligent (or semi-intelligent) scheduling can be found in literature. The first "intelligent scheduling system" to be reported, ISIS [5], also introduced scheduling (or specifically job shop scheduling) to the AI community. Over the last two decades, several research efforts have been directed at solving the scheduling problem, though most have been directed at the classical "job shop scheduling problem" [25][21][8]. Further, research in the Operations Research domain has also looked at the problem of scheduling for Operating Theatres and proposed efficient solvers [7][15][20][14] to handle the task, but most such solvers approach the problem as a centralized one. Given the need for maintaining the departmental decision control nature of the problem domain, we focus our research on distributed problem solving, specifically multiagent representations of the problem.

A study conducted as part of this research evaluated state-of-the-art commercial surgery scheduling software. Softwares like ORMIS[1], OPERA[2], and

[1] http://isoftsanidad.es/text/products/2593.asp

[2] http://www.chca.ca/opera.php?lang=en

MEDITECH Operating Room Management solution[3], provide sophisticated interfaces for users to enter scheduling decisions, and handy tools to detect conflicts and manage schedules, but decision making and optimization are largely left to the operators of the system. This results in several staff hours being spent each week on cumbersomely optimizing and aligning schedules. Krempels and Panchenko [13] reveal that in the Operation Theatre Scheduling domain they study, it takes one person 3-5 full working days to create a Nurse Roster. Several discussions and interviews with hospital administrators and schedulers also revealed that the most popular tools for departmental scheduling were still paper templates, excel spreadsheets and whiteboards, with software systems being used to record manually optimized schedules.

A review and analysis of health-related scheduling systems proposed by recent research revealed that most were based on simplistic case studies and did not map the complexities of the domain they were modeling. While several systems, including *DISA* [6], *MedPage*[18], and *Policy Agents* [12], used multiagent systems to model their domains, distributed schedule optimization was largely overlooked or proposed as one of the future aims. We also found that since transient elective surgery scheduling data is not captured in any current mechanisms, there is a lack of benchmark problems in this domain.

We believe that, while all of these methods help to improve the state-of-the-art, what is missing is an intelligent flexible methodology that can adapt itself to the complexity of the problem, without modifying or scaling it down. Optimally solving local problems and handling changes caused by the dynamic nature of the environment in a timely manner is also a non-trivial challenge. We argue thus that incorporating optimization internally for each agent and as an integral element of the inter-agent negotiation process is critical to the success of any proposed system.

2.3 Multiagent Systems and Distributed Optimization

Multiagent Systems [24] are a popular paradigm for modeling distributed systems. Intelligent autonomous agents incorporate powerful capabilities such as reactivity, proactiveness, cooperation, learning and intention management. Hospitals exhibit a high level of departmental autonomy and thus multiagent technology offers expressively rich tools for modeling the hospital scheduling environment. Further, multiagent systems also offer the Distributed Constraint Optimization Problem (DCOP) formalism for modeling and solving naturally distributed optimization problems efficiently.

Formally, we can define a DCOP as consisting of:

1. A finite ordered set of Agents $A = \{A_1, A_2, ..., A_k | k \in \mathbb{N}^*\}$, where, for each Agent A there exists :
   (a) A finite ordered set of variables $V = \{V_1, V_2, ..., V_n | n \in \mathbb{N}^*\}$,
   (b) A domain set $D = \{D_1, D_2, ..., D_n\}$, containing a finite and discrete domain D_i for each V_i,

[3] `http://www.meditech.com/ProductBriefs/pages/productpageorm.htm`

Algorithm 1. The DCDCOP Algorithm

```
Calculate static measures
Solve_local_problem
Calculate dynamic measures
Send message (DU, CurrContext) to all neighbours
Receive messages
when received (messageDU, msgContext) do
|   if msgContext and CurrContext are consistent then
|   |   add msgContext to CurrContext
|   |   if DU > msgDU then
|   |   |   Solve_local_problem
|   |   end
|   |   else if DU = msgDU and higher_order then
|   |   |   Solve_local_problem
|   |   end
|   |   Calculate dynamic measures
|   |   Send message (DU, CurrContext) to all neighbours
|   end
end

Procedure: Solve_local_problem
Branch and Bound to solve local problem
```

(c) A constraint set $C = \{C_1, C_2, ..., C_m \,|m \in \mathbb{N}^*\}$, where each $C_j, \forall j \in [1, m]$, is defined as a cost function (f) on a pair of variables (i, i'). i.e. $C_j = f_{ii'} : D_i \times D_{i'} \rightarrow \mathbb{N}$, $\forall V_i, V_{i'} \in V$, and

(d) An ordered solution set $S = \{v_1, v_2, ..., v_n | v_i \in D_i, \forall i \in [1, n]\}$ where each v_i is an instantiation of the variable V_i and the aggregate cost of the assignment $F(S) = \sum_{(x_i, x_{i'} \in V)} f_{ii'}(d_i, d_{i'}), x_i \leftarrow d_i, x_{i'} \leftarrow d_{i'} \in S$.

2. The solution set of the DCOP $S^\star$ is defined as the set of the solution sets of each agent.

Employing techniques from search, dynamic programming, and cooperative mediation, DCOP offers efficient and sophisticated algorithms like ADOPT [17], DPOP [19], and NCBB [4], to model and solve a variety of naturally distributed problems. Recent research efforts [16][3][10] have however identified shortcomings in DCOP algorithms when applied to dynamic and complex environments.

We have previously proposed DCDCOP [10] (see Algorithm 1), where agents solve their local sub-problem using a local solver of their choice and then employ a novel metric called Degree of Unsatisfaction to guide inter-agent negotiation and solve inter-agent constraints. DCDCOP has been shown [9] to outperform ADOPT, DPOP, and NCBB, by more than an order of magnitude.

3 ASES - an Automated Scheduler for Elective Surgery

3.1 Domain Mapping

The ESSP presented in Section 2.1 can be viewed as a set of departmental scheduling problems. Each department allocating staff or other resources to the surgery prepares their own schedule and then negotiates with other departments to ensure that the schedules are aligned and the resulting Operating Theatre schedule is conflict free.

To map the ESSP to a multiagent DCOP notation (Fig. 3), we assign each departmental scheduling problem to a single agent. The schedule slots are mapped to variables, and the staff and resources to be scheduled form the domain of values for the variables. Constraints between variables of the same agent represent conditions such as not being able to schedule a staff to two slots that run in parallel, while constraints between variables belonging to different agents represent conditions such as doctor-nurse team preference allocations. Domain rules and preferences are used to define cost functions for individual constraints. An optimal solution to the resultant DCOP problem will now lead to an optimal elective surgery schedule.

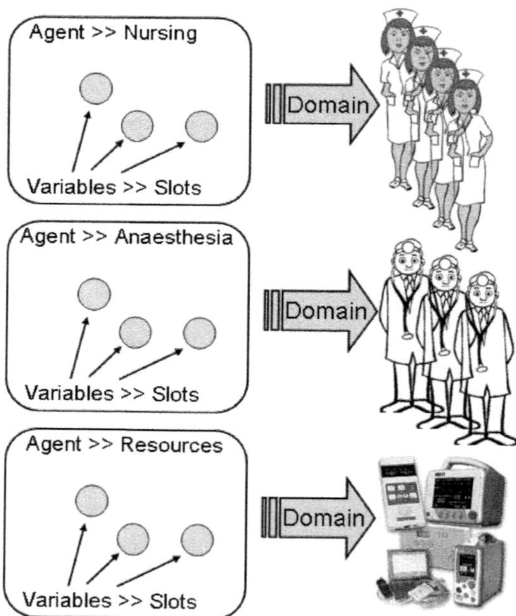

Fig. 3. Mapping the Problem

3.2 Proposed Architecture

We propose an agent-oriented methodology where each department involved in the scheduling of its resources, be they patients, staff or equipment, is represented by an intelligent agent. These agents are customized to the constraints, preference and priorities of the party they represent. It is the responsibility of the agents to react to messages from other agents and optimize their local schedule accordingly. As necessary, the agents then negotiate in a privacy-preserving manner to resolve inter-agent constraints (Fig. 4(a)). The architecture of individual agents (Fig. 4(b)) consists of a number of modules. An interface module handles communication with other agents and users. Decision support and learning is handled by the intelligence module. Negotiation and optimization is driven by the DCOP engine.

The agents thus have a number of capabilities. They can learn user preferences and domain knowledge. The environment is monitored for changes necessitating updates to the schedule. They use logical reasoning to identify the need for and to guide negotiation. An advanced DCOP algorithm is used to optimize local schedules while ensuring efficient alignment of the global schedule.

3.3 The DCOP Engine

The DCOP algorithm we utilize needs to be robust in a number of ways. It must be scalable to the variety and complexity of the involved agents' sub-problems. Negotiation resolution must be timely with respect to the environment under which the negotiation is taking place. The ability to separate the communication protocol from the details of the local solver is also essential, as this facilitates the customization of the local solver to each agent's unique problem while maintaining communication compatibility.

Given its ability to preserve the distributed sub-problem structure, and its computational superiority over ADOPT, DPOP, and NCBB, we have chosen DCDCOP to drive the DCOP engine in ASES. It is proposed to implement other key algorithms, like ADOPT, within ASES at a later stage to empirically validate our choice.

3.4 Implementation

ASES has been implemented using Jason [2]. Jason is a Java implementation of Agentspeak(L) [23]. In addition to providing extended Agentspeak(L) syntax and semantics for the development of individual agents, Jason provides facilities for the specification of multiagent systems. Crucial in so doing is the provision for speech-act-based communication. This speech-act-based communication underlies our DCOP communication implementation.

ASES models the scheduling activity of 4 agents: Bookings, Nursing, Anaesthesiology and Theatre Resources. Each agent is discussed briefly to present a better understanding of their activities.

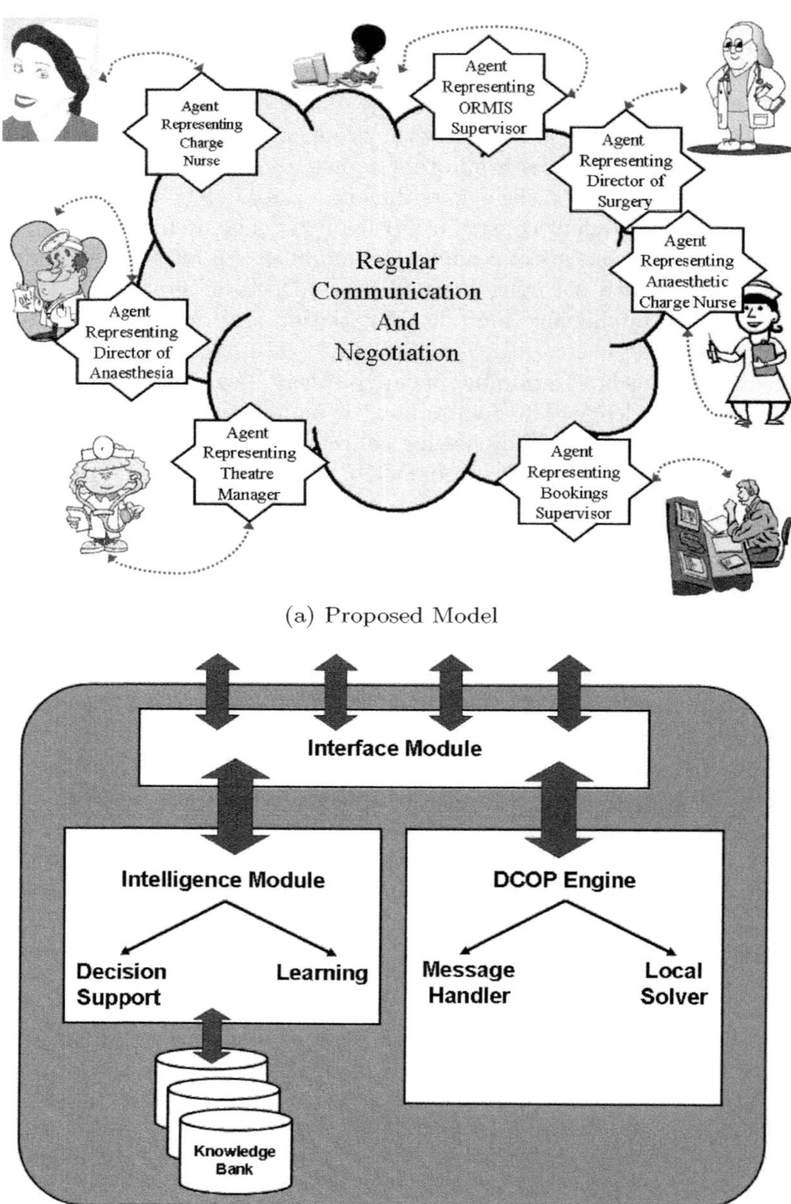

(a) Proposed Model

(b) Agent Architecture

Fig. 4. Scheduling Elective Surgery with ASES

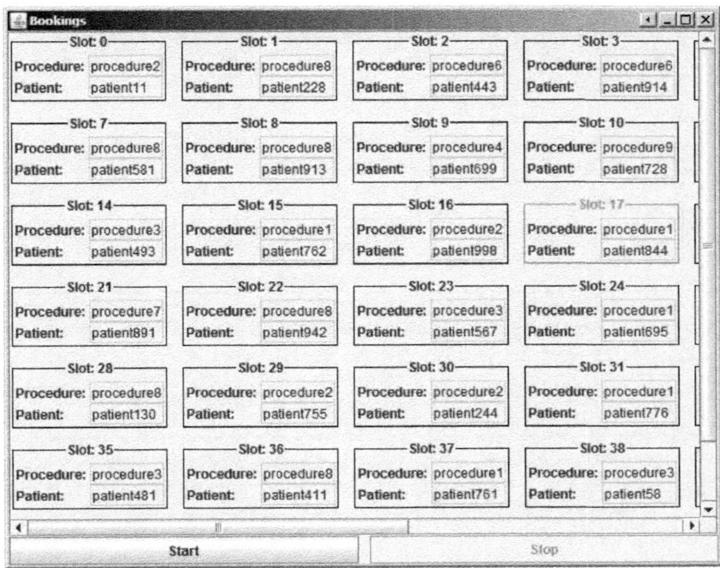

Fig. 5. Bookings Agent

The Bookings agent (Fig. 5) receives randomly generated requests to add or modify bookings. Each request includes the patient and procedure information. When a slot is allocated, the Bookings agent sends this information out to all agents concerned. If an agent is unable to provide resources, a message is returned to the Bookings agent, resulting in the allocation being cancelled and another message being sent out to all agents concerned.

The Resource agent (Fig. 6) calculates the equipment required for the procedure to schedule. If the required resources are unavailable, the Resource agent requests that the Bookings agent reschedule the procedure. Thus, equipment is allocated on a first-come first-served basis. This models the hospital's current resource allocation strategy. However, work is underway to enhance this process to utilize procedure/patient priorities if required.

The Nursing agent (Fig. 7), upon receiving notification of a new procedure allocation, must then schedule the nursing staff to accommodate the new allocation. Unlike the Resource agent, the resources available to the Nursing agent are not fixed. The Nurse Unit Manager is able to hire casual/temporary nurses when necessary. However, their use is to be minimized. This is modeled by assigning a higher cost to casual/temporary nursing staff.

In managing the nursing schedule, the Nursing agent is required to ensure that for each assignment of nurse to procedure, the nurse contributes a skill necessary to the completion of the procedure. No more nurses than necessary should be assigned to a procedure. Each procedure must have its nursing skills requirements met. Should the nursing agent be unable to allocate nurses to satisfy a procedure's requirements, a request is sent to the bookings agent to reschedule the procedure.

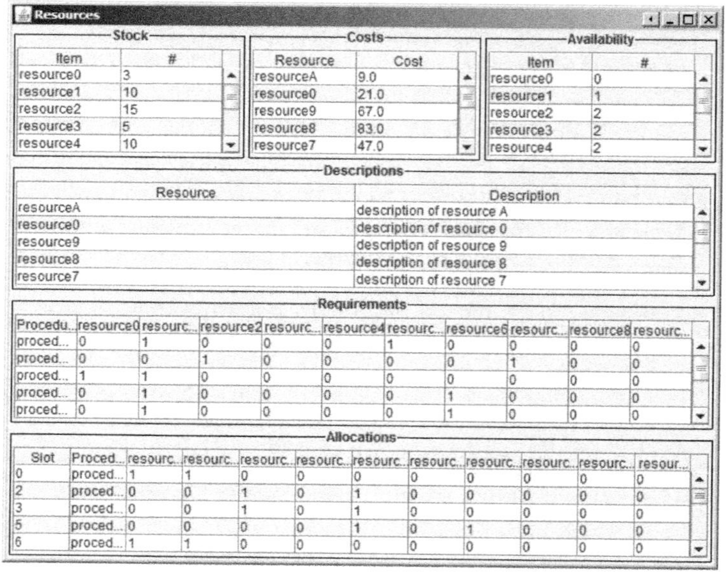

Resources

Stock

Item	#
resource0	3
resource1	10
resource2	15
resource3	5
resource4	10

Costs

Resource	Cost
resourceA	9.0
resource0	21.0
resource9	67.0
resource8	83.0
resource7	47.0

Availability

Item	#
resource0	0
resource1	1
resource2	2
resource3	2
resource4	2

Descriptions

Resource	Description
resourceA	description of resource A
resource0	description of resource 0
resource9	description of resource 9
resource8	description of resource 8
resource7	description of resource 7

Requirements

Procedu...	resource0	resourc...	resource2	resourc...	resource4	resourc...	resource6	resourc...	resource8	resourc...
proced...	0	1	0	0	0	1	0	0	0	0
proced...	0	0	1	0	0	0	0	1	0	0
proced...	1	1	0	0	0	0	0	0	0	0
proced...	0	1	0	0	0	0	1	0	0	0
proced...	0	1	0	0	0	0	1	0	0	0

Allocations

Slot	Proced...	resourc...	resourc...	resourc...	resourc...	resourc...	resourc...	resourc...	resourc...	resourc...	resour...
0	proced...	1	1	0	0	0	0	0	0	0	0
2	proced...	0	0	1	0	1	0	0	0	0	0
3	proced...	0	0	1	0	1	0	0	0	0	0
5	proced...	0	0	0	0	1	0	1	0	0	0
6	proced...	1	1	0	0	0	0	0	0	0	0

Fig. 6. Resources Agent

Additional constraints representing preference, breaks, shifts and working regulation also apply to the nursing schedule.

The Nursing agent also needs to match the allocation of nurses to procedures with other staffing agents such as Anaesthesiology. Such negotiations are often necessary to maximize the compatibility and efficiency of the operating team, and also help maintain staff morale. This is modeled using inter-agent constraints carrying appropriately high cost. An optimal solution would thus ensure that these constraints were satisfied even if it came at the cost of hiring additional casual staff.

The responsibilities of the Anaesthesiology agent largely mimic those of the Nursing agent. The differences lie in the requirements of procedures, preferences and number of staff to be assigned, use of temporary staff, and award and training requirements of the department.

Finally, all agents are able to incrementally adjust and optimize the schedules based on changing circumstances. Should a procedure be rescheduled, all schedules must reflect this in a timely manner. As scheduled procedures draw near to execution, additional constraints can be imposed to increase stability. This would reflect the difficulty of successfully accommodating last minute changes.

However, at no point prior to the scheduled time of a procedure can a procedure be confirmed. Emergency cases must be accommodated. Should theatres, staff or resources be required by such emergencies, the system must be capable of adjusting to these last minute needs.

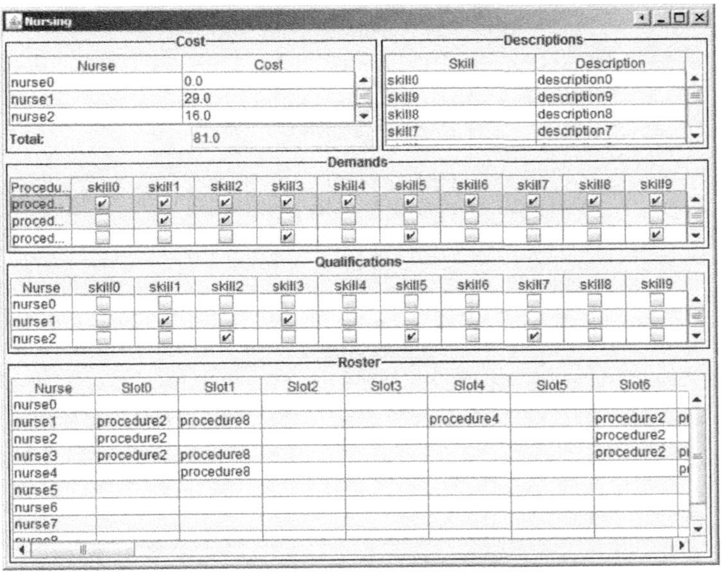

Nursing

Cost

Nurse	Cost
nurse0	0.0
nurse1	29.0
nurse2	16.0
Total:	81.0

Descriptions

Skill	Description
skill0	description0
skill9	description9
skill8	description8
skill7	description7

Demands

Procedu...	skill0	skill1	skill2	skill3	skill4	skill5	skill6	skill7	skill8	skill9
proced...	✓	✓	✓	✓	✓	✓	✓	✓	✓	✓
proced...		✓	✓							
proced...				✓		✓				✓

Qualifications

Nurse	skill0	skill1	skill2	skill3	skill4	skill5	skill6	skill7	skill8	skill9
nurse0										
nurse1		✓		✓						
nurse2			✓			✓		✓		

Roster

Nurse	Slot0	Slot1	Slot2	Slot3	Slot4	Slot5	Slot6	
nurse0								
nurse1	procedure2	procedure8			procedure4		procedure2	pr
nurse2	procedure2						procedure2	
nurse3	procedure2	procedure8					procedure2	pr
nurse4		procedure8						pr
nurse5								
nurse6								
nurse7								

Fig. 7. Nursing Agent

In many scenarios, the system needs user-input to make a decision about a negotiation request received. For example, if a slot opening permits a procedure to be brought forward, the Bookings department may request such a change. However, the Nurse Unit Manager may accommodate the change at short notice only at her discretion, or after explicit discussion with the staff involved. In situations such as this, there is no alternative to deferring the decision to the user. We are currently working on implementing an Intelligence Module within ASES that provides this decision support. The module is based on the system suggested by Khanna et al. [11]. It is designed to mimic the behaviour of the domain expert in these scenarios and to build a knowledge bank by learning from decisions taken by the domain expert. The decision flow of this module is presented in Fig. 8.

4 Evaluation

Since current hospital processes do not capture transient scheduling information, real-world data could not be used to drive the simulation. Parameters such as the number of theatre slots, average procedure time and number of staff per department were selected based on data collected from interviews with domain experts and the tools currently in the hospitals employ. These were used to generate statistically significant random test data to drive the ASES system and evaluate the feasibility of our approach. However, we did make some simplifying assumptions. We did not model all of the constraints we identified as crucial. This was due to the immaturity of the system, as this process would require

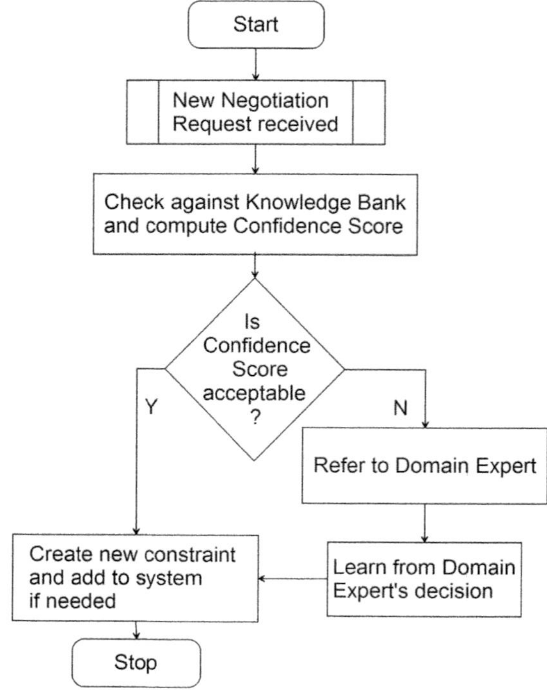

Fig. 8. Intelligent Decision Support

considerable domain expert interaction, and not to any technical difficulty. Further, given the absence of suitable comparison benchmarks, the efficiency of the DCDCOP algorithm was not specifically evaluated within the system.

As procedures were booked, the information flowed in real time to other agents, who updated their schedule accordingly. Conflicts were identified and negotiation initiated to resolve them. Similarly, cancellations resulted in resources being freed up and made available instantly. The system thus reduces inefficiencies caused by delays in current communication and negotiation procedures. With all resources and staff available, ASES reported resolving an average of 226 conflicts at 70% theatre utilization and an average of 325 conflicts at 100% theatre utilization. When available resources were reduced by 10% (to simulate situations where equipment was unavailable), the number of conflicts increased to 384 at 70% utilization and ASES managed to achieve only a maximum of 93% theatre utilization (Fig. 9).

In automating the scheduling process, thus, ASES significantly reduces delays in inter-departmental information flow and negotiation. The ability to automatically generate optimal departmental schedules also offers a saving of several hours of manual work that currently goes into preparing the schedules. For example, the Nurse Unit Manager currently spends an average of 50 hours a month creating the following month's schedule and an average of 2 hours a day han-

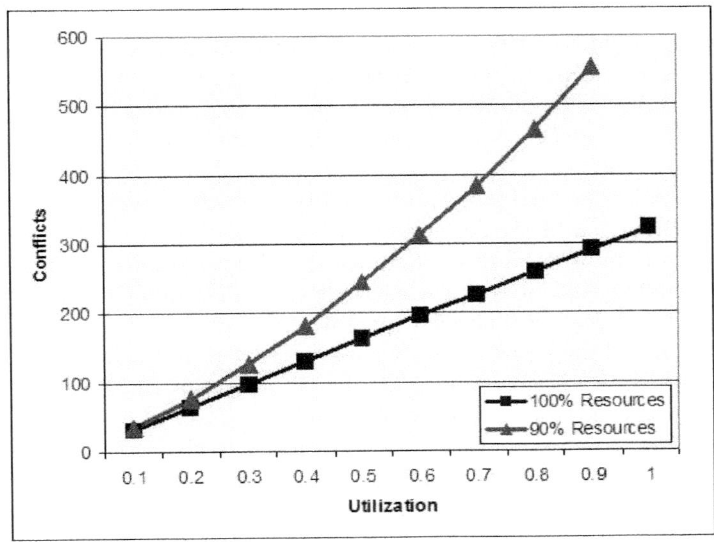

Fig. 9. Conflicts Vs Theatre Utilization

dling the rescheduling. Though delays resulting from waiting for user interaction are unavoidable, the need for such interaction will also decrease as the system learns and builds its knowledge bank for automated decision support. Further, as the departmental schedules are always maintained conflict free, ASES altogether does away with the need for weekly meetings.

Another key enhancement offered by ASES revolves around the efficient management of operating theatre resources. In the current manual system, procedures are scheduled without foreknowledge of the availability of resources, often resulting in a compromised schedule. This is corroborated in the current evaluation as we observe that unavailability of resources can quickly lead to poor theatre utilization. Integrating resource management and scheduling within the ASES system can allow sufficient time to overcome resource shortages and improve theatre utilization.

5 Conclusion and Future Work

We have presented ASES, an Automated Scheduler for Elective Surgery. ASES models the challenging Elective Surgery Scheduling Problem using the multiagent system paradigm, and is powered by a DCOP engine capable of handling the complex and dynamic nature of the problem. Through this novel integration of multiagent modeling and state-of-the-art artificial intelligence techniques, ASES represents a significant advance towards solving this particularly challenging class of complex distributed dynamic problems. Our preliminary evaluation of the system shows that automated scheduling using ASES offers real-world efficiency improvements.

We are currently working towards implementing intelligent decision support and learning within ASES. This module would gradually learn to mimic the domain expert's decision making process and help overcome delays caused by the unavailability of the domain experts. We are also implementing other DCOP algorithms within ASES to aid empirical evaluation of DCDCOP's performance within the system.

Several challenges need to be addressed before ASES can be deployed in hospitals. Firstly, much of the knowledge utilized to generate current departmental schedules is informal and undocumented. Creating domain rules that could be used to define and quantify constraint cost functions is a non trivial task. Achieving this milestone, however, would also serve the purpose of streamlining current scheduling processes. Secondly, quantifying confidence scores and managing dynamically changing priorities also poses a challenge for intelligent decision support. Manual curation of the schedules, and the system's ability to learn from this process, however, provides a mechanism for assisting with the latter. Lastly, gaining acceptance from the end-users of the system is critical, and we are working closely with these practitioners to ensure that the system optimally serves their scheduling needs.

Acknowledgments. The authors wish to thank Dr. Peter Moran and his colleagues at the Princess Alexandra Hospital for their ongoing support, for allowing us into their world, and for sharing their invaluable expertise.

References

1. Australian Medical Association: Public Hospital Report Card 2009 (2009), `http://ama.com.au/node/5030`
2. Bordini, R.H., Wooldridge, M., Hübner, J.F.: Programming Multi-Agent Systems in AgentSpeak using Jason. John Wiley & Sons (2007)
3. Burke, D.A.: Exploiting Problem Structure in Distributed Constraint Optimisation with Complex Local Problems. PhD thesis, Department of Computer Science, University College Cork, Ireland (2008)
4. Chechetka, A., Sycara, K.: An Any-Space Algorithm for Distributed Constraint Optimization. In: AAAI Spring Symposium on Distributed Plan and Schedule Management (2006)
5. Fox, M.S., Allen, B., Strohm, G.: Job-Shop Scheduling: An Investigation in Constraint-Directed Reasoning. In: 2nd Conference of The American Association for Artificial Intelligence, pp. 155–158 (1982)
6. Friha, L.: DISA: Distributed Interactive Scheduler using Abstractions, PhD thesis, University of Geneva, Geneva (1998)
7. Jebali, A., Hadj Alouane, A.B., Ladet, P.: Operating Rooms Scheduling. International Journal of Production Economics 99(1-2), 52–62 (2006)
8. Jones, A., Rabelo, J.: Survey of Job Shop Scheduling Techniques. NISTIR, National Institute of Standards and Technology, Gaithersburg, USA (1998)
9. Khanna, S.: Distributed Constraint Optimization and Scheduling in Dynamic Environments. PhD Thesis, Institute for Integrated and Intelligent Systems, Griffith University, Australia (2010)

10. Khanna, S., Sattar, A., Hansen, D., Stantic, B.: An Efficient Algorithm for Solving Dynamic Complex DCOP Problems. In: 2009 IEEE/WIC/ACM International Joint Conference on Web Intelligence and Intelligent Agent Technology (WI-IAT 2009), Milano, Italy, pp. 339–346 (2009)
11. Khanna, S., Sattar, A., Maeder, A., Stantic, B.: Intelligent Scheduling in Complex Dynamic Distributed Environments. In: 12th World Congress on Health (Medical) Informatics; Building Sustainable Health System (Medinfo 2007), Brisbane, Australia, pp. 1665–1666 (2007)
12. Krempels, K., Panchenko, A.: An Approach for Automated Surgery Scheduling. In: 6th International Conference on the Practice and Theory of Automated Timetabling, Brno, Czech Republic, pp. 209–233 (2006)
13. Krempels, K., Panchenko, A.: Dialog-Based Intelligent Operation Theatre Scheduler. In: 6th International Conference on the Practice and Theory of Automated Timetabling, Brno, Czech Republic, pp. 524–527 (2006)
14. Lamiri, M., Grimaud, F., Xie, X.: Optimization Methods for a Stochastic Surgery Planning Problem. International Journal of Production Economics, Special Issue on Introduction to Design and Analysis of Production Systems 120(2), 400–410 (2009)
15. Lamiri, M., Xie, X., Dolgui, A., Grimaud, F.: A Stochastic Model for Operating Room Planning with Elective and Emergency Demand For Surgery. European Journal of Operational Research 185(3), 1026–1037 (2008)
16. Lass, R.N., Sultanik, E.A., Regli, W.C.: Dynamic Distributed Constraint Reasoning. In: 23rd AAAI Conference on Artificial Intelligence, Chicago, USA, pp. 1466–1469 (2008)
17. Modi, P.J., Shen, W., Tambe, M., Yokoo, M.: An Asynchronous Complete Method for Distributed Constraint Optimization. In: 2nd International Joint Conference on Autonomous Agents and Multiagent Systems, Melbourne, Australia, pp. 161–168 (2003)
18. Paulussen, T., Zöller, A., Rothlauf, F., Heinzl, A., Braubach, L., Pokahr, A., Lamersdorf, W.: Agent-Based Patient Scheduling in Hospitals. In: Multiagent Engineering, Theory and Applications in Enterprises, pp. 255–275. Springer, Heidelberg (2006)
19. Petcu, A., Faltings, B.: A Scalable Method for Multiagent Constraint Optimization. In: Nineteenth International Joint Conference on Artificial Intelligence, Edinburgh, Scotland, pp. 266–271 (2005)
20. Pham, D.N., Klinkert, A.: Surgical Case Scheduling as a Generalized Job Shop Scheduling Problem. European Journal of Operational Research 185(3), 1011–1025 (2008)
21. Prosser, P., Buchanan, I.: Intelligent Scheduling: Past, Present and Future. Intelligent Systems Engineering 3(2), 67–78 (1994)
22. Queensland Health: Quarterly Public Hospitals Performance Report March Quarter 2010 (2010), http://www.health.qld.gov.au/surgical_access
23. Rao, A.S.: AgentSpeak(L): BDI Agents Speak Out in a Logical Computable Language. In: Perram, J., Van de Velde, W. (eds.) MAAMAW 1996. LNCS, vol. 1038, pp. 42–55. Springer, Heidelberg (1996)
24. Woolridge, M.: Introduction to Multiagent Systems, 2nd edn. John Wiley & Sons (2009)
25. Zweben, M., Fox, M.: Intelligent Scheduling. Morgan Kaufmann, San Francisco (1994)

Effect of Alternative Distributed Task Allocation Strategy Based on Local Observations in Contract Net Protocol

Toshiharu Sugawara[1], Kensuke Fukuda[2], Toshio Hirotsu[3], and Satoshi Kurihara[4]

[1] Department of Computer Science and Engineering
Waseda University,
Tokyo 1698555, Japan
sugawara@waseda.jp

[2] National Institute of Informatics
Chiyoda, Tokyo 100-000, Japan
kensuke@nii.ac.jp

[3] Faculty of Computer and Information Sciences
Hosei University, Tokyo, Japan
hirotsu@hosei.ac.jp

[4] Institute of Scientific and Industrial Research
Osaka University
kurihara@ist.osaka-u.ac.jp

Abstract. This paper presents a distributed task allocation method whose strategies are alternatively selected based on the estimated workloads of the local agents. Recent Internet, sensor-network, and cloud computing applications are large-scale and fully-distributed, and thus, require sophisticated multi-agent system technologies to enable a large number of programs and computing resources to be effectively used. To elicit the capabilities of all the agents in a large-scale multi-agent system (LSMAS) in which thousands of agents work concurrently requires a new negotiation strategy for appropriately allocating tasks in a distributed manner. We start by focusing on the contract net protocol (CNP) in LSMAS and then examine the effects of the awardee selection strategies, that is, the task allocation strategies. We will show that probabilistic awardee selections improve the overall performance in specific situations. Next, the mixed strategy in which a number of awardee selections are alternatively used based on the analysis of the bid from the local agents is proposed. Finally, we show that the proposed strategy does not only avoid task concentrations but also reduces the wasted efforts, thus it can considerably improve the performance.

Keywords: Distributed task allocation, Adaptive Behavior, Negotiation, Load-balancing.

1 Introduction

Recent Internet technologies enable for advanced large-scale applications, such as e-commerce, grid computing, distributed computing, and cloud computing. Within these applications, thousands of computational entities, called *agents*, have their own tasks,

N. Desai, A. Liu, and M. Winikoff (Eds.): PRIMA 2010, LNAI 7057, pp. 90–104, 2012.

such as user authentication, stock control, customer recommendation, purchasing management, and shipping control in e-commerce applications, work concurrently and collaborate with each other. In this kind of system, which can be modeled as a *large-scale multi-agent system* (LSMAS), these tasks must be appropriately assigned to the agents based on their abilities. However, they often interfere with each other. For example, if many tasks are allocated to only a few specific agents, this may lead to a delay of one of the task fragments (or subtasks), resulting in the delay of the whole task.

On the other hand, new Internet applications have been and will be more dynamic, agents will have different computational resources/abilities, and new services and new servers will frequently come and go. Of course, the agents' states will also change over time. These facts indicate that agents cannot acquire the most accurate global states of the entire system. Thus, the key issue is how the agents will effectively allocate subtasks to other agents using only locally available information so as to exploit the capabilities of the entire system. For this requirement, contract- and auction-based approaches to task and resource allocations [2] have received a lot of attention for future wide-area distributed network applications.

Although a number of researches on (distributed) task allocations have already been conducted such as Ref. [7], we first focus on a task allocation using a *contract net protocol* (CNP) because it is used in many applications [9,16]. In the CNP, an agent plays one of two roles: *managers* who are responsible for allocating tasks and monitoring processes and *contractors* who are responsible for executing the allocated tasks. A manager agent makes a task known to the contractor agents in the announcement phase, and the contractors tender the bid on the task with certain values, such as the cost, estimated duration to process, or required payment, in the bid phase. In the award phase, the manager awards the contractor (or *awardee*) who tendered the best bid.

The objective of our research is to clarify the characteristics of the CNP in a busy LSMAS and to propose contract strategy, more precisely *awarding strategy* in the award phase, resulting in a more efficient cumulative processing of the entire system than the contract strategy in a conventional CNP. This is a challenging issue because interference among agents is intricately intertwined in this kind of negotiation protocol if many managers have tasks to allocate simultaneously. In a naive CNP, a contractor agent responds to the task announcements one by one, but if many managers announce tasks simultaneously in a busy LSMAS, the managers may have to wait a long time to receive a sufficient number of bids. This significantly reduces the performance of the entire system [6]. In the original conception of CNP [12], the use of multiple bids was proposed as a way to concurrently handle many announcements. If a contractor is awarded multiple bids simultaneously, however, it may not be able to provide the quality or performance it declared in the bids. In fact, managers tend to select highly capable contractor agents. Additionally, if the task has a structure, meaning if the task consists of a number of different subtasks, the situation becomes ever more complex.

In this paper, we propose a novel awarding strategy that leads to a more efficient processing of LSMAS. This is a meta-level strategy that selects one from a set of awarding strategies on the basis of the local observations. References [14,15] already tackled this issue, but they assumed a simplified model in which the tasks have no structure, which means a task is singleton and indivisible, and have the same cost. However, our model is more general, that is, a task is plural consisting of a number of subtasks, and their method in [15] cannot be applied to plural tasks.

In addition, another significant issue, wasted efforts, appears in the plural task structure model. Of course, in both the singleton and plural models, we have to avoid task concentrations that lead to inefficient processing and many drops of subtasks. In addition, the failure (or delay) of only one subtask means the failure (or delay) of the whole task in the plural model. Therefore, the agents' resources used for other subtasks become useless. This also significantly reduces the performance of the entire LSMAS. Thus, the required strategy has to be able to reduce the number of wasted efforts as well as the task concentration so that it can considerably improve the overall performance.

This paper is organized as follows: In the next section, we explain our models, the issues to be addressed, and our simulation environment. Then, we introduce the *probabilistic awardee selection strategy*, under which an awardee is selected with certain fixed probabilities based on the bid values. We show that by changing the award strategies according to the local workload, the overall performance can be considerably improved for a specific task consisting of a number of subtasks. After that, we optimize this award strategy under which a probabilistic award strategy and the conventional award strategy are selected alternatively according to the estimated local workloads of the agents within the environments where certain tasks are blended. We experimentally show that the extended strategy can significantly improve the overall performance. Finally, we try to explain the reason for this improvement.

2 Problem Description

2.1 Model of Agents and Tasks

Let $\mathcal{A} = \{1, \ldots, n\}$ be a set of agents, $\mathcal{T}$ be a task, and $\mathcal{F} = \{f^1, \ldots, f^d\}$ be the set of skills or functions that agents can perform. We assume that task $\mathcal{T}$ consists of subtasks, $t_1, \ldots, t_l$, (i.e., $\mathcal{T} = \{t_1, \ldots, t_l\}$ and $|\mathcal{T}| = l$) and that subtask $t (\in \mathcal{T})$ requires the $s(t)$-th skill, $f^{s(t)}$, where $1 \leq s(t) \leq d$. A subtask is denoted by the lower-case letter t and is simply called a task unless this creates confusion. Agent i is expressed as a tuple, $(\alpha_i, L_i, S_i, Q_i)$, where $\alpha_i = (a_i^1, \ldots, a_i^d)$ is the set of agent's capabilities (a_i^h corresponds to the h-th skill, f^h, and $a_i^h \geq 0$; $a_i^h = 0$ indicates agent i does not have skill f^h), L_i is the location of i, and Q_i is the queue where the agent's tasks are stored, which are waiting to be executed one by one. The maximum queue length, Q_i, can be finite or infinite, but was assumed 20 in our experiments. The set $S_i (\subset \mathcal{A})$ is i's scope, i.e., the set of agents that i knows. The *metric* between the agents, $\delta(i, j)$, is based on their locations, L_i and L_j, and is used to define the communication time (or delay) of the messages between i and j.

Subtask t has an associated cost, $\gamma(t)$, which is the cost to complete it. Subtask t can be done by i in $\lceil \gamma(t)/a_i^{s(t)} \rceil$ time units, where $\lceil x \rceil$ denotes the ceiling function. The time it takes to complete t is also called the *execution time* of t by i. $\mathcal{T}$ is completed when all its subtasks are completed.

In every unit time, $\mathcal{L} (\geq 0)$ tasks on average are generated according to a Poisson distribution and are randomly assigned to different managers. The parameter $\mathcal{L}$ is called the *task load* and is denoted by $\mathcal{L}$ tasks per unit time, or simply $\mathcal{L}$ T/t.

2.2 Task Allocations for LSMAS

For CNP, we define $\mathcal{M} = \{m_j\}(\subset \mathcal{A})$ as the set of managers who allocate tasks and $\mathcal{C} = \{c_k\}(\subset \mathcal{A})$ as the set of contractors who execute the allocated tasks. Let us assume that $|\mathcal{A}|$ is large (on the order of thousands); therefore, $|\mathcal{M}|$ and $|\mathcal{C}|$ are also large; Moreover, we shall assume that the agents are widely distributed, like servers on the Internet.

In our experiments, we used a CNP modified for use in a LSMAS for the sake of efficiency. In this CNP, (1) multiple bids and *regret* and *no-bid* messages are allowed, and (2) manager m announces each subtask in $\mathcal{T}$ to the contractors that are selected from its scope, S_m, on the basis of an *announcement strategy*. This procedure can reduce the number of messages. *Regret messages* are sent in the award phase to contractors who were not awarded the contract; *no-bid messages* are sent to managers by contractors who decided not to bid on an announced task. These messages prevent long waits for bids and award messages (e.g., [9,17]).

When manager m receives $\mathcal{T}$, it immediately initiates the modified CNP for each task $\tilde{t}(\in \mathcal{T})$. It first sends announcement messages to the contractors selected from its scope. Each of these contractors sends back a bid message with a certain *bid value*. The bid values might include parameters such as the price for executing the task, the quality of the result, or a combination of these values. Since we are concerned with the efficiency of processing using multiple agents, we assume that their bid values contain the estimated required times for completing the task. Thus, the bid value of contractor c is:

$$\lceil \gamma(\tilde{t})/a_c^{s(\tilde{t})} \rceil + \sum_{t \in Q_c} \lceil \gamma(t)/a_c^{s(t)} \rceil + \beta,$$

where β is the time required to complete the task currently being executed. For multiple bidding, c might have a number of outstanding bids. These bids are not considered because it is uncertain whether they will be accepted. Then, m selects a contractor, the awardee, on the basis of the *award strategy* and sends the awardee a message along with the announced task. Selecting the best bidder is the award strategy in the naive CNP.

When contractor c is awarded a task, it immediately executes it if it has no other tasks. If c is already executing a task, the new task is stored in Q_c, and the tasks in Q_c are executed in turn.

2.3 Performance Measures

Since the queue length of agent i is finite, some allocated subtasks might not be storable in its queue and so they are *dropped*. If all the subtasks in $\mathcal{T}$ are dropped, $\mathcal{T}$ is called a *dropped task*. If $\mathcal{T}$ contains both dropped and not-dropped tasks, it is called a *wasting task*. From the viewpoints of the users and clients in actual applications such as e-commerce, dropped and wasting tasks appear as refused or non-responding requests due to the congestion of servers. From the viewpoints of the servers, and thus, the investors who prepared the equipment to provide the services, the wasting task contains wasted efforts, that is, a number of uselessly executed subtasks, whereas the dropped task does not. So, more wasting tasks lowers the performance of the entire LSMAS.

We assume that manager agents can observe, for each subtask t, the *completion time*, which is the elapsed time from the time the award message is sent, $m_s(t)$, to the time the message indicating that the subtask has been completed is received, $m_e(t)$. The completion time thus includes the communication time in both directions, the queue time, and the execution time. The completion time of $\mathcal{T}$ is defined as $\max_{t\in\mathcal{T}}(m_e(t)) - \min_{t\in\mathcal{T}}(m_s(t))$. A smaller average completion time is better. The *overall performance of a LSMAS*, denoted by $\wp$, is defined as the average of the completion times observed by all managers and used as the system's performance measure. The issues we address are thus the overall performance of a LSMAS under various award strategies and how to improve it by combining the advantages of these award strategies. Moreover, dropped and wasting tasks are counted as a separate performance measure; they are non-zero only if the systems are busy or overloaded.

2.4 Simulation Environment

We set $|C| = 500$ and $|\mathcal{M}| = 10,000$ in our simulation. The agents were randomly placed on a 150×150 grid with a torus topology, which is denoted by G. The Manhattan distance was chosen as G's metric. The communication time ranged from 1 to 14 (in *ticks*, the time unit in the simulation), in proportion to the value of $\delta(i, j)$.

We express the cost structure of the subtasks by using the superscript of $\mathcal{T}$, if necessary. For example, $\mathcal{T}^{25-5}$ consists of two subtasks, $\{t_1, t_2\}$ such that $\gamma(t_1) = 2500$ and $\gamma(t_2) = 500$.[1] Contractor c_i is assigned different capabilities so that the values of $2500/a^1_{c_i}$ $(c_i \in C)$ will be *uniformly distributed* over the range 20–100; the values of $a^1_{c_i}$ range from 25 – 125. Therefore, for $\mathcal{T}^{25-5} = \{t_1, t_2\}$, c_i can execute t_1 and t_2 within 20–100 ticks and 4–20 ticks, respectively. We assume that the manager agents can not do the tasks themselves ($a^1_m = a^2_m = 0$) forcing them to assign the tasks to agents who can, and that $a^1_{c_i} = a^2_{c_i}$; the latter condition means that a high-performance PC can effectively execute any task if the functions are defined.

The results presented here are the mean values from ten independent trials. In these trials, the maximal numbers of $\mathcal{T}$s being executed every tick, as derived from the cumulative capabilities of all contractors $\sum_{c\in C} a_c$, ranged from 8.15 to 8.30 T/t, with an average of 8.25 T/t. This is the theoretical upper limit, meaning that if the task allocation is ideal, the contractors can execute 8.25 tasks every tick.

Manager m's scope, S_m, consists of the nearest 50 contractors. More precisely, for a positive integer n, let $S_m(n) = \{c \in C | \delta(m, c) \leq n\}$. It follows that $S_m(n) \subset S_m(n + 1)$. S_m is defined as the smallest $S_m(n)$ such that $|S_m(n)| \geq 50$. Then, m announces tasks to $N (\leq 50)$ contractors who were randomly selected from S_m. The overall performance varied depending on N and was optimal when N was 20 in our simulation environment [13]. Thus, we assume $N = 20$ in what follows so we can focus on the award strategies.

3 Usage of Probability in the Award Phase

A small number of high-capability agents that receive multiple awards will likely bear an excessive workload whenever many managers simultaneously announce numerous

[1] As another example, $\mathcal{T}^{18-8-4}$ means a task consisting of three subtasks $\{t_1, t_2, t_3\}$ whose costs are 1800, 800 and 400, respectively.

tasks. A simple awarding strategy for alleviating the burden of too many awards is to allocate some tasks to the non-best contractor by introducing a probability in the award phase. In this section, we discuss the effect of this type of probabilistic award by comparing it with that for the naive CNP.

3.1 Effect of Probabilistic Award

Reference [15] reported that some degree of fluctuation in the award phase could improve the overall performance when a task has no structure. The objective of the first experiment was to verify this effect when a task consists of a number of subtasks.

Let $\{c_1, \ldots, c_p\}$ be the contractors that bid on the announced task. We denote the bid value from contractor c_i by b_{c_i}. In the naive CNP, m selects the contractor who submitted the best bid (a smaller bid is better). The first award strategy selects the awardee according to the following probability:

$$\Pr(c_i) = \frac{1/(b_{c_i})^k}{\sum_{j=1}^{p} 1/(b_{c_j})^k}. \tag{1}$$

This *probabilistic awardee selection* strategy is denoted by PAS_k. Non-negative integer k is a parameter called the *fluctuation factor*, or simply the *f-factor*. The larger the k, the smaller the degree of fluctuation: PAS_0 and PAS_∞ respectively correspond to "random selection" and "no randomness." Therefore, PAS_∞ is the award strategy in the naive CNP.

We evaluated the overall performance by gradually increasing $\mathcal{L}$ from 0.1 (idle) to 10 (extremely busy, over the cumulative capabilities) in 5-K ticks and then returning it to 0.1. The total duration was 160-K ticks. We plotted the improvement ratios $\mathcal{I}_{CNP}$ from PAS_k to PAS_∞ every 5-K ticks:

$$\mathcal{I}_{CNP}(\text{PAS}_k) = \frac{\wp(\text{PAS}_\infty) - \wp(\text{PAS}_k)}{\wp(\text{PAS}_\infty)} \times 100, \tag{2}$$

where $\wp(\mathit{str})$ indicates the overall performance when award selection strategy *str* is used. Note that $\mathcal{I}_{CNP}(\text{PAS}_\infty) = 0$.

We assumed $\mathcal{T} = \{t_1, t_2\}$ and examined $\mathcal{T}^{25-5}$ and $\mathcal{T}^{20-10}$; the results are labeled "PAS_3" and "PAS_6" in Fig. 1. The graphs also list the task loads over time along the horizontal axis. These curves indicate that when task load $\mathcal{L}$ is small (very few multiple awards occur) or very large (over the theoretical limit of cumulative capability), PAS_∞ performs well (PAS_k is worse up to 34%). When $\mathcal{L}$ is in the middle range, PAS_k ($k = 3$ or 6) improves the overall efficiency by as much as 29%. We can thus expect that when the system is busy but does not reach the theoretical limit, PAS_k can avoid the concentration of the workload and maintain the efficiency. However, this is not always true if the system is too busy to process the given tasks. When the system is extremely busy, $\mathcal{I}_{CNP}(\text{PAS}_6)$ for $\mathcal{T}^{25-5}$ is better than $\mathcal{I}_{CNP}(\text{PAS}_6)$ for $\mathcal{T}^{20-10}$, and $\mathcal{I}_{CNP}(\text{PAS}_6) > 0$ for $\mathcal{T}^{25-5}$ but $\mathcal{I}_{CNP}(\text{PAS}_6) < 0$ for $\mathcal{T}^{20-10}$. After a number of experiments, we observed that $\mathcal{I}_{CNP}(\text{PAS}_k)$ was lower in an extremely busy environment if (1) $|\gamma(t_1) - \gamma(t_2)|$ is small or (2) $\gamma(t_1) + \gamma(t_2)$ is large. For the former situation, we introduce

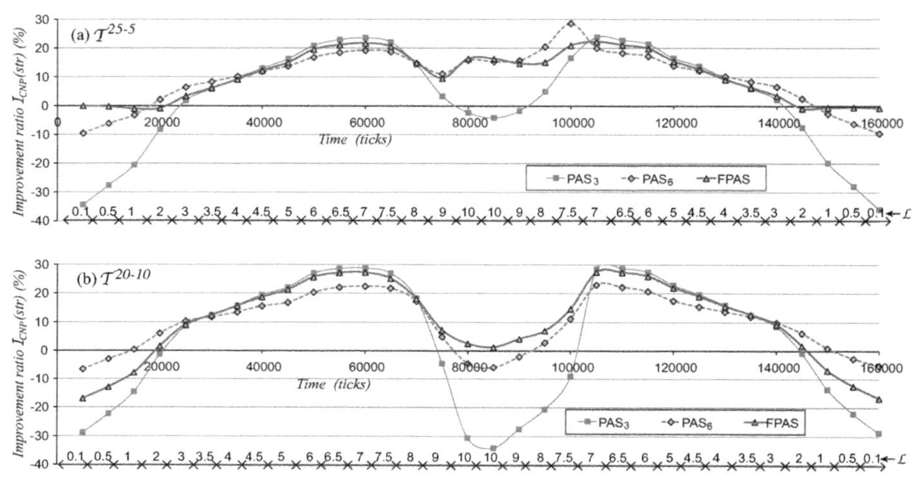

Fig. 1. Ratio of completion times $\mathcal{I}_{CNP}(\mathrm{PAS}_k)$ ($k = 3$ and 6) and $\mathcal{I}_{CNP}(\mathrm{FPAS})$

a *phantom task*, which will be discussed later. Note that the center of the curves in Fig. 1 are shifted slightly to the left because of the effect of the delay in executing tasks queuing during the overload.

3.2 'Flexible' Probabilistic Award

The f-factor of PAS_k should be adaptively controlled according to the system's task loads in order to utilize the full capabilities of a LSMAS from the experimental results in the previous section. However, it is impossible to assess the system's task load, because it is non-local information. Instead, Ref. [14] estimated the task load of the LSMAS from the average queue length of contractors. However, this estimate cannot be easily applied to our case, because if the queue is long but the costs of the queuing tasks are small, the agents cannot conclude whether the system is busy.

Our idea to resolve this issue is to estimate the situations by statistically analyzing the bid values from the local contractors. More precisely, we used the differences between the standard deviations (SDs) of the bid values for different tasks that had different costs. Assume that, for announced task t, manager m received bids whose values were $B_m(t) = \{b_1(t), b_2(t), \dots\}$. Let the SD of $B_m(t)$ be denoted by $SD_m(t)$, and $D_m^{SD}(\mathcal{T})$ be $|SD_m(t_1) - SD_m(t_2)|$ for $\mathcal{T} = \{t_1, t_2\}$. Figure 2 shows how the average values and standard deviations of $D_m^{SD}(\mathcal{T}^{25-5})$ for $\forall m \in \mathcal{M}$ vary every 5000 ticks.

When comparing Figs. 1 and 2, we see that $D_m^{SD}(\mathcal{T}^{25-5})$ can be used as the signal for optimizing the degree of fluctuation; more precisely, the f-factor k can be chosen by using the following strategy,

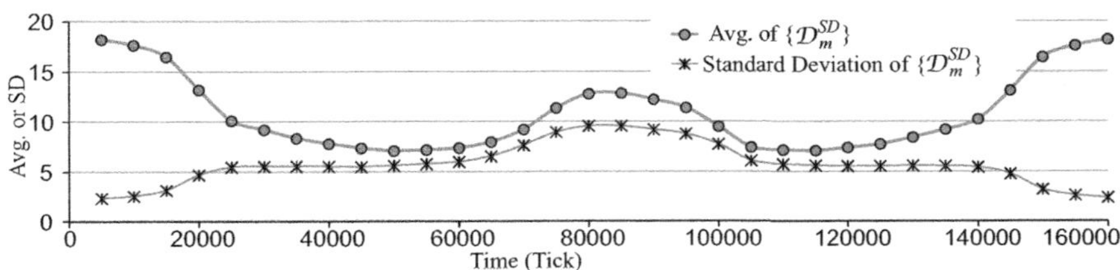

Fig. 2. Average values and SDs of $D_m^{SD}(\mathcal{T}^{25-5})$ over time

$$\begin{aligned} k &= \infty \text{ if } D_m^{SD}(\mathcal{T}) \geq 12.0, \\ k &= 6 \text{ if } 12.0 > D_m^{SD}(\mathcal{T}) \geq 8.8, \text{ and} \\ k &= 3 \text{ if } D_m^{SD}(\mathcal{T}) < 8.8. \end{aligned} \qquad \text{(S1)}$$

This is called the *flexible probabilistic awardee selection* strategy or *FPAS*. The threshold values are determined on the basis of a detailed analysis of each trial from the previous experiments, especially those of $\mathcal{T}^{25-5}$. The aim of this strategy is to combine the best from PAS_∞, PAS_3, and PAS_6.

The results for $\mathcal{I}_{CNP}$(FPAS) are also plotted in Fig. 1. Figure 1 clearly indicates that FPAS usually provides a better overall performance than the other individual strategies for $\mathcal{T}^{25-5}$ and $\mathcal{T}^{20-10}$. The improvement ratios are particularly large just before the task load reaches the theoretical limit of the LSMAS and right after the contractors surmount the overload caused by the huge number of queued tasks. This is the most important characteristic and will be discussed in Section 5.

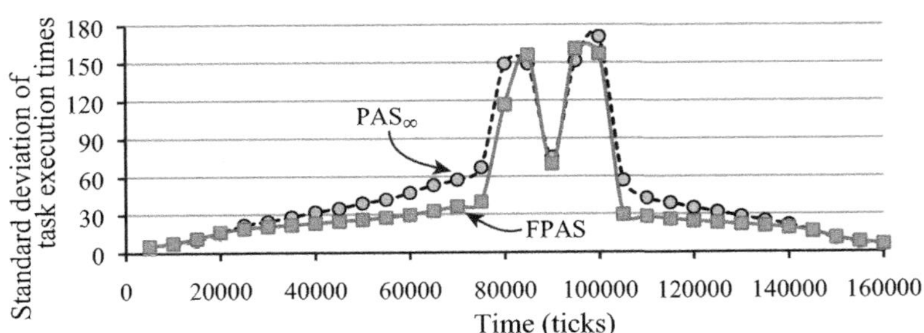

Fig. 3. Standard deviation of completion times under PAS_∞ and FPAS over time

We should also emphasize that FPAS is beneficial to any agent. Figure 3 plots the SDs of the average completion times of individual agents using PAS_∞ and FPAS. The SDs for FPAS are smaller than those for PAS_∞. Therefore, FPAS fairly and impartially performs better for almost all agents.

4 Adaptive Strategy Based on Bid Statistics

4.1 Adaptively Probabilistic Awardee Selection

Since FPAS under strategy (S1) is mainly based on the data for $\mathcal{T}^{25-5}$, it does not necessarily perform well in tasks that have other cost structures. For example, Fig. 1 (b), which indicates the improvement ratio for $\mathcal{T}^{20-10}$, shows that FPAS did not result in a better performance, especially when the task load was low. In this section, we propose a new strategy whereby managers learn how they should determine the f-factor in their environments. The aim of this strategy is to perform in a way that is comparable to that of FPAS for $\mathcal{T}^{25-5}$ and that is generally better than that of PAS$_\infty$ for all tasks.

The algorithm for selecting the f-factor is listed in Fig. 4. First, manager m calculates the SDs of the bid values for each $t_i \in \mathcal{T}$ and the maximum difference between these SDs (denoted by $D_m^{SD}(\mathcal{T})$). It also retains the maximum and minimum values of $D_m^{SD}(\mathcal{T})$ (denoted by *maxSDdiff*, and *minSDdiff*) that have been obtained thus far. It estimates the current task load using *maxSDdiff*, *minSDdiff*, and $D_m^{SD}(\mathcal{T})$. We call this award strategy *adaptively probabilistic awardee selection*, or *APAS*.

Parameter α and variable *minMaxAv* in Fig. 4 are referred to in order to determine whether *maxSDdiff* and *minSDdiff* should be revised. The SDs of $\{D_m^{SD}\}$ in Fig. 2 indicate that the minimum values of $D_m^{SD}(\mathcal{T})$, *maxSDdiff*, and *minSDdiff*, will likely be over-estimated in busy situations because the SD of D_m^{SD} increases. Condition (1) in Fig. 4 estimates this state of overestimation, so we set $\alpha = 1.5$. The constant ε in the figure is used to define the threshold *Th* to switch between award strategies. In our experiments, we chose $\varepsilon = 0.58$ on the basis of the average D_m^{SD} and the SDs of the preliminary experiment shown in Fig. 2. APAS is quite simple in that only PAS$_3$ or PAS$_\infty$ is alternatively selected. Of course, we can extend this to select the appropriate strategy from the set of awarding strategies $\mathcal{S}$, although we set $\mathcal{S}$ ={PAS$_3$, PAS$_\infty$} in our experiment.

Figure 5 plots the improvement ratios for $\mathcal{T}^{25-5}$ and $\mathcal{T}^{20-10}$ over time. $\mathcal{I}_{CNP}$(PAS$_3$) is also plotted because APAS is a mixed strategy involving PAS$_3$ and PAS$_\infty$. Figure 5 indicates that APAS performs as efficiently as FPAS for $\mathcal{T}^{25-5}$ and excellently performs even for $\mathcal{T}^{20-20}$. Note that APAS performs slightly worse than PAS$_\infty$ only when the system is not busy. The learned *Th* might not have been sufficient in this case. Nevertheless, APAS performs excellently in busier situations; it outperforms both PAS$_3$ and PAS$_\infty$, whereas it is the mixed strategy of these two.

4.2 Performance for Different Task Structures and Phantom Task

We also investigated the effect of APAS in tasks with other cost structures. The results are plotted in Fig. 6. These curves indicate that APAS outperforms PAS$_\infty$ for $\mathcal{T}^{22-8}$, $\mathcal{T}^{18-8-4}$, and $\mathcal{T}^{15-8-5-2}$. FPAS does not perform well. We fixed the sum of the costs of these tasks at 3000 to standardize the theoretical upper limit of the task executions by all agents. We used the same changes in the task loads over time because we only wanted to compare their performances under APAS and PAS$_\infty$.

Furthermore, we examined situations in which a number of different tasks occur. For the sake of convenience, let

---

Initialize:
$maxSDdiff = 0, minSDdiff = minMaxAv = \infty$.

for each $\mathcal{T}$
Manager m announces all tasks $t_1, \ldots, t_l, (\in \mathcal{T})$ to the local contractors[2], and m calculates the average value, $Av_m(t_i)$, and the SD, $SD_m(t_i)$, of bid values for t_i.

/* Then, it calculates some statistical values. */
$\overline{Av}_m(\mathcal{T}) \stackrel{\leftarrow}{=} \max_{t_i \in \mathcal{T}} Av_m(t_i)$;
$\overline{SD}_m(\mathcal{T}) \stackrel{\leftarrow}{=} \max_{t_i \in \mathcal{T}} SD_m(t_i)$;
$\underline{SD}_m(\mathcal{T}) \stackrel{\leftarrow}{=} \min_{t_i \in \mathcal{T}} SD_m(t_i)$;
$D_m^{SD}(\mathcal{T}) \stackrel{\leftarrow}{=} \overline{SD}_m(\mathcal{T}) - \underline{SD}_m(\mathcal{T})$;
$minMaxAv \stackrel{\leftarrow}{=} \min(minMaxAv, \overline{Av}_m(\mathcal{T}))$;

/* If the system is not so busy, */
if $(minMaxAv \times \alpha > \overline{Av}_m(\mathcal{T}))\{$ /* Condition (1) */
$maxSDdiff \stackrel{\leftarrow}{=} \max(maxSDdiff, \overline{SD}_m(\mathcal{T}))$;
$minSDdiff \stackrel{\leftarrow}{=} \min(minSDdiff, \underline{SD}_m(\mathcal{T}))$;
}

/* Defining threshold values: */
$Th = \varepsilon \cdot maxSDdiff + (\varepsilon - 1) \cdot minSDdiff$;
/* where $0 < \varepsilon < 1$. */

/* Then output PAS_k by following the rule: */
if $(D_m^{SD}(\mathcal{T}) \geq Th)$ $k = \infty$;
else $k = 3$;

Fig. 4. Outline of APAS strategy

$$C1 = \{\mathcal{T}^{25-5}, \mathcal{T}^{22-8}, \mathcal{T}^{20-10}, \mathcal{T}^{18-12}\}$$
$$C2 = \{\mathcal{T}^{25-3-2}, \mathcal{T}^{20-8-2}, \mathcal{T}^{18-8-4}\}.$$

$\mathcal{T}^{C1}$ (or $\mathcal{T}^{C2}$) in Fig. 6 corresponds to a situation in which the tasks in *C1* (or *C2*) are generated with equal probability. The results in the figure show that APAS performs well in these situations.

If $\mathcal{T}$ consisted of a single subtask or a number of subtasks with almost identical costs, $D_m^{SD}(\mathcal{T})$ could not be calculated or would always be small. For such tasks, we can introduce a *phantom task*, which is announced but is never awarded as a way to estimate the current local workload.

We also investigated the performance of APAS for $\mathcal{T}^{15-15} = \{t_1, t_2\}$ using phantom task t_p, whose cost is 500, and found that APAS outperforms PAS_k and PAS_∞, although the details were omitted here due to space limitations. In this case, managers with $\mathcal{T}^{15-15}$ announce t_1, t_2, and t_p and calculate $D_m^{SD}(\mathcal{T}^{15-15-5})$, but never select an awardee for t_p.

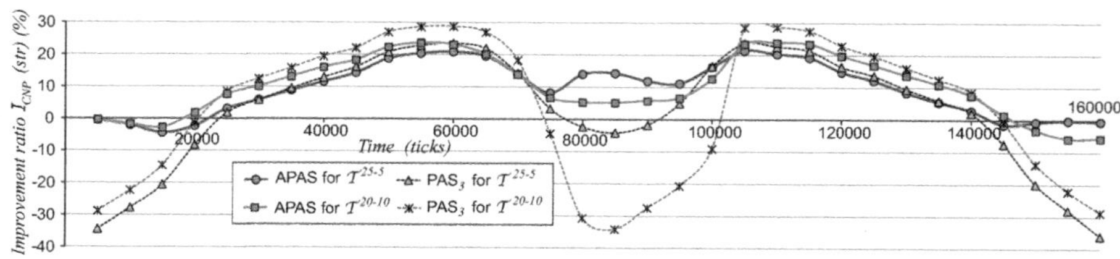

Fig. 5. Improvement ratios of APAS compared with PAS

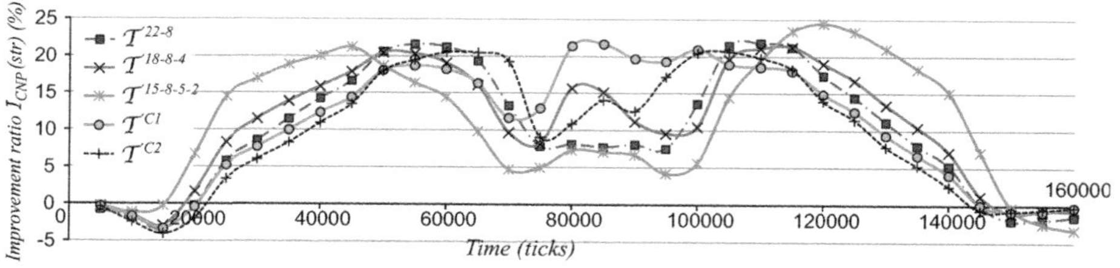

Fig. 6. Improvement ratios of APAS for various tasks

Table 1. Numbers of Dropped and Wasting Tasks

		25-5	18-8-4	15-8-5-2	C1
PAS$_\infty$	dropped	8526.4	4741.3	2538.1	8519.3
	wasting	41517.4	68230	64270.1	40457.5
	total	50043.8	72971.3	66808.2	48976.8
PAS$_3$	dropped	5473.8	1593.6	585.4	5452.1
	wasting	41383.2	66467.7	87807.8	41124.3
	total	46857	68061.3	88393.2	46576.4
APAS	dropped	8542	4655.7	2616.2	9297.9
	wasting	29211.6	47084	62123	29944.3
	total	37753.6	51739.7	64739.2	39242.2

4.3 Analysis of Dropped and Wasting Tasks

In this section we try to analyze why APAS can improve the overall performance. Table 1 lists the numbers of dropped and wasting tasks for different task types in the experiments. We can see that PAS$_3$ clearly reduces the dropped tasks, and that APAS reduces the wasting tasks. APAS also has fewer total numbers of dropped and wasting tasks compared with PAS$_\infty$ and PAS$_3$. Having fewer wasting tasks improves the efficiency of the entire system, because wasting tasks consume more of the contractors' resources.

The main reason for this phenomenon is a small spatial fluctuation in the task load in a busy environment when looking closely at the workloads in each area. As mentioned in the previous section, even in extremely busy cases (near or beyond the theoretical limit), the workload is not spatially uniform although the tasks are randomly assigned to managers. In certain parts of G, agents are overloaded and their queues are full, whereas in other parts the agents have completed some tasks and are somewhat less busy. APAS enables agents to adaptively select PAS_3 or PAS_∞ in accordance with their local conditions. When the workload is beyond the theoretical limit, PAS_∞ (and APAS usually select PAS_∞) results in a large number of dropped and wasting tasks in return for a better performance, $\wp$. In particular, many dropped tasks occur in this case. Unlike PAS_∞, PAS_3 can turn some dropped tasks into wasting ones due to the fluctuation in the award phase. However, wasting tasks are still useless. Thus, PAS_3 is less efficient but has less dropped tasks in extremely busy cases. At the moment of becoming somewhat less busy (APAS usually selects PAS_3), more wasting tasks occur than dropped ones and then PAS_3 can turn some wasting tasks into completed ones. From these results and our analysis, APAS can reduce the number of wasting tasks, comparing with those under PAS_3 and PAS_∞. The analysis in this section implies both a better performance and the presence of less wasting (and dropped) tasks when using the APAS strategy.

4.4 Effect of Maximum Queue Length

In the above experiments, we assumed that the maximum queue length of agent $|Q|$ is 20. This affects the overall performance only during extremely busy periods; the number of tasks in the queue in other situations do not increase. We investigate how the maximum queue length affects the improvement ratios in the paragraphs that follow.

Let $|Q| = \infty$ and use task $\mathcal{T}^{25-5}$ as an example. $\mathcal{I}_{CNP}(\text{PAS}_3)$ improves slightly from its value at $|Q| = 20$, whereas $\mathcal{I}_{CNP}(\text{PAS}_6)$ remains better than $\mathcal{I}_{CNP}(\text{PAS}_3)$. In extremely busy situations, PAS_6 was better than PAS_∞ when $|Q| = 20$, as shown in Fig. 1, but it was worse than PAS_∞ when $|Q| = \infty$. Thus,

$$\mathcal{I}_{CNP}(\text{PAS}_3) < \mathcal{I}_{CNP}(\text{PAS}_6) < 0$$

when $|Q| = \infty$. On the other hand, $\mathcal{I}_{CNP}(\text{APAS})$ is nearly 0 in extremely busy situation, because the queues of the contractors become very long, and none of the managers ever become less busy. Therefore, APAS almost always selects PAS_∞.

5 Discussion

First, we want to point out that the improvement elicited by the proposed strategy was at its largest just before and right after the task load reached the theoretical upper limit. We believe that this feature of our strategy is crucial for real applications. If the task load is low, any task allocation strategy can provide a satisfactory service. However, if it is extremely heavy and over the theoretical limit, no strategy leads to an acceptable performance. In other situations, the system should yield a maximum performance and perform at its fullest potential. Our experimental results revealed that our strategy is excellent in these situations.

When comparing the results in this paper with those in [15], we found that there was significant difference in the mechanism for improving the efficiency. In [15], their method improved the efficiency by avoiding excessive concentration. They dealt with a singleton task, so there was no concept of wasting tasks. In real application systems, however, many wasting tasks that heavily impair the performance are likely to actually occur when they are busy. So, our model is more realistic and from the discussion in the previous section, our proposed task allocation method can improve the performance by reducing the number of dropped and wasting tasks when the agents were extremely busy in the situations mentioned above.

To reduce the number of wasting tasks, it may be possible to propose another and more complex protocol that tracks where the tasks are allocated, monitors them, and if one of the subtask is dropped, stops other subtasks by sending messages to the concerned agents. However, a problem still remains in that the efforts by agents before the arrivals of the messages become meaningless. Another solution is to implement the schedulers that have an accurate view of the other agents and that can compass the other agents' workloads. It is, however, almost impossible to know the other agents' situations because computers may be replaced by others, and tasks are allocated and processed in a distributed way. Avoiding wasting tasks is crucial for the system's efficiency.

Our experiments suggest that autonomous local decisions are more essential for the performance improvement of the entire system. For example, APAS can perform better than PAS_3 and PAS_∞ even though it is a mixture of them. We also examined the performance when $\mathcal{S} = \{\text{PAS}_3, \text{PAS}_6, \text{PAS}_\infty\}$, like for FPAS, but we found no major differences in their performances. The possible reason for these phenomena is that the appropriate and adaptive ratios of PAS_3 and PAS_∞ are more influential. If we closely look at the results from our experiments, the tasks do not arrive at mangers uniformly as discussed in Section 4.3. This small variation is only identified by the individual agents, and only the local decisions can reflect it.

We think that the main reason of the phenomenon shown in this paper is the small communication delay that increase the chances of simultaneous awarding. In our experiments, we assume that managers announce its near agents in terms of communication costs. However, in the actual situations, agent's scope is determined the service-level or upper-level relationships. This makes communication cost larger. So we believe that the phenomena described in this paper are more strongly exposed.

6 Related Works

There is a lot of research currently focused on improving the performance and functionality of CNP. For example, reference [10] extends CNP by introducing *levels of commitment*, i.e., making a commitment breakable with some penalty. References [8,10] try to reduce the number of messages and thereby improve the performance. From the theoretical aspect, there are notable researches that discussed the algorithm of the distributed task allocation in the multi-agent contexts, such as in [7]. All these studies assume, however, that the agents are not very busy and that there are not that many of them, making any interference among them insignificant.

Reference [11] discussed the issue of the eager-bidder problem occurring in a LS-MAS, where a number of tasks are announced concurrently so that a CNP with certain levels of commitment does not work well. These authors propose another CNP extension based on statistical risk management. However, their experiments still used fewer agents than in ours. More importantly, the types of resources and tasks considered are quite different; specifically, the resources are exclusive, such as airplane seats, so they should be selectively allocated. In our case, the resources are divisible, e.g., CPUs or network bandwidth, which can accept any number of tasks simultaneously but with reduced quality.

As a result, many agents with many tasks in our experiments cause a floating uncertainty, which affects the learning, statistical estimation, and rational decisionmaking.

From an organizational perspective, reference [5] proposes an agent organizational network and investigates what features are required to effectively make teams perform a large task. In [1], the issue of an adaptive organizational structure to improve the (overall) efficiency was also addressed. However, these studies do not discuss the allocation strategies for the tasks.

Task allocation to hosts for minimizing the makespan is also one of the central research topics in other domains such as grid computing [3,4]. Programs called mappers or schedulers assign requested tasks to appropriate hosts. However, the costs of the tasks and the capabilities of the hosts are often given so that the mapper accurately knows the processing time of each host. A number of agent-based mapping methods have been proposed; reference [4] uses auction- or contract-based protocols for task allocation. However, these methods are limited to hierarchical mapping structures so they assume geographically close clusters. They also do not take into account the communication delays that may cause uncertainty between the estimated processing status and the actual status.

7 Conclusion

We proposed an optimization method for the probabilistic award strategy in CNP for a large-scale MAS to elicit the potential capabilities of all agents. In a strategy with this optimization, called APAS, a manager agent (a) announces subtasks, (b) statistically analyzes the bids for each of these, (c) estimates the current local task load, and (d) introduces an adaptive degree of fluctuation in the award phase. We experimentally demonstrated that this strategy provides considerably a better performance than the naive CNP.

Although the proposed method performs better than the naive CNP, it still might not be optimal. We must emphasize that the characteristics affecting the overall performance of a LSMAS are complicated and quite different from those of small-scale multi-agent systems, so managers should adaptively select the most appropriate strategy. The strategy presented in this paper is simple but can elicit an excellent performance in comparison with the naive CNP. We believe that we can tailor controls to improve the system's performance even further. Moreover, we have to clarify (1) how to vary task types over time and (2) how agent-agent network structures affect the performance under the strategy proposed in this paper. These issues are our future works.

We focused on CNP because it is the well-known and most useful protocol at this time, but CNP is not the only approach to task allocation. Other protocols (with some modification) need to be investigated or a new protocol for busy LSMASs needs to be created. This is also one of our future research topics.

Acknowledgement. This work is, in part, supported by KAKENHI (22300056) and Kayamori Foundation.

References

1. Abdallah, S., Lesser, V.: Multiagent Reinforcement Learning and Self-Organization in a Network of Agents. In: Proceedings of the Sixth International Joint Conference on Autonomous Agents and Multi-Agent Systems, pp. 172–179. IFAAMAS, Honolulu (2007)

2. Buyya, R., Abramson, D., Giddy, J., Stockinger, H.: Economic models for resource management and scheduling in grid computing. Concurrency and Computation: Practice and Experience 14(13-15), 1507–1542 (2003)
3. Casanova, H., Legrand, A., Zagorodnov, D., Berman, F.: Heuristics for Scheduling Parameter Sweep Applications in Grid Environments. In: Proceedings of the 9th Heterogeneous Computing Workshop, pp. 349–363 (2000)
4. Dalheimer, M., Pfreundt, F.-J., Merz, P.: Agent-Based Grid Scheduling with Calana. In: Wyrzykowski, R., Dongarra, J., Meyer, N., Waśniewski, J. (eds.) PPAM 2005. LNCS, vol. 3911, pp. 741–750. Springer, Heidelberg (2006)
5. Gaston, M.E., desJardins, M.: Agent-organized networks for dynamic team formation. In: Proceedings of 4th Int. Joint Conf. on Autonomous Agents and Multiagent Systems (AAMAS 2005), pp. 230–237 (2005)
6. Gu, C., Ishida, T.: Analyzing the Social Behavior of Contract Net Protocol. In: Perram, J., Van de Velde, W. (eds.) MAAMAW 1996. LNCS(LNAI), vol. 1038, pp. 116–127. Springer, Heidelberg (1996)
7. Kraus, S., Plotkin, T.: Algorithms of distributed task allocation for cooperative agents. Theoretical Computer Science 242(1-2), 1–27 (2000)
8. Parunak, H.V.D.: Manufacturing experience with the contract net. In: Huhns, M. (ed.) Distributed Artificial Intelligence, pp. 285–310. Pitman Publishing, Morgan Kaufmann, London, San Mateo (1987)
9. Sandholm, T.: An Implementation of the Contract Net Protocol Based on Marginal Cost Calculations. In: Proceedings of the Eleventh National Conference on Artificial Intelligence, pp. 256–262 (1993)
10. Sandholm, T., Lesser, V.: Issues in automated negotiation and electronic commerce: Extending the contract net framework. In: Lesser, V. (ed.) Proceedings of the First International Conference on Multi-Agent Systems (ICMAS 1995), pp. 328–335. The MIT Press, Cambridge (1995)
11. Schillo, M., Kray, C., Fischer, K.: The Eager Bidder Problem: A Fundamental Problem of DAI and Selected Solutions. In: Proceedings of First International Joint Conference on Autonomous Agents and Multiagent Systems (AAMAS 2002), pp. 599–606 (2002)
12. Smith, R.G.: The Contract Net Protocol: High-Level Communication and Control in a Distributed Problem Solver. IEEE Transactions on Computers C-29(12), 1104–1113 (1980)
13. Sugawara, T., Hirotsu, T., Kurihara, S., Fukuda, K.: Performance Variation Due to Interference Among a Large Number of Self-Interested Agents. In: Proceedings of 2007 IEEE Congress on Evolutionary Computation, pp. 766–773 (2007)
14. Sugawara, T., Hirotsu, T., Kurihara, S., Fukuda, K.: Adaptive Manager-side Control Policy in Contract Net Protocol for Massively Multi-Agent Systems. In: Proceedings of 7th Int. Joint Conf. on Autonomous Agents and Multiagent Systems (AAMAS 2008), pp. 1433–1436. IFMAS (May 2008)
15. Sugawara, T., Hirotsu, T., Kurihara, S., Fukuda, K.: Controling Contract Net Protocol by Local Observation for Large-Scale Multi-Agent Systems. In: Klusch, M., Pěchouček, M., Polleres, A. (eds.) CIA 2008. LNCS (LNAI), vol. 5180, pp. 206–220. Springer, Heidelberg (2008)
16. Weyns, D., Boucké, N., Holvoet, T.: Gradient Field-Based Task Assignment in an AGV Transportation System. In: Proceedings of 5th International Joint Conference on Autonomous Agents and Multiagent Systems (AAMAS 2006), pp. 842–849 (2006)
17. Xu, L., Weigand, H.: The Evolution of the Contract Net Protocol. In: Wang, X.S., Yu, G., Lu, H. (eds.) WAIM 2001. LNCS, vol. 2118, pp. 257–264. Springer, Heidelberg (2001)

Gossip-Based Self-organising Open Agent Societies

Sharmila Savarimuthu, Martin Purvis, Bastin Tony Roy Savarimuthu, and Maryam Purvis

Department of Information Science, University of Otago, Dunedin, New Zealand
{sharmilas,mpurvis,tonyr,tehrany}@infoscience.otago.ac.nz

Abstract. The objective of this work is to demonstrate how cooperative sharers and uncooperative free riders can be placed in different groups of an electronic society in a decentralized manner. We have simulated an agent-based open and decentralized P2P system which self-organises itself into different groups to avoid cooperative sharers being exploited by uncooperative free riders. This approach encourages sharers to move to better groups and restricts free riders into those groups of sharers without needing centralized control. Our approach is suitable for current P2P systems that are open and distributed. Gossip is used as a social mechanism for information sharing which facilitates the formation of groups. Using multi-agent based simulations we demonstrate how the adaptive behaviour of agents lead to self-organization.

Keywords: Self-organising systems, Gossip; Multi-agent Based Simulation, Cooperation, Sharing behavior, Peer-to-Peer, Artificial Societies.

1 Introduction

One of the most common problems in P2P networks is free riding [5, 17]. In our context, free riders are those agents that do not contribute to the collective goals of the networked society, but make use of the resources of the network [17]. These free riders decrease the overall performance of the society by degrading the common good [5].

Electronic societies suffer from these free riders who exploit the common resources (e.g. bandwidth in a file sharing system). Many existing approaches employ centralized social regulations to control free riders. Researchers have used monitoring agents or governor agents to control agent behaviour [7]. But these centralized mechanisms are computationally expensive for a system. Centralized mechanisms are known to cause performance bottlenecks and also suffer from scalability issues [17].

With the increase in processing power and storage capacity of low-cost, lightweight computing devices such as smart phones, the arena of computing is becoming much more distributed. The clients of file sharing systems are not only personal computers but also smaller devices such as smart phones. There is a need for decentralized solutions to deal with the free riders. Additionally, the openness of the Internet allows users to dynamically join and leave the system at any point of time. So, a solution to the free-riding problem should take into account the open, dynamic and distributed nature of modern software systems.

N. Desai, A. Liu, and M. Winikoff (Eds.): PRIMA 2010, LNAI 7057, pp. 105–120, 2012.

To that extent, this paper proposes a decentralized solution that makes use of social mechanisms such as gossip [10] and ostracism [11]. The inspiration to use social mechanisms for our work comes from the human societies, which have evolved over millennia to work effectively in groups. For human beings group mechanisms provide social machinery that supports cooperation and collaboration. Social control is a fundamental concept that has evolved in human societies. Social control can be employed through leadership mechanisms. For example, the leader can impose rules on his followers. The disadvantage of this approach is that it is centralized. On the other hand, social control can be achieved using a bottom up approach.

For example, a gossip-based mechanism can be used to achieve social control as it serves as a distributed referral mechanism where information about a person or a group is spread informally among the agents. This approach can be used to achieve control in agent groups. Another social mechanism that can be employed to deal with free riders is ostracism. Members that do not adhere to the values or expectations of the groups can be sanctioned by the other agents by their refusal to interact with those agents.

In this work we demonstrate how these social mechanisms can be employed in an open, dynamic and decentralized society where several groups are formed and are ranked based on their performance.

The remainder of the paper is organised as follows. The social concepts used in this work are introduced in Section 2. Our experimental setting and selected experimental results are described in Sections 3 and 4. In Section 5 we present the related work and the comparison with our previous work. Finally, Section 6 concludes the paper.

2 Modeling Social Dilemma between Sharing and Non-sharing

Our experimental model presents a social situation in which the agents have the option to share or not to share. Sharing would cost the donor who shares. But the receiver receives the benefit without incurring any cost. Non-sharing (defection) is the selfish option which benefits the individual but is not good for the society. Sharing benefits the society by improving the performance of the whole system, which leads to the overall betterment of the society. Since the donating agent spends some effort (e.g. bandwidth) in the process of donating, it incurs some cost in our model. That sharing agent could have decided to be selfish and thereby avoid incurring that cost. Thus free riding becomes a threat to the society, causing damage to the common good. This is the issue of the "Tragedy of the Commons" [5]. A brief overview of the social mechanisms used in our experiments to deal with free riding are described below.

2.1 Gossip

Gossip is a powerful social mechanism found in human societies for information sharing. Gossip is a public opinion which leads to the benefit of a social group [10].

According to research done by evolutionary biologists humans have shown more interest in gossip than the truth [16]. The research has shown that gossip is more powerful than the truth in human societies when the participants were presented with both types of information (the gossip information and the real information).

They note that "gossip has a strong influence even when participants have access to the original information as well as gossip about the same information" and also have noted that "gossip has a strong manipulative potential". There are other examples of agent based simulation and P2P systems [4, 6] which have used a gossip based protocol [3]. Gossip can be considered to be a distributed referral mechanism.

2.2 Ostracism

It has long been a feature of human and animal societies that the member of a group who do not abide by rules or norms can be punished by other members of the group (the followers of the rule/norm). One kind of punishment is ostracism [11]. Other members will stop interacting with the member who is being ostracized and don't consider that person as a part of their group by ignoring or refusing to interact. This social sanctioning mechanism works without a centralized control or authority.

3 Experimental Setup

In our experimental arrangement agents are engaged in the sharing of digital goods in a P2P environment of a simulated artificial agent society. The system is developed as a distributed system without central control.

3.1 3.1 Agent Attributes

For this experimental model we have used the agents which have fixed, randomly assigned attribute values which represent how they behave.

- **Cooperativeness value:** This attribute concerns how cooperative an agent is. Agents have a randomly assigned cooperation value between 0 and 10 that represents how much they cooperate (share), with 0 representing an agent that never cooperates and 10 representing an agent that cooperates every time. This value is known as the cooperativeness of the agent.
- **Tolerance value:** Agents have a tolerance value between 1 and 10, which characterizes how much non-cooperation the agent can tolerate before it decides to leave the group. A value of 1 identifies the least tolerant agent, and 10 identifies the most tolerant agent.
- **Rejection limit:** Rejection limit represents how many rejections the agent can face before it decides to leave for another group.
- **Gossip blackboard length:** Each agent has a gossip blackboard of certain length to store the gossip messages from other agents of its group. Each agent also has a memory of certain number of previous groups to which it belonged.

- **Life span:** Agents are set to have life spans, which determine how long the agents remain in the society (i.e. die). When an agent's life span is over it leaves the society.
- **Cost and benefit for sharing:** A sharing agent loses 0.1 as cost for sharing and the receiving agent receives 1 as benefit.

3.2 Experimental Parameters

In the initial setup agents are put into random groups. Each group can be imagined to be represented by a tag (badge). Agents within a group have the same tag. They interact within their group, and they can also move to other groups under certain conditions. In such cases they join the other, jumped-to group, and the tag changes accordingly. Agents can ask for gossip feedback about other agents' behavior. Groups are formed or dismantled based on their size. The procedure of the experiment is explained in the following sections. The experimental parameters are listed in Table 1.

Table 1. Experimental parameters

Experimental parameters	Values
Number of agents to start with	100
Number of groups to start with	5
Number of iterations	5000
Agent's cooperative value:	0-10 (random)
Agent's tolerance value:	1-10 (random)
Agent's rejection limit	10
Agent's gossip blackboard length	10
Agents group memory limit	4
Agent's lifespan	Varies
Number of gossip feedbacks	5
Group's size for dismantling	5
Group's size for splitting	40
Cost for sharing	-0.1
Benefit for receiving	1

The procedure of the experiment is explained below.

3.3 Publishing Gossip

In each iteration, a certain number of random players (agents) may ask for files from other players of their group. A player can gossip about the outcome of an interaction with another agent (random) in its group (report whether the other agent was cooperative or not). In this gossip mechanism we assume that there is no lying. Since this happens within the group (agents in a group have same tags), we have assumed that the agent has no motivation to lie. In this fashion, every transaction is reported (gossiped about) to one of the other agents in the group. Thus the overall system has some partial information about the cooperativeness of each agent, maintained in a distributed way. For further illustration, the operation of how peers publish gossip is explained in the following example. Consider A, B and C as the three random agents in a group. A is the taking-player, B is the giving-player and C is the gossip holder. A asks for a file from B. If B shares then A gossips positively about him to C, otherwise A gossips negatively about him to C.

3.4 Using Gossip

Each peer has a limited amount of memory space for storing new gossip information. After reaching the storage limit, the memory register rolls over, based on a First-In-First-Out (FIFO) algorithm. When a player requests a file, the giving-player can check with a certain number of (e.g. five) other random agents (asking them what they know from the gossip information they have received) whether this taking-player is the worst cooperator of their group. The worst player is the one who has been uncooperative most times in its group (according to the available gossip information). If the taking-player is the worst player, the giving-player refuses to interact with the taking-player (ostracism). Otherwise this giving-player interacts (sharing a file or not based on its own cooperativeness). The operation of how peers use gossip is explained by the example given below.

Assume C and D are the players in the group where C is the taking-player, D is the giving-player. D checks with five other players in the group in order to see whether C is the worst player in their group. If so D refuses to play with (share file with) C. Thus C is ostracized. Otherwise D plays with C. When only a few agents (less than five) have gossip about the taking-player, then only the available information is taken into consideration. Sometimes it can be the case that none of the players have gossip about the taking-player. In such a case the taking-player is not considered to be the worst player, a privilege similar to what happens when a new player joins a group. By this process agents share file taking gossip into consideration which is about other agents' past behaviour.

3.5 Leaving a Group

An agent can leave a group for two reasons. A player can leave a group if its tolerance level is surpassed or its rejection level is surpassed. We call this leaving agent a "hopping peer". If its tolerance limit is reached, that means this agent is in a group where others do not cooperate at the rate that meets this agent's minimum level of expectation. Thus after a number of such non-sharing events from the group members (the agent's tolerance limit is surpassed) the agent will decide to leave that group and move to another group. If its rejection limit is reached, that means this agent is in a group where it is considered to be the worst cooperator by some other agents so it has been refused a play more often than others. If the rejection level is met then the agent will leave that group and move to another group.

3.6 Choosing a New Group to Join

When an agent decides to leave a group and join another, it looks for a group that may accept it. Agents can apply to enter into other groups they choose but they get entry into a group which matches its cooperativeness. A good agent would get into a group that is better than its current group while a bad agent should get into a group that is worse than its current group. This process is explained in detail in [9]. We have restated it in the following paragraphs.

The hopping peer collects information about other groups from their group members. Then it decides to which group to request admission from. Every agent has a memory record of its most recent groups (in our experiments the memory limit was set to 4). For example, assume agent E has been in 3 other groups before, as shown below in Table 2.

Table 2. Previous group history

Group No	Iteration No	Cooperativeness
1	560	4.5
3	700	6.0
2	1200	6.4

Table 3. Latest available information

Group No	Iteration No	Cooperativeness
5	1330	8.1
3	1170	7.5
2	1200	6.4
1	1199	3.8

The first row of Table 2 shows that E has left group 1 at the 560th iteration, and the cooperation value of that group was 4.5 at that time. E left group 3 at the 700th iteration and group 2 at 1200th iteration. Since the composition of groups change over time, the cooperativeness of the group also changes. So it is likely that the most recent information will be the most accurate and useful for an agent. Since all agents have a memory of their previous groups, the hopping peer can collect this information from all its group members and calculates the latest information about other groups. In particular, the agents who moved into this group recently from other groups have the most recent information. Taking into consideration this information, the agent decides where to move. For example assuming the current iteration is 1400, the latest information collected from the group members is given in Table 3.

Assume here that agent L intends leaving group 4, and Group 4's cooperativeness is 6.6 at that moment. From the latest information agent L knows about other groups and their cooperation value. For agent L, groups 5 and 3 are better, since the cooperation value in those groups appear to be higher than L's current group. Groups

2 and 1 are lower-ranked groups. So agent L chooses to move to the groups in the order of their ranking.

If L is intolerant of its current group (which means it is not happy about the cooperativeness of its current group), it will try to enter into the best group that it can find. This is the case of an agent being "too good" for its current group and wanting to move to a more cooperative group. But if the better groups on its list does not allow entry, then the intolerant agent L may determine that there is no group available that is better than its current group, and it will remain in its current group. In this case its tolerance limit is reset to 0.

On the other hand, an agent may not be good enough for its current group i.e. it is being shunned by the other members for being the worst member of its group. Because of refusals from other agents to play, its wealth will not increase, and it will want to leave and find some another group in which it can find players to play with. If the better groups do not allow entry, the agent will go to lower groups, since it is better off moving to any new group (even if it is a lower group) rather than staying in the current group where it is known as the worst player. How a player gets entry to another group is explained in the following section.

3.7 Joining Another Group

The hopping peer asks any randomly chosen agent in the group to which it seeks entry for its permission to enter. We call this permission-granting agent in the group to which entry is sought, the "checking peer". The checking peer will accept an agent whose cooperativeness value is greater than or equal to a value calculated by a formula (given below). This formula is the same one used in our previous work [9]. This hopping peer will gain permission to enter the group whenever its cooperativeness is greater or equal to the group's entry value calculated by the following formula:

$$EV = AC - (C1 / (SL - S)\, C2) + C3(S-SU) \quad (1)$$

The group Entry Value (EV) is calculated considering the given group's Average Cooperativeness (AC) and its group Size (S). AC is the average cooperativeness of the group calculated through the gossip mechanism, and S is the size of the group. C1, C2, C3 are constants whose values in our experiments are 25, 2, 10, respectively. These constants were adjusted to make the EV expression appropriate for two\``boundary values", the upper size limit of a group (SU) and the lower size limit of a group (SL). It is inappropriate or inefficient for groups of players or traders to become too big or too small. In our experiments, SU was set to be 25, and SL was set to be 10. That means if the size of the group is 10 or below the entry qualification value is set at a low value, making entry into the group very easy to obtain. If the size is 25 or above the entry qualification value is set to a high value and that would make it difficult for any but the most cooperative agents to join. Any values of the EV expression that fall below 0 are set to 0, and entry values above 10 are set to 10. Thus a group's entry value is always between 0 and 10. A simple example illustrates the use of this formula.

Consider that a group's calculated cooperativeness (AC) is 6. When the group Size (S) is 14 the group Entry Value (EV) is 4.43. When the group Size (S) is 25 the Group Entry Value (EV) is 6.88. In our system, the checking peer needs to get an estimate of the cooperativeness of the hopping peer (the agent seeking entry). So the checking peer asks 5 randomly chosen players from the hopping peer's group about the hopping peer's cooperation. It is thus inquiring into gossip information from the hopping peer's group. Consider a case where E and F are in different groups. E is the checking peer, and F is the hopping peer that wants to enter E's group. F asks E for entry, and E asks 5 other randomly chosen players in F's group for gossip information about F's cooperativeness. The averaged value is calculated (out of 10) from this information considering the worst case scenario. This estimated cooperativeness would be a value between 0 and 10. If F's estimated cooperativeness calculated through this gossip information is greater than or equal to the entry value (EV) of its group, the checking peer allows entry for the hopping player; otherwise it denies entry. In that case the hopping peer will try to enter into other groups. The hopping peer will ultimately get into a group where its cooperativeness meets the eligibility criteria to enter. If no such group is available, the hopping peer stays in its current group.

The entire process is repeated for many iterations, and gradually, some groups will emerge as elite groups with many cooperators, and other groups will have less cooperative players. As a consequence, these mechanisms achieve a separation of groups based on performance.

3.8 Groups Splitting and Dismantling

Our aim has been to develop a self-organizing open and dynamic system, where new agents may come into the society and also agents may leave the society at any time. To start with, new peers are allowed to join the society by gaining entry into random groups in the society. They can build their way up to higher groups based on their cooperativeness. A truly open and dynamic system will allow the formation of new groups and dismantling of existing groups according to the population size. Our aim was to achieve the same in a decentralized manner without explicit control at the top level. Forming groups using tags is helpful, since it is scalable and robust [4].

The agents' lifespan determines how long the agents remain in the society and when they leave (i.e. "die"). At any time a new agent could join the society and an existing agent could leave when its lifespan is over.

Since the number of agents in the society at any time is dynamic the system adapts itself to form new groups if more agents join. It also dismantles groups if there are fewer agents in the society (less than the lower size limit of a group).

The motivation for splitting and dismantling comes from real life societies. For example, when the size of a group becomes too large, it becomes unmanageable. Larger hunter-gatherer groups split because of reasons such as seasonal change or inequality in resource sharing (e.g. when meat is not shared equally).

In our approach, a group splits into two if the size of group reaches a certain limit (40). Based on the local gossip information in the splitting group, the top cooperators (first half) form one group and the rest (second half) form the other group.

If the size of the group decreases and goes below a certain limit (5) then the group dismantles. The remaining agents in the group go to random groups where they could enter. This is similar to a society where it can be functional only if the society has a certain size. For example, in hunter-gatherer societies, in order to hunt larger preys a group has to have a minimum size. Otherwise, the prey cannot be hunted. The same holds in the context of playing a sport. For example, a team playing volleyball has to have six players. Otherwise, the team cannot exist.

It should be noted that the splitting and dismantling functionalities account for the scalability of the system and its robustness.

4 Results

Before we present the experiments we have conducted and the results obtained, we would like turn the attention of the reader to the work reported in [9] where the results of the closed society are presented. In this work, there were 5 groups. The total number of agents in the society was 100. The work shows how the agents self-organise themselves into these groups based on their cooperativeness values [12].

4.1 Experiment 1 – Self-organization in an Open Society

We have conducted experiments on an open system by varying the arrival and departure rate of the agents. For all the experiments presented in this paper we start with 100 agents in 5 groups initially. After that agents can join (new arrivals) or leave (if life span is over) the society.

Figure 1 shows two graphs which share the same x-axis. The x-axis shows the number of iterations. In the top graph y-axis shows the cooperativeness of groups. Each diamond shown in the graph represents the cooperativeness of a particular group. For a given iteration number in the x-axis, the y-axis shows the cooperativeness of all the groups that were present in that iteration. For example, in iteration 100, there were 6 groups (represented by diamonds), with different levels of cooperativeness. The graph given in the bottom of Figure 1 shows the total number of agents (alive agents) in the society for a given iteration. For example, in iteration 100 there were 130 agents in the society.

These two graphs together show the dynamic behavior of the system (the formation of new groups and dismantling of old groups). It can be observed that, at the start the groups had an average cooperativeness value of 5. As the number of agents increased, new groups were formed (iteration 100). As the number of agents decreased (iteration 200), the number of groups decreased. The separation between the good groups and the bad groups is distinct. When the total number of agents was about 40 in iteration 300, there were fewer groups. Note that the cooperativeness of these groups was about 5 at that point. As the number of agents in the societies then increased, there were more groups and the separation between the good and the bad groups is evident. We note this process can be appreciated better by viewing the video shown in link [13].

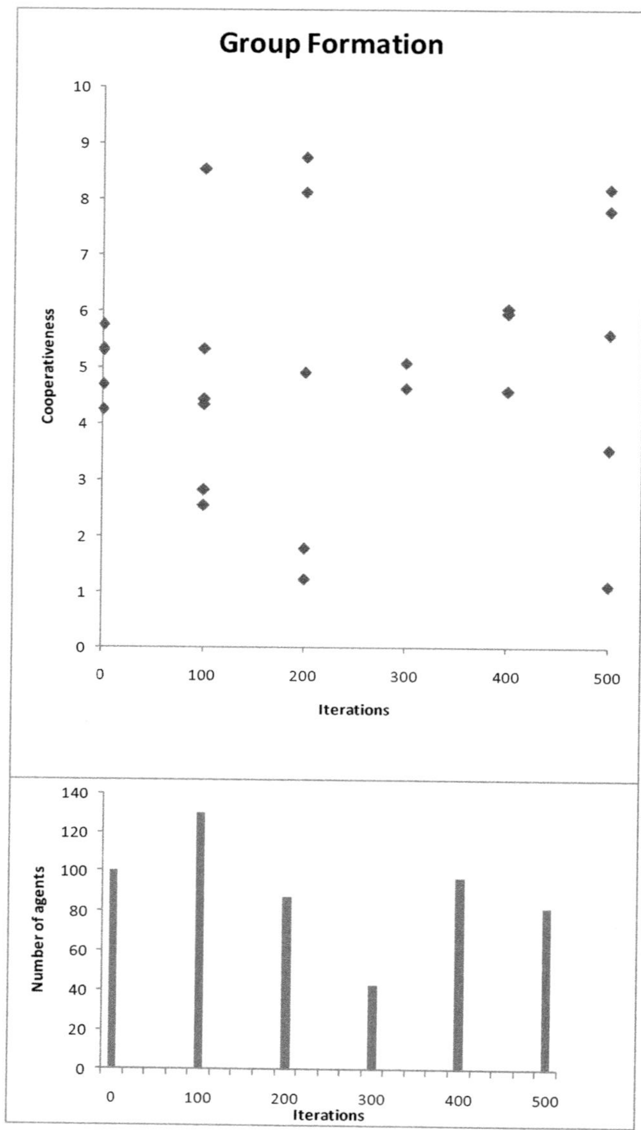

Fig. 1. Self-organisation of an open system when agents' arrival and departure rates are dynamic

There are two kinds of behavior we observe in the system. Firstly, the system dynamically enlarges or shrinks by creating more groups or dismantling existing groups based on the number of agents in the system. Secondly, it also forms groups based on cooperativeness. Cooperators move towards other cooperators and non-cooperators end up with other non-cooperators. The agents self-organize into groups that have different ranges of cooperativeness. Thus this system restricts the non-cooperators taking advantage of cooperators by restricting their access to better groups.

4.2 Experiment 2 – Arrival Rate Greater Than Departure Rate

We conducted experiments by keeping the arrival rate greater than the departure rate. A run of this experiment is shown in Figure 2. It can be observed that when the number of agents increase, the system is able to dynamically create more groups and also these groups are separated based on the cooperativeness of the agents. This shows the scalability of the system.

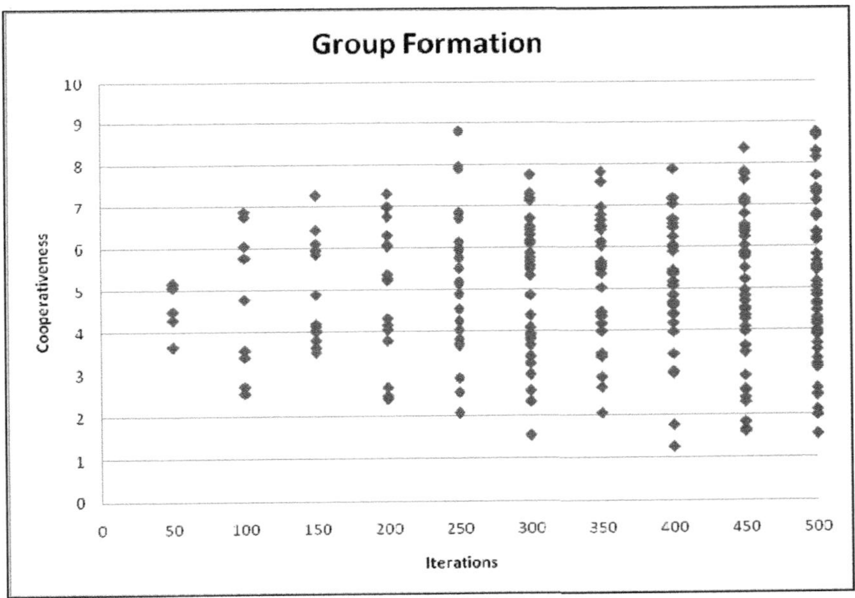

Fig. 2. Self-organization of an open system when agents' arrival rate is increased

4.3 Experiment 3 – Arrival Rate Equal to Departure Rate

When the number of new comers is roughly the same as the number of leaving agents in the system, the system will have same number of agents and the number of groups remain the same. But new agents who join the society have certain cooperativeness. Because of this the composition of groups and the cooperativeness of groups change over time. Figure 3 shows the cooperativeness of five different groups over 500 iterations. The cooperativeness of these groups varies depending upon the net effect of the cooperativeness of the agents that are present in the society. A new agent whose cooperativeness value of nine joining a group whose average cooperativeness value is five will increase the group's average. In the same way, a bad agent leaving a good group will increase the group's cooperativeness average. Figure 3 shows how the 5 groups change over time based on the number of agents (composition of the group) and the cooperativeness of agents present in the system over time.

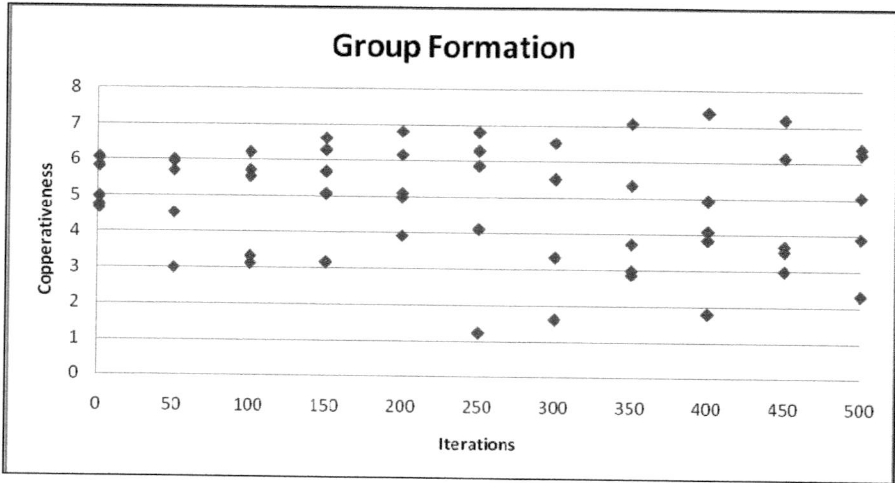

Fig. 3. Self-organization of an open system when the arrival rate is equal to the departure rate of the agents

4.4 Experiment 4 – Varying Life Spans of Agents

We varied the life span of the agents. We investigated the impact of the lifespan of agents on the system's behaviour. So we conducted two experiments by varying the lifespan. The lifespan of an agent is governed by the minimum time to live (TTL) parameter. The minimum TTL in one of the experiments was set to 300 and the other was set to 500. Figures 4 and 5 show the cooperativeness values of the groups for these two values of minimum TTL respectively.

Figures 4 and 5 show the result of groups' cooperativeness for 1000 iterations. From these results it can be observed that having longer life time (agents being in the society for longer period of time) helps to achieve better segregation of groups. This is because, when the agents live longer, they have a longer period to gather and use gossip. Additionally, when agents live for a shorter period of time, the system has a comparatively shorter period of time to segregate into groups than the system where the agents live longer. This can be observed by comparing the results for iterations 400 and 500. The separation of groups is better when minimum TTL=500. The same can also be observed in the circled regions of these two figures. The videos of these simulations can be seen in these links [14, 15].

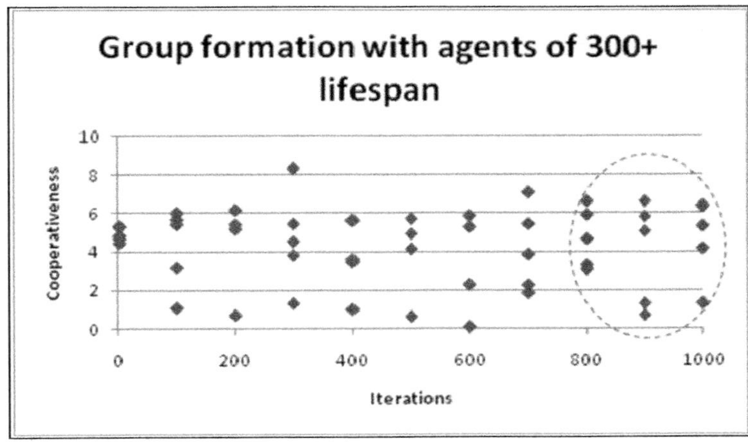

Fig. 4. Group formation with minimum TTL = 300

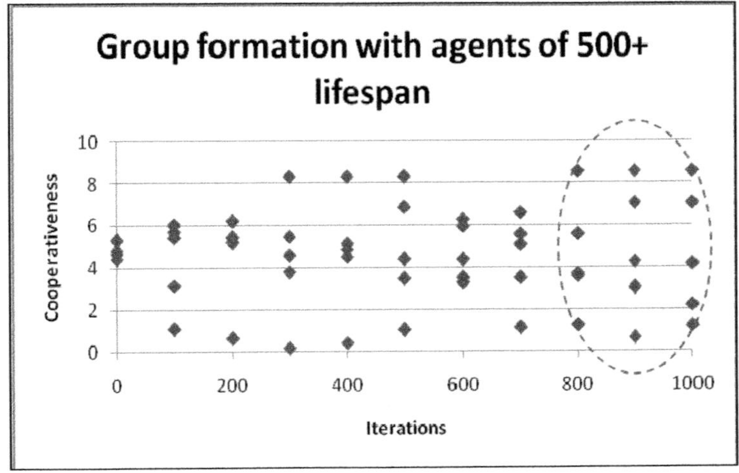

Fig. 5. Group formation with minimum TTL=500

5 Related Work and Comparison

In our previous work [7], the self-organization of peers in different groups was achieved by making use of tags and monitoring agents, where the population had a mixture of cooperators and non-cooperators. By employing a monitoring agent for each group, the system evolved into groups partitioned according to the performances of their group members. Each monitoring agent employed a voting mechanism within the group to determine which agents were the most and least cooperative members of the group. Then the most cooperative member was allowed to move to a new group, and the least cooperative member was expelled from the group. Those peers who left voluntarily or those who were expelled from their groups obtained membership in a new group only if the local monitor agent of the other (new) group accepted them. Since the local monitor agents picked players for their group based on performance, the high performing player had a good chance to get entry into the best group, and the reverse conditions applied for the worst performing player. As a result, the players entered into groups based on their performances. Though this system produced good results, this approach is semi-centralized, because it required a local monitoring agent for each group. In addition the work considered a closed society. We believe this system can be applied in a regimented, closed society but cannot be applied to the modern systems which are open and distributed.

Hales's work [4], extends his previous work on tags to networks, considers a 'neighbor list of nodes' as a tag. The 'movement of node in a network' is modeled as a mutation. His results showed that tags work well for P2P systems in achieving cooperation, scalability and robustness.

In our present work, instead of the Prisoner's Dilemma game, we have adopted the more practical scenario of sharing digital goods in electronic societies. We investigate how a society can achieve the separation or self-organization of groups in a decentralized manner in an open society. Such a system would help to protect cooperators from being exploited by the non-cooperators. It would also restrict the non-cooperators from taking advantage of cooperators by restricting their entry to better groups where the access to resources is better. Hence, the quality of service (e.g. the quality of file sharing) and the performance (e.g. utility of agents) in the better groups will be higher. By doing so, the performance of the whole system can be improved; as resources can be distributed in greater proportion to the better performing groups [1]. Otherwise, it will be difficult to shield the cooperators from the defectors who rarely or never share their resources.

For easy understanding, we differentiate our current system from our previous work [7]. First we explain the results from the earlier system [7] for comparative purposes. In that work, all the 5 groups started with a similar number of cooperators in each group. Later the groups were separated into 2 groups having most of the cooperators, 2 groups having most of the non-cooperators and the middle group having a mixed population of both. But that earlier work employed localized group monitors and was therefore less scalable and semi-centralized.

The work presented in [8] is based on a closed society but cannot be applied to systems that are open and distributed. Even though the mechanism achieves self-organization, it is suitable for systems in which the performances of the other groups are directly revealed to the agents in the society.

The work presented in [9] shows the self-organization of groups using similar mechanisms and it has been improved upon in this current work. The differences between the work presented in [9] and current work are as follows. In earlier work [9] the game was played for certain iterations and the gossip information was stored. Later the agents use the stored gossip information when they play. In the current setup, the agents start using the gossip right from the start. If there is no information the agent is considered as a new player and allowed to play or enter into any group. As they play, the gossip is also stored and used. In the earlier work wealth has been taken into account. If the wealth of an agent has not increased in the last certain number of iterations then the agent decides to move. In the current setup, instead of wealth if the rejection limit is met then the agent decides to move. We found that using a rejection limit works better for group separation than basing the decision on wealth, since it is likely that the wealth will increase for a certain number of iterations (because the agents play with bad agents if the gossip information was not available, hence the wealth of the bad players might increase).

In the earlier work [9] new players are introduced into the lowest group in the society and they are expected to build their way up to the higher groups based on their behaviour (cooperativeness). For that it was necessary to keep track of the lowest group of the system all the time, which is not a recommended practice if we want to achieve a decentralized environment. In the current setup new agents go to random groups in the society. As they are new they have no past behaviour to track and they are allowed in any group as they come in. Eventually they will end up in a group based on their behaviour by the mechanism we have in place. In the earlier work the remaining agents in a dismantling group go to the lowest performing group. In the current setup, they can apply to other groups and go to the group that accepts them. If they are not allowed then they keep trying to get entry into one of the groups.

In summary, our current work focuses on addressing the free-riding problem in an open, dynamic and distributed society. The work presented here provides an improved model when compared to the model presented in [9].

In future, we intend to include false gossip (lying) in the system and examine the mechanisms for handling the lying problem.

6 Conclusion

We have presented a gossip based decentralized mechanism to facilitate the self-organization of agent groups in open agent societies. Through agent based simulation we have demonstrated that our mechanism helps the sharing agents (cooperators) to move to better groups while the non-sharing agents are restricted from getting into the better groups. Thus, the mechanism achieves the separation of groups. The mechanism allows for dynamic group formation through the splitting and dismantling processes. We have also demonstrated that our system is scalable. Finally, we have compared our results with previous works.

Acknowledgments. Our sincere thanks to the New Zealand Federation of Graduate Women (NZFGW-Otago branch) for the NZFGW Travel Award.

References

1. Antoniadis, P., Grand, B.L.: Incentives for resource sharing in self-organized communities: From economics to social psychology. In: ICDIM, pp. 756–761. IEEE (2007)
2. de Pinninck, A.P., Sierra, C., Schorlemmer, M.: Distributed Norm Enforcement: Ostracism in Open Multi-Agent Systems. In: Casanovas, P., Sartor, G., Casellas, N., Rubino, R. (eds.) Computable Models of the Law. LNCS (LNAI), vol. 4884, pp. 275–290. Springer, Heidelberg (2008)

3. Eugster, P., Felber, P., Le Fessant, F.: The "art" of programming gossip-based systems. SIGOPS Oper. Syst. Rev. 41(5), 37–42 (2007)
4. Hales, D.: Self-Organising, Open and Cooperative P2P Societies – From Tags to Networks. In: Brueckner, S., Di Marzo Serugendo, G., Karageorgos, A., Nagpal, R. (eds.) ESOA 2005. LNCS (LNAI), vol. 3464, pp. 123–137. Springer, Heidelberg (2005)
5. Hardin, G.: The Tragedy of the Commons. Science 162, 1243–1248 (1968)
6. Jelasity, M., Montresor, A., Babaoglu, O.: Detection and removal of malicious peers in gossip-based protocols. In: FuDiCo II: S.O.S., Bertinoro, Italy (June 2004)
7. Purvis, M.K., Savarimuthu, S., De Oliveira, M., Purvis, M.: Mechanisms for Cooperative Behaviour in Agent Institution. In: Nishida, T., Klusch, M., Sycara, K., Yokoo, M., Liu, J., Wah, B., Cheung, W., Cheung, Y.-M. (eds.) Proceedings of IEEE/WIC/ACM International Conference on Intelligent Agent Technology (IAT 2006), pp. 121–124. IEEE Press, Los Alamitos (2006) ISBN 0-7695-2748-5
8. Savarimuthu, S., Purvis, M.A., Purvis, M.K.: Self-Organization of Peers in Agent Societies. In: IEEE/WIC/ACM International Conference on Web Intelligence and Intelligent Agent Technology, Milan, Italy, Los Alamitos, CA, USA, September 15-18, vol. 2, pp. 74–77 (2009) ISBN 978-0-7695-3801-3
9. Savarimuthu, S., Purvis, M., Purvis, M., Savarimuthu, B.T.R.: Mechanisms for the Self-Organization of Peer Groups in Agent Societies. In: Bosse, T., Geller, A., Jonker, C.M. (eds.) MABS 2010. LNCS, vol. 6532, pp. 93–107. Springer, Heidelberg (2011)
10. Rebecca, S.B.: Some Psychological Mechanisms Operative in Gossip. Social Forces 34(3), 262–267 (1956), Stable `http://www.jstor.org/stable/2574050`
11. Thomsen, R.: The Origins of Ostracism, A Synthesis. Gyldendal, Copenhagen (1972)
12. Savarimuthu, S.: Self-organising groups (gui for closed society). University of Otago (February 2010c), `http://unitube.otago.ac.nz/view?m=9GT31pqTPSk`
13. Savarimuthu, S.: Self-organising groups (gui for open society). University of Otago (February 2010d), `http://unitube.otago.ac.nz/view?m=HbOw1pni7qS`
14. Savarimuthu, S.: Self-organising groups (gui for lifespan=300+). University of Otago (February 2010a), `http://unitube.otago.ac.nz/view?m=JHaY1poMt9P`
15. Savarimuthu, S.: Self-organising groups (gui for lifespan=500+). University of Otago (February 2010b), `http://unitube.otago.ac.nz/view?m=7SK81pp4WP0`
16. Sommerfeld, R.D., Krambeck, H.J., Semmann, D., Milinski, M.: Gossip as an Alternative for Direct Observation in Games of Indirect Reciprocity. Proceedings of the National Academy of Sciences of the United States of America 104(44), 17435–17440 (2007), Stable `http://www.jstor.org/stable/25450253`
17. Saroiu, S., Gummadi, P., Gribbe, S.: A measurement study of peer-to-peer file-sharing systems, Technical report UW-CSE-01-06002, University of Washington (2002)

Adaptive Negotiation in Managing Wireless Sensor Networks

Thao P. Le, Timothy J. Norman, and Wamberto Vasconcelos

Department of Computer Science
King's college, University of Aberdeen, AB24 3UE, UK
{thao.le,t.j.norman}@abdn.ac.uk,
wvasconcelos@acm.org

Abstract. The allocation of resources to tasks in an efficient manner is a key problem in computer science. One important application domain for solutions to this class of problem is the allocation of sensor resources for environmental monitoring, surveillance, or similar sensing tasks. In real-world problem domains, the problem is compounded by the fact that the number of tasks and resources change over time, the number of available resources is limited and tasks compete for resources. Thus, it is necessary for a practical allocation mechanism to have the flexibility to cope with dynamic environments, and to ensure that unfair advantages are not given to a subset of the tasks (say, because they arrived first). Typical contemporary approaches use agents to manage individual resources, and the allocation problem is modelled as a coordination problem. In existing approaches, however, the successful allocation of resources to a new task is strongly dependent upon the allocation of resources to existing tasks. In this paper we propose a novel negotiation mechanism for exchanging resources to accommodate the arrival of new tasks, dynamically re-arranging the resource allocation. We have shown, via a set of experiments, that our approach offers significantly better results when compared with an agent-based approach without resource re-allocation through concurrent negotiation.

1 Introduction

When a sensor network is deployed it is typically required to support multiple simultaneous tasks. A given sensor can provide different amounts of information to each individual task. Tasks are broken down as sub-tasks and can appear at any time placing varying demands on sensor resources. In such multiple-sensor and multiple-task problems in dynamic environments, conflicts between sub-tasks may occur for the use of the same sensor resource. Thus, efficient mechanisms to allocate individual sensors to appropriate sub-tasks on the basis of information need are necessary.

The resource-task allocation problem is at least as hard as the Knapsack problem which is NP-Complete [5]. In the current state of the art, there is no generally adopted approach to solve this class of problems, and researchers have made many assumptions in order to be able to provide a solution to a subset of the generic problem (e.g. considering only systems where sensors are identical,

N. Desai, A. Liu, and M. Winikoff (Eds.): PRIMA 2010, LNAI 7057, pp. 121–136, 2012.

sub-tasks are of the same type, or systems where sub-tasks require the exclusive use of sensor resources). In an attempt to relax such assumptions, we have focused on resource allocation problems in heterogeneous and dynamic sensor networks. Specifically, we employ an agent-based approach allowing sensors to be shared between sub-tasks. In so doing, however, the success of a sub-task strongly depends on the allocation of earlier sub-tasks. Moreover, in practical scenarios not all sub-tasks will operate in a cooperative manner (i.e. the agents coordinating the sub-tasks might not be willing to participate in the reassignment of sensors without compensation).

Negotiation techniques have long been used in multi-agent systems to resolve disagreements between agents to enable them to come to agreements that all parties can live with [10]. It is, therefore, appropriate to investigate the use of negotiation mechanisms for reassigning sensor resources. In doing this, we introduce another objective for agents: maximising profit. A task (represented by a buyer agent) in need of a particular sensor might be willing to give up part of its profit to a potential seller (representing another task) in exchange for the service of that sensor. If the seller can find an alternative sensor to replace that particular sensor, it will be beneficial to do the exchange if it is able to obtain additional profit from the buyer. For the buyer, it will have a chance of completing its allocation, thus achieving the objective and also obtaining a profit that is unavailable otherwise. We further demonstrate that it is advantageous for the buyer to have a number of such negotiations concurrently because this increases its chance of being successful.

In this paper, we make the following contributions to the state of the art. First, we enhance sensor-task allocation mechanisms by employing an adaptive negotiation mechanism in the allocation process. This makes our approach more applicable in realistic situations where sub-tasks compete for resources. Additionally, to the best of our knowledge, this presents the first model introducing negotiation as a post-processing step to improve the actual allocation process. Through simulations, we empirically demonstrate that our extended model provides an improvement in the number of completed tasks.

The remainder of this paper is organized as follows: Section 2 formulates the sensor-task allocation problem. Section 3 presents our agent-based approach and Section 4 extends this model by incorporating a novel negotiation mechanism specifically for resource exchange between self-interested task-agents. We present an in-depth analysis of our experimental results in Section 5, followed by Section 6 where we relate our model to existing research in this area, discuss the shortcomings of our model and point towards avenues for future research. Finally, Section 7 concludes.

2 Sensor-Task Allocation Problem

The problem considered in this paper involves allocating a collection of sensors to a number of tasks in order to satisfy the information requirements of those tasks.

A sensor s_i is defined as a tuple $\langle \gamma_i, l_i, r_i, c_i, u_i \rangle$ where $\gamma_i \in \Gamma$ specifies s_i's type (Γ is the set of all sensor types); l_i and r_i are the location and sensing range of s_i; c_i is the cost of using s_i; and u_i is the maximum utility s_i can provide in a single time unit.

Tasks may arrive at any time and may last for any duration. A task M is defined by a specific geographic location, starting time and duration. M is composed by a set of sub-tasks T. Each sub-task $t_j \in T$ has a specific type and is defined as a tuple $\langle l_j, r_j, d_j, p_j, b_j \rangle$ where l_j and r_j specifies t_j's location and operational range; d_j is the sensing demand that t_j requires; p_j is the profit t_j will achieve if successfully allocated; and lastly, b_j is the overall budget for the sub-task. The active time for t_j is within the duration of task M. We denote u_{ij} as the utility that s_i can provide to t_j, which is defined as a percentage of u_i calculated by the ratio between the overlap of the ranges of s_i and t_j and the range of s_i. If the operational areas of s_i and t_j do not intersect, the value of u_{ij} will be 0.

Given a set of available sensors $S = \{s_1, s_2, ..., s_n\}$ for t_j at t_j's starting time, we formulate the allocation for t_j as a mathematical programming problem. Specifically, an allocation to t_j is defined as the matrix $A_j = (x_{ij})_{n\times 1}$ where $x_{ij} = \{0, 1\}$ and $x_{ij} = 1$ denotes that sensor s_i is allocated to sub-task t_j. The utility that t_j achieves is calculated as: $U_{t_j} = \sum_{i=1}^{n} u_{ij} \times x_{ij}$. The cost of t_j's allocation is calculated as: $C_{t_j} = \sum_{i=1}^{n} c_i \times x_{ij}$.

An allocation A_j is valid if, and only if:

1. the total cost of an allocation must be within budget: $C_{t_j} \leq b_j$
2. the utility achieved must greater than or equal to the sensing demand (within a threshold ξ) for t_j: $U_{t_j} \geq \xi \times d_j$,
3. the set of sensor types of the sensors allocated to t_j must cover its information requirements: for all required type $\gamma_k \exists s_i : x_{ij} = 1, \gamma_i = \gamma_k$
4. sensors cannot be allocated to more than one type of sub-task at the same time (i.e. the only permit sensors to be shared between sub-tasks of the same type): $\sum_{j\in\overline{T}} x_{ij} \leq 1$ for all set $\overline{T}$ of sub-tasks with different types.

If A_j is valid, the profit that t_j will receive is calculated as $P_{t_j} = min(U_{t_j}/d_j, 1) \times p_j$. Task M will have a successful allocation if all of its sub-tasks are satisfied (A_j is valid $\forall t_j \in T$). The profit that M receives in this case is $P_M = \sum_{t_j \in T} P_{t_j}$, $\forall t_j \in T$.

Formally, the allocation problem is defined as:

$$\begin{array}{ll} \text{max:} & \text{count}(M),\ \Sigma P_M \\ \text{s.t.:} & A_j \text{ is valid } \forall t_j \in T \end{array}$$

In other words, we aim to utilize the set of sensors to maximize the number of successful tasks as well as obtain as much profit as possible for such tasks (emphasizing the number of successful tasks).

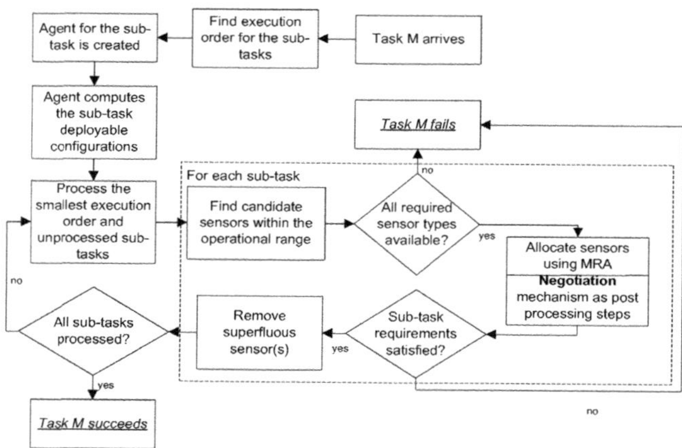

Fig. 1. Our proposed approach as a flowchart

3 Agent-Based Sensor-Task Allocation

In this section, we present an approach to continuous resource allocation problem for sensor network management that offers significant efficiency improvements over existing solutions, while generating high quality solutions.

We assume that sensors of different types are deployed in an environment in a uniformly random manner, have varying sensing ranges and each sensor provides different utilities to different sub-tasks. The utility each sensor can contribute is computed by a predefined function for each task and depends on various factors such as sensor type, range, location and so on.

By a task, we mean a sensing task that requires information of a certain type, which may be contributed by one or more sensor types. Tasks can arrive at any time, and there may be more than one task active at any given time. Tasks may consist of a set of sub-tasks and each sub-task is defined by a specific location, operational range and type. Moreover, each task has a profit representing its importance, and this profit can only be achieved if the task is successfully allocated. Tasks also require different numbers of sensing resources (i.e. it has a sensing demand) and these requirements may not be met by a single sensor type. In such cases, different sensor types should be allocated together to meet the requirements of a sub-task. We use the term *Deployable Configuration* (DC) to refer to the set of resource types that an atomic task requires.

We propose a multi-agent system where each task is represented by a task agent. The task agent is responsible for the task. If a task is composed of sub-tasks, then that task's agent delegates those subtasks to other task agents. If a task agent represents an atomic task (i.e. the task have no sub-tasks), then the agent is only responsible for the determination and allocation of resources required to execute the task. In summary, agents of tasks are responsible for the delegation of subtasks to other agents while the agents of sub-tasks are responsible for the determination and allocation of resources.

Resource determination and allocation for each atomic task is managed by the agent of that task. Hence, for a composite task, overall resource determination and allocation is achieved in a decentralized manner by the agents representing atomic tasks within the composite task. The agents of the atomic tasks first determine the necessary resource types and then interact with the resources (sensors) on the area of their interest to allocate the necessary resources. In our approach, each sensor is represented by a sensor agent, knowledgeable about the location, range, type, battery life and utility of its sensor. Therefore, in order to allocate sensors for a specific atomic task, the agent of this task should interact with the sensor agents considering its requirements and constraints. Here, we assume that task agents compete for resources while sensor agents are purely cooperative.

As mentioned earlier, a task can arrive at any time and there may be more than one task active at any given time. When a new task T arrives, T is delegated to a task agent A_T (the sensor agent closest to the central of Ts range). A_T is responsible for controlling the process of finding an allocation for T as follows (see Figure 1):

1. Establish the execution order for sub-tasks. Basically, two tasks t_i and t_j belong to the same execution set (they can be executed at the same time) if their operational ranges do not intersect or their sensor type requirements do not overlap. However, if two tasks have the same type, both will be in the same execution set. Initially, the execution set containing t_0 will be processed first and followed by the set containing the next unprocessed task until all the tasks have been handled.
2. Delegate the sub-tasks (e.g., t_j) to task agents (e.g.,A_T^j).

A_T^j is knowledgeable about the constraints and requirements of the sub-task t_j. A_T^j computes the set of deployable configurations (DCs) for t_j. These DCs are determined by a semantic matchmaking process [13] and then used as the input for the actual allocation process. The key benefit in doing so is that the search space for finding the allocation solution can be greatly reduced (A_T^j only has an interest in sensors of a specific type if the deployable configurations of its sub-task contains this sensor type).

When a DC has been selected for t_j, the actual allocation steps are as follows:

The task agent A_T^j identifies candidate sensors within the operational range of t_j. A call for bids is issued to appropriate sensors. The call for bids includes information regarding its type, location, etc. Each sensor agent then makes an independent decision on whether and what to bid based on its type and workload. A response to a call will include the utility that can be provided and the cost associated with the use of this sensor.

Once bids are received, the coordinator agent attempts to allocate sensors to the sub-task using a multi-round allocation algorithm (MRA). MRA operates in the similar way to GAP-E algorithm [8]; typically, it is in the nature of this allocation algorithm that the various agent-based techniques differ. If A_T^j fails to satisfy its information requirements, it reports failure to the agent responsible for A_T, and if the sub-task is critical to the overall task, all other task agents coordinating dependent tasks/sub-tasks will be requested to abort and release their resources. All sensor agents from which bids were received are informed of whether they are required.

In the MRA algorithm, sensors of various types are allocated to the sub-task in a number of rounds, one for each sensor type the sub-task requires. The first step is to set the order of selection of potential sensors using their priority. In this way, all sensors of the highest priority are considered first. Also, MRA introduces a budget (a constraint that governs the number of sensors that can be allocated to the atomic task) as part of its specification. From the bids received the allocation algorithm also has the costs associated with using specific sensors and the utilities they provide. The Fully Polynomial Time Approximation Scheme (FPTAS) algorithm which offers an approximation guarantee of $2 + \epsilon$ is then run with this as input along with an allocation from the remaining budget and utilities that sensors can provide to the task. This algorithm returns a revised allocation. If this allocation does not contain at least one sensor of the type being considered, the atomic task fails. Otherwise, the algorithm then reassesses the priority among sensor types (given the fact that sensors have been allocated) and proceeds to the next round if additional resources are required.

4 Negotiation for (Re-)Allocation of Resources

In this section, we detail our novel negotiation mechanism which can be used during the post-processing step in each round of the allocation algorithm outlined in the previous section. As has been argued, the problem inherent in a decentralised (or agent-based) approaches to the sensor-task allocation problem is that the order of task arrival (or, strictly, allocation by agents in the system) can significantly affect the quality of the global solution, and hence the number of tasks that are satisfied. The aim of concurrent negotiation is to alleviate the impact that task arrival has on solution quality. Specifically, it is of benefit if:

1. there are selfish coordinating agents which are not willing to cooperate without reward, and
2. a sub-task t_j of task M cannot find an available sensor of a particular type γ_i, t_j fails and, consequently, M fails. In many cases, t_j cannot satisfy its sensing requirement δ_j for sensor type γ_i not because there is no such sensor within t_j's range, but because there are sensors of type γ_i within its range that are allocated to other sub-tasks. If one such sub-tasks can find a replacement, that sensor can be allocated to t_j and, thus, t_j will succeed.

The negotiation mechanism detailed in this section allows an agent (buyer) representing a task to negotiate concurrently with other task-agents (sellers) to obtain a resource of type γ that is currently allocated to one of these other tasks in exchange for a fraction of its profit. Obviously, the buyer will only be interested in instances of resource type γ that it can make use of (i.e. utility of the resource instance to the buyer is not 0). The buyer will negotiate simultaneously with all the sellers that currently employ a resource of type γ.

The buyer and the sellers work to different negotiation deadlines, each representing availability in terms of both resource and processing power. They follow a Sequential Alternating Protocol where at each step an agent can either accept the offer from the opponent, propose a counter-offer, renege from its commitment or opt out of the negotiation (typically if its deadline is reached). At each negotiation time period, the interest of each agent is represented by a proposal ϕ, which refers to the profit that will be paid to the seller by the buyer.

The buyer agent (B) consists of two main components: a *coordinator* and a number of *negotiation threads*. The negotiation threads deal directly with the sellers (one per seller S) and are responsible for deciding what counter-offers to send and what proposals to accept. Each thread inherits the preferences from the main buyer agent, including the acceptable ranges of values for the profit, the deadline of the negotiation and the current reservation value (the highest profit value that the buyer is willing to pay). The coordinator decides the negotiation strategies for each thread. If a thread reaches a deal with a particular seller, it terminates and notifies the coordinator. The coordinator will then notify all other negotiation threads of the new reservation value.

In this way, the buyer, B, will engage in simultaneous negotiations with all the sellers that currently possess a resource of type b. In our model, the buyer can either choose to terminate all negotiation threads once an agreement has been reached (*simple negotiation mode*) or it can wait until all the negotiations have been finished and then select the agreement that is most valuable (*extended negotiation mode*) either with the smallest profit to pay or with the highest utility achieved.

For each seller, if the negotiation succeeds, it will have to give up one of its resources to the buyer. As a result, it is necessary for the seller to obtain a replacement resource before it can enter the negotiation. If there is an available and appropriate alternative resource (i.e. a resource that achieves the requirements of the task — validates the allocation — without the original resource), it can replace the previously allocated resource with the alternative. We label this situation as 1-sequence negotiation. However, there exists a more complicated case (2-sequence) in which the seller needs to negotiate with another seller for a replacement resource before it can negotiate with the buyer (i.e. buyer B and seller S are negotiating about a resource b but S needs to negotiate with seller C about resource b' which is the replacement for b). If the seller cannot manage to find the replacement resource, it will not enter the negotiation.

The agents bargain about the profit that will be paid for the resource that the seller is currently holding (the price being a share of the profit that the buyer acquires in completing its task). The buyer and sellers use different negotiation strategies that are based on the set of linear strategies as specified in [9]. This strategy family is employed because it represents the neutral stances of both the buyer and the seller, not favouring anyone in particular and allows a solution to be found that is beneficial for both parties rather than having only one better off. Furthermore, by doing so, it will increase the chance for more agents to participate and in turn, improve the global goal of maximizing the number of successful task allocations.

Specifically, a strategy is a sequence of decisions that an individual agent will make during negotiation. These decisions could be either to send an initial offer to the opponent, select an offer to propose, accept the offer proposed by the opponent or withdraw from the negotiation. Here, the value of the profit is between the minimum and the maximum limit of each agent. For the buyer, the proposed profit will increase in value over time and conversely, the seller's value will decrease. For each seller, the reservation value or the minimum profit (min_{PS}) it will accept is the difference between the profit it received by having the resource s and that received with the replacement resource *s'*. For example, if s receives a profit of 1.5 with s and a profit of 1.2 with *s'*, the minimum profit it will accept from B is 0.3. The maximum profit (max_{PS}) it can expect from the buyer is the difference between the profit with *s'* and the maximum profit it can obtain. This is the incentive for the seller agents to enter into negotiation. For a seller S, at any time t between 0 and its negotiation deadline $t_{S_{max}}$, the value of the proposal it will send to B is: $\phi(S \rightarrow B) = max_{PS} - (max_{PS} - min_{PS}) \times (\frac{t}{t_{S_{max}}})^{\frac{1.00}{\beta_S}}$ where β_S is the parameter that defines the shape of the function.

On the other hand, the buyer will attempt to give up as little of its profit as possible. Thus, its minimum profit (min_{PB}) it is willing to pay is 0. The reservation value (max_{PB}) it is willing to pay is set at half of potential profit it can obtain if s is allocated. If it is higher, the buyer might not get any profit at all and it might not be tempted to enter the bargaining process. Thus, at any time t between 0 and deadline $t_{B_{max}}$, the value of the proposal B will send to S is: $\phi(B \rightarrow S) = min_{PB} + (max_{PB} - min_{PB}) \times (\frac{t}{t_{B_{max}}})^{\frac{1.00}{\beta_B}}$ where β_B is the parameter that defines the shape of the function.

When an offer proposed by a party is between the minimum and the maximum acceptable profit of the other party, it will be accepted and a provisional agreement (or deal) is created. If the negotiation is in the simple mode, the buyer will terminate all other negotiation threads and select the resource in the deal reached with the winning seller. If, however, it is in the extended mode, the buyer will attempt to establish as many deals as possible, and then commit to the best (based on its selection criteria), declining all others. The selection criteria that the buyer has in this model are (i) the deal with the least amount of profit, and (ii) the deal that can provide the highest utility value. The final agreement and the final allocated resource plays an important role in determining the success rate of subsequent tasks and this is reflected in the results of our empirical evaluation presented in Section 5.

5 Evaluation

Having defined our negotiation mechanism, we now present a detailed discussion of our empirical evaluation aimed at assessing the benefit of employing our concurrent negotiation mechanism in sensor-task allocation.

The sensors and tasks are deployed in uniformly random locations in a 400m × 400m environment. Each sensor range (r_i) is randomized between 20m and 40m and their maximum utility is calculated as $(r_i/40)^2$, which ensures that their the values lie between 0.25 and 1. The operational ranges of the sub-tasks are set to be randomized between 40m and 80m. The values for β_B and β_S are selected randomly between 0.95 and 1.05. The threshold ξ is set at 0.75.

The task arrival rates are controlled by the *task_per_hour* parameter, which ranges from 2 to 8, and *number_of_days* parameter, which is kept at 2 days. Each task can last for an arbitrary amount of time, ranging from 5 minutes to 4 hours. There are *total_sensor_types* different sensor types, which will vary between 4 and 8 and, for each sensor type, there will be *total_sensors_per_type* sensors. For each task, the number of sub-tasks will be varied between 4 and 5. Each sub-task type will require a number of different sensor types, which varies between 1 and 4. These individual sensor type requirements are generated randomly and have the value between 1 and *total_sensor_types.*

To evaluate the negotiation mechanism, we benchmark our model with 3 different settings: *4tph 4st*, *4tph 8st* and *8tph 8st* where *tph* stands for *task_per_hour* and *st* stands for *total_sensor_types.* With each setting, we vary *total_sensors_per _type* between 30 and 250 to create additional 12 environments, each then carries further 500 experiments with randomized data sets. The results are averaged and put through a regression test to ensure that all differences are significant at the 99% confidence level.

We measure the number of successful tasks, the average profit achieved and the running time. We also measure the performance of the different negotiation modes: simple mode (terminate whenever an agreement is reached); and extended mode with either smallest profit or highest utility selection criterion. It would be reasonable to expect that the different ratios between the number of tasks and sensors leads to different improvements in the number of successful tasks between negotiation-enabled and non-negotiation models. For example, when the number of tasks remain unchanged, the more sensors there are, fewer negotiations are required and thus, any improvement due to negotiation might decrease. Hence, we explored variations in these values.

We now turn to the specific results.

Hypothesis 1. *By negotiating, agents will have a better chance of finding a successful allocation as well as increasing the total profit achieved. Moreover, the running time of the algorithm is still acceptable.*

To evaluate this hypothesis, we measure the number of successful allocated tasks and the total amount of profit achieved for the model with the 1-sequence negotiation featured in extended utility mode and the one without the negotiation feature. The differences are shown in Figure 2.

As can be seen, negotiation allows the number of successful tasks to increase in all cases, varying between 2% and 12%. This can be explained by the fact that, in many situations, a sub-task in the standard model fails because it cannot find a sensor of a particular type to satisfy its requirement. This same sub-task in the negotiation-enabled model can now bargain with another sub-task to acquire

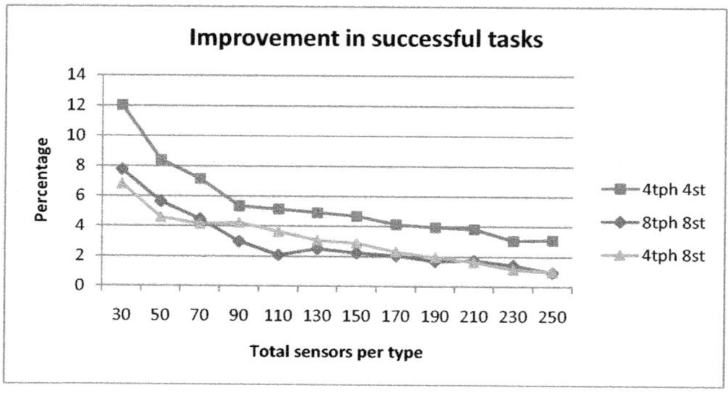

Fig. 2. The improvement of successful tasks between 1-sequence concurrent negotiation (simple negotiation mode) vs no negotiation

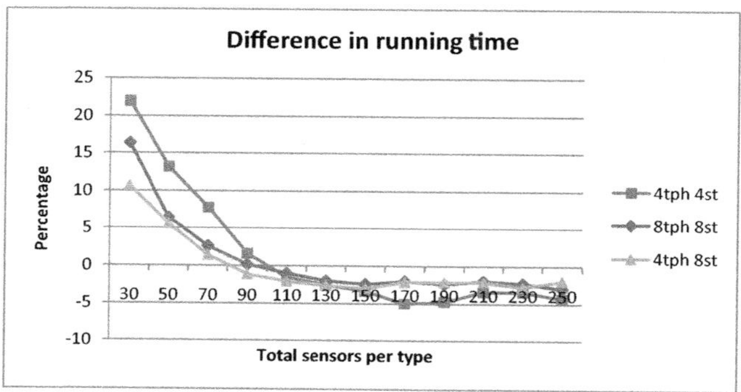

Fig. 3. The differences of the running time of the algorithm between 1 sequence concurrent negotiation (simple negotiation mode) vs no negotiation

a sensor that is unavailable otherwise and this helps it to obtain a successful allocation and, eventually in some cases, lead to a successfully allocated task. As the number of successful tasks increases, the overall profit achieved also increases.

We detail the differences between the running time of our model with and without negotiation in Figure 3. This is the actual amount of time that the machine took to solve the allocation problem. As can be seen from the graph, the negotiation-enabled model takes longer than its counterpart when the number of sensors is roughly between 5% and 22% which, we believe, is still acceptable given the more beneficial outcomes achieved. However, as the number of sensors increases, the time it took decreases such that there is a negligible impact on running time. By far, the greatest impact on running time is the number of tasks and sensors involved in a problem.

Hypothesis 2. *The overall utility achieved through the use of negotiation is higher than that without.*

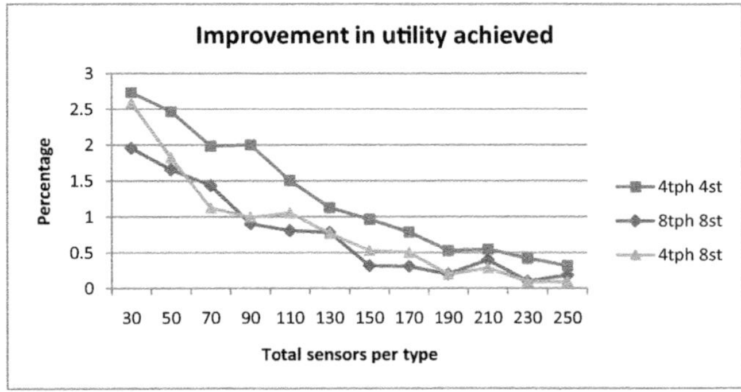

Fig. 4. The improvement of utility achieved between 1 sequence concurrent negotiation (simple negotiation mode) vs no negotiation

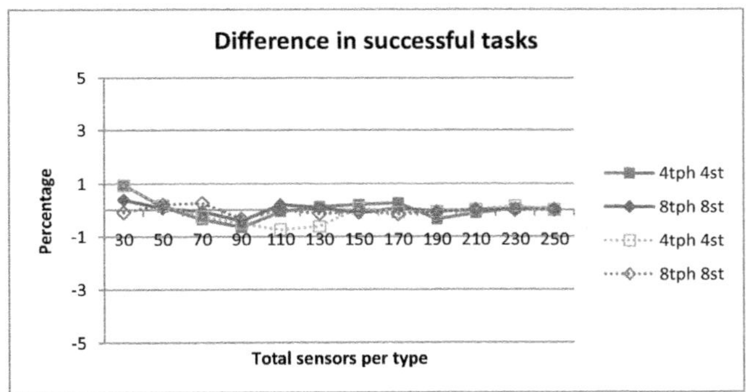

Fig. 5. The differences of the number of successful tasks between 1-sequence highest utility agreement (straight line) vs 1-sequence lowest profit (dotted line) vs simple negotiation mode

The differences between the averaged utility achieved by using model with and without negotiation feature are displayed in Figure 4. As can be seen from hypothesis 1, negotiation enabled model allows higher number of successfully allocated tasks in all situations. Consequently, the utility achieved by successful tasks is increased, leading to an increase in the averaged utility obtained by a task. Also similar to hypothesis 1, the more sensors there are, the lower this increase will be.

Hypothesis 3. *There is no clear advantage of selecting the extended negotiation mode.*

To evaluate this hypothesis, we show the difference between the performance of 1-sequence lowest profit agreement and 1-sequence highest utility agreement vs simple negotiation mode in Figure 5.

As can be seen, the difference between extended negotiation mode and the simple negotiation mode are negligible with the highest value less than 1%.

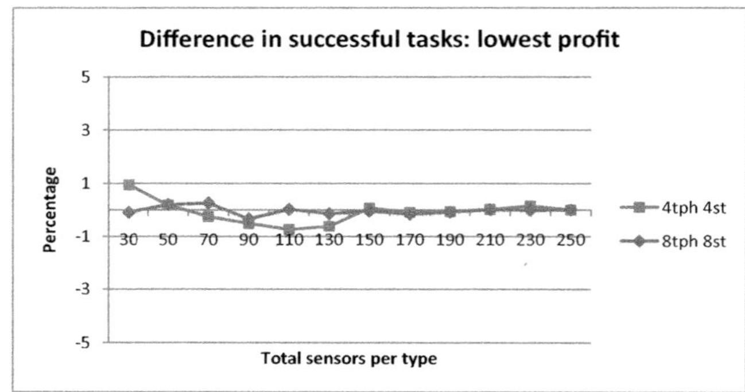

Fig. 6. The differences of the number of successful tasks between 1-sequence lowest profit agreement vs simple negotiation mode

There is no decisive pattern of which negotiation mode provides a more desirable outcome. Obviously, the extended negotiation mode strongly favours the buyer sub-task (see Section 4) whereas the simple negotiation mode treats all agents equally. Consequently, it is rational to select the simple mode as the negotiation method since the sellers will be more willing to participate (they do not have to wait for the buyer to finalize their agreements). Moreover, it will be faster for an agreement to be reached.

Hypothesis 4. *Allowing 2-sequence negotiation in the model provides higher number of successful allocated tasks than 1-sequence negotiation enabled model.*

2-sequence negotiation allows a sub-task agent to have a slightly better chance of finding a replacement sensor (see Section 4). For most sellers, instead of only finding free sensors, they can now negotiate with other potential seller for a replacement sensor, having both the roles of buyer and seller at the same time. By doing so, the chance of finding a replacement sensor for any seller is increased and that results in a higher number of negotiations for the original buyer and, consequently, a higher number of successful negotiations, eventually leading to an increase in the number of successful negotiations compared to its 1-sequence counterpart. The results are clearly demonstrated in Figure 7.

Hypothesis 5. *The running time of 2-sequence negotiation enabled model is considerably longer than that of 1-sequence counterpart.*

Even though 2-sequence negotiation mode provides better outcomes than 1-sequence mode, the running time of the algorithm is much higher (see Figure 8). In the worst case, it is nearly 2.5 times worse and even in the best case, it takes nearly 50% longer than its counterpart.

Now that the sellers can negotiate with other potential sellers, their chances of finding a replacement is increased but also the number of negotiations carried out is also increased. There is no way of knowing which negotiation will be beneficial and thus, all the negotiations will need to be carried out. As a result, there will

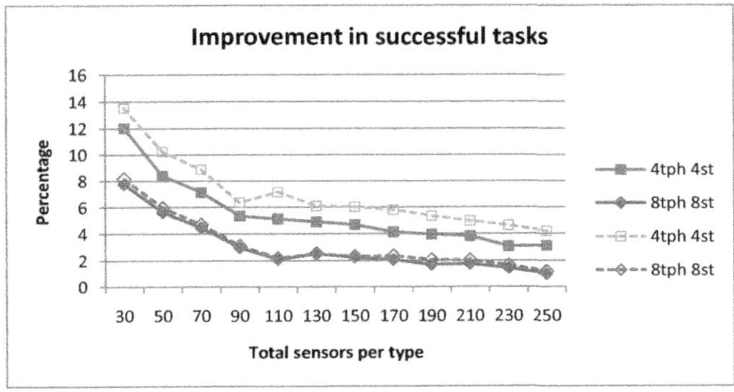

Fig. 7. The differences of the number of successful tasks between 2-sequence *vs* 1-sequence concurrent negotiation (dotted *vs* straight lines)

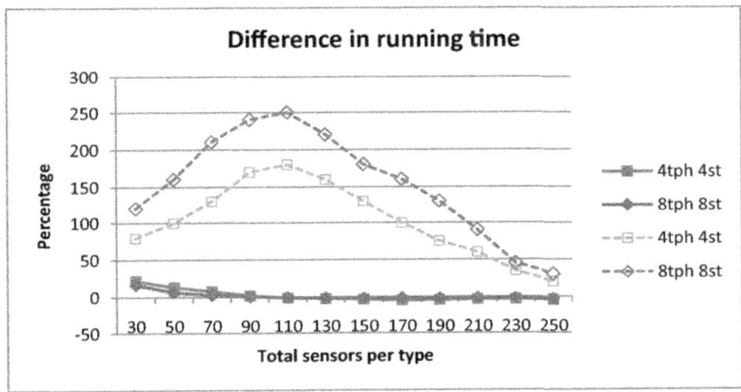

Fig. 8. The differences of the algorithm running time between 2-sequence *vs* 1-sequence concurrent negotiation (dotted *vs* straight lines)

be many unnecessary bargaining processes, leading to a dramatic increase in the running time of our model.

As can be seen, even though the number of successful tasks increases with 2-sequence negotiation, the time it takes to complete is considerably longer than that of 1-sequence counterpart. Thus, it will not be beneficial to support more than 2-sequence negotiation in our model since the trade-off between the successful task and the running time will be undesirable.

6 Discussion and Related Work

There are only a small number of sensor-task allocation studies that have considered the heterogeneous sensor, heterogeneous task case [11,5] and our work falls in this class, which can be considered the most generic version of the sensor-task allocation problem. In addition, the problem we are considering can be viewed as a more general problem of resource allocation such as scheduling jobs on unrelated parallel machines [16] (the feasible constraint is that a job may need to be performed by a set of families of machines) or the Bin Covering problem (our problem is a generalization of this problem when the item may take a different amount of space in different bins). Our MRA algorithm presented in Section 3 is an adaptation of the MRGAP algorithm proposed in [5] in which the idea is to consider tasks as knapsacks that together form an instance of the Generalized Assignment Problem (GAP).

Resource allocation models in multi agent systems have two major branches: centralised and decentralised [1,4]. Centralised systems make use of a single agent to assign resources to all tasks and optimal outcomes might be achieved because that single agent has a global view of the situation. The most successful centralised models are auctions and it comes in various form including regular or combinatorial auctions [6]. Agents may submit the "best" bid(s) serving their own interests and wait for the final allocation decided by the auctioneer. In addition, advantage of such models is that the communication protocols required are normally simpler than that of decentralised approaches [1]. Nonetheless, the central agent creates a bottleneck and generally, these solutions do not scale well. Decentralised systems are typically preferred in practical situations [4] and peer-to-peer negotiation has long been a popular technique for agent coordination in such system.

In sensor networks, various forms of negotiation have been explored. For example, Sujit *et al.* [15] employ an auction-based negotiation model for distributing UAVs (Unmanned Aerial Vehicles) to search and attack some targets in the environment. Similarly, Shima *et al.* [14] use an auction-based negotiation model to establish information regarding other neighbouring nodes and estimate costs for other members to assign to different targets in order to find an efficient solution for all the participating nodes. The DISTINCT algorithm [12] uses negotiation to distribute tasks among robots. The disadvantage of these approaches is that they cannot guarantee all the negotiations will terminate after a finite number of cycles.

Another model introduced by Howard *et al.* [3] uses a market-based approach and the contract net protocol to allocate a group of robots to a number of tasks. Each task is announced and all the robots bid for tasks. If a robot has already been allocated to another task then the robot will select the better task and broadcast the other. The major issue with this model is that there are a great deal of duplicate allocations, resulting unnecessary time and resource consumed.

In [2,7], Kulik *et al* introduce four SPIN (Sensor Protocols for Information via Negotiation) protocols for exchanging information in wireless sensor networks. They are all negotiation based and can be applied in either point-to-point or broadcast modes. In either mode, the sensor nodes use some variation of the three-stage handshake protocol to negotiate for newly discovered data. Basically, whenever a sensor discovers new data, it will broadcast its findings (ADV message) to its neighbouring sensors. These sensors, in turn, will decide whether or not to ask for the actual data to be sent to them (REQ message) based on their constraints. Finally the initiator will response to the REQ message with a DATA message containing the actual data. Even though the communication between sensors can be reduced by using these protocols, the sensors need to be equipped with large buffers to store previous requests/data to avoid duplication. Moreover, these protocols only provide best results when the topology of the network is fixed.

As can be seen, using negotiation as the sole means to allocate resources might not be beneficial. However, it is useful if negotiation is used to enhance existing allocation algorithms. There are a number of negotiation models that can be employed such as auctions, double auctions or bilateral negotiations. However in this work, we consider the application of the multiple concurrent bilateral negotiation model introduced by Nguyen *et al.* [10] since it allows the agents to engage in real time and the results obtained are close to optimum [10,9]. There are a number of shortcomings with our model, however. First, the strategies employed by the agents are linear and constant throughout each encounter. Ideally, they should adapt to their opponents so that the participating agents might be able to obtain better outcomes. Second, we consider profit to be exchangeable between tasks so that it can be used as the base for the negotiations to happen. This is not always an appropriate assumption and this issue requires further investigation.

7 Conclusion

In this paper, we have proposed a decentralised agent-based approach for handling the sensor-task allocation problem in dynamic environments where the tasks and resources can appear/disappear any time. Moreover, our model allows various tasks to compete for the same resources in a graceful manner. In particular, we have incorporated a negotiation mechanism as a post-processing stage of agent-based allocation models. The mechanism allows resources to be exchanged between self-interested agents. Specifically, a task negotiates concurrently with other tasks to obtain a resource that is currently allocated to one of these tasks in exchange for a fraction of its profit which it will receive if it can obtain a valid alternative allocation. Via empirical evaluation, we have demonstrated that this offers significantly better results when compared with an agent-based allocation model without resource re-allocation.

References

1. Chevaleyre, Y., Dunne, P.E., Endriss, U., Lang, J., Lemaitre, M., Maudet, N., Padget, J., Phelps, S., Rodrguez-aguilar, J.A., Sousa, P.: Issues in multiagent resource allocation. Informatica 30 (2006)
2. Heinzelman, W.R., Kulik, J., Balakrishnan, H.: Adaptive protocols for information dissemination in wireless sensor networks. In: Proceedings of the ACM MobiCom 1999, Seattle, Washington, pp. 174–185 (1999)
3. Howard, A., Viguria, A.: Controlled reconfiguration of robotic mobile sensor networks using distributed allocation formalisms. In: Proc. of the NASA Science Technology Conference, NSTC 2007 (2007)

4. Jacyno, M., Bullock, S., Payne, T., Luck, M.: Understanding decentralised control of resource allocation in a minimal multi-agent system. In: AAMAS 2007: Proceedings of the 6th International Joint Conference on Autonomous Agents and Multiagent Systems. pp. 208–210 (2007)
5. Johnson, M.P., Rowaihy, H., Pizzocaro, D., Bar-Noy, A., Chalmers, S., La Porta, T., Preece, A.: Frugal Sensor Assignment. In: Nikoletseas, S.E., Chlebus, B.S., Johnson, D.B., Krishnamachari, B. (eds.) DCOSS 2008. LNCS, vol. 5067, pp. 219–236. Springer, Heidelberg (2008)
6. Krishna, V.: Auction Theory. Academic Press (2002)
7. Kulik, J., Heinzelman, W.: Negotiation-based protocols for disseminating information in wireless sensor networks. Wireless Networks 8, 169–185 (2002)
8. Le, T.P., Norman, T.J., Vasconcelos, W.: Agent-based sensor-mission assignment for tasks sharing assets. In: Proceeding of the Third International Workshop on Agent Technology for Sensor Networks, Budapest, Hungary (May 2009)
9. Nguyen, T.D.: A heuristic model for concurrent bilateral negotiations in incomplete information settings. Ph.D. thesis, University of Southampton, Southampton, England (2005)
10. Nguyen, T.D., Jennings, N.R.: Coordinating multiple concurrent negotiations. In: Proceedings of the Third International Conference on Autonomous Agents and Multiagent Systems, New York, USA, pp. 1064–1071 (2004)
11. Preece, A., Pizzocaro, D., Borowiecki, K., de Mel, G., Gomez, M., Vasconcelos, M., Bar-Noy, A., Johnson, M.P., La Porta, T.L., Rowaihy, H., Pearson, G., Pham, T.: Reasoning and resource allocation for sensor-mission assignment in a coalition context. In: MILCOM 2008 (2008)
12. Salemi, B., Will, P., min Shen, W.: Distributed task negotiation in modular robots. Robotics Society of Japan, Special Issue (2003)
13. Sensoy, M., Le, T., Vasconcelos, W.W., Norman, T.J., Preece, A.D.: Resource determination and allocation in sensor networks: A hybrid approach. Computer Journal (2010) (to appear)
14. Shima, T., Rasmussen, S.J., Chandler, P.: UAV team decision and control using efficient collaborative estimation. In: Proceedings of the 2005 American Control Conference, vol. 6, pp. 4107–4112 (2005)
15. Sujit, P.B., Sinha, A., Ghose, D.: Multiple UAV task allocation using negotiation. In: AAMAS 2006: Proceedings of the Fifth International Conference on Autonomous Agents and Multiagent Systems, pp. 471–478 (2006)
16. Sung, S.C., Vlach, M.: Maximizing weighted number of just-in-time jobs on unrelated parallel machines. Journal of Scheduling 8(5), 453–460 (2005)

Negotiation Strategy for Mobile Agent-Based e-Negotiation

Raja Al-Jaljouli and Jemal Abawajy

[1] Deakin University, School of Information Technology,
Pigdons Road, Geelong,
Victoria 3217, Australia
{ralj,jemal}@deakin.com.au

Abstract. Negotiation is a vital component of electronic trading. It is the key decision-making approach used to reach consensus between trading partners. Generally, trading partners implement various negotiation strategies in an attempt to maximize their utilities. As strategies have impact on the outcomes of negotiation, it is imperative to have efficient negotiation strategies that truly maximize clients' utilities. In this paper, we propose a multi-attribute mobile agent-based negotiation strategy that maximizes client's utility. The strategy focuses on one-to-many bilateral negotiation. It considers different factors that significantly affect the scheduling of various negotiation phases: offer collection, evaluation, negotiation, and bid award. The factors include offers expiry time, market search space, communication delays, processing queues, and transportation times. We reasoned about the correctness of the proposed negotiation strategy with respect to the existing negotiation strategies. The analysis showed that the proposed strategy enhances client's utility, reduces negotiation time, and ensures minimum search space.

Keywords: Negotiation strategy, e-Trade, temporal constraints, client's utilities, end of offer validity, negotiation deadline.

1 Introduction

Automated negotiation (e-negotiation) has been proposed for e-Trade applications as a promising environment that facilitates negotiation without human intervention/supervision. It overcomes problems associated with human negotiation that includes rational and emotional responses. Moreover, it concludes verifiable agreements and optimizes negotiation outcomes [6]. Mobile agents have been employed to act on behalf of negotiators and reach a mutual agreement that satisfies their requirement profiles and maximizes their individual utilities. They exhibit special characteristics including heterogeneous execution, dynamic adaptation to environmental changes, and cooperative capacity. In addition, they build knowledge about opponents' attitudes and intensions through negotiation and can make decisions autonomously based on negotiation threads. In this paper, we focus on mobile agent-based negotiation.

N. Desai, A. Liu, and M. Winikoff (Eds.): PRIMA 2010, LNAI 7057, pp. 137–151, 2012.

In e-Trade, a client who is interested in a service such as network maintenance would place a request with a mobile agent and defines his own constraints, preferences, and priorities. Constraints may include price of service, maintenance period, penalty of breach of agreement, etc. Preferences may include payment installments, response time, etc. Priorities may include quality of service. The mobile agent would initially plan the bid and sets a deadline for bidding. It then collects offers from potential suppliers and negotiates for an offer that meets client's constraints and preferences and provides best quality of maintenance. It tries to make an extensive market search with the aim of reaching an agreement that satisfies client's requirements profile and maximizes client's utility. There exists a risk that the mobile agent collects the most advantageous offer in last few minutes of its validity and before it completes a thorough market search. The agent continues on negotiation and might abort it few minutes later than its validity. The most advantageous offer would be missed out and, hence, client's utility would not be maximized.

Negotiation strategies presented in the literature delay offer evaluation till all offers are collected. They do not consider offer expiry time and only consider particular temporal constraints such as bidding deadline, goods/service delivery deadline or negotiation deadline. Therefore, there is a need to develop a more efficient negotiation strategy that avoids delayed evaluation of collected offers and considers the effect of offer expiry time. It should also ensure accurate assessment of the market through an adequate market search without the loss of advantageous offers that might expire shortly before the negotiation deadline. The strategy should consider the risk of missing out advantageous offers that are likely to expire earlier than the bidding deadline and interrupts offer collection/negotiation earlier than the deadline, whenever, the most advantageous offer is about to expire and an adequate market search is completed. The bid may be awarded earlier than the bidding deadline. Thus, various factors including: offer expiry time, market search space, communication delays, processing queues, and transportation times should be considered to be able to maximize client's utility.

In this paper, we address the problem of limited-time offers in e-negotiation and the probable deficit in optimizing the outcomes of negotiation. We propose a negotiation strategy that overcomes the problem and maximizes client's utility. We focus on multi-attribute one-to-many bilateral negotiation.

The proposed negotiation strategy searches the marketplace for the most competitive offers, carries preliminary evaluation of each offer at collection time and computes its utility, and awards the bid to the offer that has the top utility. We show that the proposed negotiation strategy maximizes client's utility, ensures satisfactory search and negotiation spaces, shortens negotiation time, and avoids loss of the top utility offer that might expire before the negotiation deadline.

The rest of the paper is organized as follows. The background to the effect of temporal constraints on negotiation is discussed in Section 2. The existing negotiation strategies are discussed and the drawbacks as regards negotiation outcomes are highlighted. A real example is also presented for illustration. In Section 3, the system architecture of mobile agent-based one-to-many bilateral negotiation is described and various phases of negotiation are discussed. In Section 4, the proposed negotiation strategy is described in details and negotiation algorithm is outlined. Performance analysis of the proposed negotiation strategy is presented in Section 5. The conclusions and future works are discussed in Section 6.

2 Background

In this section, we present related work and illustrate the effect of negotiation strategies on the outcomes of e-negotiation.

2.1 Problem Overview

There are three negotiation strategies that mobile agents can employ based on a time constraint: anxious, patient, and partially patient strategies. Strategies are constrained by negotiation deadlines. In anxious strategy, the agent tries to settle an agreement before the negotiation deadline and the soonest possible, whereas in patient strategy it may extend negotiation till the negotiation deadline trying to settle an agreement at the most possible utility. The partially patient strategy tries to reach an agreement before the negotiation deadline and may interrupt negotiation earlier than the negotiation deadline having received a good offer. There are some problems with the existing negotiation strategies.

We present a real example that illustrates the effect of negotiation strategies on the outcomes of e-negotiation. A client agent that searches various airlines for a flight on 24th March, 2011 from Montreal, QC Canada (YUL) to Bathurst, NB Canada (ZBF). It searches for a non-stop cheap flight with a price limit of $500 and sets 14th March, 2011 00:05 EDT (Canada) as negotiation deadline. It starts the search on 13th March, 2011 11:55 EDT (Canada) being unaware of time-limited offers. It searched through Yahootravel.com, Aircanada.com, Orbitz.com, Grab2Travel.com, and Cheapoair.com. Different offers are provided for a non-stop flight with the prices of: $471, $456, $370, $355, and $261.03. The offer of $471 is the first collected offer and the offer of $261.03 is a limited-time offer that expires on 6th Sep, 2010 11.59 EDT. The query retrieval time of mobile agents, excluding time needed for verification and negotiation, varies from 125 - 450 seconds using Generic Algorithm (GA) that implements short routes of local pre-fetched servers (LP) rather than long routes [12]. Assume the retrieval query time is 420 seconds.

The decisions an agent takes are based on preferences, priorities, constraints, and implemented negotiation strategy, e.g. non-stop route as a flight preference, specific travel dates as a priority, and upper limit of ticket price as a constraint. The anxious strategy awards the bid to the first acceptable offer of $471, whereas the patient strategy completes the search of various airlines 3 minutes later than the expiry time of the best offer of $261.03. It would miss out the best offer and, thus, awards the bid to the second advantageous offer of $355. The two strategies would miss out the best offer of $261.03. Our proposed negotiation strategy would not complete the search of various airlines due to the risk of missing out the most advantageous offer priced as $261.03 that would expire before the agent completes its search plan. It interrupts the search before the expiry of the offer priced $261.03 having completed an adequate market search, e.g. four service providers and as long as the offer is the most advantageous among the so far collected offers. Our strategy in this instance provides 44.5% and 22.6% additional savings as compared to anxious and patient strategies, respectively.

The anxious negotiation strategy awards the bid to the first acceptable offer which is most probably overpriced and, hence, does not maximize client's utility as it does not give enough time for evaluating the market accurately. Whereas, the patient negotiation strategy extends search till market search is completed trying to maximize client's utility. It would miss out the best utility offer that has a short validity and would expire before the bidding deadline and, hence, would not maximize client's utility.

The partially patient negotiation strategy might interrupt offer collection if the so far most advantageous offer would expire earlier than bidding deadline regardless of satisfying a minimum market search. There is risk of interrupting negotiation at a very early stage while more advantageous offer might be forthcoming, and hence, the strategy would not maximize client utility. There is also another risk of a malicious vendor that might provide a little bit competitive offer with an expiry earlier than the negotiation deadline or would delay the agent till negotiation deadline so as to win the bid.

2.2 Related Work

Negotiation is a process in which two or more parties articulate conflicting requests and try to reach a mutual agreement by search of acceptable alternatives or concession. Negotiation can be described by cardinality (one-to-one, one-to-many, or many-to-many), negotiation issues (single issue, multiple issues), and negotiation attributes (single attribute, multi-attributes) of a particular issue. Searching for a holiday package that includes flight, accommodation, and car hire represents multiple issues negotiation, whereas, searching for a flight to a particular destination on specific date within a limited budget represents multi-attributes negotiation. In this paper, we address on one-to-many bilateral negotiation.

Research has mainly focused on one-to-one negotiation. Particular related issues have been addressed including bidding deadline [4, 10] and multi-attribute negotiation [4, 5, 7], negotiation protocols [9], and negotiation security [8, 14]. Collins et al. [3] addressed one-to-many bilateral single issue negotiation. They discussed the interdependencies between various temporal constraints and how they affect the strategic behavior of agent participating in e-negotiation. They considered sealed bid or Vickery auctions where the bids earliest evaluation time is later than the bidding deadline. They proposed to shift the offer evaluation time to be earlier than the bidding deadline, whenever, the expiry time of an offer is earlier than the bidding deadline. The approach might result in awarding overpriced bids. Assume a vendor was able to speculate that the bidding task is critical, he would then provide an offer with a short validity forcing the bidder to reason early and award the bid before waiting for more valuable offers that might be forthcoming. The approach would result in inadequate search space and, hence, may not maximize client's utility.

Si et al. [13] proposed a negotiation framework for one-to-many bilateral negotiation that maximizes client's utility. The framework coordinates negotiations of composite trading activities and models it as simultaneous one-to-one negotiations. It considered particular temporal constraints including bidding time, turnaround time for bidding, and offer expiry time. It assumed that bidding time is communicated to vendors participating in trading activities and negotiation is purely price based.

There are different negotiation strategies [11]. The anxious strategy tries to close the bidding as soon it finds an offer that meets client's preferences and constraints. It may not achieve client's maximum utility. The patient strategy waits till negotiation deadline and then chooses the best valid offer. It gives better chance for maximizing client's utility. Negotiation participants may impose a negotiation deadline as the negotiation may be endless. The optimized patient strategy evaluates the outcomes of a negotiation round and accordingly amends bidding constraints so as to improve the outcomes of the subsequent negotiation round. The negotiation continues till it reaches the most possible utility before the negotiation deadline.

The patient strategy is usually implemented in one-to-many unilateral negotiation e.g. sealed-bid auctions and in one-to-many bilateral negotiation e.g. e-commerce. A major problem in the strategy is that offers and, in particular, limited-time offers have expiry times that might be earlier than the negotiation deadline and, thus, there is a risk of losing advantageous offers and reducing the chances of maximizing client's utility. The problem has not been sufficiently addressed in the literature.

The aim of the proposed negotiation strategy is to avoid loss of top utility offer that might expire before bidding deadline. We assume that offers are non-retractable. The withdrawal of an offer results in imposing a penalty on the respective trading partner. The proposed strategy implements immediate response interaction, which evaluates an incoming offer as soon as it is received. This is different from the strategies that implement delayed response interaction [3], which delays the evaluation of offers till all offers are collected, e.g. sealed bid or Vickery auctions. The delayed response interaction does not surely maximize client's utility as a top utility offer might expire before bidding deadline.

3 System Architecture

The high-level system architecture for mobile agent-based one-to-many negotiation is depicted in Figure. 1. There are six successive and non-concurrent phases the agent passes through its lifetime. In phase 1, the client places a request with the mobile agent that describes goods/service of interest and defines expected delivery time T_{ED}, preferences, constraints, and priorities. The phase is referred to as *Initiation phase*.

In phase 2, the client agent plans a bid and sets a deadline for bidding T_{EB} to be earlier than the negotiation deadline allowing for offer negotiation and bid award. It then migrates to the marketplace to collect offers from potential vendors (S1) until bidding deadline is reached. The phase is referred to as *Bidding phase*.

In phase 3, it migrates to the trusted host, where it can securely verify and evaluate collected offers. It then shortlists acceptable offers and identifies constraints to negotiate with short-listed vendors. The phase is referred to as *Evaluation phase*.

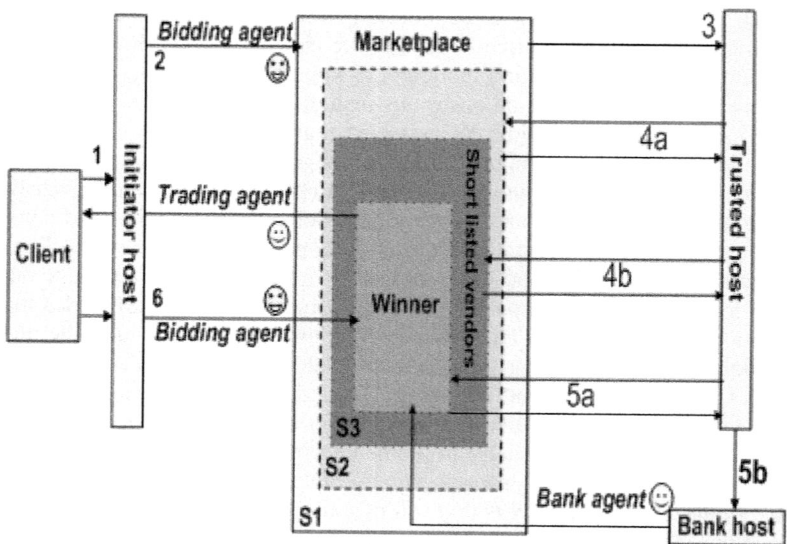

Fig. 1. High-level system architecture of mobile agent-basedone-to-many negotiation

In phase 4, the client agent sets a negotiation strategy and selects attributes to negotiate. It then runs multiple negotiation rounds as necessary e.g. a, b, c, etc. In the first round, it migrates to the marketplace to negotiate with a shortlist of vendors (S2) and collects amendments to their original offers if any exists. It would migrate back to the trusted host to evaluate outcomes of negotiation. If client's requirements are not satisfied and there is a need for more negotiation, the agent runs a second round of negotiation with a narrower shortlist of vendors (S3). It may run multiple rounds of negotiation till client's requirements are satisfied and adequate market search is completed. It then concludes the offer of maximum utility and indentifies the winning vendor. The phase is referred to as *Negotiation phase*.

Phase 5 consists of two stages. In the first stage, the client agent sends a purchase order to the winning vendor and waits for acceptance. In the second stage, it then makes a payment order to client's bank to process a payment for the winning vendor. The bank then processes the payment to the winning vendor. The phase is referred to as *Award phase*. Upon receipt of payment, the winning vendor delivers service/goods to the client.

In phase 6, the client agent receives an acknowledgement from the client confirming the receipt of service/goods. It would then pass the acknowledgement to the winning vendor and concludes the successful completion of client's request. The phase is referred to as *Acknowledgement phase*.

At initiation, the client agent sets temporal constraints defining start and end times of the different phases. During negotiation different entities: client, client agent, and vendor agents exchange messages till an agreement is congregated and service/goods are delivered to the client.

4 Negotiation Strategy

The proposed negotiation strategy focuses on one-to-many multi-constraint bilateral negotiation. The utility of an offer can be assessed by calculating the offer value. Scoring functions [14] defined in Equations: (1) – (5) estimate the value of a collected offer based on constraints the client sets e.g. price and installment plan. Upper and lower limits the client sets for each constraint (j) for ($1 \leq j \leq m$) e.g. (min_j, max_j) and the constraint (X) given in the respective offer are substituted into Equations (2) and (3) to estimate the value of each constraint $S_j(X)$. The parameter (β) defines the gradient of the scoring function. Equation (2) is used to evaluate small item values X, while Equation (3) is used to evaluate large item values X.

The value of an offer $S(X)$ is calculated based on Equation (1) as the sums of each constraint value $S_j(X)$ multiplied by its normalized constraint weight (w_j) that indicates the priority level of the constraint [16]. The more the constraint weight is the higher is the constraint priority and the less is the agent concession [16]. The sum of constraints weights (w_j) for ($1 \leq j \leq m$) complies with Equation (4). Agents can pre-define weights of constraints by implementing Q-learning approach [2].

$$S(X) = \sum_{1 \leq j \leq m} w_j \cdot S_j(X) \tag{1}$$

$$S_j(X) = \left| \left(\frac{X - min_j}{max_j - min_j} \right)^{\frac{1}{\beta}} \right| \tag{2}$$

$$S_j(X) = \left| \left(\frac{max_j - X}{max_j - min_j} \right)^{\frac{1}{\beta}} \right| \tag{3}$$

$$\sum_{j=1 \ldots m} w_j = 1 \quad \text{where } 0 < w_j < 1 \tag{4}$$

The client might only define upper or lower limit of constraints. The value of each constraint $S_j(X)$ is then calculated based on Equations (5) and (6). The proposed negotiation strategy deduces the best utility offer by sorting the collected offers by their values.

$$S_j(X) = \left| \left(\frac{X - min_j}{min_j} \right)^{\frac{1}{\beta}} \right| \tag{5}$$

$$S_j(X) = \left| \left(\frac{max_j - X}{max_j} \right)^{\frac{1}{\beta}} \right| \tag{6}$$

The algorithm in Figure 2 shows the pseudo-code of the *Proposed Negotiation_ tactic*. Firstly, a mobile agent receives a request from a client that consists of bid attributes (Y), expected delivery time T_{ED}, matrix (M) of upper and lower limits of constraints (max_j, min_j) for ($1 \leq j \leq m$).

```
Algorithm Proposed Negotiation_tactic
 INPUT: T_c , t, T_ED
 OUTPUT: V_W
 Set temporal constraints, e.g. T_EB
 Set W, S_P, N_MIN
 Q ← {Y, W, S_P, M, N_MIN, T_EB}
 Select Agent's itinerary V←{V_1 , … , V_j , … , V_z}
  FOR (V_j ∈ V) DO
     V_j ← Dispatch (MA)
     Read timer value t and store current time at V_j as T_j
     Calculate Drift time Td_j = T_c + t - T_j
     IF (T_EB ≤ (T_j + Td_j )) THEN Abort_execution
    ELSE
     Execute (MA) and collect offer (F_j)
     Compute offer's value(S_j)using scoring functions
     Compute number of visited vendors N_T = N_T +1
     IF offer F_j satisfy:
      a. Client's constraints (max_j, min_j) for (1 ≤ j ≤ m)
      b. Offer value is equal to or greater than the preferred
         offer value (S_j ≥ S_P)
     THEN
      {
       F • Append F_j ( Ȳ, V_j , S_j, T_SV, T_EV)
      Sort offers' values (S_j) and store as vector (S̄)
      IF (S[1]== S_j) AND (T_EV ≤ T_EB) THEN
       {
       Estimate award time
       T_a • award time
       Tr_j • Compute (T_EV + Td_j - T_a)//Alert period of F_j
       Set_Alert  (Tr_j , F_j)
       }
      ENDIF
      }
     ELSE Exclude offer
     ENDIF
    ENDIF
 ENDFOR
END Proposed Negotiation_tactic
```

Fig. 2. Pseudo code of the *Proposed Negotiation_tactic*

The mobile agent (MA) initially sets bidding deadline (T_{EB}), matrix of weights of constraints (W), preferred offer value (S_P), and minimum search space (N_{MIN}). It then stores the request into vector (Q). It then stores the current time at its host (T_c), and initializes two parameters: Timer (*t*) and Number visited vendors N_T and sets both to zero. It initializes two empty vectors: offers vector (S) and offer values vector ($\overline{S}$). It then selects an itinerary for the agent $\{V_1, \ldots, V_z\}$ and stores it in vector (V).

The agent would search for the most similar need pattern to the client's pattern from the prefetched servers and then compares the current need pattern to previously recorded ones. Based on similarities between the two patterns [15], they recommend the minimum search space (N_{MIN}) before a decision can be made.

The agent (MA) starts its itinerary and searches for offers. A visited vendor (V_j) may provide an offer. The negotiation strategy carries out *preliminary evaluation* of each offer as soon as it is received and computes its value (S_j) using Equations: (1) – (5) and stores it in vector ($\overline{S}$).

The mobile agent verifies if the collected offer (F_i): (1) satisfies client's constraints (max_j, min_j) for ($1 \le j \le m$); (2) has a value (S_j) equal to or greater than the preferred offer value (S_P). If the offer passes the verification, it appends the offer (F_j) to offer vector (F), otherwise it excludes the offer and migrates to the next host in agent's itinerary.

The offer (F_j) consists of: offer attributes ($\overline{Y}$), vendor identity (V_k), offer value (S_j), start of offer validity (T_{SV}), end of offer validity (T_{EV}). It then ranks the so far collected offers by their values (S_j) by sorting vector ($\overline{S}$) and short-lists the highly ranked offers.

If the offer has best value i.e. ($\overline{S}[1] == S_j$) and would expire before the end time of bidding phase, it then set a timer to signal before the so far most advantageous offer expires. It estimates the time (T_a) the client agent needs to award the bid to the winning vendor taking into consideration delays due to communication, transportation, and processing queues. It sets a timer to signal an alert at (Tr_j). It is calculated based on Equation (7) and is earlier than the expiry time (T_{EV}) of offer (F_j) to allow for awarding the bid to the winning vendor.

$$Tr_j = T_{EV} + Td_j - Ta \quad (7)$$

Whenever, the timer signals an alert at Tr_j, it indicates that an advantageous offer (F_k) is about to expire. The mobile agent sorts the vector ($\overline{S}$) to identify the utility of the top offer and then verifies if the offer (F_k) has the top utility i.e. ($S_k = \overline{S}[1]$). If the offer passes the verification, the agent verifies if the number of visited vendors satisfies the minimum number of searched vendors i.e. ($N_T \ge N_{MIN}$). If the verification passes, then the vendor (V_k) would be selected as the winning vendor. Offer collection would be interrupted and vendor (V_k) would be awarded the bid.

The agent (MA) does not immediately award the bid to the vendor (V_k) for which the alert is on as more advantageous offers may have been offered or an adequate price of first best offer, price of second best offer, offer validity, and negotiation deadline. Let market search has not yet been completed. It carries multiple verifications to ensure maximum utility is achieved. It sorts the so far collected offers and stores them in vector ($\bar{S}$) and then verifies if offer for which the alert is on has the best value i.e. ($\bar{S}[1] == S_k$). If verification fails, it excludes the offer. If verification passes, it then verifies if the constraint on minimum number of visited vendors is met i.e. ($N_T == N_{MIN}$). If the verification passes, offers collection/negotiation would be interrupted and the vendor (V_k) would be awarded the bid. Next, an agreement is settled and payment is processed for the winning vendor. If the verification fails, then the offer (F_k) would not be considered to any further extent and the client agent migrates to the next vendor's host in agent's itinerary for offer collection or negotiation.

5 Analysis of Strategy

The main objective of e-negotiation is to optimize negotiation outcomes in terms of expected utility. Negotiation outcomes depend on multiple factors such as negotiation deadline, eagerness, competition, and trading opportunities, etc [1].We measure the performance of the system based on the expected utility as being the fundamental evaluation criterion. We develop a function that computes the client's expected utility in one-to-many e-negotiation. As experiments may not fetch critical cases that deal with advantageous offer that expire before negotiation deadline, we simulate the system with all possible critical cases considering variations of four variables: offers be collected at discrete time instants $t_i^R = \{1, 2, \dots, i, \dots, n\}$ and expire at discrete time instants, $t_i^E = \{2, 3, \dots, i, \dots, n)$ with the earliest expiry of a collected offer at $n = 2$.

The negotiation deadline is at time instant n, where $n = \{10, 15, 20\}$. The price of the first best offer varies from 0.5 to 0.9 of the price upper limit and the difference in price between the first and the second best offers ranges from (5%) to (40%) with an increment of (5%). We test (40*360) states and present numerical results of expected utility that provide insight into the system performance. For simplicity, we consider price-based negotiation. Let (P_{max}) represents the price upper limit of service/goods, and represents $\left(P_{BP}^i\right)$ the bid price of vendor i. The bidding time and the end of offer validity are denoted as are denoted as (T_{EB}), and $\left(T_{EV}^i\right)$ respectively. The expected utility function is defined in Equation (8).

$$U = \left(\frac{P_{max} - P_{BP}^i}{P_{max}}\right)^{\varphi} \tag{8}$$

$$\text{where, } \varphi = \left(\frac{T_{EB}}{T_{EV}^i}\right)$$

Assume the client sets an upper-limit constraint on the price of service/goods P_{max} and a fixed bidding deadline n. The agent received offers from m vendors and intends to run a single round of negotiation. The client's utility is inversely proportional to (P_{BP}^{i}) offering better savings on purchases. Thus, the lower the bid price is as compared to (P_{max}) the better is the client's utility. Whereas, the utility is directly proportional to offer validity (T_{EV}^{i}) that allows for broader search/negotiation space. Thus, the longer the offer validity is as compared to (T_{EB}) the better is the client's utility.

We present the results of simulating a system of a negotiating mobile agent that sets n to 15. Let the price of the best offer be 0.5 of the price upper limit (P_{max}). Due to space limitations we only analyze (14*3) states where the difference in price between the first and the second best offers is as: 5%, 15% or 30% of the price upper limit.

Figure 3 shows the increase in client utility if the best offer is awarded the bid just before it expires. The utility is compared to the expected utility if negotiation continues till its deadline. The intersection of the graph with the horizontal axis shows the minimum acceptable validity of the best offer for negotiation to be interrupted. For example, the client would benefit from the interruption of negotiation if the best offer expires later than time instant $t = 5$ and there is a significant difference in price of (30%). Conversely, the client would only benefit from the interruption of negotiation if the best offer expires later than time instant $t = 14$ and there is a marginal difference in price of (5%).

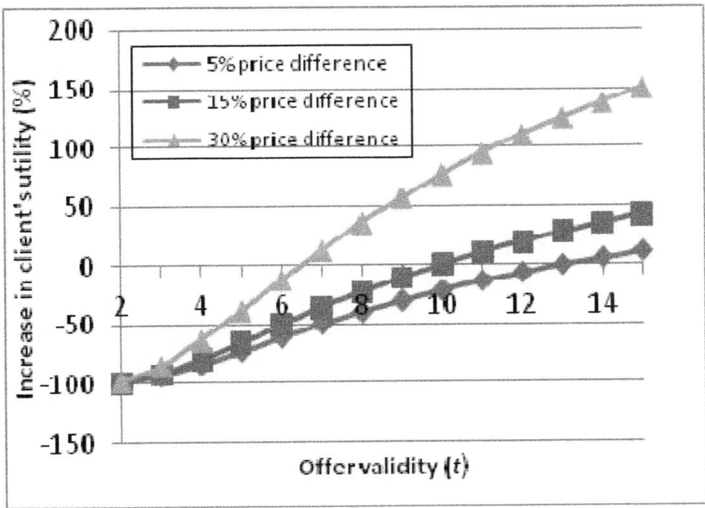

Fig. 3. Increase in expected utility (%) when negotiation ends before the best offer expires

The strategy encourages early interruption of negotiation if there is a significant difference in price, whereas if does not if there is a marginal difference in price. The more the difference in price between the first and second top offers, the earlier the

Table 1. Detailed reasoning of various negotiation strategies

Scenario	Negotiation Strategy	Criteria: $T_{EV} \leq T_{EB}$	Criteria: $T_{EV} > T_{EB}$ / $T_{EV} < T_{EB} + T_a - Td_j$	Criteria: $S[1] = S_k$	Criteria: $N_T \geq N_{MIN}$	Negotiation Outcome	Utility Enhancement	Search Adequacy
❶	*Proposed*		○			*Reject*	✓	✓
	Patient	◉		○	◉	*Reject*	×	✓
	Anxious		○			*Accept*	×	×
❷	*Proposed*		○			*Reject*	✓	✓
	Patient	◉		◉	◉	*Reject*	×	✓
	Anxious		○			*Accept*	×	×
❸	*Proposed*		○			*Reject*	✓	✓
	Patient	◉		○	○	*Reject*	×	✓
	Anxious		○			*Accept*	×	×
❹	*Proposed*		○			*Accept*	✓	✓
	Patient	◉		◉	○	*Reject*	×	✓
	Anxious		○			*Accept*	×	×
❺	*Proposed*		◉			*Reject*	✓	✓
	Patient	○		○	◉	*Reject*	×	✓
	Anxious		◉			*Accept*	×	×
❻	*Proposed*		◉			*Accept*	✓	✓
	Patient	○		◉	◉	*Reject*	×	✓
	Anxious		◉			*Accept*	×	×
❼	*Proposed*		◉			*Reject*	✓	✓
	Patient	○		○	○	*Reject*	×	✓
	Anxious		◉			*Accept*	×	×
❽	*Proposed*		◉			*Accept*	✓	✓
	Patient	○		◉	○	*Reject*	×	✓
	Anxious		◉			*Accept*	×	×
❾	*Proposed*		◉			*Accept*	✓	✓
	Patient	○		◉	○	*Accept*	×	✓
	Anxious		○			*Accept*	×	×
❿	*Proposed*		◉			*Reject*	✓	✓
	Patient	○		○	○	*Reject*	×	✓
	Anxious		○			*Accept*	×	×

negotiation can be interrupted with more gain in utility. The strategy weighs extended market search more than a marginal gain difference in price For example, interrupting negotiation before the best offer expires at time instant $t = 9$ would result in an increase in utility by 76.8% and a drop in negotiation time by 40% having a difference in price is (30%), whereas it would result in a drop in utility by 21.4% if the difference in price is (5%).

Moreover, we reason the correctness of the proposed negotiation strategy by examining the end results of various negotiation strategies for four decision-making conditions. The first condition tests if the expiry time of a limited-time offer (T_{EV}) is earlier than the bidding deadline (T_{EB}). The second condition tests if the expiry time of a limited-time offer (T_{EV}) is later than the bidding deadline (T_{EB}) but earlier than the bid award time ($T_{EB} + T_a - Td_j$) at which the winning vendor receives an award confirmation message. The third condition tests if the limited-time offer has the best utility among the so far collected offers i.e. ($S_k = S[1]$). The fourth condition tests if the number of visited vendors satisfies the minimum number of searched vendors i.e. ($N_T \geq N_{MIN}$). We examine all probable scenarios of different settings. We summarize the reasoning results in Table 1 and highlight the enhancements the proposed strategy presents as compared to patient and anxious strategies [6]. It avoids loss of the most advantageous offer that expires earlier than the bidding deadline, increases client's utility, and ensures adequacy of market search.

The reasoning shows the following:

- The *proposed strategy* carries out prompt evaluation of each collected offer and verifies if the offer satisfies client's constraints and preferences. It then tests if a collected offer has the best utility and would expire earlier than bidding deadline. If the offer passes the test, it sets an alert and extends offer negotiation/collection to (T_a) just before the expiry time of the offer. If the alert signals soon expiry of the offer, it awards it the bid if it satisfies constraint on minimum number of vendors to search and has the top utility among the so far collected offers. The strategy interrupts offer collection/negotiation and awards the bid to the vendor of the most advantageous limited-time offer in four scenarios out of the ten scenarios confirming minimum market search. Thus, the strategy improves utility while ensuring adequacy of market search. It would further interrupt offer collection/negotiation earlier than bidding deadline, which results in shortening offer collection/negotiation time.
- The *anxious strategy* in all scenarios immediately accepts the first collected offer that satisfies client's constraints and priorities. The strategy does not improve client's utility, nor confirms adequacy of market search.
- The *patient strategy* losses any advantageous limited-time offer that expires before bidding deadline or even expires later than the bidding time but before the sent bid award notification is received by winning vendor. The strategy only accepts one scenario out of the ten scenarios. It can only accept the top ranked offer only if its expiry time is later than bidding deadline by enough time for awarding it the bid. The offer has to satisfy conditions: (1) ($T_{EV} > T_{EB}$); (2) ($T_{EV} < T_{EB} + T_a - Td_j$). It only ensures adequacy of market search, but does not maximize utility.

The proposed strategy as compared to patient and anxious strategies results in: (1) Better outcomes, (2) Increase in utility, (3) Adequacy of market search, (4) shorter search time as compared to the patient strategy. It improves utility as it avoids loss of top utility offer that expires before bidding deadline and avoids early bid award that would result in overpriced bids. It also shortens the marketplace search time as the search can be interrupted and the bid may be awarded earlier than the bidding deadline, whenever, the most advantageous offer is about to expire and an adequate market search is completed.

6 Conclusion

In this paper, we proposed a mobile agent-based one-to-many bilateral negotiation strategy for e-Trade applications. The aim of the proposed strategy is to maximize client's utility. It overcomes the risk of missing out limited-time advantageous offers during offer collection/negotiation that have not been addressed in existing negotiation strategies. Moreover, it confirms adequacy of market search and considers various temporal constraints including bidding deadline, offer expiry time, award time, communication delays, processing queues, and transportation times. The negotiation strategy is more efficient than the existing negotiation strategies. It presents six advantages: (1) attenuation in offer collection/negotiation time; (2) avoidance of loss of best utility offer that would expire before offer collection or bid award is completed; (3) assurance of a satisfactory market search; (4) maximizing client utility; (5) avoidance of early bid award that would result in overpriced bids; (6) assurance of accurate comparative analysis of top ranked offers in terms of offers value and offers validity.

The future works of the paper is to extend the proposed negotiation strategy with the implementation of multi-agents that concurrently search sub-spaces of marketplace. It shortens offer collection/negotiation time and, thus, minimizes the risk of missing out the top utility offer that has a short validity.

References

1. An, B., Sim, K., Gui Tang, L., Qing Li, S., Cheng, D.: Continuous-Time Negotiation Mechanism for Software Agents. IEEE Transactions on Systems, Man, and Cybernetics, Part B: Cybernetics 36(6), 1261–1272 (2006)
2. Braun, P., Brzostowski, J., Kersten, G., Kim, J., Kowalczyk, R., Strecker, S., Vahidov, R.: E-Negotiation Systems and Software Agents: Methods, Models, and Applications. In: Intelligent Decision-Making Support Systems: Foundation, Applications, and Challenges. Decision Engineering Series. Springer, Heidelberg (2006)
3. Collins, J., Jamison, S., Gini, M., Mobasher, B.: Temporal Strategies in Mult-Agent Contracting Protocol. In: Proceedings of AAAI-1997 Workshop on Using AI in Electtronic Commerce, Virtual Organizations, Enterprise Knowledge Management to Re-enginer the Corporation, pp. 50–56 (1997)
4. Fatima, S., Wooldridge, M., Jennings, N.: Multi-Issue Negotiation with Deadlines. Journal of Artificial Intelligence Research 6, 381–417 (2006)

5. Fatima, S., Wooldridge, M., Jennings, N.R.: An Agenda Based Framework for Multi-Issue Negotiation. Journal of Artificial Intelligence 152(1), 1–45 (2004)
6. Fatima, S., Wooldridge, M., Jennings, N.R.: Bargaining with incomplete information. Annals of Mathematics and Artificial Intelligence 44(3), 207–232 (2005)
7. Kebriaei, H., Majd, V.: A Simultaneous Multi-Attribute Soft-Bargaining Design for Bilateral Contracts. Journal of Expert Systems and Applications (2008)
8. Jaljouli, R., Abawajy, J.: Secure Mobile Agent-based E-negotiation for Online Trading. In: Proceedings of the 7th IEEE International Symposium on Signal Processing and Information Technology (ISSPIT 2007), Cairo, Egypt, pp. 610–615 (2007)
9. Kersten, G.E., Lai, H.: Satisfiability and Completeness of Protocols for Electronic Negotiations. European Journal of Operational Research 180(2), 922–937 (2007)
10. Levati, M.V., Maciejovsky, B.: Deadline Effects in Ultimatum Bargaining: an Experimental Study of Concession Sniping with Low or no Costs of Delay. Journal Costs of Delay: International Game Theory Review 7, 117–135 (2001)
11. Rahwan, I., Kowalczyk, R., Pham, H.: Intelligent Agents for Automated One-to-Many e-Commerce Negotiation. In: Proceedings of the 25th Australian Conference on Computer Science, pp. 197–204. Australian Computer Society Press (2002)
12. Selamat, A., Selamat, H.: Routing Algorithm of Mobile Agents for Query Retrieval Using Generic Algorithm. Malaysian Journal of Computer Science 17(2), 1–10 (2004)
13. Si, Y., Edmond, D., Dumas, M., Hofstede, A.H.: Specification and Execution of Composite Trading Activities. Journal of Electronic Commerce Research 7(3-4), 221–263 (2007)
14. Vogler, H., Spriestersbach, A., Moschgath, M.: Protecting Competitive Negotiation of Mobile Agents. In: IEEE Workshop on Future Trends of Distributed Computing Systems FTDCS (1999)
15. Zen, Z.: An Agent-Based Online Shopping System in E-Commerce. Journal of Computer and Information Science 2(4), 14–19 (2009)
16. Zhuang, Y., Fong, S., Shi, M.: Knowledge-empowered Automated Negotiation System for e-Commerce. Journal of Knowledge and Information Systems 17, 167–191 (2008)

Adaptive Choice of Behavior and Protocol Parameters

Frank Grove, Sandip Sen, and Oly Mistry

University of Tulsa
800 South Tucker Avenue
Tulsa, OK 74104, USA
{dean-grove,sandip,oly-mistry}@utulsa.edu

Abstract. Research on interaction between multiple self-interested agents has focused on either designing rational behavior for agents given the interaction protocol or designing the interaction protocol that will promote desirable rational behavior by agents. We believe that in certain situations self-interested agents can be interested in both choosing desirable protocols and deciding effective strategies to follow under the chosen protocol. We experiment with a market situation where agents repeatedly negotiate to decide on the allocation of indivisible resources. We present a parameterized protocol selection scheme which can be used by agents to select the interaction protocol to use. We show that learning agents can greatly improve performance by adapting the protocol used and the behavior adopted against a range of opponents.

1 Introduction

The research in agent coordination can be grouped into two general areas:
Coordination protocol design: Agents typically interact within a framework that guides the nature, duration, and frequency of interaction as well as the relative roles assumed by the participants. Auction protocols, bargaining frameworks, negotiation protocols, cake-cutting protocols, etc are prominent protocols that have received widespread use in the multiagent community [15]. Protocol design has been an active and influential area of research with notable advances in key application areas like combinatorial auctions with the notion that it will incentivize social welfare maximizing behavior by rational, strategic agents.
Agent behavior design: This branch of research focuses on designing efficient and effective algorithms for agents to follow. The point of view assumed by this body of work is that often an agent will find itself in an environment where it has no control over the domain protocols or the "rules of the road" and can only seek to optimize performance by selecting and executing appropriate behaviors.

We are interested in studying the problem of repeated negotiations in agent societies when the details of the interaction protocol are themeselves "negotiable" and can be adapted online by the negotiating agengts. More specifically, agents can both jointly choose from a range of parameterized protocols for interaction and individually select their behaviors from the corresponding behavior spaces.

N. Desai, A. Liu, and M. Winikoff (Eds.): PRIMA 2010, LNAI 7057, pp. 152–165, 2012.

While mutually agreeing on an interaction protocol and then choosing appropriate behaviors is necessary in the absence of existing infrastructure, agents may prefer to negotiate details of the interaction protocol even when such facilities and services are available. This is particularly true in the presence of information asymmetry. For example, if one agent has more information about the opponent than the latter has for itself, the former may prefer to use a version of the protocol that requires less revelation of private information.

We assume that agents possess the basic communication skills and share a language and vocabulary to negotiate the domain level interaction protocol. Hence we will not address the meta-level or recursive problems of choosing a mechanism to select a domain-level protocol. Rather, we will work with a parameterized version of a protocol-selection scheme that we present in Section 3.

Our domain of application is a system for allocating non-shareable resources or services. We posit a framework where an agent requesting service or resources can submit a request with a level of urgency (or strategy or bid), i.e., the maximum amount it is willing to pay, if necessary. If there is a conflict, i.e., multiple requesters request a given item, they select a protocol that will both determine the winner, i,e, the agent who gets the item, and what payment, if any, the winner is going to pay to the system.

The protocol set available to the agents for selection ranges from the Vickrey's auction protocol at one end, where the winner has to pay the system the amount of the second highest bid, to the trusting protocol where the winner does not pay anything. We empower the agents with the ability to learn to choose the protocol parameters such that exploitative behaviors will be suppressed while rewarding agents who truthfully represented their resource requirements.

2 Related Work

In recent literature on multi-agent systems, negotiation is studied as isolated incidents in one-shot stage games. Equilibrium conditions are analyzed under different degree of available information, *e.g.*, complete information [10,11], incomplete information [5], or knowledge of a probability that they will negotiate under same condition [8]. There has been research in multi-agent systems on using helpful social attitudes [6], reciprocity mechanisms [13], and trust in negotiation [1]. There has not been any work that deals with selecting a protocol to negotiate indivisible resources utilizing trust. In particular there is very little work on studying the effect of negotiation behavior on mutual trust, future negotiation opportunities and agent utilities.

Research in economics and psychology have investigated the effectiveness of strategic negotiation behaviors [4,16]. These studies are concerned with the behavior and utility of two general types of agents: egoistic and pro-social. The goal of an egoistic agent is to maximize its own profit and it does not want to sacrifice any utility to cooperate with other agents. On the other hand, pro-social agents want to maximize the joint profit without considering their individual profitability. De Dreu *et al.* have showed that a group of pro-social agents achieve higher joint outcomes than egoistically motivated agents as the egoistic agents settle on suboptimal agreements [4]. They have considered a homogeneous group of agents, whereas real-world societies contain a great variety of negotiation behaviors. In a following paper, they demonstrated that groups with a majority of egoistic agents settle on suboptimal agreements more frequently than a group with a majority of pro-social agents. In both situations, they view the problem from the perspective of the entire society. We, on the other hand, are interested in the analysis of negotiation behavior and utility from the perspective of self-interested agents.

The CREDIT [14] trust model allows an agent to calculate the trust of other agents and uses this trust measure during negotiation. This measurement effectively decreases the uncertainty in the environment and enables the agents to reach more efficient agreements. Truth-telling behavior in the environment can be rewarded by this incentive compatible scheme. The CREDIT model is effective in producing the outcomes that maximizes all the negotiating agents' utilities and in choosing the most reliable agents in the long run. Though we also focus on utility maximization, we do not restrict the agents to playing against only related opponents. Rather, we assume that agents may have to interact with arbitrary opponents and hence must learn to play against potentially harmful opponents and yet secure higher utility than any other agent in the population.

3 Domain and Interaction Model

3.1 Domain Assumptions

We now present our domain model which describes a facility for sharing resources and services by a large agent society. We assume that resources or services are *atomic* and are *non-shareable.* Typical example of such services include libraries checking out limited copies of eBooks or organizations giving employees access to software with limited number of licenses. Users are represented by their agents who interact with similar agents to obtain the necessary resources or services. Whenever two agents request the same resource for an overlapping period of time, a *conflict-of-interest (COI)* happens and the agents need to directly resolve such a COI as resources/services are atomic and non-shareable. We assume the following characteristics of our domains of interest:

- The society is semi-stable, where users frequently request resources/services.
- The number of resources/services is limited and this leads to frequent COIs.
- The above two assumptions lead to the fact that agents with similar service/resource requirements will have a history of COIs from which they can learn about others negotiation behavior.
- Agents are interested in maximizing their satisfaction or utility but are not spiteful (deliberately trying to reduce others' utilities) or colluding to manipulate the system. Agent requirements or demands for a resource/service vary over time. In particular, an important consideration in our work is the importance, priority or urgency with which an agent requires a resource in the current time period.

• We assume an incomplete but perfect information scenario, i.e., agents will not know about the true preferences of the opponent about the resource/service under conflict but can observe the behavior or strategy chosen by other agents[1]. We also assume that each agent makes its offer without knowledge of the other agents's choices.

3.2 Trust Considerations in Protocol Selection

Trust can be key in the protocol mechanism decision. An agent with a high trust for its opponent is more inclined to prefer allocation based purely on reported urgency or priority. On the other hand, an agent with low trust for its opponent will be inclined to prefer the auction mechanism, a relatively safer bet that guards against manipulations. We want to develop a new protocol selection framework that allowed agents to range from a complete trusting to a complete distrusting protocol. Hence, we adopt a parameterized protocol selection scheme that allows selection from a continuous spectrum of protocols ranging from pure priority based allocation to the Vickrey's 2nd price auction. In this range, the winner's payment is determined by the loser's level of trust for the opponent. If the loser has high trust in it's opponent, the winner has to pay less to the system. Conversely, low trust will cause the winner's payment to the system to increase.

Note that from our perspective, we are only interested in the net utilities (valuation minus payment) of the agents and the system is viewed only as a sink and money paid to it is undesirable waste as it decreases the total utility to the agents. This is somewhat different from the view of social welfare taken in auction theory where the auctioneer is considered part of the society. To differentiate our view, we will use the term "agent welfare". Hence, while Vickrey's second price auction is the fall-back option for an agent when faced with an untrustworthy agent, this protocol reduces the overall agent welfare as payoffs to the system will reduce agent utility. If agents are mutually trustworthy, however, they can eliminate such "wasteful" payments to the system and truly maximize agent welfare. The goal of this research, therefore, is to develop a protocole selection framework by which non-manipulative agents can learn to trust each other from experience and maximize their welfare while avoiding manipulation by malevolent agents. Though manipulative agents can exploit this protocol and receive a higher payoff in the short run (also resulting in suboptimal allocations), the protocol selection framework gives adaptive agents the capability to punish the exploitive agents while reciprocating the trust of an agent that truthfully reports its priorities.

3.3 Trust-Based Protocol Selection Framework

We consider a society of N agents who repeatedly engage in resource allocation. At each iteration, each agent's valuation v_t is derived from a uniform distribution of $U(0.5, 1)$. This assures a competitive society where agents have similar

[1] We use the term behavior and strategy interchangeably.

valuations and demands for the resource. Next, each agent interacts with the rest $N-1$ agents. During an interaction between two agents i and j, each agent specifies both a bid for the contested item and a trust value in its opponent. Hence, agent i specifies a bid b_i and a trust value α_i^j representing i's trust in the truthfulness of j. If $b_i > b_j$, the resource is allocated to i.

The payment of winner, i, to the system is determined to be

$$payment_i = b_j * \alpha_j^i. \tag{1}$$

Hence, the payment of the winner is the product of the loser's bid and the loser's trust in the winner reporting truthfully. The utility u_i for the winner is defined as $u_i = v_i - payment_i$.

Each agent $j \in N$ stores a list of $\alpha_j^i \in [0,1], \forall i \in N$. $1 - \alpha_j^i$ gives the measure of actual trust value of agent j on agent i. As α_j^i increases the i must pay a greater payment. When $\alpha_j^i = 1$, the winner pays the loser's bid b_j, *i.e.*, the second highest bid, which is equivalent to the 2nd price or Vickrey's auction. Conversely, when $\alpha_j^i = 0$, representing total trust, the winner pays nothing and the protocol reverts to priority based resource allocation. Hence, we see that this protocol selection framework allows agents to use reported trust values to choose radically different protocol instantiations. We will see later that adaptive agents can learn to choose these parameters (trust values) to reward truthful agents and punish greedy or untrustworthy behavior.

Over successive iterations, agents accumulate utility, and the agent with the greatest utility is the optimal strategy within this society.

4 Strategizing over Trust

We now examine whether bidding truthfully is the dominant strategy for agents in a single interaction in this setting. To examine the ability to strategize about the opponents value of α, we must analyse whether the bidder can overbid to achieve a greater utility than it achieves by bidding truthfully. We examine the three cases where bidder i overbids. The payoff for the bidder is defined by Equation 1 if the bid $b_i > b_j$:

$b_j < v_i$ **:** In this case overbidding yields the same utility as truth telling.
$b_j > b_i$ **:** In this case regardless of overbidding the agent does not gain the good and no utility is gained or lost.
$v_i < b_j < b_i$ **:** In this case the utility is given by the payment equation. However, it is not clear where or not $v_i < b_j * \alpha_j^i$ and the subsequent utility from overbidding is greater. When $\alpha_j^i = 0$ the optimal strategy is to overbid, and the case of $\alpha_j^i = 1$ reduces to the Vickrey's Auction dominant strategy of truth telling. However in the case where $0 < \alpha_j^i < 1$ the dominant strategy is not immediately clear and depends on the opponents trust value α_j^i. If agent i could deduce the value of α_j^i and the b_j values then the agent could easily determine the optimal amount of overbidding necessary to achieve maximum utility. However the nature of the

trust protocol makes it difficult to determine α_j^i. While the Trust Based Protocol lacks the dominant strategy of truth-telling, we show that our protocol is robust against agents attempting to deduce the α values. It may be possible to elicit the mean of another bidder's α over time, especially if the agent can determine the distribution from which the opposing bidder draws its valuation. However, it is unlikely that an agent will know its opponent's valuation distribution. In most domains this is unlikely or unwanted. In fact a criticism of the standard Vickrey's Auction is that the agents are forced to make their valuations public. However, without this knowledge it is not possible to determine the valuation or the trust its opponent has. When agent i wins, it is only made aware that $b_i > b_j$ but cannot know for certain what the value of b_j actually is. For this reason we argue that our Trust based Protocol is a robust mechanism for resource allocation even though truth-telling is not always the dominant strategy. In cases where bidders prefer to keep their valuations secret, the Trust based protocol is indeed preferable. Only in trivial circumstances, where the opponent's α is static and opponent valuation distribution is known, is it possible to infer the α value and thereafter obtain utility gains through overbidding.

5 Agents

To evaluate the effectiveness of our protocol selection mechanism in effectively resolving COIs, we experiment with a variety of agent types and observe the resultant performance of these agents. We now describe the agent types used.

Bully Agent: A Bully agent always bids 1.0 irrespective of their resource need. This bid represents the strategy to attempt to obtain the resource in all interactions, regardless of another agent's valuation. They also use an α value of 1 for all the other agents in the population. Therefore, any agents that obtain the resource instead of the bully (can only happen with probability 0.5 where both agents bid 1) will have a payment of 1 according to our protocol.

Naive Agents: Naive agents always bid their true valuation for the resource. They use low α values for the other agents present in the population, *i.e.*, they trust other agents to bid their true valuation. Although this is not a rational strategy, similar agents do exist in real-world markets. We do not expect naive agents to be very successful, but it is important to study the effect of their presence in a society.

Rational Myopic Agents: These agents always bid their true valuation but always use $\alpha = 1$, *i.e.*, they do not trust other agents. This behavior is optimal for a single interaction. It defends against exploitation from bullies by ensuring that the agent never receives a negative utility. A society of rational myopic agents always select Vickrey's 2nd price auction. While this strategy is optimal from the myopic perspective, it results in agents paying to the system the sum total of the agent utilities and hence agents welfare is not maximized. The learning agents introduced next are designed to maximize agent welfare by trusting truthful agents.

α-Learning Agents: The α-learning agents always bid their true valuation. However, they adapt their reported α values over time to more accurately represent their trust for the opponents. An α-learning agent records the number of win (w) and loss (l) against each of its opponents. After every interaction, it calculates a ratio (r):

$$r = \frac{w}{(w+l)} \cdot (1-\gamma) + Result \cdot \gamma \tag{2}$$

where γ is the *forgetting factor* and *Result* is a boolean value of 1 or 0 representing win or loss in the latest interaction. Based on r, these agents adapts their α value using the sigmoid function given below:

$$\alpha = \frac{1}{1+e^{C\cdot(r-0.5)}} \tag{3}$$

where C is a constant. If $r \geq 0.5$, we set C to C_{low} and otherwise set C to C_{high}. For experiments reported in this paper, we used $C_{low} = 1$ and $C_{high} = 30$. We expect an agent to win the contested resource 50% of the time as agent valuations are drawn randomly. We used different learning rates for different regions in Equation 3 as we want the learners to respond aggressively to potentially exploitative agents but should be more cautious about adapting its α value against truthful agents.

α-Bid Learning Agents: Our next, more advanced, learning agent employs the same learning algorithm as the α-learning agent when adapting its α values. In addition, it also learns to adapt its bid to respond to exploitative agents such as the Bully. Such an agent will identify other agents in the population that are trying to corner the resources by overbidding their valuations.

If the fraction of wins in intearctions against a particulr opponent is below τ, i.e., $\frac{w}{w+l} < \tau$, the α-Bid learner agent will increase its bid against that opponent. We use the following equation to update the advanced learning agent's bid:

$$bid = (1 - valuation) \cdot \alpha^4 + valuation. \tag{4}$$

Figure 1 shows the effect of α on the reported bid given the true valuation. We used $\tau = 0.2$ in our initial simulations. The bid update equation (Equation 4) ensures that the bid increment is almost negligible against opponents for whom the learner has $\alpha < 0.5$. However, bid increment is significant against opponents for whom $\alpha \gg 0.5$. This implies that agents who are acting selfishly will be punished over time if their behavior causes the learning agent to not receive a fair share of required resources.

6 Experimental Results

Here we present our experimental results from simulations that evaluates the performances of the agent types introduced above under different environmental conditions. We observe their performances varying number and types of agents in

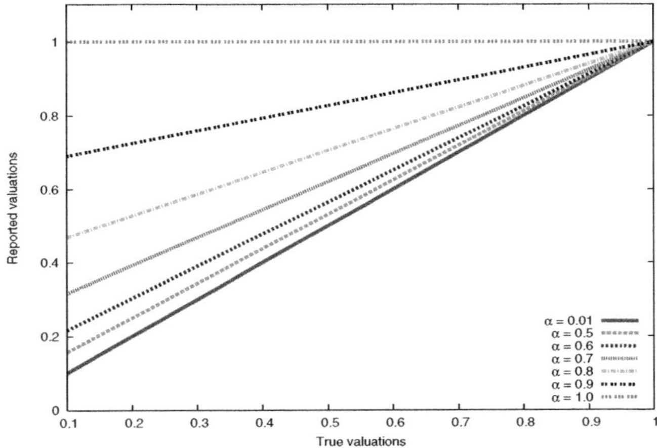

Fig. 1. Function used by α-Bid learning agents to Update bid

the population. We also compare results using our parameterized trust protocol with that using VCG auction in terms of agent welfare generated.

We sample valuations for an agent at every iteration t from a *Uniform Distribution* $U(0.5, 1)$. We initialize the α values of the *Bully*, *Naive* and *Myopic* agents at 1, 0.01 and 1 respectively. The α values of the learning agents are randomly initialized in the range $[0, 1]$.

6.1 One-on-One Interaction Results

We now discuss the performance of each learning agent type against every other agent type in a society.

Bully vs. α Learner: In this situation, the basic learning agent quickly determines its opponent is selfish and responds by increasing α value. As the α value increases, level of trust decreases, and the bully, though always winning the resource by bidding 1, is required to pay a greater percentage of the α learner's bid. Therefore, it receives mostly negatively utilities. Since all valuations are sampled from the same distribution, the bully's accumulated utility should ultimately converge to 0 after the basic learner learns not to trust its opponent. Since we consider only a finite number of iterations, the actual cumulative utility of a bully agent oscillates around 0 (see Figure 2). Since the basic learning agent will never bid greater than its valuation, the bully's selfish behavior will not be punished more aggressively to produce larger negative values.

Bully vs. α-Bid Learner: Similar to the α learner, the α-bid learner quickly learns to distrust the bully agent. In addition, the α-bid learner also increases its bid against the bully agent following Equation 4, as the win-loss ratio shows

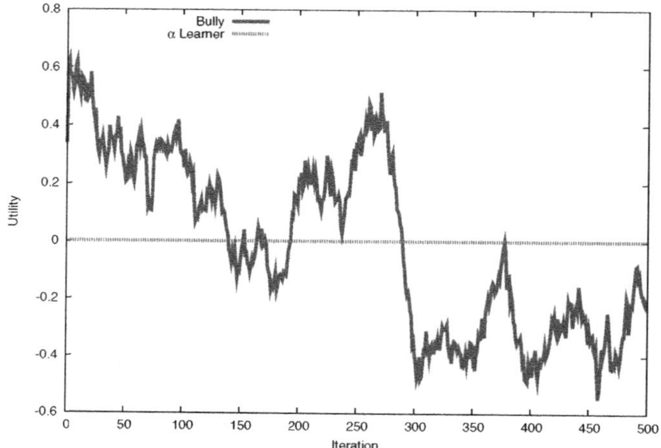

Fig. 2. Bully vs. α Learner utilities

complete monopoly by the bully. The result of this bid increase on the bully agent's utility is reflected in Figure 3. The α-bid learner increases its bid close to, but not equal to, 1 and thereby maximizes the payment for the bully with high bid and α values. This minimizes the bully's utility in every interaction and the utility of the bully agent monotonically decreases (see Figure 3).

Naive vs. α Learner: In this case, the α learner learns to trust the naive agent and its α value reaches 0. Over time their win-loss ratio reaches 0.5, resulting in a positive utility gain for both the agents. The rate of utility increase for the learning agent is found to be significantly higher than that of the Naive agent (see Figure 3). This result can be explained by the varying and static α values of learning and naive agent respectively. The learner uses a non-zero α value causing the naive agent to make a positive payment when winning, which reduces the latter's net utility.

Naive vs. α-Bid Learner: The α-bid learner also learns to trust the naive agent. Initially, it increases its bid against the naive agent but that increment is small. Also, ultimately its α value tends towards ≈ 0.0. As the win-loss ration also reaches its equilibrium value of 0.5, the α-bid learner bids its true valuation. We do not report this utility graph as it is found to be very similar to that of Figure 3.

Myopic vs. α Learner: In this case, myopic agents always accumulate higher utility than the learners by imposing a higher payment on the winner (see Figure 3). And the learners learn to trust the myopic agents from a fair win-loss ration (≈ 0.5)

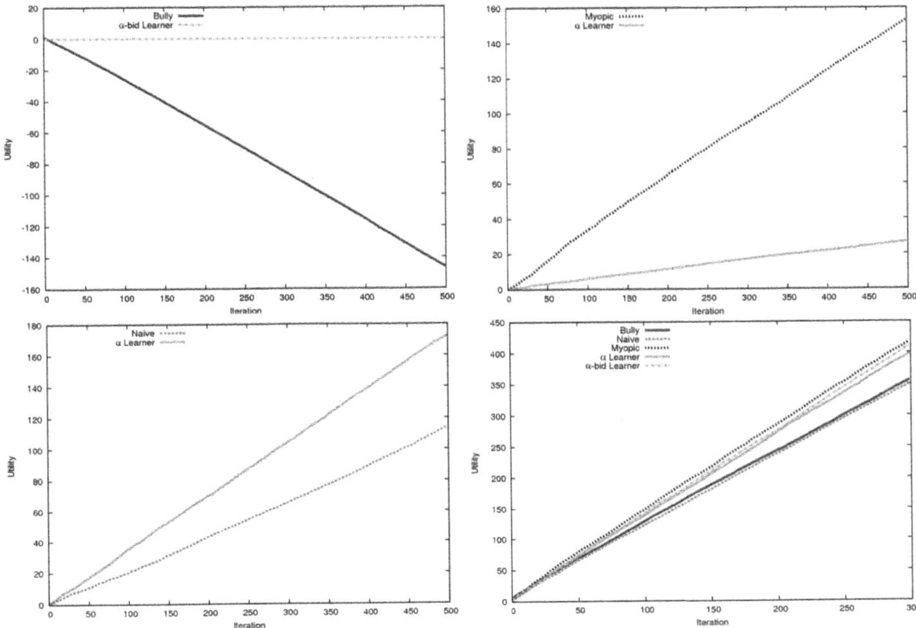

Fig. 3. Average utility over time for each agent strategy

Myopic vs. α-Bid Learner: This situation also yields similar results as shown in Myopic vs. α Learner. With a balanced win-loss ratio the advanced learner does not use its bid increment strategy and hence behaves similar to a basic learner.

6.2 Group Interaction

We now discuss the performance of the learning agents as a group in a multiagent society. We consider the average utility of the group instead of that of individual agents and observer performance trends over the course of a run.

All Agent types: We consider a population of $N = 20$ with 4 agents of each type. Figure 3 shows the average cumulative utility for each group averaged over 10 simulations. Myopic agents have very high α values for all the other agents, which incorporates higher payment in the system whenever any other agent loses against myopic agents and this reduces their utility. Myopic agents get higher utility in interactions against the naive agents because of the higher trust value of naive agents which creates lower payment for myopic agents.

Bully, Naive, and Learning Agents: For these group interactions, we used three agent types (Bully, Naive, and one learning type) with 4 agents of each type for a total of twelve agents ($N = 12$). The cumulative utility of one of the

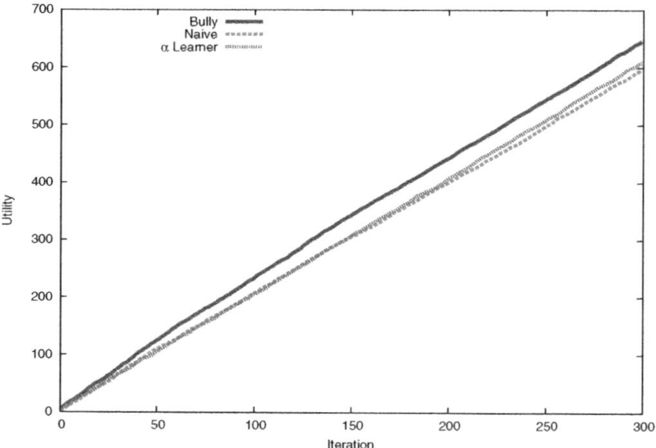

Fig. 4. Bully, Naive, and α-learners

cases is shown in Figure 4. This experiment demonstrates how bullies thrive in a society. As bullies are most successful in one-on-one interaction with a naive agent, they can utilize this advantage to outperform learning agents in a group containing naive agents. We conducted a series of experiments for this group configuration varying the ratio of bullies and naive agents in the population. Results show that the ratio of naive to rational agents within a group can significantly impact the cumulative utility of the bully agent. A larger ratio of naive to bully agents can allow the bully class to accumulate the greatest utility of all classes. However, interactions with other bullies severely impact the bully agent's cumulative utility. Since bullies always bid 1 and use $\alpha = 1$, they will never receive positive utility from interactions amongst themselves. This is why there must exist more naive agents than bullies within the population for the bullies to thrive. The learning agents are able to quickly identify the bully as selfish, and increases the α until $\alpha \approx 1.0$. They also identify the naive agents, and the respective α value quickly decreases until $\alpha \approx 0$.

When initialized with the advanced learning agent, the bully's cumulative utility is significantly worse, since the advanced learning agent will adjust both α and bid until both $\alpha \approx 1.0$ and $bid \approx 1.0$ As $bid < 1.0$ so a bully will still acquire the resource in every interaction with a learning agent, but will never receive a positive cumulative utility in its interactions with the advanced learners. In such a configuration, for the bully agents to accumulate positive utility, the number of naive agents should be a majority in the society. Such a large number of naive and irrational agents is unlikely in real world societies.

6.3 Homogeneous Populations

When the population consists of a homogeneous group of Myopic rational agents, all COIs are resolved using Vickrey's 2nd Price auction. Since the myopic agents

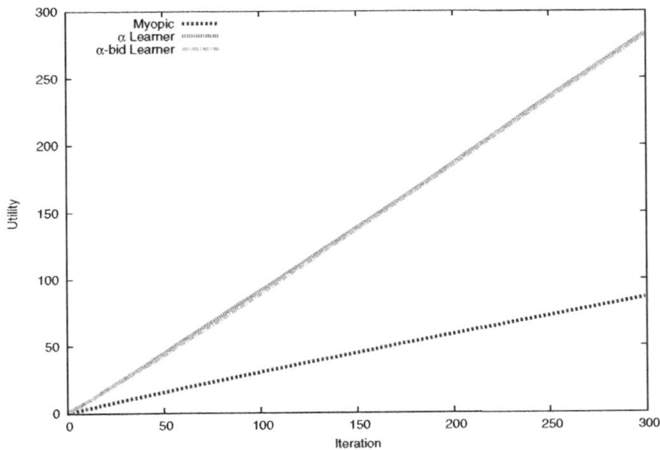

Fig. 5. Agent utilities in homogeneous populations

always report their bid truthfully from their true valuation, and the α value is always reported as 1, the winner payment is equivalent to the loser's bid.

Homogeneous groups of α as well as α-bid learners, however, adopt their α values to use the Trusting protocol and no agent pays any significant amount after some interactions. Hence these groups exhibit significantly higher agent utility compared to the homogeneous groups of myopic, rational agents (see Figure 5). This observation proves our initial claim about achieving higher social utility when using the Trust protocol than Vickrey's auction.

7 Conclusion

By using a parameterized protocol selection scheme we allow agents to negotiate domain-level or problem-solving protocols. This protocol seems best suited for negotiating the allocation of indivisible, non-shareable resources. For example, licenses and eBooks within an organization would be appropriate resources to be allocated using this protocol. From the perspective of resource allocation this allows agents to function without need for considerable amount of negotiation or communication, therefore reducing load on the system. If agents are willing to adapt their trust in other agents, they can use this framework to maximize agent welfare. The continuous range of choice from Trusting to Vickrey's 2nd price auction allows agents to effectively negotiate the appropriate type of protocol for resource allocation. This allows a simple learning agent to punish a selfish agent while reciprocating the trust of a friendly agent. Such adaptation can lead to a higher agent welfare compared to Vickrey's 2nd Price auction in homogeneous groups where the agent welfare is maximized as the protocol reverts to the Trusting protocol.

To our knowledge, this is the first attempt to implement trust within a protocol for negotiated resource allocation. Resource allocation is an important field of study, and the introduction of trust has the capability to increase the utility of all members involved in repeated resource allocation scenarios. Rational and strategic agents can take advantage of this protocol to increase their respective utilities while decreasing the utility of irrational and selfish agents.

We plan to investigate new scenarios in which we can introduce the parameterized protocol and examine the possible interactions between more strategic agent types. The development of strategic and adaptive exploitative agent is also key for a more thorough examination of this framework.

We observed that learners lose out to myopic rational agents in head-to-head interactions. This is because learners continue to trust the myopic agents while the latter did not reciprocate that trust. A more responsive bid and trust adaptation mechanism can use the actual utilities received rather than just the win-loss ratios. We plan to implement and experiment with such more "rational", utility-centric learners.

References

1. Broersen, J., Dastani, M., van der Torre, L.: Leveled commitment and trust in negotiation. In: Workshop on Deception, Fraud and Trust in Agent Societies (2000)
2. Chavez, A., Maes, P.: Kasbah: An agent marketplace for buying and selling goods. In: PAAM-1996, London, UK, pp. 75–90 (1996)
3. Chevaleyre, Y., Dunne, P.E., Endriss, U., Lang, J., Lemaitre, M., Maudet, N., Padget, J., Phelps, S., Rodriguez-Aguilar, J.A., Sousa, P.: Issues in multiagent resource allocation. Informatica 30, 3–31 (2006)
4. Dreu, C.K.D., Weingart, L.R., Kwon, S.: Influence of social motives on integrative negotiations: A meta-analytic review and test of two theories. Journal of Personality and Social Psychology 78, 889–905 (2000)
5. Fatima, S.S., Wooldridge, M., Jennings, N.R.: Bargaining with incomplete information. Annals of Mathematics and Artificial Intelligence 44(3), 207–232 (2005)
6. Glass, A., Grosz, B.: Socially conscious decision-making. Autonomous Agents and Multi-Agent Systems 6(3), 317–339 (2003)
7. Jennings, N., Faratin, P., Parsons, A.R.L.S., Sierra, C., Wooldridge, M.: Automated negotiation: prospects, methods and challenges. Group Decision and Negotiation 10(2), 199–215 (2001)
8. Kraus, S.: Strategic negotiation in multiagent environments. MIT Press, Cambridge (2001)
9. Maes, P., Guttman, R.H., Moukas, A.G.: Agents that buy and sell. Communications of the ACM 42(3) (March 1999)
10. Nash, J.: The bargaining problem. Econometrica 18(2), 155–162 (1950)
11. Rubinstein, A.: Perfect equilibrium in a bargaining model. Econometrica 50, 97–110 (1982)
12. Rubinstein, A., Wolinsky, A.: Decentralized trading, strategic behavior and the walrasian outcome. Review of Economic Studies 57, 63–78 (1990)
13. Sen, S.: Believing others: Pros and cons. Artificial Intelligence 142(2), 179–203 (2002)

14. Ramchurn, S.D.: Multi-Agent Negotiation using Trust and Persuasion PhD thesis, University of Southampton (2004)
15. Shoham, Y., Lleyton-Brown, K.: Multiagent Systems: Algorithmic, Game-theoretic, & Logical Foundations. Cambridge University Press, New York (2009)
16. ten Velden, F., Beersma, B., Dreu, C.K.D.: Heterogeneous social motives in negotiating groups: The moderating effects of decision rule and interest position. In: 17th Annual of International Association for Conflict Management (2004)

Effect of DisCSP Variable-Ordering Heuristics in Scale-Free Networks

Tenda Okimoto, Atsushi Iwasaki, and Makoto Yokoo

Kyushu University, Fukuoka 8190395, Japan
{tenda,iwasaki,yokoo}@is.kyushu-u.ac.jp

Abstract. A Distributed Constraint Satisfaction Problem (DisCSP) is a constraint satisfaction problem in which variables and constraints are distributed among multiple agents. Various algorithms for solving DisCSPs have been developed, which are intended for general purposes, i.e., they can be applied to any network structure. However, if a network has some particular structure, e.g., the network structure is scale-free, we can expect that some specialized algorithms or heuristics, which are tuned for the network structure, can outperform general purpose algorithms/heuristics.

In this paper, as an initial step toward developing specialized algorithms for particular network structures, we examine variable-ordering heuristics in scale-free networks. We use the classic asynchronous backtracking algorithm as a baseline algorithm and examine the effect of variable-ordering heuristics. First, we show that the choice of variable-ordering heuristics is more influential in scale-free networks than in random networks. Furthermore, we develop a novel variable-ordering heuristic that is specialized to scale-free networks. Experimental results illustrate that our new variable-ordering heuristic is more effective than a standard degree-based variable-ordering heuristic. Our proposed heuristic reduces the required cycles by 30% at the critical point.

1 Introduction

A surprisingly wide variety of Artificial Intelligence (AI) problems can be formalized as constraint satisfaction problems (CSPs). A CSP is a problem that finds a consistent assignment of values to variables. A Distributed Constraint Satisfaction Problem (DisCSP) is formalized as a CSP in which variables and constraints are distributed among multiple agents [1]. In DisCSP, agents assign values to variables, attempting to generate a locally consistent assignment that is also consistent with all the constraints between agents.

Asynchronous BackTracking algorithm (ABT), which was first presented by Yokoo [2], is the most basic algorithm for solving DisCSPs. It is also the first complete and asynchronous search algorithm for DisCSPs. ABT allows agents to act asynchronously and concurrently without any global control, while guaranteeing the completeness of the algorithm. Various algorithms have been developed for solving DisCSPs, e.g., Distributed BackTracking algorithm [3], an ABT

N. Desai, A. Liu, and M. Winikoff (Eds.): PRIMA 2010, LNAI 7057, pp. 166–180, 2012.

based algorithm without adding links [4], Dynamic Distributed BackJumping [5], Asynchronous Partial Overlay [6], and Dynamic ordering for ABT [7, 8].

Since the topology of real large networks like the Internet substantially differs from the topology of random graphs, new methods, tools, and models must be developed. Traditionally, a network of complex topology is described by a random graph, for example, the graph of Erdös and Rényi (ER model) [9]. One feature of the ER model is that the connectivity distribution of the network peaks at an average value and decays exponentially. Such an exponential network is homogeneous in nature. In other words, each node has roughly the same number of connections.

Recently, *scale-free graphs* in complex networks, introduced by Barabási and Albert [10, 11], has become a very popular interdisciplinary research topic. These graphs have been proposed as a generic and universal model of network topologies that exhibit power-law distributions in the connectivity of network nodes. A scale-free network is inhomogeneous in nature, i.e., there exist a small number of nodes that have many connections, while most nodes have very few connections.

There already exist several works on examining the effect of such network structures in CSPs [12, 13, 14]. For example, Walsh showed several application domains of CSPs, e.g., graph-coloring problems (which are generated from register allocation problems), time-tabling, and quasi-group problems, actually have small-world like structures, and the cost of solving such problem instances can have a heavy-tailed distribution. Later, he also showed that high-degree nodes can frequently occur these problem instances and the existence of such high-degree nodes can eliminate the long heavy tail in search costs [14]. Devlin and O'Sullivan showed that several real-world applications, such as a car configuration problem, radio line frequency assignment, and logic circuit diagnosis, exhibit degree distributions similar to scale-free graphs [12]. They also showed that the effect of standard degree-based search heuristics is greater for such problems than for problems with a uniform random structure.

However, as far as the authors aware, there exists virtually no work on examining the effect of such network structures in DisCSPs. As shown in [12, 13, 14], various CSP application problems actually have structures similar to small-world/scale-free graphs. If the knowledge of such problem instances are distributed among multiple agents, there would be a need for solving them using DisCSP techniques.

Furthermore, let us consider a situation where there exists an agent who acts as a representative/secretary for each person in a social network [15]. A social network tends to have a scale-free like structure. When solving a meeting scheduling problem [16] in such a social network, we can apply DisCSP techniques.

In this paper, as an initial step toward developing specialized algorithms/ heuristics for particular network structures in DisCSP, we examine the effect of variable-ordering heuristics of ABT in scale-free networks. Although a variety of more efficient, sophisticated algorithms have been developed for solving DisCSPs, we focus on ABT as a baseline algorithm, since it is one of the simplest algorithms and is suitable for our purpose and we are interested in developing a good variable-ordering heuristic for scale-free networks. We believe that our analysis and results can be applied to other sophisticated algorithms.

First, we show that the choice of variable-ordering heuristics is more influential in scale-free networks than in random networks. Specifically, we show that the performances of ABT in the former network depend on which variable-ordering heuristics is used much more than that in the latter network, since the degree distribution of scale-free networks is significantly different from that of random networks. This result is consistent with the result for CSPs reported in [12].

Furthermore, we examine how the performance of ABT in scale-free networks changes in terms of the depth and number of the backedges of pseudo-trees. Given a variable-ordering, ABT determines a pseudo-tree and searches for a solution from it. Since the depth and number of backedges greatly affect the network structure, it is expected that the performance of ABT changes based on those factors. However, surprisingly, our experiments reveal that the performance does not significantly change.

Finally, we develop a novel variable-ordering heuristic called Average Length between Hubs (ALH) specialized for scale-free networks. Our experiments show that ALH outperforms a standard degree-based variable-ordering heuristic in scale-free networks. As far as the authors aware, there exists virtually no work on variable-ordering heuristics specialized for scale-free networks in DisCSP, although many studies have dealt with variable-ordering heuristics [7, 17, 18, 19, 20].

The rest of our paper is organized as follows. We describe the definition of a DisCSP (Section 2) and introduce a scale-free network (Section 3). We examine the performance of ABT in scale-free and random networks (Section 4). Next, we present a novel variable-ordering heuristic that is specialized to scale-free networks and show that our new variable-ordering heuristic is effective for scale-free networks (Section 5). Finally, we give a discussion (Section 6) and present a conclusion and some future work (Section 7).

2 Distributed Constraint Satisfaction Problem

A Constraint Satisfaction Problem (CSP) [21] consists of m variables $x_1, ..., x_m$, whose values are taken from finite, discrete domains $D_1, ..., D_m$, respectively, and a set of constraints on their values. A constraint is defined by a predicate. That is, the constraint $p(k; x_{k1}, ..., x_{kj})$ is a predicate that is defined on Cartesian product $D_{k1} \times ... \times D_{kj}$. This predicate is true iff the value assignment of these variables satisfies this constraint. Solving a CSP is equivalent to finding an assignment of values to all variables such that all constraints are satisfied.

A Distributed Constraint Satisfaction Problem (DisCSP) is a CSP in which the variables and constraints are distributed among multiple agents [1, 2]. We assume the following communication model:

- Agents communicate by sending messages. An agent can send messages to other agents iff the agent knows the addresses of the agents.

– The delay in delivering a message is finite, although random. For transmission between any pair of agents, messages are received in the order in which they were sent.

Note that although algorithms for solving DisCSPs seem similar to parallel/distributed processing methods for solving CSPs, the research motivations are fundamentally different. Each agent has variables and tries to determine their values. However, there exist interagent constraints, and the value assignment must satisfy these interagent constraints. Formally, there exist m agents $\{1, 2, ..., m\}$. Each variable x_j belongs to one agent i (this relation is represented as belongs(x_j,i)). Constraints are also distributed among agents. The fact that agent l knows constraint predicate p_k is represented as know(p_k,l).

A DisCSP is solved iff the following conditions are satisfied:

– $\forall i, \forall x_j$ where belongs(x_j,i), the value of x_j is assigned to d_j, and $\forall l, \forall p_k$ where know(p_k,l), p_k is true under the assignment x_1=d_1, x_2=d_2,....., x_n=d_n.

For example, the n-queens problem is well known for CSP. If we assume there exists an agent that corresponds to a queen of each row and these queens try to find their positions so that they do not kill each other, this problem can be formalized as a DisCSP.

Asynchronous BackTracking algorithm (ABT), which was first presented by Yokoo [1, 2], is the most basic algorithm for solving DisCSPs. We make the following assumptions while describing this algorithm for simplicity. Relaxing these assumptions to general cases is relatively straightforward:

– Each agent has exactly one variable.
– All constraints are binary.
– Each agent knows all constraint predicates relevant to its variable.

In ABT, the priority order among agents is determined. First, agents instantiate their variables concurrently and send their assigned values to the agents that are connected to them by outgoing links, i.e., there exists a link between two agents who are involved by a binary constraint, and the link is directed from the higher priority agent to the lower priority agent. Then all agents wait for and respond to messages. After each update of its assignment, an agent sends its new assignment to all outgoing links. An agent that receives an assignment from an incoming link, tries to find an assignment for its variable that does not violate a constraint with the assignment it received.

The main message types communicated among agents are *ok*? messages and *nogood* messages. An *ok*? message carries an assignment of an agent. When agent A_i receives an *ok*? message from agent A_j, it places the received assignment in a data structure called Agent_View, which holds the last assignment A_i received from higher priority neighbors such as A_j. Next, A_i checks if its current assignment is still consistent with its Agent_View. If it is consistent, A_i does nothing. If not, then A_i searches its domain for a new consistent value. If it finds one, it assigns its variable and sends *ok*? messages to all lower priority agents linked to it. Otherwise, A_i backtracks.

The backtrack operation is executed by sending a *nogood* message that contains an inconsistent partial assignment. *nogood* messages are sent to the agent with the lowest priority among the agents whose assignments are included in the inconsistent tuple in the *nogood* message. Agent A_i that sends a *nogood* message to agent A_j assumes that A_j will change its assignment. Therefore, A_i removes from its Agent_View the assignment of A_j and makes an attempt to find an assignment for its variable that is consistent with the updated Agent_View.

3 Scale-Free Network

In recent years, various complex networks have been identified as having a scale-free structure [10, 11, 22, 23], e.g., the Internet, SNS, and the citation relation graphs of scientific articles. Traditionally, these networks are approximated as random graphs, but the degree distributions of these networks (and other networks in nature) are significantly different from the degree distribution of random graphs.

The term random graph refers to the disordered nature of the arrangement of edges between different nodes. In this network, the majority of nodes have approximately the same degree (symmetry of degree distribution). It starts with N nodes and connects each pair of nodes with probability p. In ER model, the probability that a node has k edges follows a Poisson distribution:

$$p(k) = e^{-\lambda}\lambda^k/k!,$$

where

$$\lambda = N\binom{N-1}{k}p^k(1-p)^{N-1-k}.$$

Several complex networks have a scale-free structure. Their degree distribution follows a power-law for a large k. Even for those real networks for which $p(k)$ has an exponential tail, the degree distribution significantly deviates from Poisson. Random graph theory is unable to reproduce this feature, which was found to be a consequence of two generic mechanisms. Networks expand continuously by the addition of new nodes, and new nodes attach themselves preferentially to sites that are already well connected. The random network models assume that the probability that two nodes are connected is random and uniform. In contrast, most real networks exhibit preferential connectivity. For example, a newly created webpage will more likely include edges to well-known, popular documents that already have high connectivity. This example indicates that the probability with which a new node connects to existing nodes is not uniform, but there is a higher probability to be linked to a node that already has a large number of connections. Because a few nodes have a large number of connections, the distribution of real networks has a power-law tail. Such a highly connected node is called a hub. The following are the typical properties of scale-free networks:

- Degree distribution $p(k)$ is approximated by a power-law that the form

$$p(k) \propto k^{-\gamma},$$

where k is a degree and γ is the exponent that depends on each network structure.
- Scale-free networks have no *scale* because there is no typical number of links (asymmetry of degree distribution).
- Scale-free networks have highly connected hubs that "hold the network together" and give the "robust yet fragile" features of error tolerance but attack vulnerability.
- Scale-free networks are self-similar.

4 Influence of Variable-Ordering Heuristics in Scale-Free Networks

In this section, we show that the choice of variable-ordering heuristics can be more influential in scale-free networks than in random networks. Furthermore, we show that the performance of ABT is not affected by the depth and the number of backedges of a pseudo-tree. First, let us explain how we measure the performance of a DisCSP algorithm. We use the number of simulated time steps (cycles), which is counted as follows.

By a discrete event simulation, each agent maintains its own simulated clock. An agent's time is incremented by one simulated time unit whenever it performs one cycle of computation. One cycle consists of reading all incoming messages, performing local computation, and then sending messages. We assume that a message issued at time t is available to the recipient at time t+1. We analyze the performance in terms of the number of cycles required to solve the problem. One cycle corresponds to a series of agent actions, in which an agent recognizes the state of the world (the value assignments of other agents), then decides its response to that state (its own value assignment), and communicates its decisions.

There are some other simulations to evaluate DisCSP algorithms, e.g., Non Concurrent Constraints Checks (NCCCs). However, we analyze different variable ordering heuristics on a single algorithm and the computational cost for each cycle is almost identical. Therefore, we believe that using only cycles rather than NCCCs is enough.

In this paper, the Java program developed by Sun Microsystems Laboratories is used as a scale-free network formation tool [24]. This program can generate scale-free networks giving the number of *nodes*, exponent γ, and the minimal degree of each agent *md*. More specifically, this program can generate a power-law list of nodes and edges.

We examine the performance of ABT in random and scale-free networks. Scale-free networks are generated by the tool with the following parameters: *nodes*=100, *md*=2, and γ=1.8. To generate random networks, we chose *nodes*=100 and *edges*=247, so that the number of constraints will resemble those of the scale-free networks [1]. We set the domain size of each variable to

[1] For γ=2.2, 2.6, 3.0, the essential results did not change.

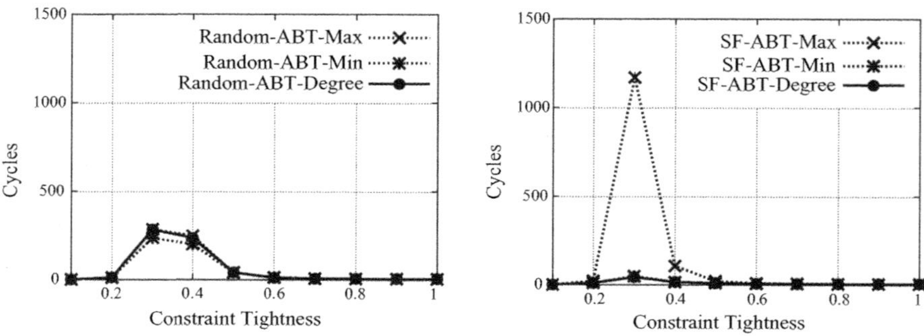

(a) Performance of ABT in random network r_1

(b) Performance of ABT in scale-free network sf_1

Fig. 1. Performance of ABT in random network r_1 and scale-free network sf_1

three, i.e., *domain*=3 which means $|D_1|$=,...,=$|D_m|$=3 for m variables $x_1, ..., x_m$. For the evaluations, we generate ten random and ten scale-free networks. Assume r_1,...,r_{10} for the ten random networks and sf_1,...,sf_{10} for the ten scale-free networks. For each network, the constraint tightness is varied from 0.1 to 0.9 by 0.1. For each constraint tightness, 100 random problem instances are generated. Thus, the results represent the averages of these 100 instances in all ten networks. For a variable-ordering of ABT, we determine ten different random variable-orderings.

In Figure 1(a)-(b), we show the performance of ABT with three different random variable-orderings in random network r_1 and scale-free network sf_1 that exhibit characteristic results. When the constraint tightness is less than 0.3 or greater than 0.3, ABT can terminate early, i.e., ABT can easily find a solution for less than 0.3, and it can easily find that the problem is unsolvable for greater than 0.3. When the constraint tightness equals 0.3, the required cycles of ABT are maximum in r_1 and sf_1. We call such a peak the *critical point.*

Random-ABT-Max (Random-ABT-Min) represents the performance of ABT in random network r_1, whose required cycles at the critical point are maximum (minimum). SF-ABT-Max and SF-ABT-Min represent the performance of ABT as above in scale-free network sf_1. In addition, Random-ABT-Degree and SF-ABT-Degree represent the performance of ABT with a standard degree-based variable-ordering heuristic. In this heuristic, the priority of nodes is determined one by one. First, we choose node n_{1st}, which has the highest degree. Second, we choose node n_{2nd}, which has the highest degree and connected to n_{1st}. Similarly, we keep on choosing a node, that has the highest degree without the nodes already chosen, breaking ties using the degree with the unchosen nodes.

The performance of ABT significantly depends on variable-ordering in scale-free networks. In random network r_1, the required cycles at the critical point vary from 235 to 283 cycles (Figure 1(a)). On the other hand, in scale-free network sf_1, the required cycles vary from 47 to 1171 cycles (Figure 1(b)). We confirmed that similar results were obtained in other networks, i.e., in r_2,...,r_{10} and sf_2,...,sf_{10}.

Table 1. Depth and number of backedges of pseudo-trees and required cycles at critical point

ABT	Depth	Backedges	Cycles
ABT 1	17	207	10253
ABT 2	14	176	7815
ABT 3	15	220	2279
ABT 4	22	327	1673
ABT 5	13	173	777
ABT 6	12	175	380

Particularly, in scale-free networks, ABT with a standard degree-based variable-ordering heuristic requires the smallest cycles at the critical point.

Additionally, we examine the effect of the depth and the number of backedges in a pseudo-tree on the performance of ABT in scale-free networks. According to a variable-ordering, a pseudo-tree is determined whose depth is the length of the longest path from the root agent to one of the leaf agents. A backedge is a link between two agents that are not in a direct parent-child relationship. Our initial expectation was that the performance of ABT would improve with shallower depth and fewer backedges. In Table 1, we show the depth and the number of backedges of the pseudo-trees and the required cycles of ABT at the critical point with six different variable-orderings, where *domain*=10. Here, we increased the domain size to make the required cycles vary significantly according to variable-orderings. As shown in Table 1, we cannot see any direct relationship between the performance and the parameters we examined (i.e., tree depth and number of backedges). For example, in "ABT 1", the required cycle at the critical point is 10253, the depth is 17, and the number of backedges is 207. On the other hand, in "ABT 4", the required cycle at the critical point is 1673, the depth is 22, and the number of backedges is 327.

The experimental results reveal that the choice of variable-ordering heuristics is influential in scale-free networks. Particularly, a standard degree-based variable-ordering heuristic is effective in scale-free networks. We don't see any direct relationship between the performance of ABT and the parameters of a pseudo-tree (i.e., depth and number of backedges).

5 A Variable-Ordering Heuristic for Scale-Free Networks

In this section, we propose a novel variable-ordering heuristic called Average Length between Hubs (ALH). Based on the results so far, since ALH focuses on the average length between hubs, it is specialized for scale-free networks. This section introduces our proposed variable-ordering heuristics and shows that ALH outperforms a standard degree-based variable-ordering heuristic in scale-free networks.

5.1 Heuristic

Let $G = (N, E)$ be a graph, where $N = \{n_i | i \in \mathbb{N}\}$ is a set of nodes (agents) and $E = \{e(n_i, n_j) | n_i, n_j \in N, n_i \neq n_j\}$ is a set of edges. The ABT for graph G needs to predetermine the variable-ordering to reach a solution. A pseudo-tree in which each hub in a graph is placed on different branches is constructed by the variable-ordering.

A node is called a hub if it has a larger number of connections than constant $c \in \mathbb{N}$. Let H be set of hubs

$$H = \{n_i | n_i \in N, deg(n_i) \geq c\}$$

where $deg(n_i)$ is the degree of node n_i. Each agent knows whether he belongs to H.

Next, we define *border-set* nodes by using the distance between nodes $dis : N \times N \to \mathbb{N}$, i.e., $dis(n_i, n_j)$ gives the number of the edges of the shortest path between n_i and n_j. For node n_i, the average distance of the shortest paths to each hub in H is defined as follows:

$$n_i^{av} = \Sigma_{n_j \in H} dis(n_i, n_j)/|H|.$$

The average distance between hubs is defined as follows:

$$h^{av} = \Sigma_{n_i \in H} n_i^{av}/|H|.$$

Then, border-set BS is defined as:

$$BS = \{n_i \mid n_i^{av} \leq h^{av}\}.$$

The priorities of agents are determined using BS. Basically, A node in BS has a higher priority than a node that is not in BS. Between two nodes in BS, the node that is not in H has a higher priority. If two nodes, n_i and n_j, in BS are also in H, then n_i has a higher priority than n_j when $deg(n_i) > deg(n_j)$ (and vice versa). If two nodes, n_i and n_j, in BS are not in H, then n_i has a higher priority than n_j when $n_i^{av} < n_j^{av}$ (and vice versa). Ties are broken using the degrees. Further ties are broken using the lexicographical order of identifiers. Then the priority among two nodes that are not in BS is determined by the total distance between BS. More specifically, for node $n_i \notin BS$, denote the total distance to the nodes of BS as $td(n_i) = \sum_{n_j \in BS} dis(n_i, n_j)$. For two nodes, n_i and n_j that are not in BS, n_i has a higher priority than n_j when $td(n_i) < td(n_j)$ (and vice versa). Ties are broken using the degrees. Further ties are broken using the lexicographical order of identifiers.

If all hubs are directly connected, ALH becomes equivalent to a degree-based heuristic, since BS contains only nodes in H. Consider a scale-free network where each hub is not directly connected. In ALH, the nodes in BS have the highest priority, i.e., the node in BS has a higher priority than the hubs. Let us consider the pseudo-tree defined by this ordering. In the pseudo-tree, the hubs are placed below the nodes in BS, i.e., the hubs are siblings of the nodes in

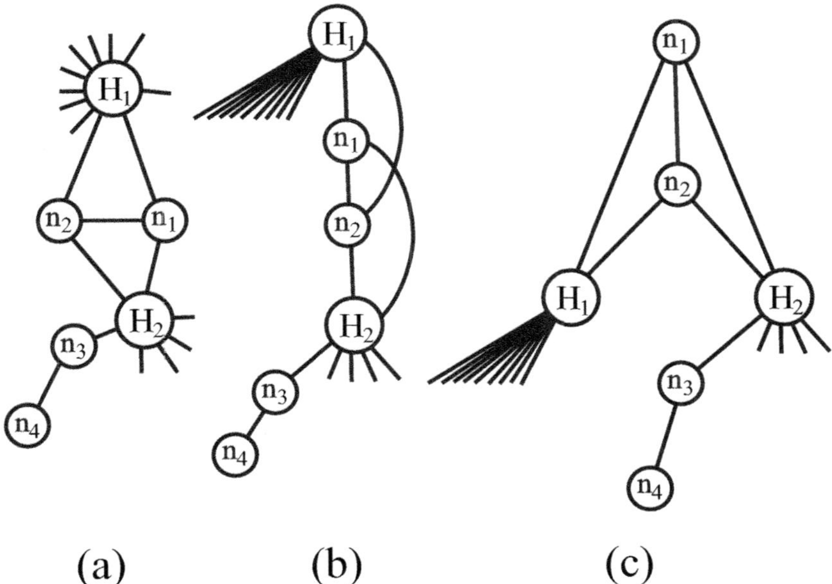

Fig. 2. (a) Constraint network representing a DisCSP where H_1 and H_2 are hubs, (b) Pseudo-tree determined by degree-based heuristic, and (c) Pseudo-tree determined by ALH

BS. Also, under each hub, we can expect that there exists a cluster of nodes, which is independent from other clusters, given that the values of variables in BS are determined. Thus, we can expect that ABT can efficiently solve such a problem instance since these clusters can be solved independently. The cost of implementing the proposed heuristic ALH is enough low compared to the cost of the ABT, since finding a shortest path can be done in O(n) time.

Let us show a simple example. A constraint network of a DisCSP represented as Figure 2(a) exists, where H_1 and H_2 are hubs. For nodes $H_1, H_2, n_1, \ldots, n_4$, their degrees satisfy the following condition: $deg(H_1) > deg(H_2) > deg(n_1) > deg(n_2) > deg(n_3) > deg(n_4)$. Figure 2(b) represents the pseudo-tree determined by a degree-based heuristic.

Since H_1 has the highest degree, it becomes the root of this pseudo-tree. Since h^{av}=1, n_1^{av}=n_2^{av}=1, n_3^{av}=2, and n_4^{av}=3, BS is determined as follows:

$$BS = \{H_1, H_2, n_1, n_2\}.$$

Thus, among these nodes, priority ordering is determined as:

$$n_1, n_2, H_1, H_2, n_3, n_4,$$

where n_1 is the highest and n_4 is the lowest.

Figure 2(c) represents the pseudo-tree determined by ALH. The nodes in BS are placed around the root of the pseudo-tree. The hubs are placed just below

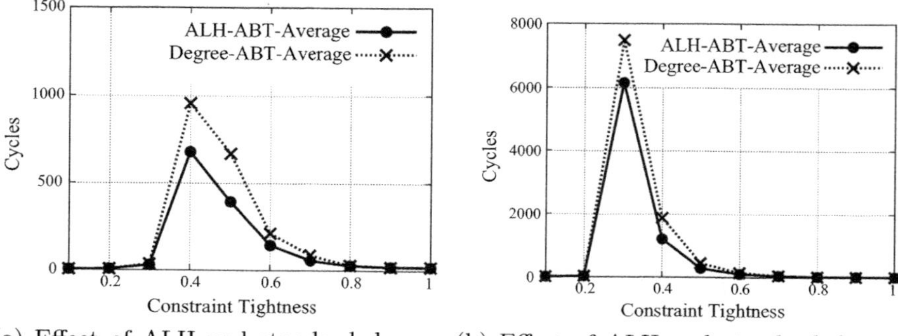

(a) Effect of ALH and standard degree-based heuristics in SFN 1

(b) Effect of ALH and standard degree-based heuristics in SFN 2

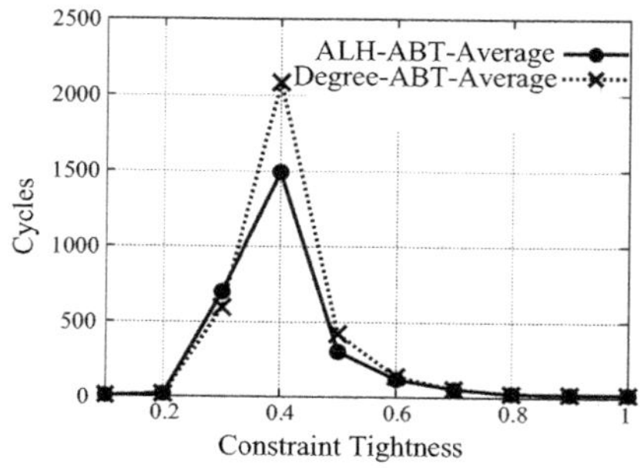

(c) Effect of ALH and standard degree-based heuristics in SFN 3

Fig. 3. Effect of ALH compared to standard degree-based heuristics in SFN 1, SFN 2 and SFN 3

the root as siblings, and in particular, hubs H_1 and H_2 are placed on different branches in this pseudo-tree.

Generally, the hubs are siblings in a pseudo-tree determined by the ALH variable-ordering heuristic, i.e., the given hubs are placed on different branches. When a pseudo-tree is determined by a standard degree-based variable-ordering heuristic, the hub with the highest degree becomes the root of the pseudo-tree. The remaining hubs become the descendant nodes of this hub. In this pseudo-tree, each hub is either the root or is placed on the upper part of the pseudo-tree. On the other hand, when a pseudo-tree is determined by the ALH variable-ordering heuristic, the nodes in the border-set are placed on the upper part of the pseudo-tree. The hubs are below the upper part of the pseudo-tree and the siblings.

5.2 Evaluations

In our evaluations, we show that ALH is effective and can reduce the required cycles at the critical point in scale-free networks. More specifically, we compare the effect of ALH with a standard degree-based heuristic in the following three kinds of scale-free networks:

(SFN 1): *nodes* =100, γ=1.8, and *md*=2,
(SFN 2): *nodes* =200, γ=1.8, and *md*=2,
(SFN 3): *nodes* =100, γ=1.8, and *md*=3.

The evaluations were conducted with *domain*=10. For each parameter we generated ten scale-free networks. For each network, the constraint tightness was varied from 0.1 to 0.9 by 0.1. For each constraint tightness, 100 random constraint instances were generated. The results represent the averages of these 100 instances for all ten scale-free networks (1000 in total). The experimental results in SFN 1 are summarized in Figure 3(a), in which ALH-ABT-Average represents the performance of ABT with ALH and Degree-ABT-Average represents the performance of ABT with the standard degree-based variable-ordering heuristic. Here, the critical point appears when the constraint tightness is around 0.4. At the critical point, ALH-ABT-Average requires 678 cycles while Degree-ABT-Average requires 955 cycles. Thus, ALH-ABT-Average performs approximately 30% better than Degree-ABT-Average at the critical point in SFN 1. We confirmed that ALH is also effective in SFN 2 and SFN 3.

The experimental results in SFN 2 are summarized in Figure 3(b). The network in SFN 2 is larger than that in SFN 1, i.e, the number of nodes in SFN 2 is 200, compared to 100 in SFN 1. ALH-ABT-Average requires 6156 cycles and Degree-ABT-Average requires 7487 cycles at the critical point. Thus, ALH-ABT-Average performs approximately 19% better than Degree-ABT-Average.

The experimental results in SFN 3 are summarized in Figure 3(c). The network in SFN 3 is more complicated than SFN 1, i.e., the minimal degree of each agent increased from *md*=2 to *md*=3. ALH-ABT-Average requires 1489 cycles and Degree-ABT-Average requires 2083 cycles at the critical point. ALH-ABT-Average performs approximately 30% better than Degree-ABT-Average at the critical point in SFN 3.

The experimental results reveal that ALH outperforms the standard degree-based heuristic in three scale-free networks, varying the number of nodes and the minimal degree. We also confirmed that fact did not change with other parameter settings.

6 Discussion

The previous section showed that the standard degree-based heuristic is outperformed by ALH. One might expect that it is also outperformed by the other simple heuristics, since ALH, particularly its way of determining the border set, is somewhat complicated. Thus, we consider a simple variable-ordering heuristic, called a *naive* heuristic described below.

Let us define a naive border-set (NBS) for that heuristic, instead of a BS for ALH. Whether a node belongs to NBS is determined by the distance between the two nearest hubs to the node. Formally, for node $n_i \in N$, denote the two

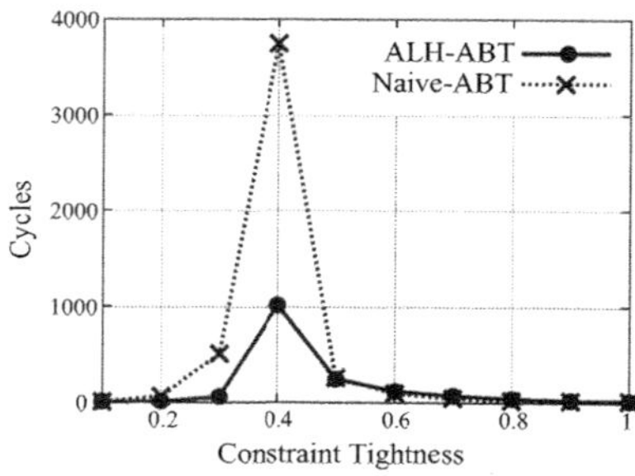

Fig. 4. Effect of ALH compared to *naive* heuristic in SFN 3

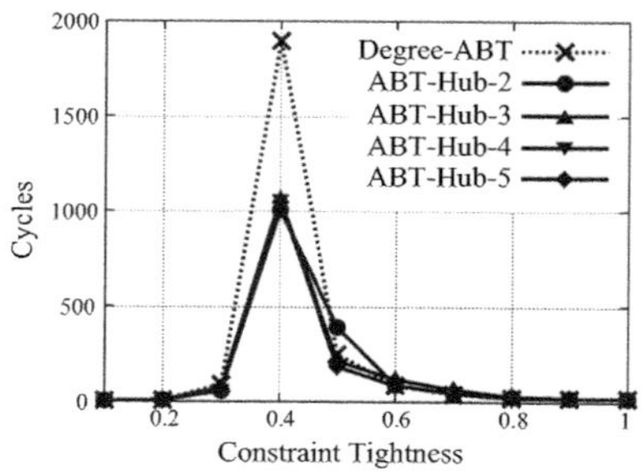

Fig. 5. Effect of ALH by increasing number of hubs from 2 to 5 in SFN 3

nearest hubs from n_i as $h_{i,1st}, h_{i,2nd} \in H$ and denote the distances to $h_{i,1st}$ and $h_{i,2nd}$ from the node as $dis_{1st}(n_i)$, $dis_{2nd}(n_i)$, respectively. Then, we define NBS as follows:

$$NBS = \{n_i \mid |dis_{1st}(n_i) - dis_{2nd}(n_i)| \leq 1\}.$$

In short, NBS contains nodes that lies exactly in the middle of the two nearest hubs. The priority among nodes is determined in exactly the same way as ALH, except that we use NBS instead of BS. The experimental result is summarized in Figure 4. Naive-ABT represents the performance of ABT with the naive heuristic. ALH-ABT performs approximately 3.7 times better than Naive-ABT at the critical point. Precisely, the required cycles for ALH-ABT is 1016, while that for Naive-ABT is 3744 at that point. As a result, we can say that the simplified version of the heuristics fails to perform as well as ALH.

We examined the reason why the performance of the *naive* heuristic is much worse than that of ALH, and found that the size of NBS of the *naive* heuristic is much larger than the size of BS of ALH. In fact, NBS contains at least twice as many agents as BS. Therefore, we conjecture that the size of BS should be small; otherwise, the priority based on BS becomes less informative.

In previous evaluations, we set the number of hubs to two. This seems to be a reasonable choice to make the size of the border-set (BS) small. We further examine the performance of ABT with ALH by varying the number of hubs from two to five. The experimental results are summarized in Figure 5, in which ABT-Hub-k represents the performance of ABT when choosing the number of hubs as k. The performance is basically unchanged even if we change the number of hubs, i.e., the required cycles at the critical point for ABT-Hub-5 is 1048, while that for ABT-Hub-2 is 1004. These results imply that the choice of the number of hubs is not so influential to the performance of ABT with ALH.

Note also that, this result does not explain how many hubs we should choose in any scale-free networks. We will research a good value for some of constants (constant for selecting hubs) as a future work.

7 Conclusions

In this paper, we showed that the choice of variable-ordering heuristics is more influential in scale-free networks than in random networks. We observed that in scale-free networks there is more significant difference between maximum and minimum of the required cycles than in random networks.

Furthermore, we examined how the performance of ABT in scale-free networks changes in terms of the depth and number of backedges of pseudo-trees. We chose six different variable-orderings, i.e., six different pseudo-trees of different of depths. We compared the differences of the depth or the number of backedges and the differences of the performances of ABT. The experimental result revealed that these parameters do not significantly affect the performance of ABT in scale-free networks.

Finally, we developed a novel variable-ordering heuristic called Average Length between Hubs (ALH) specialized for scale-free networks. We showed that ALH outperforms a standard degree-based variable-ordering heuristic in scale-free networks and can reduce the required cycles by 30% at the critical point.

As future works, we must show that our experimental results are common with other different scale-free networks, e.g., scale-free networks with 1,000 or 10,000 nodes. Furthermore, we hope to develop dynamic variable-ordering heuristics/algorithms that are specialized to scale-free networks.

References

[1] Yokoo, M., Durfee, E.H., Ishida, T., Kuwabara, K.: The distributed constraint satisfaction problem: formalization and algorithms. IEEE Transactions on Knowledge and Data Engineering 10(5), 673–685 (1998)

[2] Yokoo, M., Hirayama, K.: Algorithms for distributed constraint satisfaction: A review. Journal of Autonomous Agents and Multi-agent Systems 3(2), 189–211 (2000)

[3] Hamadi, Y.: Backtracking in distributed constraint networks. International Journal on Artificial Intelligence Tools, 219–223 (1998)

[4] Bessiere, C., Brito, I., Maestre, A., Meseguer, P.: Asynchronous backtracking without adding links: a new member in the ABT family. Artificial Intelligence 161, 7–24 (2005)

[5] Nguyen, V., Sam-Haroud, D., Faltings, B.: Dynamic distributed backjumping. In: Joint ERCIM/CoLogNet International Workshop on Constraint Solving and Constraint Logic Programming, pp. 71–85 (2004)

[6] Mailler, R., Lesser, V.: Asynchronous partial overlay: A new algorithm for solving distributed constraint satisfaction problems. Journal of Artificial Intelligence Research 25, 529–576 (2006)

[7] Silaghi, M.-C.: Framework for modeling reordering heuristics for asynchronous backtracking. In: IEEE/WIC/ACM International Conference on intelligent Agent Technology, pp. 529–536 (2006)

[8] Zivan, R., Meisels, A.: Dynamic ordering for asynchronous backtracking on DisCSPs. Constraints 11(2-3), 179–197 (2006)

[9] Erdös, P., Rényi, A.: On random graphs I. Publicationes Mathematicae Debrecen 6, 290–297 (1959)

[10] Barabási, A.-L.: Linked: The new science of networks. Perseus Publishing, Cambridge (2003)
[11] Barabási, A.-L., Albert, R.: Emergence of scaling in random networks. Science 286, 509–512 (1999)
[12] Devlin, D., O'Sullivan, B.: Preferential attachment in constraint networks. In: 21st International Conference on Tools with Artificial Intelligence, pp. 708–715 (2009)
[13] Walsh, T.: Search in a small world. In: 16th International Joint Conference on Artificial Intelligence, pp. 1172–1177 (1999)
[14] Walsh, T.: Search on high degree graphs. In: 17th International Joint Conference on Artificial Intelligence, pp. 266–274 (2001)
[15] Chalupsky, H., Gil, Y., Knoblock, C.A., Lerman, K., Oh, J., Pynadath, D.V., Russ, T.A., Tambe, M.: Electric elves: Agent technology for supporting human organizations. AI Magazine 23(2), 11–24 (2002)
[16] Brito, I., Meseguer, P.: Distributed meeting scheduling. In: Computer & Communications Industry Association, pp. 38–45 (2007)
[17] Arbelaez, A., Hamadi, Y.: Exploiting weak dependencies in tree-based search. In: 24th Annual ACM Symposium on Applied Computing, pp. 1385–1391 (2009)
[18] Ezzahir, R., Bessiere, C., Wahbi, M., Benelallam, I., Bouyakhf, E.H.: Asynchronous Inter-Level Forward-Checking for DisCSPs. In: Gent, I.P. (ed.) CP 2009. LNCS, vol. 5732, pp. 304–318. Springer, Heidelberg (2009)
[19] Hamadi, Y.: Interleaved backtracking in distributed constraint networks. International Journal on Artificial Intelligence Tools 11(2), 167–188 (2002)
[20] Sultanik, E., Lass, R.N., Regli, W.C.: Dynamic configuration of agent organizations. In: 21st International Joint Conference on Artificial Intelligence, pp. 305–311 (2009)
[21] Mackworth, A.K.: Constraint Satisfaction. In: Encyclopedia of Artificial Intelligence, pp. 285–293 (1992)
[22] Buchanan, M.: Nexus: Small worlds and the groundbreaking science of networks. W. W. Norton & Company, London (2003)
[23] Li, L., Alderson, D., Doyle, J.C., Willinger, W.: Towards a theory of scale-free graphs: Definition, properties, and implications. Internet Mathematics 2(4), 431–523 (2005)
[24] Densmore, O.: An exploration of power-law networks (2009), `http://backspaces.net/sun/PLaw/index.html`

Multi-attribute Preference Logic

Koen V. Hindriks, Wietske Visser, and Catholijn M. Jonker

Man Machine Interaction Group, Delft University of Technology
Mekelweg 4, 2628 CD Delft, The Netherlands
K.V.Hindriks@tudelft.nl, Wietske.Visser@tudelft.nl,
C.M.Jonker@tudelft.nl

Abstract. Preferences for objects are commonly derived from ranked sets of properties or multiple attributes associated with these objects. There are several options or strategies to qualitatively derive a preference for one object over another from a property ranking. We introduce a modal logic, called multi-attribute preference logic, that provides a language for expressing such strategies. The logic provides the means to represent and reason about qualitative multi-attribute preferences and to derive object preferences from property rankings. The main result of the paper is a proof that various well-known preference orderings can be defined in multi-attribute preference logic.

1 Introduction

Preferences may be associated with various entities such as states of affairs, properties, objects and outcomes in e.g. games. Our main concern here are object preferences. A natural approach to obtain preferences about objects is to start with a set of properties of these objects and derive preferences from a ranking of these properties, where the ranking indicates the relative importance or priority of each of these properties. This approach to obtain preferences is typical in multi-attribute decision theory, see e.g. Keeney and Raiffa [10]. Multi-attribute decision theory provides a quantitative theory that derives object preferences from utility values assigned to outcomes which are derived from numeric weights associated with properties or attributes of objects. As it is difficult to obtain such quantitative utility values and weights, however, several qualitative approaches have been proposed instead, see e.g. [2,4,5,6,11]. There is also extensive literature on preference logic following the seminal work of Von Wright [12,9], but such logics are not specifically suited for the multi-attribute case. To illustrate what we are after, we first present a motivating example that is used throughout the paper.

Example 1. Suppose we want to buy a house. The properties that we find important are that we can afford the house, that it is close to our work, and that it is large, in that order. Consider three houses, $house_1$, $house_2$ and $house_3$, whose properties are listed in Figure 1, which we have to order according to our preferences. It seems clear that we would prefer $house_1$ over the other two, because it has two of the most important properties, while both other houses only have one of these properties. But what about the relative preference of $house_2$ and $house_3$? $house_3$ has two out of three of the relevant properties where $house_2$ has only one. If the property that $house_2$ has is considered more important than both properties of $house_3$, $house_2$ would be preferred over $house_3$.

N. Desai, A. Liu, and M. Winikoff (Eds.): PRIMA 2010, LNAI 7057, pp. 181–195, 2012.

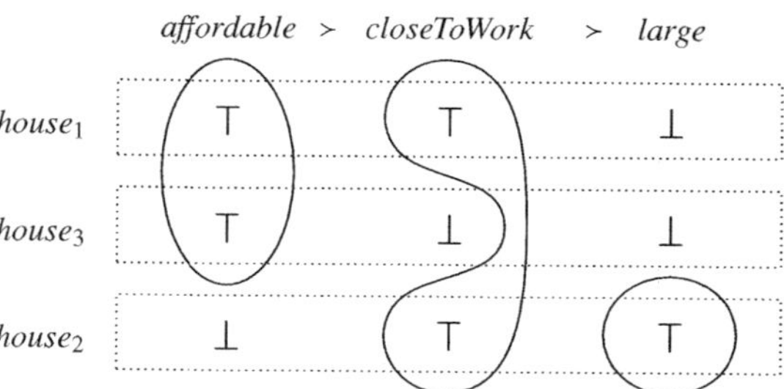

Fig. 1. Properties of three houses

Key to a logic of multi-attribute preferences is the representation of property rankings. Encodings of property rankings have been explored in Coste-Marquis *et al.* [6] where they are called goal bases, and in Brewka [4] where they are called ranked knowledge bases. Such ranked goals are binary, and in this paper we also consider desired attributes that are binary (as opposed to numeric or ordinal ones). Coste-Marquis *et al.* and Brewka moreover discuss various options, or strategies, for deriving object preferences from a property ranking. The preference orderings thus obtained are not expressed in a logic, however. Brewka *et al.* [5] propose a non-monotonic logic called qualitative choice logic to reason about multi-attribute preferences. An alternative approach towards a logic of multi-attribute preferences is presented in Liu [11] where property rankings called priority sequences are encoded in first-order logic. Both approaches are based on one particular strategy, namely lexicographic ordering, and cannot be used to reason about preference orderings.

In this paper a generic logic of qualitative multi-attribute preferences is proposed in which property rankings and associated strategies for deriving object preferences from such rankings can be defined. In Section 2 the syntax and semantics of multi-attribute preference logic is introduced. Section 3 shows how various strategies to obtain object preferences from a property ranking can be defined in the logic. Section 4 presents the main result of the paper and shows that property rankings encoded as ranked knowledge bases and a number of related strategies to obtain preference orderings can be equivalently translated into multi-attribute preference logic. Section 5 concludes the paper.

2 Multi-attribute Preference Logic

2.1 Syntax and Semantics

The logic of multi-attribute preferences that we introduce here is an extension of the modal binary preference logic presented in [7]. This logic is a propositional modal logic with a modal operator $\Box^{\leq}\varphi$, and its dual $\Diamond^{\leq}\varphi$. Here $\Box^{\leq}\varphi$ expresses that φ is true in all states that are at least as good as the current state. Binary preference relations over formulae are subsequently defined. One of the more natural binary preference statements is $\varphi <_{\forall\forall} \psi$ which expresses that any state where ψ is true is strictly better than any state where φ is true. That is, whenever φ is the case, ψ is preferred, and never vice versa. By adding a global modality U to the language, the binary preference operator $<_{\forall\forall}$ can be defined by $U(\psi \to \Box^{\leq}\neg\varphi)$, when it is assumed that the underlying order on worlds or states has been completely specified, i.e. is total.

Multi-attribute preference logic adds two operators to binary preference logic. First, multi-attribute preference logic, as in hybrid logic [1] adds names for objects to the language by adding nullary modal operators i, j to the language. The semantics of the operators introduced here, however, differs from the standard semantics of hybrid logic. Here i, j are used as names for objects which semantically are more complex entities than the usual worlds of modal semantics. In order to avoid confusion, we will refer to i, j as object names below. This language extension allows us to talk about objects and associated preferences explicitly.

Second, the logic introduces a new modal operator $\Box^{\neq}$. The language of multi-attribute preference logic consists of four unary modal operators. Instead of the single operator $\Box^{\leq}$ it is more convenient to introduce the two operators $\Box^{<}$ and $\Box^{=}$: informally, $\Box^{<}\varphi$ expresses that at all worlds that are ranked higher than the current one φ is true, whereas $\Box^{=}\varphi$ expresses that at all worlds that are equally ranked to the current one φ is true. The modal operator $\Box^{\neq}$ is introduced to inspect worlds that are not ranked equally to the current one.

Definition 1. (Language) *Let At be a set of propositional atoms with typical element p and Nom be a set of names, with typical elements i, j. The language $\mathcal{L}_{pref}$ is defined as follows:*

$$\varphi \in \mathcal{L}_{pref} ::= p \mid i \mid \neg\varphi \mid \varphi \wedge \varphi \mid \Box^{=}\varphi \mid \Box^{\neq}\varphi \mid \Box^{<}\varphi \mid U\varphi$$

Disjunction $\vee$, implication $\to$, and bi-implication $\leftrightarrow$ are defined as the usual abbreviations. $\Diamond^{<}\varphi, \Diamond^{=}, \Diamond^{\neq}$ are abbreviations for $\neg\Box^{<}\neg\varphi$, $\neg\Box^{=}\neg\varphi$, and $\neg\Box^{\neq}\neg\varphi$. $\Box^{\leq}\varphi$ is short for $\Box^{<}\varphi \vee \Box^{=}\varphi$ and $\Diamond^{\leq}\varphi$ is its dual. The dual of the global modal operator, $E\varphi$, is defined as $\neg U\neg\varphi$. We also write $U_i\varphi$ for $U(i \to \varphi)$ and $E_i\varphi$ for $E(i \wedge \varphi)$ for $i \in Nom$. Finally, the set of purely propositional formulae is denoted by $\mathcal{L}_0$ and consists of all formulae without any occurrences of modal operators or names $i \in Nom$. $\varphi \in \mathcal{L}_0$ is also called an objective formula.

The basic concepts in the semantics for multi-attribute preference logic are objects and properties those objects may have. Properties are naturally represented by sets of worlds. As we want to use properties to classify the ranking of objects, properties are ordered in correspondence with their relative importance; such an order is called a property ranking here. To order properties, i.e. sets of worlds, it is required that properties are disjoint sets of worlds. Property rankings will be derived from an order on worlds below.

Objects are also identified with particular sets of worlds. The idea is that the properties (in the sense of the previous paragraph) of an object can be derived from the worlds which define the object. To ensure that objects are coherent, that is have a uniquely defined set of properties, the worlds that define the object need to be copies of each other, which means that these worlds need to assign the same truth values to propositional atoms. Objects are identified with equivalence classes of worlds with respect to a truth assignment.

Definition 2. (Object) *Let W be a set of worlds and V be a mapping of W to truth assignments 2^{At}. An object is an equivalence class on W with respect to V. The set $\mathcal{O}_V$ denotes the set of all objects defined by W and V and is formally defined by:*

$$\mathcal{O}_V = \{[w]_V \mid w \in W\}$$

where $[w]_V = \{v \in W \mid V(w) = V(v)\}$. Whenever V is clear from the context, we drop the subscript V. As an object o is the equivalence class of a world w with respect to V, we also say that world w identifies object o.

Definition 3. (Model) *A* multi-attribute preference model $\mathcal{M}$ *is a tuple $\langle W, \precsim, V, N\rangle$ where W is a set of worlds with typical elements u, v, w, $\precsim$ is a total pre-order (i.e. a reflexive, transitive and total relation) on W, V is a valuation function mapping worlds in W onto truth assignments in 2^{At}, and N is a naming function. The strict subrelation $<$ of $\precsim$ is defined by: $v < w := v \precsim w \;\&\; w \not\precsim v$. We write $v \sim w$ whenever $v \precsim w$ and $w \precsim v$.*

Although the strict order $<$ derived from $\precsim$ indicates a ranking of worlds where $v < w$ means that w is ranked higher than v, we do not say that w is preferred over v, because we want to reserve this terminology for talking about objects. A preference between objects is derived from the ranking $\precsim$ over worlds. The naming function N maps names i to objects o.

The truth definition for propositional atoms and Boolean operators is standard. Given a model $\mathcal{M} = \langle W, \precsim, V, N\rangle$, the semantics of names $i \in Nom$ is provided by the naming function N. The truth definitions for most modal operators are also standard definitions using the associated accessibility relations for these operators. The semantic clause for $\Box^{=}$ is defined by means of the relation $\sim$, which is derived from the order $\precsim$. Similarly, the semantic clause for $\Box^{<}$ is provided by means of the strict order $<$. The global operator U simply inspects all worlds in a model.

The truth definition for $\Box^{\neq}$ is not directly defined in terms of a given relation on W. It inspects all worlds that (i) are not ranked equally as the current one, and (ii) are not copies of worlds that are ranked equally as the current one. The motivation for this definition will become clear in Section 2.2 when clusters are introduced.

Definition 4. (Truth Definition) *Let $\mathcal{M} = \langle W, \precsim, V, N\rangle$ be an MPL model and $w \in W$ a world. The truth of a formula $\varphi \in \mathcal{L}_{pref}$ in $\mathcal{M}$ at w is defined by:*

$\mathcal{M}, w \models p \quad \Leftrightarrow p \in V(w)$
$\mathcal{M}, w \models i \quad \Leftrightarrow w \in N(i)$
$\mathcal{M}, w \models \neg\varphi \quad \Leftrightarrow \mathcal{M}, w \not\models \varphi$
$\mathcal{M}, w \models \varphi \wedge \psi \Leftrightarrow \mathcal{M}, w \models \varphi \;\&\; \mathcal{M}, w \models \psi$
$\mathcal{M}, w \models \Box^{=}\varphi \quad \Leftrightarrow \forall v : w \sim v \Rightarrow \mathcal{M}, v \models \varphi$
$\mathcal{M}, w \models \Box^{\neq}\varphi \quad \Leftrightarrow \forall u \in \overline{\bigcup\{[v]_V \mid w \sim v\}} : \mathcal{M}, u \models \varphi$
$\mathcal{M}, w \models \Box^{<}\varphi \quad \Leftrightarrow \forall v : w < v \Rightarrow \mathcal{M}, v \models \varphi$
$\mathcal{M}, w \models U\varphi \quad \Leftrightarrow \forall v : \mathcal{M}, v \models \varphi$

A name $i \in Nom$ refers to an object o and, semantically, is true at a world w that identifies the object o, i.e. $w \in o$. A name thus is a special kind of operator that is true in all worlds that identify a certain object, and false in all other worlds. We can express that an object

i has a property φ by $E_i\varphi = E(i \wedge \varphi)$. As we have $E(i)$ as a validity and the worlds that identify the corresponding object o are copies of each other, we have $E_i\varphi \leftrightarrow U_i\varphi$ for objective φ. This shows that an object is coherent in the sense that an object has a consistent set of objective properties and can be uniquely identified by this set.

The language also allows us to express properties that concern comparison of objects. For example, $U(i \to \Diamond^{<} j)$ expresses that for every property of object i object j has a property that is strictly better. The formula $E(j \wedge \neg \Diamond^{\leq} i)$ expresses that object j has a property that object i cannot match, i.e. i has no property that is strictly better than this property of j. We have $E(j \wedge \neg \Diamond^{\leq} i) \to U(i \to \Diamond^{<} j)$ in multi-attribute preference logic. This validity is based on the assumption that the pre-order in models for $\mathcal{L}_{pref}$ is total.

Recall that the binary preference operator $\varphi <_{\forall\forall} \psi$ can be defined as $U(\psi \to \Box^{\leq}\neg\varphi)$. Using $<_{\forall\forall}$ it is possible to define property rankings and express that a property ψ is ranked higher than property φ. Using the truth definitions for $U\varphi$, $\Box^{=}\varphi$ and $\Box^{<}\varphi$ and the definition of $\Box^{\leq}\varphi$ as $\Box^{=}\varphi \wedge \Box^{<}\varphi$, it can be shown that $\varphi <_{\forall\forall} \psi$ has the following truth definition:

$$\mathcal{M}, w \models \varphi <_{\forall\forall} \psi \Leftrightarrow \forall u, v : \mathcal{M}, u \models \varphi \;\&\; \mathcal{M}, v \models \psi \Rightarrow u < v$$

The intuitive reading of $\varphi <_{\forall\forall} \psi$ is that every ψ-state is ranked higher than every φ-state (cf. [7]). Returning to the comparison of objects again, $i <_{\forall\forall} j$ expresses that object j is preferred over i. The preference expressed in this way is a very strong kind of preference, however. It requires that all of object j's relevant properties are considered more important than objects i's properties, which corresponds with the definition of $i <_{\forall\forall} j$ by $U(j \to \Box^{\leq}\neg i)$. In contrast, multi-attribute preference logic is able to specify principles that allow to derive preferences over objects from their properties in a weaker sense. It enables, for example, to specify orderings where object j is preferred over object i even when object i has at least one property that is considered more important than a property that object j has (compare e.g. object c and f in Figure 2). The logic thus facilitates the specification of different ordering strategies, and, given such a specification, provides the means to derive a preference of one object over another from a property ranking and an additional specification of the objects' properties.

Proposition 1 supports our claim that multi-attribute preference logic extends binary preference logic as all listed axioms of this logic are valid in multi-attribute preference logic as well (cf. [7], p. 66). We have listed only those axioms that can straightforwardly be expressed without the need to introduce additional definitions of other binary preference operators; all of the remaining axioms are valid as well in multi-attribute preference logic when such definitions are added. Below we use that $\wedge$ and $\vee$ bind their arguments stronger than $\to$ to be able to remove some brackets.

Proposition 1. *We have the following validities:*
1. $\models E_i\varphi \leftrightarrow U_i\varphi$ *for* $\varphi \in \mathcal{L}_0$.
2. $\models \varphi <_{\forall\forall} \psi \wedge U(\xi \to \psi) \to \varphi <_{\forall\forall} \xi$
3. $\models \varphi <_{\forall\forall} \psi \wedge U(\xi \to \varphi) \to \xi <_{\forall\forall} \psi$
4. $\models \varphi <_{\forall\forall} \psi \wedge \psi <_{\forall\forall} \xi \wedge E\xi \to \varphi <_{\forall\forall} \xi$
5. $\models U\neg\varphi \vee U\neg\psi \to \varphi <_{\forall\forall} \psi$
6. $\models \varphi <_{\forall\forall} \psi \to U(\varphi <_{\forall\forall} \psi)$

What multi-attribute preference logic adds to binary preference logic are names for objects, and most importantly, the $\Box^{\neq}$ operator that allows us to define clusters (see Section 2.2) that represent desirable attributes. All of the modal operators $\Box^{=}, \Box^{<}, \Box^{\neq}$ and U are normal modal operators and satisfy the K axiom. In addition, we prove some properties of the $\Box^{=}$ and $\Box^{\neq}$ operators (some of the more obvious axioms have not been listed below). Proposition 2.3 shows that multi-attribute preference logic is related to the logic of only knowing, see [8].

Proposition 2. *We have:*
1. $\models \Box^{=}\Box^{\neq}\varphi \leftrightarrow \Box^{\neq}\varphi$
2. $\models \Box^{=}\Box^{<}\varphi \leftrightarrow \Box^{<}\varphi$
3. $\models \Box^{=}\varphi \to \neg\Box^{\neq}\varphi$ *where* $\neg\varphi \in \mathcal{L}_0$ *is consistent*

Proof. We prove item 3. Suppose $\Box^{=}\varphi$ *is true at world* w*. Then* φ *is true in all worlds* $v \sim w$*. Since the truth of objective formulae is the same within an object,* φ *is also true in every world* $u \in \{[v]_V \mid w \sim v\}$*. Since* $\neg\varphi$ *is a consistent objective formula and all valuations are present in the model,* $\neg\varphi$ *must be true in some world in the model. So there must be some world in* $\overline{\{[v]_V \mid w \sim v\}}$ *that satisfies* $\neg\varphi$*, so we have* $\neg\Box^{\neq}\varphi$ *at world* w*.*

2.2 Clusters

The total pre-order $\precsim$ in a multi-attribute preference model induces a strict linear order on sets of worlds, which we call clusters. Formally, a cluster is an equivalence class induced by $\precsim$. Intuitively, such clusters represent the properties or attributes considered relevant for deriving object preferences. The order on clusters induced by $\precsim$ represents a property ranking, i.e. the relative importance of one property compared to another. The relation between objects and properties may now be clarified as follows. The idea is that if an object has a particular property it should be represented within the cluster of worlds that represents the property. Technically, this is realized by making sure that (at least) one of the copies of a world that identifies the object is an element of the cluster that represents the property. The worlds that identify an object act as representatives for the object within a certain cluster and thus indicate that the object has that property. As clusters are disjoint and objects may have multiple properties, this also explains the need for introducing copies of worlds.

Definition 5. (Cluster) *Let* $\precsim$ *be a total pre-order on* W*. A cluster* c *is an equivalence class induced by* $\precsim$*, i.e.* $c = [w]_{\precsim} = \{v \mid w \sim v\}$ *for some* $w \in W$*.*

Example 2. The relation between clusters (properties) and sets of copies (objects) is visualized in Figure 2 (this is a model of the theory in Example 4). The ellipses (columns) represent the clusters or properties and the boxes (rows) represent objects. Objects in this case are supposed to be houses. For example, the house labelled b consists of two worlds, w_4 and w_5. As these worlds are part of the same object, they must be copies of each other. One of these worlds, w_4, is also part of the cluster representing the property of being affordable. This means that house b is affordable, as *affordable* is true at w_4

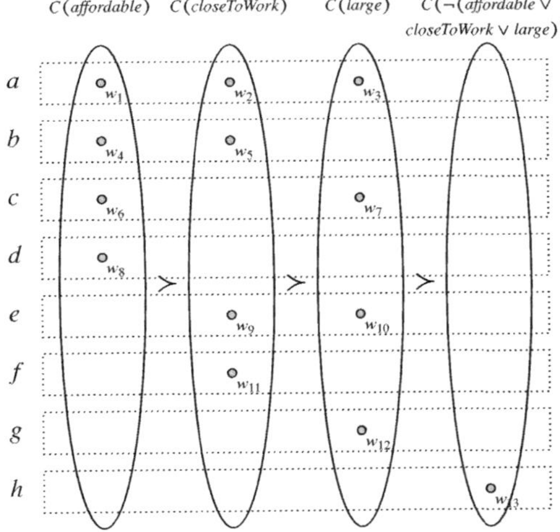

Fig. 2. Visualization of an MPL model

(and thus also at w_5). Similarly, it follows that house b is close to work, a property that is true at w_5 (and thus at w_4). As there is no world that is part of object b as well as in the cluster representing the property *large*, house b is not large. The ranking of the properties is indicated by the $\prec$ symbol: property *affordable* is more important than *close to work* which in turn is more important than *large*. As a result, in any natural preference ordering based on this ranking one would expect house b to be preferred over house c.

The modality $\Box^{=}$ can be used to express a property of a cluster. For example, $E\,\Box^{=}\varphi$ expresses that there is a cluster where φ is true everywhere. $\Box^{=}\varphi$ expresses that at least φ is true in the cluster. In Figure 2, for example, in the third cluster we have that $\Box^{=}large$ is true. This means that every object that is represented by a world in this cluster is *large*. But we also want every object that is *large* to be represented in the cluster. To specify this, we use the modality $\Box^{\neq}$. We can now explain why simply defining the truth of $\Box^{\neq}\varphi$ in terms of truth of φ in all worlds that are not equally ranked to the current one does not work. The point is that there may be copies v of worlds w that have a different ranking than world w. As copies have the same truth assignment, at such copies a propositional formula φ would be assigned the same truth value. This is illustrated in Figure 3, where *large* is true in all worlds in the shaded area. The key observation here is that worlds of a particular ranking identify a set of objects, i.e. copies of these worlds which must be part of these objects (by Definition 2 of an object). This is why $\Box^{\neq}\varphi$ evaluates φ at all objects, or, more precisely, the worlds that define these objects, that are not identified by any of the worlds that have the same ranking as the current one.

By combining both operators we are able to characterize a cluster. For the third cluster in Figure 2, we have that $\Box^{=}large \wedge \Box^{\neq}\neg large$ where *large* exactly characterizes the cluster. The characterization of a cluster by φ is abbreviated as $C\varphi$, and defined by:

$$C\varphi \ ::= \ \Box^{=}\varphi \wedge \Box^{\neq}\neg\varphi$$

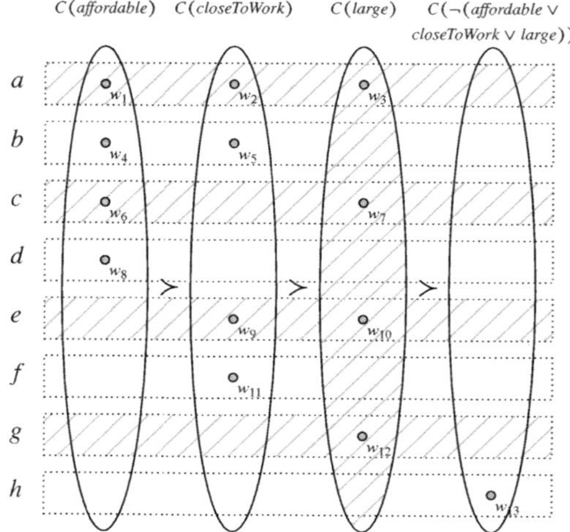

Fig. 3. Visualization of an MPL model. All worlds where *large* is true are in the shaded section.

φ is true for all objects identified by (worlds in) the cluster and not true in all worlds that identify other objects. As an object may consist of several copies to represent that it has various properties represented by different clusters, copies of such worlds outside the cluster need to be excluded in the evaluation of $\neg\varphi$ which explains the truth condition for $\Box^{\neq}$.

Proposition 3 shows that properties and objects are related in such a way that object preferences can be derived. The first item of the proposition states that if there is an object that has property φ and the current world identifies a cluster characterized by φ, then within the cluster there is a world that is named i, i.e. identifies the object i. The second item states that the converse is true for an object that does not satisfy a property φ that characterizes a cluster. That is, if object i does not satisfy φ and the current world identifies a cluster characterized by φ, then no world that identifies the object labelled i is part of that cluster. The third item generalizes the first item. It states that if there is a cluster characterized by φ, and there is an object named i that satisfies φ, then there is an i-world in that cluster. The last item states that when a world satisfies $C(\varphi)$, then all worlds within the same cluster satisfy $C(\varphi)$.

Proposition 3. *We have:*
1. $\models C(\varphi) \wedge E_i\varphi \rightarrow \Diamond^{=} i$
2. $\models C(\varphi) \wedge \neg E_i\varphi \rightarrow \neg\Diamond^{=} i$
3. $\models EC(\varphi) \wedge E_i\varphi \rightarrow E_iC(\varphi)$
4. $\models C(\varphi) \rightarrow \Box^{=} C(\varphi)$

Proof. We prove item 1. Suppose $\mathcal{M}, w \models C(\varphi) \wedge E_i\varphi$. *This means that* $\mathcal{M}, w \models \Box^{\neq}\neg\varphi$. *By the truth definition for* $\Box^{\neq}$, *this is equivalent to* $\forall u \in \overline{\bigcup\{[v]_V \mid w \sim v\}} : \mathcal{M}, u \models \neg\varphi$. *By the definition of* $E_i\varphi$ *we must also have a world* u' *such that* $\mathcal{M}, u' \models i \wedge \varphi$. *This means that we cannot have* $u' \in \overline{\bigcup\{[v]_V \mid w \sim v\}}$ *and we have that* $u' \in \bigcup\{[v]_V \mid w \sim v\}$. *It follows that* $u' \in [v]_V$ *for some* $v \sim w$*; as* u' *must be a copy of* v *this means that we have* $\mathcal{M}, v \models i$ *and, by the truth definition for* $\diamond^=$*, we have* $\mathcal{M}, w \models \diamond^= i$.

The operator C provides exactly what we need to define property rankings. Semantically, we have already seen that the pre-order $\precsim$ induces a strict linear order on clusters. The formula $C\varphi$ allows us to express that a cluster is characterized by a formula φ. Using this operator and the binary preference operator $<_{\forall\forall}$ we can express that property ψ (represented by a cluster) is ranked higher than another property φ (represented by another cluster) by $C\varphi <_{\forall\forall} C\psi$. For example, in Figure 2, we have $C(large) <_{\forall\forall} C(closeToWork) <_{\forall\forall} C(affordable)$. By combining this with specifications of particular preferences orderings and statements that an object has a particular property (cf. Proposition 3), this will allow the derivation of object preferences from a property ranking.

3 Preference Orderings

In this Section, we show how to use multi-attribute preference logic to define multi-attribute preference orderings derived from property rankings. Coste-Marquis *et al.* [6] describe three frequent orderings based on prioritized goals: best-out, discrimin and leximin ordering. Brewka [4] defines a preference language in which different basic preference orderings can be combined and identifies four 'fundamental strategies' for deriving preferences from what he calls a ranked knowledge base: $\top$, κ, $\subseteq$ and #. As best-out is the same as κ, discrimin is $\subseteq$, and leximin is #, we will base the remainder of our discussion on Brewka [4].

We first informally introduce these orderings and then present definitions for each of them in the logic. Section 4 presents the definitions of [4] and a proof that the definitions in multi-attribute preference logic match those provided in [4]. The advantage of defining preference orderings in a logic instead of providing set-theoretical definitions is that it formalizes the reasoning about object preferences. From a practical point of view, the logic allows us to provide rigorous formal proofs for object preferences derived from property rankings. From a theoretical point of view, it provides the tools to reason *about* preference orderings and allows, for example, to prove that whenever an object is preferred over another by the $\top$ strategy it also is preferred by the # strategy (see Proposition 4 below).

The two orderings $\subseteq$ and # first consider the most important property. If some object has that property and another does not, then the first is preferred over the second. So in the example, both $house_1$ and $house_2$ would be preferred over $house_3$. If two houses both have the property or if neither of them has it, the next property is considered. $house_1$ and $house_2$ are both affordable, but $house_1$ is close to work and $house_2$ is not, so $house_1$ would be preferred over $house_2$. Note that although $house_3$ satisfies two properties and house $house_2$ only satisfies one property, $house_2$ is still preferred over $house_3$ because the single property of $house_2$ is considered more important than both properties of $house_3$. The $\subseteq$ and # orderings only differ if multiple properties are equally important. As we will make the assumption that no two properties can have the same importance, we will not discuss the difference and only refer to the # ordering in the following.

The $\top$ ordering looks at the highest ranked or most important property that *is* satisfied. If that property of one object is ranked higher than that of another object, then the first object is preferred over the second. If those properties are equally ranked, then both objects are equally preferred. In our running example, $house_1$ and $house_2$ are both preferred over $house_3$, since the property ranked highest that is satisfied by both $house_1$ and $house_2$ is *affordable*, and this property is ranked higher than the highest ranked property satisfied by $house_3$, i.e. *closeToWork*. Since the most important property satisfied by $house_1$ is the same as the most important property satisfied by $house_2$, $house_1$ and $house_2$ are equally preferred.

The κ ordering looks at the most important property that *is not* satisfied. If that property of one object is less important than the property of another object, then the first object is preferred over the second. If those properties are equally important, then both objects are equally preferred. In our running example, the highest ranked property that is not satisfied by $house_1$ is *large*, that of $house_2$ is *closeToWork* and that of $house_3$ is *affordable*. Since *large* is the least important property of these properties, $house_1$ is preferred over both other houses. As *closeToWork* is less important than *affordable*, $house_2$ is preferred over $house_3$.

All preference orderings introduced can be defined in multi-attribute preference logic. We use $pref^s_\sim(i,j)$ to stand for: object i is weakly preferred over object j according to strategy s, where s is one of $\top$, κ and #; $pref^s(i,j)$ is used to express strict preference.

Definition 6. (Preference Orderings) *$pref^\kappa(i,j)$, $pref^\kappa_\sim(i,j)$, $pref^\#(i,j)$, $pref^\#_\sim(i,j)$, $pref^\top(i,j)$ and $pref^\top_\sim(i,j)$ are defined by:*

$$
\begin{aligned}
& pref^\top(i,j) :\Leftrightarrow E(i \wedge \neg\Diamond^= j \wedge \Box^<(\neg i \wedge \neg j))\\
& pref^\top_\sim(i,j) :\Leftrightarrow pref^\top(i,j) \vee\\
& \qquad U((\Diamond^= i \wedge \Box^< \neg i) \leftrightarrow (\Diamond^= j \wedge \Box^< \neg j))\\
& pref^\kappa(i,j) :\Leftrightarrow E(i \wedge \neg\Diamond^= j \wedge \Box^<(\Diamond^= i \wedge \Diamond^= j))\\
& pref^\kappa_\sim(i,j) :\Leftrightarrow pref^\kappa(i,j) \vee\\
& \qquad U((\neg\Diamond^= i \wedge \Box^< \Diamond^= i) \leftrightarrow (\neg\Diamond^= j \wedge \Box^< \Diamond^= j))\\
& pref^\#(i,j) :\Leftrightarrow E(i \wedge \neg\Diamond^= j \wedge \Box^<(\Diamond^= i \leftrightarrow \Diamond^= j))\\
& pref^\#_\sim(i,j) :\Leftrightarrow pref^\#(i,j) \vee U(\Diamond^= i \leftrightarrow \Diamond^= j)
\end{aligned}
$$

To understand these definitions, recall that we say that a world identifies an object when it is part of that object and the object consists of copies of one and the same world. These copies are used to represent that an object has a property present in a property ranking. In Figure 2, for example, world w_7 is a representative of object c for the property *large*. Thus, the formula $E_i \neg\Diamond^= j$ may be read as 'object i has a property that object j does not have'. Similarly, $\Diamond^< i$ can be read as 'there is a more important property (than the current one) that object i has'. These readings may help explain the definitions. $pref^\top(i,j)$ may be read as 'there is a property such that i has it and j does not, and for all more important properties, neither i nor j has any of them'. The second disjunct in the definition of $pref^\top_\sim(i,j)$ defines when two objects are equally preferred with respect to $\top$, and may be read as 'if there is a property that i has, but i does not have any more important properties, then j has that property too and does not have any more important properties either, and vice versa'. Similar readings can be provided for the other preference operators.

Proposition 4 shows that the relation between weak and strict preference is as usual, and, moreover, a strict preference according to $\top$ or κ implies a strict preference according to #.

Proposition 4. *We have:*
1. $\models pref^s(i,j) \leftrightarrow pref^s_{\precsim}(i,j) \wedge \neg pref^s_{\precsim}(j,i)$ *for* $s \in \{\top, \kappa, \#\}$.
2. $\models pref^{\top}(i,j) \rightarrow pref^{\#}(i,j)$
3. $\models pref^{\kappa}(i,j) \rightarrow pref^{\#}(i,j)$

Example 3. Given the model of Figure 2, we can derive that $pref^{\#}(b,d)$. By definition, this is the case when $E(b \wedge \neg \Diamond^{=} d \wedge \Box^{<}(\Diamond^{=} b \leftrightarrow \Diamond^{=} d))$ is true. This means that there must be a world w that is named b that has no equally ranked world named d, and, moreover, for every higher ranked world v there is an equally ranked world named b if and only if there is an equally ranked world with name d. By inspection of Figure 2, world w_5 fits the description.

4 MPL Defines Ranked Knowledge Bases

Here we prove that the preference orderings of Definition 6 define those of Brewka [4]. Brewka [4] calls property rankings *ranked knowledge bases*, defined as follows:

Definition 7. (Ranked Knowledge Base) *A ranked knowledge base (RKB) is a set* $F \subseteq \mathcal{L}_0$ *of objective formulae together with a total pre-order* $\geq$ *on* F. *Ranked knowledge bases are represented as a set of ranked formulae* (f,k), *where* f *is an objective formula and* k, *the rank of* f, *is a non-negative integer such that* $f_1 \geq f_2$ *iff* $rank(f_1) \geq rank(f_2)$. *That is, higher rank is expressed by higher indices.*

In the setting of [4], comparing objects given a ranked knowledge base means comparing *truth assignments* which represent these objects, analogously to the representation of the three houses used in Figure 1. It is easy to see that this example is represented by the following ranked knowledge base: $\{(\mathit{affordable},3), (\mathit{closeToWork},2), (\mathit{large},1)\}$.

Object preferences can be derived in multiple ways from a ranked knowledge base. In order to define these strategies, some auxiliary definitions are introduced next. Below, $K^n(m)$ denotes the set of properties of a certain rank n that are satisfied with respect to truth assignment m; $maxsat^K(m)$ denotes the highest rank associated with the properties that are satisfied by assignment m, and $maxunsat^K(m)$ denotes the highest rank associated with the properties that are not satisfied by m.

Definition 8. *Let* K *be a ranked knowledge base and* $m \in 2^{At}$.

$$\begin{array}{lll} K^n(m) & ::= & \{f \mid (f,n) \in K, m \models f\} \\ maxsat^K(m) & ::= & -\infty \text{ if } m \not\models f_i \text{ for all } (f_i,v_i) \in K, \\ & & max\{i \mid (f,i) \in K, m \models f\} \text{ otherwise} \\ maxunsat^K(m) & ::= & -\infty \text{ if } m \models f_i \text{ for all } (f_i,v_i) \in K, \\ & & max\{i \mid (f,i) \in K, m \not\models f\} \text{ otherwise} \end{array}$$

Using these auxiliary definitions, preference orderings $m_1 \geq^K_s m_2$ are defined which mean that object (truth assignment) m_1 is (weakly) preferred over object m_2 according to strategy s.

Definition 9. (Preference Orderings) *Let K be a ranked knowledge base. Then the following preference orderings over truth assignments are defined:*
- $m_1 \geq^K_\top m_2$ *iff* $maxsat^K(m_1) \geq maxsat^K(m_2)$.
- $m_1 \geq^K_\kappa m_2$ *iff* $maxunsat^K(m_1) \leq maxunsat^K(m_2)$.
- $m_1 \geq^K_\# m_2$ *iff* $|K^n(m_1)| = |K^n(m_2)|$ *for all* n, *or there is* n *s.t.* $|K^n(m_1)| > |K^n(m_2)|$, *and for all* $j > n : |K^j(m_1)| = |K^j(m_2)|$.

To simplify, we make the assumption here that different properties cannot have the same ranking. In that case, the set of all satisfied properties of a given rank is a singleton set or the empty set, we have that $\geq$ is a strict linear order on F - also denoted by $>$, and, as a result, the $\subseteq$ and # orderings coincide. We also assume that properties in a ranked knowledge base are consistent. Finally, we may assume that a ranked knowledge base does not contain logically equivalent properties with different ranks since such occurrences except for the one ranked highest can be discarded as it has no influence on any of the preference orderings.

Definition 10. (Translation Function) *The function τ translates ranked knowledge bases $K = \langle F, \geq \rangle$ and truth assignments m to formulae and is defined by:*
- $\tau(K) ::= \bigwedge\{EC(\varphi) \mid \varphi \in F\} \wedge$
  $U(\bigvee\{C(\varphi) \mid \varphi \in F \text{ or } \varphi = \neg \bigvee\{\chi \mid \chi \in F\}\})$
  $\bigwedge\{C(\varphi) <_{\forall\forall} C(\psi) \mid \varphi, \psi \in F \;\&\; \psi > \varphi\} \wedge$
  $\bigwedge\{C(\neg \bigvee\{\varphi \mid \varphi \in F\}) <_{\forall\forall} \psi \mid \psi \in F\} \wedge$
- $\tau_{name}(m) \in Nom$
- $\tau(m) ::= \bigwedge\{E_i\varphi \mid m \models \varphi\} \cup \{\neg E_i\varphi \mid m \not\models \varphi\}$ *with* $i = \tau_{name}(m)$

The translation of a ranked knowledge base K expresses that for each property φ in K, there exists a corresponding cluster by $C\varphi$, that there are no other clusters than those specified by the properties, and one extra cluster for the case in which none of the properties is satisfied. It forces the ranking of these clusters to be the same as the property ranking induced by K, with the added extra cluster as least important one. The translation also associates an object name with a truth assignment and states for each property whether the object (truth assignment) has the property or not.

Example 4. Using the translation function, and assuming that $\tau_{name}(house_1) = b$, $\tau_{name}(house_2) = d$ and $\tau_{name}(house_3) = e$, the RKB $\{(affordable, 3), (closeToWork, 2), (large, 1)\}$ translates into:

1. $E(C(affordable)) \wedge E(C(closeToWork)) \wedge E(C(large))$
2. $U(C(affordable) \vee C(closeToWork) \vee C(large) \vee C(\neg(affordable \vee closeToWork \vee large)))$
3. $C(\neg(affordable \vee closeToWork \vee large)) <_{\forall\forall} C(large) <_{\forall\forall} C(closeToWork) <_{\forall\forall} C(affordable)$
4. $E_b(affordable) \wedge E_b(closeToWork) \wedge \neg E_b(large)$
5. $E_d(affordable) \wedge \neg E_d(closeToWork) \wedge \neg E_d(large)$
6. $\neg E_e(affordable) \wedge E_e(closeToWork) \wedge E_e(large)$

A model of this theory is shown in Figure 2. Although only objects b, d and e are specified in the theory, for illustrative reasons this model contains all possible objects (there is a world, and hence an object, for every possible valuation of the three propositional atoms). Every property has its own cluster, which means that every object satisfying that property has a world in that cluster, and that every world in that cluster satisfies that property. No worlds exist outside the four specified clusters, and the order among clusters is fixed. The only ways a model of this theory can be structurally different from the one shown are by removing objects that are not b, d or e (but then all worlds belonging to that object have to be removed at once), or by adding more worlds, but only at the same 'places' as the worlds shown.

Theorem 1 shows that every multi-attribute preference model that is a model of the translation of a particular RKB yields the same preference ordering as the original RKB.

Theorem 1. $m_1 \geq_s^K m_2$ *iff* $\models \tau(K) \wedge \tau(m_1) \wedge \tau(m_2) \rightarrow pref^s_{\sim}(\tau_{name}(m_1), \tau_{name}(m_2))$ *where* $s \in \{\top, \kappa, \#\}$.

Proof. *Assume that* $\tau_{name}(m_1) = i$ *and* $\tau_{name}(m_2) = j$*, and observe that the translation of* $K = \langle F, \geq \rangle$ *is equivalent to:*
(1) $C(\neg(f_1 \vee \ldots \vee f_n)) <_{\forall\forall} C(f_1) <_{\forall\forall} \ldots <_{\forall\forall} C(f_n)$,
(2) $\forall f \in F : E(C(f))$ *and*
(3) $U(C(f_1) \vee \ldots \vee C(f_n) \vee C(\neg(f_1 \vee \ldots \vee f_n)))$.
For brevity, we only prove the left to right direction for the case $m_1 >_\kappa^K m_2$*. Then we have* $maxunsat^K(m_1) < maxunsat^K(m_2)$ *and* $maxunsat^K(m_2) > -\infty$*, so there is a formula* f_k *in* F *such that*
(4) $m_2 \not\models f_k$,
(5) $m_1 \models f_k$ *and*
(6) $\forall f' > f_k : m_1 \models f' \;\&\; m_2 \models f'$.
Applying the translation function τ*, we then get:*
(4) $\neg E_j f_k$,
(5) $E_i f_k$ *and*
(6) $\forall f' > f_k : E_i f' \wedge E_j f'$.
From (5), (2) and Prop. 3.3 it then follows that
(8) $E_i C(f_k)$.
From (8), (4) and Prop. 3.2 it follows that
(9) $E_i \neg \Diamond^= j \wedge C(f_k)$.
And from (6) and Prop. 3.1 it follows that
(10) $\forall f' > f_k : \Diamond^= i \wedge \Diamond^= j$.
Using (1) and (3) we obtain
(11) $C(f_k) \rightarrow \Box^<(C(f_{k+1}) \vee \ldots \vee C(f_n))$.
From (10) and (11) we obtain
(12) $C(f_k) \rightarrow \Box^< \Diamond^= i \wedge \Box^< \Diamond^= j$.
Then (9) and (12) can be combined into $E(i \wedge \neg \Diamond^= j \wedge \Box^<(\Diamond^= i \wedge \Diamond^= j))$*, which is the definition of* $pref^\kappa(i, j)$.

Example 5. We now show how to formally derive a preference statement from the formulae obtained by translating a ranked knowledge base in Example 4. As an illustration, we show that $pref^\kappa(b,d)$ can be derived.
From (4.4) $E_b(closeToWork)$, (4.1) $E(C(closeToWork))$ and Proposition 3.3 we obtain

(1) $E_b C(closeToWork)$.
From (4.5) $\neg E_d(closeToWork)$ and Proposition 3.2 it follows that
(2a) $C(closeToWork) \rightarrow \neg \Diamond^{=} d$.
From 4.3 and 4.2 we can derive that
(2b) $C(closeToWork) \rightarrow \Box^{<} C(affordable)$.
By combining (1), (2a) and (2b) we derive
(3) $E_b(\neg \Diamond^{=} d \wedge \Box^{<} C(affordable))$.
Now, from Proposition 3.1, (4.4) $E_b(affordable)$ and (4.5) $E_d(affordable)$, we derive
(4a) $C(affordable) \rightarrow \Diamond^{=} b$ and
(4b) $C(affordable) \rightarrow \Diamond^{=} b$.
Using (3), (4a), and (4b), we obtain $E_b(\neg \Diamond^{=} d \wedge \Box^{<}(\Diamond^{=} b \wedge \Diamond^{=} d))$, which is the definition of $pref^{\kappa}(b,d)$.

5 Conclusion

In this paper we introduced a modal logic for qualitative multi-attribute preferences. The logic is based on Girard's binary preference logic [7], but extends this logic with objects and clusters that introduce the possibility to reason explicitly about multiple attributes. We showed that multi-attribute preference logic is expressive enough to define various natural preference orderings based on property rankings [4,6]. The additional value of the logic is that it is possible to reason about these different preference orderings within the logic. This means we cannot only reason about which objects are preferred according to a certain ordering, but also about the relation between different orderings as is shown in Proposition 4.

One possible extension to multi-attribute preference logic is the introduction of indices for different agents. In this way, distinct preference orderings for several agents can be expressed. This introduces the possibility to reason about properties such as pareto-optimality of objects (an object is pareto-optimal if there is no other object that is better for at least one agent and not worse for the other agents), which is useful in the context of e.g. joint decision making or negotiation.

We have made the assumptions that attributes are binary, and that priority orderings are total linear orders. In future work we plan to investigate how we can loosen these assumptions. For example, if multiple attributes can have the same importance, the # and $\subseteq$ orderings will differ and we will be able to encode trade-offs between attributes.

Our main concern in this paper has been the expressiveness of multi-attribute preference logic. Other questions such as a complete axiomatization of the logic, succinctness and complexity remain future work. We plan to develop a reasoning system in which agents can reason about qualitative multi-attribute preferences in various settings. In our future work we will focus more on the reasoning mechanism and how different domains can be modelled accurately in our approach.

A more detailed comparison of multi-attribute preference logic with other preference logics such as Qualitative Choice Logic [5] is planned. Other areas for future work concern the representation of dependent properties and the relation of multi-attribute preference logic to e.g. CP-nets [3].

Acknowledgements. This research is supported by the Dutch Technology Foundation STW, applied science division of NWO and the Technology Program of the Ministry of Economic Affairs. It is part of the Pocket Negotiator project with grant number VICI-project 08075.

References

1. Blackburn, P., Seligman, J.: Hybrid languages. Journal of Logic, Language and Information 4(3), 251–272 (1995)
2. Boutilier, C.: Toward a logic for qualitative decision theory. In: 4th International Conference on Principles of Knowledge Representation and Reasoning (KR), pp. 75–86 (1994)
3. Boutilier, C., Brafman, R.I., Domshlak, C., Hoos, H.H., Poole, D.: CP-nets: A tool for representing and reasoning with conditional ceteris paribus preference statements. Journal of Artificial Intelligence Research 21, 135–191 (2004)
4. Brewka, G.: A rank based description language for qualitative preferences. In: 16th European Conference on Artificial Intelligence (ECAI), pp. 303–307 (2004)
5. Brewka, G., Benferhat, S., Le Berre, D.: Qualitative choice logic. Artificial Intelligence 157(1-2), 203–237 (2004)
6. Coste-Marquis, S., Lang, J., Liberatore, P., Marquis, P.: Expressive power and succinctness of propositional languages for preference representation. In: 9th International Conference on Principles of Knowledge Representation and Reasoning (KR), pp. 203–212 (2004)
7. Girard, P.: Modal Logic for Belief and Preference Change. PhD thesis, Universiteit van Amsterdam (2008)
8. Halpern, J.Y., Lakemeyer, G.: Multi-agent only knowing. Journal of Logic and Computation 11(1), 41–70 (2001)
9. Hansson, S.O.: Preference logic. In: Gabbay, D.M., Günthner, F. (eds.) Handbook of Philosophical Logic, 2nd edn., vol. 4, pp. 319–393. Kluwer (2001)
10. Keeney, R.L., Raiffa, H.: Decisions with multiple objectives: preferences and value tradeoffs. Cambridge University Press (1993)
11. Liu, F.: Changing for the Better: Preference Dynamics and Agent Diversity. PhD thesis, Universiteit van Amsterdam (2008)
12. von Wright, G.H.: The Logic of Preference: An Essay. Edinburgh University Press (1963)

An Empirical Study of Patterns in Agent Programs

Koen V. Hindriks, M. Birna van Riemsdijk, and Catholijn M. Jonker

Delft University of Technology, P.O. Box 5031, 2600 GA, Delft, The Netherlands
{k.v.hindriks,m.b.vanriemsdijk,c.m.jonker}@tudelft.nl

Abstract. Various agent programming languages and frameworks have been developed by now, but very few systematic studies have been done as to how the language constructs in these languages may and are in fact used in practice. Performing a study of these aspects contributes to the design of best practices or programming guidelines for agent programming. Following a first empirical study of agent programs written in the GOAL agent programming language for the dynamic blocks world, in this paper we perform a considerably more extensive analysis of agent programs for the first-person shooter game UNREAL TOURNAMENT 2004. We identify and discuss several structural code patterns based on a qualitative analysis of the code, and analyze for which purposes the constructs of GOAL are typically used. This provides insight into more practical aspects of the development of agent programs, and forms the basis for development of programming guidelines and language improvements.

1 Introduction

Shoham was one of the first who proposed to use common sense notions such as beliefs and goals to build rational agents [15], coining a new programming paradigm called *agent-oriented programming*. Inspired by Shoham, a variety of agent-oriented programming languages and frameworks have been proposed since then [3]. For several of them, interpreters and Integrated Development Environments (IDEs) are being developed. Some of them have been designed mainly with a focus on building practical applications (e.g., JACK [18] and Jadex [14]), while for others the focus has been also or mainly on the languages' theoretical underpinnings (e.g., 2APL [6], GOAL [8], and Jason [4]).

In this paper, we take the language GOAL as object of study. GOAL is a high-level programming language to program rational agents that derive their choice of action from their beliefs and goals. Although the language's theoretical basis is important, it *is* designed by taking a definite *engineering stance* and aims at providing useful programming constructs to develop agent programs. Starting with small-size applications such as (dynamic) blocks world , the language is being applied more and more in larger domains where agents have to function in *real-time and highly dynamic environments*. To be more specific, recently the language has been used in a project with first year BSc students of computer science, in which groups of students had to program a team of agents to control bots in the first-person shooter game UNREAL TOURNAMENT 2004 (UT2004).

N. Desai, A. Liu, and M. Winikoff (Eds.): PRIMA 2010, LNAI 7057, pp. 196–211, 2012.

Software engineering aspects become increasingly important as applications get more complex. For this reason, in [16] a first empirical study was presented on how the language constructs are used in practice to program agents, and how easy it is to read the resulting programs with the aim of designing a set of *best practices and programming guidelines* that support GOAL programmers. In that paper, three GOAL programs for the dynamic blocks world domain were studied.

In this paper, we take this a step further and analyze GOAL programs that were developed for UT2004 by the students of the project. This study is much more extensive than [16]: the *application domain* of UT2004 is far more challenging than the dynamic blocks world, which has resulted in much larger programs (approximately 800 lines of code per agent for the larger ones, in comparison with around 100 for the dynamic blocks world); the GOAL *language* has been *extended* significantly since the programs studied in [16] were developed; the *number of available programs* to study is much larger, namely 12 for the UT2004 domain in contrast with 3 for the blocks world domain; the programs are *multi-agent systems*, rather than single agents, which gives us the opportunity to study organization structures as used and understood by students.

The focus is on a *qualitative* study of the code of the agent programs. In addition, we analyze several metrics on the code. Due to the size of the study we do not consider run-time behavior in this paper. We identify and discuss *structural code patterns* for the programming abstractions present in the latest version of GOAL, and analyze for which *purposes* the constructs are typically used. Through this empirical software engineering, we contribute to forming a body of knowledge leading to widely accepted and well-formed theories about engineering GOAL agents.

2 The Agent Programming Language GOAL

In this study, the agent programming language GOAL has been used. GOAL is a high-level language for programming *rational agents* using cognitive concepts such as *beliefs* and *goals*. The language is similar to other agent programming languages such as 2APL, Jadex, and Jason. Due to space limitations, the presentation of GOAL itself here will be very limited and we cannot illustrate all features present in the language. For more information, we refer to [8].

GOAL agents are logic-based agents in the sense that they use a knowledge representation language to represent their knowledge, beliefs and goals to reason about the environment in which they act. The knowledge representation technology we used is SWI Prolog [1]. One of GOAL's distinguishing features is that GOAL agents have a mental state that consists of the *knowledge*, *beliefs* and *goals* of the agent. Knowledge is used to represent conceptual and domain knowledge that is static. During a computation of the agent the knowledge of that agent is never modified. As knowledge is always true, it can be used in combination with both beliefs and goals to derive new beliefs and goals, respectively. For example, if an agent has a conjunctive goal to have a weapon and ammo, and knows that that combination always results in a loaded weapon, it also has the derived goal to have a loaded weapon. The belief base and goal base are the dynamic components of an agent's mental state. Beliefs change by performing actions; GOAL also provides two built-in actions `insert(`φ`)` and `delete(`φ`)` to insert and remove information from an agent's belief base. Goals in a GOAL agent represent so-called *achievement* goals. An achievement goal is a condition that the agent wants to be true but which is currently not believed to be true by the agent. An achievement goal φ thus never follows from the agent's beliefs (in combination with its knowledge) and this constraint is enforced as a rationality constraint. The rationale is that an agent should not put time and resources into realizing an achievement goal that has already been achieved. This also means that whenever a goal has been (believed to be) *completely* realized, the goal is *automatically* removed from the goal base of the agent. GOAL also provides two built-in actions `adopt(`φ`)` and `drop(`φ`)` to, respectively, adopt a new achievement goal and drop some of the agent's current goals. The `drop` action allows an agent to revise its goals in light of, for example, changing circumstances.

Actions are selected by a GOAL agent by inspecting their mental state and by means of *rules*. GOAL agents are able to inspect their mental state by means of *mental state conditions*. Mental state conditions allow the agent to inspect both its beliefs and its goals, and provide GOAL agents with expressive reasoning capabilities. In an agent program, mental atoms of the form `bel(`φ`)` and `a-goal(`φ`)` are used to verify whether φ is believed or φ is an achievement goal.

Actions are selected in GOAL by rules of the form **if** $<$ *cond* $>$ **then** $<$ *action* $>$ where $<$ *cond* $>$ is a mental state condition. The $<$ *action* $>$ part may consist of single actions, or of multiple actions that are combined by means of the `+` operator. Rules provide GOAL agents with the capability to react flexibly and reactively to environment changes but also allow a programmer to define more complicated strategies. Rules may be located in either the *program section* or the *perceptrule section* of an agent program. In the program section, every cycle of the interpreter a *single* applicable rule is selected and rules in this section are typically used to select actions that are executed in the environment. In the perceptrule section, every cycle of the interpreter *all* applicable rules are executed in order. Rules in the perceptrule section are typically used to process percepts from the environment and messages received from other agents. All built-in actions of GOAL may occur in both sections but *user-specified* actions of both internal or environment actions may only occur in the program section. This restriction implies that the number of environment actions executed every cycle is limited to at most one.

Modules provide a means to structure action rules into clusters and to define different strategies for different situations [8]. In particular, modules facilitate structuring the tasks and role assignment of an agent, as it allows an agent to focus on some of its current goals and disregard others for the moment. Different types of modules are distinguished based on whether the module is entered by means of a trigger related to the beliefs or the goals of an agent.

Finally, *mas files* provide a recipe for launching multi-agent systems composed of several GOAL agents. A mas file specifies which environment to start and how it should be initialized, which agent source code files are used to create agents, and when to create an agent. An agent may or may not be connected to an environment. In our UT2004 case study agents may be connected to bots; an agent may be launched e.g. when a bot becomes available in the environment. Agents connected to an environment are able to execute environment actions to change the environment and receive percepts from the environment which enables an agent to monitor its environment. Percepts - received every cycle of the interpreter - are stored in an agent's percept base. At the end of each cycle this percept base is cleared again and all percepts are removed. This implies that each cycle all percepts need to be processed immediately.

Additional features of GOAL include among others a macro definition construct to associate intuitive labels with mental state conditions to increase the readability of the agent code, options to apply rules in various ways, and communication. Various communication primitives are available but the most basic action is the `send` action to send a message to another agent. Messages that are sent as well as those that are received are archived in the mailbox of an agent, and are only removed when the agent explicitly does so.

3 Experimental Setup

We perform a qualitative study (rather than a quantitative study) since it better fits the aim of this paper, namely to analyze how students use GOAL as a step towards developing programming guidelines for GOAL. Qualitative methods are used for exploratory research in which hypotheses are formed, while quantitative methods are used to test pre-determined hypothesis and produce generalizable results [12]. Our research is exploratory, since we are in the process of investigating which structural code patterns might be part of programming guidelines for GOAL, as examples of recommended or not recommended uses of the language (comparable to design patterns and antipatterns used in software engineering).

In programming language research, several *criteria for good language design* have been identified. The following are particularly relevant in the context of this paper. The value of linear flow of control was, for example, recognized, primarily for its value in program debugging and verification, it was recognized that a language must be comprehensible, so that programs written in the language can be read and maintained, and modular program structures were observed to make an important contribution to the production of large software systems [17]. Moreover, in [10] several language evaluation criteria are distinguished among which: human factors (to what degree does the language alow a competent programmer to code algorithms easily and correctly, how easy is the language to learn), software engineering (maintainability, reusability, etc.), and application domain (how well a language supports development for a specific domain).

In agent research, software engineering has mainly been studied in the context of agent-oriented software engineering methodolgies such as Prometheus [13]. These methodologies, however, are either too abstract to provide programming guidelines for concrete agent programming languages, or, to the extent to which they provide concrete implementation guidance, do not fit the programming abstractions as used in languages like GOAL. In the agent programming field, [11] focuses on structural metrics related to dependencies between abstractions, which among others indirectly predict the likelihood of bugs. This paper can be viewed as complementary to ours.

Subjects. The programmers whose code we have analyzed are first-year BSc computing science students who followed our second-semester course on Programming Multi-Agent Systems and the consecutive Project Multi-Agent Systems. These students are the subjects of our experimental research. In the course the students were trained in both Prolog as well as the agent programming language GOAL. As an indication of the level these students had, we briefly provide some observations related to their skills in Prolog which is a prerequisite for writing GOAL agents since Prolog is used as the knowledge representation language in these agents. The Prolog skills demonstrated by students are basic but sufficient. Students were, for example, able to apply negation as failure and recursion.

Project. UT2004 is an interactive, multi-player computer game where bots can compete with each other in various arenas. The game provides ten different game types. The game type that was used in the student project is called *Capture The Flag* (CTF). In this type of game, two teams compete with each other that have as main goal to conquer the flag located in the home base of the other team. Points are scored by bringing the flag of the opponent's team to ones own home base while making sure ones own flag remains in its home base. Students have to implement basic agent skills regarding walking around in the environment and collecting weapons and other relevant materials, communication between agents, fighting against bots of the other team, and the strategy and teamwork for capturing the flag. We chose CTF because teams of bots have to cooperate, which requires students to think about coordination and teamwork in a mas.

In the project, students are divided into teams of five students each. Every group has to develop a team of GOAL agents that control three UT bots in the CTF scenario. In the project manual, it was suggested that although the number of bots in the UT environment is three, students can also implement agents that do not control bots in the environment, e.g., for coordination purposes. The time available for developing the agent team was approximately two months, in which each student has to spend about 1 to 1,5 days a week working on the project. At the end of the project, there was a competition in which the developed agent teams compete against one another. The grade is determined based on the students' report and their final presentation.

For the project, an interface was designed that is suitable for connecting logic-based BDI (Belief-Desire-Intention) agents to a real-time game. Such an interface needs to be designed at the right abstraction level. The reasoning typically employed by logic-based BDI agents does not make them suitable for controlling low-level details of a bot. It makes little sense, for example, to require such agents to deliberate about the degrees of rotation a bot should make when it makes a turn. Such low-level control is better delegated to a more behavioral control layer, which was built on top of Pogamut [5]. At the same time, however, the BDI agent should be able to remain in control and the interface should support sufficiently finegrained control. Details on the interface can be found in [9].

Sample. In quantitative research, a random and relatively large sample of subjects to study is selected such that results can be generalized to the population of interest. By contrast, in qualitative research the most productive sample to answer the research question is selected, e.g., based on experience or expertise of the subjects. In our case, 12 teams of 5 students participated in the project. The focus of our qualitative analysis is on the code of Teams 1, 2, and 3 who performed best in terms of code and performance in the competition, and Team 12 who performed worst in terms of code and performance.

4 Identification of Patterns

In this section, we present the observations we made by doing a qualitative analysis of the code of our sample. We identify numerous *structural code patterns*, and augment this qualitative analysis with *metrics* concerning, e.g., the number of times certain GOAL constructs were used. Also, we analyze for which *purposes* the constructs are typically used. Sections 4.1 to 4.7 each treat a particular language element; sect. 4.8 discusses coordination and mas organization; sect. 4.9 discusses more general software engineering aspects.

4.1 Knowledge and Belief Base

The knowledge base typically was used to define predicates for computing, e.g., distances and other relevant aspects related to navigation. The belief base was used to keep track of the actual state of the environment and typical functions of code in the belief base are to (i) represent global features of the environment (e.g., where is the flag), and (ii) represent assigned tasks or roles (agents were typically assigned a single role or task at any one time). On average the knowledge base was significantly larger than the belief base (23.25 versus 15.67 clauses, with a standard deviation of 24.23 versus 8.7, respectively); moreover, the number of predicates defined in the knowledge base is larger (ranging from 7 to more than 25 predicates) than that in the belief base (about 5) with some exceptions. This suggests that most of the domain logic was located in the knowledge base, in line with its main function to represent conceptual and domain knowledge.

One observation made by inspecting the code of various teams is that this code includes predicates in the knowledge base that have motivational connotations such as `priority` to indicate relative importance and `needItem` and `wants`. The code fragments for defining these predicates are significant portions of the code, sometimes more than a 100 lines of code.

4.2 Goal Base

The use of explicit goals has been limited. On average about 1.13 initial goals were used with a standard deviation of 1.36. By inspection of code, it turns out that initial goals most of the time are abstract goals such as `visitFlags` or even `win`. These abstract goals are not actually used in action or percept rules and are never removed, neither explicitly using a drop action nor implicitly by inserting a belief into the belief base which implies the goal has been achieved. These abstract goals thus are redundant and serve no functional purpose. In 6 out of 12 teams goals are added during runtime by using the adopt action; on average 3.86 adopts are used by these 6 teams with a standard deviation of 4.29.

The goals adopted dynamically are used in context conditions of modules. In these cases, the context condition consists of a check on a single goal which forms the goal of the module, e.g., goal `protectBot` for the module `protector` (Team 3). In these cases, goals are *removed explicitly* (never implicitly) using drop actions (occurring in both action and percept rules). In Team 3, the goal of a module is removed only *after* the module was exited explicitly based on beliefs about role changes. In Team 2, an action rule `if goal( not(camp) ) then exit-module.` is present at the top of the camp module, to express that the module should be exited if the agent no longer has the camp goal. However, this behavior is already in the semantics of GOAL, and thus the rule is redundant. Another observation on the goals used by Team 3 is that some goals could naturally be modelled as *achievement goals* (even though not used as such), while others rather express an *activity over time*. For example, the goal `getFlag` (which expresses an activity) could be replaced by the achievement goal `haveFlag`. In fact, Team 3 uses an action rule to drop the goal `getFlag` if the agent believes `haveFlag`. The goal `protectBot` expresses a behavior that is not so easily transformed into an achievement goal, since it is not clear in which state the agent has "achieved" protecting a bot. Finally, Team 12 has a one-to-one relation between goals and modules where each module corresponds with a different role or task. The use of goals in conjunction with modules and their function is a recurrent pattern in the code that has been analyzed.

We investigated various hypotheses related to the use of goals, built-in goal-related actions, and modules. First, for all teams except Team 6, whenever the code contains occurrences of `drop` actions the code also contained `adopt` actions. The reason that in one agent of Team 6 only one `drop` action was used is that the agent has one goal `start` in the initial goal base that is used to *initialize* the roles of other agents and thereafter is dropped. Second, whenever an `adopt` action occurs it occurs in tandem with `drop` actions. And, finally, occurrences of `adopt` actions entail the presence of modules. The latter suggests that goals have been typically used to implement roles.

4.3 Rules

As explained, rules in a GOAL agent can be placed in the *program* and the *perceptrule* section. The former kind of rules are called *action rules* and are used among others to select actions that are performed in the environment. These rules define the agent's strategy or action selection policy, and determine what the bot that the agent controls will do in the environment. The latter kind of rules are called *percept rules* and are used, among others, to process percepts and messages. Rules can be classified along other dimensions based on their use and in comments in analyzed code we find that rules are used as *communication rules* to send messages, *exit rules* to exit a module, as *mailbox cleanup rules* to cleanup messages stored in an agent's mailbox, etc.

Some examples of patterns observed in rules are:

```
if bel(received(_, role(X)), role(Y))
  then insert(role(X)) + delete(role(Y))
```

This rule inserts an instance of a predicate `role` that has been received via communication and overwrites an old instance of that predicate.

The following rule retrieves the agent's name and communicates the role with the name to all other agents *once*:

```
if bel( me(X) ) then sendonce(allother, navServer(X)).
```

Although the last rule can only be used to select the single `sendonce` action, using the + operator multiple actions may be selected simultaneously as illustrated by the second last rule above. This feature allows an agent to execute more than one action in a cycle of the interpreter. All teams make frequent use of the + operator to execute multiple actions with one action rule.

The average number of action rules per agent over all twelve teams is approximately 28. The average number for agents that are connected to the environment is 42. The average number for agents connected to the environment for Teams 1, 2 and 3 is 65.5. As action rules determine strategy, this suggests that Teams 1, 2, and 3 have implemented the most elaborate strategies and suggests more strategic programming. This is in line with performance in the competition where Teams 1, 2, and 3 outperformed other teams. The hypothesis that Teams 1, 2, and 3 have coded more elaborate strategies is also corroborated by the fact that the number of percept rules used by these teams is only little above average.

Since goals are used to a very limited extent, the majority of mental state conditions in action rules consists of conditions on beliefs. The number of conjuncts of belief conditions varies, but typically no more than five conjuncts are used. Since most conditions are on beliefs only, never more than one belief operator is used per action rule. This holds for all twelve teams.

Percept rules, i.e. rules in the perceptrule section, are used for several main purposes: processing percepts and messages, sending messages, cleaning up the mailbox, and adoption and dropping of goals (e.g. Team 3). The average number of percept rules per agent over all twelve teams is approximately 51. The average number for agents that are connected to the environment is 69. The average number for agents connected to the environment for Teams 1, 2 and 3 is 78. Note that the number of percept rules overall is higher than the number of action rules per agent. This probably is related to the fact that *all* applicable percept rules are executed in every cycle of the interpreter whereas only *one* applicable action rule is executed in that same cycle. The perceptrule section thus allows to process *all* incoming percepts and *all* received messages. It also facilitates updating mental states in other ways, for example, to adopt a goal when the agent learns the environment has changed.

4.4 Program Section

The program section contains all the action rules, from which exactly one of the applicable action rules is selected for execution. This section comes with the option to evaluate rules randomly or in linear order. When rules are evaluated randomly, a rule is chosen randomly, and the conditions associated with the rule and action(s) are evaluated; in case these conditions hold, the action(s) is executed, otherwise randomly another rule is chosen. Linear order evaluation means that rules are evaluated in order. This type of evaluation is deterministic and potentially ease programming as conditions of rules that have been evaluated but failed can be assumed to be false in rules below these rules. Linear order may provide a programmer thus with a greater sense of control. It turns out that all teams use the option `order=linear` to enforce linear execution of action rules.

The management bot of Team 1 does not have action rules in the program section. All other agents have (functional) action rules in the program section. The number of action rules on top level, i.e., not within modules, is typically small (ranging from 0 to 2 in Teams 1, 2 and 3).

4.5 Modules

Modules facilitate structuring code as well as the behavior of agents and are used by all teams. A module may be entered when an associated context condition holds and thereafter only *action* rules inside the module are executed. A module can be exited automatically or by means of selecting and executing an `exit-module` action. Automated exit of modules works differently for the two types of modules, namely *reactive* and *goal-based* modules. Reactive modules have a context condition that does not check whether goals are present but does inspect the beliefs of the agent; such modules are automatically exited when there are no options anymore to execute an action. Goal-based modules have context conditions that inspect the goal base of an agent and after entering the module focus on goals that satisfy the context condition; such modules are automatically exited when all goals have been achieved. Note that the semantics of exiting a module is built-in but is a delayed effect. That is, exiting may happen after a number of cycles of the interpreter that is not easily predicted.

Teams 1, 2, and 12, who make use of a management agent, have significantly fewer (sub)modules for this agent (0, 1, and 0 respectively) than for the agents that are connected to bots (13, 7, and 4, respectively). The average number of (sub)modules used in the agents of all twelve teams is approximately 3. Although a module may contain the same sections as a GOAL agent except for the perceptrule section, often, only the program section is used in modules.

Modules are used to encapsulate behavior for *roles or (high-level) tasks*. For example, Team 2 distinguishes the modules defender, assault, bodyguard, flag-carrier, and hunter on top level, which form the roles as indicated by corresponding context conditions such as `bel ( role(defender) )`. Team 1 distinguishes capture, defend, attack, and waitAtEnemyBase, which form tasks as indicated by corresponding context conditions such as `bel(task(capture(_)) )`.

If submodules are used, they are used one level deep, i.e., a module within a module. Team 1 makes frequent use of submodules (1 to 3 per top level module) and Team 2 uses one submodule (`camp` as a submodule of `defender`). Teams 3 and 12 do not make use of submodules.

Several patterns can be observed concerning strategies for *entering and exiting modules*. The context condition usually consists of a single belief or goal condition, expressing the *task* (Team 1 uses, e.g., `bel(task(capture(_))` and similarly for other modules) as the context condition for the module `capture`), the *role* (Team 2 uses, e.g., the context condition `bel ( role(defender) )` in the module `defender` and similarly for other modules), or the *goal* of the module (Team 3 uses, e.g., the context condition `a-goal ( getFlag )` in the attacker module and similarly for other modules). Teams 1, 2, 3 and 12 use the `exit-module` action to explicitly specify when to exit the module. Modules typically start with such an action rule, which has as the condition the negation of the context condition of the module, e.g., Team 2 uses `bel( not(role(defender)) )` in the defender module where the context condition is `bel ( role(defender) )`. Sometimes, additional action rules for explicitly exiting modules are introduced. For example, Team 1 uses rules that allow the agent to exit the module because it has a more important task (if the agent sees an item it needs, it will get it and afterwards continue).

Interestingly, Team 6 uses modules for initialization purposes. Their management agent uses a single goal `start` which is present in the initial goal base of that agent to enter a module that contains some initialization code; after executing that code the initial goal `start` is dropped and the module is exited. (Recall that Team 6 also is the only team that has an agent with a `drop` action without an `adopt` action; this explains why.)

4.6 Actions Specification

The action specification section needs to contain specifications for all actions that are used in the agent program but not built-in into GOAL. Such actions are called *user-specified* actions, and can be actions with effects only on the mental state, called *internal actions*, as well as actions which also change the environment, called *environment actions*. In principle there is no need to introduce *internal actions* as whatever can be achieved with such actions can be achieved with the built-in actions of GOAL but introducing such actions may increase readability.

Concerning *internal actions*, i.e., actions that are not executed in the environment, we observe that only Teams 1, 2 and 4 have used these. Team 1 only implements a dummy `nothing` action. Teams 2 and 4 implement internal actions only in the management bot which is not connected to the environment.

All agents that are connected to the environment contain action specifications for *environment actions*. The interface to the UT2004 environment made available in the student project [9] provides 9 different actions with a range of different parameters to select from. Actions, without mentioning parameters, include, for example, `selectWeapon`, `goto`, `pursue`, `lookAt`. On average the `goto` and `halt` actions are used 23 times versus 13 times that other actions are used.

The `goto` and `halt` actions thus are used about 4 to 5 times more often than other actions. This suggests that navigational issues are dominant in the project.

In action specifications, we make several observations concerning the use of *pre- and postconditions* in environment actions. First, we can distinguish actions for moving around in the environment, namely `goto`, `pursue`, `halt` and `respawn`, from other actions such as `selectWeapon`. For moving actions, Teams 1, 2, and 3 use pre- and postconditions that express how to change the agent's moving state. The moving state is expressed by all three teams as `state(moving(Route))`, `state(pursue)`, or `state(reached([])`. This is related to the fact that moving actions are typically *durative* (except for the `halt` action), and it needs to be recorded whether the agent is currently executing such an action. For *instantaneous* actions, postconditions typically express the (immediate) effect of the action, such as the current weapon for `selectWeapon` (Teams 2 and 3), or the postcondition `true`, in which case percepts are used for observing the effect of the action in the agent's next reasoning cycle (Team 1).

4.7 Communication

Plain communication in which send actions of the form `send(A,Proposition)` are used is distinguished from *advanced* communication with mental models in which actions of the form `send(A,:Proposition)`, `send(A,!Proposition)`, `send(A,?Proposition)` are used. Mostly plain communication is used. Team 3 uses a few messages with :, e.g., `send( allother, :myTeam(MyName, MyRole))`. The management agent of Team 1 uses a few instances of messages with `!`, e.g., `send(Bot, !task(capture(return)))`, to tell other agents what to do.

Two main ways of *handling received messages* can be distinguished. The first is by *preprocessing* messages using percept rules, which insert the received information into the belief base and delete the received message. The following pattern for preprocessing messages is used by Teams 1 and 3, and the agent connected to the environment of Team 2.

```
if bel(received(A,Proposition))
then insert(Proposition) + delete(received(A,Proposition))
```

The second is by using the received messages directly in conditions of action rules to select the next action (the management agent of Team 2), without preprocessing them. Team 2 also uses the `received` predicate in the knowledge base of the management agent. The first method yields better readable code because action rules and knowledge base are not cluttered with `received` predicate, and allows reasoning with the added propositions using the knowledge and belief base. The second method may have efficiency benefits since no preprocessing is needed, and is simpler since no preprocessing rules have to be written.

4.8 Coordination and MAS Organization

The *organisation structures* chosen by the students were hierarchical and network [7]. Irrespective of the organisation structure the teams used roles (or tasks) to differentiate in behaviour and let the bots change their behaviour over time, with the exception of Team 11. Team 11 had a static role division over the bots. Team 7 uses a bit of a mixture; two of their bots have to change roles depending on the game state, the third always has to defend the flag.

The hierarchical models all consist of one management agent and three team member bots, where the team members were just copies of each other. The bots in the teams using a network organisation (Teams 3, and 11) did not collectively deliberate about strategy and tactics. Each bot decides for itself when to switch roles and only informs the others of its new role. In the hierarchical teams the management agent gets progress information from the team member bots and on the basis of that information decides on role changes for the bots.

The initialisation differed at bit over the teams. Some had the management agent assign the roles arbitrary over the bots (e.g., Team 12), some initially gave the bots a kind of `nothing` role (e.g., Team 1), some intially gave each of the bots a specific active rol like defender, attacker (e.g., Team 3), and Team 11 used three differently coded bots (an attacker, a defender and a support bot).

The roles and their number in different teams vary. The smallest number of roles used is two: attacker and defender (Team 5). Some introduced three roles: hunter, defender, and supporter. Typically, however, a bit more variation was used, as for example by Team 2 who used: attacker, bodyguard, defender, flagcarrier, hunter, and none. The more roles, the more rules were defined to switch between behaviours, and in general the more sophisticated the code to determine the expected behaviour for the various roles.

4.9 Human Factors and Software Engineering

We make several observations concerning human factors and software engineering, in particular with respect to readability, maintainability, and reusability.

We observe that none of the teams have used *macros*. Readability of mental state conditions in rules might have been improved by the use of macros, since the number of conjuncts in these conditions can become relatively large (see Section 4.3). A large number of conjuncts can make it difficult to grasp what is expressed by the condition. Macros may not have been used because they received little attention in the lectures preceding the project, since their definition and meaning is relatively simple. Another reason may be related to the fact that the students used only one belief operator per rule. This may make it less natural to use macros, since one might expect that multiple macro definitions would be used to replace belief conditions with many conjuncts. This would then require the use of multiple macros in rules, instead of using a single belief condition.

Another observation related to human factors and software engineering is that we found frequent occurrences of *duplicate code*. The most notable example was found in the code of Team 3, which coded two agent files that are almost exact duplicates (lines of code = 884). The only difference seems to concern the initial role of the agents. Duplicates are undesirable since it makes it more difficult to understand resulting programs (readability), as it is often not easy to identify the differences between very similar pieces of code. Also, it has a negative influence on maintainability, since changes have to be duplicated too.

Further, we observe that Team 1 uses *hardcoding of agent names* both in the manager agent as well as in the agent program that is used to launch agents that are connected to a bot in the environment. This introduces dependencies between these files which are hard to maintain as, for example, such hardcoding makes it difficult to extend or reduce the number of agents launched in a mas file. Reducing the number of agents would cause runtime errors (as messages are being sent to agents that do not exist) and extending the number of agents would decrease the functionality of these new agents as messages will never be sent to these additional agents. An example of the use of hardcoded agent names is the following. In the agent program that is connected to the environment, percept rules are used to store information about the environment in the belief base, and to send this information to the manager agent. The information sent to the manager agent is divided over the other agents, yielding the following patterns for percept rules, where `zombieA` is the name of an agent connected to the environment, and `godMother` is the name of the manager agent:

```
if bel (me(zombieA), percept(<Percept>))
   then insert(<Percept>) + send(godMother, :<Percept>)
if bel (not(me(zombieA)), percept(<Percept>) )
   then insert(<Percept>).
```

5 Discussion

Explicit Control Several of our observations suggest that programmers prefer *explicit control* over *built-in semantics with delayed effects*. In particular, determinism (by selecting *linear rule order* evaluation, Section 4.4) is preferred over non-determinism (random action option selection). This is related to linear flow of control, which has been proposed as a criterion for good language design (see Section 3). Another well-known paradigm of computing that involves non-determinism is concurrent programming. Non-determinism in concurrent programming stems from the fact that it is unknown how much of one process is executed during the time another one executes an instruction. Interestingly, high-school students of concurrent programming were found to avoid using concurrency [2]. Another observation related to explicit control is that explicit strategies for exiting modules were programmed using the `exit-module` action, rather than relying on the automatic exit mechanisms of the language (see Section 4.5). Also, goals were not used as often as could have been. What's more, if goals *were* used, automatic goal deletion upon achievement was not exploited, since corresponding beliefs were never added to the belief base.

We conjecture that these findings are on the one hand due to an *inherent preference for explicit control*, and on the other hand due to *lack of understanding* of these mechanisms. Exam results indicate that students were more competent in explaining and/or applying action rules, action specifications, linear rule order option and basic Prolog than they were able to do so for modules and subtle differences between communication primitives (`send` versus `sendonce` command). Scores on questions related to the former were significantly higher than those related to the latter. Moreover, the use of explicit module exit strategies in cases where use of built-in mechanisms would have been simpler, also suggest a lack of understanding. To some extent, lack of understanding of the nature of achievement goals is indicated by the fact that corresponding beliefs are never inserted into the belief base, but more research is needed to explain the code fragments in some agent programs related to motivational notions in the knowledge base instead of the goal base. These findings provide valuable input for teaching the language, since it suggests more time needs to be devoted to explaining and practicing with the features of GOAL that have built-in semantics with delayed effect. In particular, programming examples and patterns will have to be developed to demonstrate possible uses of the language.

A possible *pattern for using modules*, derived from the observations and discussion above, is the following. For each role that the agent should be able to take, create a module with the goal of the module as the context condition. If the goal of the module is adopted, the agent can enter the module to perform the corresponding role. The program rules of the module should aim at achieving the goal of the module. If the goal is reached, the agent will automatically exit the module. If the agent should no longer pursue the goal because, e.g., more important goals should be pursued, percept rules can be used for specifying when the goal should be dropped, in which case the agent would also exit the module automatically. It is important to specify such *goal revision policies*, due to incomplete information and incomplete control over the environment. New observations of or changes in the environment may cause an adopted goal to become obsolete, requiring the need for specifying when the goal should be dropped. A similar observation about dropping of goals being used for dealing with dynamics of the environment was made in [16].

Language Design. The idenfication of patterns has yielded not only insights on how GOAL constructs are (to be) used, but also gives rise to multiple possibilities for *language improvement* and further investigation of *language design choices.* For reasons of space, we briefly discuss some of them.

Mailbox clean-up as performed in percept rules suggests investigation of whether keeping `received` and `sent` messages by default in the mailbox is to be preferred over cleaning up the mailbox in every cycle. This can be done by introducing these modes as an option in an agent program. In this way, we can find out by experience and practice what is preferred by the programmer.

One of the difficulties of continuous language design is to monitor whether code parts keep providing useful functionality throughout the changes that are made to the language. For example, the GOAL syntax requires agent files to provide an agent name. However, this agent name is just a label at the top of an agent file which is never used as the functionality of naming and making agent names public has been delegated to the mas file. Using these labels in agent files thus only creates confusion and it is better to remove these agent names.

Similarly, early requirements on syntax may not be so useful anymore as the language is extended. In particular, after introducing the perceptrule section the requirement to have at least one action rule in the program section seems not as useful anymore (Team 1 introduced a trivial 'obligatory' rule in the program section in their management agent). We plan to remove this requirement and allow an empty program section, and only generate a warning at parse time.

We will consider the introduction of warnings and automatic dependency analysis and checks: check on whether goals can ever become beliefs of the agent (to indicate proper use of achievement goals); check for single `send` actions in the program section, since these could just as well have been added in the percept rules; automated support for dependency analysis to identify duplicate code, etc. Also, support will have to be added to prevent duplicate code, e.g., by providing import and extension functionalities.

6 Conclusion

In this paper, we have studied GOAL programs that were written by first year computer science students for the domain of UT2004. This study is far more extensive than a previous study of GOAL programs for the dynamic blocks world. It has provided insights into how students use GOAL to program agent teams for a real-time dynamic environment. Overall, we can conclude that GOAL and the interface that was provided between GOAL and UT2004 allow students to program multi-agent systems in which high-level team strategies are used, in combination with navigation and interaction with the virtual environment.

Our analysis has identified patterns that seem to be very useful, such as the use of modules to implement agent roles; patterns that indicate a preference for explicit control and lack of understanding of implicit built-in semantics, such as use of the `exit-module` action to explicitly exit modules; patterns that suggest improvements to the language are needed, such as the frequent occurrence of duplicate code; patterns that require further analysis, such as the use of preprocessing of received messages versus direct use of messages, and the limited use of goals. One issue that is hard to disentangle is whether problems we identified in the source code are due to programming skills and teaching effort, or rather due to the design and semantics of the language studied. To deal with this issue, here we have tried to establish by looking at exam results, for example, if code practices could be related to skills. More research is needed to get a better grip on this issue, however. It remains to be established, for example, why students use the knowledge base in ways not envisaged at design time.

Through this analysis, we have come closer to the development of best practices and programming guidelines for GOAL, we have identified aspects that can be improved in the language, and we have gained a better understanding of which aspects of the language are easy to use and which are more difficult to grasp. A better understanding of problems that programmers face when using the language will help us make better debugging and development software. Note also that some of our main findings seem applicable to other agent programming languages as well. E.g. the use of modules to program roles has also been suggested elsewhere [3]. Our method and the results obtained may extend in particular to languages such as 2APL and *Jason* as the components in these languages are similar in many respects, but, of course, more research is required.

In future work, we plan on improving GOAL along the lines suggested in this paper, using the identified patterns to improve teaching of how to use GOAL and studying the effects of this, and further investigating the hypotheses formed through our analysis, e.g., concerning the reasons for the use of explicit control rather than built-in semantics.

References

1. SWI Prolog, `http://www.swi-prolog.org/`
2. Ben-Ari, M., Ben-David Kolikant, Y.: Thinking parallel: The process of learning concurrency. In: Fourth SIGCSE Conference on Innovation and Technology in Computer Science Education, pp. 13–16 (1999)
3. Bordini, R.H., Dastani, M., Dix, J., Seghrouchni, A.E.F.: Multi-Agent Programming: Languages, Tools and Applications. Springer, Heidelberg (2009)
4. Bordini, R.H., Hübner, J.F., Wooldridge, M.: Programming Multi-agent Systems in AgentSpeak using Jason. Wiley (2007)
5. Burkert, O., Kadlec, R., Gemrot, J., Bída, M., Havlíček, J., Dörfler, M., Brom, C.: Towards Fast Prototyping of IVAs Behavior: Pogamut 2. In: Pelachaud, C., Martin, J.-C., André, E., Chollet, G., Karpouzis, K., Pelé, D. (eds.) IVA 2007. LNCS (LNAI), vol. 4722, pp. 362–363. Springer, Heidelberg (2007)
6. Dastani, M.: 2APL: a practical agent programming language. JAAMAS 16(3), 214–248 (2008)
7. Dignum, V.: A Model for Organizational Interaction: Based on Agents, Founded in Logic. PhD thesis (2004)
8. Hindriks, K.V.: GOAL Programming Guide (2010), `http://mmi.tudelft.nl/~koen/goal`
9. Hindriks, K.V., Birna van Riemsdijk, M., Behrens, T., Korstanje, R., Kraaijenbrink, N., Pasman, W., de Rijk, L.: Unreal GOAL agents. In: Proc. of AGS 2010 (2010)
10. Howatt, J.: A project-based approach to programming language evaluation. ACM SIGPLAN Notices 30(7), 37–40 (1995)
11. Jordan Howell, R., Collier, R.: Evaluating agent-oriented programs: Towards multi-paradigm metrics. In: Proc. of ProMAS 2010, pp. 63–79 (2010)
12. Marshall, M.N.: Sampling for qualitative research. Family Practice 13(6), 522–525 (1996)
13. Padgham, L., Winikoff, M.: Developing Intelligent Agent Systems: A Practical Guide. Wiley Series in Agent Technology. John Wiley and Sons (2004)
14. Pokahr, A., Braubach, L., Lamersdorf, W.: Jadex: a BDI reasoning engine. In: Multi-Agent Programming. Springer, Berlin (2005)
15. Shoham, Y.: Agent-oriented programming. Artificial Intelligence 60, 51–92 (1993)
16. van Riemsdijk, M.B., Hindriks, K.V.: An Empirical Study of Agent Programs: A Dynamic Blocks World Case Study in GOAL. In: Yang, J.-J., Yokoo, M., Ito, T., Jin, Z., Scerri, P. (eds.) PRIMA 2009. LNCS, vol. 5925, pp. 200–215. Springer, Heidelberg (2009)
17. Wasserman, A.I.: Issues in programming language design— an overview. SIGPLAN Notices (1975)
18. Winikoff, M.: JACK^{TM} intelligent agents: an industrial strength platform. In: Multi-Agent Programming: Languages, Platforms and Applications. Springer, Heidelberg (2005)

A Modelling Language to Represent and Specify Emerging Structures in Agent-Based Model

Duc-An Vo[1,2], Alexis Drogoul[1,2], Jean-Daniel Zucker[1,2], and Tuong-Vinh Ho[2]

[1] IRD, UMI UMMISCO 209,
32 avenue Henri Varagnat, 93143 Bondy, France
[2] IFI, MSI, UMI 209,
ngo 42 Ta Quang Buu, Hanoi, Vietnam
{alexis.drogoul,jdzucker}@gmail.com, voducanvn@yahoo.com,
ho.tuong.vinh@auf.org

Abstract. All modellers have come across, one day, one of these popular toy agent-based models (ABMs), like "Ants", for instance, which depicts the appearance of pheromone trails built by simulated ants. They are simple, but representative of the way "real", more complex, ABMs are designed: in addition to explicitly describe the individual entities used to represent the system, modellers make implicit references to abstractions corresponding to the emerging structures they are tracking in the simulations. Yet, these abstractions are not represented in the models themselves as first-class entities: they are either hidden in ex-post computations or only part of visualization tasks, as if an explicit representation could somehow damage the processes at work in their emergence. This clearly constitutes an obstacle to the development of multi-level models, where emergence is likely to occur at different levels of abstraction of the system: if some of these levels are not represented in the models, the emergence of higher-level structures is not likely to be observed. This paper describes a modelling language that allows a modeller to represent and specify emerging structures in agent-based models. Firstly, to ease the description, we present these structures and their properties in four toy ABMs: Schelling, Boids, Collective Sort and Ants. Then we define the operations that are needed to represent and specify them without sacrificing the properties of the original model. An implementation of these operations in the GAML modelling language (part of the GAMA agent-based platform) is then presented. Finally, two simulations of the Boids model are used to illustrate the expressivity of this language and the multiple advantages it brings in terms of analysis, visualization and modeling of multi-level ABMs.

Keywords: Agent-based modelling, modelling language, emergence, GAMA simulation platform.

1 Introduction

When developing agent-based models (ABMs), modellers represent explicit entities of the system modelled as agents. The choice of entities depends on the level of

N. Desai, A. Liu, and M. Winikoff (Eds.): PRIMA 2010, LNAI 7057, pp. 212–227, 2012.

abstraction of the reference system the modeller is working with, and this in turn depends on the question he/she wants to answer with the model, on the data available at hand, on the scale at which this data is described, etc.

What is remarkable in ABMs, however, contrary to other modelling techniques, is that at least two different scales are involved in the modelling process: the scale at which the agents are described, and the scale at which the simulations are to be observed and their results analysed. This is especially true when modellers try to capture and understand the emergence of functions (social, biological, ecological, etc.) structures or functions by means of simulation [10]. These structures, emerging in the course of the simulations, are often the result of non-linear interactions between the agents defined in the model and they can play significant roles in its dynamics by providing feedback constraints on the behaviour of the underlying agents composing them.

As we will see in the presentation of the toy agent-based models in section 2, these emerging structures are normally not explicitly represented in the models as agents. They are either hidden in ex-post computations or only part of visualization tasks, as if an explicit representation could somehow damage the processes at work in their emergence. This deliberate choice may lead the modeller to the following difficulties:

- If certain structures emerge during the simulation, for example groups of agents having certain common similarities or spatial-temporal regularities, they can be only identified posteriorly (using classification method or analyzing statistic for example) and hence play no role in the dynamic of the simulation.
- If the data, possessed by the modeller, are distributed on several levels of abstraction (for example the data of individual, the data of group and the data of the population level), it is not evident to simultaneously represent them in the model.

Currently, there is no explicit support in term of agent-based modelling language for representing the relationships and interactions between multiple levels of abstraction in the model. To remedy this deficiency of current agent-based platforms, the modeller can develop his multi-level model from scratch. He thus has to develop a set of proprietary abstractions representing explicit entities and emerging structures concerned. Several multi-level agent-based models are developed this way such as [8], [9]. This approach has several drawbacks. Firstly, the modeller doesn't take advantage of all the services offered by an agent-based modelling platform. Secondly, he has to manually manage all issues specific to multi-level model, which is in fact an error prone process. Hence these drawbacks raise the question of reusability and ease of modelling. So the goal of this work is to propose a modelling language to assist the modeller in representing and specifying emerging structures in an agent-based model.

When working with emerging structures in agent-based models, we propose the modeller a process with two complementary tasks as depicted in figure 1:

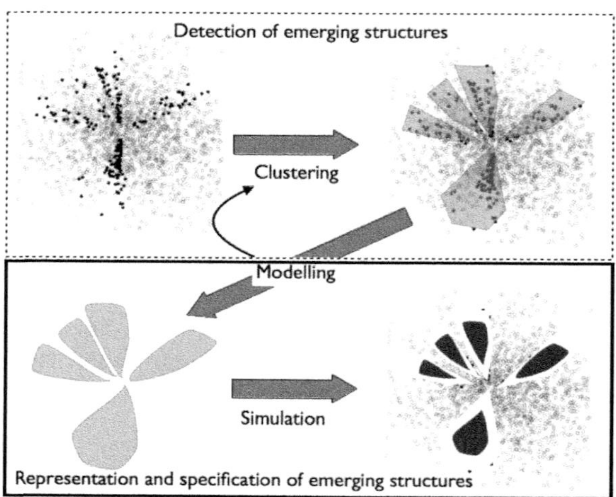

Fig. 1. Detection and Representation of Emerging Structures

Detection of emerging structures. This task, illustrated in the upper-box of figure 1, concerns the detection of emerging structures in the course of a simulation. An emerging structure normally consists of a group of interacting agents sharing certain similarities. This detection task uses several clustering techniques [11] that classify agents into groups according to certain criteria. These criteria depend of course on what the modeller wants to observe.

Representation and specification of emerging structures. This task, depicted in the lower-box of figure 1, concerns the representation and specification of emerging structure in an agent-based model. The modeller describes what he expects as emerging structures. He specifies the conditions under which a group of interacting agents is considered to form an emergent structure. In order to describe the emerging structure, the modeller employs a set of representing abstraction. He models also the relationships and interactions between the emerging structure and the composing agents.

Figure 1 separates the two tasks a modeller deals with when working with emerging structures in an agent-based model. Some existing works aim at addressing the first task such as [7]. They propose techniques to detect emerging structures in an agent-based simulation. Emerging structures vary a lot according to the concerning model. Each detection technique may adapt well to certain emerging structures and not well to other ones. This is understandable because a detection technique is normally developed to address a precise problem [11]. In this context, the author may make certain "optimizations" to adapt the technique to the characteristics of the emerging structures he is interested in.

The modelling language proposed by this work aims at addressing the second task, which corresponds to the lower-box of the figure. For the detection task, we would like to reuse the existing detection techniques of the communities. We integrate our work, focusing on the description level of emerging structures, with existing detection techniques. With this integration, the way that a modeller models (represents and specifies) emerging structures remains (almost) intact as he changes the underlying clustering techniques employed to detect these structures. The modeller can thus "switch back and forth" opting for a detection techniques optimal to his problem. This modular approach of separating the detection task and the representation task has two significant advantages: 1) It favours the reusability of existing detection techniques; 2) It abstracts the modeller from the internal detail of how a detection technique functions which rather interests computer scientists.

To ease the description of the language, in the second section, we present four toy agent-based models along with the corresponding emerging structures. Then in the third section, we point out the common characteristic of the presented emerging structures. From this common characteristic, we discuss the operations a modeller needs in order to work with these structures in an agent-based model. After that, we describe how the operations discussed in the third section are implemented in the GAML modelling language of the GAMA agent-based modelling platform [1], [2]. In the experimentation section, we illustrate the expressivity of GAML language through some demos of the representation of emerging structures in the Boids model. Finally, we conclude this article by resuming the initial contribution and discussing some future works.

2 Emerging Structures in Some Toy Agent-Based Models

We present in this section four popular toy agent-based models. With each model, we introduce briefly its origin and purpose. Then we indicate the emerging structures in the simulation that may interest the modeler.

2.1 "Schelling" Model of Segregation

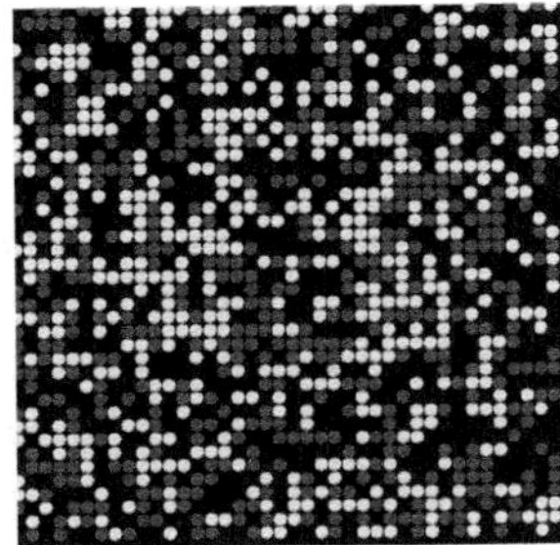

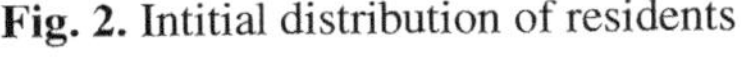

Fig. 2. Intitial distribution of residents

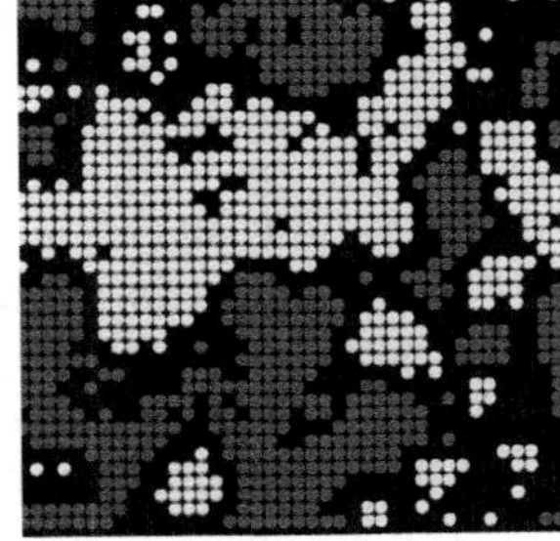

Fig. 3. Groups of same colour residents appear as emerging structures

This model, proposed by Thomas Schelling in 1969, attempts at understanding the phenomenon of residential segregation in cities [4] by seeing it as an aggregated result of the decisions of residents in choosing their housings. Residents are represented explicitly as agents in the model. Residents having certain similarities are classified as belonging to the same class. In reality, criteria used to classify resident may be educational level, religion, annual income, skin colour, political point of view, ... Same class residents are represented by same colour agents. When the simulation runs, we see groups of nearby same colour residents appear. We call these groups emerging structures because they are not explicitly represented in the model as agents.

As soon as these emerging structures appear in the simulation, isolated residents tend to be attracted to them. Isolated residents move to join group of other residents similar to them. The forming of such emerging structures is the result of residents' decision in choosing places where they live in a city. Vice-versa, these emerging structures have certain feedback influences on the behaviours of the residents.

2.2 "Boids" Model

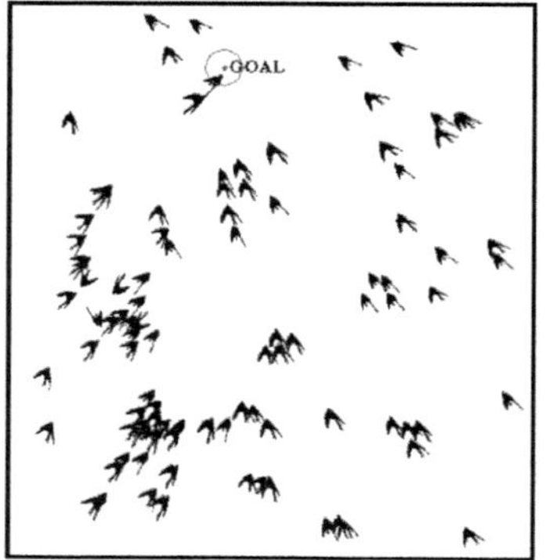

Fig. 4. Formation of bird flock

"Boids", proposed by Craig Reynolds in 1986, is a model of coordinated animal motion such as bird flocks or fish schools [3]. The behaviour of each agent is represented by simple rules: separation, alignment, cohesion and obstacle avoidance. There is no group leader, but when the simulation runs, depending on the parameters chosen, coherent flocks appear. They are coherent in space, coherent in time, but yet the result of only local interactions between bird agents. In that sense, they can be considered as emerging structures.

2.3 "Collective Sort" Model

The "Collective Sort" model concerns the activity of agents in gathering objects of different types scattered in an environment [5]. Objects of the same type have the same colour. Agents move in the environment picking up and dropping down objects. Their behaviour is simple. Let us call *similarity_index* the number of objects of the same colour around one object in the environment. Agents move the objects in order to locally increase the *similarity_index* of each object. When the simulation runs, groups of objects of similar colour appear. The larger a group becomes, the higher the probability that a robot drops an object on it is. This is similar to the influence of groups of birds on the behaviours of individual birds. If the simulation runs long enough, all the objects of the same colour end up gathered in one group. In this case, as groups result from the interactions between robots, objects and the environment, they can be considered as emerging structures.

Fig. 5. Scattered objects at t = 0

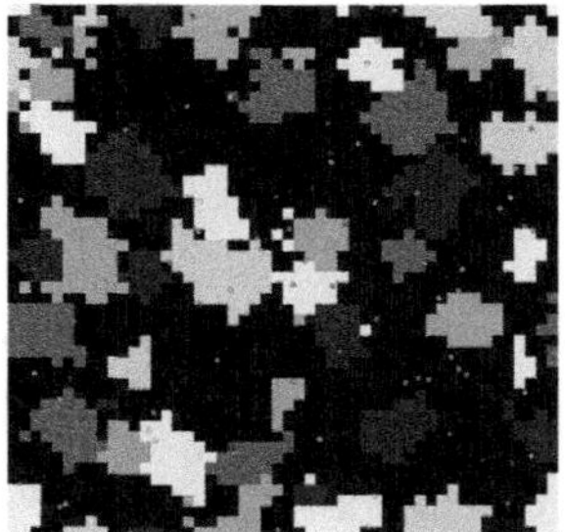

Fig. 6. Same color (type) objects aggregate into groups

2.4 "Ants" Model

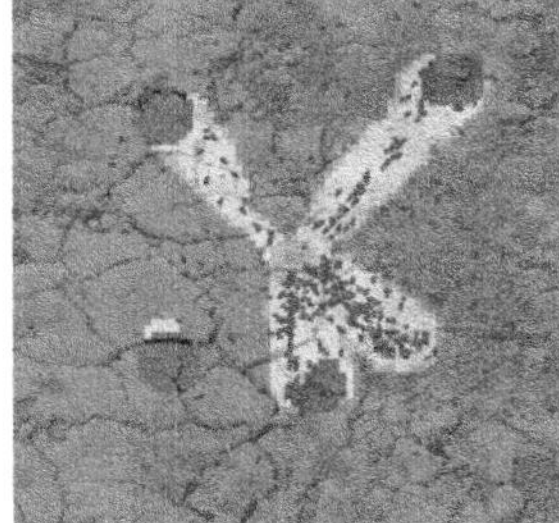

Fig. 7. Ants foraging for food

The "Ants" model mimics the foraging activity of an ant colony [10]. Around a nest, where the ants are located at the beginning of simulations, sources of food are placed in an environment. Ants initially move at random, searching for food. If they detect some, they pick it and bring it back to the nest. On the returning journey, they deposit a "signal" on the ground (pheromone) that other agents can detect and follow to the food.

As the simulation runs, it is easy to see "roads" of pheromone built by ants bringing food back to nest. The larger this road, the higher the probability ants will follow it. Pheromone roads and groups of ants following them are emerging structures resulting from the interactions between ants with their environment.

3 Representing Emerging Structures

All the emerging structures described in the previous section are implicit entities resulting from interactions between explicit entities, and they only appear in the course of the simulation. The modeller somehow implicitly "waits for" their emergence, and they are sometimes the goal of the simulation itself. Yet, these structures are not represented in the model as explicit entities. Thus it is impossible for a modeller to track what is happening in the run of a simulation in terms of emergence. The visual feedback provided by the user interface is a poor and imprecise substitute for this.

In our proposal, in order to let modellers dynamically track the emergence of these structures, we let them represent these structures as explicit (albeit potential) entities in the model. We call these entities "emergent agents". They are regular agents (which can be provided with their own attributes or behaviours if necessary), except that their instantiation is dependent on the appearance of certain properties during the simulation.

In this section, we describe the common features of these agents. Then we discuss the operations that a modeller needs in order to represent and specify them in an ABM.

First of all, the emergent agents found in the previous models can be described as composed of several other agents *(micro-agents)* that appear to share certain similarities: a segregated group is composed of multiple inhabitants located close to each other and sharing some characteristics (at least the colour); a flock contains several birds flying in the same direction within a certain distance; a pile of objects is exclusively composed of nearby objects of the same colour; a pheromone trail is a group of adjacent cells in the environment that are provided with a pheromone signal and an ant group is a group of ants that follow the same pheromone trail.

In addition to the attributes and behaviours a modeller might provide them with, and in order to manage both their instantiation and the relationships with their micro-agents, emergent agents have then to be provided with the five following behaviours, specific to their lifecycle: creation, update, merge, disposal and top-down feedback control.

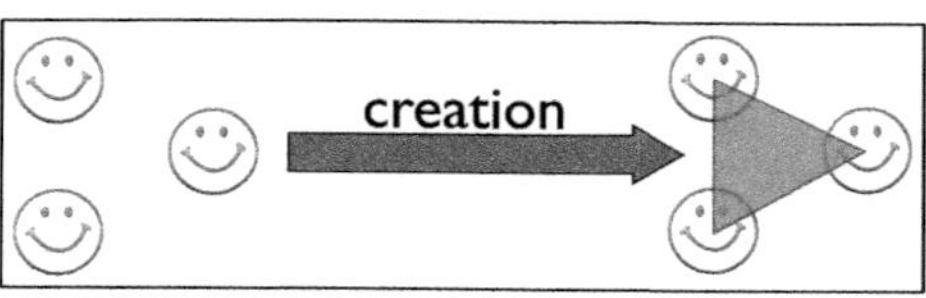

Fig. 8. Creation of an emergent agent

The "creation" operation helps to specify when an emergent agent representing an emerging structure is created. For instance, it might be the case that, when the spatial distance between three flying birds in the Boids model is less than 10 meters, an emergent agent composed of these three birds is created in the simulation. This operation allows the modeller to express the rule governing the instantiation of emergent agents during the simulation. Figure 8 illustrates this operation. An emergent agent representing the emergent structure is created with three micro-agents as components.

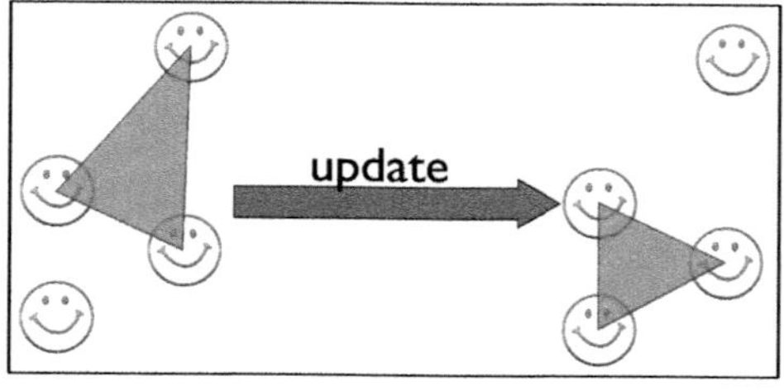

Fig. 9. Update of an emergent agent

The "update" operation describes how micro-agents are added to or removed from an emergent agent. Some micro-agents may no longer satisfy a condition to belong to an emergent agent, while others, still "free" may now fulfil it: this operation helps to specify how these agents are added or removed from the structure.

Figure 9 illustrates the "update" operation. On the left side, we have one free micro-agent and one emergent agent with three micro-agents. The "update" operation helps the modeller in describing when one micro-agent, already part of the emergent agent, doesn't satisfy the condition to be considered as a component anymore and when, possibily at the same time, one free micro-agent meets the condition to become a component. Its purpose is to keep the list of components up-to-date with respect to the meaning of the emergent agent.

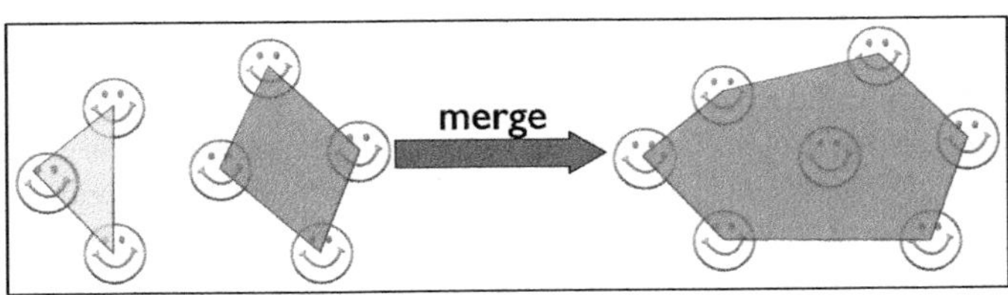

Fig. 10. Fusion of different emergent agents

The "merge" operation allows the modeller to specify how several emergent agents representing different structures can be merged into one unique emergent agent. The fusion of their respective components then becomes the components of the new unique emergent agent.

Figure 10 illustrates the "merge" operation. On the left, we have two emergent agents representing two emerging structures. Supposing that these two emergent agents satisfy certain predefined criteria, the "merge" operation then merges these two emergent agents into one unique emergent agent.

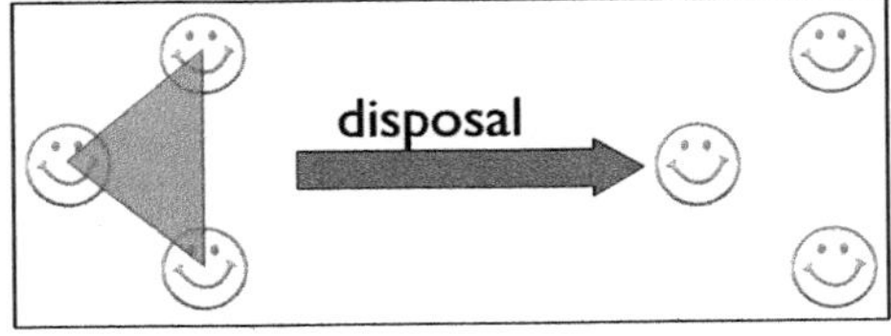

Fig. 11. Destruction of an emergent agent

The purpose of the "disposal" operation is to express when an emerging structure should not considered to be an agent in the simulation anymore. The emergent agent representing the structure is cleared out of the simulation and its components become free.

Figure 11 illustrates the "disposal" operation. On the left, we have an emergent agent with three micro-agents. If the corresponding emerging structure doesn't meet a predefined condition anymore, then the "disposal" operation helps to specify how the emergent agent is cleared out of the simulation.

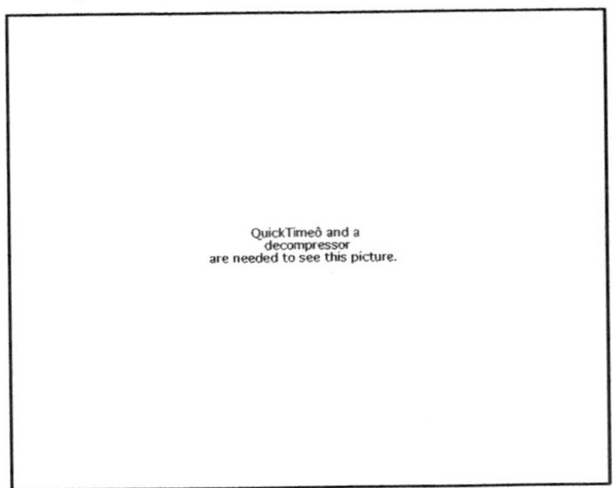

QuickTimeô and a
decompressor
are needed to see this picture.

Fig. 12. Feedbacks between micro- and emergent agents behaviour

The top-down feedback control finally allows the modeller to describe which feedback constraint an emergent agent is exercising on its underlying micro-agents. As emergent agents usually emerge because of the interactions of certain micro-agents, these agents have an influence on its attributes and behaviour. Vice-versa, an emergent agent may also provide a feedback on the behaviour of its components, either implicitly or explicitly [10]. In order to describe it when it is necessary to do so, the modeller needs to have some way to alter the behaviour of a micro-agent (by changing parameters, adding, or removing entire behaviours) before and after it enters an emergent agent.

4 Representing Emergent Agents in GAMA

We describe in this section how the operations introduced in the previous section are implemented as commands in the GAML modelling language. We begin with a brief introduction of the GAMA agent-based platform and the GAML modelling language. Then we detail how the ability of working with emergent agent is taken into account in the GAML modelling language.

GAMA (**G**eneric **A**gent-based **M**odelling **A**rchitecture) is an agent-based modelling platform, developed by the MSI research team (part of UMI 209 UMMISCO research unit) since 2007 [1] [2]. GAMA aims at providing field expert, modeller and computer scientists with a complete modelling and simulation development environment for building spatially explicit multi-agent simulation.

GAML (**GAMA M**odelling **L**anguage) is the modelling language used to develop agent-based models in the GAMA platform. Besides some common concepts for modelling agent and environment, GAML supplies a large and extensible library of commands, primitives and expressions facilitating the model development task. Because of the space limitation, we don't elaborate on the detail of GAML, interested readers can refer to [2] for a detailed tutorial of this language.

An emergent agent composes of constituent agents. Constituent agents can be considered as micro-agents compared to the emergent agent. Then the emergent agent can be seen as a macro-agent compared to its constituent agents. In turn, several emergent agents can be merged to form another emergent agent at a higher level of abstraction. Thus an agent in GAMA can play the role of macro-agent in one level of abstraction and micro-agent in another (higher) level of abstraction. This design aims at permitting the modeller to represent as many levels of abstraction as he needs in his model.

To manipulate the five specific operations in the lifecycle of an emergent agent (*create*, *update*, *merge*, *disposal, top-down constraint control*), six new GAML commands are introduced: *creation*, *update*, *merge*, *disposal*, *enable and disable*.

- **The "creation" command** helps to specify when emergent agents are created in the simulation.
- **The "update" command** describes how the constituent micro-agents are added and removed from an emergent agent.
- **The "merge" command** determines how several emergent agents are merged.
- **The "disposal" command** indicates when an emergent agent is cleared out of the simulation.
- **The "disable" command** permits the modeller to disable certain behaviour units appropriately. While **the "enable" command** helps the modeller to enable the inactive behaviour units.

These GAML commands help the modeller to model/describe the life-cycle of an emergent agent. They aim at addressing the task (of representing and specifying the emerging structure) depicted in the lower-box of figure 1. Through the GAML language, we would like to offer a set of abstractions and "vocabulary" that are usable for describing the relationship and interactions between multiple levels of abstraction in an agent-based model.

As mentioned in the introduction section, concerning the task of detecting emerging structure (corresponding to the upper-box in figure 1), we integrate, in the

GAMA platform, a set of existing clustering techniques of the community [10]. Through the primitive mechanism of GAML language, the modeller can invoke these clustering algorithms directly from his/her model (depicted by the black upper-arrow in figure 1) in order to initialize, update, merge and dispose emergent agents appropriately during the course of the simulation.

5 Experimentations

This section shows how to use the GAML commands presented in the last section to represent the emerging structure in the Boids model. Continuing section 2.2, we detail a little bit more about how Craig Reynolds models the behaviour of each bird in a flock. Let consider a flock of birds, each bird has a perceptional radius within which it reacts on the behaviour of others neighbours. Motion of bird is modelled by the following rules:

- **Separation** rule helps a bird to maintain a minimum distance with its neighbours so that they don't collide.
- **Alignment** rule permits a bird to maintain the same flying direction with its neighbours.
- **Cohesion** rule ensures that a bird is not left far away from its neighbours.
- **Obstacles avoidance** rule helps a bird to avoid obstacles in the environment.

Table 1. Behaviour of birds [3]

Separation	Alignment	Cohesion	Obstacles avoidance

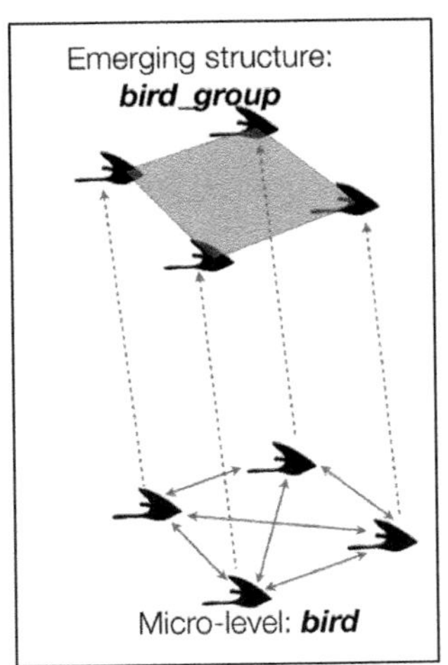

Fig. 13. Boids model with two levels of organization

As mentioned in section 2.2, a group of birds is an emerging structure formed by nearby flying birds within a predefined distance. We would like to capture its dynamic in the simulation. Basing on the GAML commands proposed in section 4, the following modification is introduced to the original version of Boids model.

A new species, named bird_group, is introduced to the model, representing a group of nearby birds. An agent of bird_group species is considered as an emergent agent and contains birds as constituent micro-agents.

With the bird_group species, we have now a new version of Boids model with two levels of abstraction. At the micro-level, we have bird species. At the macro-level, we have bird_group species. As described in figure 13, interactions between birds at micro-level result in the emergence of groups of bird, represented as bird_group emergent agents, at macro-level.

The four operations of creation of a bird_group agent, update of a bird_group agent, merge between bird_group agents and disposal of a bird_group agent are represented in GAML language as following:

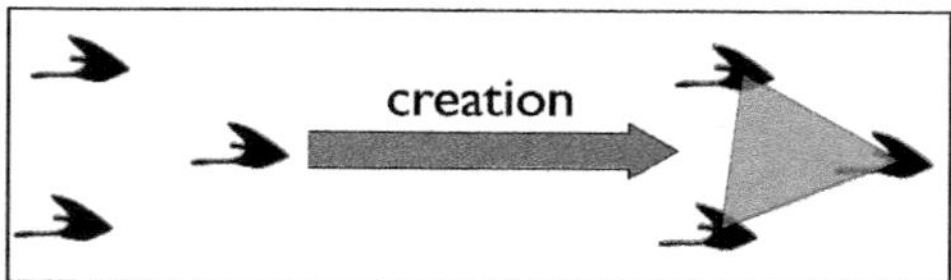

Fig. 14. Creation of a bird_group agent

- **Creation of a bird_group agent:** The "creation" command is used to model the creation of bird_group emergent agents. When birds are found flying near together within a predefined distance and these birds haven't belong to any bird_group agent yet, a bird_group emergent agent is initialized representing these nearby birds.

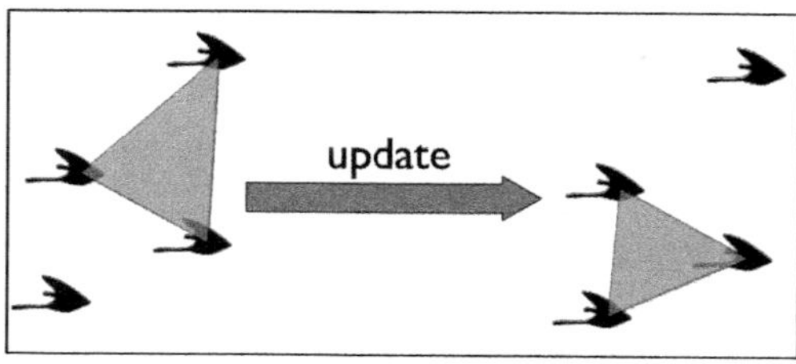

Fig. 15. Update of a bird_group agent

- **Update of a bird_group agent:** As birds move, separate birds can enter an existing group of bird. Birds belonging to an existing group can leave group. The "update" command is where the code to add birds to and remove birds from a bird_group agent is implemented.

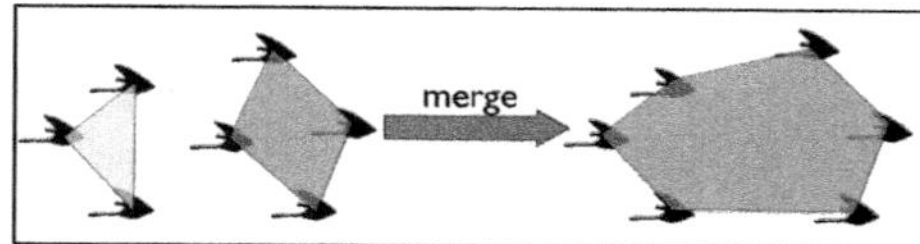

Fig. 16. Fusion between bird_group agents

- **Merge between bird_group agents:** When several bird_group emergent agents are found near together in a predefined distance, then these bird_groups will be merged into one unique bird_group. In this case, our implementation approach is to keep the biggest bird_group emergent agent. Constituent birds of others bird_group agent will become constituents of this biggest bird_group agent. Other bird_group agents are cleared out of the simulation. This operation is implemented in the "merge" command.

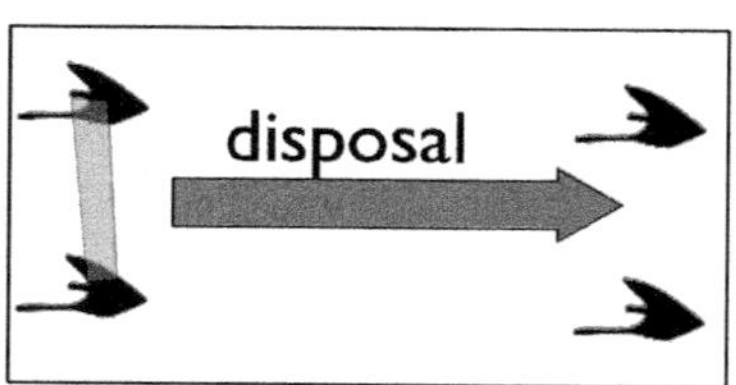

Fig. 17. Disposal of a bird_group agent

- **Disposal of a bird_group agent:** when a bird_group agent has less than two constituent birds then we don't consider it as an agent anymore. This bird_group agent will be cleared out of the simulation. Corresponding bird agents will become free. We specify this operation in the "disposal" command.

First simulation. We run several simulations of this model in the GAMA platform to test the operation of the four commands "creation", "merge", "update" and "disposal". Main parameters of one simulation are as following:

- The number of bird agents: 200
- The distance within which two birds are considered as nearby: 10 meters
- Update radius: a dynamic value basing on size of the bird_group agent. This plays the role of the perceptional radius of the bird_group agent.
  - If free birds are found within this radius, they will become constituents of the corresponding bird_group.
  - If a bird of a bird_group has no other constituents as neighbours within this radius, it won't be considered as member of the bird_group anymore.
- Merge distance: the distance within which two bird_group agents are merged is 10 meters
- If a group of bird has less than two birds, the corresponding emergent agent will be cleared out of the simulation.

Figure 21 captures the variation of the number of bird_group emergent agent and micro-agent bird during 280 steps of the simulation is captured. This chart is quite intuitive. The horizontal axis represents the simulation step. The vertical one signifies the number of agent of each species. The red line captures the number of bird_group emergent agent. While the green one indicates the number of free bird agent. Bird agent is represented graphically by a black bird-shape image. Emergent agents, bird_group, are represented as polygons covering all the constituent birds. At the beginning of the simulation, as bird agents are scattered in the environment so there are not many bird_group agents. There is an agent representing a target point (goal) that birds follow in the simulation. This target point (represented graphically as circle) periodically changes its position and colour after certain random amount of simulation step. As the simulation runs, bird_group emergent agents are created, updated, merged and disposed dynamically.

We see the significant change in the number of birds and groups of bird between two consecutive steps of the simulation. Whenever number of free birds decreases, the number of bird groups increase and vice-versa. This explains that the creation of new bird_group emergent agents diminishes the number of free birds because when a bird agent becomes the constituent of a bird_group agent it isn't considered as free bird anymore. And the disposal of bird_group emergent agents makes the number of free birds increase. From step 240 to step 280 of the simulation, although the significant change between two consecutive simulation steps continues, we see that both the number of free birds and the number of bird groups follow the decreasing trend. Because all birds are approaching the goal at the upper left corner of the environment (figure 20), so the distance between them decreases. Hence all the emergent agents are thus merged into a big one making the number of emergent agent decrease. The bigger the emergent agent, the more attractive this agent has on others free birds. Hence others free birds will join this emergent agent easier and/or faster making the number of free birds decrease to almost 0.

Second simulation. The previous simulation shows that interactions between birds at micro-level make groups of birds emerge at macro-level. However, such emergent agents, bird_group, have no explicit influence on the behaviour of constituent micro-agents. As described in figure 12 and [10], when interactions between micro-level agents result in the emergence of dynamic structures, these structures often have influences on the behaviour of constituent agents through some feedback constraints.

Fig. 18. Snapshot of the simulation at step 0

Fig. 19. Snapshot (focus on certain bird_gorup agents) of the simulation at step 70

Fig. 20. Snapshot (focus on the biggest bird_group agent) of the simulation at step 280

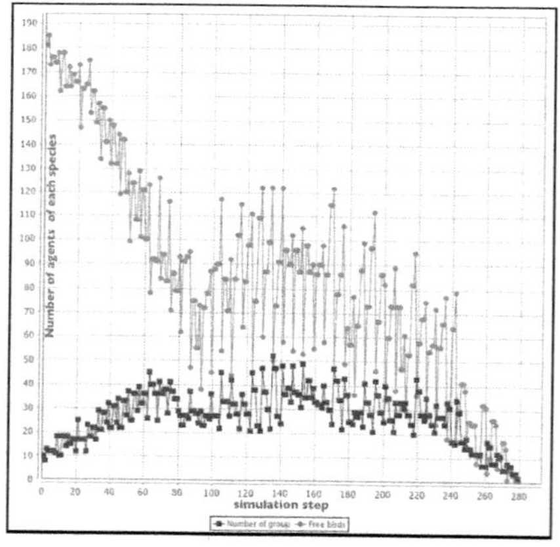

Fig. 21. Number of bird_group agents and free bird agents

To model this feedback constraint, we use two GAML commands "enable" and "disable". Some modifications are introduced to the model used in previous simulation. A species name "obstacle" is introduced to represent obstacles in the environment. Agents of obstacle species move slowly in the environment in order to perturb the birds. There is a small modification on the behaviour of bird_group species. A bird_group agent has a perceptional radius calculated dynamically basing on the number of constituent birds. If a bird_group agent doesn't "perceive" any obstacles within its perceptional radius, it will deactivate the behaviour model of its constituent birds using the "disable" command. Movement of constituent birds will be governed rather by the macro-agent bird_group. The macro-agent simply asks its constituent birds to move towards the goal agent. We call this macro-agent active bird_group. Vice-versa, if a bird_group agent "perceives" obstacles within its perceptional range, it will withdraw its influence from the constituent birds using the "enable" command. Hence bird agents are become autonomous and interact with others neighbours through their local perception in order to move towards the target point. We call this macro-agent passive bird_group. This simulation uses the same principal parameters like the previous one. We create additionally 40 agents representing 40 moving obstacles in the environment. Obstacles are visually represented as red squares in the environment. Figure 23 captures the number of active bird_group agents (red line) and passive bird_group agents (green line). At the beginning of the simulation, like the previous one, the number of both active and passive bird_group agents is almost 0 because bird agents are scattered in the environment. As the simulation runs, the number of active bird_group agents increases fast and is a lot more than the number of passive bird_group agents. This is quite intuitive because the obstacles are distributed sparsely in the environment (Figure 22, 23). So not many bird_group agents "perceive" obstacles within their perceptional radius. This results in less passive bird_group agents and more active bird_group agents.

Fig. 22. Snapshot of the simulation at step 0

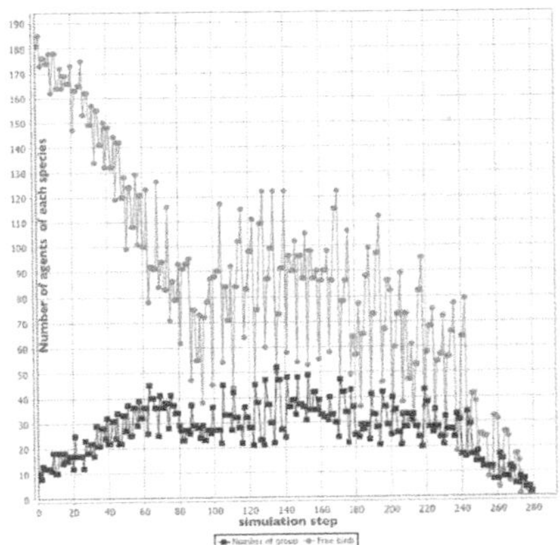

Fig. 23. Number of active and passive bird_group agents

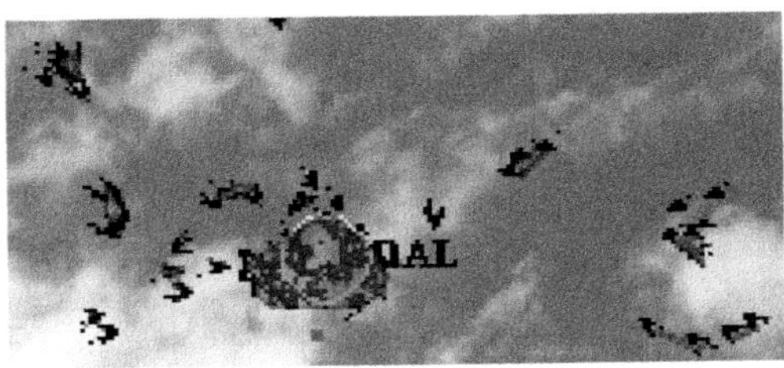

Fig. 24. Snap shot (focus on certain bird_group agents) of the simulation at step 120

6 Conclusion and Future Work

We have introduced a modelling language to represent and specify emerging structure in agent-based model. We begin by describing the two complementary tasks a modeller deals with when working with emerging structure: (1) Detection of emerging structure; (2) Representation and specification of emerging structure. The proposed language aims at addressing the second task. For the first task, we integrate in GAMA platform a set of clustering techniques, which the modeller can use if necessary to detect emerging structures during the course of the simulation. After presenting emerging structures in four toy agent-based models, we discuss the operations a modeller needs in order to model the lifecycle of an emergent agent. We implement these operations as commands of the GAML language. These commands are employed to represent the emergent agent (bird_group) in the Boids model. We explore also the possibility of modelling the top-down feedback constraint of the emergent agents at macro-level on agents at the micro-level (birds). As we see in the experimentation section, emergent agents are created, merged, updated, disposed in a dynamical way.

With the proposed commands as initial result of the work, we supply the modeller with some basic "bricks" he can use to represent the emerging structure in some simple agent-based models. This opens several interesting problems to tackle. As we would like to develop GAML as a multi-level agent-based modelling language, so more test should be done on multi-level models, which have more than two levels of abstraction. When there are multiple levels of abstraction, there will be conflicts in time-scale, space-scale, data and concurrent interactions between different levels of abstraction [12]. We need to supply in GAMA a framework to maintain the consistency between agents at different levels of abstraction. Basing on this framework, through the GAML language, the modeller should be able to express in the model how the consistency is ensured between different abstraction levels.

References

1. Amouroux, E., Chu, T.-Q., Boucher, A., Drogoul, A.: GAMA: An Environment for Implementing and Running Spatially Explicit Multi-Agent Simulations. In: Ghose, A., Governatori, G., Sadananda, R. (eds.) PRIMA 2007. LNCS, vol. 5044, pp. 359–371. Springer, Heidelberg (2009)
2. GAMA platform, http://gama-platform.googlecode.com
3. Reynolds, C.: Boids, Background and update, http://www.red3d.com/cwr/boids
4. Schelling, T.: Schelling Segregation model, http://web.mit.edu/www/alife/schelling.html
5. Deneubourg, J.-L., Goss, S., Franks, N., Sendova-Franks, A., Detrain, C., Chrétien, L.: The Dynamics of Collective Sorting Robot-Like Ants and Ant-Like Robots (1991)
6. Grimm, V., Railsback, S.F.: Individual-based Modelling and Ecology (2005)
7. Moncion, T., Amar, P., Hutzler, G.: Automatic characterization of emergent phenomena in complex system. In: JBPC 2010 (2010)

8. Servat, D., Perrier, E., Treuil, J.-P., Drogoul, A.: When Agents Emerge from Agents: Introducing Multi-Scale Viewpoints in Multi-Agent Simulations. In: Sichman, J.S., Conte, R., Gilbert, N. (eds.) MABS 1998. LNCS (LNAI), vol. 1534, pp. 183–198. Springer, Heidelberg (1998)
9. Breton, L., Zucker, J.-D., Clément, E.: A Multi-Agent Based Simulation of Sand Piles in a Static Equilibrium. In: Moss, S., Davidsson, P. (eds.) MABS 2000. LNCS (LNAI), vol. 1979, pp. 108–118. Springer, Heidelberg (2001)
10. Camazine, S., Deneubourg, J.-L., Franks, N.R., Sneyd, J., Theraulaz, G., Bonabeau, E.: Self-Organization in Biological Systems (2001)
11. Witten, I.H., Frank, E.: Data Mining: Practical Machine Learning Tools and Techniques (2005)
12. Natrajan, A.: Doctoral thesis: Consistency Maintenance in Concurrent Representations (2000)

Multi-model Based Simulation Platform for Urban Traffic Simulation

Yuu Nakajima, Shohei Yamane, and Hiromitsu Hattori

Department of Social Informatics, Kyoto University
Yoshida-Honmachi, Sakyo-ku, Kyoto, 606-8501, Japan
{nkjm,hatto}@i.kyoto-u.ac.jp
yamane@ai.soc.i.kyoto-u.ac.jp

Abstract. Multiagent-based simulations are regarded as a useful technology for analyzing complex social systems; for example, traffic in a city. Traffic in a city has various aspects such as route planning on the road network and driving operations on a certain road. Both types of human behavior are being studied separately by specialists in their respective domains. We believe that traffic simulation platforms should integrate the various paradigms underlying agent decision making and the target environment. We focus on urban traffic as the target problem and attempt to realize a multiagent simulation platform based on the multi-model approach. While traffic flow simulations using simple agents are popular in the traffic domain, it has been recognized that driving behavior simulations with sophisticated agents are also beneficial. However, there is no software platform that can integrate traffic simulators dealing with different aspects of urban traffic. In this paper, we propose a traffic simulation platform that can execute citywide traffic simulations that take account of the aspects of route selection on a road network and driving behavior on individual roads. The proposed simulation platform enables the multiple aspects of city traffic to be reproduced while still retaining scalability.

1 Introduction

Multiagent-based simulations are increasingly seen as the most attractive approach to reproducing and analyzing diverse social systems including autonomous and heterogeneous decision making entities, *i.e.*, humans [5]. The multiagent-based simulation is a paradigm that can reproduce macroscopic complex phenomena through localized interactions among heterogeneous agents. Multiagent-based simulations have been applied in various fields in the city, examples include traffic planning, rescues, and pandemic responses[1,8,4]. Although numerous attempts have been made to conduct multiagent-based simulations in various domains, no study has fully captured and analyzed social systems from various aspects.

The challenge tackled in this paper is a massive urban traffic simulation platform based on the multi-model approach to agent decision making and the target

N. Desai, A. Liu, and M. Winikoff (Eds.): PRIMA 2010, LNAI 7057, pp. 228–241, 2012.

environment in a city. Traffic, which is one of the most complex systems in modern society, is a highly suitable target for our research because vehicular traffic is a phenomenon that includes various aspects: route selection and driving behavior.

While traffic flow simulations using simple agents are popular in the traffic domain, it has been recognized that driving behavior simulations with sophisticated agents provide many additional benefits for analyzing the relation between local driving behaviors and global traffic flow in a city. However, no published software platform can integrate traffic simulators dealing with different aspects of urban traffic. We design an architecture and develop a framework to integrate multiple simulators founded on different paradigms. The proposed platform provides a collaborative environment to experts who traditionally use different simulators in different domains. We also propose a traffic simulation platform that can execute citywide traffic simulations that include the aspects of route selection aspect and driving behavior.

More specifically, this paper has three goals:

1. Design multiagent simulation platform based on multi-model of a city
   The phenomena that occur in a city cannot be captured with a single model. For realizing traffic simulations of a whole city, it is required that the platform enable us to integrate different aspects of agent decision making and the target environment in the relevant areas. It is also necessary that the platform take advantage of multiple models proposed in different works.
2. Implement urban traffic simulation capturing various aspects of a city and agents
   We develop an urban traffic simulator based on the proposed architecture. In this platform, we focus on two aspects of the traffic domain in a city: global route processing and local driving behavior.
3. Evaluate platform performance
   We investigate the potential of the developed platform to realize more realistic urban traffic simulations. We verify that the simulation platform enables the introduction of multiple aspects of traffic while still retaining scalability. We also conduct an experiment that demonstrates how the number of agents impacts simulation results such as traffic flow.

The remainder of this paper is as follows. Section 2 describes our approach to designing the multi-model traffic simulator platform. Section 3 shows the implementation of the platform. Section 4 describe an analysis of the platform's performance and Section 5 demonstrates the effects of the number of agents.

2 Architecture

We consider that agents in the traffic simulation should be covered by flexible combinations of various decision-making models. This is because agents face various situations and make decisions according to their current situations while they move around the city. In addition, the simulation has to include traffic

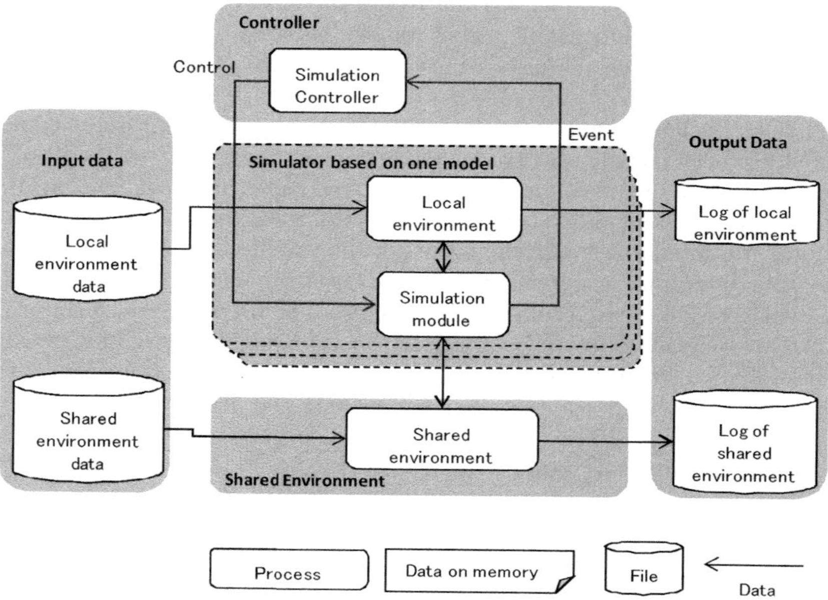

Fig. 1. Architecture for Multi-model Simulation Platform

systems such as traffic control systems and car navigation systems. The platform must integrate various aspects of the city environment.

Figure 1 shows the architecture proposed in this paper. This architecture includes multiple simulators and each simulator captures a specialized aspect of the traffic domain (*e.g.* route selection aspect and driving behavior aspect).

Settings unique to the environment covered by each simulator and the environment settings shared by the simulators are input. When the result of a certain simulator influences another simulator, the result is stored in the shared environment. On the other hand, information that is unique to one simulator cannot be accessed by other simulators. Such data is accumulated in the corresponding local environment.

Simulation controller should manage the simulation processes in order to combine the multiple simulators. The controller requests simulators to calculate the state of the next step. Basically, the simulators receive a request to output a result for the next time step. When an event that should be sent to another simulator occurs in the calculation, the event is sent to that simulator through the simulation controller.

When all simulations finish, the logs of local environments and the logs of the shared environment are written to external files.

Some platforms that combine multiple simulators have been proposed, but these platforms mainly focus on use in a distributed environment [11].

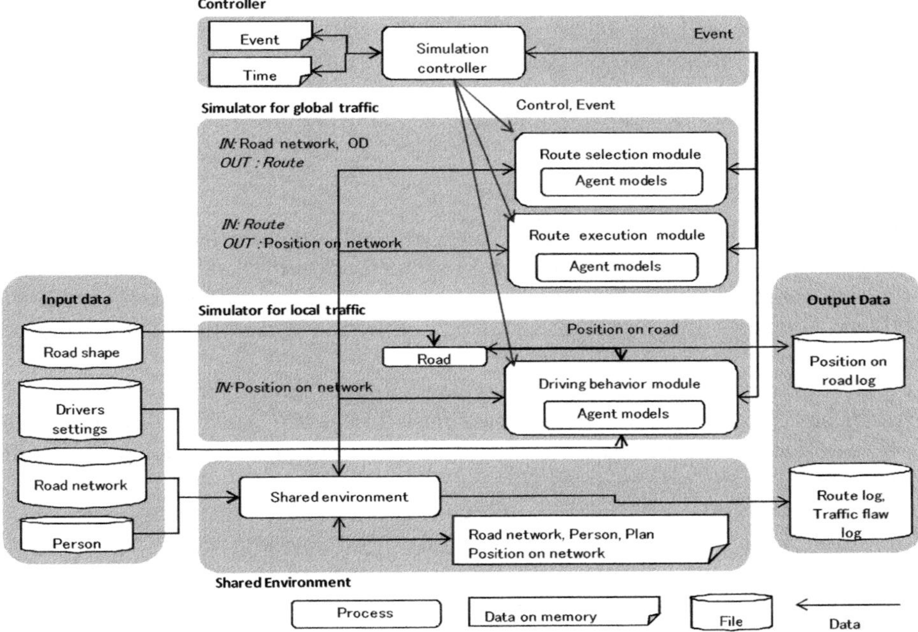

Fig. 2. System Diagram of Platform

3 Implementation

Previous traffic simulation research consists of either route selection on a road network or local driving behavior on single roads. Research on route selection has lead to the modeling of decision processes and route utility functions. Research on local driving behavior has considered the observation of and responses to road geometry, signals, and surrounding cars. There are gaps between the global traffic flow based on route selection and local traffic flows based on driving behavior.

Nagel and his colleagues worked on global traffic flow in a city with multiagent-based traffic simulators based on the queue model [1]. However, their approach fails to support realistic driving behavior simulations on particular roads. This is because details of the road structure (*e.g.*, the width of lanes) or surrounding environment including neighboring vehicles cannot be represented, so that the simulated driving behavior fails to consider such local factors.

We assume that there is some interaction between local driving behavior and global route selection. What we need to do is to analyze how local driving behavior impacts citywide traffic patterns. Therefore, the simulation platform must be able to incorporate both driving behavior models and route selection models.

We implemented a traffic simulation platform on the proposed architecture. Figure 2 depicts the system diagram of the platform. We used the open source traffic simulation tool kit MATSim[1] to create the platform. We select MATSim because it has been applied to various traffic simulations and its source codes are completely open [7,2,3]. The global traffic simulation part of our platform is mainly owe to MATSim.

In the following sections, each module is described precisely.

3.1 Simulator for Global Traffic

Route Selection Module. The route selection module reads road network data and OD (Origin-Destination) data of agents from the shared environment. Road network data mainly describes the structure of the road network while the OD data consists of tuples of the starting point and the destination point of each agent.

The road network has travel times of each link; we use either initial default values or the results of the traffic flow simulation of the previous day. The route selection module calculates the average trip time of each road based on the traffic information of the previous day.

In the route selection module, an agent is regarded as the entity performing route selection. The agent selects the route that has minimum cost considering map information and the average trip time of each road. A route plan consists of paths, mode choice, daily activity, and so on.

This module outputs the routes selected by the agents to the shared environment.

Route Execution Module. The route execution module deals with abstracted road networks, not two-dimensional spaces. The route execution module is implemented for handling a queue-based simulator; that is, the road network is represented as a network of FIFO (First-In, First-Out) queues. Each agent moves over this queue-network between queues according to its scheduled routing plan given vacancies in the next queue. Traffic flows in this platform are composed of agent transfers between queues.

The route execution module reads the route plan of each driver agent from the shared environment. In the route execution module, the agent is regarded as the plan executor.

The road network is abstracted as a network consisting of nodes and links. The agent acquires location information on the basis of nodes and links. A road node pops a driver agent from the waiting queue and pushes it onto the running queue of the next road link, if the running queue on the next road link has enough space.

The route execution module writes agent positions, using node and link descriptions, to the shared environment.

---

[1] MATSim (Multiagent Transport Simulation Toolkit: (`http://sourceforge.net/projects/matsim/`) is an open source toolkit developed by the Technical University Berlin and the Swiss Federal Institute of Technology Zurich for conducting large-scale agent-based traffic simulations. Revision 7476 is used in this paper.

3.2 Simulator for Local Traffic

Driving Behavior Module. In order to achieve traffic simulations that cover the driving behavior level, we add a driving behavior module. In the driving behavior module, the agent is regarded as a virtual driver and vehicle. They move in a two-dimensional space rather than the abstract road network.

The driving behavior module starts calculating driving behavior when an agent enters a link in the route execution module. The module reads agent ID and road ID from the shared environment and gets details of the road's structure and surrounding environment including neighboring vehicles from the road module in the local environment.

Data that is used by only one simulator must be accumulated in the local environment for the simulator. Other simulators do not use specific road details such as width and slope, but deal with more abstract data such as transit time or link loads. Accordingly, these elements are stored in the road module of the local environment.

The execution process of agents in the driving behavior module is summarized as follows.

1. Observation
   Controller requests the driving behavior module to determine the next operation. At first, the driver agent demands information on the surrounding environment, *i.e.*, sensor data. He observes state of own car, surrounding cars, and the roads in the immediate vicinity.
2. Recognition
   Drivers may not be able to recognize all observed information. This step filters the observed information based on the driver's characteristic. For example, an aged driver is unable to mentally map the surrounding traffic situation as quickly as a young driver.
3. Decision
   Driver agents decide which driving behavior should be executed next considering the recognized information. They determine their acceleration/brake/steering operations.
4. Execution
   The driver agents execute the acceleration/brake/steering operations. This involves not only setting the accelerator/brake/steering values directly but also the execution of sequential acts such as changing lanes. The driver agent has own vehicle module which holds car specifications, such as size, maximum speed, car type and so on. The vehicle module converts the operations set by the driver agent into direction and acceleration/deceleration values.
5. Update location
   Vehicle module calculates the vehicle's next state, such as its speed, velocity, and direction, based on the driving operation. Vehicle module updates the location information for the road module by accumulating the positions of vehicles in the local environment.

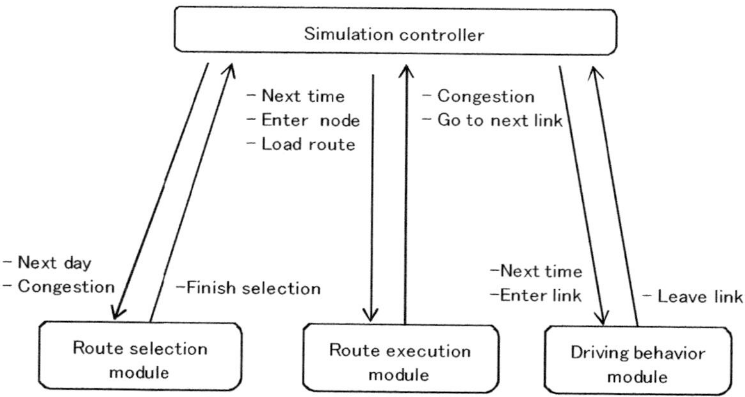

Fig. 3. Message Control Provided by Simulation Controller

Using the location information, the driving behavior module checks whether the driver agent should be transferred to the next link or not. The result is then reported to the route execution module via the simulation controller.

3.3 Simulation Controller

The simulation controller administers the entire simulation process. Simulator communication is based on message passing. At the beginning of a city traffic simulation, the route selection module is called to create a route from starting point to goal point for each agent. After that, the traffic simulation is started. The route execution module is called every second to calculate the route traces of agents on the abstracted road network. The driving behavior module can be called on shorter periods, such as 0.1 seconds.

Figure 3 shows how the simulators work together by sending messages.

- When a simulation is started, the controller requests the route selection module to calculate a route from starting point to goal point ("Next Day"). When congestion occurs on an intersection, the route selection module receives a "Congestion" message from the route execution module and rerouting is begun. The route selection module returns "Finish selection" message. After that, the controller sends "Load route" to the route execution module which triggers the module into reloading the appropriate routes.
- When the route execution module receives "Next time" message, the module calculates the state expected at the next time step. If the route execution module receives "Enter node" message which is raised by the "Leave link" message sent by the driving behavior module, the route execution module registers the agent mentioned in the message as an object to calculate the route trace of the agent on the road network. The agents on the route execution module decide the next link toward their goals and send "Go to next link" messages with agent ID and road ID to the simulation controller.

– When the driving behavior module receives "Next time" message, the module calculates the state expected at the next time step. If the driving behavior module receives "Enter link" message which is raised from "Go to next link" from the route execution module, the driving behavior module registers the agent mentioned in the message as an object to calculate its driving behavior. The driver agents in the driving behavior module check whether they have reached the end of the link or not. If they have arrived at the end of the link, "Leave link" messages are sent to the route execution module via the simulation controller.

In this manner, our platform for traffic simulations can integrate the simulators that reflect different aspects of driving in a city, *i.e.*, global route planning-execution and local reactive behavior.

3.4 Shared Environment

The shared environment manages data shared by agents on different simulators. This technique allows transitions in the data to be handled. At the step of time t, all agents read data at time t and decide actions for time t. At the end of the step, the shared environment fixes the data for time $t+1$. In doing so, the simulators do not need to consider the order in which agents are processed.

In general, several simulators may access the shared environment simultaneously, so we need to implement the lock and rollback functions for the shared environment. At present, the shared environment does not have facilities for lock and rollback because these agents on the simulator do not write to the shared environment simultaneously and so do not cause conflicts in terms of the results of actions in our traffic simulation[2]. If the actions of the agents cause a conflict, for example the agents intend to occupy the same spatial position at the same time step in the driving behavior module; the shared environment rollbacks the data and requests the agents to recalculate. With the conflict in mind, they recast their operations at time t all over again.

When other simulation modules are added in this platform, the simulation modules have to implement the interfaces that support event control and data sharing, which are defined by the simulation controller and the shared environment.

4 Performance Analyses

It is important to achieve adequate scalability as well as the ability to handle multiple aspects of traffic. This is because traffic is a phenomenon that emerges from the mass actions of agents.

[2] In the driving behavior module, driver agents can recognize surrounding agents and they move only a short distance from one time step to the next because the time offset is small. Therefore, agents should not collide with each other.

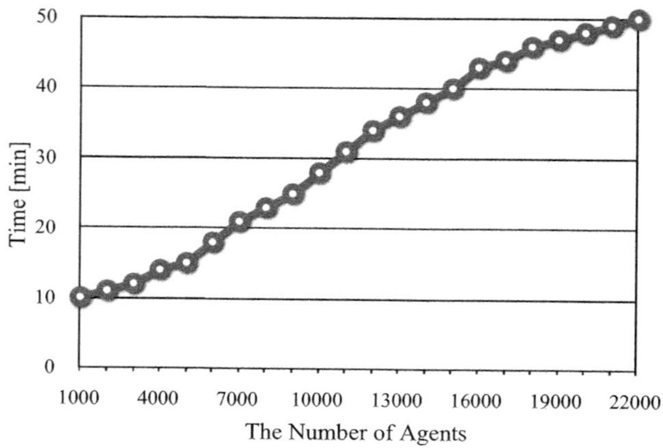

Fig. 4. Computation Time

For example, Paruchuri *et al.* reproduced some traffic situations with around 30 vehicles [9]. Increasing the number of vehicles yielded different results. Agent-based auction simulations were executed in [12], this research indicated that the simulation results were affected by the number of agents.

The challenge tackled in this paper is to achieve massive urban traffic simulations based on the multi-model simulator. In this section, we show that the implemented simulation platform has sufficient scalability. This is because there is a trade-off between the scale of multiagent-based simulations and the diversity of traffic models (decision making of agent and the target environment) in terms of the computation time.

In this experiment, we generated 100 ODs (origin-destination) by pairing two randomly selected points from 25 main intersections within an area that represents the heart of the city of Kyoto (2km x 2km square with 1700 links). For simplicity, all agents used the same route selection model and the same driving behavior model. The simulation time was 2 hours. We ran our experiments on a desktop computer with a Core2Duo 2.53 GHz CPU and 3GB of main memory.

Figure 4 plots the computation time versus the number of agents. As you can see, the computation time is directly proportional to the number of agents. In fact, with the largest number of agents (22,000), the computation time is around 50 minutes.

5 Effect of the Number of Agents

As shown above, we implemented a traffic simulation platform and in this section, we experimentally confirm that our platform has the ability to reproduce actual urban traffic created by a large number of agents. As an example, we investigated how the number of agents impacted city traffic.

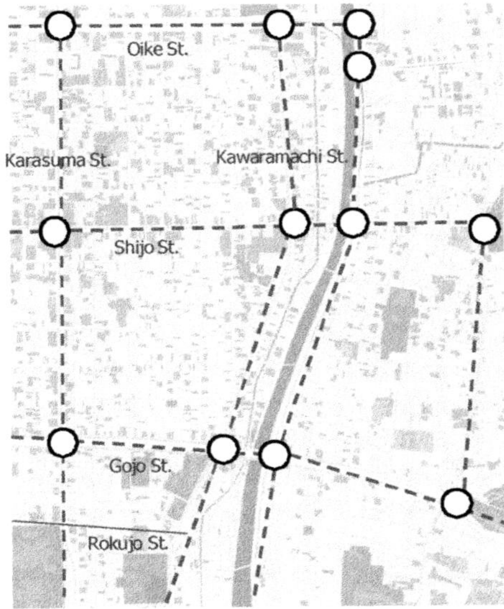

Fig. 5. Simulation Target Area

5.1 Settings

We conducted simulations with 8000 vehicle agents, each of which was assigned an OD selected from 36 types of ODs. We prepared an OD set considering two types of traffic, *i.e.*, traffic in the central part of the target area of the experiment and traffic through the central area. The simulation period was set to 90 minutes and the simulation was iterated 50 times following [10].

Figure 5 shows the simulation target area, which is the central part in the city of Kyoto. Circled points are big intersections. Agents mainly depart from and arrive at these big intersections. The dashed red lines are main streets. We applied the road network data, including all road links in Kyoto city, prepared for commercial programs. Figure 6 shows a screen shot of a simulation experiment. Red rectangles are simulated vehicles.

The aim of this experiment was to investigate how the number of agents influences global traffic flow via agents' route selection.

5.2 Execution

In this platform, multiagent-based urban traffic simulations are conducted with agents who can make decisions on both global route planning-execution and local driving operation. An agent has functions to interact with both simulation modules so that it can determine the most suitable route to the destination and run on that route while expressing its preferred driving behavior (accelerating, braking, lane-changing) given the surrounding environment. The agents decide their behavior according to the assigned models.

Fig. 6. Simulations of the Traffic in the heart of Kyoto city

Within a simulation, the agents iteratively execute the day-to-day re-planning process which consists of route-planning, traffic flow simulation, and scoring. The traffic flow simulation is calculated every second. The details of the process are as follows:

1. At the initial step, a set of initial plans (routes) is generated based on free speed travel times in the route selection module.
2. The traffic simulation is run using the generated plans in the route execution module and the driving behavior module.
3. Each agent calculates the score of his/her plan based on the performance identified by the simulation at end of the day in the route selection module.
4. In the route selection module, some of the population (10% is used in this paper) explore new plans based on the updated travel times resulting from the last simulation. The remaining agents use the previously executed plan.
5. Step 2 to step 4 must be iterated many times before the optimized demand can be identified.

In this paper, we iterated steps 2 to 4 over 50 days and the length of step 2 was 90 minutes.

5.3 Results

We investigate how the number of agents affects the outcome of the simulation, such as visible traffic flows. In order to analyze the effect of the number of agents, we changed only the number of agents; from 2,000 to 12,000 in steps of 2,000.

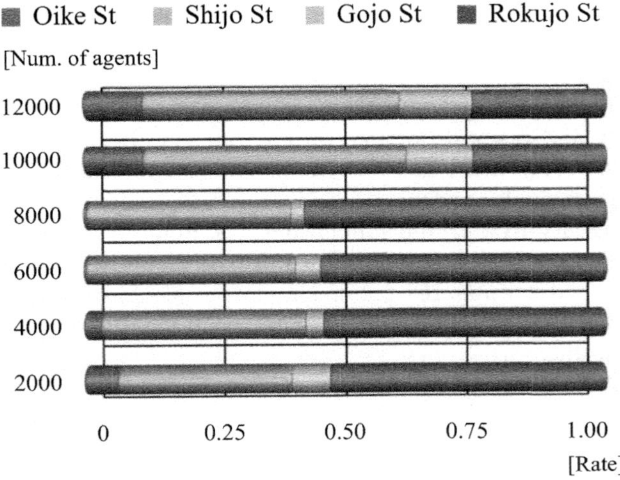

Fig. 7. Impact of the Number of Vehicle Agents: Traffic Share Rate of Four Streets

We counted the number of vehicles that drove through four streets (Oike St., Shijo St., Gojo St., and Rokujo St.) from Karasuma St. to Kawaramachi St. (accordingly, we did not count vehicles which changed their route in the middle of the streets). Rokujo St. is relatively narrow and the three other streets are main streets in the city.

Figure 7 shows the traffic share rates of these four streets in the result of simulation iteration 50. Starting from the left, each column lists the share rates of Oike St., Shijo St., Gojo St. and Rokujo St. Because Rokujo St. is rather a short route between Kawaramachi St. from Karasuma St. (see Figure 5), the share rate of Rokujo St. was high. As shown in the figure, this situation, traffic flows are biased to Rokujo St., is unchanged regardless of the number of agents. However, the share rate of Rokujo St. is reduced at agent numbers of 8000 and 1,0000, while the rates of Oike St., Shijo St and Gojo St. are increased. These results presumably mean that Rokujo St. becomes full and the agents avoid it by selecting other routes including the three other streets even though the routes are longer than routes through Rokujo St.

The important point is that these results are obtained by only changing of the number of the agents. These results indicate that traffic modality patterns do depend on simulation scale. Thanks to the scalability of our simulation platform, we can capture the effect of volume of agents on the city traffic.

6 Conclusion

Multiagent-based simulations yield multiagent societies that well reproduce human societies, and so are seen as an excellent tool for analyzing the real world.

Although numerous attempts have been made to conduct multiagent-based simulations in the traffic domain, it has, up to now, been impossible to reproduce and analyze the traffic from various aspects.

Existing research on city traffic falls into two camps; research focused on global route selection and research focused on local driving behavior. However, these two behaviors clearly affect each other. Phenomena that occur in a city cannot be captured with single model.

For realizing city-wide traffic simulations, the different aspects of agent decision making and the target environment must be integrated. Toward our objective, we developed a wide-area traffic simulation platform based on the multi-model approach that enables us to execute social simulations from various aspects of city traffic.

Our contributions are as follows.

1. Designed multiagent simulation platform based on multi-model approach
   For realizing city-wide traffic simulations, we designed a multi-model platform for urban traffic simulations that can take account of the different aspects of the decision making of agents and the target environment. The platform allows us to take advantage of the multiple models proposed in related works.
2. Implemented urban traffic simulation capturing various aspects
   We developed an urban traffic simulator based on the proposed architecture. This integrated simulator includes two models; route processing and driving behavior.
3. Evaluate platform performance
   We evaluated the scalability of the platform. As a simulation example, we examined how the number of agents impacts simulation results such as traffic flow.

One future direction of this study is to create more sophisticated behavior models. It is clear that human drivers have very diverse driving behaviors with complicated decision making processes. We are going to use participatory modeling methodologies to extract more realistic driving behavior models [6].

Acknowledgment. This work was supported by Panasonic Corp. - Kyoto University Joint Research: Crowd Navigation for Region EMS Considering Individual Behaviors and Preferences and Kyoto University Global COE Program: Informatics Education and Research Center for Knowledge-Circulating Society.

References

1. Balmer, M., Cetin, N., Nagel, K., Raney, B.: Towards truly agent-based traffic and mobility simulations. In: The 3rd International Conference on Autonomous Agents and Multiagent Systems (AAMAS-2004), pp. 60–67 (2004)
2. Balmer, M., Meister, K., Rieser, M., Nagel, K., Axhausen, K.W.: Agent-based simulation of travel demand: Structure and computational performance of matsim-t. In: The 2nd TRB Conference on Innovations in Travel Modeling (2008)

3. Balmer, M., Rieser, M., Meister, K., Charypar, D., Lefebvre, N., Nagel, K.: MATSim-T: Architecture and Simulation Times. In: Multi-Agent Systems for Traffic and Transportation Engineering, pp. 57–78. IGI Global (2009)
4. Deguchi, H., Kanatani, Y., Kaneda, T., Koyama, Y., Ichikawa, M., Tanuma, H.: Social simulation design for pandemic protection. In: The First World Congress on Social Simulation (WCSS-2006), vol. 1, pp. 21–28 (2006)
5. Epstein, J., Axtell, R.: Growing Artificial Societies: Social Science from the Bottom Up. MIT Press (1996)
6. Hattori, H., Nakajima, Y., Ishida, T.: Learning from humans: Agent modeling with individual human behaviors. IEEE Transactions on Systems, Man, and Cybernetics, Part A 41(1), 1–9 (2011)
7. Illenberger, J., Flotterod, G., Nagel, K.: Enhancing matsim with capabilities of within-day re-planning. In: The IEEE Intelligent Transportation Systems Conference, pp. 94–99 (2007)
8. Kitano, H., Tadokor, S., Noda, H., Matsubara, I., Takahasi, T., Shinjou, A., Shimada, S.: Robocup rescue: search and rescue in large-scale disasters as a domain for autonomous agents research. In: The IEEE Conference on Systems, Men, and Cybernetics, Tokyo, vol. VI, pp. 739–743 (October 1999), `citeseer.ist.psu.edu/kitano99robocup.html`
9. Paruchuri, P., Pullalarevu, A.R., Karlapalem, K.: Multi agent simulation of unorganized traffic. In: The 1st International Joint Conference on Autonomous Agents and Multiagent Systems (AAMAS-2002), pp. 176–183 (2002)
10. Raney, B., Nagel, K.: Iterative route planning for large-scale modular transportation simulations. Future Generation Computer Systems 20(7), 1101–1118 (2004)
11. Scerri, D., Hickmott, S., Padgham, L., Drogoul, A.: An Architecture for Modular Distributed Simulation with Agent-Based Models. In: Ninth International Joint Conference on Autonomous Agents and Multiagent Systems (AAMAS-2010), pp. 541–548 (2010)
12. Yamamoto, G., Tai, H., Mizuta, H.: A Platform for Massive Agent-Based Simulation and Its Evaluation. In: Jamali, N., Scerri, P., Sugawara, T. (eds.) MMAS 2006, LSMAS 2006, and CCMMS 2007. LNCS (LNAI), vol. 5043, pp. 1–12. Springer, Heidelberg (2008)

GAMA: A Simulation Platform That Integrates Geographical Information Data, Agent-Based Modeling and Multi-scale Control

Patrick Taillandier[1,2], Duc-An Vo[1,2], Edouard Amouroux[1,2], and Alexis Drogoul[1,2]

[1] IRD, UMI UMMISCO 209, 32 avenue Henri Varagnat, 93143 Bondy, France
[2] IFI, MSI, UMI 209, ngo 42 Ta Quang Buu, Hanoi, Vietnam
voducanvn@yahoo.com, edouard.amouroux@ird.fr, {patrick.taillandier,alexis.drogoul}@gmail.com

Abstract. The agent-based modeling is now widely used to study complex systems. Its ability to represent several levels of interaction along a detailed (complex) environment representation favored such a development. However, in many models, these capabilities are not fully used. Indeed, only simple, usually discrete, environment representation and one level of interaction (rarely two or three) are considered in most of the agent-based models. The major reason behind this fact is the lack of simulation platforms assisting the work of modelers in these domains. To tackle this problem, we developed a new simulation platform, GAMA. This platform allows modelers to define spatially explicit and multi-levels models. In particular, it integrates powerful tools coming from Geographic Information Systems (GIS) and Data Mining easing the modeling and analysis efforts. In this paper, we present how this platform addresses these issues and how such tools are available right out of the box to modelers.

Keywords: Simulation platform, Agent-based modeling, Geographical vector data, Multi-level control.

1 Introduction

The agent-based modeling has brought a new way to study the complex systems. It allows to take into account different levels of interactions as well as the heterogeneity of the entities composing the system.

Even if numerous simulation platforms exist, most of the complex models are still developed from scratch. Indeed, very few platforms allow to directly work with geographical vector data (series of coordinates defining geometries) and/or to define multi-level models. Moreover, these platforms are often complex to use and their understanding can require a time investment from the modeler that can be similar to the one needed to develop a model from scratch.

N. Desai, A. Liu, and M. Winikoff (Eds.): PRIMA 2010, LNAI 7057, pp. 242–258, 2012.

In this paper, we present the GAMA agent-based simulation platform [1], [2]. This platform provides a complete modeling and simulation development environment for building spatially explicit multi-agent simulations. Many models have already been implemented using this platform (e.g. [3][4][5][6]). Its main advantages come from its versatility (domain independent) and the simplicity to define a model with it. Indeed, GAMA provides a rich, yet accessible, modeling language based on XML, GAML, that allows to define complex models integrating at the same time entities of different scales and geographical vector data.

The paper is organized as follow. In Section 2, we present the capabilities of GAMA concerning the integration of geographical vector data. Section 3 is dedicated to the presentation of its multi-scale modeling capabilities. In Section 4, we investigate a way to couple the use of geographical data and multi-scale modeling. Section 5 discusses about the contributions of this paper. At last, Section 6 concludes.

2 Integrating Geographical Vector Data in Simulation

2.1 Why Using Geographical Vector Data in Models?

These last years have seen the development on a large scale of geographical vector datasets. Today, most of the decision makers use this type of data when they have to face a problem integrating a spatial dimension.

In the context of simulations, using this type of data allows to make the simulations closer to the field situation. In addition, it allows to use tools, like spatial analysis, coming from Geographic Information Systems (GIS) to manage these data.

2.2 Use of Geographical Data in Models

If more and more models integrate geographical vector data, their use can take different forms. In the following sections, we present three different ways of using vector data, from the simplest (reading/writing of geographical data) to the most complex (agentification of geographical data).

2.2.1 Reading and Writing of Geographical Vector Data

The most basic functions concerning the use of geographical vector data are the reading and the writing of geographical data from files and from database. The goal is to integrate seamlessly the vector data as the simulation's environment (input) and to store the resulting environment (output).

Once geographical vector data has been read, several uses can be made of them. The most straightforward one consists in translating them as a grid where agents are localized.

2.2.2 Using Geographical Vector Data as Background Layers

A more complex use consists in using these data as a "background layer" constituted of geographical objects: the agents will be able to move according to this layer.

For example, some agents will be able to move along a network of road, or inside a complex polygon (e.g. inside a forest represented by a polygon.

This use requires the integration in the simulator of GIS specific primitives such as moving an agent inside a geometry, computing a shortest path between two points of this geometry (or on a network), etc.

2.2.3 Agentification of Geographical Vector Data

A richer ways of integrating geographical vector data in a model is to consider each geographical object as an agent. Thus, a road will be an agent, a building or a city, and each object contained in a geographical dataset will also be represented by an agent. Remark that this kind of geographical data agentification was already used for other application contexts such as cartographic generalization [7]. In the context of simulation, the advantage of this approach is to give the possibility to manage geographical objects exactly like other agents in the simulation: it will be possible to give them an internal state and a behavior.

Reciprocally, it is possible to go further and to consider that every "spatialized" (localized and with a geometry) agents of the simulation has a geometry and can be viewed as a geographical object in a geographical dataset. In this way, the management of agents and geographical objects is equivalent and trouble-free. Indeed, no difference is made anymore between agents and geographical objects.

2.3 Geographical Vector Data in Existing Simulation Platforms

2.3.1 Simulation Platforms with Basic Support of Geographical Vector Data

Swarm [8] is a well-established simulation platform and inspiration for many others. Its original version does not allow to integrate geographical vector data. However, a library called Kenge [9] allows to load layers of geographical vector data. Practically, this extension allows to create a cellular automata from a shape file. In addition, an ad hoc access to geographical data has been developed for specific models (e.g. [10]). Unfortunately, they do not provide any spatial primitives neither the possibility to store the resulted environment.

Netlogo [11] is also a well-established simulation platform. It is largely used for educational purpose and for research. The GIS support has been added recently through an extension [12]. It allows import and export of vector data and support the projection system (the method used to represent the geographical data on a plane). The attributes of the vector data are made accessible as well as their geometrical characteristics (centroid, list of vertex, etc.). Some basic geometrical operations are also available (bounding rectangles, union of polygons, etc.). However, many more advanced spatial analysis operation are not offered.

CORMAS [13] is a platform dedicated to the modeling in ecology and especially the natural resources management where space representation and interaction is essential. It proposes two environment modes: vector and raster. They share the same organization of 3 classes «spatial entity», «agent», and «object». This organization, though being rigid, ease the development of model by abstracting the interaction with environment, thus allows to switch from a discrete environment to a continuous (or vector) one. Unfortunately, CORMAS provides only basic services for the discrete environment. Moreover, GIS support is limited to loading and storing shapefiles (a popular vector data format) and creating elementary areas. GIS primitives (union, intersection, shortest path, etc.) and access to polygon attributes have to be programmed.

In 2008, Urbani proposed the SMAG (portmanteau word from SMA-SIG or MAS-GIS in English) architecture linking a GIS and MABS simulator for decision support system. The author implemented it over CORMAS, calling it CORMGIS [14]. The integration is relatively basic as access to geo-referenced data is done through a data-connection to ArcGIS. In addition, no GIS primitive (union, intersection, etc) is available.

2.3.2 Simulation Platforms with Advanced Support of Geographical Vector Data

Repast J [15] is a modeling toolkit inspired by Swarm. As a toolkit, it provides a structure with only basic services readily available. Different grids are implemented (hexagonal or rectangular, torus or not, etc.) but agents are not (only an interface is given). The GIS support is done through the OpenMap library. It provides the minimal services of a GIS: importing/exporting shapefiles and raster data, some geometrical operations, access to data attributes, etc. Nevertheless, as Repast J provides access to OpenMap, the modeler can implement more complex operations. Unfortunately, this programming is far from reach of the vast majority of modelers.

Repast Symphony (Repast S) [16] is the up-to-date version of the Repast toolkit. It provides the same basic features as Repast J, but is based on a more advanced GIS library, Geotools, which provides additional GIS services. In particular, Repast S allows to directly model a network of lines as a graph and to compute the shortest paths from one point to another. It allows as well to visualize and manage 3D data. Nevertheless, the number of GIS operations available is still fairly limited and localized agents are still to be programmed. More advanced operations have to be programmed (using the Geotools librabry) which is again, evidently, far from reach for many modelers.

2.4 Geographical Vector Data in GAMA

In order to address these shortcomings we developed the GAMA platform, which goes much further by making available many more GIS services and operations and especially an advance management of geographical vector data.

The first version of GAMA that was presented in [1] proposed the idea of using a continuous environment to serve as a reference for all other environments (e.g. grid environment). In this former version, all situated agents had a point for geometry. The use of geographical vector data was very limited: there were just to initialize the initial location of the agents and as a background layer.

If the new version of GAMA (GAMA 1.3) kept the same idea of a reference environment, it goes further by providing a true geometry to all situated agents. This geometry, which is based on vector representation, can be simple (point, polyline or polygon) or complex (composed of several sub-geometries).

The geometry of the agents can be defined by the modeler (a list of points) or directly loaded from a shapefile. Indeed, GAMA allows to use geographical vector data to create agents of a specific species (a prototype of agents that defines both the agent internal state and their behavior): each object of the geographical data will be automatically used to instantiate an agent, GAMA taking care of managing the spatial projection of the data and, if necessary, of reading the values of the attributes. Consequently GAMA considers localized agents and geographical objects in the exact same way.

Example: the following GAML lines allow to create a set of *building* agents from the shapefile *shape_file_building.shp* and to set the value of the attribute *nature* of each created *building* agent according to the attribute *NATURE* of the shapefile:

```
<create species="building" from="shape_file_building.shp"
 with="[nature:: read 'NATURE']"/>
```

Figure 1 gives an example of the agentification of 4 buildings from a shapefile.

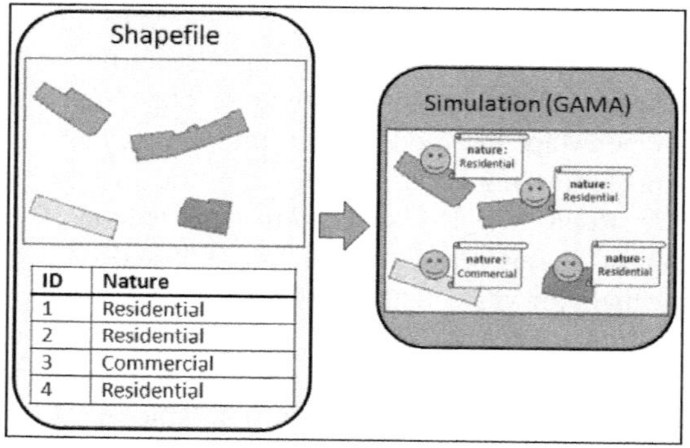

Fig. 1. Example of geographical data agentification

In the same way, GAMA allows to save a set of agents in a shapefile.

Example: the following GAML lines allow to save all the agents of the species *building* in the shapefile *shape_file_building.shp* and to set the value of the attribute *NATURE* of each geographical object according to the attribute *nature* of the agents:

```
<save species="building" to="shape_file_building.shp"
 with="[nature:: 'NATURE']"/>
```

In order to ease the manipulation of the vector geometries, GAMA integrates different GIS features that are directly available through the GAML language. Thus, GAMA allows to:

- Compute the area and the perimeter of a geometry.

Example: The following GAML line allows to compute the area of the geometry of the agent *ag*:

```
<let name="the_area" value="ag.area" />
```

- Test if two geometries intersect, touch, cross, overlap each other.

Example: The following GAML lines allow to test if the geometry of the agent that is applying the action intersects the geometry *geom*:

```
<do action="interection" return="is_true">
   <arg name="geometry" value="geom" />
</do>
```

- Compute the convex hull and the buffer geometry of a geometry (Figure 2).

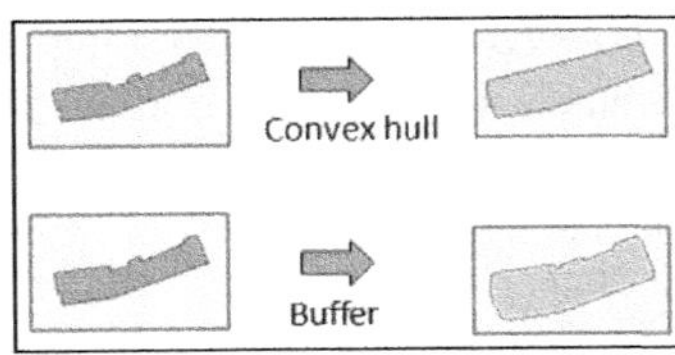

Fig. 2. Example of convex hull and buffer actions

Example: The following GAML line allows to compute the convex hull of the geometry of the agent that is applying the action:

```
<do action="convex_hull" return="result"/>
```

- Apply translation, rotation and scaling operations on a geometry (Figure 3).

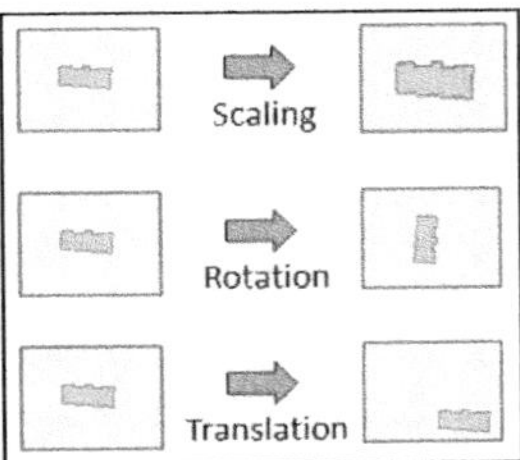

Fig. 3. Example of scaling, rotation and translation actions

Example: The following GAML lines allow to rotate the geometry of the agent that is applying the action with an angle of 90°:

```
<do action="rotation ">
   <arg  name="angle" value="90" />
</do>
```

- Compute the geometry resulting from the union, intersection or difference of two geometries (Figure 4).

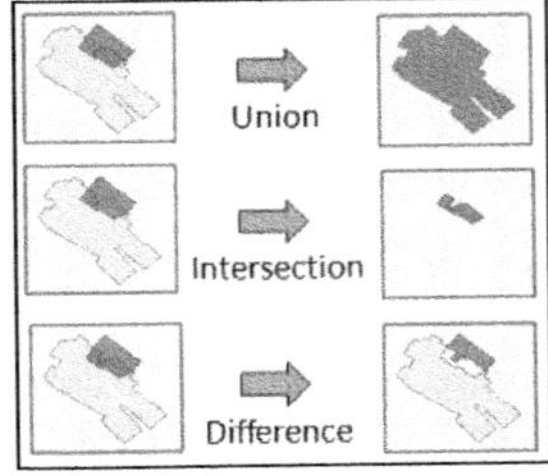

Fig. 4. Example of union, intersection and difference actions

Example: The following GAML lines allow to compute the difference between the geometry $geom_1$ and the geometry $geom_2$:

```
<do action="difference" return="result">
   <arg name="geometry1" value="geom1" />
   <arg name="geometry2" value="geom2" />
</do>
```

- Compute the distance between two geometries (minimal distance).

Example: The following GAML lines allow to compute the distance between the geometry of the agent that is applying the action and the geometry *geom*:

```
<do action="distance_geometry" return="result">
   <arg name="geometry" value="geom" />
</do>
```

- Compute the neighborhood of an agent, i.e. all the agents that are localized at a distance lower than a given thresholds to the agent.

Example: The following GAML lines allow to compute the neighborhood of the agent *ag*:

```
<let name="neighborhood" value="ag.neighbours_geometry "/>
```

- Compute a random point inside a geometry.

Example: The following GAML lines allow to compute a random point inside the geometry *geom*:

```
<do action="place_in" return="result">
   <arg name="geometry" value="geom" />
</do>
```

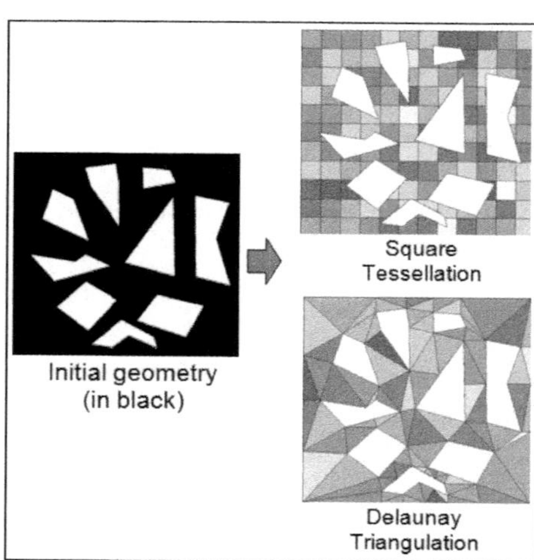

Fig. 5. Example of Tessellations (square and triangle)

- Compute the point of a geometry that is the closest to the agent location.

Example: The following GAML lines allow to compute the point of the geometry *geom* that is the closest to the agent that is applying the action.

```
<do action="closest_point_in" return="result">
   <arg name="geometry" value="geom" />
</do>
```

- Apply a tessellation operation (square or triangle) on a geometry (Figure 5).

Example: The following GAML lines allow to compute the Delaunay triangulation of the geometry (polygon) *geom*:

```
<do action="triangulation" return="result">
   <arg name="geometry" value="geom" />
</do>
```

- Compute the skeleton of a geometry (Figure 6).

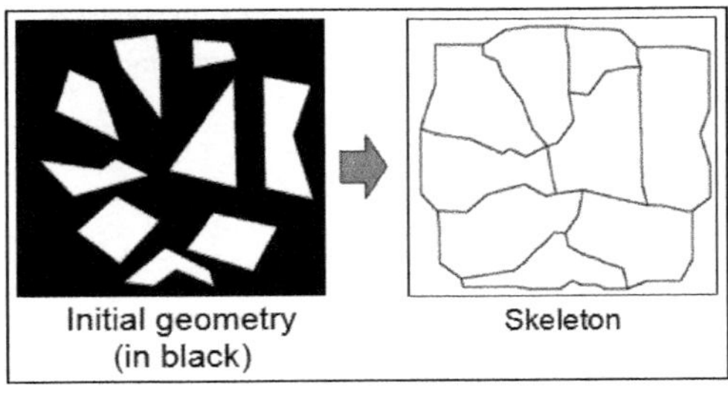

Fig. 6. Example of Skeletonization

Example: The following GAML lines allow to compute the skeleton of the geometry (polygon) *geom*:

```
<do action="skeletonization" return="result">
   <arg name="geometry" value="geom" />
</do>
```

- Compute the shortest path (or the distance) inside a geometry (line network or polygon) between two points located in the geometry. For this computation, our approach consists in modeling the geometry as a graph, and in computing from it the shortest path linking the two points. In the context of a line network, the modeling as a graph is trivial. In the context of a polygon, this one is based on a Delaunay triangulation of the geometry: each triangle resulting from the triangulation is modeled as a node and an edge represents the fact that two triangles are adjacent. Figure 7 shows an example of graph computation. Two algorithms are implemented for the shortest path computation: Dijkstra [17] and Floyd Warshall [18].

Example: the following GAML lines allow to move the agent that is applying the action toward the point *the_target*, at a speed of 5 km/h, inside the geometry *geom (which can be a graph or a polygon)*:

```
<do action="goto">
   <arg name="target" value="the_target" />
   <arg name="speed" value="5 km/s" />
   <arg name="geometry" value="geom" />
</do>
```

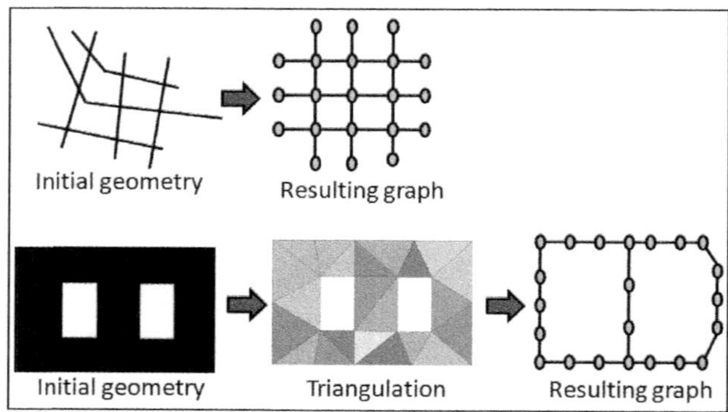

Fig. 7. Example of graph computation

3 Multi-scale Modeling

3.1 Context

Another advantage of the agent-based modeling approach is its representation versatility. Indeed, an "agent" can represent any individual or aggregation/structure of individuals of the reference system, at any spatial scale and across different time horizons. Thus the modeler is free in her/his choice of the entities of the reference system that will be represented by agents. This choice will depend on the level of abstraction of the reference system the modeler is working with. This, in turn, depends on the question he/she wants to answer with the model, on the data available at hand, on the scale at which this data is described, etc.

In addition to the agent representing entities of the reference system, the modeler can need to explicitly represent emergent structures. Indeed, during the simulation stage (execution of the model), some structure can emerge: appearance of pheromone trail built by ant [19], evolution of social group within a population [20], formation of arches in granular environment [21], etc. These structures are often the result of non-linear interactions between the agents defined in the model and can play a significant role in the model dynamics. They can be considered as a higher level of abstraction (upper scale) compare to the underlying agents composing them. It is important, if not crucial, to be able to detect and to generate them dynamically (i.e. might simplified the simulation run).

Current agent-based modeling platforms lack support in term of agent-based modeling language to represent these structures as explicit entities in the model and tools to detect them. Thus, modelers face difficulties when they need to represent them and to follow their dynamics during the course of the simulation.

3.2 Multi-scale Modeling in GAMA

In GAMA, in order to let modelers dynamically track the emergence of dynamic structures, we let them represent these structures as explicit entities in the model. We call these entities “emergent agents”. As regular agent, an emergent agent can have attributes and behaviors. Beside, its instantiation depends on the appearance of certain properties during the simulation and its life-cycle possesses some specific operations.

3.2.1 Representing Emergent Structure

The “creation” operation helps to specify when an emergent agent is instantiated. This operation allows the modeler to express in an explicit way the rules governing the instantiation of emergent agents during the simulation. For example, consider a simulation of city dynamics: a modeler can decide to instantiate an emergent agent of species *building block* when two or more *building* agents are close enough. Figure 8 illustrates this example: an emergent agent *(building block)* representing the emergent structure is created with six micro-agents *(building)* as components.

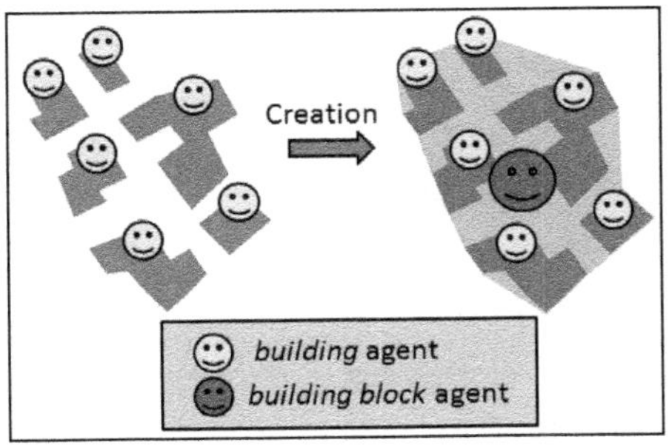

Fig. 8. Creation of an emergent agent (*building block* agent)

The “update” operation describes how micro-agents are added to or removed from an emergent agent. Some micro-agents may no longer satisfy a condition to belong to an emergent agent, while others, still “free” may now fulfill it: this operation allows to specify how these agents are added or removed from the structure. The purpose of this operation is to keep the list of components up-to-date with respect to the meaning of the emergent agent.

Figure 9 illustrates the “update” operation. It follows the example of city dynamic simulation presented Figure 8. We consider that a building block agent composes of three *building* agents. One building agent doesn’t satisfy the condition to belong to the building block agent anymore. A free building agent satisfies the condition to become a member of the building block agent. This operation helps the modeler to remove one building agent from the building block agent and add one building agent to the building block agent.

The “merge” operation allows the modeler to specify how several emergent agents representing different structures can be merged into one unique emergent agent. The fusion of their respective components then becomes the components of the new unique emergent agent.

Figure 10 illustrates the “merge” operation using the same example as Figure 8 and 9. We consider a new *building block* agent (in yellow) has been created. This agent is close enough to the existing *building block* agent (in green) to merge with it. The resulting agent will be composed of the 5 *building* agents composing the two *building block* agents.

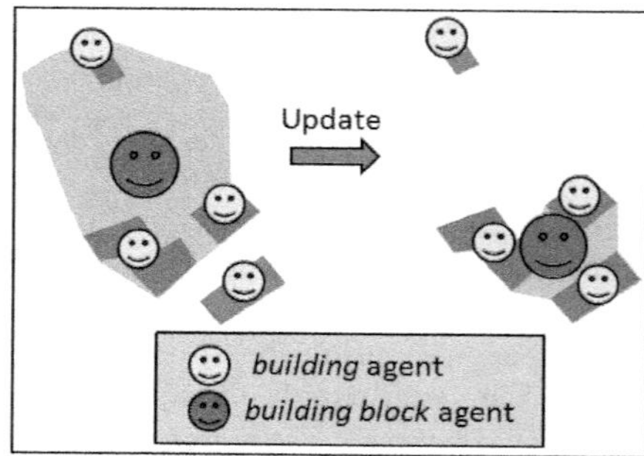

Fig. 9. Update of an emergent agent (*building block* agent)

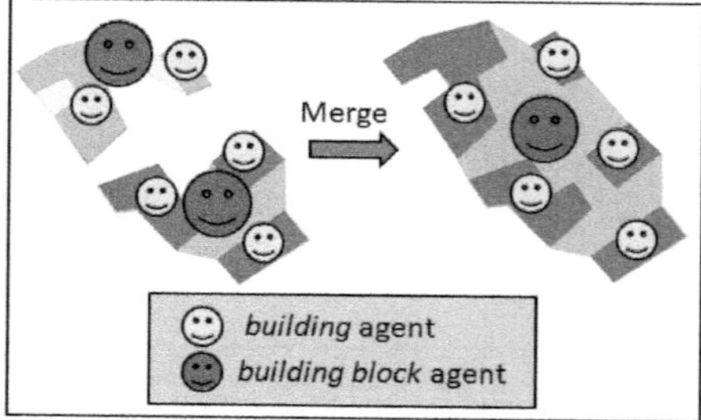

Fig. 10. Fusion of different emergent agents

The purpose of the "disposal" operation is to express when an emerging structure should not consider to be an agent in the simulation anymore. The emergent agent representing the structure is cleared out of the simulation and its components become free.

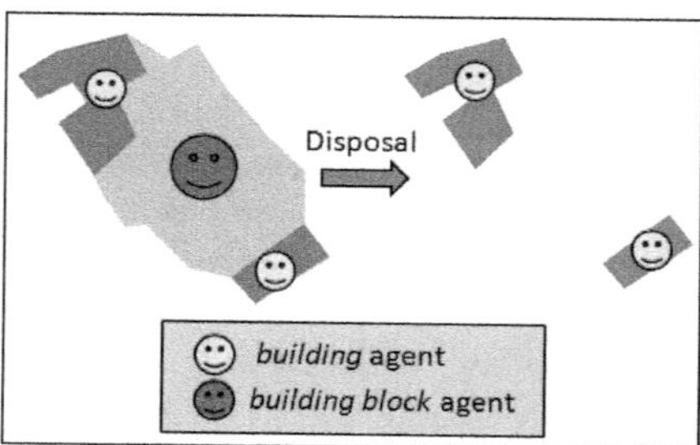

Fig. 11. Death of an emergent agent

Figure 11 illustrates the "disposal" operation. Following the example presented Figure 10, we consider that three of the *building* agents composing the *building block* agent died. Now, the remaining *building* agents are too far from each other to compose a *building block* agent. Then, the *building block* agent is going to die.

The top-down feedback control allows the modeler to describe which feedback constraint an emergent agent is exercising on its underlying micro-agents. As emergent agents usually emerge because of the interactions of certain micro-agents, these agents have an influence on its attributes and behavior. Reciprocally, an emergent agent may also provide a feedback on the behavior of its components, either implicitly or explicitly. In order to describe it, the modeler needs to have some way to alter the behavior of a micro-agent (by changing parameters, adding, or removing entire behaviors) before and after it enters an emergent agent.

Typically, in our city dynamic simulation example, a *building* agent, once part of *building block* agent, has more chance to attract residents to live in, and thus to lead to construction of new buildings in the neighborhood (for example, shops).

3.2.2 Representing Emergent Agents in GAMA

An emergent agent is composed of constituent agents. Constituent agents can be considered as micro-agents compared to the emergent agent. Reciprocally, the emergent agent can be seen as a macro-agent compared to its constituent agents. In turn, several emergent agents can be merged to form another emergent agent at a higher level of abstraction. Thus, an agent in GAMA can play the role of macro-agent in one level of organization and micro-agent in a higher level of abstraction. This design aims at permitting the modeler to represent as many levels of abstraction as he needs in his model. Figure 12 shows an example of abstraction level hierarchy for the city dynamic simulation problem: a *city* agent is composed of a set of *district* agents that are each composed of a set of *building block* agents that are at their turn composed of a set of *building* agents.

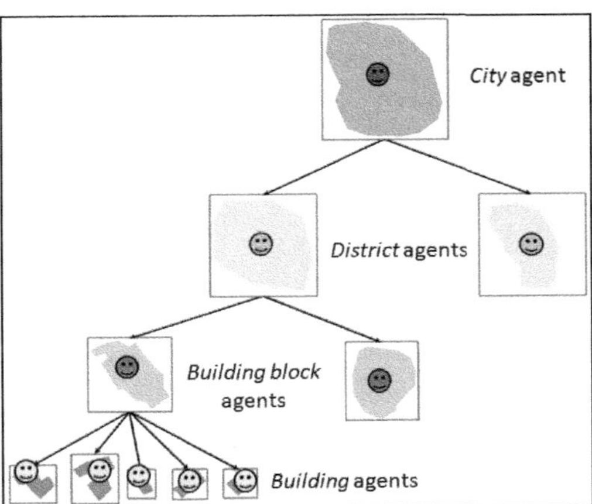

Fig. 12. Example of level of abstraction hierarchy

To manipulate the five specific operations in the lifecycle of an emergent agent (create, update, merge, disposal, top-down constraint control), six GAML commands are defined: *creation, update, merge, disposal, enable* and *disable*.

- The *creation* command allows to specify when emergent agents are created in the simulation.

Example: the following GAML lines create a *building block* agent which has for components the *building* agent contained in the list *list_buildings*:

```
<creation>
   <create with="[components::list_buildings]"
    species="building" />
</creation>
```

- The *update* command allows the modeler to define how the constituent micro-agents are added and removed from an emergent agent.

Example: the following GAML lines update the components of the *building block* agent that is applying this command by adding the *building* agents contained in *added_buildings* and removing the ones contained in *removed_buildings*:

```
<update>
  <set name="components" value ="components + added_buildings -
      removed_buildings"/>
</update>
```

- The *merge* command allows the modeler to define how several emergent agents are merged.

Example: the following GAML lines allow to merge several *building block* agents (the ones contained in the *nearby_bb* list) with the *building block* agent applying this command. All the constituent *building* agents of the *building block* agents contained in the *nearby_bb* list are added to the component list of the one applying the command. Then, the other *building block* agents die (i.e. are removed from the simulation):

```
<merge>
  <loop over="nearby_bb" var="one_bb">
     <set name="components" value ="components +
       one_bb.components"/>
     <ask target="one_bb">
        <do action="die">
     </ask>
  </loop>
</merge>
```

- The *disposal* command allows the modeler to specify when an emergent agent is cleared out of the simulation.

Example: the following GAML line specifies that a building *block agent* will be removed from the simulation if it contains less than two *building* agents:

```
<disposal when="(length components) < 2"/>
```

- The *disable* command allows the modeler to disable certain behavior units appropriately. While the *enable* command allows the modeler to enable the inactive behavior units.

Example: the following GAML lines enable the behavior "expansion" and disable the behavior "destruction" of the *building* agent *one_building_agent*:

```
<ask target="one_building_agent">
   <enable behavior="'expansion'">
   <enable behavior="'destruction'">
</ask>
```

Note that GAMA provides several clustering algorithms (e.g. hierarchical clustering, X-Means [22], Cobweb [23]) that can be used to dynamically detect if an emergent agent has to be instantiate. For example, these algorithms can be used to detect groups of close agents, or agents sharing some specific attributes.

Example: the following GAML lines allows to regroup the *building* agents contained in the *buildings* list into a set of groups; each group being composed of *building* agents of which the distance to each other is lower or equal to 10m:

```
<do action="simple_clustering_by_distance" return="groups">
   <arg name="agents" value="buildings" >
   <arg name="dist_max" value="10m" >
</do>
```

4 Coupling Geographical Vector Data and Multi-scale Modeling

In Section 2.4, we presented the GIS capacities and in Section 3.2 its multi-scale modeling capacities of GAMA. In this section, we investigate a way to couple the use of geographical data and multi-scale modeling: we propose to decompose an agent into a set of constituent agents on geometric basis. One of the main interests of such decomposition is to improve the dynamicity of the special operations applied on the agent.

Indeed, consider an agent with a geometry, which is used to constraint the movement of other agents: for example, a *road network* agent on which some *people* agents are moving, a *forest* agent in which *animal* agents are moving, etc.. Moving agents on this geometry requires to compute a new graph from the geometry each time it is modified. This computation can be very time consuming if the geometry is complex. An approach to face this problem is to decompose the agent in a set of constituent agents on a geometric basis: each constituent agent will represent a part of the macro agent geometry (for example, a line in the context of line network, or a triangle in the context of a polygon). Instead of computing the new graph each time the geometry is modified, the complete graph will be computed only once and each constituent agent will remember its role in the graph. Then, each time the macro agent geometry is modified, it will locally update its list of micro agents (delete the micro agents which geometry is no more part of the global geometry, create new ones if necessary and modify the geometry of existing ones), and each micro agent will update its role in the graph. Figure 13 gives an example, where a graph was already computed for a geometry, and where the modification of the geometry has lead to a local update of the graph.

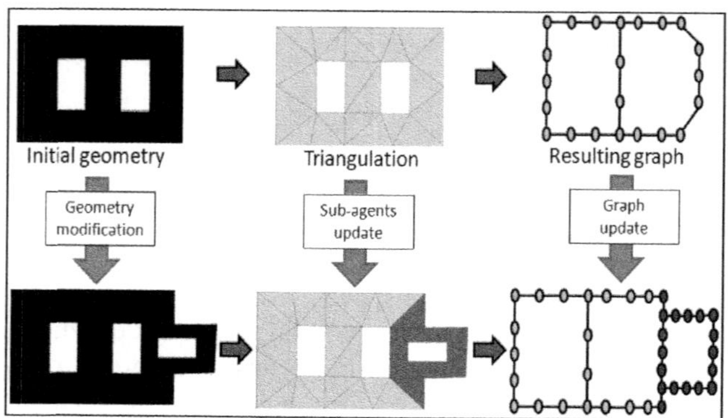

Fig. 13. Example of a local modification of a graph

In GAMA, using such an approach can be easily achieved. Indeed, in Section 2.4, we presented how GAMA allows to compute the square or triangle tessellation of a geometry and a graph from a geometry. More-over, as seen in Section 3.2, GAMA allows to define macro-agents (emergent agent). Thus, GAMA provides all the features that are required to apply this approach.

5 Discussion

We see the contributions of this work as threefold:

1. There is a difference between an idea and its implementation. What we incorporate into GAMA are implementations of ideas that may have been (or not) already proposed by other people but rarely found their way into operational instances. They are implemented into the platform and linked with the modeling language, so that they can be used by anyone building a model in GAMA. In our point of view, these implementations are contributions to the field, because they eliminate the ambiguities and the lack of formalism often found in ABM/MAS contributions and, most important, can be experimented.
2. Integrating existing techniques in a framework and enabling the researchers to easily choose the most appropriate is a delicate exercise. In GAMA, we have ensured that all the proposed techniques are tightly coupled, and that they are usable even by novice users through GAML. This allows us to build, in the same platform, simple models (a la NetLogo) alongside more complex models. Actually, our efforts of integration tend to the point that there are no real differences between a "simple" and a "complex" model. So, while it is true that, for instance, we did not invent graph-related techniques, we believe we contribute to the field by providing a way, for researchers, to use the most appropriate, transparently, into their models.
3. Following the previous point, we see GAMA as a contribution by itself, filling the gap between NetLogo, interesting for prototyping small models, but which does not scale well when it comes to real ones, and RePast, more a complete toolbox than a platform. The fact, for instance, that every agent in GAMA is provided with

a geometry, and that any environment can be discretized, means that researchers can begin with a simple prototype (where agents are points on a grid, like in Netlogo) to test the logic of a model, and turn this model into a more realistic one, for example by loading data from a GIS base, without having to change anything to the logic. This radically transforms the experimental processes of ABM.

6 Conclusion

In this paper, we present the new advance features included in the last version of the GAMA platform (version 1.3)[2]. These features concern the use of geographical vector data and the definition of multi-scale models.

This version of GAMA is already used in several projects related to different application domains such as the avian flu local propagation in North Vietnam, the rift valley fever in Senegal, the brown hopper invasion in South Vietnam, the effect of emotions on waves of panic.

The next version of GAMA, version 1.4, is going to include a new integrated development environment (IDE) with a new modeling language. The goal is to ease the work of the modelers by providing a less extensive and easier to learn language. This version will also include all the classic features provide by most of the modern IDE (auto-completion, automatic detection of errors, etc.). In addition, we plan to improve the integration of the approach proposed in Section 4. Practically, for the moment, the use of this approach with GAMA is still complex and require much GAML code. Methods allowing to automate this approach are required.

References

1. Amouroux, E., Chu, T.-Q., Boucher, A., Drogoul, A.: GAMA: An Environment for Implementing and Running Spatially Explicit Multi-agent Simulations. In: Ghose, A., Governatori, G., Sadananda, R. (eds.) PRIMA 2007. LNCS, vol. 5044, pp. 359–371. Springer, Heidelberg (2009)
2. GAMA platform, `http://gama-platform.googlecode.com`
3. Amouroux, E., Desvaux, S., Drogoul, A.: Towards Virtual Epidemiology: An Agent-Based Approach to the Modeling of H5N1 Propagation and Persistence in North-Vietnam. In: Bui, T.D., Ho, T.V., Ha, Q.T. (eds.) PRIMA 2008. LNCS (LNAI), vol. 5357, pp. 26–33. Springer, Heidelberg (2008)
4. Nguyen Vu, Q.A., Gaudou, B., Canal, R., Hassas, S.: Coherence and robustness in a disturbed MAS. In: IEEE-RIVF, Danang, Vietnam. IEEE (2009)
5. Chu, T.Q., Drogoul, A., Boucher, A., Zucker, J.: Interactive Learning of Independent Experts' Criteria for Rescue Simulations. Journal of Universal Computer Science 15(13), 2701–2725 (2009)
6. Taillandier, P., Buard, E.: Designing Agent Behaviour in Agent-Based Simulation Through Participatory Method. In: Yang, J.-J., Yokoo, M., Ito, T., Jin, Z., Scerri, P. (eds.) PRIMA 2009. LNCS, vol. 5925, pp. 571–578. Springer, Heidelberg (2009)

7. Ruas, A., Duchêne, C.: A prototype generalisation system based on the multi-agent system paradigm. In: Generalisation of Geographic Information: Cartographic Modelling and Applications, pp. 269–284. Elsevier Ltd. (2007)
8. Minar, N., Burkhart, R., Langton, C., Askenazi, M.: The Swarm Simulation System: A Toolkit for Building Multi-Agent Simulations, SFI Working Paper 96-06-042 (1996)
9. Box, P.: Spatial Units as Agents. In: Integrating GIS and Agent-Based Modelling Techniques, Oxford (2002)
10. Haklay, M., O'Sullivan, D., Thurstain-Goodwin, M., Schelhorn, T.: So Go Downtown: Simulating Pedestrian Movement in Town Centres. Environment and Planning B: Planning and Design 28(3), 343–359 (2001)
11. Wilensky, U.: NetLogo. In: Center for Connected Learning and Computer-Based Modeling. Northwestern University, Evanston (1999), http://ccl.northwestern.edu/netlogo/
12. Russell, E., Wilensky, U.: Consuming spatial data in NetLogo using the GIS Extension. In: The Annual Meeting of the Swarm Development Group, Chicago, IL (2008)
13. Bousquet, F., Bakam, I., Proton, H., Le Page, C.: Cormas: common-pool resources and multi-agents systems. In: IEA/AIE, vol. 2, pp. 826–837 (1998)
14. Urbani, D., Delhom, M.: Analyzing Knowledge Exchanges in Hybrid MAS GIS Decision Support Systems, Toward a New DSS Architecture. In: Nguyen, N.T., Jo, G.-S., Howlett, R.J., Jain, L.C. (eds.) KES-AMSTA 2008. LNCS (LNAI), vol. 4953, pp. 323–332. Springer, Heidelberg (2008)
15. North, M.J., Collier, N.T., Vos, J.R.: Experiences Creating Three Implementations of the Repast Agent Modeling Toolkit. ACM Transactions on Modeling and Computer Simulation 16(1), 1–25 (2006)
16. North, M.J., Tatara, E., Collier, N.T., Ozik, J.: Visual Agent-based Model Development with Repast Simphony. In: Conference on Complex Interaction and Social Emergence (2007)
17. Dijkstra, E.W.: A short introduction to the art of programming. Technological Univ. Eindhoven, Rep. EWD316 (1971)
18. Floyd, R.W.: Algorithm 97: Shortest Path. Communications of the ACM 5(6), 345 (1962)
19. Camazine, S., et al.: Self-Organization in Biological Systems. Princeton University Press, Princeton (2001)
20. Schelling, http://web.mit.edu/www/lab/alife/schelling.html
21. Breton, L., Zucker, J.-D., Clément, E.: A Multi-Agent Based Simulation of Sand Piles in a Static Equilibrium. In: Moss, S., Davidsson, P. (eds.) MABS 2000. LNCS (LNAI), vol. 1979, pp. 108–118. Springer, Heidelberg (2001)
22. Pelleg, D., Moore, A.W.: X-means: Extending K-means with Efficient Estimation of the Number of Clusters. In: International Conference on Machine Learning, pp. 727–734 (2000)
23. Gennari, J.H., Langley, P., Fisher, D.: Models of incremental concept formation. Artificial Intelligence 40, 11–61 (1990)

Ao Dai: Agent Oriented Design for Ambient Intelligence

Amal El Fallah Seghrouchni[1], Andrei Olaru[1,2,*], Nga Thi Thuy Nguyen[1,3], and Diego Salomone[1]

[1] Laboratoire d'Informatique de Paris 6, University Pierre et Marie Curie, 4 Place Jussieu, 75005 Paris, France
[2] Computer Science Department, University Politehnica of Bucharest, 313 Splaiul Independentei, 060042 Bucharest, Romania
[3] Institute of French-Speaking Countries for Informatics, 42 Ta Quang Buu, Hanoi, Vietnam
ngaagn@gmail.com, amal.elfallah@lip6.fr,cs@andreiolaru.ro, diego.salomone@sma.lip6.fr

Abstract. In this paper we present mobile Multi-Agent Systems (MAS) as a specific paradigm to design intelligent and distributed applications in the context of Ambient Intelligence (AmI). We discuss how mobility, coupled with MAS, can be useful to meet the requirements of AmI. Indeed, the main features of mobile MAS, such as natural distribution of the system, inherent intelligence of the agents, and their mobility help to address a large scope of distributed applications in the domain of AmI. Other features of MAS, like multi-agent planning, context-awareness and self-adaptation are also very useful to bring an added value to AmI applications. They allow the implementation of both intelligent and collaborative agent behavior. This paper presents the Ao Dai project, that employs the mobile MAS paradigm, and serves as a prototype AmI environment. We also illustrate the functioning of the application through a scenario of user guidance in a smart environment.

Keywords: Ambient Intelligence, Mobile Multi-Agent Systems, Context-Awareness.

1 Mobile Multi-Agent Systems

A Multi-Agent System (MAS) is an organization of a set of autonomous and potentially heterogeneous agents acting in a shared and dynamic environment. MAS represents (e.g. manages, models and / or simulates) physical systems (in robotics) or, more often, software systems. The MAS keystone is the double inference mechanism that is used by the agents. Agents, unlike other design paradigms such as objects or components, distinguish the level of task completion (or problem solving) from the level of solution control. Thus, they may act,

* This author is a PhD student in cotutelle between University Politehnica of Bucharest and University Pierre et Marie Curie.

N. Desai, A. Liu, and M. Winikoff (Eds.): PRIMA 2010, LNAI 7057, pp. 259–269, 2012.

observe their actions and change their own course of action. Agents have specific properties such as autonomy (an agent controls its condition and its actions regardless of any outside intervention); reactivity (an agent senses its environment and reacts to its changes); pro-activity (an agent tends to generate and achieve goals all by itself); and sociability (an agent interacts with other agents in the system). Within a MAS, agents interact to achieve cooperative (e.g. distributed problem solving) or competitive (e.g. coalition formation, auction) group behavior. Finally, a MAS is deployed in a environment that impacts its dynamic behavior.

The agent-based paradigm is particularly appropriate for the implementation of Ambient Intelligence [6,16], because agents offer features that originate from the field of Artificial Intelligence and that are vital to the needs of Ambient Intelligence [11]. Autonomy is useful because individual devices in an Ambient Intelligence environment must be able to act on their own, without the need for user intervention or permanent control from centralized components. Learning can serve to adapt to the user's habits. And reasoning – as well as the capability to make plans – is what makes a system appear intelligent to the user.

The agent-oriented paradigm is also useful in modeling real-world and social systems, where optimal solutions are not needed and problems are solved by cooperation and communication, in a fully distributed fashion [11]. Currently, several agent-oriented programming languages exist [2], that allow the programmer to describe an application only by specifying the behaviour of individual agents.

Such an agent-oriented programming language is CLAIM, that also features a deployment platform for agents, called Sympa [14]. In CLAIM, each agent has a knowledge base, offers to the exterior a certain number of capabilities and is capable of both reactive (by means of rules) and proactive behaviours. More importantly, the multi-agent system has a structure that is inspired from ambient calculus [3]: agents are placed in a hierarchical structure and an agent can have another agent as parent, as well as several other agents as children. Agents in CLAIM are mobile – they are able to change the host on which they are executing, and they are also able to change their place in the hierarchical structure. Moreover, when an agent moves, its children move with it automatically.

Mobility means that agents can move (or migrate) within the organization of their associated MAS. In our framework, migration allows for dynamics that cover several aspects:

- the structure of the MAS (the organization of agents) may change over time due to openness (arrival and departure of agents) and to the evolution of functional requirements (creation / removal of agents).
- the dynamics of acquaintances between agents may appear (arrival or creation of agents), others may disappear (departure or removal of agents) and / or change (e.g. for mobile agents).
- the environment of the MAS may change which requires that agents perceive the changes and take them into account incrementally.

It is the hierarchical structure of CLAIM, as well as the strong mobility that it offers, that makes it especially appropriate for the implementation of an Ambient Intelligence system. That is because CLAIM makes it easier to implement context-awareness. An agent's ambient – formed by itself and all if its children – can represent a context. Agents can represent smart places, can manage smart devices, or can offer services.

The next section discusses several aspects in the implementation of Ambient Intelligence, like context awareness and representation. Section 3 describes the scenario and the implementation of the Ao Dai project – a proof-of-concept Ambient Intelligence systems implemented in CLAIM. The last section draws the conclusions.

2 Context-Awareness

One of the central features that makes distributed systems "intelligent" is *context awareness*. One of the definitions of context is *the set of environmental states and settings that either determines an application's behaviour or in which an application event occurs and is interesting to the user* [4]. One important point in the above definition is the relevance to the user. Either an event must be relevant to the user, or the application's behaviour must change so that it becomes relevant to the user. Context-awareness is the characteristic of an application that makes it change its behaviour depending on, and according to, context.

Research in the domain of context awareness has shown that there are many aspects of context. One classification of context [4] divides it into computational context – available computing and networking resources, including the cost for using them; user context – user's profile, location, people and objects nearby, social situation; physical context – light and noise levels, temperature, traffic conditions, etc; and time context – the current time coordinate of the user and related information (like the season, for instance). Context can be further classified [5] as primary – sensed directly by sensors and specialized devices – and secondary – which is inferred from the primary context.

If many authors consider context as merely a set of sensed values [1,7], a particularly interesting approach to context-awareness is taken by Henricksen et al [8,9], that model context as associations between entities or between entities and attributes, where an entity can be a person, a place, a communication device, etc. These associations can be of different types: static – associations that remain fixed for the lifetime of the entity; dynamic and sensed – obtained from sensors, usually transformed afterwards, changing frequently and subject to sensing errors; dynamic and derived – information that is inferred, usually from sensed or static associations; dynamic and profiled – introduced explicitly by the user, leading to greater reliability, but also subject to staleness.

In a context-aware system, there are several layers that deal with context information. One possible organization [15] uses three layers: data acquisition, data interpretation and data utilization. However, considering that much context information is volatile (e.g. user's location and time), a context-aware system must also feature components for the degradation of context information.

Another important point in context-aware applications is the representation of context information. The choice of the representation technique is closely related to the system itself but some approaches are more appropriate to the field of AmI, like ontology-based models. This technique is the most promising for context modeling in ubiquitous environments [13]. It combines the assets of logic-based models and object-oriented technology [10], showing a higher level of robustness and expressiveness with the possibility of semantic representation.

In AmI systems, the heterogeneity of entities makes the global context representation more difficult due the differences between the context models of each agent. The ontology-based approach allows the different representations since it permits the agents to compare and share information. We need to process the information to compare the similarities between the possible representations to eventually arrive at a common understanding [12]. To avoid this problem, the most part of the implemented projects of Ubiquitous Computing usually work with a smaller part of a bigger scenario. For the sake of simplicity, they cover a closed environment with a global ontology as the base for context representation.

The main drawback of this approach is the definition of a centralized and universal ontology to be used by the system and all of its agents. In open AmI applications, the sensing capacity and incoming agents may change over time, affecting the system's needs. Thus, the MAS should be able to absorb, in some way, the new ontology information and, also, provide tools for the new agents' communication. This distributed ontology issue is an active research domain in part because of the Semantic Web [1] requirements.

3 Ao Dai Project

3.1 Ao Dai Project Scenario

In this project, we have studied several scenarios including the following (see also Figure 1): a user has a meeting in a building that he / she does not previously know. When arriving at the right floor, the user's PDA automatically connects to a local wireless access point. A CLAIM agent executes on the user's PDA – we will call this agent *PDA*. Another agent executes on a local machine and manages the context of the building's floor – call it *Floor*. *Floor* detects the presence of the user's PDA, and instructs the *PDA* agent to move in the agent structure and become a child of *Floor*. The movement is only logical: the agents keep executing on the same machines as before.

When *PDA* enters the floor, *Floor* also spawns a new agent – called *Navigator* – and instructs it to move as a child of *PDA*. This time, the movement is not only logical: *Navigator* is a mobile agent that actually arrives on the user's PDA and will execute there for all the time during which the user is on the floor. The *Navigator* can provide *PDA* (and, inherently, the user) with a map of the floor, can translate indications of the floor's sensors (sent to *Navigator* by *Floor*, and through *PDA*) into positions on the graphical map, and can calculate paths

[1] Semantic Web: http://www.w3.org/2001/sw/

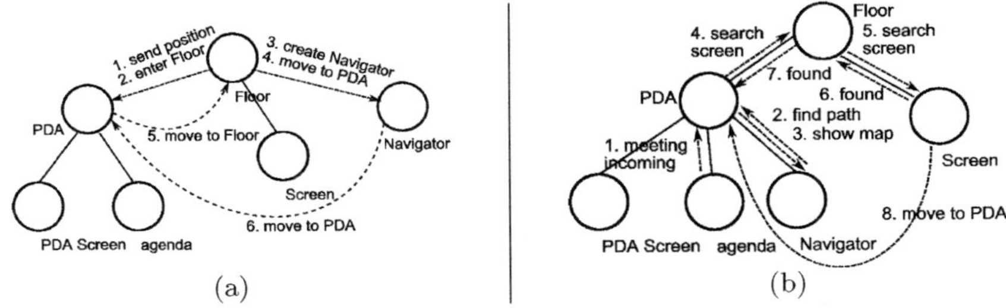

Fig. 1. Sequences of messages exchanged between agents: (a) *Floor* announces *PDA* of its new position, and instructs it to move as its child, then creates a *Navigator* that will offer services to *PDA*; (b) *Agenda* announces a new meeting, *PDA* asks a path from *Navigator*, which in turn requires a larger screen – which is searched on the floor, and found, then *Screen* moves as a child of *PDA*

between the offices on the floor. *Navigator* is an agent that offers to the user services that are available and only makes sense in the context of the floor.

For displaying the map, *PDA* may detect that its screen is too small too appropriately display the map, so *PDA* will proactively initiate the search for a larger screen in the nearby area. The search can have several criteria: the space in which the search will take place (the current office, a nearby office, the whole floor), the range in which to search, and the minimal size of the searched screen. Devices are searched by the capabilities they offer – in this case the *display* capability is needed. *PDA* sends the query to its parent – *Floor* – which in turn locates among its children an agent *Screen*, that manages a physical screen that fits the requirements: it is located near the user and it is available. *Screen* answers the query and *PDA* asks it to move to become its child. Being a child of *PDA* also marks the fact that *Screen* is in use by the user, and *PDA* gains control over the displayed information. Agent *Screen* may either run on the actual intelligent screen, or may only manage the screen while being executed on a server. When the user moves farther from the screen, the PDA will detect that the context is no longer compatible and will free *Screen*, which will return to be a child of *Floor*.

3.2 Implementation

In the Ao Dai project, we have implemented a prototype of multi-agent system that handles several aspects of context-awareness, like user's location, available resources and user preferences. We have based ourselves in an extension of the scenario defined above. The project has been developed by Thi Thuy Nga Nguyen, Diego Salomone Bruno and Andrei Olaru, under the supervision of Prof. Amal El Fallah Seghrouchni.

The prototype is implemented in CLAIM and executes on the Sympa platform. It features several types of agents: *Site*, which is used for "smart" places like *Floor* and *Office*; *PDA*, which directly assists the user from his personal

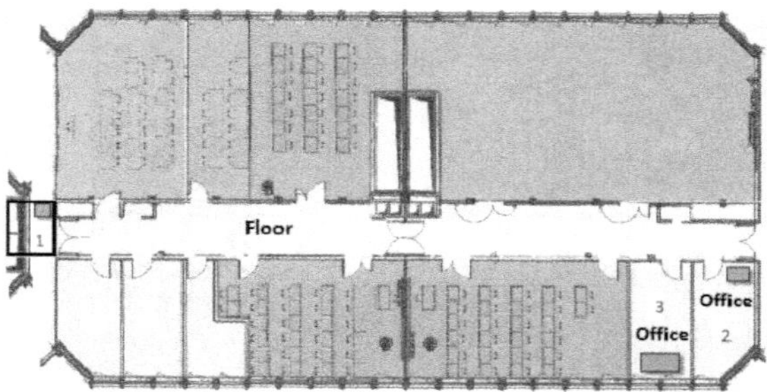

Fig. 2. The map shown by different screens in Ao Dai. There are three *Site* agents: *Floor* and two *Office* agents. Each one has a child of type *Screen*, representing the screens in the different places. The user starts on the floor (1) then moves to one office (2) and then to the other (3).

device; *Navigator* and *Agenda*, which offer services to the user; and *Screen*, which represents a "smart" device with the capability of displaying information.

The prototype has been demonstrated during the 5th NII-LIP6 Workshop held on June 21-22 in Paris, France. The prototype was run on 2 machines. The *Floor* agent (of type *Site*) ran on one machine, and two *Office* agents (also of *Site* type) ran on the other machine. The floor and the two offices all featured screens of different sizes, managed by *Screen* agents (see Figure 2). During the demonstration, a *PDA* agent entered the floor, becoming a child of the *Floor* agent. A *Navigator* was created and sent to *PDA*. When the time of the meeting approached, *Agenda* announced *PDA*, which asked *Navigator* to find the path to the right office. *PDA* also searched for a larger screen, and found one near to the user, and automatically used it to display the map and the path. When the user – together with the PDA – moved to an office, the screen was freed and *PDA* with all children (*Agenda* and *Navigator*) moved to the other machine. There, the user explicitly requires a large screen, and *PDA* finds an appropriate one in the next room, and announces the user. The user then moves to the other office and *PDA* and all of its children move to become children of the agent managing that office. To simulate the interaction between the user and his personal agent *PDA*, an interface was created in Java (see Figure 2).

3.3 Programming in CLAIM

As an agent-oriented programming language, CLAIM [14] eases the task of implementing MAS. It works on top of Java, giving direct access to Java resources if needed. This language is based on explicit declaration of agent's characteristics. The following code shows a part of the definition of agent *PDA* in the Ao Dai project.

```
defineAgentClass PDA(?w,?h,?x_i,?y_i){
   authority = null;
   parent = null;
```

```
  knowledge = {location(?xi,?yi); type(1);}
  goals = null;
  messages = null;
  capabilities = {
     message = PDAatLoc (?name,?xnew,?ynew);
        condition = null;
        do{send(this,migrateTo(?name))}
        effects = null;
     }

     migrate{
        message = migrateTo(?name);
        condition = not(Java(PDA.isParent(this,?name)));
        do{send(this,removeOldNavi(?name))
           .moveTo(this,?name).send(this,demandNavi(?name))}
        effects = null;
     }
     ...
  processes = {send(this,starting())}
  agents = null;
}
```

When the agent *PDA* (the PDA is initially characterized by its location and the size – w, h – of its screen) receives a message about its new location, it will execute the action "migrate". In this action, it checks if its actual location is already the location in the message (the variable $?name$). If it is, the agent ignores the message. Otherwise, it moves to the new site by calling the function "moveTo()". If the new site is located in another computer in the network, the agent and its children will migrate to the new computer.

These characteristics are used to build the hierarchical relationship between agents in CLAIM. As a result, the MAS will be a set of hierarchies distributed over a network [14]. In the Ao Dai project, the agents of type Floor and Office ran on different machines to simulate the agents' migration.

The developer, in this case, need not to worry about the code migration and registration problems that may arise. The language takes care of it, concentrating the agents' information on the *Administration System* (see Figure 3). To address the security issues concerning mobile code, CLAIM offers some features like the agent's authority validation. The language also allows the developer to decide if an agent must have some special access or if an agent must have some resource denied. The sum of these features creates a powerful platform to the development of agent-oriented mobile applications.

3.4 Ao Dai Agents

The given scenario has three major types of agents: Site agent (Floor, Office), Device / Service agent (Navigator, Agenda, Screen) and PDA agent. The latter with the specific role of representing the user during the simulation.

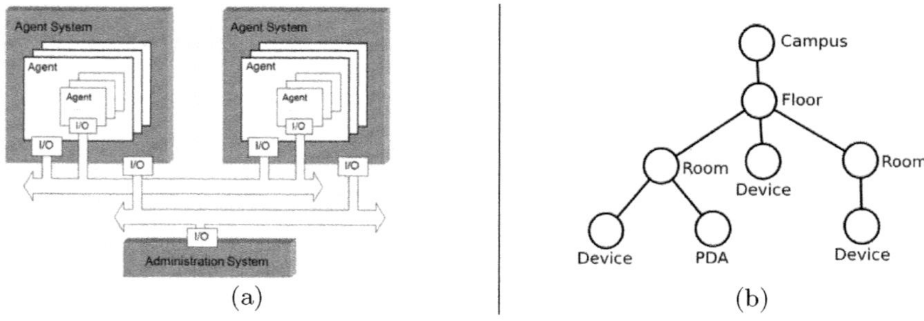

Fig. 3. System distribution in CLAIM: (a) Distribution over the network with each system deployed on a different machine; (b) An example hierarchy in Ao Dai.

- The *Site* agent is used to determine the physical relationship between the agents. It means that an Office agent is a child of a Floor agent only if it is physically located on the given floor.
- The *Service* (or *Device*) agent has the capability to offer to the other agents some specific service. It may be in a direct or indirect way, like showing some information on the screen or advising other agents of the user meeting.
- The *PDA* agent works like a personal device that follows the user through his tasks. The most important features of this agent are that the PDA moves physically with user and has the CLAIM capability of managing requests for services or devices. It also stores the user's preferences.

3.5 Context Representation in Ao Dai

Location is, notably, the most used type of context in applications [5], because it reflects an important set of physical contents. In the Ao Dai project, besides location, we also consider, as part of the user's context, the available computing resources around him and his preferences.

In the first version of this project, the context is directly sensed (in a simulated manner) by the *PDA* and the *Site* Agents, but it is known that, in real applications, an additional layer is needed to capture the sensor information and translate it in useful data.

The context-awareness in Ao Dai is done by exploiting the particular hierarchical agent structure that is offered by the CLAIM language. In CLAIM it is very easy for the developer to instruct agents to move from one parent to another, and an agent moves automatically along with its entire sub-hierarchy of agents. This resembles the mobile ambients of Cardelli [3] and is an essential advantage when implementing context-awareness. That is because agents, while representing devices or locations, can also represent contexts, allowing the developer to describe, in fact, a hierarchy of contexts.

For example, when the user is inside a room, its *PDA* agent is a child of the respective *Site* agent. The children of *PDA* – devices or services – are also in the same context. When the user moves to another room, the *PDA* agent changes parent and, along with it, its children move as well, therefore changing context. Some devices may not be able to move along with the user (e.g. fixed screens, etc.) so they will determine that the new context is incompatible with their properties, moving away from *PDA*.

But context is not only about location, and the hierarchical structure that is offered by CLAIM can be used for easy implementation of other types of context. One of them is computational context. When the user uses a service, a *Service* agent is created and becomes a child of *PDA*. It is easy for the service to interrogate its parent in order to find out more about its capabilities. Conversely, it is easy for *PDA* to check on its children – *Services* or *Devices* – in order to find the resources and capabilities that the user is able to use.

One last type of context that is handled in Ao Dai is user preferences. The user is able to input preferences on the capabilities of devices that it needs to use. These preferences are then integrated in the queries that are launched by the PDA (see Section 3.1). While the structure offered by CLAIM is not directly useful for this aspect, the preferences help find not only the closest device with the required capability, but also the closest device that fulfills certain user requirements. Preferences can also be used to limit the range of the search, which is meaningful from the context-aware point of view: a *Device* that is closer in the agent hierarchy also shares more context with the user.

3.6 Interaction Protocol

In a highly distributed AmI environment, a good representation of context and context-related relations between devices means that most of the communication will happen only at a local level, within the structure formed by these relations. In Ao Dai, the CLAIM agent hierarchy facilitates this: agents sharing a parent share a context.

To preserve the hierarchy, agents interact only with their parent and their children. Take for example the search for devices (see Figure 1). When agent *PDA* wants to search for a device with a certain capability and certain criteria, it must send a request to its parent, for example agent *Floor*. Once the request is received, agent *Floor* searches itself to see if it has the requested capability and satisfies the criteria. If it does, *Floor* answers immediately to agent *PDA*, in the other case, it searches in all of its children (if any) except the agent who invoked the search (agent *PDA*). After all of its children have answered, agent *Floor* checks if there are one or more children that have the capability requested and satisfy the criteria. If it has a confirmation answer, it sends the search result which contains the information about the found device(s) to agent *PDA* and the search is finished. If not, agent *Floor* has to search in its parent (if any). After the parent has answered, agent *Floor* sends the search result to agent *PDA* and finishes the search. The process is executed recursively. User preferences can be used to limit the range of the search to closer contexts.

The advantage of using such a protocol in conjunction with mapping context over the agent hierarchy is that the search will usually end very quickly, assuming the user will most times ask for devices that are likely to exist in his context. The search is executed in the current context first, and then in the parent context and sibling contexts.

4 Conclusion

In this paper we have discussed the use of Mobile Multi-Agent Systems for Ambient Intelligence. Features like distribution, inherent intelligence of the agents, and mobility make MMAS a natural solution for the problems raised in the implementation of Ambient Intelligence environments. Other features of MAS, like multi-agent planning, collective learning and adaptation bring added value by allowing intelligent collaborative behaviour.

Additional challenges that MAS have to deal with in the context of Ambient Intelligence are issues like context-awareness, anticipation and user modeling. The paper discusses some of these issues and then presents the Ao Dai project, a prototype AmI environment, implemented as a multi-agents system, using the agent-oriented language CLAIM.

Ao Dai project is a preliminary work that will serve as a foundation of an international collaboration between four teams [2].

The prototype has been developed as a proof of concept and gave promising results. It shows that the hierarchy of the CLAIM language is very useful to capture different aspects of context-awareness. CLAIM also provides native primitives that allow agents to move – in a single step – between contexts, while their own context follows their movement.

As future steps in our research, integration of better mechanisms of anticipation, more types of contexts and improved context representation into the project will bring it closer to dealing with realistic requirements.

References

1. Baldauf, M., Dustdar, S., Rosenberg, F.: A survey on context-aware systems. International Journal of Ad Hoc and Ubiquitous Computing 2(4), 263–277 (2007)
2. Bordini, R.H., Braubach, L., Dastani, M., El Fallah-Seghrouchni, A., Gómez-Sanz, J.J., Leite, J., O'Hare, G.M.P., Pokahr, A., Ricci, A.: A survey of programming languages and platforms for multi-agent systems. Informatica (Slovenia) 30(1), 33–44 (2006)
3. Cardelli, L., Gordon, A.D.: Mobile ambients. Theor. Comput. Sci. 240(1), 177–213 (2000)
4. Chen, G., Kotz, D.: A survey of context-aware mobile computing research. Technical Report TR2000-381, Dartmouth College (November 2000)
5. Dey, A.K., Abowd, G.D.: Towards a better understanding of context and context-awareness. In: CHI 2000 Workshop on the What, Who, Where, When, and How of Context-Awareness, pp. 304–307 (2000)

[2] MAS team from Paris 6, AIMAS from Politehnica of Bucharest, IFI form Hanoi and PUC-Rio from Brazil.

6. Ducatel, K., Bogdanowicz, M., Scapolo, F., Leijten, J., Burgelman, J.: Scenarios for ambient intelligence in 2010. Technical report, Office for Official Publications of the European Communities (February 2001)
7. Feng, L., Apers, P.M.G., Jonker, W.: Towards Context-Aware Data Management for Ambient Intelligence. In: Galindo, F., Takizawa, M., Traunmüller, R. (eds.) DEXA 2004. LNCS, vol. 3180, pp. 422–431. Springer, Heidelberg (2004)
8. Henricksen, K., Indulska, J.: Developing context-aware pervasive computing applications: Models and approach. Pervasive and Mobile Computing 2(1), 37–64 (2006)
9. Henricksen, K., Indulska, J., Rakotonirainy, A.: Modeling Context Information in Pervasive Computing Systems. In: Mattern, F., Naghshineh, M. (eds.) PERVASIVE 2002. LNCS, vol. 2414, pp. 167–180. Springer, Heidelberg (2002)
10. Krummenacher, R., Lausen, H., Strang, T., Kopeckỳ, J.: Analyzing the modeling of context with ontologies. In: International Workshop on Context-Awareness for Self-Managing Systems (2007)
11. Ramos, C., Augusto, J.C., Shapiro, D.: Ambient intelligence - the next step for artificial intelligence. IEEE Intelligent Systems 23(2), 15–18 (2008)
12. Sansonnet, J.-P., Valencia, E.: Terminological heterogeneity between agents using a generalized simplicial representation. In: Gleizes, M.P., Kaminka, G.A., Nowé, A., Ossowski, S., Tuyls, K., Verbeeck, K. (eds.) EUMAS, pp. 363–374. Koninklijke Vlaamse Academie van Belie voor Wetenschappen en Kunsten (2005)
13. Strang, T., Linnhoff-Popien, C.: A context modeling survey. In: Workshop on Advanced Context Modelling, Reasoning and Management as Part of UbiComp, pp. 1–8 (2004)
14. Suna, A., El Fallah Seghrouchni, A.: Programming mobile intelligent agents: An operational semantics. Web Intelligence and Agent Systems 5(1), 47–67 (2004)
15. Viterbo, J., Mazuel, L., Charif, Y., Endler, M., Sabouret, N., Breitman, K., El Fallah Seghrouchni, A., Briot, J.P.: Ambient intelligence: Management of distributed and heterogeneous context knowledge. In: Ambient Intelligence: Management of Distributed and Heterogeneous Context Knowledge. CRC Studies in Informatics Series, pp. 1–44. Chapman & Hall (2008)
16. Weiser, M.: The computer for the 21st century. Scientific American 272(3), 78–89 (1995)

Probabilistic Approaches to Tag Recommendation in a Social Bookmarking Network

Oly Mistry and Sandip Sen

University of Tulsa
800 South Tucker Avenue
Tulsa, OK 74104, USA
{oly-mistry,sandip}@utulsa.edu

Abstract. Tagging has become increasingly popular with the explosion of user-created content on the web. A 'tag' can be defined as a group of keywords that makes organizing, browsing and searching for content more efficient. Users apply tags to a variety of web-based, shareable content including photos, videos, news articles, bookmarks, friends, etc. Tag suggestions for blog posts or web-pages have changed the focus of the tagging process from generation to recognition, thus making it less time and effort intensive. We propose tag recommendation algorithms for personalized agents, that recommend tags for bookmarks stored in a popular social bookmarking website, *Del.ici.ous* [6]. Our tag recommender agents learn to classify the tags according to their semantic similarity based on collaborative tagging by the users. Hence this approach can be used to facilitate folksonomy formation for the social network. In this paper, we first empirically verify our hypothesis that web pages with similar content are tagged with similar tags. We compare both Content-based and Collaborative approaches to recommend tags to the users. We analyze the performance of two probabilistic approaches to recommend tags from users with similar tagging behavior.

1 Introduction

Tags are labels or keywords associated with items that facilitates organizing, browsing and searching for information [17]. Tags are used for diverse items including photos, URLs, blogs, etc. The use of tag suggestions for blog posts or web-pages has changed the focus of the tagging processes from generation to recognition, thereby making tagging less time and effort intensive [8]. In addition to this immediate tangible benefit of tag recommendation, it has greater impact on online information distribution and sharing. Efficient tag recommendation algorithms can also facilitate emergence of folksonomies for a web-environment, *e.g.*, blog and bookmark sharing.

Researchers have posited that tagging bridges the gap between *browsing* and *searching* [21]. When a web-environment allows free-form tagging for articles, it creates the possibility of formation of Tag-Clouds [5]. A Tag Cloud represents

N. Desai, A. Liu, and M. Winikoff (Eds.): PRIMA 2010, LNAI 7057, pp. 270–287, 2012.

the popularity of different tags based on their frequency of use. This is the most primitive building block for folksonomy formation in a collaborative web environment. Folksonomy is viewed as a type of classification achieved by collaborative effort. T. Vander [19] describes folksonomy as "result of personal free tagging of information and objects for one's own retrieval". This collaboration is driven by the bias of the user pool. Using tag recommendations from the system will provide an added measure to facilitate the emergence of folksonomy. It will also provide consistent definition and scope for particular tags.

The magnitude of information content including social bookmarking makes the tag recommendation problem significantly harder. Another challenge for building tag recommendation systems is the limited access to data in these domains. Fortunately, the *Del.ici.ous* website allows extensive data access.

We propose a personalized agent based system for recommending appropriate tags to users in the online bookmarking website, *Del.ici.ous*. Users can apply any tag(s) to classify these bookmarks. These bookmarks can also be used for searching by other users in the social network. Users typically tag the saved bookmarks for easy access and retrieval. We develop tag recommender agents that are dedicated to each user and maintains a history of bookmarks tagged by the user with the list of tags for each such bookmark, thereby, learning users' tagging behavior. We assume that there is a central repository that stores the bookmarks in the system and the users who tagged them. Each user agent can query this repository to get a list of other users who has tagged a particular document, and then can query the agents of those users to get the tag lists for that document. Then it uses collaborative filtering mechanism to recommend tags to the user. We suggest two variations of collaborative filtering for these tag recommender agents to recommend tags to users.

In one approach we directly estimate the probability of one user using a tag given other users using that same tag for a common URL or document. In the other approach, we compute the likelihood that a user is going to use a tag depending on the position of the tag on the tag list of another user for the same document. This approach uses an ordered list of tags associated with documents or links. We also propose a content based recommendation technique. We base our approach on the following hypothesis: *Similar documents are tagged by similar tags.* We provide empirical verification of this hypothesis. The success of our approach for developing the tag recommendation system opens up the possibility of using this approach for diverse item recommendation. For example, this approach can be used for recommending tags for blogs or even other non-textual items. In this paper we refer to agents associated with individual users as the recommendation agents and the central repository as the recommendation system.

2 Related Work

In recent years, tagging has become extremely popular in online communities with the increase in user-created content on the web. Though self interest is the primary driving factor for tagging, tags have an important and potential effect on online information clustering and sharing. Tagging has the potential to facilitate folksonomy formation and this process can be influenced by intelligent tag suggestion or recommendation engines. Moreover, tags may be suggested for different types of media: photos, videos, news, blogs, web-pages, users (in a social network). There has been a vast quantity of research on this area over the past decade. To automate the tagging process, researchers have used and verified various techniques, e.g., information retrieval, support vector machines, clustering, probabilistic reasoning, etc [21], [14], [15],[18], [11].

Xu *et al* [21] has suggested a set of desired criteria for "good tags": high popularity, least effort and uniformity. They suggest that a good tagging system should allow the free-form of tagging. Based on those criteria, Xu *et al* developed a collaborative tag suggestion system. The "goodness"of a <tag(t), object(o)> tuple is defined as the sum of the authority scores of all users who have tagged the object o with the tag t. The authority score of a user is iteratively computed by the average "goodness"of the used tags. The authority computation process implements collaborative filtering in their system. This algorithm does not facilitate the emergence of new tags, as it analyzes only existing tags. Such shortcomings can be overcome by incorporating significant term determination using Information Retrieval (IR) techniques.

Sigma and Andy [14] presents a collaborative tagging approach for automatic tag suggestions for blog posts based on their semantic content using a hybrid artificial neural network (ANN). Their algorithm consists of two stages: the training phase of the ANN followed by the execution phase for tag suggestion. After retrieving blog-posts, the algorithm performs key-word extraction from the documents using the popular TF/IDF technique for both unigrams and bi-grams. These keywords are then organized into a synonymous set (synset) using WordNet [7]. This keyword set with its synset is then used to construct the first layer of the neural network, followed by the hidden layer and the suggested tag layer. Instead of selecting one tag from this ANN, they modified the back propagation algorithm to sort them according to the activation value of the link (connecting the nodes). To achieve this, they also modified the error calculation-propagation algorithm. This paper demonstrates a unique approach for automatic tag recommendation by incorporating neural network training for blog posts and validating it on a subset of blogs from the Technorati API [2]. However, this approach needs to be modified to recommend tags in real-time for larger-scale data.

Song [15] addresses the automatic tag recommendation problem from a machine learning perspective. Researchers generally use either a document-centered or a user-centered approach for tag recommendation. The document centered approach uses analysis of documents grouped by broader topics while the user centered approach uses the historical tagging behavior of similar users or user groups.Using empirical analysis of large-scale dataset, Song has shown that the user-centered approach is not as effective as the document-centered approach. The user-centered approach is not very effective because the distribution of users vs. the number of tags used by them follows a long-tail power law distribution.

The reuseability of the tags is also very low. Even if the users are clustered to overcome the sparseness it is highly inefficient to cope with the changing interest of users.

Song *et al* have suggested two document-centered approaches: Graph Based and Prototype Based.The former is comprised of four basic steps: Step 1 represents the relationship between documents, words and tags by two bipartite graphs (followed by their Singular Value Decomposition (SVD) to lower the order of the adjacency matrix), which are subsequently partitioned into sub-graphs creating topic based clusters using Spectral Recursive Embedding (SRE). Step 2 calculates the ranks of the tags found in those clusters as a function of their average frequency of occurrence given the cluster (N-Precision) and their posterior probability of occurrence in the cluster (N-Recall). Step 3 learns the document distribution over the words using the Poisson mixture model (PMM). Finally, step 4 performs a soft classification over the new document and recommends the highest probability tag to that.The first three steps of their algorithm are offline, and the final step is performed online with the appearance of a new document.This graph based approach uses techniques like SVD, SRE and PMM to make it scalable for real world data.

In the prototype-based approach, they reduce the training data by selecting a representative subset to reduce the learning complexity. This supervised learning approach classifies the documents into some predefined categories where these categories are determined by the popularity of existing tags. Then tags are ranked in a manner similar to the graph-based approach and recommended for a new document based on their joint probability.

To make the prototype selection process efficient for online recommendation, Song has proposed a Sparse Gaussian Process (GP) framework [15]. Song has successfully extended the multi-class GP classifier for multi-label (tag) scenarios. This classification expedites the process of searching for the most suitable prototype and suggests the highest-ranked tags. The non-parametric nature of GP makes their approach model-independent and hence it does not suffer from performance degradation for false model assumptions, unlike Naive-Based approaches.

Song performed their experiments on *Del.ici.ous*, CiteULike and BibSonomy datasets. They presented a range of performance measures, i.e., Top-k accuracy, Exact-k accuracy and Tag precision to validate the efficiency and effectiveness of their algorithm. They provide a comparison of tags suggested by their algorithm to those assigned to them by actual users in those networks. The precision and recall value of their approaches are found to be better than the other existing approaches in the literature. This paper contributes to the literature by validating the mechanisms suitable for analyzing real-world data.

Tso-Sutter [18] introduced a tag-aware recommendation system to recommend items. The authors use the tagging information of a user to determine the correlation between the users and the items they like. Tso-sutter provides a 3-dimensional correlation between the users, items and tags as $<$ *user, item, tag* $>$. This 3-dimensional matrix is decomposed into 3 two-dimensional matrices:

$< user, tag >$, $< item, tag >$ and $< user, item >$. This matrix decomposition is performed after the user profile U and the item profile I are extended by the tags as follows: $U_{extended} = U + T_i$, where T_i is the set of tags that describe item i by users, and$I_{extended} = I + T_u$, where T_u is the set of tags that are used by u.

They perform collaborative filtering in the extended $< user, item >$ matrix for item-based and user-based recommendations. Results from these two collaborative filtering systems are then fused using an algorithm developed by Wang *et al* [20]. This fusion system is basically a computation of conditional probabilities. Their algorithm performs better in terms of *Recall* value than the algorithm that does not use tag information. However, their decomposition of the ternary relationship between user, tag, and items can be improved as suggested by Liang [11]. Liang proposes a modification for user modeling. Users are modeled by using three aspects, i.e., the tags used by the users, the items tagged by the users and the relations between the tags and the items tagged. A user profile is described by the formulation $E(u_i, t_j, p_k) = \{0, 1\}$ where $E(u_i, t_j, p_k) = 1$ indicates that u_i has used the tag t_j for item p_k. Liang et. al proposes three similarity measures to determine similar users:

- $UTsim(u_i, u_j)$: Percentage of common tag used by users i and j,
- $UPsim(u_i, u_j)$: Percentage of common items tagged by users i and j, and
- $UTPsim(u_i, u_j)$: Percentage of common items tagged using common tags by users i and j.

These measures are averaged using weights wUT, wUP and $wUTP$ that add up to 1. Liang also describe the similarity between items in a similar way. The user similarity is combined with the item similarity to produce the recommendation. Liang's method for both item-based and user-based recommendation outperforms Tso-sutter's method.

Song suggests a clustering approach for real time tag recommendation in [16]. After training the documents are treated as triplets < docs, words, tags >. The authors breaks this graph into two bi-partite graphs of < docs, tags > and < docs, words >. A Bipartite graph is represented by very sparse adjacency matrix. Song *et al* use Lanczos algorithm [9] to lower the rank of this adjacency matrix. They perform multi-clustering on these graphs to cluster the documents according to the *topic* by applying Spectral Recursive Embedding (SRE) algorithm [22]. They determine the effectiveness of this clustering using *N-Precision* and *N-Recall*. N-Precision measures the importance of a node (document) in a cluster (topic space) in comparison to other nodes. N-Recall determines the posterior probability of a node (document) for a given cluster. Combining these two metrics produces the *Rank* of a node (document). They use the Poisson Mixture Model [10] to classify a new document in the trained cluster of documents. Closest neighbors of the document are located in the cluster and tags are recommended from the tag list of that document.

3 Tag Recommendation Approaches

In this section, we describe the tag recommendation problem with respect to a specific domain. We describe the features of the domain and behavior of the users pertinent to our research. We also introduce a hypothesis we believe applies to domains similar to the one we have considered. We formally present our tag recommendation approaches. We also introduce metrics to evaluate the performance of the proposed recommendation approaches.

3.1 Del.ici.ous Dataset

We propose a tag recommendation system for the online social bookmarking website *Del.ici.ous* [6]. *Del.ici.ous* provides an open network for storing and sharing URLs as bookmarks. Users can apply various tags to organize and search their own bookmarks. The *Del.ici.ous* website first opened on March 2005 and currently serves more than 5 million users and contains 150 million bookmarks. We have used a part of the dataset provided by the *Information Retrieval & Machine Learning* department of the *Berlin Institute of Technology* [4]. The complete dataset contains about 132 million public bookmarks, 420 million tag assignments by 950,000 users retrieved from *Del.ici.ous* between Sepetember 2003 and December 2007. Each line of these datafiles contains one instance of tag assignment described by the following tuple, $[date, userName, URL, tag]$.

Due to computational constraints, we have only used the data from November 2007 for training (2.4 GB in size) and a part of the data from December 2007 for testing the accuracy of our recommendation algorithms. We scraped the webpages specified by the URLs in the datafiles and stemmed the contents using the Porter-Stemmer's stemming algorithm [1]. We used Python and MySQL to manage the corresponding databases and Java to perform analysis on the dataset.

3.2 Hypothesis: Correlating Tag and Document Similarity

We hypothesize that in a social networking site that encourages tagging and sharing of articles (photos, videos, bookmark etc.), similar groups of articles are tagged with similar sets of tag. To investigate the correlation of tag-similarity and document-similarity between the bookmarks, we have considered a subset of the bookmarks from the *Del.ici.ous* dataset: we consider only the bookmark that was tagged by "programming".

Each webpage or document d_i has multiple lists of tags assigned to them by different users. We create the combined tag set for each document d_i as $tag_{d_i} = \{tag_1^i, tag_2^i, \ldots tag_n^i\}$. All the tags that are used by users are considered to create this tag set but each tag is considered only once in this set. We compute the tag similarity, $TS_{i,j}$ between these tag sets tag_{d_i} and tag_{d_j} associated with documents d_i and d_j respectively, using the following:

$$TS_{i,j} = \frac{|tag_{d_i} \bigcap tag_{d_j}|}{|tag_{d_i}| + |tag_{d_j}|}. \tag{1}$$

This formulation limits the maximum value of tag similarity to 0.5. Using Equation 1, we segregate the documents d_i into 5 groups. These groups are based on the $TS_{i,j}$ values of the documents, and contain either lists of documents having $TS_{i,j}$ within that range. These groups are $[(0.49-0.4), (0.39-0.3), (0.29-0.2), (0.19-0.1), (0.09-0.01)]$. We determine the document similarity $DS_{i,j}$ of the documents belonging to each of these sub groups.

To obtain the correlation between the tag similarity $TS_{i,j}$ and document similarity $DS_{i,j}$ for the documents, we use the bag of word representation of documents approach. This representation involves the use of the following terms:

Term Frequency: For a document d_i, we calculate the term frequency, tf_{w_j,d_i}, which is the frequency of occurrence of the term w_j in document d_i. However, in order to compute $DS_{i,j}$ between two documents, all terms should not be considered equally important. To consider only the relevant terms we need to incorporate their *Inverse Document Frequency* $idf_{w,D}$ [12].

Inverse Document Frequency: $idf_{w,D}$ is the inverse of the frequency of occurrence of the term w in the entire document corpora $D = \bigcup_j d_j$.

Term Weight: Combining $tf_{w,d}$ and $idf_{w,D}$ for a term, we calculate the Term Weight $tw_{w,D}$ of each term w_j as follows:

$$tw_{w,D} = tf_{w,d} \cdot idf_{w,D}. \tag{2}$$

This is a standard procedure for preparing document vectors for similarity computation [12] that consider only relevant terms. Given a document we first eliminate the most commonly occurring English stopwords (Such as prepositions, articles and pronouns). Then we follow the procedure mentioned above to represent the document vector $\vec{d_i}$ in terms of the $tw_{w,D}$ of the constituent terms:

$$\vec{d_i} = [(w_1, tw_{w_1,D}), (w_2, tw_{w_2,D}), \ldots (w_n, tw_{w_n,D})]. \tag{3}$$

The use of term weight ensures that the components of the document vector consists of the terms that are relevant. We use this form of the document vector shown in Equation 3 to measure the document similarity, $DS_{i,j}$ using the cosine similarity measure as follows:

$$DS_{i,j} = \frac{\vec{d_i} \cdot \vec{d_j}}{|\vec{d_i}| \cdot |\vec{d_j}|}. \tag{4}$$

As mentioned earlier, we have grouped documents with high tag similarity $TS_{i,j}$ between them. We find out the fraction of documents that have higher $DS_{i,j}$ as for each of these groups. We present the results in the Figure 1.

In Figure 1 we plot the $DS_{i,j}$ on the horizontal axis and the percentage of document with corresponding $DS_{i,j}$ on the vertical axis. We plot the $DS_{i,j}$ for three of the groups with different $TS_{i,j}$ values. We find that documents that have high $DS_{i,j}$ also typically have high $TS_{i,j}$ values (for $DS_{i,j} > 0.5$). This is particularly true for $DS_{i,j} = 1$. This proves our hypothesis that similar documents are tagged with similar tags.

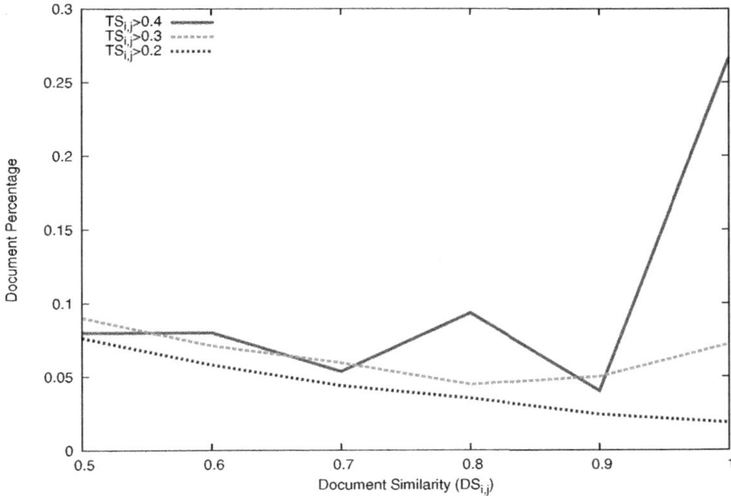

Fig. 1. Document Similarity vs. Tag Similarity

3.3 Content-Based Recommendation

A content based recommendation system recommends items similar to the one the user has already liked. In the case of tag recommendation, this process involves the recommendation of tags from the previously used tag set of a particular user. Different heuristic and probability based approaches can be used for selecting the appropriate tags to be recommended for a document. In our research we use probabilistic approaches for recommending tags for new documents. Given the new document d, we represent it in the form of document vector as shown in equation 3. Using equation 4 we rank the documents that were previously tagged by user i. We then recommend tags from similar documents until the recommended tag list reaches a length close to the average tag list length used by this user.

3.4 Collaborative Recommendation

A collaborative recommender system suggests items that are liked by users similar to the target user. In our tag recommendation framework, we determine the similarity between the users using two different algorithms. We recommend tags to user u from the tag list of the users similar to u for the given document. In the following Sections 3.4 and 3.4 we formally specify the algorithms we have developed for recommending tags using the collaborative approaches.

Tag Based Approach. In this algorithm, we determine users that are similar to our target user based on their choice of tags for the same documents.

We follow a Bayesian approach to determine this similarity. For two users i and j that have tagged some common document, we compute the probability that user i will use tag t given that user j has used it as $P(i \mid j, t)$. We calculate $P(i \mid j, t)$ for all the tags t that have been used by users i and j for the set of common documents. Using Bayes Theorem we can rewrite this probability as:

$$P(i|j,t) = \frac{P(j|i,t) \cdot P(i|t)}{P(j|t)} = \frac{P(i,j|t)}{P(j|t)}. \tag{5}$$

Now,

$$P(i,j|t) = \frac{\#\text{ documents where both } i \text{ and } j \text{ used tag } t}{\#\text{ documents where tag } t \text{ was used}}. \tag{6}$$

and

$$P(j|t) = \frac{\#\text{ documents where } j \text{ used tag } t}{\#\text{ documents where tag } t \text{ was used}}. \tag{7}$$

Combining Equation 5, 6 and 7, we get:

$$P(i|j,t) = \frac{\#\text{ documents where both } i \text{ and } j \text{ used tag } t}{\#\text{ documents where } j \text{ used tag } t}. \tag{8}$$

As mentioned earlier, given our user i, we determine the probabilities $P(i|j,t)$ for each tag t for all user j. For a target user i we calculate a user similarity score $SU_{i,j}$ for user j as follows:

$$SU_{i,j} = (1 - \prod_{\forall t \text{ common between } i \text{ and } j} (1 - P(i|j,t))). \tag{9}$$

In Equation 9, $(1 - P(i|j,t))$ is the probability that user i will not use tag t given user j has used it. The quantity $\prod_t (1 - P(i|j,t))$ denotes the probability that none of the tags used by user j will be used by user i. And the similarity score, $SU_{i,j}$, quantifies the probability that at least one tag that has been used by j will be used by i. However, this score does not immediately suggest which of user j's tag will be used by user i. Users j with $SU_{i,j} > \delta$ are selected for recommendation of tags.

For any user i we extract all the documents tagged by user i with their corresponding tag list.

Document Set(D^i): Document Set D^i is the set of all the documents tagged by user i.

Tag List Set($TagList^i_d$): Tag List $TagList^i_d$ consists of the list of tags that user i assigned to a document d, where $d \in D^i$.

Given a new document d for our target user i, we first find all sufficiently similar users j, i.e., $SU_{i,j} > \delta$, who have also tagged that document, $U^d_{i,\delta}$. We then find all the tags used by those users on this document, $TagList^d_{i,\delta} = \bigcup_{j \in U^d_{i,\delta}} TagList^j_d$. For each such tag $t \in TagList^d_{i,\delta}$ we calculate the probability, $P(i|t, U^d_{i,\delta})$, that user i will use that t given its use by other users in $U^d_{i,\delta}$ for document d as follows:

$$P(i|t, U^d_{i,\delta}) = (1 - \prod_{j \in U^d_{i,\delta}} (1 - P(i|j,t))). \tag{10}$$

This is essentially the probability of user i using the tag based on the "recommendation" from one of the users with sufficiently similar tagging behavior, $U^d_{i,\delta}$. Using Equation 10, we get a list of tag, probability pairs $< t, P(i|t, U^d_{i,\delta}) >$ where, $t \in$ {Set of all tags t assigned to document d by sufficiently similar users $j \in U^d_{i,\delta}$}. We sort these tags in descending order of $P(i|t, U^d_{i,\delta})$ and recommend a subset of them that are likely to be used by user i.

Position Based Approach. In the Tag-Based approach to collaborative recommendation, to identify users with similar tagging behavior, we locate those users that have applied the same tag t to the same document d. We have also investigated the presence of additional factor in the tagging behavior of other users that may help us recommend appropriate tags for our target user. We surmise that the position of a tag in the tag list may be predictive of its usefulness, *i.e.*, it might be that one user always uses the first few tags used by given user on a common document.

In this approach, we find the probability $P^n_{i,j}$ that user i will use user j's n^{th} tag for a common document d. To determine $P^n_{i,j}$ we first find the set of documents D_{ij} that has been tagged by both users i and j. For any document $d \in D_{ij}$, let the list of tags used by j indexed by their position n be

$$TagList^j_d = [(t_1, pos_1), (t_2, pos_2), \ldots (t_n, pos_n)]. \tag{11}$$

For the document set D_{ij}, we denote the number of times i has used the nth tag in j's taglist as $Used_{i,j}[n]$ and number of times i has not used the nth tag in j's taglist as $NotUsed_{i,j}[n]$ for all the common documents that are tagged by both i and j. The ratio $\frac{Used_{i,j}[n]}{Used_{i,j}[n]+NotUsed_{i,j}[n]}$ for each position of the tag list then provides an estimate of $P^n_{i,j}$. This estimate of $P^n_{i,j}$, however can be poor when $Used_{i,j}[n]+NotUsed_{i,j}[n]$ is very small. In that case $\frac{Used_{i,j}[n]}{Used_{i,j}[n]+NotUsed_{i,j}[n]}$ produces a biased estimate that can skew the *Bayesian* probability calculation. To alleviate this bias, we use the *m-estimate* approach [13] and calculate $P^n_{i,j}$ as follows:

$$P^n_{i,j} = \frac{Used_{i,j}[n] + mp}{Used_{i,j}[n] + NotUsed_{i,j}[n] + m}, \tag{12}$$

where $p = 0.5$ is the *prior probability* estimate of $P^n_{i,j}$ and m is a constant called the *equivalent sample size*. The value of m determines how much the *prior estimate* should be weighted relative to the observed data. The information required to determine $P^n_{i,j}$ for user i is similar to the one explained for the Tag Based Approach in 3.4. However, as shown in Equation 11, we also store the position of the tags in the $TagList^j_d$.

Once we have determined these probabilities $P^n_{i,j}$, given a new URL d we first form the list of tags $TagList^j_d$ assigned to the document d by other similar users who have tagged d. Let, $Users(d,t)$ be the users who have tagged d with tag $t \in TagList_d$, the list of all tags used for document d. Let $index(t, TL)$ be the position of tag t in the ordered taglist TL, *i.e.*, $index(t_x, TagList^j_d) = pos_x$ from Equation 11. We determine the $TagScore^t_d$ of all tags $t \in TagList_d$ as follows:

$$TagScore^t_d = (1 - \prod_{u \in Users(d,t)} (1 - P^{index(t,TagList^u_d)}_{i,u})). \tag{13}$$

where, $P^{index(t,TagList^u_d)}_{i,u}$ is estimated using Equation 12. Using the tag scores calculated using Equation 13 we construct a list of tuples $< t, TagScore^t_d >$. We the sort this list in the descending order of the tag scores and recommend a subset of the tags with high tag scores to the user. This subset is determined by using different thresholds for probability $P^n_{i,j}$ or by restricting the number of recommendations to some multiple of the average number of tags, avg_i, used by the user i.

We have used this position based approach for tag recommendation because the tags assigned by users in online social networks are generally ranked by their importance. The tag assignment process has been identified by recent researchers as a type of classification process where an article is classified by users using different tags [19]. Users generally provide a tag to associate an article with a pre-existing group of articles. These tags range from general to specific keywords. Often the first tag gives the general identification of the article. Tags tends to become more specific further along the tag list. As user's tagging behavior suggests the importance of tag position in a tag list, we conjectured that a position based approach can be useful for recommending tags.

3.5 Evaluation Metrics

The efficiency of any recommendation system is generally computed using two metrics **Precision** and **Recall** [3]:

Precision corresponds to the fraction of the recommended items that were actually used by the user

$$Precision = \frac{\text{Set of items recommended} \bigcap \text{Set of items used}}{\text{Set of items recommended}}. \tag{14}$$

Recall corresponds to the fraction of items that are used by the user that were recommended by the recommendation system.

$$Recall = \frac{\text{Set of items recommended} \bigcap \text{Set of items used}}{\text{Set of items used}}. \tag{15}$$

4 Experimental Results

In this section we present the results from the evaluation of the tag recommendation approaches discussed in Section 3. We also present a comparison between the proposed recommendation approaches. As mentioned in Section 3.1, we have used part of the November 2007 dataset for training our recommendation system. For computational reasons, for most of the experiments we have considered only those bookmarks that are tagged with "programming". Before building the recommendation system, we have collected some statistics about the user behavior from the training data. There are 82631 users who has tagged 15060 distinct links in November 2007.

To test the efficiency of our recommendation systems we consider the most active users: we have selected only those users who have tagged more than 50 bookmarks. There are 32 such users in this dataset. An extremely active user has tagged over 250 documents and used over 200 unique tag on those documents over a period of a month. For each user i, we stored all the bookmarks and corresponding list of tags. We also extracted the other users who have tagged any of the bookmarks tagged by i and their corresponding tag lists. We refer to these users as the neighbors of user i.

To construct the test dataset, we collected the bookmarks tagged by these users in December 2007. For any user i we have considered only those bookmarks for testing that were also tagged by the neighbors of this user.

4.1 Content-Based Recommendation

Figure 2 shows the results for our content based recommendation system (described in Section 3.3). Recall values are better than precision values for most of the users. This is due to the reduced data set we have used. We have considered the bookmarks tagged by these users in only one month. However,

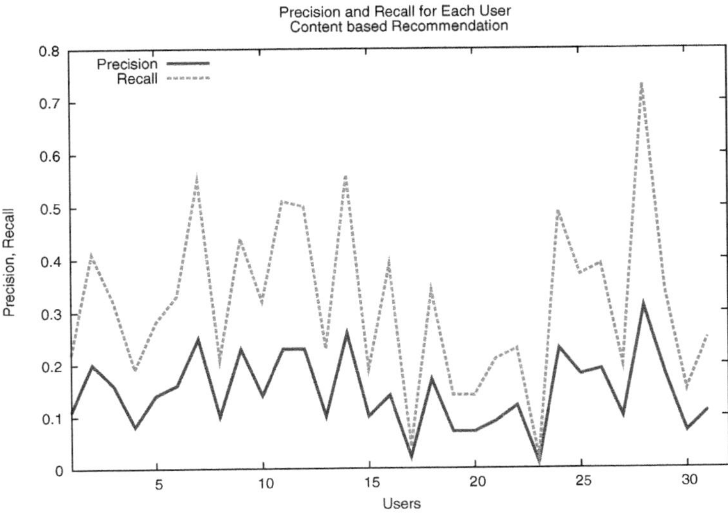

Fig. 2. Precision and Recall for Content Based Recommendation

utilizing larger training data for each of the users will lead to better precision values.

4.2 Collaborative Recommendation

Tag Based Approach. We have tested the collaborative recommendation mechanism with tag based approach using different thresholds. We determine the similarity $SU_{i,j}$ between user i and j using Equation 9. To recommend tags for user i, we select all those user j who has $SU_{i,j} > 0$ ($\delta = 0$). We then calculate the probability $P(i|t, U^d_{i,\delta})$ for all the tags that are used by these j users and recommend tags using different tag thresholds. A tag threshold of τ means a tag t is recommended if $P(i|t, U^d_{i,\delta}) > \tau$. We recorded the maximum, minimum, and average precision and recall values for the 32 users with three different tag thresholds τ: 0.0, 0.3 and 0.5. As the number of tags satisfying the threshold criterion can be large, we considered further limits on the number of tags recommended based on the average number of tags used by a user i for his/her bookmarks, avg_i. For each threshold value, we consider the following number of recommended tags: no limit, avg_i, $1.5 * avg_i$. We expected to see an increase in the precision values and decrease in the recall values when we reduce the number of recommended tags. Figure 3 shows the precision and recall values for the 32 users where the threshold for $P(i|t, U^d_{i,\delta})$ was $\tau = 0.0$. The plots are consistent with our expectations. Precision value is maximized when we restrict the recommendation length to be equal to avg_i, whereas recall is highest when all tags are recommend. We have found similar results for other τ.

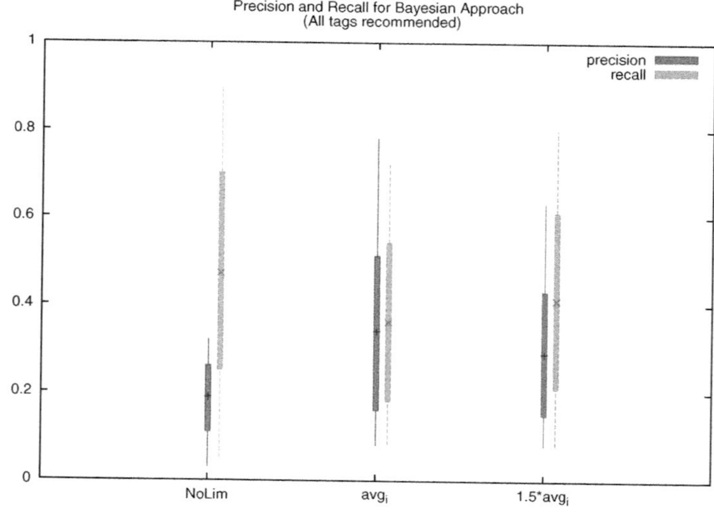

Fig. 3. Precision and Recall for Collaborative Recommendation using Tag Based Approach

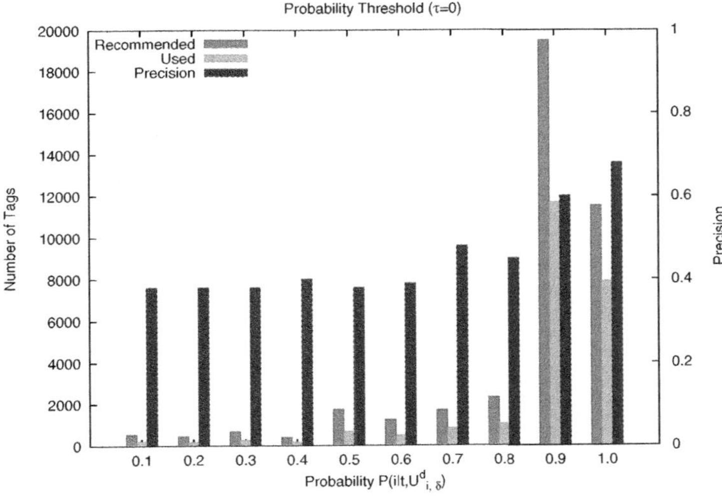

Fig. 4. Histogram for Collaborative Recommendation using Tag Based Approach (Number of Recommendations=avg_i)

We also plot the number of tags recommended and tags actually used for different $P(i|t, U^d_{i,\delta})$ values in Figure 4. For drawing histograms we have rounded up the $P(i|t, U^d_{i,\delta})$ values to the nearest 10th decimal place. Note that as $P(i|t, U^d_{i,\delta})$ increases, the precision values increase. This fact confirms the effectiveness of the tag recommendation scheme. We observed similar trends for the other two cases (no limit and $1.5 * avg_i$). Only the number of tags recommended in the no limit scenario is significantly higher than that of Figure 4.

Position Based Approach. To evaluate the recommendation efficiency for the position based approach, we present the precision and recall values in Figure 5. In our experiment, we have used $m = 5$ as the *equivalent sample size*. We have suggested two different approaches using the probabilities $P^n_{i,j}$ estimated using Equation 12:

Thresholding: In this case, for each position n we only recommend any tag t such that $P^n_{i,j} > \tau$, for some j. We do not restrict the length of the recommended tag list. The τ levels we have used for experiments are 0.25, 0.5, 0.75 and 0.9. Precision and recall values for these schemes are represented as *Th 25*, *Th 50*, *Th 75* and *Th 90* respectively in Figure 5.

Weighted: In this case we calculate the $TagScore^t_d$ of each tag t using Equation 13. Then we rank these tags according to the tag scores and recommend only the first x tags. We have used two different values for x: avg_i and $1.5 * avg_i$. Precision and recall values for these schemes are represented as *Wt* avg_i and *Wt* $1.5 * avg_i$ in Figure 5.

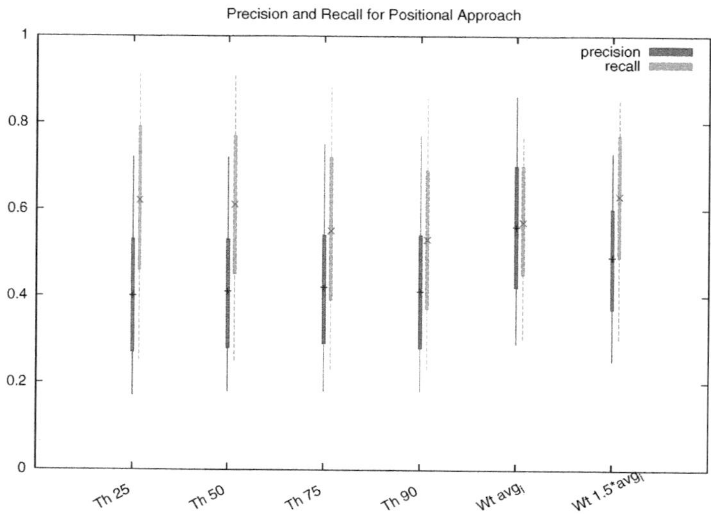

Fig. 5. Precision and Recall for Collaborative Recommendation using Position based Approach

We expected that the precision values will increase and the recall values will decrease for the Thresholding approach as we increase the thresholds. We also expected the precision to be significantly higher for avg_i than $1.5avg_i$ for the Weighted scheme. The plots in Figure 5 confirms our expectation.

We also noted the correlation of $P^n_{i,j}$ values of recommended tags with their adoption by the target user. From Figure 6 we see that as $P^n_{i,j}$ increases, the precision values increase. However, fewer tags have higher $P^n_{i,j}$ values and hence the number of total recommendation for higher $P^n_{i,j}$ values decreases. We also collect and analyze data to see whether tags higher in tag lists are used more often or not. Figure 7 shows that higher position tags are recommended more often (as they have higher conditional probability of being used by the user) and are also used more frequently.

4.3 Comparison of Proposed Recommendation Approaches

In this section we present a comparison of the recommendation systems described earlier. We have shown the precision and recall values for the different recommender approaches in Figures 2, 3 and 5. In Figure 3, we see that the precision and recall values are maximum when recommendation length is restricted to avg_i. In Figure 5, we observe that the precision and recall values are maximized for the weighted scheme with avg_i recommendation length. In Table 1 we present the precision and recall values from content based and the collaborative systems selecting the best performance from each. We see that the position based collaborative recommender performs better than the content based and the tag based

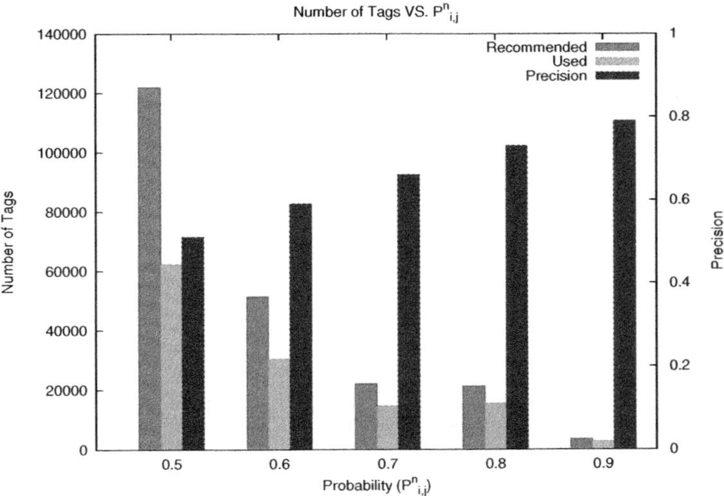

Fig. 6. Histogram for Collaborative Recommendation using Position based Approach

collaborative approach. This observation was based on the bookmarks that had a "programming" tag associated with them. We observer that the position based system performs significantly better than the other two. Moreover, the Position based system can actually recommend tags that had never been used by the target user but can be appropriate for the current document. The Tag based approach lack this capability.

Table 1. Comparison of Recommendation Systems

	Content Based	Collaborative Tag Based $\tau = 0, avg_i$	Collaborative Position Based $Wt\ avg_i$
Precision	0.15	0.34	0.56
Recall	0.31	0.36	0.58

5 Conclusion

We have successfully demonstrated a tag recommendation system that suggests tags using probabilistic analysis of past user behavior. We have observed distinctive user behavior for tag assignment in a social bookmarking website *Del.ici.ous.* Some of the tags provided by the users are more general than others, and their tag lists are generally sorted from general to specific according to the cardinal position of the tags. We have shown the correlation between document similarity and tag similarity in a social-tagging environment. We introduce two collaborative tag recommendation approaches and empirically demonstrate higher precision and recall of recommendation of the position-based approach compared to

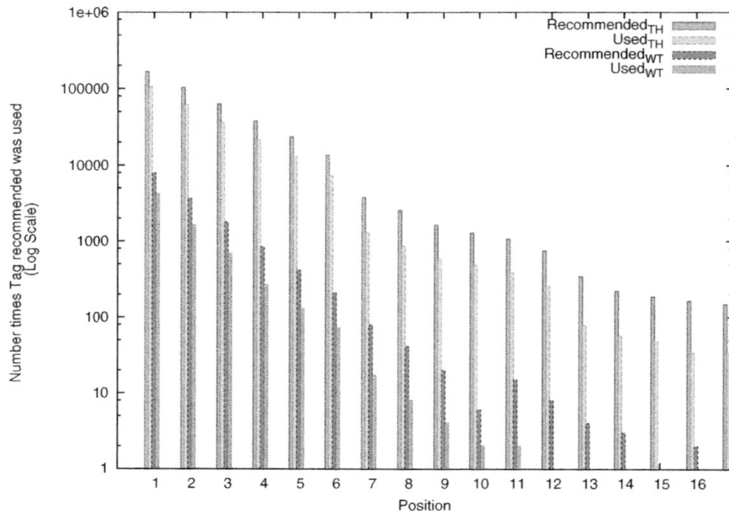

Fig. 7. Histogram for Collaborative Recommendation using Position based Approach

the tag-based approach. We compare the effectiveness of the content-based and the collaborative approach and find that the collaborative approaches perform better.

We want to compare our approach with some of the existing approach mentioned in the Section 2. We also want to test the performance of our recommendation system using data from other online bookmarking websites.

References

1. P. S. Algorithm. Stemming algorithm, `http://en.wikipedia.org/wiki/Stemming`
2. T. API. Technorati was founded to help bloggers succeed by collecting, highlighting, and distributing the global online conversation, `http://technorati.com/`
3. Basu, C., Hirsh, H., Cohen, W.W.: Recommendation as classification: Using social and content-based information in recommendation. In: AAAI/IAAI, pp. 714–720 (1998)
4. I.R. .M.L.D.D.-L. Berlin Institute of Technology. Dai labor, berlin, `http://www.dai-labor.de/en/competence_centers/irml/datasets/`
5. T. Cloud. Delicous, `http://delicious.com/tag`
6. Delicious. Social bookmarking website, `http://www.delicious.com`
7. Fellbaum, C.: WordNet: An Electronical Lexical Database. The MIT Press, Cambridge (1998)
8. Goldstein, D.G., Gigerenzer, G.: The recognition heuristic: How ignorance makes us smart. In: Gigerenzer, G., Todd, P.M., The ABC Research Group (eds.) Simple Heuristics That Make Us Smart, ch. 2, pp. 37–58. Oxford University Press, New York (1999)

9. Golub, G.H., Van Loan, C.F.: Matrix Computations (Johns Hopkins Studies in Mathematical Sciences). The Johns Hopkins University Press (October 1996)
10. Li, J., Zha, H.: Two-way poisson mixture models for simultaneous document classification and word clustering. Computational Statistics & Data Analysis 50(1), 163–180 (2006)
11. Liang, H., Xu, Y., Li, Y., Nayak, R.: Collaborative filtering recommender systems using tag information. In: Web Intelligence/IAT Workshops, pp. 59–62. IEEE (2008)
12. Manning, C.D., Raghavan, P., Schütze, H.: Introduction to Information Retrieval, 1st edn. Cambridge University Press (July 2008)
13. Mitchell, T.M.: Machine Learning. McGraw-Hill Science/Engineering/Math (March 1997)
14. Sigma, Andy: Automatic tag recommendation for the web 2.0 blogosphere using collaborative tagging and hybrid ann semantic structures. In: ACOS 2007, pp. 88–93. WSEAS, Stevens Point (2007)
15. Song, Y.: Automatic tag recommendation algorithms for social recommender systems - microsoft research. ACM Transactions on Web (2009)
16. Song, Y., Zhuang, Z., Li, H., Zhao, Q., Li, J., Lee, W.C., Giles, C.L.: Real-time automatic tag recommendation. In: SIGIR 2008, pp. 515–522. ACM, New York (2008)
17. Sood, S., Owsley, S., Hammond, K., Birnbaum, L.: Tagassist: Automatic tag suggestion for blog posts
18. Tso Sutter, K.H.L., Marinho, L.B., Thieme, L.S.: Tag-aware recommender systems by fusion of collaborative filtering algorithms. In: SAC 2008, pp. 1995–1999. ACM, New York (2008)
19. Wal, T.V.: Folksonomy definition and wikipedia :: Off the top :: vanderwal.net.
20. Wang, J., de Vries, A.P., Reinders, M.J.T.: Unifying user-based and item-based collaborative filtering approaches by similarity fusion. In: SIGIR 2006, pp. 501–508. ACM Press, New York (2006)
21. Xu, Z., Fu, Y., Mao, J., Su, D.: Towards the semantic web: Collaborative tag suggestions. In: WWW 2006: Proceedings of the Collaborative Web Tagging Workshop, Edinburgh, Scotland (2006) æ
22. Zha, H., He, X., Ding, C., Simon, H., Gu, M.: Bipartite graph partitioning and data clustering. In: CIKM 2001, pp. 25–32. ACM Press, New York (2001)

Complex Task Allocation in Mixed-Initiative Delegation: A UAV Case Study*

David Landén, Fredrik Heintz, and Patrick Doherty

Dept. of Computer and Information Science, Linköping University, Sweden
{david.landen,fredrik.heintz,patrick.doherty}@liu.se

Abstract. Unmanned aircraft systems (UAS's) are now becoming technologically mature enough to be integrated into civil society. An essential issue is principled mixed-initiative interaction between UAS's and human operators. Two central problems are to specify the structure and requirements of complex tasks and to assign platforms to these tasks. We have previously proposed Task Specification Trees (TST's) as a highly expressive specification language for complex multi-agent tasks that supports mixed-initiative delegation and adjustable autonomy. The main contribution of this paper is a sound and complete distributed heuristic search algorithm for allocating the individual tasks in a TST to platforms. The allocation also instantiates the parameters of the tasks such that all the constraints of the TST are satisfied. Constraints are used to model dependencies between tasks, resource usage as well as temporal and spatial requirements on complex tasks. Finally, we discuss a concrete case study with a team of unmanned aerial vehicles assisting in a challenging emergency situation.

1 Introduction

Unmanned aircraft systems (UAS's) are now becoming technologically mature enough to be integrated into civil society. Principled interaction between UAS's and human resources is an essential component in the future uses of UAS's in complex emergency services scenarios. Mixed-initiative interaction between human operators and such systems will be central. By mixed-initiative, we mean that interaction and negotiation between a UAS and a human will take advantage of each of their skills, capacities, and knowledge in developing a mission plan, executing the plan, and adapting to contingencies during the execution of the plan. In developing a principled framework for such sophisticated interaction in complex scenarios, a great many interdependent conceptual and pragmatic issues arise and need clarification both theoretically and pragmatically in the form of demonstrators.

Two central problems are to define complex mixed-initiative missions and given a mission find platforms which together can execute it. We have previously proposed Task Specification Trees (TST's) as a highly expressive specification language for multi-agent tasks that supports mixed-initiative delegation and adjustable autonomy (3). A

* This work is partially supported by grants from the Swedish Foundation for Strategic Research (SSF) Strategic Research Center MOVIII, the Swedish Research Council (VR), the VR Linnaeus Center CADICS, the ELLIIT Excellence Center at Linköping-Lund for Information Technology, and the Center for Industrial Information Technology CENIIT.

N. Desai, A. Liu, and M. Winikoff (Eds.): PRIMA 2010, LNAI 7057, pp. 288–303, 2012.

task is recursively defined as a tree of tasks where temporal requirements and interdependencies among tasks are specified as constraints. In this paper we describe an allocation algorithm for TST's together with a concrete unmanned aerial vehicle (UAV) case study. The allocation algorithm assigns platforms to tasks and instantiates the parameters of the tasks such that all the constraints of the TST are satisfied. The algorithm recursively searches among the potential allocations in a distributed manner and uses distributed constraint satisfaction techniques to check if an allocation satisfies the task and platform constraints. The case study gives a detailed example of the allocation algorithm applied to a team of UAV's assisting in a challenging emergency services scenario involving delivery of food and medical supplies to injured people.

2 The Delegation Framework

To support cooperative goal achievement among a group of agents a delegation framework has been developed (3, 4). It provides a formal framework for describing and reasoning about what it means for an agent to delegate an objective, which can be either a goal or a plan, to another agent. The concept of delegation allows for studying not only cooperation but also mixed-initiative problem-solving and adjustable autonomy.

By delegating a partially specified objective the delegee is given the autonomy to complete the specification itself. By making the objective more specific the autonomy is limited. If the delegated objective is completely specified then the agent has no autonomy when it comes to achieving the objective. By allowing both agents and human operators to partially specify an objective, mixed-initiative problem-solving is supported.

2.1 Task Specification Trees

A *Task Specification Tree* (TST) is a distributed data structure with a declarative representation that describes a complex multi-agent task. Each node in a TST corresponds to a task that should be performed. Each node has a *node interface* consisting of a set of parameters called *node parameters* that can be specified for the node. The node parameters determine task specific details of the node.

Nodes in a TST either specify actions or goals. Actions can either be elementary or composite. A *elementary action* is a leaf node in the TST while a *composite action* is an interior node. Action nodes can be executed when instantiated, whereas goal nodes first require a plan to be generated. The plan then becomes a new TST branch that in turn can be instantiated and executed. A TST without any goal nodes is called *fully expanded.* Nodes can also be removed and added during execution, for example, to repair a TST after a failure. When a TST has been executed, the resulting TST represents the history of the mission, including concrete task instantiations, errors, and repairs.

Figure 1 shows an example TST for first scanning Area_A and Area_B concurrently and then flying to Dest_4. Nodes N_0 and N_1 are composite action nodes, sequential (S) and concurrent (C), respectively. Nodes N_2, N_3 and N_4 are elementary action nodes. Each node specifies a task and has a node interface containing node parameters. In this case only temporal parameters are shown representing the respective intervals a task should be completed in.

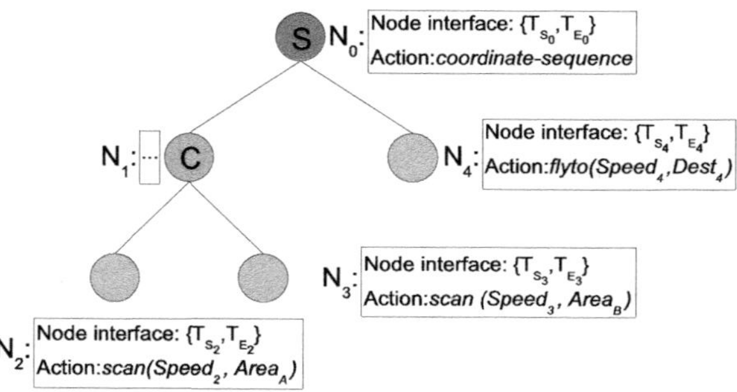

Fig. 1. An example TST for first scanning Area_A and Area_B concurrently and then flying to Dest_4

Each node can have constraints associated with it, called *node constraints*. These constraints limit the valid values of the node parameters. A TST can also have *tree constraints*, expressing precedence, dependence, and organizational relations between the nodes in the TST. Together the node parameters and the constraints form a constraint network. Setting the value of a parameter constrains not only the network, but implicitly, also the degree of autonomy of an agent. Figure 2 shows the constraint network defined by the TST in Figure 1.

3 Allocating TST Specified Tasks

Given a TST representing a complex task, an important problem is to find a set of platforms that can execute these tasks according to the specification. The problem is to allocate tasks to platforms and assign values to parameters such that each task can be carried out by its assigned platform and all the constraints of the TST are satisfied.

For a platform to be able to carry out a task, it must have the *capabilities* and the *resources* required for the task. A platform that can be assigned a task in a TST is called a *candidate*. The capabilities of a platform are fixed while the available resources will vary depending on its commitments, including the tasks it has already been allocated. The resources and the commitments are modeled with constraints. Resources are represented by variables and commitments by constraints. The resources used by a platform when executing a particular action are represented by a parameterized set of constraints. The action parameters must be part of the node interface for any node containing that action. These constraints are local to the platform and different platforms may have different constraints for the same action. Figure 3 shows the constraints for the scan action for platform P_1.

When a platform is assigned an action node in a TST, the constraints associated with that action are instantiated and added to the constraints of the platform. The platform constraints are connected to the constraint problem defined by the TST through the node parameters in the node interface. Figure 4 shows the constraint network after allocating node N_2 from the example TST to platform P_1.

A platform can be allocated more than one node. This may introduce implicit dependencies between the actions since each allocation adds constraints to the constraint

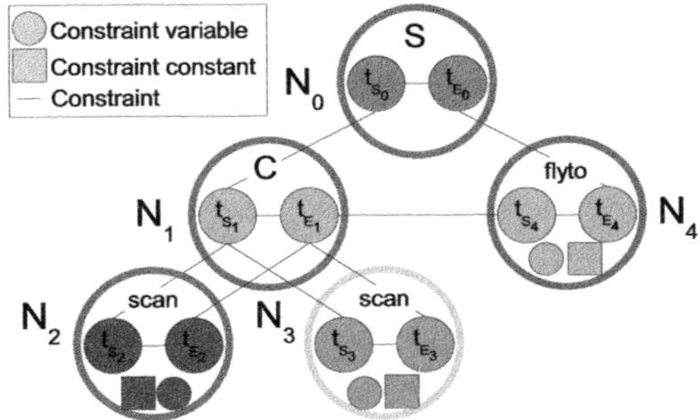

Fig. 2. The constraint network defined by the TST in Figure 1

problem of the platform. There can for example be a shared resource that both actions use. Figure 5 shows the constraint network of platform P_1 after it has been allocated nodes N_2 and N_4 from the example TST. In this example the position of the platform is implicitly shared since the first action will change the location of the platform.

A *complete allocation* is an allocation which allocates every node in a TST to a platform. A completely allocated TST defines a constraint problem that represents all the constraints for this particular allocation of the TST. As the constraints are distributed among the platforms it is in effect a distributed constraint problem. If the constraint problem is consistent then a *valid allocation* has been found and each solution can be seen as a potential execution schedule of the TST. The consistency of an allocation can be checked by a distributed constraint satisfaction problem (DCSP) solver such as the Asynchronous Weak Commitment Search (AWCS) algorithm (17) or ADOPT (12).

4 Multi-Robot Task Allocation

Multi-robot task allocation (MRTA) is an important problem in the multi-agent community (6, 7, 11, 15, 18). It deals with the complexities involved in taking a description of a set of tasks and deciding which of the available robots should do what. Often the problem also involves maximizing some utility function or minimizing a cost function. Important aspects of the problem are what types of tasks and robots can be described, what type of optimization is being done, and how computationally expensive the allocation is. In this section we discuss the MRTA problem and how it relates to allocating complex tasks specified as TST's. In the process, we extend the classification introduced by Gerkey and Matarić (6, 8) with four new dimensions.

The task allocation problem can be traced back to the Optimal Assignment Problem (OAP) (5). In OAP, m workers should be assigned to n jobs, one worker per job, where the worker-job combinations have different utilities depending on how well suited the worker is for the job. The problem is to find the optimal allocation.

The following assumptions are made in OAP: A worker can only have one job at a time. A job only needs one worker. The assignment is instantaneous. There are no more jobs to take care of later. The jobs are atomic in the sense that they do not relate to each other. Both utilities and jobs are independent. Since assigning a worker to a job does not

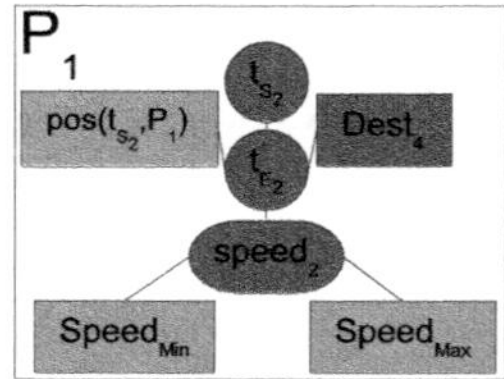

Fig. 3. The parameterized platform constraints for the scan action

change the utilities of other workers, the jobs can be assigned in any order. One can see that the problem has three dimensions: worker capacity, job complexity, and allocation horizon.

4.1 Classifying Multi-Robot Task Allocation

The multi-robot task allocation problem is in its simplest form equal to the OAP. By varying the problem along the three OAP dimensions Gerkey and Matarić define seven more complex variants (8). Single task robots (ST) vs. multi-task robots (MT), i.e. can a robot execute one or many tasks at the same time (worker capacity). Single robot tasks (SR) vs. multi-robot tasks (MR), where SR means that each task can be executed by a single robot, while with MR a task may need more than one robot (job complexity). The final dimension, allocation horizon, is instantaneous assignment (IA) vs. time-extended assignment (TE). In IA there is no information available to reason about further allocations, instead an allocation can be done directly with the information that is available. For TE there is more information such as information about all tasks that need to be assigned or a model of how tasks are expected to arrive in time.

In his thesis (6), Gerkey points out that the classification does not really apply to tasks that have interrelated utilities (e.g., the utility of task 1 for platform A is dependent on whether it is also allocated task 2) and tasks that have constraints between them (e.g., a TST with sequential tasks). To cover these cases we extend the classification model with the dimensions unrelated utilities (UU) vs. interrelated utilities (IU) and independent tasks (IT) vs. constrained tasks (CT).

Another aspect of the task allocation problem is *who* is making the task allocation. In OAP, solving the allocation problem is separate from executing the allocated tasks. The allocation itself is not seen as something that has to be done by a worker, instead it is an external process. If the allocation is done by a worker, then both the tasks and the task allocation are tasks for the multi-agent system. Making task allocation a task is part of the delegation concept. A delegation is a task allocation performed by a particular platform. We call this new dimension external allocation view (EV) vs. internal allocation view (IV). Whether IV is harder than EV depends on how much information about the task allocation problem that the allocator has. In EV it is assumed that all the information can be given to the external allocator. This does not have to be the case for IV.

Related to, but not directly included in the task allocation problem is the task allocation environment dimension. A task allocation environment can be even more challenging than TE, if the task allocator not only has to take into account future tasks to

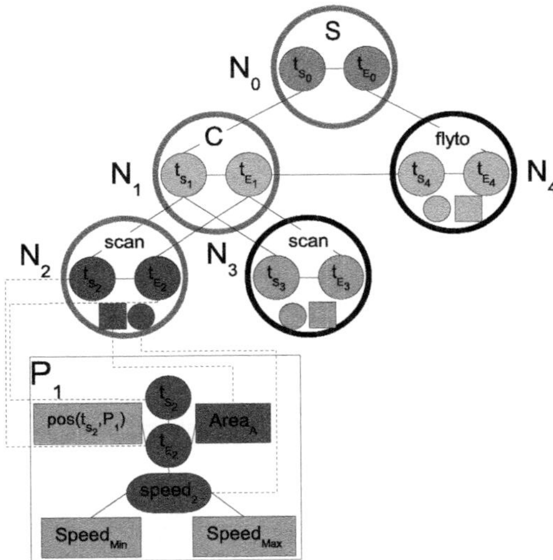

Fig. 4. The combined constraint problem after allocating node N_2 to platform P_1

allocate, but also that the task allocation problem can change unexpectedly. Changes could include addition or removal of robots, changes to constraints, and changes to variables. Such environments introduce the additional problem of task re-allocation. We call this extra dimension static allocation environment (SA) vs. dynamic allocation environment (DA).

4.2 Classifying Allocating TST Specified Tasks

Following the above classification, the problem of allocating a complex task according to a TST is classified as a MT-SR-TE-IU-CT-IV-DA problem. Each platform can do more than one task at a time (MT) since it is only restricted by its resources. Only one platform is needed (SR) for each task if we view each node in the TST as an individual task. If we view the entire TST as a task, then it is in the MR class. This shows that specifying a multi-robot task as a TST avoids the problem of allocating multiple robots to the same task. More generally, the class SR-CT includes parts of the MR class. Since a TST models the tasks that should be allocated and how they relate to each other the problem is in TE. Since a TST can specify constraints such as execution order and global timing, the problem is in CT. The problem is also in IU due to shared resources for example. Since allocating tasks is an active part in the delegation, the problem is in IV. In addition, the problem is in DA, meaning that we also have to think about task re-allocation.

5 An Algorithm for Allocating Complex Tasks Specified by TST's

This section presents a heuristic search algorithm for allocating a fully expanded TST to a set of platforms. A successful allocation allocates each node to a platform and assigns

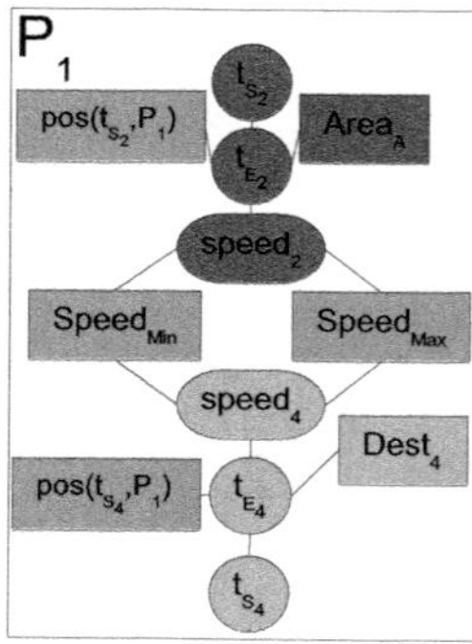

Fig. 5. The constraints of platform P_1 when allocated nodes N_2 and N_4

values to parameters such that each task can be carried out by its assigned platform and all the constraints of the TST are satisfied. During the allocation, variables will be instantiated resulting in a schedule for executing the TST.

The algorithm starts with an empty allocation and extends it one node at a time in a depth-first order over the TST. To extend the allocation, the algorithm takes the current allocation, finds a consistent allocation of the next node, and then recursively allocates the rest of the TST. Since a partial allocation corresponds to a distributed constraint satisfaction problem, a DCSP solver is used to check whether the constraints are consistent. If all possible allocations of the next node violate the constraints, then the algorithm uses backtracking with backjumping to find the next allocation.

The algorithm is both sound and complete. It is sound since the consistency of the corresponding constraint problem is verified in each step and it is complete since every possible allocation is eventually tested. Since the algorithm is recursive the search can be distributed among multiple platforms.

To improve the search, a heuristic function is used to determine the order platforms are tested. The heuristic function is constructed by auctioning out the node to all platforms with the required capabilities. The bid is the marginal cost for the platform to accept the task relative to the current partial allocation. The cost could for example be the total time required to execute all tasks allocated to the platform.

To increase the efficiency of the backtracking, the algorithm uses backjumping to find the latest partial allocation which has a consistent allocation of the current node. This preserves the soundness as only partial allocations that are guaranteed to violate the constraints are skipped.

The AllocateTST algorithm takes a TST rooted in the node N as input and finds a valid allocation of the TST if possible. To check whether a node N can be allocated to a specific platform P the TryAllocateTST algorithm is used. It tries to allocate the top node N to P and then recursively finding an allocation of the sub-TST's.

AllocateTST(Node N)

1. Find the set of candidates C for N.
2. Run an auction for N among the candidates in C and order C according to the bids.

3. For each candidate c in the ordered set C:
   (a) If TryAllocateTST(c, N) then return success.
4. Return failure.

TryAllocateTST(Platform P, Node N)

1. AllocateTST P to N.
2. If the allocation is inconsistent then undo the allocation and return false.
3. For each sub-TST n of N do
   (a) If AllocateTST(n) fails then undo the allocation and do a backjump.
4. An allocation has been found, return true.

The implementation of TryAllocateTST is based on the contract-net protocol (14). For a platform A to try to allocate a TST rooted in N to platform B it sends a *call-for-proposal* (cfp) message containing the TST to platform B. If TryAllocateTST is successful then A will send a *propose* message back to A otherwise it will send a *refuse* message.

5.1 Node Auctions

Broadcasting for candidates for a node N only returns platforms with the required capabilities for the node. There is no information about the usefulness or cost of allocating the node to the candidate. Blindly testing candidates for a node is an obvious source of inefficiency. Instead, the node is auctioned out to the candidates. Each bidding platform bids its marginal cost for executing the node. I.e., taking into account all previous tasks the platform has been allocated, how much more would it cost the platform to take on the extra task. The cost could for example be the total time needed to complete all tasks. To be efficient, it is important that the cost can be computed by the platform locally. We are currently only evaluating the cost of the current node, not the sub-TST rooted in the node. This leaves room for interesting extensions. Low bids are favorable and the candidates are sorted according to their bids. The bids are used as a heuristic function that increases the chance of finding a suitable platform early in the search.

5.2 Distributed Backjumping

A dead-end is reached when a platform is trying to allocate a node N_k but there is no consistent allocation. The platform must then undo previous allocations until a partial allocation is found where N_k can be allocated. This is the backjump point where the backtracking will start.

More formally, the current partial allocation can be seen as the assignment $A_1, \ldots, A_k$ of platforms to each node in the sequence $N_1, \ldots, N_k$. Instead of backtracking over the next allocation for $N_1, \ldots, N_{k-1}$ as in normal chronological backtracking, the algorithm finds the node N_j with the highest index j such that a consistent allocation for N_k can be found given the partial allocation $A_1, \ldots, A_j$. The node N_j is called the *backjump point*. Using the fact that N_k must be allocated we can skip all partial allocations of $N_{j+1}, \ldots, N_{k-1}$ that do not lead to a consistent allocation of N_k.

The backjump point is found by disconnecting parts of the DCSP network and then trying all possible allocations for N_k. When the node can be allocated with parts of the network disconnected, it means that the backjump point resides in the disconnected part of the network. The localization of the backjump point continues in the previously disconnected network by recursively dividing it into smaller parts. Each new partial allocation is checked by trying to extend it with an allocation of N_k. Since the task allocation process is distributed the backjump process must also be distributed.

To describe the algorithm, the following definitions are used. A platform is *in charge* of all nodes below a node it has been allocated. The node that could not be allocated is called the *failure point*. The platform trying to find an allocation for the failure point is called *failure point allocator*. *Disconnecting* a network means temporarily removing the variables in the network from the DCSP which is equivalent to removing the corresponding allocations. When a platform disconnects networks and checks for consistency, an *activation* message is sent from the platform to the failure point allocator. The failure point allocator will then try applicable platforms for the failure point until an allocation is found or none exists. The failure point allocator sends an *allocation succeed* if an allocation is found, otherwise an *allocation failed* message.

The procedures *Search Upwards* and *Search Downwards* are used to find the backjump point, beginning with the *Search Upwards* procedure. Two different search procedures are necessary since we first have to find which platform is in control over the backjump point, and second to find the actual backjump point.

Search Upwards

1. Disconnect all child branches (that have been allocated) except the branch that contains the failure point. Signal the failure point allocator to start finding an allocation for the failure point.
   (a) If the failed node can be allocated, reconnect all child branches and start searching for the backjump point by calling Search Downwards.
   (b) If no allocation can be found, then do a Search Upwards starting from the parent of the node. If the node has no parent then there is no allocation.

Search Downwards

1. Disconnect child branches one at the time in the reverse order they were allocated and check the consistency. If the network is consistent then the backjump point is in that branch.
2. When a branch containing the backjump point is located, check if the child branch has a composite action node as the top-node. In that case, do a recursive Search Downwards starting at that node. Otherwise, the backjump point has been found.

6 A Collaborative UAV Case Study

On December 26, 2004, a devastating earthquake of high magnitude occurred off the west coast of Sumatra. This resulted in a tsunami which hit the coasts of India, Sri Lanka, Thailand, Indonesia, and many other islands. Both the earthquake and the tsunami caused great devastation. During the initial stages of the catastrophe, there was a great deal of confusion and chaos in setting into motion rescue operations in such wide geographic areas. The problem was exacerbated by a shortage of manpower, supplies, and machinery. The highest priorities in the initial stages of the disaster were searching for survivors in many isolated areas where road systems had become inaccessible and providing relief in the form of delivery of food, water, and medical supplies. Similar real-life scenarios have occurred more recently in China and Haiti where devastating earthquakes have caused tremendous material and human damage.

Let us assume that one has access to a fleet of autonomous unmanned helicopter systems with ground operation facilities. How could such a resource be used in the real-life scenario described?

A prerequisite for the successful operation would be the existence of a multi-agent software infrastructure for assisting emergency services. At the very least, one would require the system to allow mixed-initiative interaction with multiple platforms and ground operators in a robust, safe, and dependable manner. As far as the individual platforms are concerned, one would require a number of different capabilities, not necessarily shared by each individual platform, but by the fleet in total. These capabilities would include: the ability to scan and search for salient entities such as injured humans, building structures, or vehicles; the ability to monitor or survey these salient points of interest and continually collect and communicate information back to ground operators and other platforms to keep them situationally aware of current conditions; and the ability to deliver supplies or resources to these salient points of interest if required. For example, identified injured persons should immediately receive a relief package containing food, water, and medical supplies.

To be more specific in terms of the scenario, we can assume there are two separate legs or parts to the emergency relief scenario in the context sketched previously.

Leg I. In the first part of the scenario, it is essential that for specific geographic areas, the unmanned aircraft platforms cooperatively scan large regions in an attempt to identify injured persons. The result of such a cooperative scan would be a saliency map pinpointing potential victims and their geographical coordinates and associating sensory output such as high resolution photos and thermal images with the potential victims. The saliency map could then be used directly by emergency services or passed on to other unmanned aircrafts as a basis for additional tasks.

Leg II. In the second part of the scenario, the saliency map from Leg I would be used for generating and executing a plan for the UAV' to deliver relief packages to the injured. This should also be done in a cooperative manner.

We will now consider a particular instance of the emergency services assistance scenario. In this instance there is a UAS consisting of two UAV platforms (P_1 and P_2) and an operator (OP_1). In the first part of the scenario the UAS is given the task of searching two areas for victims. The main capability required by the platforms is to fly a search pattern scanning for people. It is implemented by looking for salient features in the fused video streams from color and thermal cameras (13). In the second part the UAS is given the task to deliver boxes with food and medical supplies to the identified victims. To transport a box it can either be carried directly by an unmanned aircraft or it can be loaded onto a carrier which is then transported to a key position from where the boxes are distributed to their final locations. In this scenario, both platforms have

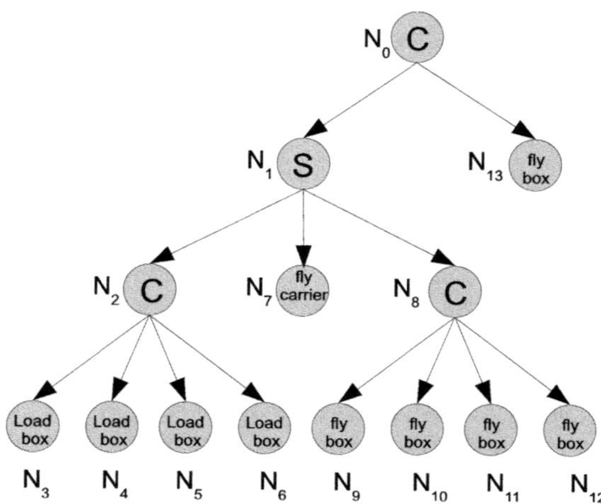

Fig. 6. The TST for the supply delivery case study

the capability to transport a single box while only platform P_1 has the capability to transport a carrier. Both platforms also have the capabilities to coordinate sequential and concurrent tasks.

In this paper, we will focus on the second part of the emergency services assistance scenario, the supply delivery. One approach to solving this type of logistics problems is to use a task planner to generate a sequence of actions that will transport each box to its destination. Each action must then be executed by a platform. We have previously shown how to generate pre-allocated plans and monitor their execution (2, 10). In this paper we show how a plan without explicit allocations expressed as a TST can be co-operatively allocated to a set of UAV's which where not known at the time of planning.

In this particular scenario, five survivors (S_1–S_5) are found in Leg I, and there are two platforms (P_1–P_2) and one carrier available. At the same time another operator OP_2 is performing a mission with the platforms P_3 and P_4 north of the area. P_3 is currently idle and OP_1 is therefore allowed to borrow it if necessary.

To start Leg II, the operator creates a TST, for example using a planner, that will achieve the goal of distributing relief packages to all survivor locations in the saliency map. The resulting TST is shown in Figure 6. The TST contains a sub-TST (N_1–N_{12}) for loading a carrier with four boxes (N_2–N_6), delivering the carrier (N_7), and unloading the packages from the carrier and delivering them to the survivors (N_8–N_{12}). A package must also be delivered to the survivor in the right uppermost part of the region, far away from where most of the survivors were found (N_{13}). The delivery of packages can be done concurrently to save time, while the loading, moving, and unloading of the carrier is a sequential operation.

To delegate the TST, the Delegation Agent of OP_1 searches for a platform that can achieve the TST. It starts by finding all platforms that have the capabilities for the top node N_0, which is both platforms. It then auctions out N_0 to both platforms to find the best initial choice. In this case, the marginal cost is the same for both platforms and the first platform, P_1 is chosen. The Delegation Agent of OP_1 then sends a *call-for-proposal* message with the TST to the winner, P_1.

P_1 is now responsible for N_0 and for recursively delegating the nodes in the TST that it is not able to do itself. The allocation algorithm traverses the TST in depth-first order. P_1 will first find a platform for node N_1. When the entire sub-TST rooted in N_1 is allocated then it will find an allocation for node N_{13}. Nodes N_1 and N_2 are composite action nodes which have the same marginal cost for all platforms. P_1 therefore allocates N_1 and N_2 to itself. The constraints from nodes N_0–N_2 are added to the constraint network of P_1. The network is consistent because the composite action nodes describe a schedule without any restrictions.

Below node N_2 are four elementary action nodes. Since P_1 is responsible for N_2, it tries to allocate them one at the time. For elementary action nodes, the choice of platform is the key to a successful allocation. This is because of each platform's unique state, constraint model for the action, and available resources. The candidates for node N_3 are platforms P_1 and P_2. P_1 is closest to the package depot and therefore gives the best bid for the node. P_1 is allocated to N_3. For node N_4, platform P_1 is still the best choice, and it is allocated to N_4. Given the new position of P_1 after being allocated N_3 and N_4, P_2 is now closest to the depot resulting in the lowest bid and is allocated to N_5 and N_6. The schedule initially defined by nodes N_0–N_2 is now also constrained by how long it takes for P_1 and P_2 to carry out action nodes N_3–N_6. The constraint network is distributed among platforms P_1 and P_2.

The next node to allocate for P_1 is node N_7, the carrier delivery node. P_1 is the only platform that has the capabilities for the fly carrier task and is allocated the node. Continuing with nodes N_8–N_{12}, the platform with the lowest bid for each node is platform P_1, since it is in the area after delivering the carrier. P_1, is therefore allocated all the nodes N_8–N_{12}. The final node, N_{13}, is allocated to P_2 and the allocation is complete.

The only non-local information used by P_1 was the capabilities of the available platforms which was gathered through a broadcast. Everything else is local. The bids are made by each platform based on local information and the consistency of the constraint network is checked through distributed constraint satisfaction techniques.

The total mission time is 58 minutes, which is much longer than the operator expected. Since the constraint problem defined by the allocation of the TST is distributed between the platforms, it is possible for the operator to modify the constraint problem by adding more constraints, and in this way modify the resulting task allocation. The operator puts a time constraint on the mission, restricting the total time to 30 minutes.

To re-allocate the TST with the added constraint, operator OP_1 sends a *reject-proposal* to platform P_1. The added time constraint makes the current allocation inconsistent. The last allocated node must therefore be re-allocated. However, no platform for N_{13} can make the allocation consistent, not even the unused platform P_3. Backtracking starts. Platform P_1 is in charge, since it is responsible for allocating node N_{13}. The N_1 sub-network is disconnected. Trying different platforms for node N_{13}, P_1 discovers that N_{13} can be allocated to P_2. P_1 sends a *backjump-search* message to the platform in charge of the sub-TST with top-node N_1, which happens to be P_1. When receiving the message, P_1 continues the search for the backjump point. Since removing all constraints due to the allocation of node N_1 and its children made the problem consistent, the backjump point is in the sub-TST rooted in N_1. Removing the allocations for sub-tree N_8 does not make the problem consistent so further backjumping is necessary.

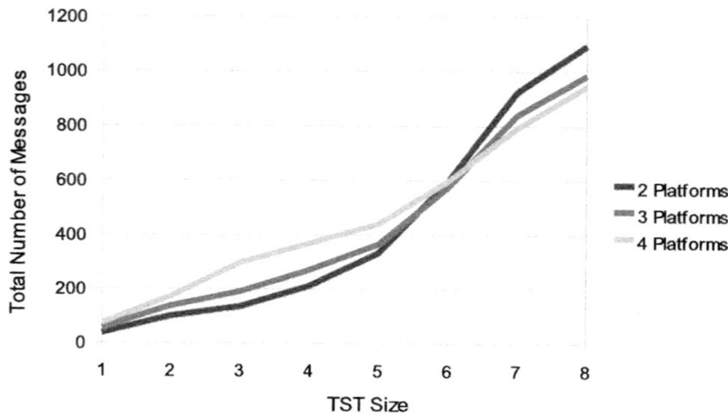

Fig. 7. Allocation time for each group of platforms, when extending the size of TST

Notice that with a single consistency check the algorithm could deduce that no possible allocation of N_8 and its children can lead to a consistent allocation of N_{13}. Removing the allocation for node N_7 does not make a difference either. However, removing the allocations for the sub-TST N_2 makes the problem consistent. When finding an allocation of N_{13} after removing the constraints from N_6 the allocation process continues from N_6 and tries the next platform for the node, P_1.

When the allocation reaches node N_{11} it is discovered that since P_1 has taken on nodes N_3–N_8, there is not enough time left for P_1 to unload the last two packages from the carrier. Instead P_3, even though it makes a higher bid for N_{11}–N_{12}, is allocated to both nodes. Finally platform P_2 is allocated to node N_{13}. It turns out that since platform P_2 helped P_1 loading the carrier, it has not enough time to deliver the final package. Instead, a new backjump point search starts, finding node N_5. The search continues from N_5. This time, nodes N_3–N_9 are allocated to platform P_1, platform P_3 is allocated to node N_{10}–N_{12}, and platform P_2 is allocated to node N_{13}. The allocation is consistent. The allocation algorithm finishes on platform P_1, by sending a *propose* message back to the operator. The operator inspects the allocation and approves it, thereby confirming the delegation and starting the execution of the mission.

6.1 Empirical Evaluation

As an initial evaluation of the task allocation algorithm it has been applied to different instances of the logistics task described above. To evaluate the scalability we varied the size of the TST (number of boxes to be delivered), the number of available platforms and the total time available to achieve the task. The task to be allocated is described by the TST in Figure 6 without the last fly box action (N_{13}). To vary the TST size, the load–move–unload carrier pattern corresponding to the sub-TST rooted in N_1 is repeated. The TST with n carriers is called Cn, consists of $12n + 1$ nodes and moves $4n$ boxes.

In the first experiment, the size of the TST and the number of available platforms is varied. The number of carriers varied between 1 and 8 (C1–C8), corresponding to between 4 and 32 boxes and between 13 and 97 nodes. The number of platforms varied between 2 and 4. For each combination, the total number of messages exchanged

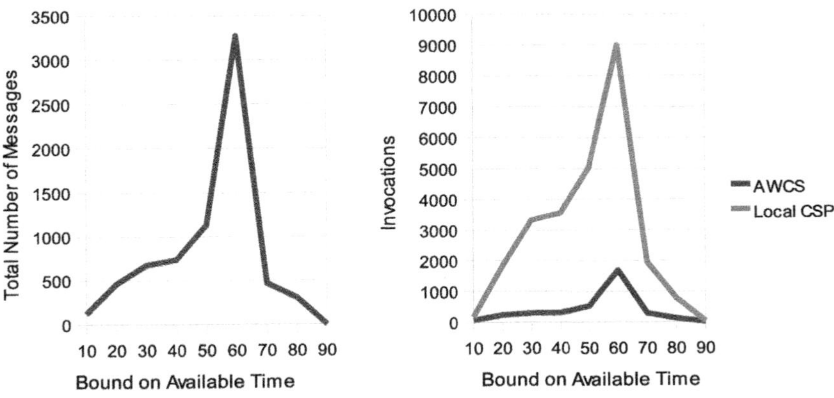

Fig. 8. The number of messages sent (left) and the constraint solver activity (right) for allocating the C1 TST to 2 platforms when the bound on the available time to complete the task varies

is measured when the algorithm allocated the TST to the available platforms using chronological backtracking. The time available to complete the task is unlimited.

The result of the experiment is shown in Figure 7. As expected, the number of messages increases more or less exponentially with the size of the TST while the number of platforms does not significantly influence the number of messages. It should be noted that a TST with n carriers corresponds to a constraint satisfaction problem with $33n+2$ variables. To solve constraint problems with hundreds of variables is currently not feasible with distributed constraint solvers. The results are therefore quite good.

In the second experiment the total time available to complete the task is varied while the size of the TST is fixed to C1 and the number of available platforms is fixed to 2. The available time, called the *bound*, is varied between 10 and 100. When the total time is limited the constraint problem becomes harder and there are fewer solutions. The optimal solution, with respect to the total time used to complete the task, is 65. This means that for bounds less than 65 there is no solution.

The result of the experiment is shown in Figure 8. The left graph shows the total number of messages sent and the right the number of invocations of the AWCS algorithm and calls to the local constraint solvers. As expected, the number of messages is high when there is no solution and the bound is close to the lowest value. As the bound increases the algorithm uses relatively few messages to find an acceptable solution.

The experiments show that the algorithm is capable of allocating relatively large TST's and that the number of platforms does not significantly influence the number of messages sent when there is no bound on the available time. They also show that global constraints, such as bounds on the time to complete a task, is a highly significant factor.

7 Related Work

The closest work to allocating TST's is the work on task allocation for task trees (18). In task trees, tasks are related to each other either by precedence constraints or by compositions as expressed by logical connectives. The authors call this "complex task allocation". A major difference is that these task trees can not express interrelated utilities (IU), which TST's can.

Many task allocation algorithms are auction-based (1). There, tasks are auctioned out and allocated to the agent that makes the best bid. Bids are determined by a utility function. The auction concept decentralizes the task allocation process which is very useful especially in multi-robot systems, where centralized solutions are impractical. For tasks that have unrelated utilities, this approach has been very successful. The reason is that UU guarantees that each task can be treated as an independent entity, and can be auctioned out without affecting other parts of the allocation. This means that a robot does not have to take other tasks into consideration when making a bid.

In complex task allocation sub-tasks may not be independent. A complex task has structure and there are relations between its atomic tasks. It is also often the case that a complex task must be allocated to a group of agents, creating relations between the agents relative to the task. Complex task allocation must therefore take into account synergy effects between allocations which influence the bids for tasks. A bid could for example be different depending on other commitments of the platform.

More advanced auction protocols have been developed to handle dependencies among tasks. These are constructed to deal with complementarities (substitution effects, which we call interrelated utilities). Examples are sequential single item auctions (9) and combinatorial auctions (16). These auctions typically handle that different combinations of tasks have different bids, which can be compared to our model where different sets of allocations result in different restrictions to the constraint network between the platforms.

The sequential single item (SSI) auction (9) is of special interest as it is similar to our algorithm. In SSI auctions, the tasks are auctioned out in sequence, one at a time to make sure the new task fits with the previous allocations. Normally SSI auctions are applied to problems where it is easy to find a solution but it is hard to find a good solution. They are therefore normally not complete for problems where it is hard to find a solution, like with TST allocation.

Combinatorial auctions deal with complementarities by bidding on bundles containing multiple items. Each bidder places bids on all the bundles that are of interest, which could be exponentially many. The auctioneer must then select the best set of bids, called the winner determination problem, which is NP-hard (16). I.e., even in the best case there is a very high computational cost involved in using combinatorial auctions.

8 Conclusions

Two central problems in our research with collaborative unmanned aerial vehicles are to define complex mixed-initiative missions and given a mission find UAV platforms that can execute it. We have previously introduced a formal delegation framework and within that proposed Task Specification Trees as a highly expressive specification language for multi-agent tasks that supports mixed-initiative delegation with adjustable autonomy. In this paper we have discussed the problem of allocating complex tasks to robots. We extended the multi-robot task allocation classification introduced by Gerkey and Matarić (8) with four new dimensions and argued that allocating Task Specification Trees is more challenging than most allocation problems currently considered. The problem of allocating TST's to robot platforms was defined and a heuristic algorithm for finding a consistent allocation was presented. The heuristic is based on auctions. The algorithm recursively searches among the potential allocations in a distributed manner and uses distributed constraint satisfaction techniques to check if an allocation satisfies the constraints. We also presented a detailed case study with a team of unmanned aerial vehicles assisting in a challenging emergency services scenario.

In conclusion, specifying and allocating complex tasks are important research problems in multi-agent systems, especially when dealing with real world robotic agents. The presented approach takes another step towards practical multi-robot collaboration.

References

1. Dias, M., Zlot, R., Kalra, N., Stentz, A.: Market-based multirobot coordination: a survey and analysis. Proc. of IEEE 94(1), 1257–1270 (2006)
2. Doherty, P., Kvarnström, J., Heintz, F.: A temporal logic-based planning and execution monitoring framework for unmanned aircraft systems. Journal of Automated Agents and Multi-Agent Systems 19(3), 332–377 (2009)
3. Doherty, P., Landén, D., Heintz, F.: A Distributed Task Specification Language for Mixed-Initiative Delegation. In: Desai, N., Liu, A., Winikoff, M. (eds.) PRIMA 2010, vol. 7057, pp. 42–57. Springer, Heidelberg (2011)
4. Doherty, P., Meyer, J.-J.C.: Towards a Delegation Framework for Aerial Robotic Mission Scenarios. In: Klusch, M., Hindriks, K.V., Papazoglou, M.P., Sterling, L. (eds.) CIA 2007. LNCS (LNAI), vol. 4676, pp. 5–26. Springer, Heidelberg (2007)
5. Gale, D.: The Theory of Linear Economic Models. McGraw-Hill Book Company, Inc. (1960)
6. Gerkey, B.: On multi-robot task allocation. Ph.D. thesis (2003)
7. Gerkey, B., Mataric, M.: Sold!: Auction methods for multi-robot coordination. IEEE Transactions on Robotics and Automation (2001)
8. Gerkey, B., Mataric, M.: A formal analysis and taxonomy of task allocation in multi-robot systems. Int. Journal of Robotic Research 23(9), 939–954 (2004)
9. Koenig, S., Keskinocak, P., Tovey, C.: Progress on agent coordination with cooperative auctions. In: Proc. AAAI (2010)
10. Kvarnström, J., Doherty, P.: Automated planning for collaborative systems. In: Proceedings of the International Conference on Control, Automation, Robotics and Vision (2010)
11. Lemaire, T., Alami, R., Lacroix, S.: A distributed tasks allocation scheme in multi-uav context. In: Proc. ICRA (2004)
12. Modi, P., Shen, W.-M., Tambe, M., Yokoo, M.: Adopt: Asynchronous distributed constraint optimization with quality guarantees. AI 161 (2006)
13. Rudol, P., Doherty, P.: Human body detection and geolocalization for UAV search and rescue missions using color and thermal imagery. In: Proc. IEEE Aerospace Conference (2008)
14. Smith, R.: The contract net protocol. IEEE Transactions on Computers C-29(12) (1980)
15. Viguria, A., Maza, I., Ollero, A.: Distributed service-based cooperation in aerial/ground robot teams applied to fire detection and extinguishing missions. Adv. Robotics 24 (2010)
16. de Vries, S., Vohra, R.: Combinatorial auctions: A survey. J. on Computing 15(3) (2003)
17. Yokoo, M.: Asynchronous weak-commitment search for solving distributed constraint satisfaction problems. In: Proc. CP (1995)
18. Zlot, R., Stentz, A.: Market-based multirobot coordination for complex tasks. International Journal of Robotics Research 25(1) (2006)

Affordance-Based Intention Recognition in Virtual Spatial Environments

Michal Sindlar and John-Jules Meyer*

University of Utrecht, The Netherlands
{michal,jj}@cs.uu.nl

Abstract. In applications for entertainment or training, behavior of characters often takes place in virtual environments with spatial dimensions that incorporate both agents and objects. Situated virtual characters can employ knowledge of their environment in reasoning about the goals or intentions of other characters, virtual or human, contributing to their believability. This paper presents lightweight techniques to that extent, utilizing object affordances and observed behavior of characters to define an observer reasoning about that behavior. In case an observer reasons about the behavior of virtual autonomous agents, knowledge of behavior-producing rules can also be employed. This is formalized by extending earlier work on mental state abduction of BDI-based agents with the techniques presented here. The presentation is technical, illustrated with practical examples.

1 Introduction

Computer video games quite often take place in spatial virtual environments which are inhabited by virtual characters; e.g. first-person shooters (F.E.A.R. [17]), platform games, real-time strategy games, and role-playing games (The Elder Scrolls: Oblivion [4]). The same holds for training applications that are used by the military or civil services if those incorporate representations of the environment where personnel is to operate. In case one or more human participants are involved in aforementioned applications, the role of virtual characters is typically secondary to that of humans: video games require that characters contribute to players' enjoyment of the game, and training applications require that their behavior benefits achievement of training objectives. Both kinds of applications require characters to exhibit believable behavior, and in this respect it can be worthwhile to consider automating aspects of that behavior.

Loyall [15] mentions several requirements for virtual characters' believability which pertain to social interaction, and user feedback indicates that players of role-playing games are not satisfied with the believability of virtual non-player characters in that respect [1]. Social skills — inferring and reacting to

* This research has been supported by the GATE project, funded by the Netherlands Organization for Scientific Research (NWO) and the Netherlands ICT Research and Innovation Authority (ICT Regie).

N. Desai, A. Liu, and M. Winikoff (Eds.): PRIMA 2010, LNAI 7057, pp. 304–319, 2012.

the presumed beliefs and goals of others — can be simulated in various ways: e.g. characters can be scripted to make their behavior appear social; characters' motion can be determined in relation to that of others to simulate awareness of others' goals (flocking/avoidance); or characters can be given information of the actual beliefs/goals of other virtual characters and use this information in their own decision-making, possibly with a margin of error so as not to seem omniscient [20,16,9]. In this paper, it is assumed that characters receive knowledge-level perceptory data (i.e. objects, actions), and use that data for intention recognition (i.e. inferring the intentions/goals and predicting future behavior of other characters). Focus is on formalization of a virtual observer.

The main contribution of the paper is a model for intention recognition that utilizes a priori available data, in the sense that it is non-probabilistic and mostly based on geometric calculations. This work is to be considered 'early innovation' because it presents a framework of which the theoretical and conceptual foundations are clear and which is mathematically defined, but for whose deployment empirical evaluation is required. The paper is structured as follows. The environment model of the observer is described in Section 2. Given this model and the fulfillment of particular assumptions, Sections 3 and 4 formalize the observer reasoning about the behavior of characters based on knowledge of afforded actions and the character's *spatio-temporal behavior.* If the character observed by the observer is virtual (i.e. non-human), then it is possible that it is instantiated as an autonomous virtual agent that plans its actions in order to achieve its goals (an approach recently adopted successfully in games [17]). In Section 5 the computational approaches of preceding sections are applied to our earlier work on (BDI-based) intention recognition [18,19], yielding a hybrid model. Section 6 then discusses related work in some detail, and Section 7 concludes the paper.

2 Environment Model

This section describes the environment model used by an observer to explain/predict observed characters' behavior.

2.1 Agents and Objects

Many applications — e.g. games, simulations, training environments — involve virtual environments that have a *spatial* component. In the present context, this means that they can be represented as a 2-dimensional (2D) or 3-dimensional (3D) vector space, such that entities situated in those environments can be assigned coordinates in that space. It is assumed that there are two classes of entities in the environment which are of interest to the observer: *agents* and *objects.* Let Ag be the set of agents and Obj the set of objects, and let $\mathbb{R}^d$ be a vector space of dimensionality d. The function $\mathsf{p} : (\mathsf{Ag} \cup \mathsf{Obj}) \longrightarrow \mathbb{R}^d$ then assigns a spatial position (i.e. coordinate vector with dimension d) to an entity x. It should be noted that this function is partial if the observer does not (always) have information about every entity's position, and that it is assumed for simplicity that position can be represented with a single coordinate.

Agents and objects play different roles in the environment; agents are entities which can perform actions, and objects are entities on which actions can be performed. The above view on objects is in line with the psychologist James Gibson's concept of *affordance* [11], which can be defined as "action possibilities latent in the environment" and which is here applied to objects. Note that the extensions of the concepts 'agents' and 'objects' are not per definition mutually exclusive: an entity can have both the role of agent (acting itself) and object (being acted upon). Affordance is also used in the context of human-machine interaction, where it refers to an object's action possibilities *as perceived by an agent*; under this latter definition it is usually referred to as *perceived affordance*. In the present context we take the affordance of an object to mean the action possibilities provided by that object *according to the observer*. Because different agents might have different capabilities, the affordance of objects is here considered relative to agents; a formal definition is given in Section 2.3.

2.2 Regions

The vector space that represents the environment may consist of many individual points, and sometimes it can be useful to think of multiple points as forming a coherent whole. If $\mathbb{R}^d$ is a d-dimensional vector space, then a collection of points $R \subseteq \mathbb{R}^d$ is referred to as a *region* if those points are appropriately related; in this paper, it is required that they are adjoining. Considering regions can be a useful heuristic in reasoning about observed behavior, for example if the agent is situated in an enclosure (e.g. a room) where it is non-sensical to treat adjoining coordinates as unrelated.

For example, Figure 1 shows a 2D grid environment with a walled enclosure in which a bomb and a trashcan are positioned. If $(0, 0)$ denotes the bottom left square, then the trashcan is positioned at $(3, 3)$ and the bomb at $(7, 8)$. Should regions be marked out in this environment, then a probable choice is to consider the square with $(5, 5)$ at bottom left and $(9, 9)$ at top right as a whole. This region can be extended to include the cells $(3, 3)$, $(4, 3)$, $(5, 3)$, and $(5, 4)$. However, it is also justifiable to consider the square and $(3, 3)$–$(5, 3)$ as two different regions, and $(5, 4)$ as yet another region that connects those two. This illustrates that defining regions is often a matter of design choice.

2.3 Weighted Affordance

In Section 2.1 the concept of affordance was introduced, and an informal definition was given. Here, the function aff is defined to return the set of actions that some object affords to some agent *according to the observer*. The perspective-relativity of affordance is furthermore illustrated by the fact that an action afforded by some object to a particular agent may be 'more interesting' to the observer than other actions this object affords to that same agent, or those afforded by other objects. Regardless of specifics, it is here assumed that the observer's affordance function assigns a weight to each action representing the observer's interest therein, such that it is defined as $\mathsf{aff} : \mathsf{Obj} \times \mathsf{Ag} \longrightarrow$

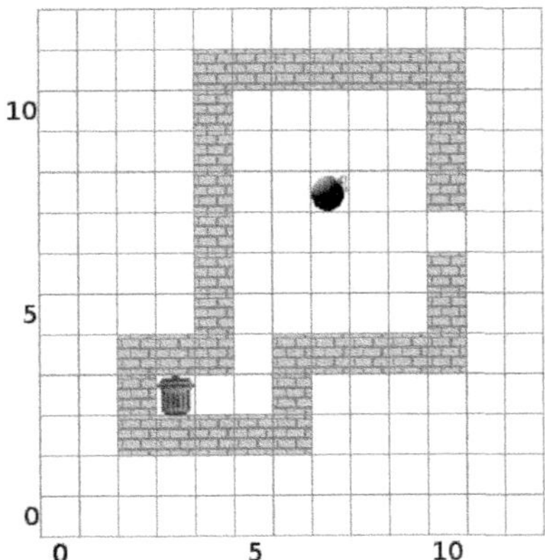

Fig. 1. A simple 2D grid environment

$\wp(\mathsf{Act} \longrightarrow \mathbb{R})$. Note that aff maps to a set of functions, as it is assumed that per object/agent pair a single weight is assigned to each of the afforded actions.

The semantics of weights are context-dependent; for example, if weight differs across objects but is constant for every action afforded by individual objects then it can represent the salience of objects to the observer and/or focus of the observer's attention. Alternatively, if it varies across actions but is constant for objects then it might represent the (un)desirability, from the point of view of the observer, of actions being performed. This paper does not delve into semantics of weights, but shows how these integrate with the topic of this paper: modeling an observer that explains or predicts the behavior of agents. A final note concerns objects, which can abstractly be viewed as *locations* in the environment that afford actions to agents.

3 Position-Based Prediction

The observer described in this paper focuses on agents in a spatial environment. Prediction of future actions is an aspect of reasoning about those agents' behavior, and in this section it is shown how the observer can utilize the position of an observed agent to that extent. Inspiration is recent work of Doirado and Martinho [8], which focuses on motion-based calculations but gives less — if any — attention to contextual information (such as affordance).

3.1 Perception Radius

In some situations it cannot be assumed that the observer has full perception of the agent and its surroundings, either from a physical point of view (e.g. if the observer is situated in the environment together with the agent and its vision is obscured) or because of restricted resources (if the observer can process only a certain amount of perceptual data). And even if full perception is feasible in principle, it may not be desirable to realize it; for instance in games where a sense of realism can be maintained by giving the observer incomplete perception. The latter is referred to as *sensory honesty* [13], meaning that characters are provided with perceptual data deemed similar to what humans perceive.

A possible approach to model perception of the observer is to consider regions in the observed agent's vicinity, so let the function $\mathsf{vic} : \mathbb{R}^d \longrightarrow \wp(\mathbb{R}^d)$ return the region(s) — i.e. an adjoining set of points — that surround a point in the vector space. The specifics of this function are left implicit: if perception is complete then it might return the entire space, if it is not then only part of this space might be returned. Factors that possibly determine those specifics are mentioned in the previous paragraph. In any case, the regions returned by vic represent the *perception radius*[1] of the observer with regard to some point in the vector space, determining what it sees (i.e. its 'field of view').

3.2 Distance and Affordance

Prediction of an agent's actions is done on grounds of its position in the environment; specifically, its vicinity to objects that afford specific actions. Let $\mathsf{d} : \mathsf{Ag} \times \mathbb{R}^d \times \mathbb{R}^d \longrightarrow \mathbb{R}$ be the function that per agent returns the distance between two points in the vector space. Note that this distance need *not* be the Euclidean distance! Even though it might be the Euclidean distance in certain cases, in many environments other distance measures (such as the shortest path) are more practical.[2] Many games employ path planning algorithms like A^* for planning character's paths, which can also be used in determining d. Computational cost need not be prohibitive: if path planning is used (in the case of virtual agents), then outcomes of the path planning process can be reused in the observer's distance function. In case of non-virtual characters Euclidean distance can be used if more refined measures prove too costly, a measure which is known to involve little computational overhead [8].

Based on the observed agent's position, its distance to objects in its vicinity can be determined by the observer. In environments where interaction with objects presents a significant part of character behavior, such distance measures give an indication for the characters' expected behavior. Let $\mathsf{obj} : \wp(\mathbb{R}^d) \longrightarrow \wp(\mathsf{Obj})$ be the function that returns the set of objects that are situated in some region (where it is assumed that objects do not span across regions). Given the aforementioned formal ingredients, it is possible to define the following position-based prediction function.

Definition 1 (position-based prediction). *Let* $i \in \mathsf{Ag}$ *be an observed agent,* $\mathsf{aff}, \mathsf{d}, \mathsf{obj}, \mathsf{p}, \mathsf{vic}$ *as defined before, and* $A = \{(x, \alpha, w) \mid x \in \mathsf{obj}(\mathsf{vic}(\mathsf{p}(i))) \;\&\; (\alpha, w) \in \mathsf{aff}(x, i)\}$ *a set of tuples of object, afforded action, and*

[1] The term 'radius' here has its general meaning of 'area'; i.e. it can be non-circular.

[2] In a grid environment as depicted in Figure 1 the shortest path from any square to any diagonally adjoining square (e.g. from $(0, 0)$ to $(1, 1)$) is not $\sqrt{2}$ (which is the Euclidean distance) but 2, for agents that move only horizontally and vertically.

affordance weight. $\mathcal{P} : \mathsf{Ag} \longrightarrow \wp(\mathsf{Obj} \times \mathsf{Act} \times \mathbb{R})$ *is then the position-based prediction function.*

$$\mathcal{P}(i) = \{\ (x, \alpha, r) \mid (x, \alpha, w) \in A \ \& \\ r = (w \cdot f(\mathsf{d}(i, \mathsf{p}(i), \mathsf{p}(x))))\ \}$$

Note in the function $\mathcal{P}$ defined in Def. 1 that $r \in \mathbb{R}$ is derived from the multiplication of w, the affordance weight of an object, with a function f of the agent's distance to that object. The function $f : \mathbb{R} \longrightarrow \mathbb{R}$ models the fact that 'influence' of an object *decreases* with distance. An example of this degradation function is $f(d) = (1/d)$, but more sophistication is of course possible. Tuples (x, α, r) that are returned by the function $\mathcal{P}$ then give rise to a partial ordering on pairs (x, α) that follows the ordering on the reals $r \in \mathbb{R}$. Let $\mathcal{P}_{\leqslant}(i)$ be this poset for some agent i, which then represents the object/action pairs the observer predicts for this agent, based on the agent's observed position with respect to those objects, in ratio to their weighted affordance.

3.3 Example

In this example the 2D grid of Figure 1 is used for illustration. Assume the observer to observe an agent i located at coordinate $P_i = (6, 6)$. The coordinates of the bomb and trashcan are as the figure shows, i.e. $P_b = (7, 8)$ and $P_t = (3, 3)$, respectively. Let i be a hostile agent, and let $\mathsf{aff}(\mathsf{bomb}, i) = \{(\mathsf{pickup}, 1), (\mathsf{detonate}, 4)\}$ be the actions afforded by the bomb to the agent. The perceived region returned by $\mathsf{vic}(P_i)$ is the set of accessible cells in a 2-cell radius around the agent (i.e. the square from $(4, 4)$ to $(8, 8)$ minus the walls), such that $\mathsf{obj}(\mathsf{vic}(P_i)) = \{\mathsf{bomb}\} = O$. Let $A = \{(\mathsf{bomb}, \mathsf{pickup}, 1), (\mathsf{bomb}, \mathsf{detonate}, 4)\}$, as in Def. 1, noting $\mathsf{d}(i, P_i, P_b) = 3$, which given $f = (1/d)$ yields the prediction $\mathcal{P}(i) = \{(\mathsf{bomb}, \mathsf{pickup}, \frac{1}{3}), (\mathsf{bomb}, \mathsf{detonate}, \frac{4}{3})\}$.

Alternative to the above, let j be an agent with position $P_j = (5, 5)$ for which it holds that $\mathsf{aff}(\mathsf{bomb}, j) = \{(\mathsf{pickup}, 1), (\mathsf{disarm}, 1)\}$. Furthermore, assume that *only if* the observer is convinced the agent has already picked up a bomb it holds that $\mathsf{aff}(j, \mathsf{trashcan}) = \{(\mathsf{deposit}, 1)\}$. Note $\mathsf{d}(j, P_j, P_b) = 5$ and $\mathsf{d}(j, P_j, P_t) = 4$, and assume the observer is convinced that j has not yet picked up a bomb so that $\mathcal{P}(j) = \{(\mathsf{bomb}, \mathsf{pickup}, \frac{1}{5}), (\mathsf{bomb}, \mathsf{disarm}, \frac{1}{5})\}$. On the other hand, if the observer is convinced the agent did already pick up a bomb, then $\mathcal{P}(j)' = \mathcal{P}(j) \cup \{(\mathsf{trashcan}, \mathsf{deposit}, \frac{1}{4})\}$ such that the latter is the better prediction.

3.4 Reflection

The function $\mathcal{P}$, as defined above, takes a single-step approach. An algorithmic approach could implement this function iteratively; in the first step the regions "very close" to the agent can be considered, in the second step further outlying regions can be considered, etc. Thus, the observer can consider the vicinity of the observed agent in a piecemeal fashion, so if the observer is under pressure its attention for the agent and its surroundings is limited. This is plausible if the observer is to be believable, given that human perceptual processing capacity is known to decrease with increased demand on cognitive resources [10].

4 Motion-Based Prediction

Using the $\mathcal{P}$ function defined in Section 3 the observer can determine a partially ordered set of actions it expects an observed agent to perform on particular objects. This set is based on a 'snapshot' of the agent and its surroundings. It is useful to formalize this notion if the observer's perception is fragmentary. If it is not then the observer can consider movement of the observed agent, as formalized in the current section incrementally to the previous section, in the sense that several of the functions defined there are employed.

4.1 Modeling Dynamics

The notion of *dynamics* is fundamental to this section and deserves explicit mention. If the observer considers motion of the agent, then change of state must be modeled. To this extent *time* is introduced into our model, which is conceptualized as an additional dimension such that spatio-temporal behavior can be represented as a sequentiation of 'snapshots' of the vector space. If the observer is certain about the past and does not consider future states in prediction, as we assume, then time is a *linear sequence of states.*

Let $t_{now} \in \mathbb{R}$ be the present time, and let S_{now} be the present state (i.e. vector space with objects, etc., as described in Section 2). The observer presumedly also has representations of past states at past times, which can be represented as tuples (S_{past}, t_{past}), for which it holds that $t_{past} < t_{now}$. For simplicity, it is assumed here that the only (relevant) difference between S_{past} and S_{now} is the position of some observed agent. This assumption entails that most of the information in S_{past} need not be 'remembered' by the observer, except for the position of the agent at t_{past}.[3]

4.2 Displacement: Change of Position

As explained in Section 4.1, change between past and present states considered by the observer is restricted to the observed agent's position. In order to calculate position at a particular time, let $\mathsf{p} : (\mathsf{Ag} \cup \mathsf{Obj}) \times \mathbb{R} \longrightarrow \mathbb{R}^d$ be a partial function that extends the position function defined in Section 2, mapping pairs of entities (i.e. agents or objects) and time points $t \in \mathbb{R}$ to coordinates in the vector space, where objects — as noted before — are static, and entities' position can be represented with a single coordinate. In mechanics, *displacement* describes an

[3] This abstraction has multiple interpretations: the environment might be of such a nature that objects hardly change position at all; or the observer considers only those past states which differ from the present in regard to the agent's; or the observer restricts its attention to regions in which only the agent position changes with respect to other entities in the environment.

entity's position relative to some initial position. Here, interest is in agents' displacement relative to objects, so let $\Delta : \mathsf{Ag} \times \mathsf{Obj} \longrightarrow \mathbb{R}$ be the function that calculates that displacement. For simplicity, the observer considers a single past state at some t', so that past and present remain implicit in the signature of Δ. This implies no lack of generality, since temporal arguments can be incorporated.

Let i be the observed agent, t the present time and t' some past time, such that the agent's position at those times is $P_t = \mathsf{p}(i,t)$ and $P_{t'} = \mathsf{p}(i,t')$. This agent's displacement with respect to some object x is then defined as $\Delta(i,x) = \mathsf{d}(i,P_t,P_x) - \mathsf{d}(i,P_{t'},P_x)$, where $P_x = \mathsf{p}(x,t) = \mathsf{p}(x,t')$ in accordance with the assumption that objects don't move inbetween the time points considered for motion-based prediction. In other words, Δ returns the *signed* change in distance from an agent to some object; if it is negative then the agent is closer to the object at time t (it has come closer), if it is positive then the agent is farther away (has distanced itself). It should once more noted that distance need not be Euclidean, in which case Δ might map to, for example, displacement in terms of the (shortest) path from i to x.

4.3 Incorporating Motion

In Section 4.2 the function Δ was defined to return the (signed) displacement of agents in relation to objects, with negative displacement indicating approach and positive displacement indicating distancing. Those ingredients are used to define a motion-based prediction function.

Definition 2 (motion-based prediction). *Let $i \in \mathsf{Ag}$ be an observed agent, P_t the agent's position and $P_{t'}$ its past position, such that $O = (\mathsf{obj}(\mathsf{vic}(P_t)) \cup \mathsf{obj}(\mathsf{vic}(P_{t'}))$ and $A = \{(x,\alpha,w) \,|\, x \in O \,\&\, (\alpha,w) \in \mathsf{aff}(x,i)\}$ is a set of tuples of object, afforded action, and affordance weight; given the functions defined earlier. The function $\mathcal{M} : \mathsf{Ag} \longrightarrow \wp(\mathsf{Obj} \times \mathsf{Act} \times \mathbb{R})$ is then the motion-based prediction function, defined as follows.*

$$\mathcal{M}(i) = \{ \ (x,\alpha,r) \,|\, (x,\alpha,w) \in A \ \& \\ r = w \cdot g(\Delta(i,x), |\, t - t' \,|) \ \}$$

As with $\mathcal{P}$ which relied on f, the function $\mathcal{M}$ also relies on an additional function, namely g, modeling the fact that the (weighted) affordance of objects is influenced in some way by the motion of the agent, according to the observer. The specifics of the function $g : \mathbb{R} \times \mathbb{R} \longrightarrow \mathbb{R}$ depend on various factors. To wit, in classical mechanics, *velocity* is the rate of change of position that some entity exhibits, whose derivative is *acceleration*, i.e. the object's rate of change in velocity. The average velocity and acceleration of some object during some time interval can be expressed if the object's displacement during this interval is known, and either can be used in defining g. For example, g can model the fact that if the agent approaches some object with high velocity and/or acceleration it is 'likely' to perform some action associated with that object, such that through g the (weighted) affordance of this object is influenced positively.

Fig. 2. Displacement relative to objects in a 3D virtual environment

The converse may hold if the agent distances itself from some object. Similar functions have been considered in literature; cf. [8]. The motion-based prediction function of Def. 2 yields similar output to the position-based prediction function of Def. 1, such that it also allows for a derived definition of $\mathcal{M}_{\leqslant}(i)$, which maps to a partially ordered set for which the ordering on pairs (x, α) is provided by the ordering on r for corresponding $(x, \alpha, r) \in \mathcal{M}(i)$.

4.4 Example

Figure 2 illustrates the approach of this section with two images of an observed agent, to be interpreted as snapshots at t_{past} (left) and t_{now} (right), and two objects in its vicinity, a potion and a sword, situated in a 3D environment.[4] The white ellipses mark those (motionless) objects in the environment, the white dot in the left part of the image marks the agent's position at t_{past}, the lower left and upper right dots in the right part mark the agent's position at t_{past} and t_{now}, respectively, indicating its displacement. Even without formal illustration, Figure 2 should make clear that considering the agent's motion, based on snapshots at t_{past} and t_{now}, relative to the objects in its vicinity arguably indicates intentions concerning the sword (assuming, for the sake of the example, the weight of afforded actions to be equal).

4.5 Reflection

If it is assumed that objects are only influenced by actions of agents, then the assumption made in Section 4.1 — of agents' positions being the only relevant factor of change — is valid. After all, if the observer is concerned with *predicting* actions of agents on objects, then it is reasonable to consider those successive states in which only movement of agents has occurred and no objects have been

[4] The image is composed of two modified screenshots of a setting in the game Oblivion, opened for editing in the T.E.S. Construction Set [4].

acted upon. Note, though, that in scenarios where agents (acting) can also be considered as objects (acted upon), then the assumption might not be sensible. An example of such a scenario is interaction between agents involving those agents' movements. In such a case our model should be extended to deal with 'moving objects', which has not been done at present for technical simplicity and to maintain a clear relation between motion and the concept of 'agency'.

5 Intention Recognition

This section extends our earlier work on *mental state abduction* [18,19], which deals with inference of a software agent's mental state on grounds of actions it is observed to perform, and is an instance of keyhole plan/intention recognition [7]. Agents are assumed to programmed in a BDI-based [6] agent programming language that allows for developing software in mentalistic terms [5]. The basic idea is that if the behavioral rules of the agent are known and certain assumptions hold with regard to its operation, then matching observed action sequences against those generated by the agent's plans allows for defeasibly inferring the mental state (pair of achievement goal and initial belief forming a rule's precondition) if the observation matches.

In the approach presented here, abduced goals are considered in regard to the agent's intention, focusing on specific actions, and assigned a numerical value based on the approach presented in Sections 3 and 4. Thus, a hybrid model is obtained which incorporates defeasible information regarding the agent's mental state, scored on grounds of an observer's knowledge of the agent's environment and its behavior. Among the assumption made with regard to the agent's operation are the fact that its rules are known to the observer, and that it does not interleave plans (i.e. has only a single intention). Those assumptions may seem strong, but are feasible in the context of games or training applications where the designer's objective is to create believable virtual characters, and are also not uncommon in literature on plan/intention recognition (e.g. [12,7]).

5.1 Simplifying Plans

Plans of BDI-based software agents typically utilize programming constructs like sequential composition, conditional choice and iteration. Let $\pi \in \mathcal{L}_\Pi$ be the typical element of agents' plans, defined by the BNF grammar below, where $\alpha \in \mathsf{Act}$ in the definition of plans is the typical element for observable actions, and $\phi \in \mathcal{L}_0$ is a propositional logical expression.

$$\pi \ ::= \ \alpha \,|\, \pi_1; \pi_2 \,|\, \textbf{if } \phi \textbf{ then } \pi_1 \textbf{ else } \pi_2 \,|\, \textbf{while } \phi \textbf{ do } \pi$$

In order to perform intention recognition, the observer must relate actions it perceives to plans it presumes the agent to have at its disposition. Often an observer can only observe a subset of the agent's actions (it will not observe internal updates or tests, for example) and of the actions it can observe it will only be interested in some. The actions the observer is interested in are here referred to as *key actions*, and it is assumed for the sake of technical exposition that those are associated with objects in the environment. It is useful, from a computational point of view, to have a simplified representation of the agent's plans available for recognition, specifically one which does not contain iteration (the **while/do** construct). Here, it is assumed that no key actions occur in the scope of iteration, such that plans the observer considers are given by typical element $\dot{\pi} \in \mathcal{L}_{\dot{\Pi}}$, where $\mathcal{L}_{\dot{\Pi}} \subseteq \mathcal{L}_{\Pi}$.

$$\dot{\pi} \ ::= \ \alpha \,|\, \dot{\pi}_1; \dot{\pi}_2 \,|\, \textbf{if } \phi \textbf{ then } \dot{\pi}_2 \textbf{ else } \dot{\pi}_2$$

Thus, the plans of observed agents can contain iteration, but the observer ignores those iterative parts in attempting to relate observed actions. The actions the observer is interested in do not appear inside the scope of iteration anyway, and simplification in such a case does not pose technical problems. It is furthermore justifiable because repetitive actions often concern movement, which this approach deals with numerically. Also, in games plans can be restricted to allow for simplification. It should be noted that iteration is only ignored by the observer on the level of plans; in agent programming iteration also occurs on the level of rules (e.g. if a rule is applied repeatedly), which our model does account for. Given the above, it is feasible to perform intention recognition by relating observed actions to *finite observable traces* of plans by filtering out any unobservable and some of the non-key actions from simplified plans in $\mathcal{L}_{\dot{\Pi}}$.

5.2 Key Sequences

Observable sequences of key actions can be derived by simplification of agents' plans, as described in Section 5.1. Let α be an observable key action, such that the domain $\mathcal{L}_{\Sigma} \subseteq \mathcal{L}_{\dot{\Pi}}$ of observable *key sequences* is defined through its typical element $\sigma \in \mathcal{L}_{\Sigma}$ as $\sigma \ ::= \ \alpha \,|\, \sigma_1; \sigma_2$. The observer then uses a representation of a plan as a set of key sequences of interesting actions in its intention recognition process. It was assumed that the agent does not interleave its plans, and since those plans contain only sequential composition the observer also perceives an agent's actions sequentially; i.e. not concurrently. It is furthermore assumed that the observer sees *all* (key) actions of the agent, so that in relating observed sequences to key sequences derived from plans it does not have to take 'gaps' into account.[5] This entails that both an actual observed sequence and key sequences derived from a simplified plan are in $\mathcal{L}_{\Sigma}$, and here we assume the function $KS : \mathcal{L}_{\dot{\Pi}} \longrightarrow \wp(\mathcal{L}_{\Sigma})$ to translate a simplified plan to its set of key sequences by filtering out unobservable elements (cf. [18,19]). The assumption of complete observation also entails that, because every action the agent performs is observed by the observer, that the observed sequence σ must be a *prefix* of some $\sigma' \in \Sigma$.

[5] This is assumed mainly for technical simplicity; our earlier work [18] does deal with incomplete perception.

5.3 Explaining and Predicting Actions

Let Γ be a set of pairs $(\phi, \dot{\pi})$ that are the observer's representation of an agent's behavioral rules, where $\phi \in \mathcal{L}_0$ is an expression from the propositional language $\mathcal{L}_0$ which represents the achievement goal for which the rule applies, and $\dot{\pi}$ is the observer's simplified representation of the plan that can be selected by the agent to achieve ϕ. The belief condition under which a plan can be selected is ignored in our model, because focus is only on observable actions in relation to agents' presumed goals. If, however, the observer keeps track of agents' presumed beliefs as well — i.e. has a theory of mind — then this information can be used to select a subset of rules the observer considers applicable.

An observed sequence of actions is taken to be *explained* by the observer in terms of a presumed goal for which it applies, if it can be prefix-matched with a key sequence of a plan that can be selected for that goal [18,19]. Given such an explanation the observer can furthermore *predict* the agent to perform the subsequent actions of that key sequence.

Definition 3 (rule-based explanation/prediction). *Let $i \in \mathsf{Ag}$ be an observed agent, $\sigma \in \mathcal{L}_\Sigma$ its observed actions, and Γ_i its rules as known to the observer. The function $\mathcal{R} : \mathsf{Ag} \times \mathcal{L}_\Sigma \longrightarrow \mathcal{L}_0 \times \mathcal{L}_\Sigma \times \mathbb{R}$ is then the rule-based explanation and prediction function, defined as follows.*

$$\mathcal{R}(i,\sigma) = \{ \ (\phi, \sigma', r) \mid \exists (\phi, \dot{\pi}) \in \Gamma_i : (\sigma;\sigma' \in KS(\dot{\pi}))\ \& \\ r = h(\sigma', \mathsf{cost}(i, \sigma', \mathsf{p}(i))) \ \}$$

In Def. 3, $\phi \in \mathcal{L}_0$ is agent i's presumed goal, which explains the observed sequence of key actions $\sigma \in \mathcal{L}_\Sigma$ based on the fact that σ is the prefix of some key sequence σ'' of some (simplified) plan $\dot{\pi}$ for achieving ϕ, i.e. $\sigma'' = \sigma;\sigma'$ such that σ' is a suffix. Naturally, σ' is then the predicted sequence. It should be noted that in our earlier work [18,19] the non-strict prefix was considered, in which case σ' would be the empty suffix (i.e. the prediction of no further key actions). In light of technical simplicity prefixes are at present required to be strict, though. It is not uncommon for multiple distinct explanations to exist (and/or multiple corresponding predictions), in which case it is useful for the observer to have some measure of plausibility of those explanations such that it can select the 'best' one. The rank r fulfills this role, based on a function $h : \mathcal{L}_\Sigma \times \mathbb{R} \longrightarrow \mathbb{R}$ of a sequence σ' and some $\mathsf{cost} : \mathsf{Ag} \times \mathcal{L}_\Sigma \times \mathbb{R}^d \longrightarrow \mathbb{R}$, i.e. the cost, according to the observer, of the agent performing that sequence. In line with the functions defined earlier, $\mathcal{R}$ gives rise to $\mathcal{R}_\leqslant(i,\sigma)$ which maps to a partially ordered set of pairs (ϕ, σ'), following the order on corresponding $r \in \mathbb{R}$.

The rationale behind cost is as follows: because actions are associated with objects and possibly require the agent to move within the environment, it takes the agent a certain amount of effort to perform a sequence of actions. In some scenarios object/action associations may be such that the cost of a sequence can be calculated from its actions alone; in other cases such calculation is better performed on-the-fly, depending on the (possibly changing) state of agent and environment. For the particular cost function used here, it is assumed that the agent's position determines the outcome of this function. A possible instantiation is then as follows, where functions p and d are as defined before, and $\mathsf{fno} : \mathsf{Ag} \times \mathsf{Act} \times \mathbb{R}^d \longrightarrow \mathsf{Obj} \times \mathbb{R}$ is a function that maps a tuple of agent, action and coordinate to the object nearest to that coordinate which allows that agent to perform that action, along with its affordance weight. Note that the definition of cost given below is recursive, and somewhat naive in that it does not take change of the environment into account. Also note that the cost is divided by the affordance weight, reflecting the assumption of the observer that the cost of performing more important actions is less significant.

$$\mathsf{cost}(i, \sigma, P) = \begin{cases} \mathsf{d}(i, P, P') \cdot (1/w) + & \\ \quad \mathsf{cost}(i, \sigma', P') & \textit{iff } \exists \alpha \in \mathsf{Act} \exists \sigma' \in \mathcal{L}_\Sigma : (\sigma = \alpha; \sigma') \\ \mathsf{d}(i, P, P') \cdot (1/w) & \textit{iff } \exists \alpha \in \mathsf{Act} : (\sigma = \alpha) \end{cases}$$
$$\textit{where } \mathsf{fno}(i, \alpha, P) = (O, w) \,\&\, \mathsf{p}(O) = P'$$

The function h is a degradation factor that depends on the length of a sequence and its cost, reflecting the fact that shorter predicted sequences (i.e. those with less actions) are 'closer' to achieving a goal then longer ones. A possible instantiation of this function is $h(\alpha_1 \cdots \alpha_n, c) = 1/(n \cdot c)$.

5.4 Example

For this example, the 2D environment of Figure 1 is once more considered. Assume an agent is observed by the observer, who knows it to be a BDI-based software agent with the following rule (listed here in terms of the goal for which it applies, the belief condition under which it can be selected, and the plan to achieve the goal).

GOAL: $\mathsf{bomb\_disposed}$ BELIEF: $\mathsf{bomb\_at}(X, Y)$
PLAN: **while** $(\mathsf{bomb\_at}(X, Y) \wedge \neg\mathsf{at}(X, Y))$ **do** $\{\mathsf{move\_towards}(X, Y)\}$;
if $\mathsf{standing\_on\_bomb}$ **then** $\{\mathsf{pickup};$ **while**$(\mathsf{trash\_at}(A, B) \wedge \neg\mathsf{at}(A, B))$ **do** $\{\mathsf{move\_towards}(A, B)\}; \mathsf{deposit}\}$ **else** $\{\}$

Let π be the above plan, in which case its simplification into key actions is $\dot{\pi} =$ **if** $\mathsf{standing\_on\_bomb}$ **then** $\{\mathsf{pickup}; \mathsf{deposit}\}$ **else** $\{\}$ and thus $KS(\dot{\pi}) = \{\mathsf{pickup}; \mathsf{deposit}\}$. A second rule of the agent is the following, of which disarm is the only key action.

GOAL: $\mathsf{bomb\_disarmed}$ BELIEF: $\mathsf{bomb\_at}(X, Y)$
PLAN: **while** $(\mathsf{bomb\_at}(X, Y) \wedge \neg\mathsf{at}(X, Y))$ **do** $\{\mathsf{move\_towards}(X, Y)\}$;
if $\mathsf{standing\_on\_bomb}$ **then** $\{\mathsf{disarm}\}$ **else** $\{\}$

Assume the agent is the friendly agent j in Section 3.3, i.e. $\mathsf{p}(j) = (5, 5)$, and assume the observer's perceived affordance (the output of aff) is the same as in that example. The observer's prediction, based on the observed agent's position, is then as follows, where ϵ is a special element denoting the 'empty observation' which prefixes any sequence.

$$\mathcal{R}(j,\epsilon) = \{(\mathsf{bomb\_disposed},\ \mathsf{pickup};\mathsf{deposit},\ 1/28),\\ (\mathsf{bomb\_disarmed},\ \mathsf{disarm},\ 1/5)\}$$

The derived function $\mathcal{R}_{\leqslant}(j,\epsilon)$ leads to $(\mathsf{bomb\_disarmed},\ \mathsf{disarm})$ being ranked as the best explanation/prediction, followed by $(\mathsf{bomb\_disposed},\ \mathsf{pickup};\mathsf{deposit})$. After observing pickup, given that $\mathsf{p}(j)(9,9)$, note the following outcome.

$$\mathcal{R}(j,\mathsf{pickup}) = \{(\mathsf{bomb\_disposed},\ \mathsf{deposit},\ 1/12)\}$$

This example is limited in size and scope because of space restrictions, but should give an idea of how explanation and prediction based on spatial metrics (as presented in Sections 3 and 4) can complement symbolic approaches to yield hybrid models of intention recognition.

5.5 Evaluation and Reflection

An in-depth comparison between the hybrid approach presented in this section and pure symbolic approaches [12,18] is outside the scope of this paper. Nevertheless, in light of the fact that the approach presented in this section builds upon our earlier work, we can claim that it improves upon that work. Most of all, it is useful that explanation/prediction pairs are ordered such that 'better' and 'worse' conjectures can be distinguished. However, empirical evaluation of the approach is required if it is to be deployed in a practical setting, such as a game or training application. In any case, it is our conviction that a mixture of symbolic and computational methods will prove a useful level of abstraction, as on the one hand it allows for an observer that employs high-level reasoning about objects and key actions, possibly on grounds of structured intentions in relation to goals and plans, while abstracting from repetitive actions by means of spatial metrics which provide grounds for ordering explanations. It should be noted that in the function $\mathcal{R}$ of Def. 3 the factor r is defined with respect to the agent's *position*, and does not consider its motion.

6 Related Work

There exists much work on plan/intention recognition, see [7] for an overview. In this section main focus is on two recent papers which are close to our work, because they involve spatial metrics in the recognition of symbolic intentions, are based on games, and do not employ a probabilistic model.

Doirado and Martinho [8] share our goal of creating believable virtual characters, and share our belief that intention recognition is a step in this direction. Their model employs solely Euclidean metrics of agents' relative distance and acceleration, along with measures of unexpectedness of those values. Their model of intention recognition is somewhat simplistic: it is claimed that "intent results from a natural combination of movement and target", and no formal notion of affordance or goals is utilized. Instead, all information about intention is gathered from avoidance or approach behavior of agents. In that respect the use of (weighted) affordance is more sophisticated, as it allows for discriminating multiple uses of objects. Furthermore, because actions are formalized in our model, it is possible to relate observed sequences to structured intentions (i.e. plans); something that the model of Doirado and Martinho does not allow and which they themselves consider a shortcoming. A pro of their approach is that it deals with inter-agent movement. In a settings where intentions are clear (e.g. combat scenarios where the only intentions are 'fight' and 'flee') this is a useful alternative or complement to our approach.

Kiefer and Schlieder [14] explore context-sensitivity in spatial intention recognition by modeling recognition as an instance of parsing and reducing ambiguity through the use of spatial grounding. Their work targets a real-world game involving the use of GPS navigation, in which behavior consists of shorts sequences of simple (object-independent) actions. This approach and ours are complementary, in the sense that real-world applications like theirs could be expanded and improved on the basis of our techniques, if the appropriate information (i.e. object affordances and/or plans) is available. Use of GPS ensures the availability of spatial metrics. Probabilistic approaches to intention recognition abound [7], some specific to games [2], but are not primarily relevant here given our assumption that statistical data is not available. In a two-tiered approach, as mentioned by [3], our numerical model could substitute a probabilistic model for ranking the filtered output of a symbolic recognizer.

7 Conclusion

This paper presents techniques for intention recognition that involve particulars of the environment where an observed agent is situated. A formal environment model is presented, comprising agents and objects, spatial regions, and afforded actions that may be assigned weights. Ensuing sections employ this model in formalizing position-based and motion-based intention recognition, by considering the distance/motion of the observed agent in regard to objects in its vicinity. It is also shown how the framework is symbiotic with our earlier work on intention recognition of BDI-based agents, leading to a hybrid model that maintains the expressivity of symbolic approaches and combines it with a numerical abstraction over spatial actions, inducing an ordering on explanations.

Future research should focus on implementing the proposed model for empirical evaluation. The model based on spatial metrics should be evaluated on its own accord after refinement on grounds of empirical feedback; possibly also in combination with statistical (learning) methods. It is furthermore noteworthy that an implementation of mental state abduction in logic programming has been put forward [19], which can form the basis for a hybrid model based on the approach presented in this paper. Last but not least, partial observation of agent's behavior should be taken into account, possibly along the lines of [18].

References

1. Afonso, N., Prada, R.: Agents that Relate: Improving the Social Believability of Non-Player Characters in Role-Playing Games. In: Stevens, S.M., Saldamarco, S.J. (eds.) ICEC 2008. LNCS, vol. 5309, pp. 34–45. Springer, Heidelberg (2008)
2. Albrecht, D., Zukerman, I., Nicholson, A.: Bayesian models for keyhole plan recognition in an adventure game. User Modeling and User-Adapted Interaction 8(1-2), 5–47 (1998)
3. Avrahami-Zilberbrand, D., Kaminka, G.A.: Fast and complete symbolic plan recognition. In: Proc. of the 19th International Joint Conference on Artificial Intelligence (IJCAI), pp. 653–658 (2005)
4. Bethesda Game Studios. The Elder Scrolls IV: Oblivion (2006), `http://www.elderscrolls.com/`
5. Bordini, R., Dastani, M., Dix, J., El Fallah Seghrouchni, A. (eds.): Multi-Agent Programming: Languages, Tools and Applications. Springer, Heidelberg (2009)
6. Bratman, M.: Intentions, Plans, and Practical Reason. Harvard University Press, Cambridge (1987)
7. Carberry, S.: Techniques for plan recognition. User Modeling & User-Ad. Interaction 11(1-2), 31–48 (2001)
8. Doirado, E., Martinho, C.: I mean it! Detecting user intentions to create believable behaviour for virtual agents in games. In: Proc. of the 9th International Conf. on Autonomous Agents and Multiagent Systems (AAMAS), pp. 83–90 (2010)
9. Funge, J.: Artificial Intelligence for Computer Games: An Introduction. Peters Corp. (2004)
10. Gazzaniga, M.S., Ivry, R.B., Mangun, G.R.: Cognitive Neuroscience: The Biology of the Mind. W. W. Norton & Company (1998)
11. Gibson, J.J.: The theory of affordances. In: Shaw, R., Bransford, J. (eds.) Perceiving, Acting, and Knowing. Lawrence Erlbaum (1977)
12. Goultiaeva, A., Lespérance, Y.: Incremental plan recognition in an agent programming framework. In: Proceedings of the AAAI Workshop on Plan, Activity and Intent Recognition (PAIR), pp. 52–59 (2007)
13. Isla, D., Blumberg, B.: New challenges for character-based AI for games. In: Proc. of the AAAI Spring Symp. on AI and Interactive Entertainment, number SS-02-01 in AAAI Tech. Rep. (2002)
14. Kiefer, P., Schlieder, C.: Exploring context-sensitivity in spatial intention recognition. In: Proc. of the Workshop on Behaviour Monitoring and Interpretation (BMI), pp. 102–116 (2007)
15. Loyall, A.B.: Believable Agents. PhD thesis, Carnegie Mellon University (1997)
16. Millington, I.: Artificial Intelligence for Games. Morgan Kaufmann, San Francisco (2006)
17. Orkin, J.: Agent architecture considerations for real-time planning in games. In: Proc. of the First AI and Interactive Digital Entertainment Conference (AIIDE), pp. 105–110 (2005)
18. Sindlar, M.P., Dastani, M.M., Dignum, F.P.M., Meyer, J.-J.C.: Mental state abduction of BDI-based agents. In: Baldoni, M., Son, T.C., van Riemsdijk, M.B., Winikoff, M. (eds.) DALT 2008. LNCS (LNAI), vol. 5397, pp. 161–178. Springer, Heidelberg (2009)
19. Sindlar, M.P., Dastani, M., Meyer, J.-J.C.: Programming mental state abduction. In: Proceedings of the 10th International Conference on Autonomous Agents and Multi-Agent Systems, AAMAS (2011) (forthcoming)
20. West, M.: Intelligent mistakes: How to incorporate stupidity into your AI code. Gamasutra (March 2009)

A Robust Multi-unit Ascending-Price Auction with Complementarities against Strategic Manipulation*

Masabumi Furuhata

Computer Science Department, University of Southern California,
Los Angeles, CA 90089, USA

Abstract. Auctions have become enormously popular in recent years. A typical example is spectrum auction for distributions of licenses for electromagnetic spectrum based on simultaneous ascending-price auction. Even though this auction is popular, it is not robust against some strategic manipulations of buyers. While allowing buyers to submit alternative choices (due dates in this paper) in XOR bids, we propose a new auction mechanism called *simultaneous ascending-price auction with option proposal* (SAA-OP). One of the important characteristics of this mechanism is that there are two types of auction winners: an auctioneer chooses winners (exact fulfillments) or buyers take options proposed by the auctioneer (partial fulfillments). Due to this characteristic, the proposing mechanism implements an ex-post efficient equilibrium.

1 Introduction

With the emergence of Internet and electronic commerce, auctions have been enormously popular in recent years. In AI community, combinatorial auctions have particularly attracted attention due to their practical advantages and issues such as computational complexity [11], bidding protocols to describe alternative options [9,11], and preference elicitation of buyers [10]. In practice, spectrum auction is a successful example under which the government distributes licenses for the electromagnetic spectrum use to telecommunication companies. Starting in 1994, the FCC in US uses a simultaneous ascending-price auction (SAA) under which multiple goods are offered for sale, and the process involves several rounds of bidding [4,8]. In a typical ascending-price auction, the auctioneer commences the auction by calling a low price which is incremented with a progress of rounds. Corresponding to the called price, the buyers declare their demands to the auctioneer. The auction is iterated unless the overall demand does not exceed the total selling unit.

Practices of spectrum auctions for "third-generation" mobile phones in six European countries in 2000 are lessons of strategic manipulations of buyers [7]. One of the strategic manipulations is addressed by Ausubel and Cramton [2] which is *demand reduction* of buyers under uniform price auction. Against this problem, Ausubel proposes a new auction [1], however this mechanism raises another problem *over declaration*. Iwasaki

* This material is based upon work supported by Innovation Creation Project of the Ministry of Education, Culture, Sports, Science and Technology-Japan while serving at Japan Advanced Institute of Science and Technology.

N. Desai, A. Liu, and M. Winikoff (Eds.): PRIMA 2010, LNAI 7057, pp. 320–335, 2012.

et al. [5] propose ascending-price option allocation protocol (AOP) to solve these two problems in a single-item multi-unit case. We further detail these problems and existing solutions in Section 3.

The presence of complementarities and substitutability in auctions arise an issue of preference elicitation of buyers. In some cases, the buyers may necessary to consider valuations of all combinations of choices that may not be wholly considered in the auctions. Against this issue, ascending-price auctions or iterative auctions reduce the cost of preference elicitation of buyers, since the buyers only provide focused elicitation corresponding to the calling price [10]. Another issue regarding to complementarities is a bid language which has enough expressive power to describe complicated preference of buyers and enables effective communication with the auctioneer. An *XOR* bid aka *XOR-of-OR* bid is a popular language in which the set of purchasing alternatives has semantics "a buyer will purchase at most one of these alternatives" [9,10,11].

While allowing XOR bids of buyers, we propose a new ascending-price mechanism which is robust against strategic manipulations of buyers in this paper. In order to prevent the over declaration problem, the payment rule of this mechanism is uniform price under which an auction winner pays the same unit price for all units unlike Ausubel's auction [1]. In order to prevent the demand reduction problem, the allocation rules of this mechanism are either an exact fulfillment with an immediate execution of a transaction or a partial fulfillment with an option proposal to a buyer. While the output of this mechanism is a straightforward similarly to AOP, the winner determination process is complicated in order to avoid conflictions among proposing options and situations of future disadvantages of other buyers.

We emphasize that the proposing mechanism is positioning in between typical combinatorial auctions and single item auctions. While this auction is able to handle substituting items at once similarly to typical combinatorial auctions, a calling price is raised uniformly like single item auctions. In general, it is not practical to use the same calling price for totally different items. However, this auction mechanism is targeting on items having slight differences on characteristics or delivery conditions. For a clarification, representative examples of characteristics are color, quality and specs of items. Even though these differences are not significant for all buyers, these items are normally sold at different auctions in practice. The proposing mechanism intends to improve allocation efficiency by consolidation of these auctions. Probably, due date is one of the most extensive aspect among these slight differences and we demonstrate the proposing mechanism using due date as an example of substitutable dimensions of auction items.

This paper is organized as follows. In Section 2, we describe the model. We address some problems of ascending-price auctions and existing solutions in Section 3. Based on the model, we introduce our proposing mechanism in Section 4. Then, we present properties of this mechanism in Section 5. We show a numerical example how this mechanism works for the over declaration problem in Section 6. In Section 7, we show simulation results in order to compare the performances of our proposing mechanism and an existing mechanism. Finally, we conclude this paper in Section 8.

2 The Model

We consider a multi-unit ascending-price auction with strategic complementarities. Using due dates as strategic complementarities, we demonstrate our model in this paper. We remark that our model is not restricted on due dates and it is possible to replace with other kinds of complementarities like colors of auction items as mentioned above.

Let $\mathcal{T} = \{0, 1, 2, \ldots, T\}$ be discrete time periods in which a single type of identical peishable commodities is traded in an auction. In each time period, there are upper limits of supply, namely capacities. Let $\boldsymbol{k}$ be a vector of capacity in time horizon T, i.e., $\boldsymbol{k} = (k_0, k_1, \ldots, k_T) \in \Re^{T+1}$. We assume that each capacity is only available in the respective period. Hence, there is no carry over of the capacity. Each capacity possibly consists of capacities of several different sellers, i.e., several different sellers are consolidated in a single auction. In other words, we assume that the buyers only concern price, quantity and avaibale time of the commodities. In this sence, the buyers make decisions according to the overall capacity $\boldsymbol{k}$.

Let $\mathcal{B}$ be the set of all potential buyers. We assume that each buyer $i \in \mathcal{B}$ has the set of all possible demand vectors $\mathcal{D}_i$. Let $\boldsymbol{d}_i = (d_{i,0}, \ldots, d_{i,T}) \in \mathcal{D}_i$ be a demand vector for buyer i. Let us denote $D_i = \sum_{t \in \mathcal{T}} d_{i,t}$ be the overall demand in the time horizon. We assume that valuation of a demand vector is obtained from a private valuation function v_i. Notice that the value of an item may not be unique for all due dates for a buyer. We also assume that $v_i(\boldsymbol{d}_i) = 0$ if $\boldsymbol{d}_i = (0, \ldots, 0)$; $v_i(\boldsymbol{d}_i) \leq v_i(\boldsymbol{d}'_i)$ if $\boldsymbol{d}_i \leq \boldsymbol{d}'_i$, which means $d_{i,t} \leq d'_{i,t}$ for all $t \in \mathcal{T}$. We assume a quasi-linear utility for each buyer

$$u_i(\boldsymbol{d}_i, p) = v_i(\boldsymbol{d}_i) - p \tag{1}$$

where p is a payment to purchase $\boldsymbol{d}_i$.

Let $\boldsymbol{x}_i \in \mathcal{D}_i$ be a purchase plan and we denote the overall planned quantitiy $X_i = \sum_{t \in \mathcal{T}} x_{i,t}$. Let $\mathcal{X}_i$ be the set of alternative purchase plans of buyer i. With these plans, we consider exclusive-or (XOR) bids defined as follows:

Definition 1. *Let $\mathcal{X}_i = \{\boldsymbol{x}_i^1, \ldots \boldsymbol{x}_i^Z\}$ be the set of alternative purchase plans of buyer i where Z is the number of alternative plans. An exclusive-or (XOR) bid is said to be accepted by an auctioneer if at most one of the set of alternative purchase plans is accepted:* $(\ldots((\boldsymbol{x}_i^1 \text{ XOR } \boldsymbol{x}_i^2) \text{ XOR } \boldsymbol{x}_i^3) \text{ XOR } \ldots) \text{ XOR } \boldsymbol{x}_i^Z$.

In XOR bids, the different purchase plans are processed through a cascade of binary exclusive-or operations: the first two plans are fed into an XOR operation, then the output of that operation is fed into a second XOR operation together with the third plan, and so on for any remaining plans. For instance, if a buyer submits $\mathcal{X}_i = \{\boldsymbol{x}_i^1, \boldsymbol{x}_i^2, \boldsymbol{x}_i^3, \boldsymbol{x}_i^4\}$, it means that the buyer requests one of the four alternative purchase plans be accepted: $((\boldsymbol{x}_i^1 \text{ XOR } \boldsymbol{x}_i^2) \text{ XOR } \boldsymbol{x}_i^3) \text{ XOR } \boldsymbol{x}_i^4$. In the following, we may use a symbol $\oplus$ to describe XOR as well. The truthful order quantity may change how amount of payment is calculated in Equation (1). If a payment p is calculated by unit price γ times the overall quantity D_i, the utility is $u_i(\boldsymbol{d}_i, \gamma) = v_i(\boldsymbol{d}_i) - \gamma D_i$. Hence, we obtain the set of sincere purchase plans of buyer i,

$$\mathcal{X}_i^{Sin} = \{\boldsymbol{x} : \arg\max_{\boldsymbol{x} \in \mathcal{D}_i} \{u_i(\boldsymbol{x}, \gamma)\}\}. \tag{2}$$

We assume that buyers are rational. Hence, each plan $\boldsymbol{x}_i$ satisfies the following condition, $u_i(\boldsymbol{x}_i, \gamma) > 0$, at unit price γ.

We focus on design of iterative auctions or more specifically ascending-price auctions where an auctioneer calls a bidding price incrementally in each round and buyers correspond to the called price by submissions of alternative purchase plans. Let $l = \{1, 2, \ldots\}$ be a round of auctions. At the beginning of each round l, there is a remaining capacity plan $\boldsymbol{k}^l$. Let $\mathcal{T}^l = \{t \in \mathcal{T} : k_t^l > 0\}$ be a remaining planning periods and $\mathcal{B}^l$ be the set of active buyers.

Prior to submit alternative purchase plans, we assume that each buyer knows the rules of the auction, i.e., auction mechanism. Let $\mathcal{A}$ be a mechanism that consists of an allocation rule g and a payment rule h, i.e., $\mathcal{A} = (g, h)$ where $g : \prod\limits_{i \in \mathcal{B}} \mathcal{D}_i^Z \rightarrow \Re^{n \times (T+1)}$ and $h : \prod\limits_{i \in \mathcal{B}} \mathcal{D}_i^Z \rightarrow \Re^n$ if there are n potential buyers. Let us denote

$$\mathcal{J} = \prod_{i \in \mathcal{B}^l} \mathcal{X}_i^l \tag{3}$$

as the set of Cartesian products of alternative plans. Let $\boldsymbol{j} \in \mathcal{J}$ be a choice which is $|\mathcal{B}|$-tuples of purchase plans. We focus on mechanisms that are feasible, i.e.,:

Definition 2. *(Feasible Mechanism) Given capacity* $\mathbf{k}$*, the set of alternative plans of all buyers* $\mathcal{X}$ *and its Cartesian products* $\mathcal{J}$*, a mechanism* $\mathcal{A} = (g, h)$ *is feasible if the following condition is satisfied:*

1. $g_i(\mathcal{X}) \leq \boldsymbol{j}_i$ *for all* $i \in \mathcal{B}$ *where* $\boldsymbol{j} \in \mathcal{J}$*,*
2. $\sum\limits_{i \in \mathcal{B}} g_i(\mathcal{X}) \leq \boldsymbol{k}$.

The first condition specifies that each allocation does not exceed a choice of each buyer at each time period. The second condition does not allow the auctionner to allocate quantities exceeding the overall capacities at each time period.

Among feasible auctions, we focus on mechanisms that implement *ex-post equilibrium* defined as follows,

Definition 3. *(Ex-post Equilibrium) Mechanism* $\mathcal{A} = (g, h)$ *is said to implement ex-post equilibrium if the following holds:*

$$u_i(g_i(\mathcal{X}^{Sin}), h_i(\mathcal{X}^{Sin})) \geq u_i(g_i(\mathcal{X}_i', \mathcal{X}_{-i}^{Sin}), h_i(\mathcal{X}_i', \mathcal{X}_{-i}^{Sin}))$$

for all $i \in \mathcal{B}$ and for all $\mathcal{X}_i^{Sin}$ and $\mathcal{X}_i'$. Hence, if an auctioneer uses such a mechanism and all buyers submit their sincere plans, the utility of each buyer according to the output of the mechanism is maximized.

3 Problem Specification

Now, we address a few problems in iterative auctions using three typical mechanisms.

3.1 Demand Reduction and Uniform-Price Auction

Uniform-price auction is one of the simplest auctions among the iterated auctions. We present this mechanism to sell K units in a single time period. In each round l, an auctioneer calls a unit-price γ^l and each buyer $i \in \mathcal{B}$ submits an order x_i simultaneously and independently. If the overall orders do not exceed K, the market is cleared at γ^l and the auction is terminated. Otherwise, the auctioneer proceeds a successive round with an increased unit price γ^{l+1}. A well-known problem of uniform-price auction is a *demand reduction* problem which occurs if the utility of a partial fulfillment of an order at a certain round exceeds the utility of an exact fulfillment at a future unit-price. In such a case, buyers reduce their declaring demands to increase their utilities.

3.2 Over Declaration and Ausubel Auction

Ausubel auction [2], which is an ascending-price format, is one of solutions of the demand reduction problem shown in the previous section. A key point of this auction is the winner determination process which includes partial fulfillments of orders. In round l, an auctioneer provides a right to purchase $y^l_{-i}(\gamma^l)$ units at γ^l if an order of buyer i is able to be partially fulfilled $x^l_i(\gamma^l) > y^l_{-i}(\gamma^l) > 0$ where $y^l_{-i}(\gamma^l) = \max\left\{k^l - \sum_{\iota \in \mathcal{B}\setminus\{i\}} x_\iota(\gamma^l), 0\right\}$ is a residual supply without an order of buyer i. Notice that this right and price are valid in the future round. This pricing rule is called as a *clinch* which works for a problem of demand reduction. However, there is another problem called *over declaration*. This problem occurs if one buyer aims to prevent a clinch of opponents by inflating his order.

3.3 Acending-Price Option Allocation Protocol

Iwasaki et al. [5] propose ascending-price option allocation protocol (AOP) for the problems specified in Section 3.1 and 3.2. A key idea of AOP is to provide clinching options similarly to Ausubel auction; however the clearing price of each buyer is uniform like uniform-price auction. In each round, an auctioneer provides a paired clinching option for buyer i, (γ^l_i, o^l_i), where γ is a unit price and o is the maximum quantity to take the option. Among the set of proposed options, the buyer i may take an option.

While all the above auctions correspond to multi-unit auctions, they do not deal with the presence of complementarities and substitutability. If an auctioneer accepts XOR-bids, which is the input of mechanisms, auction mechanisms are necessary to be redesigned. In the following section, we detail our proposing mechanism dealing with substitutability with respect to time. Similarly to the AOP, our mechanism proposes some options in some cases in order to be robust against the demand reduction problem and the over declaration problem. However, our mechanism does not propose options in the same way due to corresponding to some complex situations with complementarities. While efficient options without conflictions are easily obtained without considering XOR bids, it requires some treatments to deal with alternative plans. Hence, our proposing mechanism has different procedures to determine auction winners from the ones under AOP.

4 Simultaneous Ascending-Price Auction with Option Proposal

In this section, we propose a new ascending-price auction, simultaneous ascending-price auction with option proposal (SAA-OP), which is able to accept XOR bids from buyers and robust against the demand reduction problem and the over declaration problem. We present an overview of this mechanism in Section 4.1 and the rest of this section covers detailed procedures of this mechanism.

4.1 Overview of SAA-OP

Similarly to other ascending-price auctions, an auctioneer calls a unit price in each round. Buyers may submit several alternative purchase plans corresponding to this unit price that are exclusively accepted. Since SAA-OP accepts XOR bids, the winner determination processes are complex. There are three ways to win under this auction and the winner determination conditions are sequential as follows:

WC1. If the auctioneer is able to find a feasible allocation choice, buyers are exactly fulfilled. If there are multiple choices, the auctioneer randomly selects a choice.

WC2. If there is an allocation choice for particular buyers which may not disturb plans of other buyers, the auctioneer selects these buyers as winners with exact fulfillments.

WC3. The auctioneer proposes an option if the residual supply is independent from requirements of other plans of other buyers. The buyer may take an option if it maximizes his utility.

The procedure of SAA-OP is briefly shown:

1. An announcement of an opening round.
2. Submissions of alternative purchase plans by buyers and a calculation of residual supplies by the auctioneer. If there is no submission, the auction terminates.
3. The auctioneer checks WC1. If there is an allocation choice, the auctioneer allocates the capacity with exact fulfillments and terminates the auction.
4. The auctioneer checks WC2. The auctioneer allocates capacities to buyers satisfying WC2.
5. The auctioneer proposes options to buyers if they satisfy WC3.
6. Taking an option if it maximizes a utility of a buyer.
7. A procedure for the successive round if there is a remaining capacity, otherwise terminates the auction.

The clearing price is uniform in the above three winning cases.

4.2 Announcement of Opening Round

In step 1, an auctioneer announces an opening of round l in order to synchronize activities of buyers and an auctioneer. In addition to the announcement of opening round, unit price γ^l and remaining capacity $\boldsymbol{k}^l$ are announced to active buyers $\mathcal{B}^l = \left\{i : i \in \mathcal{B} \setminus \bigcup_{\lambda=1}^{l-1} \hat{\mathcal{B}}^\lambda \text{ if } l > 1;\ i \in \mathcal{B} \text{ otherwise}\right\}$ where $\hat{\mathcal{B}}^\lambda$ is the set of auction winners in round λ. In the initial round, active buyers are the set of all buyers $\mathcal{B}$. In other rounds, active buyers are remaining buyers that have not been allocated until the previous round. Hereafter, we may omit the symbol of round l for the ease of readbility if it is obvious.

4.3 Submission of Purchase Plans and Calculation of Residual Supplies

In step 2, each active buyer $i \in \mathcal{B}^l$ submits the set of alternative purchase plans $\mathcal{X}_i^l$ in order to maximize his utility. The auctioneer realizes the set of allocation choices $\mathcal{J}^l$ as shown in Equation (3). If there are no active choices $\mathcal{J}^l = \{\emptyset\}$, the auction is terminated. Once the auctioneer receives the set of alternative purchase plans, the auctioneer checks all residual supplies. Let $\boldsymbol{y}_{-i}(\boldsymbol{j}) = \big(\max\{0, k_0 - \sum_{\iota \in \mathcal{B}^l \setminus \{i\}} j_{\iota,0}\}, \ldots, \min\{0, k_T - \sum_{\iota \in \mathcal{B}^l \setminus \{i\}} j_{\iota,T}\}\big)$ be the residual supply of buyer i if choice $\boldsymbol{j} \in \mathcal{J}^l$ is taken. Let us denote $\mathcal{Y}$ as the set of residual supplies. Based on the residual supply, the auctioneer is able to calculate all potential choices that are feasible $\boldsymbol{\Psi}_{Pot}^l$:

$$\begin{aligned}\boldsymbol{\Psi}_{Pot}^l = \Big\{\boldsymbol{\psi} : \{((\min\{j_{1,0}, y_{-1,0}(\boldsymbol{j})\}, \ldots, \min\{j_{1,T}, y_{-1,T}(\boldsymbol{j})\}), \ldots,\\ (\min\{j_{|\mathcal{B}^l|,0}, y_{-|\mathcal{B}^l|,0}(\boldsymbol{j})\}, \ldots, \min\{j_{|\mathcal{B}^l|,T}, y_{-|\mathcal{B}^l|,T}(\boldsymbol{j})\}))\}\\ \text{for every } \boldsymbol{j} \in \mathcal{J}^l\Big\}\end{aligned} \tag{4}$$

4.4 Exact Fulfillments

The potential choices in Equation (4) may not always fully fulfill the requirements of buyers. In the following condition (WC1), we check if the potential choices are exact fulfillments of requirements:

$$\boldsymbol{\Psi}_{WC1}^l = \{\boldsymbol{\psi} \in \boldsymbol{\Psi}_{Pot}^l : \boldsymbol{\psi} = \boldsymbol{j} \in \mathcal{J}^l\}$$

If there is only one choice in $\boldsymbol{\Psi}_{WC1}^l$, an allocation $\hat{\boldsymbol{\psi}}$ is simply determined. If there are some choices, the auctioneer randomly chooses one allocation $\hat{\boldsymbol{\psi}}$ among $\boldsymbol{\Psi}_{WC1}^l$. Let us denote $\mathcal{B}_{\hat{\boldsymbol{\psi}}}^l$ as the set of auction winners according to an allocation $\hat{\boldsymbol{\psi}}$. A buyer $i \in \mathcal{B}_{\hat{\boldsymbol{\psi}}}^l$ is allocated $\hat{\boldsymbol{x}}_i = \hat{\boldsymbol{\psi}}_i$ at unit price $\hat{\gamma}_i = \gamma^l$. If there is at least one choice in $\boldsymbol{\Psi}_{WC1}^l$, the auction is terminated.

4.5 Additional Winners

A feasible allocation investigated in the previous step is able to satisfy the requirements of all buyers. This allocation is not always found. In some cases, there are some allocations that are able to fulfill the requirements of part of buyers. If such allocations do not conflict with requirements of others, the auctioneer is able to set those buyers as auction winners.

Let us denote $\mathcal{B}_{\boldsymbol{\psi}}^{l,Ful}$ as the set of buyers that are fully allocated if $\boldsymbol{\psi}$ is taken. In addition, let $\mathcal{T}_{\mathcal{B}_{\boldsymbol{\psi}}}^l = \{t \in \mathcal{T}^l : \sum_{i \in \mathcal{B}} \psi_{i,t} > 0\}$ be the effective time periods of the set of buyers $\mathcal{B}$ if a potential choice $\boldsymbol{\psi}$ is taken. Among the potential choices, the auctioneer checks candidate choices $\boldsymbol{\Psi}^l_{Can1}$ in which allocations of auction winners do not conflict with requirements of others:

$$\boldsymbol{\Psi}^l_{Can1} = \{\boldsymbol{\psi} \in \boldsymbol{\Psi}^l_{Pot} : \mathcal{T}^l_{\mathcal{B}^{l,Ful}_{\boldsymbol{\psi}}} \bigcap \mathcal{T}^l_{\mathcal{B}^l_{\boldsymbol{\psi}'} \setminus \mathcal{B}^{l,Ful}_{\boldsymbol{\psi}}} = \{\emptyset\} \text{ for any } \boldsymbol{\psi}' \in \boldsymbol{\Psi}^l_{pot} \setminus \{\boldsymbol{\psi}\}\}$$

The effective time periods of winners under a certain candidate should not conflict with the effective time periods of the rest of buyers. Notice that candidate choices in the set of candidates $\boldsymbol{\Psi}^l_{Can1}$ may not maximize the total allocation of fully fulfilled buyers. Hence, the auctioneer checks the candidates according to the second winner determination condition $\boldsymbol{\Psi}^l_{WC2}$:

$$\boldsymbol{\Psi}^l_{WC2} = \Big\{\boldsymbol{\psi} \in \boldsymbol{\Psi}^l_{Can1} : \sum_{i \in \mathcal{B}^{l,Ful}_{\boldsymbol{\psi}}} \sum_{t \in \mathcal{T}} \psi_{i,t} \geq \sum_{i \in \mathcal{B}^{l,Ful}_{\boldsymbol{\psi}}} \sum_{t \in \mathcal{T}} \psi'_{i,t} \text{ for any } \boldsymbol{\psi}' \in \boldsymbol{\Psi}^l_{Can1} \setminus \{\boldsymbol{\psi}\}\Big\}.$$

According to the above condition, the auctioneer obtains the set of feasible and efficient allocation among the choices for buyers having locally independent requirements. If there is at least one allocation choice $|\boldsymbol{\Psi}^l_{WC2}| \geq 1$, the auctioneer (randomly) determines one allocation choice $\hat{\boldsymbol{\psi}}$. Hence, an allocation for winning buyer $i \in \mathcal{B}^{l,Ful}_{\hat{\boldsymbol{\psi}}}$ is $\hat{\boldsymbol{x}}_i = \hat{\boldsymbol{\psi}}_i$ at unit price $\hat{\gamma}_i = \gamma^l$. If there is at least one winner in this step, the auctioneer updates the set of active buyers $\mathcal{B}^l := \mathcal{B}^l \setminus \mathcal{B}^{l,Ful}_{\hat{\boldsymbol{\psi}}}$ and goes to the following step.

4.6 Proposal of Options

This step is executed if the auctioneer is not able to find any allocation choices in step 3. The auctioneer chekcs whether he is able to propose some options that are partial fulfillment of requirements of buyers. These options should not conflict with other options.

First the auctioneer prepares all the potential choices for proposing options. Let $\tilde{\psi}$ be a partitioned choice of $\boldsymbol{\psi} \in \boldsymbol{\Psi}^l_{Pot}$ such that, for all $i \in \mathcal{B}^l$, $\tilde{\psi}_{i,t} = \psi_{i,t}$ for all $t \in \mathcal{T}_{\tilde{\psi}} \subset \mathcal{T}$ and $\tilde{\psi}_{i,t} = 0$ for all $t \in \mathcal{T} \setminus \mathcal{T}_{\tilde{\psi}}$. The set of these partitioned choices are: $\boldsymbol{\Psi}^l_{Pot2} = \{\tilde{\psi} : \tilde{\psi}_{i,t} = \psi_{i,t}$ for all $i \in \mathcal{B}^l$ and for all $t \in \mathcal{T}_{\tilde{\psi}} \subset \mathcal{T}$; $\tilde{\psi}_{i,t} = 0$ for all $i \in \mathcal{B}^l$ and for all $t \in \mathcal{T} \setminus \mathcal{T}_{\tilde{\psi}}$, where $\boldsymbol{\psi} \in \boldsymbol{\Psi}^l_{Pot}\}$. Then, among the partitioned choices in $\boldsymbol{\Psi}^l_{Pot2}$, the auctioneer investigates choices that do not conflict with other choices. Let $\boldsymbol{\Psi}^l_{Can2}$ be the set of independent partitioned choices:

$$\boldsymbol{\Psi}^l_{Can2} = \{\tilde{\psi} \in \boldsymbol{\Psi}^l_{Pot2} : \sum_{i \in \mathcal{B}^l \setminus \mathcal{B}^l_{\tilde{\psi}}} \psi_{i,t} = 0 \text{ for all } t \in \mathcal{T}_{\tilde{\psi}} \text{ and for all } \boldsymbol{\psi} \in \boldsymbol{\Psi}^l_{Pot}\}$$

The candidate choices $\boldsymbol{\Psi}^l_{Can2}$ are obtained if effective time periods of $\hat{\psi}$ do not conflict with requirements of the rest of buyers in $\boldsymbol{\Psi}^l_{Pot}$. Notice that the candidate choices $\boldsymbol{\Psi}^l_{Can2}$ may contain some choices that are not efficient. Hence the auctioneer investigates efficient choices $\boldsymbol{\Psi}^l_{WC3}$ according to the following third winner determination condition:

$$\boldsymbol{\Psi}^l_{WC3} = \{\tilde{\psi} \in \boldsymbol{\Psi}^l_{Can2} : \text{there does not exist } \tilde{\psi}' \text{ such that } \tilde{\psi}' \geq \tilde{\psi} \text{ for all } \tilde{\psi}' \in \boldsymbol{\Psi}^l_{Can2} \setminus \{\tilde{\psi}\}\}$$

According to the partitioned choices $\boldsymbol{\Psi}^l_{WC3}$, each buyer $i \in \mathcal{B}_{\tilde{\psi}}$ where $\tilde{\psi} \in \boldsymbol{\Psi}^l_{WC3}$ is proposed an option $\boldsymbol{o}_i = \tilde{\psi}_i$. Let $\mathcal{O}^l$ be the set of options.

4.7 Exercise of Option

Corresponding to the proposed options in the previous step, buyer i may choose an option $\boldsymbol{o}_i \in \mathcal{O}_i^l$ if it maximizes the utility of buyer i. In this step, we detail the decision process of buyers. Notice that buyer i may have already been proposed several different options in other rounds. These options are still active for those buyers. Buyer i may choose one of these options if it exceeds the maximum utility possibly obtained in the successive round.

Let $\mathcal{Q}_i^l$ be a set of utility maximizing quantities in round l, i.e.,

$$\mathcal{Q}_i^l = \left\{ \boldsymbol{q}_i \in \Re^{T+1} : \arg\max_{\boldsymbol{q}_i} \{ u_i(\boldsymbol{q}_i, \gamma^l) \} \text{ where } \boldsymbol{q}_i \leq \boldsymbol{o}_i \text{ for any } \boldsymbol{o}_i \in \mathcal{O}^l \right\}$$

Let $\mathcal{Q}_i = \bigcup_{\lambda \in \{1,\ldots,l\}} \mathcal{Q}_i^\lambda$ be the set of utility maximizing quantities of each round up to round l. Let $\hat{\mathcal{L}}_i$ be the set of rounds that is able to maximize the utility of buyer i, i.e.,

$$\hat{\mathcal{L}}_i = \left\{ \lambda \in \{1, \ldots, l\} : \arg\max_{\lambda} \{ u_i(\boldsymbol{q}_i^\lambda, \gamma^\lambda) \} \text{ where } \boldsymbol{q}_i^\lambda \in \mathcal{Q}_i \} \right\}$$

Let $\hat{l}_i = \inf\{\hat{\mathcal{L}}_i\}$ be the best candidate round for buyer i among the set of options. Buyer i takes an option $\boldsymbol{q}_i^{\hat{l}_i}$ at unit price $\gamma^{\hat{l}_i}$ if there does not exist $\boldsymbol{x}_i^{l+1}$ such that

$$u_i(\boldsymbol{x}_i^{l+1}, \gamma^{l+1}) > u_i(\boldsymbol{q}_i^{\hat{l}_i}, \gamma^{\hat{l}_i}) \tag{5}$$

for $\boldsymbol{x}_i^{l+1} \leq \boldsymbol{x}_i^l$ for any $\boldsymbol{x}_i^l \in \mathcal{X}_i^l$. Hence, the allocation of buyer i is $\hat{\boldsymbol{x}}_i = \boldsymbol{q}_i^{\hat{l}_i}$ at price $\hat{\gamma}_i = \gamma^{\hat{l}_i}$. Once the option is taken, the auctioneer updates both remaining capacities: $k_t^l := k_t^l - \hat{x}_{i,t}$ for all $t \in \mathcal{T}$ and active buyers $\mathcal{B}^l := \mathcal{B}^l \setminus \{i\}$.

4.8 Procedures for the Successive Round

In this step, the auctioneer checks whether he terminates the auction. The condition is $\mathcal{T}^l = \{\emptyset\}$. If the condition is not satisfied, the auction goes back to step 1 with the succesive round $l+1$.

4.9 The Output of the Auction

According to the above steps, the output of the mechanism is as follows. If a buyer i is a winner in round l, an allocation is $g_i(\mathcal{X}^l) = \hat{\boldsymbol{x}}_i$ and the payment is $h_i(\mathcal{X}^l) = \hat{\gamma}_i \sum_{t \in \mathcal{T}} \hat{x}_{i,t}$ that are determined either in step 3, 4, or 5. Otherwise, the allocation is $g_i(\mathcal{X}) = 0$ and the payment is $h_i(\mathcal{X}) = 0$.

5 Theoretical Results

We show how SAA-OP prevents strategic manipulations of buyers. In addition to the quantity-dependent manipulations presented in Section 3, there are time-dependent manipulations in our model.

With respect to available due dates, there are two types of insincere plans: restriction and relaxation of available due dates. First, we check the effect of the former behavior. Let us consider the case where buyer i has the following alternative purchase plans $\mathcal{X}_i = \{\boldsymbol{x}_i^1, \ldots, \boldsymbol{x}_i^Z\}$. Let $\mathcal{T}_{\mathcal{X}_i}$ be an effective time periods of plans $\mathcal{X}_i$ such that $\mathcal{T}_{\mathcal{X}_i} = \{t \in \mathcal{T} : \sum_{z=1}^{Z} x_{i,t}^z > 0 \text{ where } (x_{i,0}^z, \ldots, x_{i,T}^z) \in \mathcal{X}_i\}$. Let $\mathcal{X}_i'$ be alternative restricted due-dates plans of $\mathcal{X}_i$ such that $\mathcal{T}_{\mathcal{X}_i} \supseteq \mathcal{T}_{\mathcal{X}_i'}$ and $X_i = X_i'$. For such $\mathcal{X}_i$ and $\mathcal{X}_i'$, a mechanism is said to be *available due date-monotonic* if the following inequation holds

$$\sum_{t \in \mathcal{T}} g_{i,t}(\mathcal{X}_i, \mathcal{X}_{-i}) \geq \sum_{t \in \mathcal{T}} g_{i,t}(\mathcal{X}_i', \mathcal{X}_{-i})$$

for all $\mathcal{X}_{-i}$ and for all i. Hence, due-date monotonic mechanisms allocate greater quantities on alternative purchase plans having greater flexible due-dates. In the following lemma, we show that SAA-OP satisfies this property.

Lemma 1. *SAA-OP is available due date-monotonic.*

Proof. Consider that there are two sets of alternative purchase plans $\mathcal{X}_i$ and $\mathcal{X}_i'$ such that $\mathcal{T}_{\mathcal{X}_i} \supseteq \mathcal{T}_{\mathcal{X}_i'}$; for any $\boldsymbol{x}_i \in \mathcal{X}_i$ and $\boldsymbol{x}_i' \in \mathcal{X}_i'$ satisfying $X_i = X_i'$. Under this auction mechanism, there are two ways to win: meeting one of purchase plans (in step 3 or 4 of the protocol) or choosing an option (in step 6). Since $\mathcal{X}_i$ and $\mathcal{X}_i'$ have differnet avaliable due dates $\mathcal{T}_{\mathcal{X}_i} \supseteq \mathcal{T}_{\mathcal{X}_i'}$, if x_i is chosen as an allocation in round l, there are three different cases of results for the buyer would have submitted $\boldsymbol{x}_i'$: (i) $\boldsymbol{x}_i'$ is chosen as an allocation in the same round, (ii) an option $\boldsymbol{q'}_i^{\hat{l}_i}$ is chosen in the same round, (iii) the output quantitiy $\hat{\boldsymbol{x}}'_i$ is determined in the future round. Similary, if an option $\boldsymbol{q}_i^{\hat{l}_i}$ is chosen in step 6, there are two cases for the buyer would have submitted $\boldsymbol{x}'_i$: (iv) an option $\boldsymbol{q'}_i^{\hat{l}_i}$ is chosen in the same round, and (v) the output quantity $\hat{\boldsymbol{x}}'_i$ is determined in the future round. Therefore, it is enough to show that $\hat{X}_i \geq \hat{X}'_i$ for all the five cases above. In case (i), it is obvious $\hat{X}_i = \hat{X}'_i$. In case (ii), it must be $X_i^l > Q_i^\lambda$ for any $\lambda = \{1, \ldots, l-1\}$, since buyer i would not have taken any options in the previous round according to Equation (5). According to step 6, there does not exist an option $\boldsymbol{o}_i \in \mathcal{O}_i^l$ such that $O_i \geq X_i$ for all $x_i \in \mathcal{X}_i^l$. Therefore, we have $\hat{X}_i > \hat{X}_i'$. In case (iii), it must be $\boldsymbol{x}_i \notin \mathcal{X'}_i^l$ and any other $\boldsymbol{x}_i' \in \mathcal{X}_i'$ does not meet in either case (i) or (ii). Therefore, in future rounds, any X'^{λ}_i where $\lambda > l$ does not exceed X_i^l. This implies that $\hat{X}_i > \hat{X}'_i$. In case (iv), it is obvious that $\hat{X}_i = \hat{X}'_i$. In case (v), buyer i chooses an option in round l means that there are no plans such that $u_i(\hat{\boldsymbol{x}}_i^l, \gamma^l) < u_i(\boldsymbol{x}_i^{l+1}, \gamma^{l+1})$ according to Equation (5). Therefore, we obtain $\hat{X}_i \geq X'^{l+1}_i$ for any $\boldsymbol{x'}_i^{l+1} \in \mathcal{X'}_i^{l+1}$. This impies that $\hat{X}_i^l \geq \hat{X'}_i^{\lambda}$ where $\lambda > l$.

This lemma shows that this mechanism assigns more allocations if purchase plans have more flexibility on due dates. This is because this mechanism searches feasible allocations and options from all the possible combinations of purchase plans. Therefore, buyers do not need to restrict their due dates.

A disadvantage of monotonicity with respect to due dates is realized if buyers have benefit by declaring phantom due dates. In the following lemma, we show that such a behavior does not increase the utility of buyers under this mechanism.

Lemma 2. *Buyer i does not increase his utility by relaxing his available due dates of sincere orders $\mathcal{X}_i^{Sin}$ under SAA-OP.*

Proof. Let $\boldsymbol{x}'_i \in \mathcal{X}'_i$ be a purchase plan having a relaxed due date of a sincere plan $\boldsymbol{x}_i^{Sin} \in \mathcal{X}_i^{Sin}$ satisfying $X'_i = X_i^{Sin}$. In order to prove this lemma, we show that the following inequation does not hold,

$$u_i(g_i(\mathcal{X}'_i, \mathcal{X}_{-i}), h_i(\mathcal{X}'_i, \mathcal{X}_{-i})) > u_i(g_i(\mathcal{X}_i^{Sin}, \mathcal{X}_{-i}), h_i(\mathcal{X}_i^{Sin}, \mathcal{X}_{-i})) \tag{6}$$

for any $\mathcal{X}'_i$, $\mathcal{X}_{-i}$ and $\mathcal{X}_i^{Sin}$. Hence, it is necessary that either $\boldsymbol{x}'_i$ is allocated or an option $\boldsymbol{o}'_i$ based on $\boldsymbol{x}'_i$ is chosen, meanwhile $\boldsymbol{x}_i^{Sin}$ is not allocated in the same round. In the former case, an option $\boldsymbol{o}_i^{Sin}$ such that $o_{i,t}^{Sin} = x'_{i,t}$ for all $t \in \mathcal{T}_{x_{i,t}^{Sin}} \bigcap \mathcal{T}_{x'_{i,t}}$ and $o_{i,t}^{Sin} = 0$ for all $t \in \mathcal{T} \setminus \mathcal{T}_{x_{i,t}^{Sin}} \bigcap \mathcal{T}_{x'_{i,t}}$ must be proposed according to step 6 in this auction. In the latter case, an option $\boldsymbol{o}_i^{Sin}$ such that $o_{i,t}^{Sin} = o'_{i,t}$ for all $t \in \mathcal{T}_{x_{i,t}^{Sin}} \bigcap \mathcal{T}_{x'_{i,t}}$ and $o_{i,t}^{Sin} = 0$ for all $t \in \mathcal{T} \setminus \mathcal{T}_{x_{i,t}^{Sin}} \bigcap \mathcal{T}_{x'_{i,t}}$ must be proposed. Hence, we have $v_i(g_i(\mathcal{X}'_i, \mathcal{X}_{-i})) - v_i(g_i(\mathcal{X}_i^{Sin}, \mathcal{X}_{-i})) = v_i(\boldsymbol{x}'_i) - v_i(\boldsymbol{x}_i^{Sin})$. Recall the definition of sincere plan in Equation (2), it must be $v_i(\boldsymbol{x}_i^{Sin}) - \gamma X_i^{Sin} > v_i(\boldsymbol{x}'_i) - \gamma X'_i$ which implies $v_i(\boldsymbol{x}_i^{Sin}) > v_i(\boldsymbol{x}'_i)$. Hence, we have $v_i(g_i(\mathcal{X}'_i, \mathcal{X}_{-i})) - v_i(g_i(\mathcal{X}_i^{Sin}, \mathcal{X}_{-i})) < 0$. Since $g_i(\mathcal{X}'_i, \mathcal{X}_{-i}) \geq g_i(\mathcal{X}_i^{Sin}, \mathcal{X}_{-i})$ according to Lemma 1, we have $h_i(\mathcal{X}'_i, \mathcal{X}_{-i}) \geq h_i(\mathcal{X}_i^{Sin}, \mathcal{X}_{-i})$. This leads to a contradiction of Equation (6) due to the following case holds $u_i(g_i(\mathcal{X}'_i, \mathcal{X}_{-i}), h_i(\mathcal{X}'_i, \mathcal{X}_{-i})) < u_i(g_i(\mathcal{X}_i^{Sin}, \mathcal{X}_{-i}), h_i(\mathcal{X}_i^{Sin}, \mathcal{X}_{-i}))$.

The above proof is obtained according to a contradiction of inequality indicating that the utility regarding to the auction output based on a purchase plan having a relaxed due date exceeds the one corresponding to a sincere plan. A key difference of the outputs between two plans is relevant to time periods that are not covered by the sincere plan. According to the definitions of valuations and the sincere plans, the allocation corresponding to these periods have a negative effect with respect to utilities. Hence, we obtain a contradiction.

Based on the above two lemmas, we show that the proposing mehcnaism is a robust mechanism for a multi-period case in the following theorem.

Theorem 1. *Sincere bidding by every buyer is an equilibrium under SAA-OP.*

Proof. According to the definition of ex-post equilibrium, it is sufficient to contradict that insincere plans increases the utilities of buyers. In Lemma 1 and 2, we have shown that insincere plans with respect to due dates do not increase the utilities of buyers. Hence, within the same due dates, we focus on the effects of changing plans that are dropping a plan from $\mathcal{X}_i^{Sin}$ and adding a plan to $\mathcal{X}_i^{Sin}$.

In the set of sincere plans $\mathcal{X}_i^{Sin}$, there are two types of plans: rapping plans $\mathcal{X}_i^{RP} = \{\boldsymbol{x}_i : \text{there exists a plan } \boldsymbol{x}'_i \text{ such that } \boldsymbol{x}_i \geq \boldsymbol{x}'_i \text{ where } \boldsymbol{x}'_i \in \mathcal{X}_i^{Sin} \setminus \{\boldsymbol{x}_i\}\}$ and non-rapping plans $\mathcal{X}_i^{NP} = \{\boldsymbol{x}_i : \boldsymbol{x}_i \in \mathcal{X}_i^{Sin} \setminus \mathcal{X}_i^{RP}\}$. If buyer i drops a non-rapping plan, it decreases a chance to win by this non-rapping plan which does not increase the utility of the buyer. Similarly, if buyer i drops a rapping plan, let us consider a special case where a rapping plan $\boldsymbol{x}_i^{l,RP}$ in round l is an only plan that conflicts with a plan of other buyer i' having no options and planning to decline the auction in the following round. In this case, dropping a plan decreases an opportunity of buyer i to win in the following round. Hence, dropping a sincere plan of either type does not increase the utility of the buyer.

Let us consider an effect of adding an insincere plan. The utility of the buyer changes if this plan is a reason to win the auction. If it is selected in step 3 or 4, the same plan is proposed in step 5 at least in the case without adding an insincere plan. Hence it does not increase the utility. If an option based on the insincere plan is selected in step 6, there are no choices of exact fulfillments in step 3 or 4. Therefore, the selected option based on the insincere plan does not exceed a plan of sincere plans. Hence, the same plan is proposed in step 5 at least in the case without adding an insincere plan which does not increase the utility.

The above proof is obtained since there are no ways to increase the utility of buyers to submit insincere plans. While the cases of the time-dependent strategic manipulations are proved in Lemma 1 and 2, the proof of this theorem focus on the cases of the quantity-dependent strategic manipulations. Due to the three different winner determination conditions, the buyer is not able to increase his utility by those manipulations.

6 Numerical Analysis

We demonstrate how SAA-OP works using some numerical examples. Example 1 includes a case of the demand reduction problem under uniform price auction 3.1; Example 2 includes a case of the over declaration problem under Ausubel auction 3.2. These numerical examples are based on the examples in [5] that are extended for cases of complementarities. In Example 3, we show how SAA-OP deals with locally independent requirements. This case is a specific issue under consolidated auctions.

The following example shows a procedure of SAA-OP which is relevant to demand reduction problem under uniform auction.

Example 1. Let us consider SAA-OP with the initial calling price \$1 and a price-tick \$1 in each round. We assume that $\mathcal{T} = \{0, 1\}$, $k = (1, 1)$ and $\mathcal{B} = \{1, 2\}$. The valuations of the buyers are as follows: $v_1((1, 0)) = v_1((0, 1)) = \$5, v_1((1, 1)) = \$8;$

Table 1. Procedure of Example 1 under SAA-OP (Robust against Demand Reduction)

Round	1	…	3	4	5
$\mathcal{X}_1$	$(1,1)$	…	$[(1,1) \oplus (1,0)]$ $\oplus(0,1)$	$(1,0) \oplus (0,1)$	$(0,0)$
$\mathcal{X}_2$	$(1,1)$	…	$(1,1)$	$(1,1)$	$(0,0)$
$\sum \mathcal{X}_i$	$(2,2)$	…	$[(2,2) \oplus (2,1)]$ $\oplus(1,2)$	$(2,1) \oplus (1,2)$	$(0,0)$
k	$(1,1)$	…	$(1,1)$	$(1,1)$	$(1,1)$
$\mathcal{Y}_{-1}$	$(0,0)$	…	$(0,0)$	$(0,0)$	$(0,0)$
$\mathcal{Y}_{-2}$	$(0,0)$	…	$[(0,0) \oplus (0,1)]$ $\oplus(1,0)$	$(0,1) \oplus (1,0)$	$(0,0)$
$\mathcal{O}_1$		…			
$\mathcal{O}_2$		…		$(0,1) \oplus (1,0)$	

$\mathcal{T} = \{0, 1\}, k = (1, 1), \mathcal{B} = \{1, 2\},$
$v_1((1, 0)) = v_1((0, 1)) = \$5, v_1((1, 1)) = \$8;$
$v_2((1, 0)) = v_2((0, 1)) = \$6, v_2((1, 1)) = \$12.$

Table 2. Procedure of Example 2 under SAA-OP(Robust against Over Declaration)

Round	1	2	…	5
$\mathcal{X}_1$	$[(1,1) \oplus (1,0)]$ $\oplus(0,1)$	$(1,0) \oplus (0,1)$	…	$(1,0) \oplus (0,1)$
$\mathcal{X}_2$	$(1,1)$	$(1,1)$	…	$(0,0)$
$\sum \mathcal{X}_i$	$[(2,2) \oplus (2,1)]$ $\oplus(1,2)$	$(2,1) \oplus (1,2)$	…	$(1,0) \oplus (0,1)$
k	$(1,1)$	$(1,1)$	…	$(1,1)$
$\mathcal{Y}_{-1}$	$(0,0)$	$(0,0)$	…	$(1,1)$
$\mathcal{Y}_{-2}$	$[(0,0) \oplus (0,1)]$ $\oplus(1,0)$	$(0,1) \oplus (1,0)$	…	$(0,1) \oplus (1,0)$
$\mathcal{O}_1$			…	$(1,0) \oplus (0,1)$
$\mathcal{O}_2$		$(0,1) \oplus (1,0)$	…	

$\mathcal{T} = \{0, 1\}, k = (1, 1), \mathcal{B} = \{1, 2\},$
$v_1((1, 0)) = v_1((0, 1)) = \$7, v_1((1, 1)) = \$8;$
$v_2((1, 0)) = v_2((0, 1)) = \$0, v_2((1, 1)) = \$10.$

$v_2((1,0)) = v_2((0,1)) = \$6, v_2((1,1)) = \$12$. Hence, buyer 1 values the commodity to obtain 1 unit as \$5 at time period either 0 or 1 and to obtain 1 unit each at time period 0 and 1 as \$8. A procedure of this example is shown in Table 1. In the first round, both buyers submit purchase plans $(1,1)$, since this plan maximizes the utilities: $u_1((1,1),2) = 8 - 2 = 6 > u_1((1,0),1) = u_1((0,1),1) = 5 - 1 = 4$; $u_2((1,1),2) = 12 - 2 = 10 > u_2((1,0),1) = u_2((0,1),1) = 6 - 1 = 5$. In this case, the aggregated purchase plans of buyers exceed the overall capacity. Hence, the auctioneer proceeds to round 2 in which both buyers take the same actions as in round 1. Buyer 1 changes its action in round 3 in which the utility function is $u_1((1,1),6) = u_1((1,0),3) = u_1((0,1),3) = 2$. Hence, buyer 1 submits a purchase plan $\{[(1,1)\ \text{XOR}\ (1,0)]\ \text{XOR}\ (0,1)\}$ instead of a single plan $(1,1)$. These alternative purchase plans mean that buyer 1 will purchase at most one of these plans. There are three types of the aggregated purchase plans. In all three cases, all of them exceed the capacity plan. Hence, the auctioneer proceeds to the next round. In round 4, buyer drops a plan $(1,1)$ from the plans in the previous round. In this case, there are residual supplies for buyer 2 either $(0,1)$ or $(1,0)$. Hence, buyer 2 is proposed options $(0,1)$ XOR $(1,0)$. Taking an either option exceeds the maximum utility obtained in the successive round. Hence, a buyer takes one option and the remaining capacity becomes either $(1,0)$ or $(0,1)$. In round 5, buyer 1 declines their plans since there are no ways to earn positive profit.

This example illustrates a procedure under SAA-OP. A key point is that buyer 2 is proposed some options and takes an option either $(0,1)$ or $(1,0)$ in round 4 which is a partial fulfillment of a plan $(1,1)$. If we consider a case of unifrom auction with the same setting, buyer 2 reduces plans $(1,0)$ XOR $(0,1)$ from the truthful demand $(1,1)$ in round 4, since this reduction exceeds a case where buyer 2 obtains 1 unit in round 5 at \$5. Hence, this example shows how SAA-OP solves a problem of demand reduction under uniform auction.

The following example includes *all-or-nothing* plan of a buyer which is relevant to over declaration problem under Ausubel auction.

Example 2. Similarly to Example 1, the procedure and the parameters of this example are presented in Table 2. In round 1, buyer 1 submits alternative purchase plans $\{(1,1),(1,0),(0,1)\}$ which means an XOR bid and buyer 2 submits a plan $(1,1)$. Since all the potential choices conflict each other, there are not feasible allocations or proposals of options. In round 2, buyer 1 drops a plan $(1,1)$ and buyer 2 submits the same plan. In this case, the auctioneer is able to propose options $(1,0)$ XOR $(0,1)$. However, these options are not taken, since buyer 2 prefers all-or-nothing. All buyers behave similarly until round 4. In round 5, buyer 2 declines his plan and buyer 1 wins 1 unit at \$5.

This example shows a situation where a buyer does not take any proposed options, since his requirement is all-or-nothing. The consequence of this example is buyer 1 obtains 1 unit at round 5, since buyer 2 declines his plan in this round. If we consider a case of Ausubel auction, buyer 2 clinches 1 unit in round 2; buyer 2 wins two units in round 7 with a payment $\$9 = \$2 + \$7$. Buyer 1 is able to increase his utility by over declaration. If he submits a plan $(1,1)$ until round 4, buyer 2 is not able to clinch and declines his plan in round 5. Hence, buyer 2 obtains 1 unit in round 5 according to a misrepresentation of his requirement. SAA-OP obtains the same consequence without the problem of over declaration.

7 Simulation

We present how complementarities and substitutability of buyers influence on performance of our proposing mechanism (the SAA-OP). For this purpose, we conduct simulation analysis with the existing mechanism, the AOP presented in Section 3.3. As we have mentioned, the AOP does not deal with the complementing choices of buyers.

In the simulation analysis, we model an identical scenario where an auctioneer runs the SAA-OP or sequentially opening (and closing) auctions for complimenting choices on the AOP for a perishable item. In this case, a buyer is able to bid substituting item in the successive auction if the buyer could not win an item in the preceding auction. Of course, the SAA-OP is run for complementing items at once. We consider a single auction item with different due dates in $\mathcal{T} = t_0, t_1$. For each buyer, we assign an independent integer valuation drawn from a given uniform distribution ranging from \$ 1 to \$ 20 for each unit and for each due date. We consider two types of buyers, *complementarity buyer* and *straight buyer*. The former buyer has a substitutable choice on due date, and the latter buyer has a strict single due date only. We assume production capacity for 4-unit per day.

We test the following 5 cases for simulations based on the ratio of complementarity buyers: (i) 0 %, (ii) 25 %, (iii) 50 %, (iv) 75 %, and (v) 100 %. For an ease of comparison, we set the maximum purchase quantity as 4-unit per buyer and assign 4 buyers in each due date. Hence, for the case (ii), we assign 3 straight buyers on due date t_0 and t_1, respectively; 2 comlementarity buyers. For the respective 5 cases, we run simulations 1,000 times. We compare the performances of the SAA-OP and AOP on social surplus and profit of sellers that are obtained by the ratio of the actual social surplus including profits of sellers to the Pareto efficient social surplus, and the overall profits of sellers. Notice that we use the same valuations for buyers to run two types of auction mechanisms in each simulation.

Based on the above settings, we conduct the simulation analysis. First, we present how the average social surplus is given impact by the auction mechanisms in Figure 1. Notice that the SAA-OP and the AOP has the same results if all buyers are straight buyers (ratio of complementarity buyers = 0), since the winner determination process in the SAA-OP for complementing choices is not used. While the SAA-OP increases its performance with respect to social surplus as the increase of complementarity buyers, the AOP decreases its performance in contrast. Main reasons of these observations are two-folds: (i) the SAA-OP is able to determine auction winners more efficient if buyers have greater number of alternative choices, and (ii) the buyers under the AOP are more competitive, since the auction losers in the preceding auction submit different orders in the successive auctions.

Next, we focus on the overall profit of sellers. We depict the overall profit of sellers in Figure 2. The overall profit of sellers indicates that the performances of the SAA-OP and the AOP are significantly different for the comlementarity buyers. Under the SAA-OP, there is a strict difference on the overall profit of sellers between all straight buyers and other cases. In our simulation settings, the number of choices of a complementarity

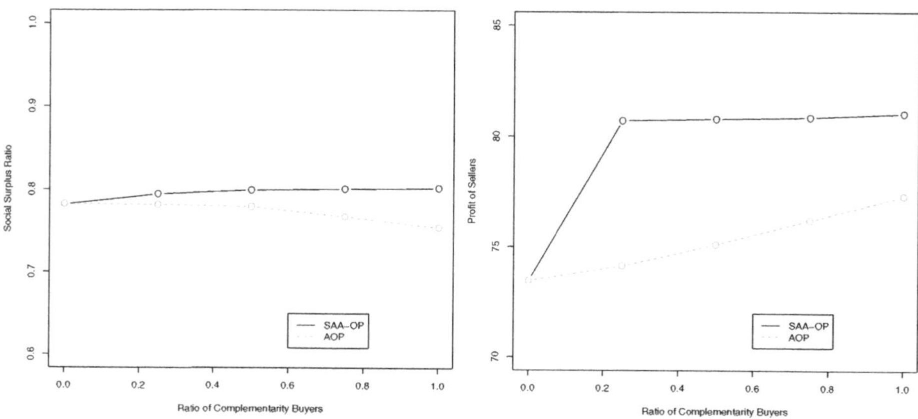

Fig. 1. Social Surplus

Fig. 2. The Overall Profit of Sellers

buyer is double compared to the one of a straight buyer. Subsequently, the complementarity buyers tend to sustain bidding at higher prices than the straight buyers. Hence, the SAA-OP corresponds to this difference efficiently in its winner determination process unlike the AOP, which is observed in the figure. While there is a jump under the SAA-OP at 0.25 of the ratio of complementarity buyers, similar phenomenon is not observed under the AOP.

Overall, the SAA-OP is able to efficiently allocate auction items for complementarity buyers without decreasing the profit of sellers and buyers. In contrast, the AOP for comlementality buyers compels competition for bidding prices. As a result, the overall profit of buyers is decreased.

8 Conclusions and Future Work

An allowance of multiple choices gives buyers expressive power of their complex preferences in auctions. These choices are significant if auctions are simultaneously undertaken with respect to multiple time periods, since valuations depend on available due dates. This scenario is important for corporate buyers concerning long-term procurements with several different business plans. A typical example is in device industries, such as chemical, papers, steels and mills industries, in which a change of production schedules or capacities is not simple due to contamination problems and production device installation lead-times and costs, while demands of customers change over time. In such a case, a flexible auction is a candidate solution to deal with a gap between supply and demand. As a solution for the scenario, this paper proposes a new multi-unit simultaneous ascending-price auction with option proposal (SAA-OP) with XOR bids in Section 4. To prevent strategic manipulations of buyers, this mechanism has complex winner determination processes. We have shown that SAA-OP implements an ex-post efficient equilibrium in Section 5. Therefore, this mechanism provides the efficient outcomes as long as all buyers submit sincere plans. We have also presented a numerical example how SAA-OP solves the over declaration problem in Section 6.

AOP proposed by Iwasaki et al. [5] and an option-based auction proposed by Juda and Parkes [6] are similar auctions to ours. The former is for a multi-unit without complementarities and the latter is for a sequential auction in a single-unit case. Our auction is for a multi-unit with complementarities.

In this paper, we have not discussed about susceptibility to *collusion* and *false-name* bid. The collusion problem occurs if buyers are able to agree to misrepresent their demands and share the gained benefits among them. Against this problem, Che and Kim [3] propose a collusion-free mechanism for a single item auction. A false-name bid, which is a loophole in the electronic business era addressed by [12], is effective if a trader gains additional profits by splitting his orders using several different identities such as free e-mail addresses. Iwasaki et al. [5] prove that AOP is a false-name-proof mechanism in a single-item auction. We will consider how to extend their ideas to multi-item auctions.

References

1. Ausubel, L.M.: An efficient ascending-bid auction for multiple objects. The RAND Journal of Economics 94(5), 1452–1475 (2004)
2. Ausubel, L.M., Cramton, P.: Demand reduction and inefficiency in multi-unit auction. Working paper no. 96-07, Department of Economics, University of Maryland (1996)
3. Che, Y.K., Kim, J.: Robustly collusion-proof implementation. Econometrica 74(4), 1063–1107 (2006)
4. Günlü, O., Ladányi, L., de Vries, S.: A branch-and-price algorithm and new test problems for spectrum auctions. Management Science 51(3), 391–406 (2005)
5. Iwasaki, A., Yokoo, M., Terada, K.: A robust open scending-price multi-unit auction protocol against false-name bids. Decision Support Systems 39, 23–39 (2005)
6. Juda, A.I., Parkes, D.C.: An options-based solution to the sequential auction problem. Artificial Intelligence 173(7-8), 876–899 (2009)
7. Klemperer, P.: What really matters in auction design. Journal of Economic Perspectives 16(1), 169–189 (2002)
8. Milgrom, P.: Putting auction theory to work: The simultaneous ascending auction. Journal of Political Economy 108(2), 245–272 (2000)
9. Nisan, N.: Bidding and allocation in combinatorial auctions. In: Proceedings of EC-2000, pp. 1–12 (2000)
10. Parkes, D.C.: Iterative combinatorial auctions. In: Cramton, P., Shoham, Y., Steinberg, R. (eds.) Combinatorial Auctions, ch. 2. MIT Press (2006)
11. Sandholm, T.: Algorithm for optimal winner determination in combinatorial auctions. Artificial Intelligence 135, 1–54 (2002)
12. Yokoo, M., Sakurai, Y., Matsubara, S.: Robust combinatorial auction protocol against false-name bids. Artificial Intelligence 130(2), 167–181 (2001)

Mobile Agent Cloning for Servicing Networked Robots

W. Wilfred Godfrey and Shivashankar B. Nair

Department of Computer Science & Engg., Indian Institute of Technology
Guwahati-781039 India
{w.godfrey,sbnair}@iitg.ernet.in

Abstract. In this work we present how the concept of cloning of mobile agents can aid in enhancing the performance of a multi robot system by providing faster services to the robots. The mobile agents carry solutions to problems faced by robots, as their payload. These agents move conscientiously in the network till they sense a pheromone gradient formed by a Robot Requesting Service (RRS) and its neighbours. Mobile agents tend to clone when they discover pheromones diffused by different RRSs thereby resulting in a faster and concurrent service. Simulation results have shown that cloning agents in high density RRS areas greatly decreases the waiting times for a service.

Keywords: Mobile Agents, Multi-Robot Systems and Pheromone Diffusion.

1 Introduction

An architecture for a multi-robot system based on mobile agents has been proposed by Godfrey and Nair [1]. The major objective of the work is to realize a multi-robot system, wherein robots need not initially have programs to execute every task they are capable of. Instead, mobile agents which carry these programs, written and deployed by a third party, could on-demand, arrive at such robotic nodes and provide for the relevant code to effect a task. Such a framework will allow even novice robotics enthusiasts to attach robots onto this network and make them execute commands for which they have not embedded the relevant program. The work reported herein describes the strategies by which a robotic node requiring a service (or a program) attracts mobile agents that carry the relevant programs needed to execute the task at hand.

2 Mobile Agent Based Multi-robot System

Fig. 1 depicts the architecture of the system being developed. It consists of multiple robots connected to one another by wireless links. A robot can thus communicate directly only with its immediate neighbours which are within the wireless range. Every robot has a platform capable of hosting mobile agents.

N. Desai, A. Liu, and M. Winikoff (Eds.): PRIMA 2010, LNAI 7057, pp. 336–339, 2012.

When a robot is issued a command to perform a task for which it does not have the relevant code, it sends out a pheromone-like volatile signal which tends to diffuse into the network through its immediate neighbours. As they diffuse their concentration decreases at each hop. When the mobile agents carrying the specific code for this task, sense these pheromones at a robotic node, they are guided directly towards the Robot Requesting their Service (RRS) along the increasing pheromone gradient. In contrast to the conventional virtual pheromone [2,3] where trails are left out by a moving agent, these pheromones are generated by a robotic node. These nodes proactively diffuse by themselves onto the neighbours till their concentration finally reduces to zero. In our scenario, the mobile agents forage for RRSs while the latter diffuse their aroma to attract the former much like what has been reported in [4].

An RRS starts diffusing a pheromone once it knows that it needs a service. A service could mean a (i) Request for a code required to accomplish a specific task which the robot is unaware of, (ii) Rules or information that could improve the performance of a robot or (iii) Information on how it could overcome a trap or an undesired situation. The RRS diffuses pheromone onto its immediate or one-hop neighbours with the maximum concentration. In subsequent time steps these neighbours diffuse the pheromones to their one-hop neighbours with a decreased concentration. The process continues till the concentration of pheromone dies down to zero.

Apart from the RRS, each robotic node also ensures the diffusion and evaporation of the pheromones. An RRS proactively attracts the mobile agents that in turn provide the relevant service. The mobile agents in turn also move in a proactive fashion towards the robot along the pheromone gradient. Both the robots and the mobile agents thus actively involve themselves in a parallel and bidirectional search for one another in the network.

The mobile agents are hosted by a platform within the robotic nodes. While pheromones are diffused radially, the agent migration is based on a combination of conscientious [5] and pheromone oriented strategies. The mobile agent normally uses conscientious strategy when it finds itself in non-pheromoned robotic nodes. The absence of pheromones at a node indicates that it is not within the near vicinity of an RRS. The agent thus opts for a conscientious strategy by migrating to a neighbouring node that it has not visited recently. It thus maintains a list of nodes visited as it migrates and tries to uniformly distribute its frequency of visits to the nodes comprising the network. When an agent finds itself within a node that has pheromones diffused onto it, it uses a pheromone tracking strategy. It tries to find whether it can service the RRS that diffused it, based on specific parameters embedded in the pheromone. If so, the agent chooses the pheromone link that has maximum concentration and migrates to the node pointed by it.

3 Cloning of Agents

When several RRSs diffuse pheromones for the same service, an agent may perceive pheromones directing it along multiple paths leading these RRSs. The

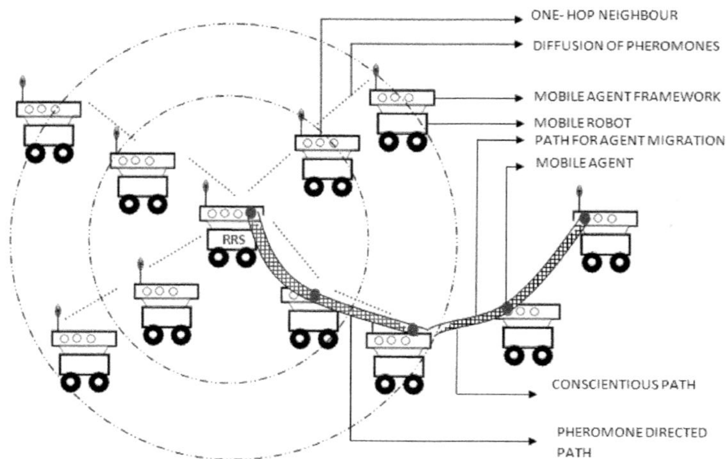

Fig. 1. Architecture of the Mobile Agent based Multi-robot system using pheromones

mobile agent needs to decide as to which RRS should be serviced first. The decision could be made based on either a random or conscientious strategy.

If an RRS were to be randomly selected and serviced, then there would be no streamlined way of finding the other RRSs requiring its service. To avoid a redundant service, the agent stays within the RRS till the time its pheromones have evaporated. The agent thus has no real means of finding the other RRSs and therefore switches back to the conscientious strategy of discovering RRSs without any memory of the previous dilemma encountered.

One solution to this problem would be to make the agent remember its path back to the node where it detected multiple pheromone paths to other RRSs and then retrace them after the first RRS is serviced. This may decrease the waiting times of the other RRS to some extent.

The best option under such conditions would be to trigger the cloning mechanism within the agent and then send each of the clones along pheromones diffused by the other RRSs. This will lead to a parallel service of all the RRSs thereby improving performance. Cloning can be beneficial in the sense that while more RRSs can be serviced in parallel, it greatly reduces the repeated diffusion of the pheromones by the other RRSs, thereby saving bandwidth as also resources consumed in pheromone diffusion.

3.1 Clonal Model

Though cloning can easily lead to better performance, there are several issues to be handled. Each clone generated is embedded with the following information:

Lifetime. If clones contained the same logic as their parent, they would further clone when faced with a similar situation. This could lead to an avalanche of clones infesting the network finally choking the bandwidth. This is why a lifetime is conferred on every clone so that they live just about as long as they are needed.

The lifetime of the clone is fixed at a value which is not more than the total pheromone spanning length. Further clones are rendered sterile, in the sense that their cloning logic is inhibited at the time when they are created. This ensures that they do not clone like their parent agents.

Service Information. When the parent clones, it embeds within the clone information regarding the RRS it needs to track down and service. Its pheromone tracking behavior is fixed to enable it to track and service only a specific RRS. However it may happen that en route to the RRS, such a clone may find that the pheromone trail has evaporated. Under such conditions, it may fail to reach the specific RRS and die a natural death when its lifetime equals zero.

4 Conclusion

In this paper, we described how mobile agents, coupled with their abilities to clone and carry service-oriented programs, can be used to service robots within a network. We also discussed how cloning significantly decreases RRSs waiting times in a network of robots. Mobile agents carry service programs as payload and search for RRSs that need a service within the network, using a conscientious algorithm. When they sense an RRS initiated pheromone diffused area, they tend to take a path along its concentration gradient and are thus directly guided to the RRS. On encountering pheromones from different RRSs requesting the same service the agent clones thereby effecting a parallel search and service procedure and decreasing waiting times on part of the RRS.

The use of a combined Conscientious and Pheromone based strategy results in a sort of bidirectional parallel search on part of the agent and the robots forming the network. Blending this approach with cloning can further improve performance over a mere conscientious approach. We are in the process of realizing the entire servicing model using real networked robots and mobile agents. Preliminary results using this blended approach on the real network of robots and mobile agents are encouraging.

References

1. Godfrey, W.W., Nair, S.B.: An Immune System Based Multi-robot Mobile Agent Network. In: Bentley, P.J., Lee, D., Jung, S. (eds.) ICARIS 2008. LNCS, vol. 5132, pp. 424–433. Springer, Heidelberg (2008)
2. Payton, D., Daily, M., Estowski, R., Howard, M., Lee, C.: Pheromone Robotics. J. Autonomous Robots 11(3), 319–324 (2001)
3. Purnamadjaja, A.H., Andrew, R.: Bi-directional pheromone communication between robots. Robotica 28(1), 69–79 (2010)
4. Li, Z., Zhou, W., Xu, B., Li, K.: An Ant Colony Genetic Algorithm Based on Pheromone Diffusion. In: Proceedings of the 4th International Conference on Natural Computation, ICNC 2008, Jinan, China, October 18-20, vol. 7, pp. 471–474 (2008)
5. Minar, N., Kwindla, H.K., Maes, P.: Cooperating Mobile Agents for Mapping Networks. In: Proceedings of the 1st Hungarian National Conference on Agent Based Computing, Hungary, pp. 34–41 (1999)

Towards Distributing Agent Intelligence: Using Decentralized Software Services for the Creation of Complex Problem Modelling

Quintin J. Balsdon and Elize M. Ehlers

The University of Johannesburg, Corner of Kingsway and University Road, Auckland Park, 2006, South Africa
qbalsdon@gmail.com, emehelers@uj.ac.za

Abstract. Autonomous agents are often restricted by the programs that make up their 'intelligence' because they are installed on the same hardware as the agent. Since intelligence is software and therefore abstract, it is possible to separate the components which 'create' the agent's intelligence from the agent itself. The disembodiment of intelligence allows agents to access components that may not be suited to their hardware for physical reasons, such as storage capacity or computational complexity.

It has been long established that humans find solutions to problems by dividing a problem into a series or smaller sub-problems [1; 2]. Using web services, 'intelligence components' can be created which perform a simple generic task on behalf of a client agent. These components may be used in different combinations in order to create customized solutions for particular problems.

Intelligence components may be distributed across servers in different locations, allowing other agents to benefit from the differing implementations. In addition, software may be updated remotely by updating individual components. The model is aimed at creating a repository of useful functionality which may enable intelligent agents to focus on the process of intelligence rather than processing individual environmental states.

The solution presented demonstrates that an agent may access distributed components in order to control behaviour, taking into consideration that components themselves have no concept of the environment in which the requesting agent exists. The problem of translating a 'model' solution into the environment-specific solution is therefore left to the agent.

Keywords: Coordination and Concurrency Runtime, Distributed Software Services, Microsoft Robotics Developer Studio, Serialization.

1 Introduction

In the field of robotics, two types of software components are required: those that interface with the hardware and those that process the information gathered from sensors [3; 4; 5]. It is often difficult to manage all the incoming information with the processes that are designed to handle that information. A robotic entity would have to wait for all the required inputs to be received before continuing with a particular task, whilst at the same time being plagued with continuous information that requires

N. Desai, A. Liu, and M. Winikoff (Eds.): PRIMA 2010, LNAI 7057, pp. 340–354, 2012.

processing. The Concurrency and Coordination Runtime (CCR) [4; 5; 6] enables a programmer to run threaded tasks without concerning themselves with the timing of thread completion, using delegates to run a particular subroutine when all the required inputs have been gathered. In addition components have been separated into Decentralized Software Services (DSS), software components which allows for processing to continue within an agent while the data manipulation occurs in a separate thread, possibly on a separate processor [4; 5].

It has been shown that these services may even be utilized to distribute behaviour of the effectors of a robotic agent [7], however, these services could also be used in the problem solving process of all types of agents, robotic and software-oriented. The distributed nature of the components also allows for functional elements of code to be shared amongst different agents.

In any problem solving process, the problem must be broken down into a series of sub-problems[1; 2]. These sub-problems can then be solved using different methods, but will always refer to axioms which define the problem space. A system which controls individual components that perform smaller tasks on behalf of agents will allow the computationally complex aspects of intelligent agents to be distributed across various platforms. The agents which use such a system must appropriately model the environment (also known as a belief state, in the *Belief-Desire-Intention* or *BDI* model) in which it exists (the model must not exclude information that is imperative to the solution [1]) and properly sub-divide its problems. In addition, a formal method of model representation and communication is required, which will enforce standards in intelligent agents to be created and maintained [8].

The Microsoft Robotics Developer Studio (MRDS) provides the ideal platform not only for embeddable intelligence, but also for the proposed agent model. A state object is used for transferring of behavioural suggestions and changes within an agent's internal structure. In addition, the C# language provides many interesting aspects for artificial intelligence. For example, delegates allow for functions to be passed like parameters and when combined with services, allow for embeddable intelligent behaviour using the predefined state transfer mechanisms.

The purpose of the following paper is to propose a method of utilizing Decentralized Software Services for the purpose of creating components which solve a particular problem independent of agent hardware and environment. These components may then be strung together in such a fashion that various types of problems may be solved in variable degrees of complexity.

2 Model

Intelligence is not simply the ability to achieve the task that is presented. The aim of intelligent systems is to achieve a solution that is adaptable to all the complexities that surround a particular problem. While systems are capable of self modification it has been proven that a no system will be so complete in its knowledge that it is capable of solving any problem [2; 9], as in human intelligence. The resulting system, therefore, is not an attempt to solve all problems but rather an experiment to evaluate the degree to which a system may increase complexity while maintaining autonomy.

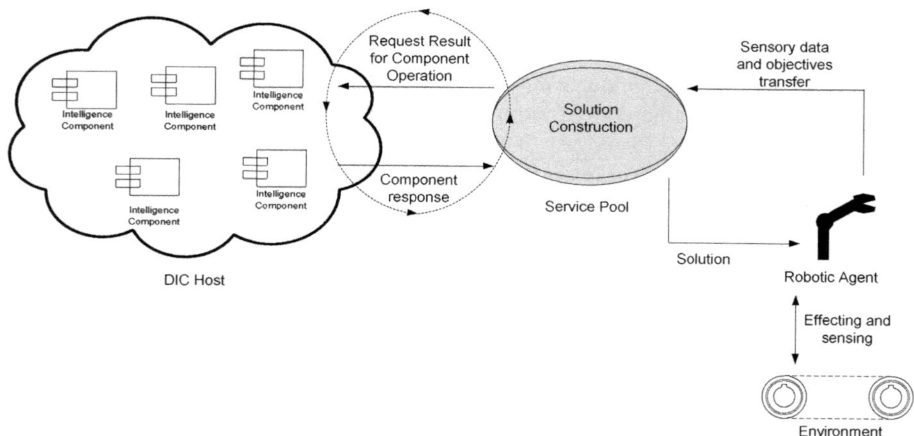

Fig. 1. The manner in which a robotic agent relates to individual intelligence components

The goal of the agent model is to prove that systems are capable of real-time self modification that will enable them to access remote components, which provide 'elemental' solutions to problems. The framework will enable any intelligent agent to solve basic problems and problems that it is capable of sub-dividing. As discussed earlier, many problems are solved by breaking down the problem into a series of sub-problems until the sub-problems may be solved by elementary processes [1 ;2]. Figure 1 depicts a robotic agent making use of the framework. Each Distributed Intelligence Component (DIC) is accessible to any agent requesting its use, making the system advantageous to multi-agent settings and those where agents exist in entirely different environments and in different systems.

In order to distribute components, some mechanism by which components may be accessed needs to be created. Since agents will be distinct from the components that they use to create their 'intelligence' [10; 11], the means by which they will gain access to these components is known as the 'component pool,' which is actually a distributed component itself. Agents will be required to register with one service which will in turn have registered with all the other services, leaving the burden of service discovery outside of the agent. The manner in which the component pool operates is discussed in section 2.2.

The agent is responsible for perceiving the environment in the correct manner. It will be required to remove noise from the environment and develop an appropriate internal model of the environment. In addition, the problem space needs to be correctly mapped including only the correct aspects of the problem, i.e. by not removing so much as to make the problem unsolvable, but not putting so much detail in to the model that every problem becomes unique. The particular problem that an agent is dealing with at the time needs to be more generic than that of the entire world space. Some problems may be more complex than others. However, it is possible that the underlying solution will not change, because the environmental factors creating the perceived complexity do not necessitate a change in problem approach (figure 1).

Agents in an environment like figure 2 (a) will have far less problems than agents existing in figure 2 (b) in terms of perception and noise reduction, however the nature

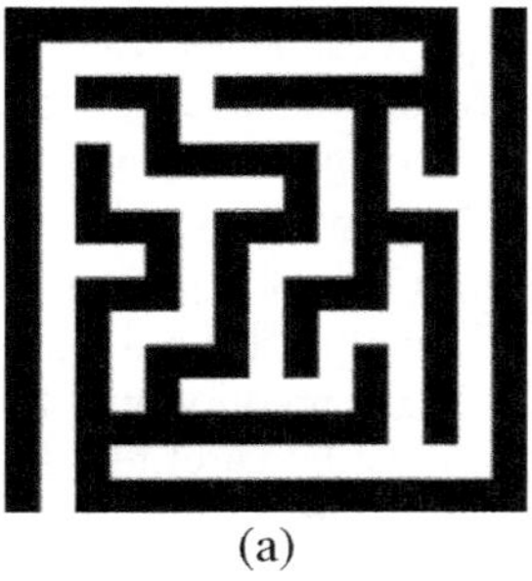

(a)

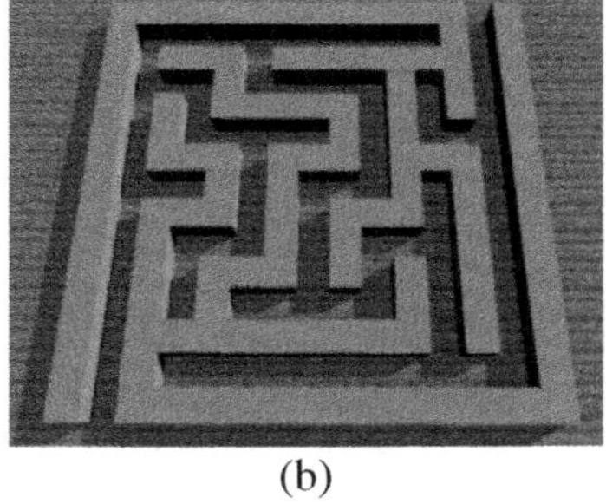

(b)

Fig. 2. Distinction of problem and environment: the figures represent that the change from two dimensional (a) to three dimensional (b) environment while the underlying problem remains the same

of solution that the agent employs (A* search, depth-first search etc.) is not required to differ. Intelligent agents, as long as their problem representation remains consistent, could employ the same components in both environments [7].

For example agents may be required to navigate through a maze (such as in figure 2). While mazes may differ in their setting, the problem has been solved via breadth-first, A* and other uninformed search strategies [10; 11; 12]. Whatever strategy an agent may wish to employ is insignificant to the environment in which it is placed. Any agent, whether in a two or three dimensional space, for example, is able to apply the same strategies based on the type of problem being solved. It can be seen from figure 2 that whilst the environment may change in its own complexity, the nature of the problem may not be as different. Therefore components for intelligence need not be situated inside an agent, but can be placed inside service components divorced from the environment.

The agent model aims to provide all agents with ubiquitous components that may be 'strung' together in any fashion [7; 12], allowing them to construct novel solutions to the challenges they face, while removing the non-essential complexities of the environment (figure 3).

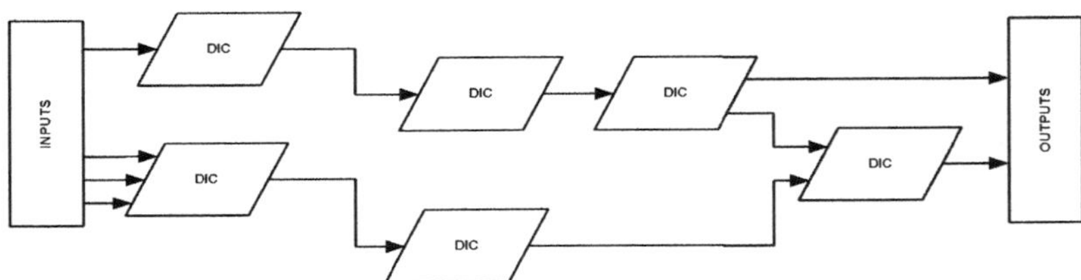

Fig. 3. A possible network of DIC components forming a complex behaviour

The solution to more complex problems is also the task of the agent. The agent must be able to map problems to some series of steps that will result in the solution. The agent must also be capable of constructing the entire solution from a sequence of sub-solutions. However is possible that the task of problem sub-dividing and solution construction can become components themselves.

An agent making use of these distributed components must be able to send and receive data to and from these components in such a manner that the solution provided by the component is of practical value to the agent. There are therefore six stages that have been determined that an agent will advance through in order to ensure the utility of a solution:

1. Filter the environment. The environment must be correctly perceived by the agent. The agent then is required to remove any noise from the perception that does not contribute to the problem at hand. The perception will be required to remove elements from the problem, but this must be carefully done so as not to modify the problem in any way. It is vital that an appropriate model is formed by the agent without adding or removing essential information [1].
2. Format the input. The filtered data must be represented in standard manner in order that it may be communicated effectively with other components. For example, a robot navigating a factory floor can represent its problem space using the same data structures as the agent in a GPS navigation application.
3. Fragment the problem. The problem needs to be broken down into a series of sub-problems (stages). These sub-problems must be ordered so that when solutions are found, the complete solution may be re-constructed by ordering the solutions to sub-problems. It is in this stage that components will be put together in order to form solutions.
4. Find the sub-solutions. Each component will start attempting solutions to each sub-problem assigned to it. In this stage the components are executing their functionality. The results are returned to the calling agent.
5. Fit the solution. Once a solution has been found, the agent must be capable of taking the generic information provided by the components and applying the solution to the particular environment in which the agent exists. This is the reverse procedure of stage two.
6. Finalize. The agent must not assume that a goal has been attained simply because it attempted a solution. The agent must once again perceive the environment and check that the goal state has in fact been reached. Once stage six is completed, the agent may be faced with other factors that have been created by 'side-effects' to the solution.

These stages define the manner in which the distributed components will integrate with modern artificial intelligence techniques. The following section will highlight the individual components themselves and in what manner they fit together.

2.1 Distributed Intelligence Components

Each intelligence component in the model will be implemented inside a separate DSS. The DSS Intelligence Components (DIC) may be combined in various arrangements to create solutions more complex than any individual component. If the DIC inputs and outputs are defined in a machine-readable manner, a network of DICs may be formed by an agent (figures 1 and 3), and all the components have a full listing of the inputs required by other components, combined with the ability to be 'aware' of what manner of output is expected [13].

DICs may be hosted locally or on a server, which describe some basic behaviour that may be performed by any artificially intelligent entity. These DICs will be loaded by an agent's component pool [7; 12], which handles the manner in which DICs are used (figure 1). The agent is responsible for determining the nature of the surrounding environment, and 'cleaning' the information in such a way that the data may be sent to the DIC in a standard format, see code sample (1).

The definition of the inputs of the DIC is required so that the agent has the ability to properly utilize the DIC functionality. This is usually done programmatically, in other words, by writing and compiling code. However, since the construction of these networks must be dynamically (done by the agent) the program may define the inputs and outputs in another manner, such as XML (and thus utilized at run time) so that the desired network of components is generated by the agent.

The DICs will allow any intelligent agent system, robotic and software, to interchange components at runtime for any purpose. Further advantages include:

- Fast process change without compilation. Since each DIC is a separate embeddable component, the manner in which a problem is solved may be modified to suite the agent.
- Component reuse. Many agents may access the host for any purpose and there is no requirement for every solution to have the same algorithms implemented in the same manner.
- Platform independence. Intelligence should not need to exist based on the environment in which it is required to operate.
- Distinction of problem from environment. The obstacle facing the agent will be differentiated from the environmental aspects and challenges the agent faces.

Each DIC will correlate to an individual function that may be performed by any agent. These DICs may be hosted on some network, for example the Internet, in order to increase availability.

(1)

```
[DataContract]
public class BehaviourRequest
{
     private object _input;
     private Type _type;

     /// <summary>
     /// Returns the object-typed input from source
     /// </summary>
     [DataMember]
     public object Input
     {
         get { return _input; }
     }

     /// <summary>
     /// Returns the type of the input
     /// </summary>
     [DataMember]
     public Type Type
     {
         get { return _type; }
     }
}
```

2.2 The Component Pool

MRDS services are modules designed for reuse in several different robotics applications. In addition, Microsoft has made provision for services to be hosted by a single service. The component pool is therefore a service utilised as a platform for other services. The advantage of using a pool as the host, rather than the agent, is that the additional layer of abstraction makes the agent 'unaware' of the explicit components provided by the pool. The agent's code does not have to be recompiled after a new component is created. Instead, the component just needs to be added to the pool of existing services, as seen in figure 1.

The purpose of the component pool is to load and group specific DICs which relate to the function of the agent itself. The component pool is used by the agent for achieving its goals. The component pool does not only host components for use in the solution of a particular problem, but is also able to construct a solution to more complex problems by combining different components' functionality together.

The component pool may host DICs in a certain manner for a number of reasons. For example, if the agent has only simple goals (or the problems are easily broken down into simple goals), and a corresponding set of DICs exist to solve the agent's problems, then it is best for the component pool to host the DICs based on solution, requiring the agent to formulate the inputs for each individual component. However, if the agent requires a specific solution based on a set of data or based on specific data representation models, the component pool is better off grouping the available components by input, in order to minimize communication. The timing of a solution may also become an issue: perhaps a rating system may be required so that agents will select a component based on the turnaround time of particular DICs. There may be multiple implementations of certain algorithms which have been optimised with different design goals (for example, time versus accuracy). However, when DICs are grouped by input, it needs to be noted that:

1. The correct DIC may not be chosen based on solution, and the agent must therefore take care to ensure the correct DIC is chosen.
2. Many DICs may be able to produce a solution, and so the agent must be sure to have a mechanism by which it can select a single DIC, based on some measurement of utility.

The services are hosted using the proxy that is produced at compilation, which contains the 'contract' of the service. This allows messages to be marshalled and passed between the two services[5]. After the services have been registered using their proxy, commands are sent to the service requesting their state. The state is then transferred to the host and may be manipulated and used.

3 Implementation

3.1 Creating Generic Behaviours

Every service that is created for MRDS must register the operations that are to be used in the PortSet [6]. The PortSet class encapsulates several ports so that multiple messages may be sent in a queue [4; 5; 6]. DIC components designed in MRDS for the component pool must have a common agreement on structure since the detection of method signatures is significantly more difficult than the detection of output types. The UML diagram shown in figure 4 depicts all the operations for the behaviours that were created. It is important to note that it is normal to leave the operations class blank (in this case, *BehaviourOperations*) as the messages that can be passed are described by the inherited PortSet. The operations class serves solely to register the operations provided by the DIC hosted on the DSS. The function of the operations is defined in a customised handler implemented in the DICBehaviour1Service class.

For a particular *Behaviour* to exist, an encapsulation class must be declared, in which the message may be passed. The *BehaviourRequest* class must be declared with the **[DataContract]** attribute, which registers the class as part of the contract that is passed using REprestational State Transfer, or REST [5; 6]. MRDS has been designed in such a manner that properties may also be passed as part of the REST, using serialisation. A property method may be written for each attribute in a class and, depending on the type, may be registered for serialisation using the **[DataMember]** attribute. In this manner the data type may be communicated to another DIC.

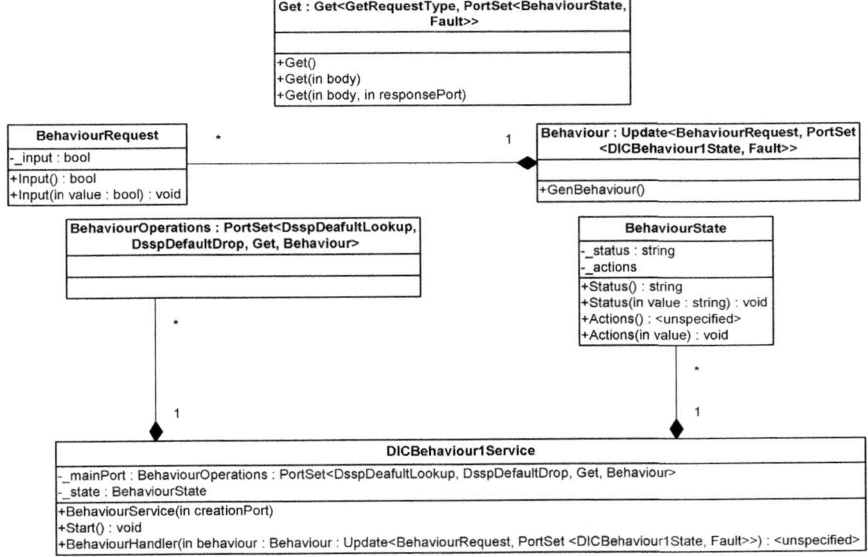

Fig. 4. UML Diagram describing the structure of an individual behaviour

The BehaviourHandler method in the DICBehaviour1Service class is the core functionality of the service. In this method, input is received and may be processed in order to generate a solution to a problem. The solution may be as simple as a calculation or as complex as an array of behavioural steps for a robotic agent to follow. This is the manner in which a problem may be resolved. The solution must be returned via the _state object declared within the DICBehaviour1Service. The _state of the service has two types returned: object and a type. The type field specifies the data type in which to cast the object variable. The object variable can be an array of more objects (each with a corresponding type array) or simply one solution for the recipient.

3.2 The Component Pool: DIC Hosting

In order to effectively create networks of DICs, each DIC must be hosted by a pool. The possibility exists for multiple pools to be created, in order to differentiate between types of DICs. Each sub-pool could then be hosted by an overall pool. The pool is designed to be a static container of DICs to which any agent may connect. The pool is responsible for communication between the agent and the DICs contained within the pool. The simplest approach for grouping behaviours at the moment is to sort them based on their input, however many options remain (output, implementation, problem type). Upon receiving a message, the pool may forward it to all the hosted DICs, or a specified DIC, specified by some variable. These messages would be passed in the same way as any other messages described in the model. Figure 5 indicates the class diagram for the component pool. An agent utilizing the model only hosts the pool service and makes use of the function calls provided by that service to access DICs.

It is important to note that certain Behaviours may be specific to the type of agent requesting the solution, i.e. that some solutions may result in an operation tailored for a specific environment. For example, a type of Behaviour in the pool may require that the agent has a (physical) differential drive. The differential drive is run by setting each wheel to a specific power (a real value ranging from -1 to 1) in which differing powers allow a robot with such hardware to turn. In addition, the differential drive must be permitted to run for a certain time before the next request is made. The reason for ensuring such an action is that the CCR does not guarantee the order in which requests are received, but only that it will wait until all messages have been received. Therefore the robot must wait between the executions of behavioural steps. Since the time it takes for a robot to drive one metre is different from the time it would take the same robot to drive ten metres, the time is as variable as the distance that the robot is requested to drive. Thus the time or distance may be abstracted to the pool as well, depending on the particular component.

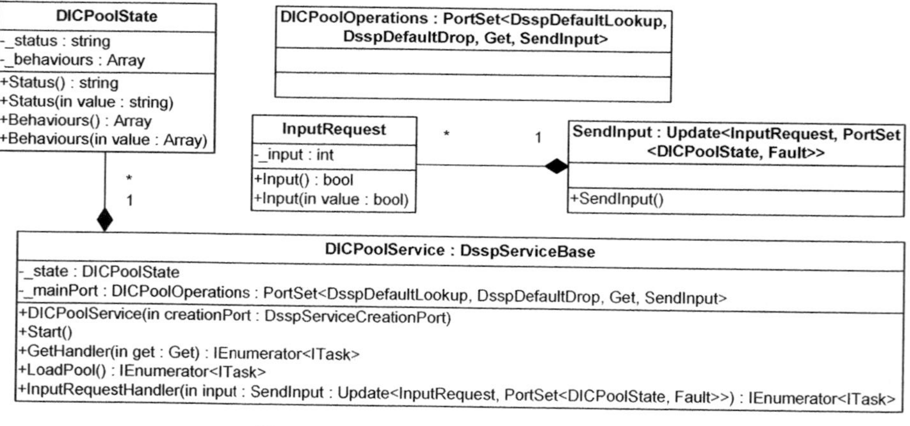

Fig. 5. Structure of the Component pool

3.3 Agent-Pool Interaction

The interaction sequence diagram (figure 6) describe the message passing between the three basic components, namely the behaviours, the pool and the agent entity. However, control needs to be carefully handled within the agent owing to the Concurrency and Coordination (CCR)-managed threading. Every threaded method has a return type of *IEnumerator<ITask>*. The robot will read its environment (*read_environment*); seek the embedded objects output (*send_inputs*) and may then issue actuator commands (e.g. *driveRobot*). The Behaviour of the entity is centrally controlled by the *perform_behaviour* method.

It is important to note that the agent is never locked in a particular behaviour, since the methods are threaded using the CCR library. This allows the agent to continue with other internal operations, such as reactive control, even when in the middle of requesting an embedded behaviour.

The start up sequence is the process where an agent invokes the pool service, which in turn invokes the behavioural services (DICs). This is accomplished using the managed asynchronous message passing of the CCR. Figure 8 depicts the message passing when the agent is in normal operating mode.

The agent is only aware of the pool service. After the pool service is loaded, the pool becomes responsible for loading and hosting the services. The agent loads the pool service which makes all the embeddable components available. The agent now has access to all the DIC components that are hosted by the pool service. Code sample (2) is the implementation of the agent calling the *Get()* method of the pool. In the same manner, sensor input can be sent through to the pool to the hosted services using the Component Pool's *SendInput* method.

The agent may load the pool service which makes all the embeddable components available. The agent will then have access to all the Distributed Software Service Protocol (DSSP) operations that are implemented in the pool service, which can access the DSSP operations in each hosted service. In the same manner, sensor input is sent through to the pool to the hosted services. Since the behaviour of the services is input driven, it is advisable that pools only associate with services (for the moment) that have the same inputs so that the Behaviour remains abstracted from the agent.

Upon an execution, the thread is able to return its control to the agent, thereby completely managing the threading issues. This obviates the need for the programmer to release locks or determine the schedule of other threads. Similarly, all the levels of the internal element component, including the reactive components, may be implemented. With the pools implemented to handle their specific behaviour and inputs, the framework will successfully embed components. The CCR manages all incoming messages, and so the order of incoming messages is not an issue since the agent can continue operation while different components execute remotely.

In order to run a certain behaviour as the result of a DSSP operation, such as Get(), the agent may simply spawn a thread to execute the Behaviour, while remaining in control of the Behaviour that is being executed. In this way, the agent is not simply executing a Behaviour blindly, but rather runs a result step by step, inside a thread that may be interrupted – for safety purposes. Figure 8 is the method that is run inside a thread, executing a specific behaviour.

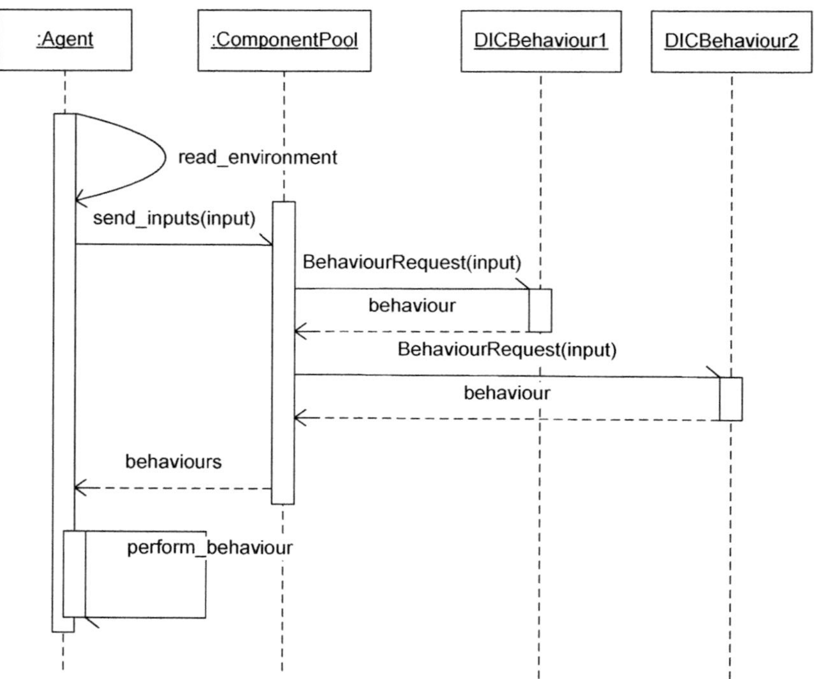

Fig. 6. The manner in which messages are passed

```
read_environment();//percieve the environment
yield return Arbiter.Choice(DICpool.Get(),                    (2)
  delegate(behaviourPool.BehaviourPoolState success)
   {
      LogInfo("AGENT: GetPool: ServicePool loaded: "
          + success.Status);
      LogInfo("AGENT: GetPool: number of activities
          in pool: " +
          success.Behaviours.GetLength(0));
      _state.Pool = success;
      agent_initiate();//use DIC components
  },
  delegate(W3C.Soap.Fault failure)
  {
      LogError("AGENT: GetPool: Could not retrieve
          pool state");
      agent_fail();//report the failed load
  }
);
LogInfo("AGENT: Get sequence complete");
```

The agent may also send messages to the services inside the pool. The DICs may then alter their behaviour based on these inputs. The ability to alter behaviour based on inputs within hosted services allows the DICs to remain unacquainted with the particular environment, but able to provide functional intelligence on the behaviour that should follow certain inputs. Code sample 3 presents how the service pool receives a message from an agent and encapsulates the message that must be forwarded to the hosted service.

4 Challenges

Communication must always be handled with great care in such models, since there is the added complexity of distribution. In modular programmed systems, complex data types (classes and objects) are shared by the entire system, however in distributed models, custom complex data types are not. It is entirely possible that a valid communication is created by the agent with a custom data type, which is passed through the component pool to a DIC that does not recognize the data type of the parameter. The problem may also occur in the DIC, where a solution is represented within a customized data type. A method of distributing complex custom data types must be implemented in order for the solution to be completely generic in terms of transferrable data types.

Since any solution that is presented by an agent is dependent on the model of the environment that is created by the agent, that model becomes an important aspect of the system in two aspects: first, that the manner in which environmental models are created is incorrect. This implies that the agent is either overloading a model with too much information or is culling information that is vital to the solution. Secondly, models are created with certain assumptions in mind, and these assumptions may or may not reflect reality [1], as a bias may have been programmed into the system. There may be an axiom within the agent system used to generate a model which creates a distorted view of reality for the agent.

(3)

```
[ServiceHandler(ServiceHandlerBehavior.Exclusive)]
public IEnumerator<ITask>
    InputRequestHandler(SendInput ipt)
{
      bh1.BehaviourRequest b1req = new
                              bh1.BehaviourRequest();
      b1req.Input = ipt.Body.Input;

      yield return
         Arbiter.Choice(pool_1.GenBehaviour(b1req),
          delegate(bh1.Behaviour1State success)
          {
              LogInfo("Pool load Successful");
              _state.Status += " ServicePool: " +
                  success.Status;

             _state.Behaviours.SetValue
                                (success.Actions, 0);
```

```
            },
            delegate(W3C.Soap.Fault failure)
            {
                LogError("Pool state fail");
            }
        );

        LogInfo("Sequence Complete");
        ipt.ResponsePort.Post(_state);
    }
```

One of the issues for consideration is that the DIC model requires a mechanism for effective component grouping. As the number of components available increases, there will need to be a mechanism by which agents can identify and use components. In addition, agents may wish to rate components on their utility. For example, one implementation of the breadth first search algorithm will have a complexity of $O(n^2)$, while another may have O(n+m), depending on the data representation [14]. Components may either be grouped by solution or by input [7; 12]. Grouping of DICs, for now, is static and controlled by the programmer on an individual basis.

In addition, components must be made available to agents. If an agent is reliant on hosted services to solve a problem, these services need to be present and available. Presence is an issue since agents cannot solve a particular problem using only one solution method. If the agent only has a hammer, ever problem may be treated as if it were a nail [1].

5 Conclusion

Components have been created which take an external stimulus from an agent, perform a function and return a result which the agent may then act upon. This behaviour demonstrates the concept of distributing intelligent behaviour in the form of embeddable components. Agent and robotic systems can now be developed where the robotic entity is responsible for perceiving and acting in the environment, but the task of processing the perceptions may be passed onto another component, which may not even operate on the same machine, or even in the same location as the robot itself. The implication is that intelligent behaviour may be generated as a result of combinations of small algorithms, rather than one consistent algorithm attempting to solve all problems. The usage of services allows for agent entities to be created independently of the software algorithms they are running. The agents need only be concerned about the particular environment in which they will be placed.

The concept that an agent may be independent of its software places a burden of reliance on the sensors of the agent. Sensors will be required to 'clean' the received information in such a manner that the perceptions may be fed into a standard algorithm for processing. However, the cost is minimal when the agent is made capable of solving a wide variety of problems rather than simply building a robotic system designed to solve one problem.

The demonstration of services being capable of receiving input is in itself significant. Customised services were originally intended to produce output, but input sent from the robotic entity means that behaviour may be adjusted in response to particular situations, not the direct environment. In other words, the services may be completely independent of the environment, should the designers wish to employ services in this manner.

MRDS as an agent platform has been discussed, as well as the agent model operating as an orchestration service within MRDS. It has been demonstrated that the proposed framework operates successfully within the bounds of the DSSs and managed threading run-times provided by MRDS. It has also been demonstrated successfully that the agent entity is capable of operating in such a manner that intelligence may be embedded into agent entities.

The agent model presented is capable of distributing software components tailored to enabling agents to embed the functions which assist in the problem solving process. The model does not attempt to create intelligence in computational or robotic entities but rather provide a strong platform by which agents may begin solving larger problems due to more available resources.

The model demonstrates that the creation of intelligence is not in the production of components, but in the effective use of problem-solving techniques. The model allows an agent to focus more of its local (on-board) processing power to real problem solving techniques than having to perform all the mundane tasks of solution discovery.

There are still many opportunities for the model to expand upon, such as formalising a standard by which agents represent their belief states, creating a mechanism by which components are effectively grouped and implementing a system where components may be rated for specific use, such as accuracy versus time-sensitivity.

References

1. Michalewicz, Z., Fogel, D.B.: How to Solve It: Modern Heuristics, vol. 2. Spriger, Heidelberg (2004) 3-540-22494-7
2. Li, D., Du, Y.: Artificial Intelligence with Uncertainty. CRC Press, Oxon (2008) 1-28488-998-5
3. Matarić, M.J.: The Robotics Primer. The MIT Press, Cambridge (2007) 978-0-262-63354-3
4. Morgan, S.: Programming Microsoft Robotics Studio. Microsoft Press, Redmond (2008) 978-0-7356-2432-0
5. Johns, K., Taylor, T.: Professional Microsoft Robotics Developer Studio. Wiley Publishing, Inc., Indianapolis (2008) 978-0470-14107-6
6. Chrysanthakopoulos, G., Singh, S.: An Asynchronous Messaging Library for C#, California, USA (2005)
7. Balsdon, Q.J., Ehlers, E.M.: Agent Framework for Self-Embedding Intelligence Components Using Simulated Robotics as a Test bed, pp. 1–200. The University of Johannesburg, Johannesburg (2009); Masters Dissertation

8. Poslad, S.: Specifying protocols for multi-agent systems interaction. ACM, New York (2007) 1556-4665
9. Russell, S., Norvig, P.: Artificial Intelligence: A Modern Approach, 3rd edn., 1152 pages. Prentice-Hall (2009) 978-0136042594
10. Gui, N., De Florio, V., Sun, H., Blondia, C.: A hybrid real-time component model for reconfigurable embedded systems, pp. 1590–1596. ACM, Fortaleza (2008)
11. Peper, C., Schneider, D.: Component engineering for adaptive ad-hoc systems, pp. 49–56. ACM (2008)
12. Balsdon, Q.J., Ehlers, E.M.: A Robust, Modular Agent Architecture With Embeddable Components for use In Various Multi-Agent Environments: Applying Simulated Robotics, vol. 2. The Faculty of Industrial Design Engineering, Delft University of Technology, Izmir, Turkey (2008) 978-90-5155-044-3
13. Burmester, S., Giese, H., Oberschelp, O.: Hybrid UML Components for the Design of Complex Self-Optimizing Mechatronic Systems, pp. 281–288. Springer Netherlands (2006)
14. Goodrich, M.T., Tamassia, R.: Data Structures and Algorithms in Java, 5th edn. Wiley (2010) 978-0470383261
15. Capretz, L.F., Capretz, M.A.M., Li, D.: Component-Based Software Development, pp. 1834–1837. Industrial Electronics Society (2001)
16. Guerrouat, A., Richter, H.: A component-based specification approach for embedded systems using FDTs. ACM, Lisbon (2005) 1-59593-371-9

Averting the Tragedy of the Commons by Adapting Aspiration Levels

Onkur Sen[1] and Sandip Sen[2]

[1] Rice University
Houston, TX, USA
onkursen@gmail.com
[2] University of Tulsa
Tulsa, OK, USA
sandip@utulsa.edu

Abstract. The Tragedy of the Commons involves a community utilizing a shared resource (the "commons") which can sustain a maximum load capacity beyond which its performance degrades. If utility received is proportional to the load applied on the system, individuals will maximize their applied load. Such greedy behavior will eventually lead to the total load exceeding the capacity of the commons. Thereafter, individuals will get less for adding more load on the system, which signifies a social dilemma. We develop a distributed solution approach to the tragedy of the commons that require individuals in the society to adapt their aspirations and apply loads based on their own aspirations. An aspiration level corresponds to the satisficing return for an individual, which is adjusted based on experience. In our model, individuals choose the load applied on the system based on their aspiration levels, thereby affecting the stability and performance of the "commons." We evaluate two different aspiration and load adjustment policies as well as effects of asynchronous decision making on the stability and performance of populations of varying sizes. Interesting results include mitigation of free-riding for larger populations. We also develop a mathematical model to predict the convergence time for such populations and verify the predictions experimentally.

Keywords: Aspiration levels, Tragedy of the Commons, free-riding.

1 Introduction

In a society, the common infrastructures, goods, and services are typically shared between members. Often the shared resource has a fixed capacity, and if the load exceeds its capacity, the resource performance, or its perceived utility to the users, decreases sharply. For example, if we consider the problem of city traffic, we find that congestion problems arise out of self-interested drivers sharing common resources like roads and bridges.

In a society of self-interested, rational members, each individual will try to maximize its utility via more extensive use of the shared resource. We focus on resources where the utility returned is proportional to load when the total load

N. Desai, A. Liu, and M. Winikoff (Eds.): PRIMA 2010, LNAI 7057, pp. 355–370, 2012.

on the system is below the threshold and decreases rapidly when the threshold is crossed. In a distributed scenario, each individual will have an incentive to myopically increase its load and hence the combined load will exceed the capacity of the common resource and everyone's utility will be adversely affected. This situation corresponds to the well-recognized *social dilemma* known as the *Tragedy of the Commons* (TOC) [9]. TOC represents critical problems for large-scale systems with multiple independent actors (henceforth referred to as *agents*) as individual behavior based on short-term gains leads to long-term global losses [13].

Real-world examples of the TOC are increasingly recognized at different scales and societal contexts, e.g., unsustainable agricultural practices, habitat destruction, traffic congestion. A case of the Tragedy of the Commons lies in the case of network congestion if every packet is sent with highest possible priority. Suppose a network contains some routes of different quality. If all agents behave selfishly, they will try to use the best possible route, leading to a congestion which worsens every routing through that route.

More recently, attention has been drawn to the Tragedy of the Commons in the context of autonomous agent systems [21]. Such problems arise in multiagent societies [16] as multiple distributed decision-makers try to maximize local utility based only on limited global knowledge. We are particularly interested in Tragedy of the Commons situations in distributed computational frameworks, such as computer networks, peer-to-peer (P2P) and grid systems, modem pools, shared databases, printers, and servers. The adverse effects of Tragedy of the Commons often lead to reduced throughput, system inefficiency and failure, and undermine user satisfaction and trust in such distributed systems. For example, when the number of users connecting to a fixed-size modem increases, the time required to connect increases, which leads individuals to hog available resources, i.e., users tend to maintain their connection rather than logging off after finishing their work. This, in turn, leads to further delays in establishing a connection.

We propose and evaluate a distributed computational approach to solve the TOC, where each agent maintains an *aspiration level* that is adapted based on observed utilities and is used to determine the load the agent applies on the system. The goal is to evaluate if the use of aspirations can suppress greedy behavior and allow agents to choose effective loads, based only on local information, that will provide satisfactory performance [5]. We assume agents have very limited information about the system, e.g., the agent does not know the number of agents in the system, the load other agents apply, or the total load. An agent adjusts its load on the commons based only on its own experience of applying loads and receiving corresponding utilities. Our research goal is to develop local decision-making procedures that will allow the system to work at near-optimum capacity without the total load being significantly higher than the threshold, thus avoiding the Tragedy of the Commons.

The rest of the paper is organized as follows: Section 2 discusses some related work; Section 3 presents our problem formulation; Section 4 discusses our proposal for adapting the load to be applied and aspiration levels; Section 5 presents a mathematical model which predicts convergence times for one decision procedure; Section 6 outlines our experimental framework; Section 7 analyzes our experimental results and their implications; in Section 8 we form a conclusion about our results and propose future work.

2 Related Work

2.1 Social Dilemmas

A social dilemma arises when agents have to decide whether or not to contribute towards a public good without the enforcement mechanism of a central authority [7]. Individual agents have to trade off local and global interests while choosing their actions. A selfish individual will prefer not to contribute towards the public good but utilize the benefits once the service is in place. If enough agents choose selfishly, the public good may not survive, causing everyone to suffer. In general, social laws, taxes, etc., are enforced to guarantee the preservation of necessary public goods. In the following, we present two quintessential social dilemmas:

Consider a scenario where a public good is to be initiated. Public goods are benefits produced by the society and available to all of its members regardless of individual contribution. Examples of public goods in human societies include provision of parks, roads, a clean environment, and national defense. Furthermore, any public good needs the contribution of a certain percentage of the populace to be initiated and maintained. Therefore, if enough agents in the populace make the selfish choice, the public good may not be produced. Every agent then faces the dilemma of whether to contribute or to exploit. Let us assume that the public good $\mathcal{G}$ incurs a cost C, and the benefit received by each individual in the populace is B. Let us also assume that in a society of N agents, $P < N$ individuals decide to contribute to the public good. Assuming that the cost is uniformly shared by the contributors, each contributing agent incurs a personal cost of $\frac{C}{P}$. If enough agents contribute, we have $\frac{C}{P} < B$, i.e. even the contributors will benefit from the public good since the cost incurred per individual is less than the benefit received. However, since we do not preclude non-contributors from enjoying the public good in this model, they will benefit more than the contributors. If we introduce a ceiling M on the cost that any individual can bear, then the public good will not be offered if $\frac{C}{P} > M$. In this case, everyone is denied the benefit from the public good.

Similarly, in a resource-sharing problem, the cost of utilizing a resource increases with the number of agents sharing it (for example, congestion on traffic lanes). Assume that initially the agents are randomly assigned to one of two identical resources. Now, if every agent opts for the resource with the least current usage, the overall system cost increases [10]. So, the dilemma for each agent is whether or not to make the greedy choice.

2.2 Tragedy of the Commons

In his book *The Wealth of Nations*, Adam Smith conjectured that an individual is prompted by an "invisible hand" to benefit the group [19] for his own gain. As a rebuttal to this theory, William Forster Lloyd presented the *Tragedy of the Commons* scenario in 1833 [14]. Lloyd's scenario consisted of a pasture shared by a number of herdsmen for grazing cattle. This pasture has a capacity L such that each time a cattle added by a herdsman results in a gain as long as $x \leq L$, where x is the total number of cattle in the pasture. When $x > L$, each addition of a cattle results in a decrease in the quality of grazing for all. Lloyd showed that when the utilization of the pasture gets close to its capacity, overgrazing is guaranteed to doom the pastureland. For each herdsman, the incentive is to add more cattle to his herd as he receives the full proceeds from the sale of additional cattle, but shares the cost of overgrazing with all herdsmen. Whereas the common resource could have been reasonably shared if the herdsmen exhibited restraint, instead, they make greedy, locally optimal choices which quickly lead to overgrazing and destruction of the pasture. The question each herdsman faces is "What is the utility of adding one more animal to my herd?" [9]. Lloyd observes that "Freedom in a commons brings ruin to all," and convincingly argues that enforced laws, and not appeals to conscience, are necessary to avoid the Tragedy of the Commons.

Recent literature about the Tragedy of the Commons is extensive [9]. Diecidue and van de Ven show how aspiration levels are linked to expected utility [5]. Gilboa and Schmeidler extend on this and provide mathematical procedures to adjust aspiration levels based on utility returned [8]. Macy and Flache indicate how agents learn over time in social dilemmas [16]. Researchers have also discussed the existence of the Tragedy of the Commons in computational systems [3,12,21]. Muhsam [15] has shown that if some or all other herdsmen add cattle when $x > L$, a rational, utility-maximizing agent will have no choice but to add to the herd to reduce the loss suffered as a result, while contributing to the overall deterioration of the resource performance. This means that it is only possible to reach a *co-operative equilibrium*. Our contribution is to successfully adapt the aspiration level mechanism to solve the Tragedy of the Commons.

2.3 Computational Approaches

Multiagent systems researchers have addressed the problem of effectively sharing common resources [2] by proposing a planner agent who makes all resource allocation decisions. However, this central planning approach requires nearly perfect global knowledge of all agents and the environment, which is not very reasonable in complex, distributed and dynamic domains. Durfee and Lesser proposed a distributed partial-global planning [4] approach for coherent coordination between distributed problem solvers through the exchange of partial local plans.

Approaches that emphasize economic mechanisms, such as contracting and auctions, allocate resources based on perceived utility [18]. While economic approaches are interesting, we believe that they do not provide a satisfactory resolution to social dilemma problems without an adequate discussion of varying individual wealth and interpersonal utility comparisons. The *COIN* approach to solving social dilemmas allows distributed computation but requires an "omniscient" agent to set up the utility functions to be optimized locally [20]. Glance and Hogg [6] observe that computational social dilemmas can produce situations where globally optimal system configurations are impossible to reach via distributed, rational decision-making with only local knowledge. They contrast such computational problems with traditional complexity analysis in algorithm theory where solutions are hard, but not impossible, to find.

The motivation of our work on computational social dilemmas has been to investigate mechanisms to resolve conflicts while requiring minimal global knowledge and imposing minimal behavioral restrictions on the agents. For example, in [1] it is shown that a genetic algorithm (GA)-based optimization framework can solve a well-known social dilemma problem, the Braess' Paradox [11]. The GA-based function optimization approach is a centralized mechanism. Mundhe *et. al.* used a more decentralized, adaptive systems approach using GAs, to address both the Braess' paradox and the Tragedy of the Commons [17]. Though decision-making is decentralized in this approach, the survival of individuals, as determined by fitness-proportionate selection scheme, is a centralized procedure. Though the latter procedure can be approximated in a decentralized manner, a further criticism of the approach, the somewhat altruistic decision procedure used by the distributed agents, is difficult to address.

3 Problem Formulation

We now formalize the Tragedy of the Commons problem used in our experimentation. For an agent $a \in N$, where N is the set of all agents, we denote U_t^a, h_t^a, and L_t^a as the *utility*, *aspiration level*, and *load*, respectively, at time t. In addition, let $\mathcal{L}_t = \sum_{a \in N} L_t^a$ be the *total load* of the system at time t. Let ϕ be the *threshold load* and $n = |N|$ be the *population size*. The function to calculate an agent a's utility can be expressed as:

$$U_t^a = \begin{cases} L_t^a; \mathcal{L}^t < \phi \\ L_t^a \times \delta e^{-k(\mathcal{L}_t - \phi)}; \mathcal{L}_t > \phi \end{cases}$$

where k is the *environmental factor*, which is an exponential factor determining the rate at which system performance deteriorates after the threshold is crossed.

4 Adjusting Aspiration Levels and Loads

The load applied by an agent on the system depends on their aspirations which are updated based on utilities received from their loads. The initial load used by an agent $a \in N$, L_0^a, is selected from the interval $\left(0, \frac{L_0^{max}}{n}\right)$ and the initial load increment is a constant, δ_0. Agents increase loads by δ_0 as long as utility received is higher than aspiration level. But once utility received does not match aspirations, loads are reduced. In the following, we present two schemes for adjusting aspiration levels and loads and refer to the corresponding agent types as *eager* and *prudent* agents.

4.1 Eager Agents

If $U_t > h_t$, eager agents adjust their aspirations as follows:

$$h_{t+1} = \alpha U_t + (1 - \alpha)U_{t-1},$$

where $\alpha \in (0, 1]$ is the *learning rate*, which is used to weigh the utility immediately received with the previous utility. The initial load applied by an agent is chosen randomly from the range $(0, \frac{L_0^{max}}{n})$. An agent subsequently increases its applied load by a constant δ as long as utility received is higher than its aspiration level. However, once the utility drops below the aspiration level, an agent chooses the next load to be the average of the current load and L_τ, where τ is the last time its aspiration level increased. Therefore,

$$L_{t+1} = \begin{cases} L_t + \delta; U_t > h_t \\ \frac{L_t + L_\tau}{2}; U_t < h_t \end{cases}$$

Each time the agent experiences utility less than aspiration, i.e., when reverting back to a lower load, the agent reduces its load increment by a constant factor of $\rho < 1$.

The algorithm used by eager agents at time step t is:

Data: Aspiration level, load, utility
U_t = getUtility();
if $U_t < h_t$ **then**
  $h_{t+1} = h_t$;
  $L_{t+1} = \frac{L_t + L_\tau}{2}$;
  if $\tau = t - 1$ **then**
    $\delta_{t+1} = \rho\delta_t$;
  end
else
  $h_{t+1} = \alpha U_t + (1 - \alpha)U_{t-1}$;
  $\tau = t$;
  $L_\tau = L_t$;
  $L_{t+1} = L_t + \delta$;
end

4.2 Prudent Agents

If $U_t > h_t$, prudent agents adjust their aspiration level and load as follows:

$$U_t > h_t \Longrightarrow h_{t+1} = \alpha U_t + (1 - \alpha)h_t.$$

$$L_{t+1} = \begin{cases} L_t + \delta; U_t > h_t \\ L_{t-1}; U_t < h_t \end{cases}$$

We see that while setting the aspiration level, the prudent model takes the previous aspiration level into account whereas the eager model simply weights the utility received in the current and immediately previous time steps. When utilities are steadily rising, i.e., $U_t > U_{t-1}$, an eager agent will have a higher aspiration level as aspiration levels typically trail utilities in such scenarios, i.e., $h_t \leq U_{t-1}$.

Furthermore, prudent agents err on the side of caution when utility received is less than the aspiration by immediately reverting to the previous load, which saw a rise in aspiration level. In contrast, eager agents reduce load optimistically and approach that previous level only asymptotically.

We now present the algorithm used by a prudent agent at each time step t:

```
Data: Aspiration level, load, utility
U_t = getUtility();
if U_t < h_t then
  | L_{t+1} = L_{t-1};
  | h_{t+1} = h_t;
  | if τ = t − 1 then
  |   | δ_{t+1} = ρδ_t;
  | end
else
  | h_{t+1} = αU_t + (1 − α)h_t;
  | L_{t+1} = L_t + δ_t;
end
```

5 Convergence Model

We present a mathematical model that determines an upper bound on convergence time.

First we model the initial load on the system, $\mathcal{L}_0$, and the initial total load increment before the threshold is crossed, Δ_0:

$$\forall_{a \in N} L_0^a \in \left(0, \frac{L_0^{max}}{n}\right) \Longrightarrow \mathcal{L}_0 \in (0, L_0^{max}).$$
$$\Delta_0 = n\delta_0.$$

Let t_f be the first time step when the total load crosses the threshold, i.e., t_f is the smallest t for which $\mathcal{L}_t > \phi$. As initial agent loads are uniformly selected from the interval $\left(0, \frac{L_0^{max}}{n}\right)$, the expected initial total load is $\bar{\mathcal{L}_0} = \frac{L_0^{max}}{2}$. Then:

$$\bar{\mathcal{L}_0} + \Delta_0 t_f > \phi \Longrightarrow t_f > \frac{\phi - \bar{\mathcal{L}_0}}{\Delta_0} \Longrightarrow t_f > \frac{2\phi - L_0^{max}}{2\Delta_0}$$

For our model we adopt the strategy of the prudent agent, who adjusts load such that when the threshold is crossed at $t = t_r$, $L_{t_r+1}^a = L_{t_r-1}^a$. In addition, each agent a reduces δ^a by a factor ρ at $t = t_r$. This leads to a reduction of the total load increment Δ in the system. We denote by $\Delta_s = \Delta_0 \rho^s$ the total load increment after the sth such reduction. We define the system to be approximately stable when $\Delta_s < \Delta_{min}$. Therefore:

$$\Delta_0 \rho^s < \Delta_{min} \Longrightarrow s < \log_\rho \frac{\Delta_{min}}{\Delta_0}.$$

Now, after the system threshold is crossed for the first time, all agents reduce load, and, hence, the total load falls back under the threshold. At this time, agents again increase their loads, albeit by a smaller amount, until the threshold is again breached. This cycle repeats[1] but the amount by which the threshold is breached decreases over time as individual load increments and hence the total load increment per time step decreases every time the threshold is crossed. A key observation here is that the number of time steps between successive threshold crossings, t_c, is a constant, $\frac{1}{\rho} + 1$: though the load increments become smaller with each additional threshold crossing, the load difference to be added to cross the threshold, after the agents revert back to their loads prior to the last crossing, is proportionately shorter.

We now derive an upper bound on convergence time t_{conv}:

$$t_{conv} < st_c + t_f \Longrightarrow t_{conv} < \left(\log_\rho \frac{\Delta_{min}}{\Delta_0}\right)\left(\frac{1}{\rho} + 1\right) + \frac{2\phi - L_0^{max}}{2\Delta_0}.$$

For our experiments, we have used the following parameter values: $\delta_0 = \frac{1}{100} \Longrightarrow \Delta_0 = \frac{n}{100}, L_0^{max} = 2, \phi = 7.5, \rho = \frac{1}{2}, \Delta_{min} = \frac{1}{1000}$. This reduces the inequality for the convergence time to:

$$t_{conv} < 3\log_2(10n) + \frac{650}{n} \Longrightarrow t_{conv}^{max} = \lfloor 3\log_2(10n) + \frac{650}{n} \rfloor.$$

where t_{conv}^{max} gives an upper bound on the time required by the system to attain stability. Note that our mathematical model produces this bound based only on the population size n and without considering the environmental factor k.

6 Experimental Framework

We introduce the performance metrics used and the different scenarios we use to evaluate our approach to solving the Tragedy of the Commons.

6.1 Performance Metrics

We have used the following ealuation metrics:

Social Welfare: Social welfare, $\mathcal{U}_t = \sum_{a \in N} U_t^a$, is the total utility received by all agents and captures the overall system performance. This was our primary metric.

Total Load: To evaluate system efficiency, we attempted to minimize $|\mathcal{L}_t - \phi|$. A truly efficient system will have a load close to but below the threshold.

[1] This is only approximately true as it assumes the absence of free riders.

6.2 Base Case Scenario

To help better understand the underlying system dynamics and the working of our approach, we created and experimented with a base case scenario. We chose parameters that would allow us to perform representative experiments while still allowing us to inspect individual behavior and environment modules. For the base case, we choose $\underset{a \in N}{\forall} \alpha = 1, \delta_0^a = 0.01$, and $h_0^a = 0$. In addition, we used $n = 10$ and $k = 3$ as our default system parameters.

6.3 Parameters for Other Scenarios

In addition to the base case, we generated a large variety of environments to evaluate the strengths and weaknesses of our proposed approach. To create these environments, we vary the following parameters over the stated ranges.

Environmental Factor: $k \in \{0.25, 0.5, 1, 3, 5\}$.
Population Size: $n \in \{10, 100, 1000\}$.
Learning Rate: $\alpha \in \{0.5, 0.75, 1\}$.

For statistical verification, we averaged results over 10 independent runs.

6.4 Asynchronous Decisions

With prudent agents, another aspect of the Tragedy of the Commons which we tested was the concept of *asynchronicity*, i.e., not all agents update their load at the same time. We simulate this by assigning each agent a probability $\epsilon \in \{0.1, 0.25, 0.5, 0.75, 0.9, 1\}$ of acting at each time step.

7 Results and Discussion

7.1 Eager Agents

Base Case. As seen in Figure 1, initially agents receive higher utility with increased load, resulting in increased aspirations. With increasingly higher individual loads applied by agents on the system, $\mathcal{L}$ surpasses ϕ between iterations 65 and 70, and the social welfare drops immediately. Correspondingly, individual agent utilities drop below their aspiration levels, and they revert back to applying lower loads. Hence, $\mathcal{L}$ drops under ϕ, then goes back over by a smaller margin between iterations 70 and 85. There are further overshoots and undershoots until the system stabilizes with $\mathcal{L} \approx \mathcal{U} \approx \phi$. Therefore, the social dilemma was successfully solved by adapting aspiration levels in the base case.

Varying Environmental Factor (k). As seen in Figure 2, for $k \neq 0.25$, the system stabilizes at ϕ. However, when $k = 0.25$, some agents acting as *free riders* are able to increase their load and utility while others decrease their load. This is because while others are decreasing their load, a free rider can still receive utility higher than its aspiration level and, hence, increase its load. This process occurs

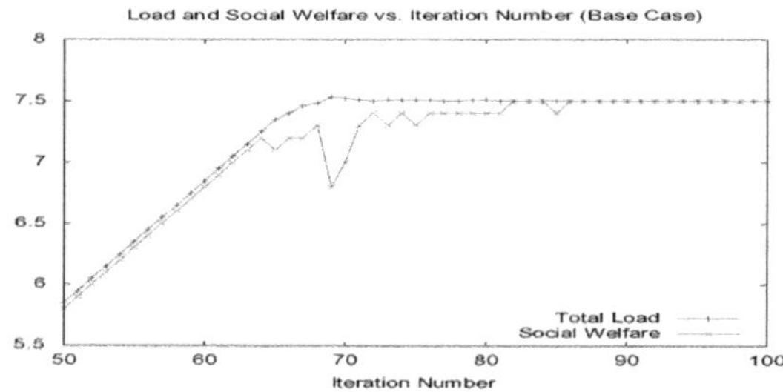

Fig. 1. Total Load and Social Welfare for the base case

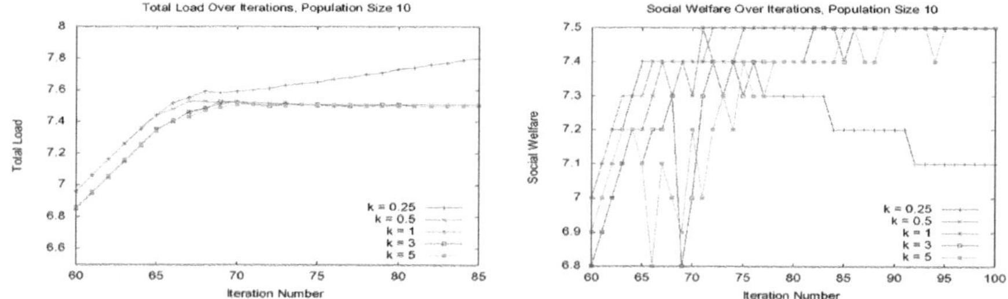

Fig. 2. Total Load (left) and Social Welfare (right) for various k ($n = 10$)

in a cycle, which leads the system to increase its load until the other agents can no longer decrease their load, at which point the free-riding stops and the total load and social welfare plateau at a suboptimal level.

Essentially, for $k = 0.25$, the utility of free riders does not decrease rapidly enough as they apply more load. Hence, such environments sustain a minority of free riders at the expense of the majority. This result is an intriguing outcome of the dynamics of aspiration level adaptation and environmental characteristics that deserve further investigation.

Varying Population Size (n). Figures 3 and 4 show graphs for total load and social welfare for different population sizes with different k values. For $n = 100$, we see a similar converging pattern as for $n = 10$, i.e., for all $k \neq 0.25$, the system stabilizes; else, the presence of free riders at $k = 0.25$ causes the load on the system to increase and the utility to decrease.

When $n = 1000$, however, we do not observe runaway free-riding with social welfare plummeting. Rather, the social welfare of the system stabilizes quickly, albeit suboptimally. This intriguing result can be explained by observing that free-riding can only occur if a small number of agents attempt it. However, in a larger society, there are more free riders, which means that the number of "victimized", non free-riding agents is smaller. Therefore, free-riding can only occur for a short period of time until the system reaches a state where further increase

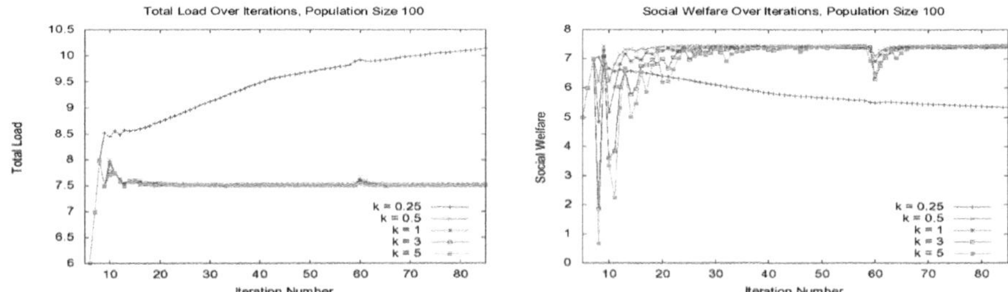

Fig. 3. Total Load (left) and Social Welfare (right) for various k ($n = 100$)

of load is detrimental for all. Hence, though free-riding is not eliminated, its effect is curtailed. This self-stabilizing nature of the system for larger population sizes is a very interesting and unexpected property of the use of aspiration levels. It would be worthwhile to further study this phenomenon to see if the drop in system performance can be minimized while avoiding free-riding.

Additionally, populations with 100 and 1000 agents fare better with $k = 0.25$ than with $k = 0.5, 1$. However, the total load on the system when $k = 0.25$ is actually higher than when $k = 0.5, 1$ (Figure 4). This can be mathematically explained in general. Suppose we have two systems $S_1 = (\mathcal{L}_1, \mathcal{U}_1, k_1)$ and $S_2 = (\mathcal{L}_2, \mathcal{U}_2, k_2)$ such that $\mathcal{L}_2 > \mathcal{L}_1 > \phi$. Then:

$$\mathcal{U}_1 > \mathcal{U}_2 \Longrightarrow \mathcal{L}_1 e^{-k_1(\mathcal{L}_1 - \phi)} < \mathcal{L}_2 e^{-k_2(\mathcal{L}_2 - \phi)}. \Longrightarrow e^{k_2(\mathcal{L}_2 - \phi) - k_1(\mathcal{L}_1 - \phi)} < \frac{\mathcal{L}_2}{\mathcal{L}_1}.$$

$$k_2(\mathcal{L}_2 - \phi) - k_1(\mathcal{L}_1 - \phi) < \ln \frac{\mathcal{L}_2}{\mathcal{L}_1}. \Longrightarrow k_2 < \frac{\ln \frac{\mathcal{L}_2}{\mathcal{L}_1} + k_1(\mathcal{L}_1 - \phi)}{\mathcal{L}_2 - \phi}.$$

Thus, although $\mathcal{L}_2 > \mathcal{L}_1$, $\mathcal{U}_2 > \mathcal{U}_1$ is possible if k_2 is sufficiently small.

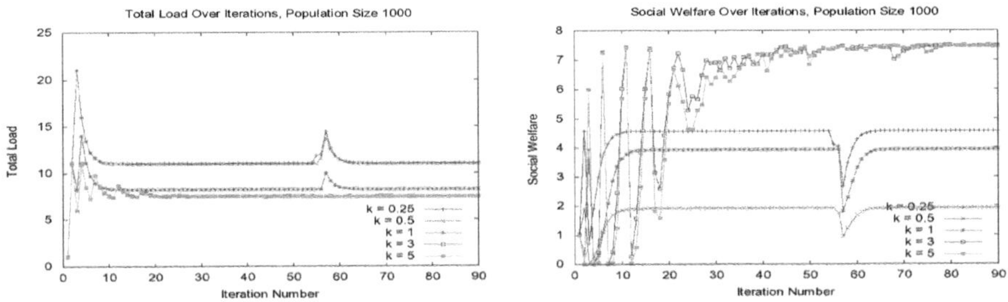

Fig. 4. Total Load (left) and Social Welfare (right) for various k ($n = 1000$)

Varying Learning Rate (α) The graphs in Figure 5 show a substantial difference in the system when α is changed. The system stabilizes optimally when $\alpha = 1$, performs slightly worse when $\alpha = 0.75$, and degrades further when $\alpha = 0.5$. This is because the aspiration level is not being adjusted quickly enough towards the current utility level. This suggests that fast learners will be able to avoid social dilemmas more consistently.

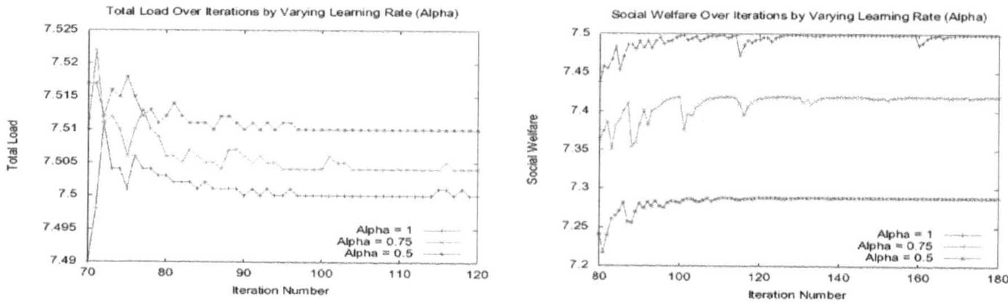

Fig. 5. Total Load (left) and Social Welfare (right) for Various $\alpha, k = 3, n = 10$

7.2 Prudent Agents

As seen in Figure 6, which shows the social welfare for a society of prudent agents for $n = 10, 100, 1000$, the prudent agents' performance is similar to that of the eager agents. However, we notice that a prudent society does perform better in larger populations, where the stabilization is not as suboptimal as in the case of a society of eager agents. In addition, we do not see any attempts of free-riding in large populations for the prudent model, which is another reason to favor the prudent society in terms of performance.

Verification of model predictions. As discussed before we developed a mathematical model to predict convergence times for a society of prudent agents. We now present data to verify those predictions. The predicted convergence times, t_{conv}^{max} was 84, 36, and 40 for $n = 10, 100, 1000$. The corresponding approximate convergence times t_{conv} from experiments were 80, 32, and 35 respectively. Thus, we conclude that our mathematical model was quite successful in predicting convergence times, with $t_{conv}^{max} - t_{conv} < 5$ for all cases.

Asynchronous decisions. We examined how asynchronicity of decisions affected system performance in a prudent society. For $n = 10$, higher asynchronicity, i.e., smaller ϵ, delays convergence without affecting performance at convergence (see Figure 7). Only a fraction of the population, i.e., $m = \epsilon n$ agents, acts each time step in the asynchronous mode. Therefore, if the convergence time for $\epsilon = 1$ is t_1, one would expect that the convergence time for $\epsilon < 1$ would be $t_\epsilon \approx \frac{t_1}{\epsilon}$.

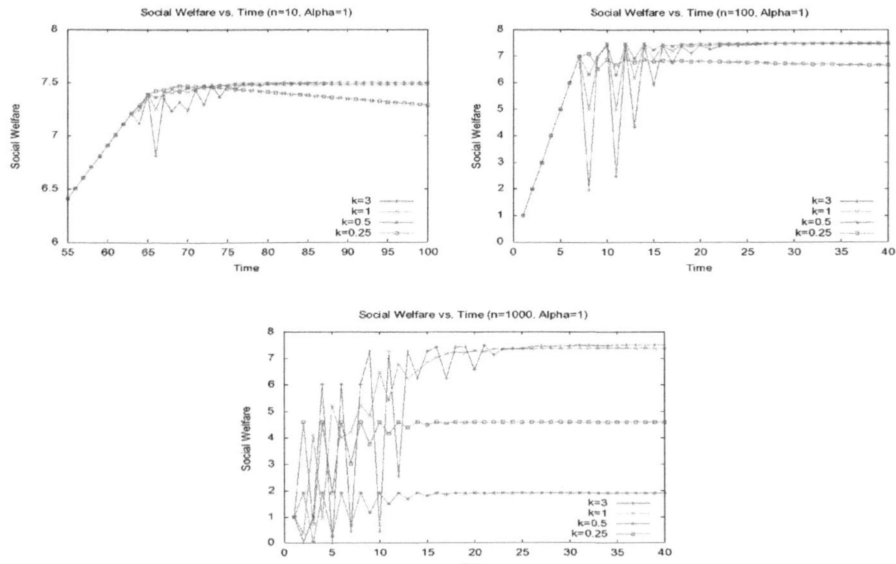

Fig. 6. Social welfare for the prudent model for $n = 10, 100, 1000$ (top left, top right, bottom)

However, we noticed that if we maintain the asynchronicity and environmental factor constant ($k = 3$ and $\epsilon = 0.1$) and increase the population size, system performance became increasingly suboptimal (see Figure 8). This is because asynchornicity acts as an avenue for free-riding in very small increments by a multitude of individuals. We first observe that the probability that the same agent acts for t successive time steps is ϵ^t, which decreases rapidly with t for ϵ values not very close to 1. Thus, at each time step, there is minimal or very low overlap between the subsets of m agents acting in successive generations, i.e., no agent can continually free ride as was the case in the previous examples. Instead, some agents see an opportunity for free-riding whenever they are able to act and hence exploit the system for one time step. This small increment is countered by other agents bringing their loads down as they are suffering. When the free-rider acts again (not necessarily in the near future), it may be the case that the system is performing much more poorly and thus that agent is inclined not to increase its load any further. Hence, over time, continually increasing load will become unattractive since an agent cannot benefit from it for a sustained period of time. Though free-riding stops, the system does not revert back to loads below the threshold. Rather, with more agents, the convergence occurs at higher total loads producing lower agent utilities.

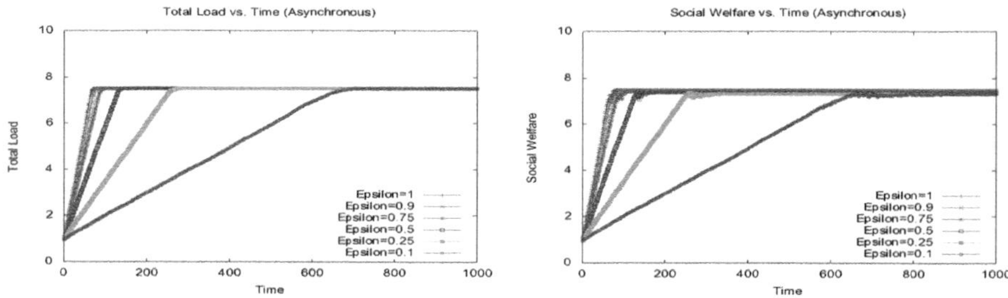

Fig. 7. Total load (left) and social welfare (right) for prudent agents with asynchronicity ($n = 10$)

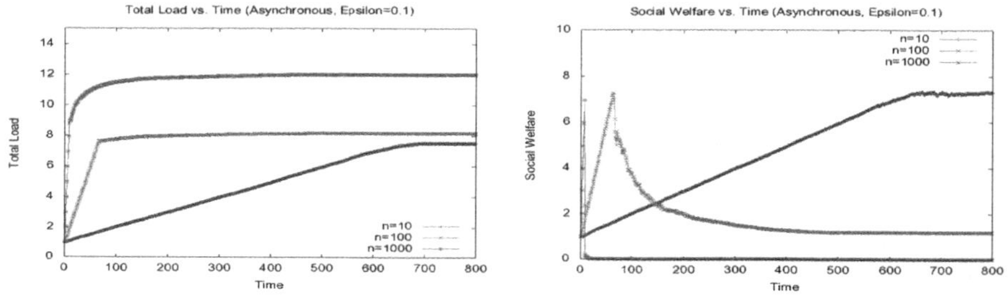

Fig. 8. Population effects on convergence for prudent agents with asynchronicity

8 Conclusions and Future Work

Our research goal is to develop a distributed computational approach to solve the Tragedy of the Commons. We investigate distributed solution for this social dilemma with two types of agents who adapt their aspiration levels based on limited, local information about the system. The aspiration levels were adjusted based on utility returned after applying load on the system. In addition, we developed a mathematical model which successfully predicted convergence times for a society of prudent agents. We systematically varied environmental factors as well as an agent's behavioral parameters to observe and analyze the scope and the effectiveness of our approach. An interesting result was that in benign environments where the system degrades slowly above its threshold load, a minority of free riders was able to benefit at the expense of the community. For large systems with many agents, however, free riders limit each others' exploitation and mitigate the adversarial effect on the system. We also observed that faster learners were more robust in avoiding the social dilemma. In addition, we noted that asynchronicity in the system prolonged convergence in smaller systems while hindering large populations. We plan to run experiments to evaluate our proposed mechanism in the following scenarios:

Dynamically Changing Population: We plan to investigate situations where agents may enter and leave the population, thereby changing the population size.

Irreversible Systems: In the environments we studied, system performance returns to its previous level if the load is reduced after crossing the threshold. We plan to study environments where crossing the threshold causes irreversible damage, i.e., the maximum utility cannot be regained after crossing the threshold.

References

1. Arora, N., Sen, S.: Resolving social dilemmas using genetic algorithms: Initial results. In: Proceedings of the 7th International Conference on Genetic Algorithms, pp. 689–695. Morgan Kaufman, San Mateo (1997)
2. Cammarata, S., McArthur, D., Steeb, R.: Strategies of cooperation in distributed problem solving. In: Proceedings of the Eighth International Joint Conference on Artificial Intelligence, Karlsruhe, Federal Republic of Germany, pp. 767–770 (August 1983)
3. de Cote, E.M., et al.: Learning to cooperate in multi-agent social dilemmas. In: Proceedings of the Fifth International Joint Conference on Autonomous Agents and Multiagent Systems, pp. 783–785 (2006)
4. Durfee, E.H., Lesser, V.R.: Using partial global plans to coordinate distributed problem solvers. In: Proceedings of the Tenth International Joint Conference on Artificial Intelligence, Milan, Italy, pp. 875–883 (August 1987)
5. Diecidue, E., van de Ven, J.: Aspiration Level, Probability of Success and Failure, and Expected Utility. International Economic Review 49(2), 683–700 (2008)
6. Glance, N.S., Hogg, T.: Dilemmas in computational societies. In: First International Conference on Multiagent Systems, pp. 117–124. AAAI Press/MIT Press, Menlo Park, CA (1995)
7. Glance, N.S., Huberman, B.A.: The dynamics of social dilemmas. Scientific American 270(3), 76–81 (1994)
8. Gilboa, I., Schmeidler, D.: Reaction to price changes and aspiration level adjustments. Review of Economic Design 6, 215–223 (2001)
9. Hardin, G.: The tragedy of the commons. Science 162, 1243–1248 (1968)
10. Hogg, T., Huberman, B.A.: Controlling chaos in distributed systems. IEEE Transactions on Systems, Man, and Cybernetics 21(6), 1325–1332 (1991) Special Issue on Distributed AI
11. Irvine, A.D.: How Braess' paradox solves Newcomb's problem. International Studies in the Philosophy of Science 7(2), 141–160 (1993)
12. Ito, A.: How do autonomous agents solve social dilemmas? In: Cavedon, L., Wobcke, W., Rao, A. (eds.) PRICAI-WS 1996. LNCS, vol. 1209, pp. 177–188. Springer, Heidelberg (1997)
13. Kollock, P.: Social Dilemmas: The Anatomy of Cooperation. Annual Review of Sociology 24, 183–214 (1998)
14. Lloyd, W.F.: Two Lectures on the Checks to Population. Oxford University Press, Oxford (1833)
15. Muhsam, H.V.: A world population policy for the World Population Year. Journal of Peace Research 1(2), 97–99 (1973)

16. Macy, M.W., Flache, A.: Learning Dynamics in Social Dilemmas. Proceedings of the National Academy of Sciences of the United States of America, 7229–7236 (May 14, 2002)
17. Mundhe, M., Sen, S.: Evolving agent societies that avoid social dilemmas. In: Proceedings of the Genetic and Evolutionary Computation Conference, GECCO-2000, pp. 809–816 (2000)
18. Sandholm, T.W., Lesser, V.R.: Equilibrium analysis of the possibilities of unenforced exchange in multiagent systems. In: 14th International Joint Conference on Artificial Intelligence, pp. 694–701. Morgan Kaufmann, San Francisco (1995)
19. Smith, A.: The Wealth of Nations, 10th edn. A. Strahan, Printer-stree; for T. Cadell Jun. and W. Davies, in the Strand, Boston, MA (1802)
20. Tumer, K., Wolpert, D.H.: Collective intelligence and Braess' paradox. In: Proceedings of the Seventeenth National Conference on Artificial Intelligence, pp. 104–109. AAAI Press, Menlo Park (2000)
21. Turner, R.M.: The tragedy of the commons and distributed AI systems. In: Working Papers of the 12th International Workshop on Distributed Artificial Intelligence, pp. 379–390 (May 1993)

The Role of Agents in Adaptive Service Oriented Architectures

Fernando Koch, Frank Dignum, Marcel Hiel, and Huib Aldewereld

Department of Information and Computing Sciences
Utrecht University
Utrecht, The Netherland
{fkoch,dignum,hiel,huib}@cs.uu.nl

Abstract. This work analyses the role of agent-based software and organisation theoretical solutions in the development of Adaptive Service Oriented Architectures. This solution aims to support integrated, scalable, and re-usable information delivery systems. This technology is required in applications that operate in complex service delivery environments, such as Electronic Government (eGov) systems, emergency response coordinators, social networks, and mobile services. In these scenarios, the intricacy of service orchestration strategies grows proportionally with the number of operational components, complexity of interactions, and degree of dynamism of the environment. We argue that strategies based on fixed workflows are insufficient to support complex content delivery services. To that end, we propose a solution that encompasses an organisation-based system architecture enacted by agent-based software components. It inherently provides the features of contextualisation, adaptiveness, flexible workflow mechanism, and proactiveness based on desirable characteristics of the agent technology. We introduce a conceptual model, detail the technical proposal, and demonstrate how the solution supports the demands of complex content delivery services.

1 Introduction

Web-Services [3], Service Oriented Architectures [10], and Mashup Environments [13] have the potential to increase significantly the utilisation, compatibility and interoperability of information and communication systems. Research has focused on designing efficient content delivery platforms based on methods of service orchestration. These developments aim to improve the performance of content composition systems in scenarios that involve dynamic environments and complex information gathering. The challenge is to support contextualisation, re-usability, and quality of services in solutions where the designer lacks complete *a priori* knowledge of the service availability and composition.

For example, eGov systems must provide end-user tailored information across diverse societal groups distinguished by location, demographic, cultural background, technology availability, and other cultural factors. Similarly, solutions for emergency coordination support require highly degree of on-line adaptability and

N. Desai, A. Liu, and M. Winikoff (Eds.): PRIMA 2010, LNAI 7057, pp. 371–386, 2012.

promote local control in order to cope with the often chaotic and unpredictable environmental behaviour. Both these solutions must integrate information from multiple sources, be robust, scalable, flexible, and deliver quality information. This scenario imposes three major challenges:

1. *the balance between adaptation and robustness*, i.e. the system must be able to adapt its internal functioning on-line in order to cope with the dynamic environment.
2. *the balance between reactive and proactive behaviour*, i.e. the system must be able to respond to both complete as well as acting upon incomplete conditions in order to improve quality of service.
3. *the balance between component autonomy and controllability*, i.e. the solution must provide the means to guarantee the performance, controllability and predictability of the system while promoting a component autonomy and local adaptation.

Given these challenges, we propose an agent organisation based solution for an Adaptive Service Oriented Architecture. This proposal extends the work in [6]. It uses a type of service orchestration based on organisation models regulating the behaviour of autonomous components (agents). Software agent components provide innate support to adaptiveness, autonomy, situatedness, proactiveness, and knowledge representation, addressing the issues of (1) adaptation and (2) balance between reactiveness and proactiveness. Additionally, the organisation model directs their behaviours promoting (3) the balance between component autonomy and controllability. The integration of these technologies along with practical solutions from Web Services and Mashup Environments leads to an extended model of information delivery.

We leverage from previous work that promoted the integration of agent technology and service composition. For instance, [5] considers the several levels of interaction between agents and web-services arguing for conceptual distinction between the two classes of components and proposing a model of integration. This work emphasises the desirable characteristics of agent technology, namely: autonomy, sociability, knowledge representation, and adaptiveness. We extend these models by incorporating higher-level coordination strategies in form of organisational structures, where one can think in terms of why, what, and how the system must behave. In this environment, system administrators define decision-making actions for workflow components and service providers. This feature addresses the main concerns related to the use of autonomous components: controllability, robustness, and quality assurance.

This development is part of a larger research programme covered in the ALIVE project[1] [2,12], which combines existing work in coordination and organisational models with the state-of-the-art in service-oriented computing. The definitions inherited from ALIVE provide the framework of the proposed model.

This work is structured as follows. Section 2 introduces a motivating scenario. Section 3 details the role of intelligent agents and organisation model technologies

[1] ALIVE Project: http://www.ist-alive.eu/

in supporting this development. Section 4 outlines the system design for the use case. We give some conclusions in Section 5.

2 Motivation

In this section, we motivate our research by describing a use case in e-government and highlighting the role of agent-based solutions in combination with services.

Figure 1 depicts a complex service delivery scenario. It involves a combination of (1) *Service Providers* that vary in terms of format, stability, and availability, and; (2) *User Environment*, that varies in terms of context, profile, and access technology, between others. The role of the (3) *Content Provisioning Service*, which implements the *workflow engine* that conciliates the variations and provide stable services and coherent results.

For example, let us consider the case of an eGov system. This service aims to improve information delivery on government initiatives and community issues, and to provide better community engagement.

In this context, let us consider two variants of end-users in this context: *User 1*, 55-years old dairy farming business man living in the rural area, and; *User 2*, 30-years old entrepreneur living in the inner-city. Intuitively, the information needs for both users accessing intuitively differ. *User 1* will be looking for regional weather information, development of the dairy industry market, and governmental incentives for that industry. *User 2* will be looking for weather information for leisure purposes, and governmental incentives for the ICT industry. So, although both users want weather info, the type of info they need might differ and thus the service they would need also might be different. Nonetheless,

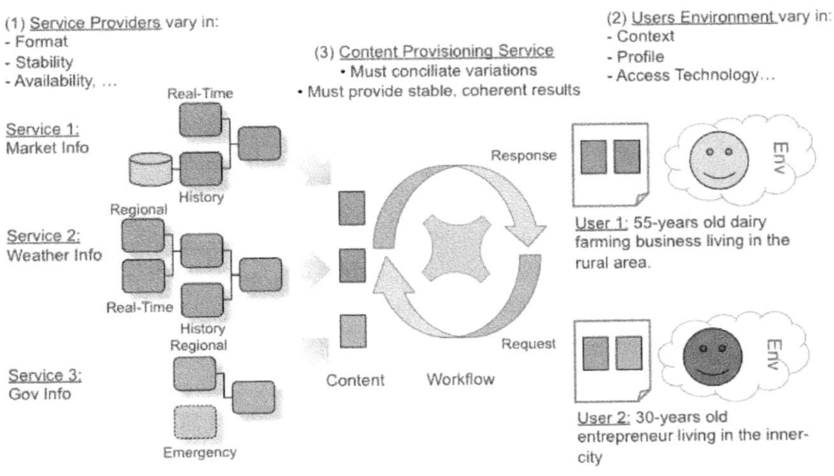

Fig. 1. Complex Service Delivery Scenario

if the system implements a normal Web-service solution, then it will provide the same content to both users. This situation happens because this solution does not take into account extensive contextual information while selecting the content to deliver.

Moreover, the information needs during state-wide emergency situation are also widely different. For example, depending on the location, there is a need to deliver tailored emergency response coordination information to *User 1*, whilst *User 2* is interested in generic news on the event. Also on the supply side things change. In this exceptional circumstances several regional government bodies will be delivering emergency coordination information, while standard services might fail or not suffice for the kind of information that is needed in this circumstances and replacements have to be used. The (3) *Content Provisioning Service* must consider these new content provisioning facilities and select the relevant ones depending on the environment, end-user's profile, and location. Because the inherent chaotic nature of the scenario, it is not possible to consider the combinations of environment and services availability beforehand.

A solution based on run-time adaptation in SOA has been proposed in [7]. This environment can adapt the composition rules in response to variations of external information – i.e. change of context, such as location, end-user profile, etc. What is not provided is a run-time selection and composition of services that are available and can be selected based on the current situation and the *purpose* of the service.

Therefore, both rigid workflow mechanisms implemented in Web-services and inflexible mechanisms implemented in SOAs fail to adapt to the evolving situation. They require continuous reconfiguration of the content provisioning component, context evaluation rules, and (most likely) the workflow rules by system administrators (usually off-line). We propose a solution where adaptation happens on-line , emerging from component level, providing an answer to this problem scenario.

2.1 Problem Analysis

The scenario described above is prototypical for situations occurring in social networks, mobile content provisioning, and emergency response coordination. Their defining characteristics are: evolving environments; modifying elements, and; evolving organisation relationships and regulations, which is the requirement to deliver contextualised, relevant information, any time, any where, minding the end-users' profiles. We distill the following *requirements* based on these characteristics:

- (a) *Contextualisation* is indispensable to support the requirement for information quality and to provide solutions for a changing environment. For example, an eGov portal must provide information most suitable to the target audience, contextualised to different locations and demographic groups. Similarly, emergence response systems must consider the current situation and target work group when delivering personal assistance information.

- (b) *Adaptiveness* is required to provide solutions for changing environments, modifying elements, and heterogeneity. It supports both the requirements for quality of information and the way in which information is presented. For example, service composition must adapt in response to variations of content provisioning facilities, like new governing bodies adding or removing services and changing of services' operation parameters. Likewise, the system must adjust the provisioning rules depending on the evolution of societal relations, as changes of circumstances impact end-user expectations.
- (c) *Knowledge accessibility* implies methods of dynamic content provisioning and composition. This is required to support quantity of information and better ways to provide content. It addresses the challenges of evolving societal relationships and technology heterogeneity. For example, methods to support the on-line inclusion of governing bodies as content providers into the system.
- (d) *Technology heterogeneity* impacts the ways in which information is provided. For example, eGov Systems that operate in developing countries where the penetration of mobile devices supersedes other forms of Internet access must consider ways to provide eGov information through this technology. Moreover, issues of human-computer-interfacing (e.g. user familiarity, pervasiveness, easy to use, etc.) and software engineering (e.g. re-usability, development costs, operation costs, etc.) must not be overlooked.

These requirements seem to point in the direction of agent-based solutions that are capable of creating flexible workflows that can adapt to the current situations. In the next section we sketch some of these elements as used in the ALIVE project.

2.2 Solution Analysis

We propose an agent-based approach using Organisational models. We use the definitions of the ALIVE project. The project extends current trends in service-oriented engineering by adding three extra layers [1]:

- The *Organisation Layer* provides context for the other levels, specifying the organisational roles, objectives and rules that govern interaction and using developments in organisation dynamics to allow structural adaptation of distributed systems over time.
- The *Coordination layer* provides the means to specify, at a high level, the patterns of interactions between services, using a variety of coordination techniques. At this level the agent technology is used.
- The *Service layer* augments the existing service models with semantic descriptions to make components aware of their social context and rules of engagement with other services.

Figure 2 depicts the information provision part of the proposed eGov service in terms of organisation theoretical elements, simplified for the sake of this analysis.

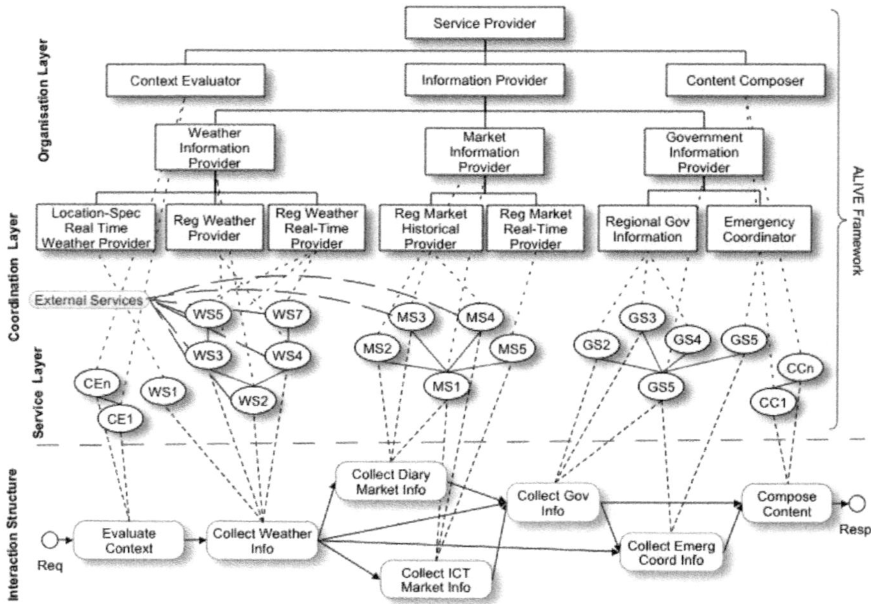

Fig. 2. Service Organisation Structure

The *Organisation Layer* describes the roles. We focus on the description of the *Information Provider* in this section (the description of the *Context Evaluator* and *Content Composer* roles will be detailed in Section 4). Let us consider three classes of *Information Providers*:

- *Weather Information Provider* summarises weather information from more detailed services, namely: *Regional Historical Weather Provider*, which provides historic regional weather information and trends, and; *Regional Real-Time Weather Providers*, which provides information being collected from weather stations in real-time.
- *Market Information Provider* summarises market information in specific niches, such as dairy industry, ICT, etc, collected from services that provide data on specific activities. For example, information on consulting and professional services activities in the ICT market, and farming and veterinarian information in the dairy industry.
- *Government Information Provider* summarises the information that governing bodies want to publicise. Information is collected from two more detailed classes of services, namely: *Regional Government Information*, which provides regional government information and; *Emergency Coordinator*, which provides coordination information on state-wide emergency situations.

The components of the *Services Layer* can consist of more detailed services, which is not represented in the figure for the sake of conciseness. In this view, service components are used by agents that manage the communication to external information providers, like web-services, RSS feeds, and other communication technologies. This way we promote the integration of diverse information sources and create a "common interface" (proxying) to external information access using agent technology. Moreover, we consider that services can be entering and leaving the system on-line, such as *emergency coordination* services entering the system when a state-wide crises erupt. The agents use their goals to determine which alternative services and service compositions are acceptable with respect to the goals they try to achieve. Figure 2 depicts WS services that enact the weather provider roles; MS services that enact the market information roles, and; GS_i services that enact the government information roles. Moreover, there are the CE services for context evaluation and CC services for content composition. The *Coordination Layer* with the agents themselves is implicit in this representation for the sake of conciseness.

Finally, the workflow mechanism that is enacted by the agents interacts with multiple services to coordinate content gathering. Its behaviour is described by the scenes in the *Interaction Structure*, represented in Figure 2. These scenes "play" the scenario and are depicted below the other levels in the figure for conciseness and explanation purposes. They are, however, specified in the organisation level.

Because of the dynamic nature of the environment – i.e. changing situation, modifying services, variations in availability, etc – it is not possible to define the workflow rules *a priori*. In this context, *situatedness* is characterised by the workflow actors' ability to reason autonomously respecting local representation of the environment and varying service availability. *Adaptiveness* is characterised by the actors' ability to reconsider ongoing workflow plans and adjust the interaction patterns in response to changes in service availability. For example, during the interaction step *Collect Weather Information* the workflow actor may find that the real-time regional weather providers are unavailable. This generates an execution exception that must be treated with plan reconsideration.

There are three key issues that are solved by using agent (organization)-based solutions in this system:

1. *The balance between adaptation and robustness*, i.e. the system must be able to adapt its internal functioning on-line in order to cope with dynamic environments. That is, solutions based on *a priori* descriptions are inclined to produce undesirable results as the environment evolves in the short- and long-term. It encompasses issues of monitoring, coordination, learning, and structural adjustment.
   In the illustrative example, the workflow actors must be able to adapt their behaviour in reaction to varying service availability and changing circumstances. This can be achieved by both dynamic variation of workflow rules and extended evaluation of the contextual information (implemented by the *Evaluate Context* service). However, the actors must avoid to compromise the overall system's performance by respecting the system's objectives and constraints. For example, they must refrain from collecting and/or providing

out-of-context information, and; misbehaving such as waiting too long for a specific processing.

2. *The balance between reactive and proactive behaviour*, i.e. the system must be able to respond to both complete as well as acting upon incomplete conditions in order to improve quality of service. If the system is "too reactive", acting on complete conditions and in response to external actions, it implies shorter response intervals, which means that it must compromise on quality eventually. However, if the system is "too proactive", acting with incomplete information, it implies waste of resources utilisation when, e.g. pro-actively computed information is not used.
   In the example, the high-level information providers (i.e. *Weather Information Provider*, *Market Information provider*, and *Government Information Providers*) can pro-actively contact the regional counter-parts to collect and cache relevant information, aiming at improving performance and stability. Moreover, the system can implement notification actors that continuously evaluate the environment and issue notification to selected end-users based on determined rules. In both cases, it is expected that the majority of the time the processed information will not be used by consumer actors, representing wasted resource utilisation.
3. *The balance between component autonomy and controllability*, i.e. a solution that implements components able to reason autonomously, as proposed above, must consider the issue of controllability and performance. Whilst autonomy is a desirable feature to support both novel and exceptional situations, it can yield unpredictable results if carelessly defined. That is, the ability of adapting the workflow rules on-the-fly to cope with variations in service availability can compromise the quality of information being provided.
   For example, in the normal scenario it is acceptable that if the *Collect Weather Information* actor cannot establish a connection to the *Regional Real-Time Weather Provider*, then it can rely on information from the *Regional Historical Market Information* to provide trend information. However, for users located in the affected areas, the weather information must be more precise and the actor must insist in providing real-time information as trend analysis of historic information are irrelevant in this context.

Motivated by this scenario, we propose a model of service composition based on adaptive components (agents) regulated by a central structure (organisation model). In the scope of this paper, we focus on describing the role of intelligent agents in this environment. At the same time, we acknowledge the crucial importance of the regulating structure in controlling their behaviour.

3 The Role of Agents

The role of agent-based software solutions is to support the desirable features of components' autonomy, adaptivity, and proactiveness. Thus, it counter-balances

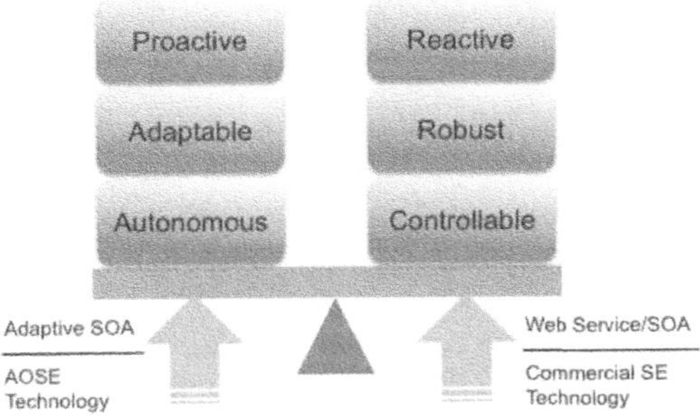

Fig. 3. The Role of Agents

(and complements) the support provided by other commercial software engineering technologies (*e.g.* Object-oriented methodologies) that focus on controllability, robustness, and reactiveness. The combination of different software development techniques has the potential to answer the aforementioned "balance issues".

In practical terms, agent solutions combined to organisation structures facilitate the implementation of purpose-oriented workflow mechanisms. The organisation model defines the purpose of the content composition – e.g. metrics for quality of information, interaction patterns, acceptable processing time, etc. The workflow actors inherit the goals and plan rules to implement these characteristics from the organisation structure. This way, the system administrators can define the purpose and methods of operation at a high-level and the agent structures enforce the operation in order to fulfil the specifications. Moreover, it facilitates the implementation of the following techniques in order to support the requirements mentioned above:

- *Flexible workflow* supporting adaptation at the service orchestration level to cope with changes of the environment. This technique can be implemented by autonomous modules that adapt their operation aiming to improve the overall system's performance. This supports (a) contextualisation, (b) adaptiveness, and (at a certain extend) (d) technology heterogeneity.
- *Advanced Context Evaluation* allowing assessment of the situation and augmenting contextual information based on a holistic view of internal and external conditions and data sources. It must also support adaptation of the evaluation rules in order to cope with evolving environments aiming at coherence and quality of service. This feature enhances (a) contextualisation and (at a certain extend) supports (b) adaptiveness and (c) knowledge accessibility.
- *Adaptable Service Provisioning* promoting integration of information from multiple sources that can be entering and leaving the system on-line. The ar-

chitecture must provide both the interface to interact with these components and an adaptable coordination strategy that considers the new configuration on-line. This feature supports (b) adaptiveness, (c) knowledge accessibility, and (d) technology heterogeneity.
- *Advanced Content Composition* in order to provide the methods for composing content that best suit the target audience and artefacts' availability. This feature supports the requirement for (c) knowledge accessibility and (d) technology heterogeneity and it is essential in promoting the ways in which information is presented and made available.
- *Proactiveness* is the ability to prescribe solutions that deal with foreseeable or unfolding situations, increasing the overall effectiveness of content delivery strategies. Proactive solutions can work on behalf of the user without requiring a direct command to execute an action. This feature aims to improve system's performance by supporting quantity and quality of information.

Research in agent based technology provides the following desirable features to support this development:

- *Advanced structures for knowledge representation* provide an answer to representing the situation, which is essential for contextualisation and knowledge accessibility. Research in agent technologies has produced a variety of methods for explicit representation of the environment, and for reasoning about this environment to produce decisions. It supports flexible workflow structure and advanced context evaluation mechanisms.
- *Responsiveness and adaptivity* are inherent features of agent components, which are designed to adapt to constantly changing execution environment, as pointed out by [8]. Agent technologies provide solutions for adaptation of the deliberation process in several levels, as described in [9]. This feature support the development of flexible workflows and enhanced context evaluators.
- *Locality of interaction* is a feature of agent technology where the components are designed to interact and cooperate. Research provides diverse mechanisms for information exchange, coordination, collaboration, and negotiation. Such mechanisms offer great potential to address the local interaction requirement in complex service composition as well as knowledge accessibility by end-users.
- *Autonomy and Proactiveness* are inherent features in agent technology, where implementations vary from reactive architectures (based on pre-determined rules) to mechanisms for proactive behaviour [4]. These features contribute to support the requirements across the board, mainly to adaptiveness and proactiveness.

Belief-Desire-Intention (BDI) agent models [11] provide desirable features in supporting situatedness and adaptive processing. Agents can dynamically adapt workflow rules based on the representation of the conditions (beliefs) and planning strategies. Moreover, this technology inherently provides plan reconsideration strategies, required to support exceptional situations. For example, the workflow threads are dynamically adjusted to consider change of resources when new service providers are added to the system. This condition is represented in the agent's belief base and considered during the plan formation process. Similarly, the agent's belief base represents the external environment. If the conditions change during the processing, then the deliberation process triggers plan reconsideration rules to automatically review the composed choreography. These features address the issues *component autonomy* and *adaptation to evolving environment*.

In addition, BDI-based agents provide a sound solution to compose personal assistants. These are applications that take actions proactively on behalf of the user. Instead of user-initiated interaction via commands and/or direct manipulation, the user is engaged in a cooperative process in which human and computer agents both initiate communication, monitor events and perform tasks. It can be applied to monitor events and procedures, help different users collaborate, and support user interactions, providing support to proactive behaviour.

Finally, organisation-based approaches addresses the requirement for overall system control [1]. The organisation-based framework applies *substantive norms* that define commitments agreed upon agents and are expected to be enforced by authoritative components, imposing repair actions and sanctions if invalid states are reached. Using this technology, system architects can define service-oriented solutions based on the definition of organisational structures and how their components should interact. That is, they can think in terms of why, what, and how when defining the actions of workflow components and service providers.

Next, we introduce the system design, demonstrating the elements and interactions.

4 Design and Implementation

Figure 4 depicts the system design for the organisation-based solution outlined in Section 2.2. The figure highlights the fact that although we use agent organisations for the conceptual design of the system, the actual software consists for a large part of (existing) services. For the sake of modularity, we divide the services in three groups, aligned to the required techniques introduced in the previous section: *Context Evaluation Services* (CE_SRV); *Content Provisioning Services* (CP_SRV) and *Content Composition Services* (CC_SRV). The agents are constituting the *Workflow Engine* (WF). *User Representation Services* (USR) support service pro-activeness by supplying user profile data.

The *System Organisation Model* SYS_MD and workflow rules WF_RL define the roles, norms, planning rules, and interaction patterns of the components, related to the definitions of the *Organisation layer*. The system works by transforming the incoming request and context information (step (1)) into responses containing the augmented context information and composed content (step (5)). The *Workflow Engine* coordinates the processing through the several service groups. The system encompasses two kinds of interactions: (i) *reactive requests*, in response to actions from end-users through the protocol interface (e.g. re-

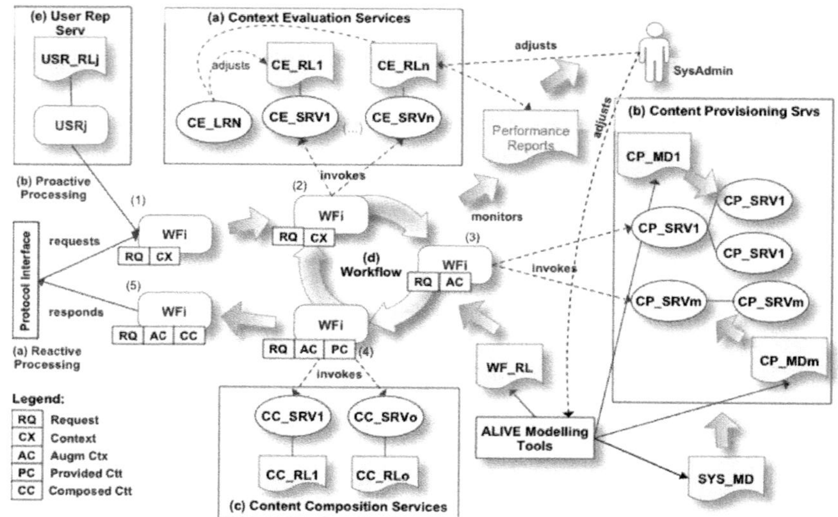

Fig. 4. System Design

quests from a web-browser), and; (ii) *proactive requests*, in response to actions from the *User Representation* agents.

The (a) *Context Evaluation Services* CE_SRV facilitates the analysis of the contextual information CX supplied along the request RQ. They serve the *Context Evaluator* role represented in Figure 2. The agents invoke a sub-set of the CE_SRV based on the processing rules and interaction patterns. This module also includes a *Context Learner Service* (CE_LRN) that supports learning of the best information to provide based on feedback from end-users interactions.

The (b) *Content Provisioning Services* CP_SRV integrate information from multiple sources (the *Information Providers* depicted in Figure 2). The services are invoked by the agents but always considering norms and interaction patterns defined by the *System Organisation Model* SYS_MD. Multiple content provisioning services will compete to provide content and the agents have plans for selecting the provider(s).

The (c) *Content Composition Services* CC_SRV implement the *Content Composer* role depicted in Figure 2.

The (d) *Workflow Mechanism* is implemented by the agents which enact the interaction structure depicted in Figure 2. The interaction rules are determined by the *System Organisation Model* SYS_MD. The agents thus inherit their "operation purpose" from the organisation structure. That is, the organisational model defines the purpose of the information provision, which is reflected in the agents rules of operations, i.e. belief representation, plan rules, and reconsideration strategies. This way, the system administrators can define the purpose and methods of operation at a high-level.

We introduce the concept of (e) *User Representation Services* (USR) to promote proactive content delivery. This facility represents individual and collective end-user information desires within the system. They are aligned to the idea of personal assistants that take actions on behalf of the user proactively. The *User Representation Rules* USR_RL are BDI-based agent abstractions that represent end-users' beliefs, desires, and plans.

Finally, the system produces *Performance Reports* summarising the system performance. This information can be used by system administrators and/or other regulating structures to adjust the operational parameters (e.g. SYS_MD and WF_RL). This feature supports the requirements for responsiveness, adaptiveness, and learning.

4.1 Use Case

Let us see how the proposed solution enacts the eGov scenario described in Section 2. We recall that in this scenario there are two different end-users (i.e. *User 1*, 55-years old dairy farming business man living in the rural area and accessing through a desktop-based web-browser, and; *User 2*, 30-years old entrepreneur living in the inner-city and accessing through an iPhone device) interacting with the system in two situations: normal conditions and during a state-wide crisis. Let us consider that in both cases, both users issue the same request for information RQ to the eGov System's (i.e. request for the web-site's root address). Moreover, let us say that the context information CTX contains information about the device profile, subscriber identification, and access location.

Initially, the agent in the MAS enacting the context evaluator role invokes context evaluation services CE_SRV to augment the information, such as extending the user's profile with information from a database; translating absolute location information with situational information in that location, and; consulting artefact's capabilities from a database. Next, the agent fulfilling the information provider role will coordinate with the set of content service providers CP_SRV that are meaningful in this context.

For example, in normal conditions, *User 1* is interested in dairy industry information. After evaluating the context, the agent communicates with weather providing agents that collect real-time regional weather information that might be useful for farming and, in parallel, coordinate with the dairy market information providers to collect relevant information. This information can be combined with other relevant information to form the final content. During this processing, it is possible that certain services are unavailable or become conflicting. The agents adjust the internal processing rules in response to these exceptional conditions. Accesses by *User 2* trigger a similar processing line, but in this context the agents collect higher-level (informative) weather information, news from the ICT industry market with specific information on his areas of interest, like support to Consulting and Professional Services. The information can be augmented by relevant government information.

Now, let us consider the scenario of a state-wide emergency situation. In this exceptional scenario, several government bodies will be entering the system to provide emergency coordination information as part of the *Government Information Provider* roles. The agent enacting the information provider must consider this new content provisioning services and select the relevant ones depending on end-user's profile and location. Because the inherent chaotic nature of the scenario, it is not possible to consider the combinations of environment and services availability *a priori*. In this case, the facilities to augment the context information and dynamic planning supports quick reaction to the changing circumstances. For example, *User 1* will receive emergency coordination information tailored to his location and current situations (e.g. the need to evacuate the region), whilst accesses by *User 2* will be responded (in lower priority) with informative news.

Finally, the system can implement *User Representation Agents* USR to enact end-user's interests, such as an agent that notifies the users' groups on relevant information of their industries. In addition, emergency coordination personal assistants can support decision making by notifying users on potentially hazardous situations in the surrounding area and coordinate the information flow.

We conclude that the proposed technology provides a sound solution by delivering flexible workflow mechanisms, advanced context evaluation, and proactive behaviour. Overall, it provides a better solution for scenarios that require contextualisation, adaptiveness, knowledge accessibility, and technology heterogeneity.

5 Conclusion

The objective of this work was to outline an extended computational model to support the development of Adaptive Service Oriented Architectures. We demonstrated that the combination of intelligent software agents and regulating organisation models provides a solution to the problem of highly adaptive content provisioning systems.

We conclude that the proposed solution addresses the three requirement drivers in this problem scenarios as follows.

- *(i) the requirement for adaptation*: software agents dynamically adapt the workflow plans based on the representation of the conditions and planning rules. In addition, rules for plan reconsideration support handling of exceptional situations, complement the process. This feature provides innate support to local control and responsiveness, allowing the implementation of advanced contextualisation techniques and flexible workflows.
- *(ii) the balance between reactive and proactive behaviour*: software agents provide a solution to deliver personal assistants. This solution can be applied to monitor events and procedures, help different users collaborate, and support user interactions, providing inherent support to end-user oriented proactive behaviour.
- *(iii) the balance between component autonomy and quality assurance*: approaches for organisation-based agent framework provide solutions for overall system control. Agents provide a sound solution for promoting the balance between component autonomy and stability, providing controllability and performance management.

We conclude that the proposed technology complements Web-Service and SOA solutions by extending their capabilities with flexible mechanisms, advanced context evaluation, and proactive behaviour. These features allow these systems to better operate in scenarios that require contextualisation, adaptiveness, knowledge accessibility, and technology heterogeneity, as demonstrated in Section 4.1

We envision this technology being applied to a new generation of user-centric information systems. The problem classification presented in this work will help future research in the area by enabling the identification of opportunities and novel uses of the proposed technology.

References

1. Aldewereld, H., Penserini, L., Dignum, F., Dignum, V.: Regulating Organizations: The ALIVE Approach. In: Proceedings of the International Workshop on Regulations Modelling and Deployment (ReMoD 2008/CAiSE 2008), pp. 37–48 (2008)
2. Alvarez-Napagao, S., Cliffe, O., Vázquez-Salceda, J., Padget, J.: Norms, organisations and semantic web services: The alive approach. In: Workshop on Coordination, Organization, Institutions and Norms at MALLOW 2009 (2009)
3. Booth, D., Haas, H., McCabe, F., Newcomer, E., Champion, M., Ferris, C., Orchad, D.: Web Services Architecture. W3C Working Group Note 11, The World Wide Web Consortium (W3C) (February 2004)
4. Dastani, M., Dignum, F., Meyer, J.-J.: Autonomy and Agent Deliberation. In: Rovatsos, M., Nickles, M. (eds.) Proceedings of the First International Workshop on Computatinal Autonomy - Potential, Risks, Solutions (Autonomous 2003), Melbourne, Australia, pp. 23–35 (July 2003)
5. Dickinson, I., Wooldridge, M.: Agents are not (just) Web Services: Considering BDI Agents and Web Services. In: Proceedings of the Workshop on Service-Oriented Computing and Agent-Based Engineering, SOCABE 2005 (2005)
6. Hiel, M.: An Adaptive Service-Oriented Architecture - Automatically Solving Interoperability Problems. PhD thesis, Tilburg University (2010)
7. Irmert, F., Fischer, T., Mayer-Wegener, K.: Runtime adaptation in a service-oriented component model. In: Proceedings of the 2008 International Workshop on Software Engineering for Adaptive and Self-Managing Systems, pp. 94–104. ACM, New York (2008)
8. Jennings, N.R.: Agent-Oriented Software Engineering. In: Garijo, F.J., Boman, M. (eds.) MAAMAW 1999. LNCS, vol. 1647, pp. 1–7. Springer, Heidelberg (1999)
9. Koch, F., Dignum, F.: Enhanced deliberation behaviour for BDI-Agents in mobile services. In: Proceedings of the 8th International Conference on Practical Applications of Agents and Multi-Agent Systems (PAAMS 2010), Salamanca (May 2010)
10. Papazoglou, M.P., Heuvel, W.-J.: Service oriented architectures: approaches, technologies and research issues. The VLDB Journal 16(3), 389–415 (2007)

11. Rao, A.S., Georgeff, M.P.: BDI-Agents: from theory to practice. In: Proceedings of the First International Conference on Multiagent Systems, San Francisco, USA (1995)
12. Vazquez-Salceda, J., Dignum, F., Vasconcelos, W., Padget, J., Clarke, S., Ceccaroni, L., Nieuwenhuis, K., Sergean, P.: ALIVE: Combining Organizational and Coordination Theory with Model Driven Approaches to develop Dynamic, Flexible Distributed Business Systems. In: Proceedings of the First International ICST Conference on Digital Business (2009)
13. Zhao, Q., Huang, G., Huang, J., Liu, X., Mei, H.: A web-based mashup environment for on-the-fly service composition. In: Proceedings of the 2008 IEEE International Symposium on Service-Oriented System Engineering, pp. 32–37. IEEE Computer Society, Washington, DC (2008)

Agent-Based Development for Business Processes

Hoa Khanh Dam and Aditya Ghose

School of Computer Science and Software Engineering
University of Wollongong
Northfields Av, Wollongong, NSW 2522, Australia
hoa@uow.edu.au, aditya@uow.edu.au

Abstract. Due to the ever-changing business environment, the supporting IT-systems that execute business processes within organisations must be increasingly flexible and adaptable if those organisations are to remain competitive in today's environment. On the other hand, despite offering promising solutions to autonomy, flexibility and adaptability, intelligent agent technology still faces many challenges in being adopted by the industry. Due to their distinct properties, agent-based systems provide a powerful platform for business process execution. Our work focuses in this area with the aim to bridge the gap between business process modelling and agent-oriented development, and consequently contributes to bring benefits to both communities. More specifically, we propose a method for a seamless transition from business process models in Business Process Modelling Notation (BPMN) to agent-oriented models in the Prometheus methodology.

1 Introduction

Business process management (BPM) refers to all activities that support the design, modelling, execution, monitoring and optimisation of business processes. In recent years, the ever-changing business environment demands constant and rapid evolution of an organisation. The flexibility in process execution through IT-systems has significant impact on the success of an organisation's business operations. Existing BPM systems, which require a priori representation of a business process and all potential deviations from that process, however, do not provide adequate support to achieve these requirements in a satisfactory way [1]. On the other hand, despite its popularity and attractiveness as a research area, agent technology still faces many challenges in being adopted by the industry [3]. Multi-agent systems (MAS) provide powerful and flexible execution platform for business processes. Therefore, closing the gap between the business community, BPM in particular, and agent technology can bring substantial benefits to both sides: agents gaining better industry traction whilst BPM having a powerful solution to deal with its current challenges.

In this paper we will propose a mapping between business process models specified in BPMN to concepts and artefacts of the Prometheus agent-oriented

N. Desai, A. Liu, and M. Winikoff (Eds.): PRIMA 2010, LNAI 7057, pp. 387–393, 2012.

methodology [2]. We have chosen BPMN since it is a standard for business process modelling and has been widely used and supported in numerous modelling tools. Figure 1 shows a BPMN diagram describing a typical process of a conference management system (CMS). This translation is a starting point towards the development of an agent system based on business processes and the use of new, alternative, behaviours discovered from such an agent-based system to enrich the original business processes.

2 BPMN to Prometheus Mapping

We now propose how details contained in BPMN models can be directly translated to Prometheus concepts and/or be used to help develop Prometheus artefacts.

Non-system Pool to Actor: A non-system pool in BPMN represents a business entity or a participant of a process. In this sense, a pool can represent either a human, an organisation or another software system. Non-system pools that interact (e.g. having message exchanged) with the pool representing the system (i.e. the system pool) are candidates for an actor in Prometheus. For example, in Figure 1 the pool "CMS" is a system pool while "Author" is a non-system pool which can be mapped to an actor in Prometheus.

Lanes situated in System Pool to Roles: a lane is situated in a pool and also stands for a process participant. Therefore, a lane represents the two-tier hierarchy within a process participant. A lane can be mapped to a system role in

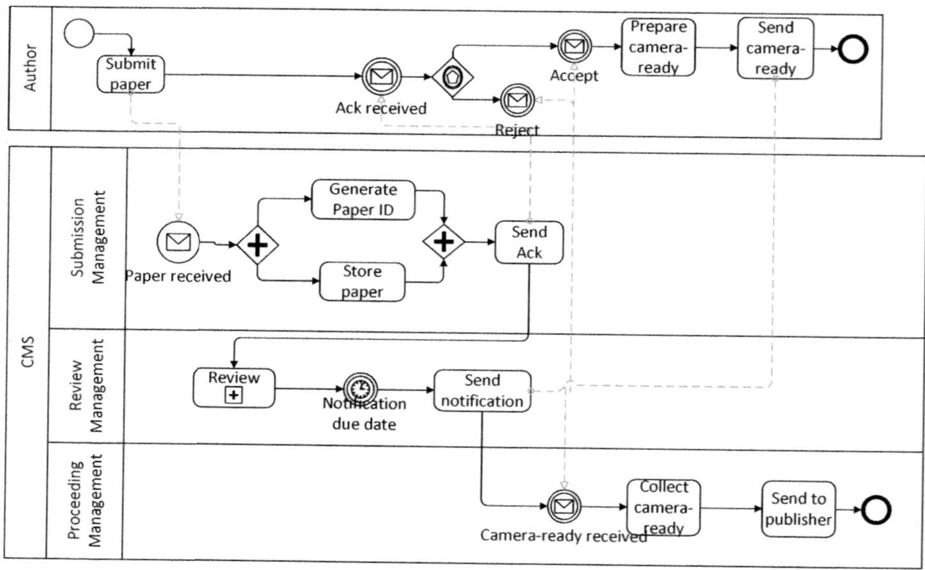

Fig. 1. A process between an author and the conference management system (CMS)

Prometheus. For example, the three swimlanes in the CMS pool, namely "Submission Management", "Review Management" and "Proceeding Management", can be translated into three equivalent roles.

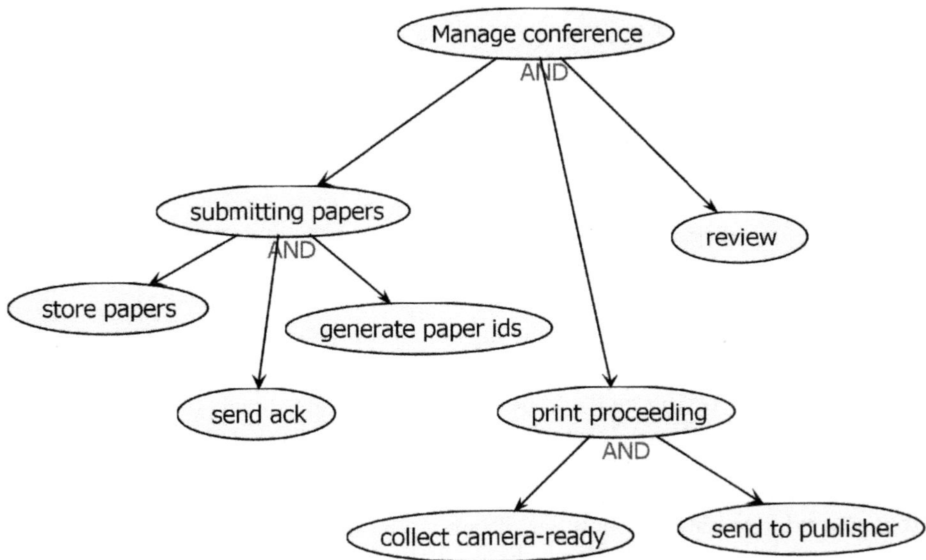

Fig. 2. A goal overview diagram for the CMS

Message Events to Percepts: Message Event which represents the arrival of a message from a participant (i.e. a pool) may trigger the start of the process (Start Event) or cause the process to continue (Intermediate Event). Such message events, if takes place within a system pool, represent information from the environment that the system receives. Hence, those message events can be transformed into percepts in Prometheus. Start Message Events can be translated to percepts that trigger a particular scenario while Intermediate Message Events are mapped to other types of percepts. There are two Message Events in the CMS pool (Figure 1) which can be translated to Prometheus percepts: "paper received" and "camera-ready received"

Message Events to Actions: The sending of a message to a process participant is represented as an Intermediate Message Event in BPMN. If the sender is the system pool and the receiver is a non-system pool, then such a message event represents an output from the system to an actor. Therefore, those events can be transformed to actions. For example, in figure 1 there are two Message Events in the CMS pool which can be translated to Prometheus actions: "ack received", "accept", and "reject".

Processes and Activities to Goals: A complete (sub-)process in a business process model leads to the achievement of a goal. Each activity within a

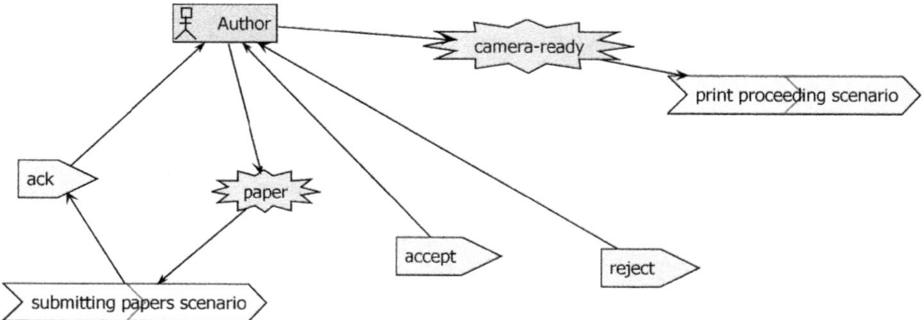

Fig. 3. An analysis overview diagram for the CMS

(sub-)process represents a certain things that need to be done to contribute to the achievement of the goal of the process. Therefore, each (sub-)process can be mapped to a goal in Prometheus and each activity within the process can be mapped to a (sub-)goal of the goal corresponding to the process. Figure 2 shows a goal diagram for the CMS. As can be seen, "manage conference" is the top goal which contain a number of sub-goals, including "submitting papers", "print proceeding" and "review". Each of these sub-goals are translated from a corresponding process or sub-process. For instance, the sub-process "review" is mapped to a sub-goal.

Processes to Scenarios: Business process models represent and support the dynamic co-ordination of activities by having decision gateways. This allows the model to represent many process instances, each of which contain a unique and supported sequence of activity execution. Each process corresponds to a scenario in Prometheus. An task can be transformed into a goal step whilst a sub-process may be mapped to a sub-scenario. A message event can be mapped into either a percept step or an action step, depending whether it is related to a sending or receiving message. The path resulting from an exclusive (XOR) gateway can be translated to a variation scenario, which represents alternative scenario to a use case. In addition, the transformation from BPMN processes to Prometheus scenarios should also preserve the order of activities and events.

Based on the previous transformation techniques, we can develop an analysis overview diagram in Prometheus as shown in figure 3. The "Author" actor interacts with the system by providing "paper" percepts that contain a paper. The analysis overview diagram also shows which percepts are required by which scenarios, e.g. the "submitting papers" scenario includes the "paper" percept. It is noted that a message flow also implies a link in Prometheus. For example, a message flow from the "submit paper" task in the "Author" pool to the "paper received" event in the CMS pool indicates a link between the "Author" actor and the "paper" percept.

3 Discussion

In the previous section, we have proposed an approach to translate business requirements in the form of business process models into a system specification using Prometheus notation. We have used a conference management as an example to illustrate our approach. From such a system specification, one can follow the process proposed in the Prometheus methodology to further design and implement an agent-based system that meets the original business requirements. For instance, a similar conference management system has been developed and presented in [5].

Business process models like BPMN tend to be initially designed in a high-level, abstract manner which covers only the normal scenarios. Such business process models do not provide in depth understanding of the processes and their ability to achieve desired goals since they are developed at the analysis level. Further details tend to be added as we move to the later stages of the software development, i.e. design and implementation phases. For instance, at the detailed design level in Prometheus (following a BDI style), we may need to define collection of pre-defined plan recipes (or types) for an agent. Each plan consists of: (a) an invocation condition which defines the event that triggers this plan (i.e. the event that the plan is *relevant* for); (b) a context condition which defines the situation in which the plan is *applicable*, i.e. it is sensible to use the plan in a particular situation; and a plan body containing a sequence of primitive actions and subgoals that are performed for plan execution to be successful. It should be noted that subgoals can trigger further plans.

At run time on a BDI platform [4], the agent achieves responds a particular event by selecting from its plan library a set of plans that are relevant (i.e. match the invocation condition) for handling the event (by looking at the plans' definition). The agent then determines the subset of the relevant plans that is applicable in terms of handling the particular event. The determination of a plan's applicability involves checking whether the plan's context condition holds in the current situation. The agent selects one of the applicable plans and executes it by performing its actions and sub-goals. A plan can be successfully executed, in which case the (sub-)goal is regarded to have been accomplished. Execution of a plan, however, can fail in some situations, e.g. a sub-goal may have no applicable plans, or an action can fail, or a test can be false. In these cases, if the agent is attempting to achieve a goal, a mechanism that handles failure is used. Typically, the agent tries an alternative applicable plan for responding to the triggering event of the failed plan. It is also noted that failures propagate upwards through the event-plan tree: if a plan fails its parent event is re-posted; if this fails then the parent of the event fails and so on.

BDI plans tend to correspond to business processes, e.g. a paper assignment plan corresponding to a process of allocating papers to reviewers. Due to such a flexibility of BDI plan composition at run-time which discussed above, the plan/process execution at run-time may deviate from the original process specification, i.e. the business process models. More specifically, new behaviours which were not previously specified in the BPMN models can be arisen. Therefore, by capturing those new behaviours we may be able to refine the original business process models. For this reason, agent-based systems can also be used a simulation environment to validate business processes and assist business process redesign. Further investigation on this area is a topic of our future work.

4 Conclusions and Future Work

On the one hand, the BPM community is facing challenges in modelling and implementing business processes that are able to adapt themselves to a changing environment. On the other hand, although multi-agent systems potentially provide a powerful and flexible platform for process execution, they still fail to attract a wide industry adoption. Therefore, it is very important to bridge the gap between the BPM community and agent technology. This paper has aimed to contribute to such an effort.

We have argued that providing mapping that automatically transforms business languages directly to an agent platform is not feasible due to the significant gap between the two different models and levels of abstraction. Therefore, we have proposed to translate business languages in a form of BPMN models to artefacts of Prometheus, a prominent agent-oriented methodology. Such artefacts are then used to implement an agent system that realizes those business requirements.

There is a number of directions for future work. Firstly, we plan to develop a more complete mapping from BPMN and Prometheus that covers other concepts in the two modelling languages. More specifically, we would like to explore how other types of events (e.g. timer, error, cancel) and decision gateways can be translated to the internal of a plan in Prometheus (e.g. triggering events, context conditions). Secondly, we plan to develop a tool which can be integrated to the Eclipse-based version of the Prometheus Design Tool to support the automation of a mapping between BPMN and Prometheus models. Another major topic for our future work involves further investigation of how new behaviours discovered from the execution of the agent-based system help improve the original business process models that it implements.

References

1. Burmeister, B., Arnold, M., Copaciu, F., Rimassa, G.: BDI-Agents for agile goal-oriented business processes. In: Padgham, Parkes, Müller, Parsons (eds.) Proceedings of the 7th International Conference on Autonomous Agents and Multiagent Systems (AAMAS 2008), Estoril, Portugal, pp. 37–44 (May 2008)
2. Padgham, L., Winikoff, M.: Developing intelligent agent systems: A practical guide. John Wiley & Sons, Chichester (2004) ISBN 0-470-86120-7

3. Weyns, D., Parunak, H.V.D., Shehory, O. (eds.): International Journal of Agent-Oriented Software Engineering (IJAOSE) - Special Issue on the Future of Software Engineering and Multi-Agent Systems, vol. 3. Inderscience Publishers, Geneva (2009)
4. Rao, A.S., Georgeff, M.P.: BDI-agents: from theory to practice. In: Proceedings of the First Intl. Conference on Multiagent Systems, San Francisco (1995)
5. Padgham, L., Thangarajah, J., Winikoff, M.: The Prometheus Design Tool – A Conference Management System Case Study. In: Luck, M., Padgham, L. (eds.) Agent-Oriented Software Engineering VIII. LNCS, vol. 4951, pp. 197–211. Springer, Heidelberg (2008)

TwitAg: A Multi-agent Feature Selection and Recommendation Framework for Twitter

Frank Grove and Sandip Sen

University of Tulsa
800 South Tucker Avenue
Tulsa, OK 74104, USA
{dean-grove,sandip,oly-mistry}@utulsa.edu

Abstract. With increasing number of users using social networking, there has been a considerable increase in user-generated content. Social networking is often used to connect with others, but in some domains such as microblogging social networking is primarily used to find interesting content. With the diversity of information sources available in microblogs, it becomes difficult for users to find interesting information sources. Recommendation engines have been developed to mitigate the problem of interesting content location in many domains, however recommendation engine research within the domain of microblogs has not been significantly explored. A key characteristic for any recommendation system is the ability to accurately classify users. Within the field of classification research feature selection is a widely used technique for improving classification accuracy. We demonstrate Unique Feature Selection (UFS), an agent based feature selection mechanism which parallelizes feature selection within the microblogging site Twitter. We show the effectiveness of UFS in both minimizing the feature space and improving classification results.

1 Introduction

Microblogging sites like Twitter are growing rapidly and people use these services to gather news and opinion concerning many types of content. Effectively searching the network to find other users that provide interesting content is a difficult problem in the context of social networks. To locate interesting users, one can browse the local network of relations, e.g., followees of followees, or one can search by keyword and manually select from the list of users that have recently posted content relevant to that keyword. These techniques are not effective in a network with millions of users. We seek the development of a novel technique for identifying users in a large social network. Classification of user's by content type is the first important mechanism of a recommendation engine. Our method is based on the Bag of Words model (BoW) where keywords are stored as an unordered set. The BoW model has been applied in information retrieval and natural language processing and is used as the underlying assumption for naive Bayes [6]. Each label, or single content type, is associated with a bag of

N. Desai, A. Liu, and M. Winikoff (Eds.): PRIMA 2010, LNAI 7057, pp. 394–397, 2012.

words and each keyword within the bag is assumed to be conditionally independent. For this work we utilize the keywords from Tweets, or short posts, posted by labeled users in the network. We facilitate mining of labels in the Twitter network through *Twitter Lists*. Lists segregate followees (friends) of users into semantic categories to allow for ease in browsing each category visually in the user interface. While these list names emerge from the network organically, and lack any structured folksonomy, Twitter Lists have been shown to be coherent labels for identification of users [2]. While the network lacks a structured folksonomy, a number of Twitter lists names are commonly used within the network. For example list names such as *tech*, *politics*, or *travel* are found often within the network. The existence of common labels allows us to train our classification model with multiple, independently generated instances. In this work we demonstrate a multi-agent feature selection technique that dynamically builds a feature space for classification. This feature space consists of keywords found within th Tweets of labeled users.

2 Related Work

Previous research in Twitter has focused on network and community structure analysis. Java et al. states that there exists three types of users within Twitter: information seeking, information sources, and social users [3]. Krishnamurthy et al. performed general analysis of the network structure, geographical, behavioral, and growth patterns [5]. There has been less work analyzing Twitter from a content perspective. Ramage et al. characterizes content based upon 6 categories such as *substance* or *style* derived from surveys with Twitter users [1]. Dong Woo et al. showed that Twitter lists were a useful source of information for identifying latent characteristics of users [2].

3 Data Gathering

For results presented in this paper, we use a data set aggregated over the course of 2 days with 10,908 users, 1,240,196 posts, and 193,714 lists (including 46,230 unique lists). Posts are tokenized on whitespace and we remove URLs, @replies, retweet symbols and users with a majority of non-Latin characters. From the data we filtered 60 users that had been listed with the content type *food*, *politics*, *travel*, *music* or *tech*. This set of labels varies in the amount of data for each label. *Music* has 320 users while *food* only has 20 users. This allows us to test the effectiveness of our feature selection technique on labels of diverse popularity. This is an important requirement because in open social networks there often exists a highly diverse set of content with varying degrees of popularity.

4 Unique Feature Selection

To facilitate accurate classification of users within the Twitter Network we developed a simple yet effective multi-agent feature selection technique. We want three primary advantages with this feature selection technique: dynamic aggregation and selection of salient features corresponding to labels, ease of parallelization and integration into task distribution managers, and improved classification performance. We show in this work that the Unique Feature Selection (UFS) satisfies each of these objectives. The UFS technique attempts to minimize the feature space, selecting features which primarily correspond to a single label. For this reason UFS considers only unique features, or features that only correspond to a single label. For instance, the keyword *CouchDB* does not appear outside of discussions within users labeled as *programming.* While many unlabeled users that are interested in programming may use the keyword *CouchDB*, users that are labeled with a different label such as *politics* will likely not use the keyword *CouchDB.* This process also significantly reduces the size of the feature space. The Twitter network is large and to effectively characterize millions of users the effort must be parallelized. Additionally the feature selection technique must be a integrated part of the classification and data aggregation system. Therefore the classification model created by UFS must dynamically grow as data is aggregated from the Twitter API, rather than requiring a batch process for selecting features. The UFS method is by nature easily parallelizable and can be integrated into a dynamic classification model. This also allows recommendation engines employing this algorithm to utilize existing resource constraint satisfaction algorithms for multi-agent systems to maximize data throughput for often recommended labels.

We now describe UFS in more detail. For each label L_j, a unique bag of words L_j^{uni} is computed. L_j^{com} is the union of the keywords of the n user's keyword sets with label L_j. Each user u consists of a bag of m keywords $U_u = (k_1, k_2, k_3, ...k_m)$. For each keyword k_i, L_j^{uni} contains the number of times it has occurred, c_i^u, and the set of users (screen names), sn_i, that have used this keyword.

$$L_j^{com} = (u_1 \cup u_2 \cup u_3 \cup ... \cup u_{n-1} \cup u_n) \tag{1}$$

L_j^{uni} represents the features that only occur within label L_j's complete set of keywords L_j^{com}. To compute L_j^{uni} keywords that intersect across multiple labels must be removed. L_j^{uni} is computed as the difference of L_j^{com} and the union of the m intersected keyword sets for each label.

$$L_j^{uni} = L_j^{com} - ((L_j^{com} \cap L_1^{com})... \cup (L_j^{com} \cap L_m^{com})) \tag{2}$$

5 Classification Experiment

We show through a k-fold classification experiment, that UFS more accurately characterizes users when compared to using the entire feature space. Through this classification experiment we also demonstrate the increase in accuracy using the Unique Feature Selection method over the complete feature set with Twitter data. We use Multinomial Bayes with 10-fold cross validation [4]. Table 1 shows that the UFS feature selection technique gives a 18.9 % increase over the full

Table 1. Classification Accuracy For Multinomial Bayes

Method	Pol	Trav	Mus	Tech	Food
All	0.435	0.459	0.572	0.918	0.5
UFS	0.682	0.639	0.900	0.818	0.599

feature space. The UFS approach more accurately classifies each label except the *tech* label, which suffers a 10 % decrease. However the accuracy for *music* label, containing the largest feature space, is significantly increased. The accuracy of classifying users with labels *travel*, *food*, and *politics* are also increased. Increase in classification accuracy for labels with various number of instances is an important requirement for social network applications.

6 Conclusion and Future Work

We have demonstrated Unique Feature Selection, a multi-agent feature selection technique designed for social networks. We have shown that this algorithm both decreases the size of the feature space and improves classification accuracy. A primary advantage of the UFS technique is it's ease of integration into existing multi-agent recommendation engines and ability to dynamically construct the feature space. In future work we will analyze UFS more extensively with new classification techniques and compare it against other feature selection techniques. We also hope to utilize this technique within a recommendation engine for Twitter.

References

1. Ramage, D., Dumais, S., Liebling, D.: Characterizing microblogs with topic models. In: ICWSM (2010)
2. Dongwoo, K., Yohan, J., Il-Chul, M., Alice, O.: Analysis of twitter lists as a potential source for discovering latent characteristics of users (2010)
3. Java, A., Song, X., Finin, T., Tseng, B.: Why we twitter: Understanding microblogging usage and communities. In: WebKDD/SNA-KDD. ACM (2007)
4. Kang, D.-K., Zhang, J., Silvescu, A., Honavar, V.: Multinomial Event Model Based Abstraction for Sequence and Text Classification. In: Zucker, J.-D., Saitta, L. (eds.) SARA 2005. LNCS (LNAI), vol. 3607, pp. 134–148. Springer, Heidelberg (2005)
5. Krishnamurthy, B., Gill, P., Arlitt, M.: A few chirps about twitter
6. McCallum, A., Nigam, K.: A comparison of event models for naive bayes text classification. In: AAAI-1998 Workshop on Learning for Text Categorization (1998)

Automated Multi-agent Simulation Generation and Validation

Philippe Caillou

LRI, Universite Paris Sud, F-91405 Orsay France
caillou@lri.fr
http://www.lri.fr/~caillou

Abstract. Multi-agent based simulation (MABS) is increasingly used for social science studies. However, few methodologies and tools exist. A strong issue is the choice of the number of simulation runs and the validation of the results by statistical methods. In this article, we propose a model of tool which automatically generates and runs new simulations until the results are statistically valid using a chi-square test. The choice of the test configuration allows both a general overview of the variable links and a more specific independence analysis. We present a generic tool for any RePast-based simulation and apply it on an Academic Labor Market economic simulation.

Keywords: Multi-Agent Based Simulation, Simulation Validation, Simulation Tool, Chi-square test, statistical test.

1 Introduction

Multi-Agent Based Simulations (MABS) are increasingly being considered as flexible and versatile modeling frameworks, enabling positive and normative investigations of phenomena out of reach when one uses analytical studies[1,2]. However, few methodologies exist on MABS usage. The main problem of MABS is validation: since simulations are by definition too complex to be validated analytically (otherwise they are only useful to inspire analytical analysis), other methods have to be considered. The result of a simulation is a set of observations (for example a set of evacuation times for a simulation of a stadium fire evacuation). As for empirical observations, statistical tools can be used to validate results obtained by the simulation[1]. Their usage is growing, even if the expert validation is still mainly used [3]. One important condition to be able to apply most statistical tests is to have a large enough number of observations. Compared to empirical observations or biological experimentations, MABS has a big advantage: it is easy and almost free to generate new simulation results. Our goal here is to use this advantage to generate automatically new simulations until observed results are statistically valid.

An ideal tool would work with any simulation framework and would select the best statistical test considering the experimenter goal. As a first step, we will however begin

[1] We consider here the validation of the results considering the model is sound. For example, statistical tests can validate the fact that the most important variable for the evacuation time is the number of exits in the simulation. However the model in itself - the agent behaviors, the stadium model - needs to be validated separately.

N. Desai, A. Liu, and M. Winikoff (Eds.): PRIMA 2010, LNAI 7057, pp. 398–412, 2012.

with a single test and a single framework. The chosen framework is RePast[4] as one of the most used framework for MABS. To be generic, we aim to keep the interaction with the framework minimal: the tool reads and write parameter files, starts the simulation program and analyzes result logs.

One of the first results of any MABS is usually the link between the observed variables and the parameters, which ones are the most important parameters and which ones have an influence on the final result. As our goal is to propose a generic tool, we consider here a test with a small number of hypotheses on the tested variables: the Pearson's Chi-square test. It tests if two observed variables/parameters are independent or not with a known percentage of error (by comparing the observed distribution of data with an expected distribution obtained from the distribution of the two tested variables considered independently).

Our objective here is to propose a model for a generic tool which automatically run new simulations from any RePast simulation until the independence results (obtained by chi-square tests) on selected variables are statistically valid. To test and illustrate our method, we apply a corresponding tool on a simulation of the French Academic Labor Market (presented - without statistical validation - in [5,6]). The main parameters describe the hiring system properties and the candidates and universities utility functions, while the observed variables measure the quality of the hiring and the rate of jobs fulfilled by local candidates.

In the following, we present the state of the art in simulation methodology and tools in section 2. Then we describe the method, the chi-square test, propose some heuristics to increase the analysis efficiency and discuss the possible applications of our tool in section 3. The simulation of the French academic labor market is introduced in section 4, some results are presented in section 5 and finally we conclude.

2 Related Work

A variety of social and economic problems have been investigated using multi-agent systems (MAS) [1]. MAS have demonstrated their ability to represent (cognitive) agents and constrained interaction rules, and provide insightful pictures of the dynamics of the system [7]. Several frameworks are available, such as RePast[4], NetLogo[8] and ModulEco[9] (see a review in [10]). The use of automated simulation generation and analysis is not yet integrated in these frameworks. NetLogo has the *BehaviorSpace* tool (and its corresponding API), but it is mainly the equivalent of RePast parameter files: it allows the user to choose parameter ranges to launch multiple experiments. An alternative approach is the LEIA tool from the IODA Framework[11], which is able to reverse-engineer agents and to explore there parameter space[12].

The closest approach to our work is the "robot scientist"[13] developed to achieve biological experiments autonomously. Our approach represents the equivalent for Multi-Agent Simulation, and improves it with efficiency heuristics and the statistical tests both for analysis and as a termination criterion. Another similar approach is the SimExplorer project [14]. Its goal is to manage simulations parameters and results with a generic framework. It is an ongoing project, with many limitations on parameter values, no possibility to "program" simulation runs with stopping criteria. Their work is very complementary to our objective, since they have no specific analysis tool in their system. An extension of our work would be to integrate it into SimExplorer to improve its interface with our goal-oriented statistical analysis.

Calibration and validation have always been a serious issue for MABS. Few general methodologies have been proposed, due to the huge variety of simulation types. Some classifications of empirically observed methods have been done ([15][16]). A survey of methods used from 1998 to 2008 [3] shows that usage of statistical tools for validation stays marginal (less than 10%) even if it has increased since 1998. The chi-square test is one of the most used for simulation analysis since it has very few requirements. A good introduction to chi-square test can be found in [17] and a more precise discussion on the test in [18].

3 Model

In this section we will first make a general presentation of our model (3.1), then we will precise the notations (3.2) we use. The Chi-squared test is described (3.3), then we detail the method algorithms (3.4), we propose some heuristics to improve our tool efficiency (3.5), and finally we discuss the objectives achievable with our tool (3.6).

3.1 Presentation

The global objective is simple and is summarized Fig.1: on a simulation model, the user chooses some parameters and observed variables, and the tool has to run simulations and make statistical tests until the tests are valid for each couple of parameters/variables. It finally indicates to the user which couple of variables are not independent and the error margin.

More precisely, we can distinguish between four main steps:

- **Parameters and variables extraction**: Starting with an existing Parameter file and result log, the tool extracts the set of parameters and variables used by the simulation and their past values.
- **Configuration and objective choice**: The user chooses which observed variables and parameters he wants to test, and gives eventually more configuration details (specific number of classes, specific parameter ranges, ...).
- **Parameter file generation and simulation run**: The tool generates a new parameter file and starts the simulation.
- **Results update**: The observed data set is updated from the result log. For each couple of variables/parameters a Chi-square test is made. If it is valid for every couple, the results are presented, otherwise the previous step is executed again.

3.2 Notation

The following notations will be used in this article:

- $V = \{v^1..v^{p+r}\}$ for the set of variables, including[2]:

[2] Since the test is identical and we study both parameter/observed variable and observed variable/observed variable independence, we use the same notation for parameters and observed variables

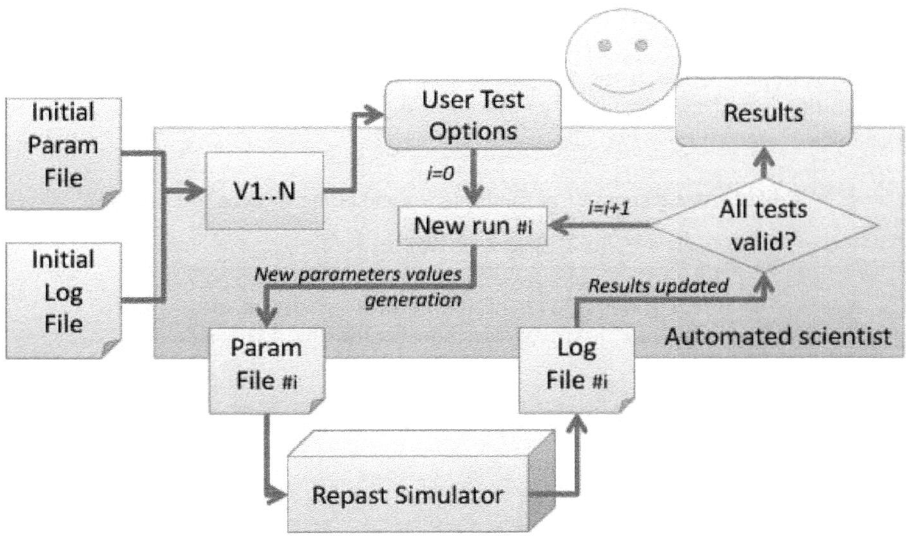

Fig. 1. Model overview: Starting with a configuration and a result file, the tool extracts the model variables. The user chooses the configuration. The tool generates, runs and analyzes new simulations until results are statistically valid, and finally present the results to the user.

- $v^1..v^p$ for the simulation parameters.
- $v^{p+1}..v^{p+r}$ for the observed variables.
- $U \subseteq V$ for the set of selected variables for the independence tests (an independence test is made for every couple $v^i \times v^j$ with $v^i \in U$ and $v^j \in U$.
- $x^1..x^{p+r}$ for observed values for variables $v^1..v^{p+r}$ after a simulation run.
- c^i for the number of classes used for variable v^i.
- l_t^i and l_{t+1}^i for the lower and upper bounds for class t of variable v^i.
- $n.$ for the total number of observations.
- n_t^i for the number of observations for class t of variable v^i.
- $n_{tt'}^{ij}$ for the number of observations simultaneously for class t of variable v^i and class t' of variable v^j.
- $e_{tt'}^{ij}$ for the number of expected observations for class t of variable v^i and class t' of variable v^j.
- Pr^{ij} is the probability for variable v^i and v^j for not being independent according to Chi-square test.
- $nbrun$ for the number of simulation runs between each result update and statistical test.

3.3 Chi-Square Test

The Pearson's Chi-square test of independence applies to two binned variables (variables put into classes). The tested hypothesis is H_0: Variable v^1 is independent from v^2. Simply put, it tests if the lines and the columns of a contingency table are independent. To test the hypothesis, the observed distribution (the contingency table) is compared to the expected distribution if the variables were independent. If H_0 is true, then $P(v^1 \bigcup v^2) = P(v^1) \times P(v^2)$.

For example, to test if the sex of the candidate (v^1) has an impact on the hiring probability as assistant professor (v^2), we consider the data presented table 1. The two variables v^1 and v^2 have two classes: $c^1 = c^2 = 2$.

Table 1. Assistant professor candidate sex and hiring success, France, 2007

$n^{12}_{tt'}$	Men	Women	Total $n^2_{t'}$
Hired	1081 (11.7%)	725 (7.9%)	1806 (19.6%)
Not Hired	4234 (46.0%)	3173 (34.4%)	7407 (80.4%)
Total n^1_t	5315 (57.7%)	3898 (42.3%)	9213 (100%)

From this observed distribution, we compute in table 2 the expected distribution (if H_0 is true) : $e^{12}_{tt'} = \frac{n^1_t * n^2_{t'}}{n.}$

Table 2. Expected distribution

$e^{12}_{tt'}$	Men	Women	Total $e^2_{t'}$
Hired	1041,9	764,1	1806
Not Hired	4273,1	3133,9	7407
Total n^1_t	5315	3898	9213

The value of the test can be computed from the sum of the squared differences divided by the expected distribution value:

$$X^2 = \sum_{t,t'} \frac{(n^{12}_{tt'} - e^{12}_{tt'})^2}{e^{12}_{tt'}}$$

Here, $X^2 = 4,317$. This test value has to be compared to the Chi-square law value $\chi^2_{df,\alpha}$ to know if the hypothesis can be rejected or not with $\alpha\%$ probability (see for example [17] for a mathematical definition of the $\chi^2_{df,\alpha}$ function). The number of degree of freedom is the product of the number of classes minus 1 : $df = (c^1 - 1)(c^2 - 1)$. Here df=1. With an error margin of 5%, the value of the Chi-square function is $\chi^2_{1,0.95} = 3.84$. We can thus reject the hypothesis "The sex of the candidate has no impact on the hiring" with only a 5% error margin. We could not have done it with an error margin of only 1%, since $\chi^2_{1,0.99} = 6,63$.

One advantage of this test is the absence of hypothesis on the form of the variable distribution. To apply it on continuous variables, the only requirement is to sample them by defining automatic or user-defined classes.

To be valid, the test has 2 requirements: the independence of the observations and a sufficiently large data set. A usual condition [19] is that the expected population has to be greater than one ($e^{12}_{tt'} > 1$) for every cell of the contingency table and greater than 5 ($e^{12}_{tt'} > 5$) for 80% of the cells. We use this condition, applied on every analyzed variable couple, to determine when to stop the simulations.

3.4 Model

The main algorithm of our tool model (Alg. 1) follows the basic steps presented in section 3.1 :

```
ExtractVariables();
ChooseObjective();
ChooseConfig();
ResValid=false;
while ResValid=false do
    GenerateRunSimulation() → ResFile;
    UpdateResults(ResFile);
    UpdateClasses();
end
ShowResults();
```

Algorithm 1. Global simulation analysis algorithm

$ExtractVariables()$ is mainly a parsing function that extract parameters names $v^1...v^p$ and values from a parameter file and variables names $v^{p+1}...v^{p+r}$ and values from a result log file.

$ChooseObjective()$ let the user choose the variables that will be tested (U) and, eventually, to set manually the number and bounds of the initial classes for each variable ($c^1...c^{p+r}$). By default, the first simulation run is used to determine $c_{default}$ uniform classes for each variable. The choice of classes uniform in size rather than uniform in observation number is made for two reasons: first, the number of observations is low at the beginning of the process and the distribution is very likely to change. Second, it is very common to have very concentrated variables (for example, 75% of the observations have an unique value for one of the observed variable of our application example). To use very small classes for v around a concentrated value x would influence the results of the test, because the variables which influence v around x would have more influence on the independence test than variables which influence v only for other values than x (because classes will switch very quickly around x, whereas bigger changes are needed to switch classes elsewhere). More discussions about user-defined classes can be found in section 3.6.

$ChooseConfig()$ let the user choose the parameters values for the simulations. RePast parameter files accept sets and loops (For..step..until). For the test to be valid, experiments have to be independent, which is not true for loops. For this reason, we replace loops by random choices between possible values. For each parameter, the user can choose between a set (containing one or several values) and a random value with or without steps (a random value without steps is a continuous uniform random variable). By default, the values are the ones used in the current parameter file. More discussion about user-defined parameter values can be found in section 3.6.

$GenerateRunSimulation()$ creates a new parameter file using the chosen values for $nbrun$ new simulation runs, creates the adapted script file (to save the results in a new file) and starts the simulations. To increase the tool efficiency, the random values for one parameter can be biased (see section 3.5).

```
while new res x^1..x^{p+r} in ResFile do
    inc(n.);
    for each v^i, v^j with v^i ∈ U and v^j ∈ U and i <= j do
        for each class c^i_t do
            if l^i_t ≤ x^i < l^i_{t+1} then inc(n^i_t)
        end
        for each c^i_t × c^j_{t'} do
            if l^i_t ≤ x^i < l^i_{t+1} and l^j_{t'} ≤ x^j < l^j_{t'+1} then inc(n^{ij}_{tt'})
        end
    end
end
ResValid = true;
for each v^i, v^j with v^i ∈ U and v^j ∈ U and i <= j do
    Nb5 = 0;
    for each c^i_t × c^j_{t'} do
        e^{ij}_{tt'} = (n^i_t * n^j_{t'}) / n.;
        if e^{ij}_{tt'} < 1 then ResValid = false;
        if e^{ij}_{tt'} < 5 then inc(Nb5);
    end
    X^{ij} = Σ_{t,t'} (n^{ij}_{tt'} - e^{ij}_{tt'})^2 / e^{ij}_{tt'};
    Pr^{ij} = pr with χ^2_{(c^i-1)(c^j-1),pr} = X^{ij};
    if Nb5 > 0.2c^i c^j then ResValid = false
end
```

Algorithm 2. $UpdateRes(ResFile)$ algorithm

$UpdateRes(ResFile)$ function is described in Alg. 2. It updates the observation contingency tables (the $n^{ij}_{tt'}$) in the while loop and computes the Chi-square value and check the test validity criteria in the For loop. The program stopping criteria ($ResValid$) is the Chi-square validity criteria: each expected distribution value ($e^{ij}_{tt'}$) has to be greater than 1 and 80% have to be greater than 5 for every selected variable couple. The Pr^{ij} value is the minimum error margin to reject the hypothesis H_0 (v^i and v^j are independent). This value gives more information than a binary answer independent/not independent since the user can compare the values between variables.

$UpdateClasses()$ is used to merge or create new classes in case the user didn't define specific classes. Classes are added when an observed value is out of the lowest/highest bounds, if the user did not choose infinite boundaries or force fixed classes.

Both options allow the user to keep a fixed number of classes, without losing any observation (infinite boundaries) or by focusing on a specific range (fixed classes). A class merging heuristic can also be used to increase the class definition efficiency (see section 3.5). The reason why new uniform classes are not redefined at each loop is that it would suppose to consider all the past results again (since the only information kept is the contingency tables with the populations in each class).

$ShowResults()$ finally presents the Pr^{ij} (which can be interpreted as probability of not being independent) for each couple of selected variable to the user. The user can have the detail of observed/expected observations for every couple by selecting it (see Fig. 2 and 3).

3.5 Heuristics

The total time required for one simulation run is usually low, but not negligible, and for some models it can even be relatively high. Moreover, several thousand simulations may be required to obtain statistically valid results. For these reasons, we propose two heuristics to decrease the required number of simulations without losing the statistical properties:

The **class merging** heuristics: During the *UpdateClasses()* step, one class is merged with its smallest neighbor when its population is lower than $minclass\%$ the average class size. This heuristic is here to prevent a class existing only because of an exceptional configuration/error to block the test and the program (if a class population is very small, expected values will be lower than 1 and the process will never stop). The main advantage of this heuristic is its efficiency (see results in section 5.4). Its downside is that it can not be applied to not orderd/string variables (because it is impossible to know which classes to merge) or when classes are fixed (when the user wants to analyze fixed classes).

The **biased values** heuristic: During the *GenerateRunSimulation()* step, the idea is to identify the most problematic variable and class (the one with the lowest number of observations), the parameter which will increase its population with the highest probability (the one with a high proportion of observations in the selected class) and to bias its values accordingly. Formally:

- Choose class t and variable i with $n_t^i = \min_{j,t'} n_{t'}^j$.
- For each continuous parameter v^j, give a score to each of its classes: $s_{t'}^j = (\frac{n_{tt'}^{ij}}{\sum_t n_{tt'}^{ij}})^2$.
- For the next simulations set generation, choose the biased parameter v^j with the highest total score $s^j = \sum_{t'} s_{t'}^j$.
- For each random value of this parameter, choose the class t' of v_j with probability $\frac{s_{t'}^j}{\sum_t s_t^j}$. The final value is selected uniformly in class t'.

The main advantage of this heuristic is that it can be applied to any variable. It can however be applied to only one parameter for each simulation generation: To apply it to several parameter at the same time may introduce artificial relations and would invalidate the statistical validity of the test.

3.6 Discussion

The main objective of our method is to test the independence of variables. However, several more precise objectives can be achieved:

- The first intuitive objective is to present a global overview of the variable interactions in the simulations. Simulations can use hundreds of parameters and variables and a first overview of the important parameters for each variable is already very useful and not trivial to obtain with current simulations framework. This is the default objective, with all default parameter values and all variables selected (see section 5.1 for an illustration).
- To change the parameters values may have a huge impact on the results. Specific submodels can thus be analyzed, for example with a fixed parameter. More interestingly, to limit the parameter range for all the parameters may give significantly different results: some variables may be interdependent only for very specific and unrealistic parameter values. With these constraints, it is possible to study the variables relations around a specific point (for example with +/- 10% variation only - see section 5.2).
- Finally, it is possible to manually define some variable classes number/range to alter the results. To choose more classes means a more precise test. But it may be interesting to know what are the variables which have the *highest influence* on a specific variable v^1 by decreasing its number of classes. The effect will be that only the variables which have an important impact on v^1 will influence the observed classes, and thus be considered as not independent by the test (see section 5.3).

4 Application Example: The French Academic Labor Market

Our application is a simulation of the French assistant professor academic labor market. As it is just an illustration for our simulation tool, a precise understanding of the model is not necessary (interested reader may refer to [5,6]) and we will just give a brief overview here.

Let $\{u_1, \ldots, u_U\}$ and $\{c_1, \ldots c_C\}$ respectively denote the set of universities and candidates, listed according to their quality. University u_t is characterized from four parameters. The first two parameters (in $[0, 1]$) govern his preference ordering: i) elitism e_t stands for its bias toward the best candidate; ii) locality l_t stands for its bias toward local candidates. Lastly, a random perturbation modeled as $(1 - e_t)V$ with V uniformly drawn in $[0, 1]$, accounts for the "subjective" preferences of university u_t. Overall, the quality $r(i, t)$ of candidate c_i for university u_t is:

$$r(i,t) = (r_t \times \frac{i}{C} + (1 - e_t)V)(1 - l_t.L(i,t))$$

where $L(i, t)$ is 1 iff c_i is local to u_t and 0 otherwise.

University u_t uses its risk-adversity parameter r_t to decide which candidates will be interviewed among those applying to u_t. Its strategic ordering is defined as:

$$s(i,t) = r_t \times r(i,t) + (1 - r_t) \times \frac{|i - (t)|}{C}$$

The candidates parameters, quality function $r'(i,t)$ and strategic ordering $s'(i,t)$ are symmetrical.

Interaction Rules. Every candidate c_i applies for positions after its preference ordering, and to his home university with probability h_i. Every university u_t produces a shortlist of 5 candidates. Every candidate c_i thereafter ranks the universities having shortlisted him. Eventually, the candidate and university ranking are aggregated by a variant of Stable Marriage algorithm [20], an optimal matching is derived, and the recruitment decisions are made accordingly.

Agents parameters are defined as random uniform variables, the boundaries are the parameters of the simulation. For example:

- Application number $NbApp_i \sim U[MinApp, MaxApplication]$,
- Risk factor $r_t \sim U[MinUnivRisk, MaxUnivRisk]$

The two main observed variables are the number of positions fulfilled ($NbHire$) and the number of positions fulfilled by local candidates ($NbLocalHire$). Two other variables evaluate the quality of the hiring process: the rank of the last hired candidate ($LastRelACand$) and the rank of the first university with no hired candidate ($FirstRelNAJob$).

5 Results

To illustrate our tool model, we used it on the simulation application with the three possible objectives described in section 3.6. First, we get a global overview of the simulation, then we try a more precise test around the equilibrium and we test the influence of class number on the results. Finally, we test the efficiency of the proposed heuristics[3].

5.1 Global Overview

With all default parameters, all parameters and four observed variables selected for test, we obtain a global view of the simulation (Fig. 2). On the top of the window is indicated the number of simulations runs completed until all tests were valid (4182)[4]. Each line and column corresponds to a variable, with the first four lines for the observed variables (results of the simulation), and the next lines for the parameters. Each cell contains the test results. The meaning of a positive test value (value higher than 0.95 on the figure, signaled with a star) is that the two variables are not independent with 5% of error margin. Interestingly, the test values for parameter/parameter couples (all values except the first four lines) are not all low. The parameter values are all random variables (using Java standard Random function - similar results were obtained with other random number generators). Nevertheless, for several parameters, the hypothesis that they are independent has to be rejected for a high enough error margin (15% for the couple MaxLocalBonus/SendApplicationHome). The lesson here is that it is important to take a very low error margin to be sure that the independence is rejected (5%, 1% or less).

[3] For each test, we use $nbrun = 102$ runs for each step and $c_{default} = 10$ classes by default for each variable.

[4] The whole analysis, with the 4182 simulations and 250 agents took approximately 6 minutes with our test configuration.

Population

Nb. XP							
4182	SendApplicationHome	MaxApplication	DistanceWeight	RankWeight	MinCandRisk	MaxCandRisk	MinUnivRisk
LastRelACand	0.52819	*1.0	*1.0	*0.98911	0.94453	0.16809	0.86364
FirstRelNAJobs	0.86139	*1.0	*1.0	*1.0	0.19615	0.22345	0.84257
NBLocalHire	*1.0	*1.0	*0.98337	*1.0	0.66491	0.5987	0.31528
NBHire	0.93636	*1.0	0.07526	0.1797	0.45918	0.31576	*0.97833
MaxLocalBonus	0.86105	0.20626	0.2597	0.46154	0.07444	0.34659	0.37135
MinLocalBonus	0.16485	0.78863	0.3636	0.66905	0.84726	0.40142	0.90696
UnivRankWeight	0.08951	0.51596	0.44967	0.20327	0.88975	0.44966	0.3017
MaxUnivRisk	0.34731	0.57991	0.22055	0.15469	0.81108	0.78509	0.70703
MinUnivRisk	0.8062	0.71874	0.34139	0.89567	0.67724	0.94328	*1.0
MaxCandRisk	0.22829	0.6967	0.117	0.1204	0.18872	*1.0	
MinCandRisk	0.03377	0.18427	0.59667	0.71646	*1.0		
RankWeight	0.75229	0.89915	0.29689	*1.0			
DistanceWeight	0.4226	[illegible]	*1.0				

Fig. 2. Result window with default parameters: each cell value is the probability for the couple of variables not to be independent. Stars indicate interdependent variables with an error margin lower than 5%.

For the user, the figure gives a good insight on the simulation behavior: the parameter $MaxApplication$ has clearly the most influence on the observed variables. Interestingly, this was one of the result of the initial analysis ([5]), but without statistical proof, only with "clear evidence" on a plot. Here, it is possible to say that this is the only parameter for which the independence hypothesis can be rejected for all observed variable with the lowest margin of error. Other analysis can be maid with statistical proof : for example, the fact that the candidates are risk-taker or risk-adverse ($MinCandRisk$ and $MaxCandRisk$ parameters) have very low influence on the result.

Detail

Nb. XP						
Dif sum	1402.958591343494					
DL	99					
Proba indep.	0.0					
Proba not indep.	1.0					
NBHire	MaxApplication	10.0>	18.7>	27.4>	36.1>	44.8>
4182	4182	420	422	413	395	455
0.15>	93	0.0/9.52683	0.0/9.5722	0.0/9.36805	0.0/8.95976	7.0/10.3
0.19>	61	0.0/6.24878	0.0/6.27854	0.0/6.14463	1.0/5.87683	4.0/6.76
0.21>	175	0.0/17.92683	0.0/18.0122	2.0/17.62805	10.0/16.85976	23.0/19.
0.239>	239	0.0/24.48293	0.0/24.59951	5.0/24.07488	14.0/23.02561	18.0/26.
0.268>	328	0.0/33.6	3.0/33.76	10.0/33.04	16.0/31.6	45.0/36.
0.297>	353	0.0/36.16098	4.0/36.33317	12.0/35.55829	38.0/34.00854	64.0/39.
0.326>	303	0.0/31.03902	8.0/31.18683	40.0/30.52171	43.0/29.19146	49.0/33.
0.355>	288	3.0/29.50244	27.0/29.64293	39.0/29.01073	51.0/27.74634	35.0/31.
0.384>	302	8.0/30.93659	50.0/31.0839	62.0/30.42098	33.0/29.09512	32.0/33.
0.413>	311	26.0/31.85854	53.0/32.01024	51.0/31.32756	36.0/29.9622	32.0/34.
0.442>	454	84.0/46.50732	74.0/46.72878	51.0/45.7322	42.0/43.73902	47.0/50.
0.471>	1193	299.0/122.20976	203.0/122.79171	141.0/120.17293	111.0/114.93537	99.0/13

Fig. 3. Detailed view for the independence test of parameter $MaxApplication$ and observed variable $NBHire$: each cell contains the observed and expected observation count

To have more details about the observed values and the test, the user can select any cell to obtain the contingency table with both the degree of freedom (DL), X^{ij} value (Dif Sum), observed and expected values (in each cell). For example, Fig. 3 details the observations for parameter $MaxApplication$ (maximum number of applications sent by a candidate) and $NbHire$ (hiring rate). It is possible to see that the parameter has a negative impact on the observed variable.

5.2 Parameters Influence

The previous analysis was global, every parameter explored its whole definition space. To know which variables have an influence around a specific point, it is possible to limit the parameter range. We have tried here to test all parameters and variables, but to limit the parameter range to a 10% variation around a specific equilibrium (the empirically observed equilibrium, see [5]). Results are presented Fig. 4. In this situation, some variables (like the first one, $SendApplicationHome$) have disappeared because their value is fixed.

In this situation, the variables influences are clearly different. The impact of $MaxApplication$, for example, is very different because its range dropped from [10,97] to [18,22]. Excessive values which conduct to a saturation of the hiring process are eliminated. Interestingly, even without this saturation effect, this parameter has still influence on some qualitative ($FirstRelNAJob$) and quantitative ($NBHire$) observed variables. Moreover, with the elimination of excessive values, some influences which were previously hidden because they were too small may appear: The influence of $MinCandRisk$ is low compared to the global influence of other variables (Fig. 2), so low that the independence hypothesis can not be rejected. But around the equilibrium this low influence becomes the strongest (Fig. 4).

Population

Nb. XP 3468	MaxApplication	DistanceWeight	RankWeight	MinCandRisk	MaxCandRisk	MinUnivRisk
LastRelACand	0.91423	0.7009	*1.0	*1.0	*1.0	0.70544
FirstRelNAJobs	*0.99992	0.79006	0.82513	*1.0	0.84114	0.79328
NBLocalHire	0.8412	*1.0	0.84399	*0.98821	0.67382	0.23346
NBHire	*0.9991	*0.99963	*1.0	*1.0	0.20851	0.90913

Fig. 4. Result window for a limited parameter range around a specific point

5.3 Variables Classes Influence

Finally, it is possible to study more precisely some variables by manually choosing the classes used for the analysis. Lowering the number of classes decreases the precision of the test, but this "blurredness" can help to identify the variables which have the strongest influence. For example, Fig. 5 details the observations for parameter $RankWeight$ (the importance of the quality of the university for the candidate) and the observed variable $NBLocalHire$ (number of hired local candidates) in two experiments: in experiment

1 (corresponding to the experiment of section 5.1, top figure), the default number of classes is 10. For experiment 2 (bottom figure), it is set to 3. Moreover, for each experiment, some classes where automatically merged because their observed population was too small. In the experiment 1, even if the variables are statistically not independent (with a very low error margin, less than 0.1%), the influence doesn't appear clearly when looking directly at the observed and expected population values (Fig. 3 is an opposite example of apparent interactions between the variables). The decrease of the observation precision in experiment 2 confirms this observation: with few classes, the independence hypothesis can not be rejected anymore.

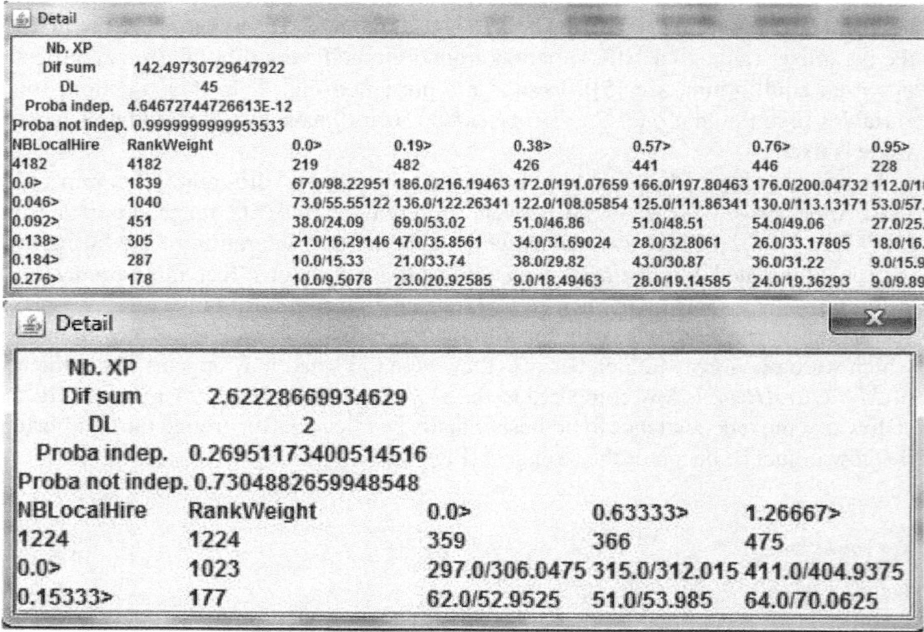

Detail

Nb. XP
Dif sum 142.49730729647922
DL 45
Proba indep. 4.64672744726613E-12
Proba not indep. 0.9999999999953533

NBLocalHire	RankWeight	0.0>	0.19>	0.38>	0.57>	0.76>	0.95>
4182	4182	219	482	426	441	446	228
0.0>	1839	67.0/98.22951	186.0/216.19463	172.0/191.07659	166.0/197.80463	176.0/200.04732	112.0/1
0.046>	1040	73.0/55.55122	136.0/122.26341	122.0/108.05854	125.0/111.86341	130.0/113.13171	53.0/57.
0.092>	451	38.0/24.09	69.0/53.02	51.0/46.86	51.0/48.51	54.0/49.06	27.0/25.
0.138>	305	21.0/16.29146	47.0/35.8561	34.0/31.69024	28.0/32.8061	26.0/33.17805	18.0/16.
0.184>	287	10.0/15.33	21.0/33.74	38.0/29.82	43.0/30.87	36.0/31.22	9.0/15.9
0.276>	178	10.0/9.5078	23.0/20.92585	9.0/18.49463	28.0/19.14585	24.0/19.36293	9.0/9.89

Detail

Nb. XP
Dif sum 2.62228669934629
DL 2
Proba indep. 0.26951173400514516
Proba not indep. 0.7304882659948548

NBLocalHire	RankWeight	0.0>	0.63333>	1.26667>
1224	1224	359	366	475
0.0>	1023	297.0/306.0475	315.0/312.015	411.0/404.9375
0.15333>	177	62.0/52.9525	51.0/53.985	64.0/70.0625

Fig. 5. Detailed view for independence test of parameter $RankWeight$ and observed variable $NBLocalHire$. In experiment 1 (top window), the number of classes is 10 for $RankWeight$ and 6 for $NBLocalHire$. In experiment 2 (bottom window), it is respectively 3 and 2. Each cell contains the observed and expected observation count.

5.4 Heuristic Efficiency

To evaluate the heuristics efficiency, we have applied our tool on the same configuration with each heuristic enabled/disabled (10 times for each situation). The selected configuration used 10 classes for each variable, some of these classes were rather rare and thus difficult to obtain. The average number of required simulations and the variance are given Table 3. The heuristic efficiency was statistically tested (with a Chi-Squared test, of course) and every hypothesis "The heuristic HC/HB has no effect on the number of required simulations" can be rejected with less than 1% of error probability.

Table 3. Average number of simulation runs (and variance) with/without the Class-merging heuristic (HC) and the biased-values heuristic (HB)

	HC	$\overline{HC}$
HB	4760(1517)	16442(1943)
$\overline{HB}$	6800(1819)	24112(579)

The HC (class merging) heuristic appears to be the most efficient and decreases significantly the number of required simulations. When this heuristic can not be used (for example with string variables), the HB heuristic may still be useful. Even if its efficiency is lower, it does not require any specific configuration to be applied.

6 Conclusion

In this paper, we have presented a tool model to help the scientist using Multi-Agent Based Simulation to explore its simulation and obtain statistically valid results. We applied a corresponding tool on an Academic market simulation, and we have shown that it successfully generates and runs new simulations until Chi-square independence tests on selected variables are valid. It presents a global overview of the simulation results with the most important variables and the main interactions. It can also be used to obtain more precise results on the simulation behavior for specific parameter ranges, or focus on a specific couple of parameters/variables. We proposed heuristics to decrease the number of required simulations and tested their efficiency.

The first step to continue this work will be to generalize it to other statistical tests and simulation frameworks. A complementary goal would be to integrate this tool in the project of generic simulation explorer SimExplorer.

References

1. Axelrod, R.: Advancing the art of simulation in the social sciences. Advances in Complex Systems 7(1), 77–92 (2004)
2. Tesfatsion, L.S.: A constructive approach to economic theory. In: Handbook of Computational Economics. Agent-Based Computational Economics of Handbooks in Economic Series, vol. 2. North-Holland (2006)
3. Heath, B., Hill, R., Ciarallo, F.: A survey of agent-based modeling practices (January 1998 to July 2008). Journal of Artificial Societies and Social Simulation 12(4), 9 (2009)
4. North, M.J., Collier, N.T., Vos, J.R.: Experiences creating three implementations of the repast agent modeling toolkit. ACM Transactions on Modeling and Computer Simulation 16(1), 1–25 (2006)
5. Caillou, P., Sebag, M.: Modelling a Centralized Academic Labour Market: Efficiency and Fairness. In: ECCS 2008. Complex Systems Society, Jerusalem Israel (2008)
6. Caillou, P., Sebag, M.: Pride and Prejudice on a Centralized Academic Labor Market. In: Artificial Economics 2009. LNEMS, pp. 29–40. Springer, Valladolid Espagne (2009)
7. Phan, D., Amblard, F.: Multi-agent Modelling and Simulation in the Social and Human Sciences. Bardwell Press (2007), http://www.bardwell-press.co.uk/
8. Wilensky, U.: http://ccl.northwestern.edu/netlogo/

9. Phan, D.: From agent-based computational economics towards cognitive economics. In: Cognitive Economics. Handbook of Computational Economics, pp. 371–398. Springer, Heidelberg (2004)
10. Railsback, S.F., Lytinen, S.L., Jackson, S.K.: Agent-based simulation platforms: Review and development recommendations. Simulation 82(9), 609–623 (2006)
11. Kubera, Y., Mathieu, P., Picault, S.: Interaction-oriented agent simulations: From theory to implementation. In: Ghallab, M., Spyropoulos, C., Fakotakis, N., Avouris, N. (eds.) Proceedings of the 18th European Conference on Artificial Intelligence (ECAI 2008), pp. 383–387. IOS Press (2008)
12. Gaillard, F., Kubera, Y., Mathieu, P., Picault, S.: A Reverse Engineering form for Multi Agent Systems. In: Artikis, A., Picard, G., Vercouter, L. (eds.) ESAW 2008. LNCS, vol. 5485, pp. 137–153. Springer, Heidelberg (2009)
13. Soldatova, L., Clare, A., Sparkes, A., King, R.D.: An ontology for a robot scientist. Bioinformatics 22, 464–471 (2006); ISMB 2006
14. Amblard, F., Hill, D.R.C., Bernard, S., Truffot, J., Deffuant, G.: `http://www.simexplorer.org/`
15. Windrum, P., Fagiolo, G., Moneta, A.: Empirical validation of agent-based models: Alternatives and prospects. Journal of Artificial Societies and Social Simulation 10 (2007)
16. Moss, S.: Alternative approaches to the empirical validation of agent-based models. Journal of Artificial Societies and Social Simulation 11 (2007)
17. Wonnacott, T.H., Wonnacott, R.J.: Introductory statistics, 5th edn. Wiley, New York (1990)
18. Greenwood, P.E., Nikulin, M.S.: A Guide to Chi-Squared Testing. Wiley, New York (1996)
19. Cochran, W.G.: Some methods for strengthening the common chi-square tests. Biometrics (10), 10–417 (1954)
20. Baiou, M., Balinski, M.: Student admissions and faculty recruitment. Theor. Comput. Sci. 322(2), 245–265 (2004)

Inferring Equation-Based Models from Agent-Based Models: A Case Study in Competition Dynamics

Ngoc Doanh Nguyen[1,2], Patrick Taillandier[1,2], Alexis Drogoul[1,2], and Pierre Auger[2,3]

[1] MSI, IFI, 42 Ta Quang Buu Street, Hai Ba Trung District, Hanoi, Vietnam
[2] UMMISCO, UMI 209, IRD/UPMC, 32 Henri Varagnat,93143 Bondy Cedex, France
[3] LMPD, University Cadi Ayyad, Marrakech, Morocco
{doanhbondy,patrick.taillandier,alexis.drogoul}@gmail.com,
pierre.auger@ird.fr

Abstract. Two types of model, equation-based models (EBMs) and agent-based models (ABMs) are now widely used in modeling ecological complex systems and seem not to be reconciled. While ABMs can help in exploring and explaining the local causes of global phenomena, EBMs are useful for predicting their long-term evolution without having to explore them through simulated experiments. In this paper, we show that it is possible to use an ABM to infer an EBM. Base on the case study, a dynamics of two competing species, we illustrate our methodology through the presentation of two models: an ABM and an EBM. We also show that the two models give the same results on coexistence of the two competing species.

Keywords: Agent-Based Models, Equation-Based Models, Population Dynamics, Complex Systems.

1 Introduction

In modeling ecological complex systems, two widely accepted models coexist: agent-based models (ABMs) and equation-based models (EBMs). Each of these two models has its own strengths and weakness ([1], [2]) depending on the purpose of study. EBMs, on one hand, play as compartment models and operate on global laws generally, defined by the equations that apply to all members of the compartments. For example, in early ecological models, the state variables (compartments) in the models of population dynamics was often chosen as the total population densities and the model was a set of nonlinear, coupled, ordinary differential equations or discrete equations [3]. In such classical models, the agents (individuals) are assumed to be homogenous and well mixed: they are all treated as identical. The benefit of these simple EBMs is that they can be handled analytically. However, given this previous assumption, they cannot be very realistic. In recent years, some "more realistic" EBMs have been developed, which are aimed at taking different categories of agents into account. These EBMs involve a large number of variables and are in general difficult to handle analytically. However, in most cases, it is possible to consider different time scales: a fast one for processes operating at the agent level; and a slow one at the levels of the pop-

N. Desai, A. Liu, and M. Winikoff (Eds.): PRIMA 2010, LNAI 7057, pp. 413–427, 2012.

ulation and the community. It is then possible to use the "variable aggregation" method, deriving a reduced model which governs a few global variables at the slow time scale while taking into account all the processes going on at the agent level [4]. One can also find in [4] some interesting examples of EBMs in which different categories of agents were considered, and for which aggregation methods were used successfully to proceed analysis of the EBMs.

ABMs, on the other hand, are natural representations of real ecological systems [5]. The obvious reason for using ABMs to model a real ecological system is that agents are building blocks of ecological systems. The properties and behaviors of agents determine the properties of the systems that the agents compose. In ecological systems, agents are not identical and do not stay the same all their life: all that an agent does-grow, develop, acquire resources, reproduce, interact - depends on its internal and external environments and it modifies both with its actions. ABMs are then particularly adapted to represent and understand the emergence of global dynamics among heterogeneous agents sharing common environmental constraints. In comparison to EBMs, ABMs are much more realistic with respect to the data available in the field and thus are easier to test in scientific process. But being closer to reality usually means having to define, calibrate and determine much more parameter values than in EBMs and analysis problems then arise.

To summarize, both ABMs and EBMs address, with its own point of view, the same problems in ecological complex systems. Each of these modeling approaches answers different, yet complementary, questions. While ABMs can help in exploring and explaining the local causes of global phenomena, EBMs are useful for predicting their long-term evolution without having to explore them through simulated experiments.

Therefore, it is primary to couple these two modeling approaches when studying ecological complex systems. There are many alternative ways for coupling these two approaches. For instance, the process can be completely top-down: by distributing global parameters of a given EBM to obtain local parameters of a related ABM. We refer to our previous contribution [2] for this way. It can also be bottom-up, by extracting local parameters of a given ABM to obtain global parameters of inferred EBM. Several studies seem to be related to this way can be found in ([6], [7]). In these contributions, the authors tried to abstract ABMs by introducing mathematical formalism [6] as well as moment approximations of ABMs [7].

In this paper, the novel issue we explore is closed to the "bottom-up" way. Based on the case study, a dynamics of two competing species, we represent how to infer an EBM from a given ABM. Unlike in the previous studies ([6], [7]), we extract local parameters to obtain global ones. For instance, we show that an EBM can be built from a given ABM by considering ABM as a virtual laboratory to test and to see effects of parameters. Once we observe the effects of parameters, we choose parameters to build EBMs. We also show that the two models give the same results on coexistence of the two competing species.

The paper is organized as follows. In section 2, we present the case study -the dynamics of two competing species. The ABM implemented for the case study is presented in section 3. In section 4, we present our methodological steps to reach to EBM from a given ABM. We then present in section 5 how we extract global parameters in order to build an EBM. We present the EBM and its result in section 6, we also comparison result of the inferred EBM and the ABM. Section 7 is dedicated for conclusion and perspectives.

2 Case Study: Competition Dynamics

We consider a system of two species competing for a common resource. We are interested in pre-emptive competition, i.e., one of the two species will end up extinction if it has smaller number of individuals at the beginning. There are a lot of such complex systems in the reality where two species coexist. The aim is to figure out under which conditions two species coexist in the pre-emption dynamics.

In the next sections, we shall present two models which can explain the coexistence of two species in pre-emption dynamics. To do that, we first present an ABM for dynamics of two competing species. We then test the ABM to figure out parameters and conditions under which two species coexist. We based on these results to build an EBM which has provable result on coexistence of two competing species.

3 Agent-Based Model

In this section, we propose a description following the ODD protocol [8] of our ABM.

3.1 Overview

Purpose. The purpose of the model is to study the dynamic of two species when these ones are in competition and when the total quantity of food existing in the environment is stable.

State variables and scales. In our model, each individual of each species is represented as an "agent" that is located in a continuous environment. The food patches are also modeled as agents.

Environment. We chose to model the environment as a 2D plane of a specific size (300×300). The agents can not go out this environment.

Food patch agent (FPA). Each food patch is represented by an agent (FPA). A FPA has for geometry a circle of which the area depends of the quantity of food contained in the food patch. The attributes of FPAs are described in Table 1.

Species individual agent (SIA). Each species individual is represented by an agent (SIA) that has a point for geometry. The attributes of these agents are described in Table 2.

Table 1. Attributes of the food patch agents

Attribute name	Brief description	Value
Location	X and Y coordinates of the food patch (its center)	Random
Food production	quantity of food produced at each simulation step (in the food patch)	30
Food	current quantity of food contained in the food patch (when null, the agent dies)	-
Max food	maximal quantity of food in a food patch	100
Food area coefficient	coefficient that links the food quantity to the food patch area	5
Area	area of the food patch	-

Process Overview and Scheduling. At each simulation step, the SIAs act, then the FPAs evolve. The evolution of the FPAs is very simple (Fig. 1): if there is no more food in the food patch, the agent dies, otherwise, the quantity of food evolves according to the food production attribute. Then the new area of the food patch is computed. When a FPA dies, a new one is created (at a random location). This mechanism allows to keep a stable quantity of food in the environment.

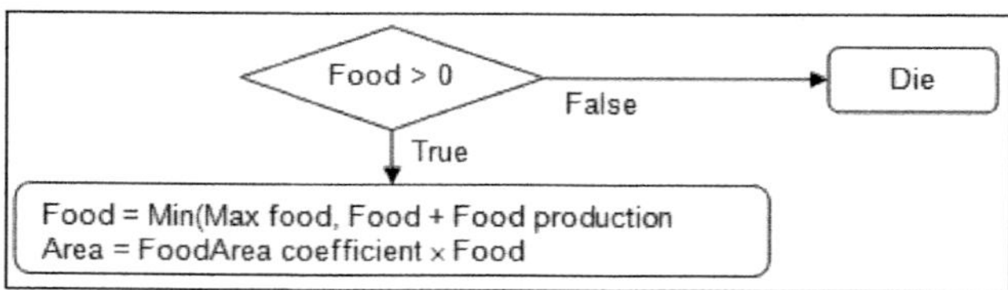

Fig. 1. Food patch agent evolution (at each simulation step)

Concerning the SIAs, their general behavior consists in trying to survive (Fig. 2). They have the capacity to move, to eat and to reproduce. They gain energy by eating food (in a food patch) and lose it, when fighting on a patch with member of the other species. When a SIA finds a food patch, it remains in this one as long as the proportion of agents of the same species is high enough. The choice of a new food patch is done randomly between the food patch perceived by the agent.

Table 2. Attributes of the species individual agents

Attribute name	Brief description	Value
Location	X and Y coordinates of the agent	-
Displacement range	maximal distance of displacement per step	100
Energy	quantity of energy (when null, the agent dies)	-
Max energy	maximum quantity of energy	30
Energy consumption	quantity of energy consumed at each simulation step	2
Extra competition coefficient	coefficient of energy lost per simulation step due to competition with individuals of the other species	10
Energy reproduction	energy lost during the reproduction (the energy of the offspring will be equal to the energy reproduction / number of offspring)	10
Reproduction probability	probability that an individual reproduces at each simulation step	0.01
Reproduction Time	minimal number of steps between two reproductions	20
Max offspring	maximal number of offspring that an individual can have when reproducing	3
Max consumption	maximal quantity of food that an individual agent can eat at each simulation step	4
Tolerance for other species	proportion of individual agents of other species from which the agent is going to leave a food patch. Defined the strategy of the agent	0.3

3.2 Design Concept

Emergence. In this model, the emergent aspect concerns the population dynamics resulting from the interaction between the two species of SIAs and the FPAs; in particular the creation of groups of individual of the same species in a same food patch. It is influenced by different parameters: the extra competition coefficient, the tolerance for others, the food production, etc.

Fitness. Each individual does not have an explicit fitness function to optimise. However, the implicit fitness of a species concerns its survival. Thus the more agents of this species, the higher the fitness for this species will be.

Adaptation. The adaptive trait of the SIAs comes from their capacity to not tolerate a high proportion of agent of other species. This property allows them to avoid food patches with too much competition.

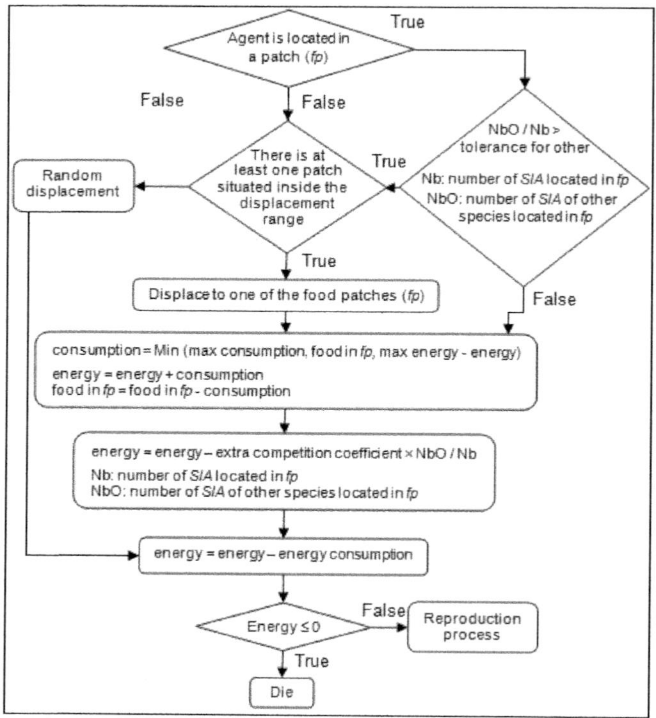

Fig. 2. Species individual agent behavior (at each simulation step)

Interaction. There are two kinds of interaction between agents: the interaction between the SIAs and the FPAs (the SIAs eat food contains in FPA) and the interaction between SIAs of different species (competition and non tolerance to agents of other species).

Sensing. The SIAs know the number of agents (of the same species and of other species) that share the same food patch as them. They can detect food patches which geometry overlaps their seeing range (displacement range).

Stochasticity. The stochasticity is involved in the repartition of the food patches in the environment. It is also involved in the initial food contained in the food patches. At last, it is involved in the choice of a food patch by the SIA: these ones randomly choose a food patch among the perceived ones.

Collectives. SIAs of the same species sharing a same food patch formed an implicit group. Higher the number of agents in this group, the stronger will be its defense against SIAs from other species, but more quickly the food contained in the food patch will be consumed.

Observation. Various observations are available in this model from an omniscient perspective. However, as we study the population dynamics, a first observation is the evolution of the number of agents of the two species. The repartition of the species in the different food patches is as well an interesting observation.

3.3 Details

Initialisation. At the initialisation, the FPAs and the SIAs are randomly placed in the environment. The quantity of food in each food patch is randomly drawn between [1, max food]. In the way the quantity of energy of each SIA is randomly drawn between [1, max energy]. The initial number of SIAs of each species is 50. The number of FPAs (which is constant) is equals to 10.

Simulation implementation. Since few years, many simulation platforms dedicated to the implementation of agent-based models have been developed. We can cite as examples GAMA [9], Mason [10], Repast [11], NetLogo [12]. In this work, we chose to develop our simulation with the GAMA platform. This platform provides a complete modeling and simulation environment for building spatially explicit multi-agent simulations. In particular, it integrates powerful spatial analysis tools coming from Geographic Information Systems (GIS) allowing to give agents a geometry and spatial analysis capacities.

Test the model. Fig. 3 shows examples of results concerning the distribution of individuals at several simulation steps. This figure shows that at step 1, the individuals are randomly located in the food patches; then at step 3, groups of individuals of the same species are beginning to form; at last, at step 20, these groups are uniform (only composed of individuals of the same species). Fig. 4 gives the simulation results obtained for the population evolution during the first 20 steps. In order to build this graphic, we carried out 30 simulations and we computed the means. The goal was to limit the stochastic bias of the model. First, one can observe that the two populations similarly evolve. The population is stable during the first three steps, and then it decreases until reaching an equilibrium point.

Remarks. We pay our attention on the key result concerning to the parameter "tolerance for other species". Actually, this parameter, which defines the strategy used by the SIs to survive, has a deep impact on the generation of SIs aggressive/defensive groups. When the value of this parameter is high enough we can observe the formation of groups composed of SIs of the same species.

These groups can allow to the IC to survive by combining their strength. The IC individuals tend to form big groups that "invade" patches without SC individuals. The parameter "tolerance for other species" of the IC individual equals to 0.3, IC individuals are likely to distribute on food patches where there are few SC individuals.

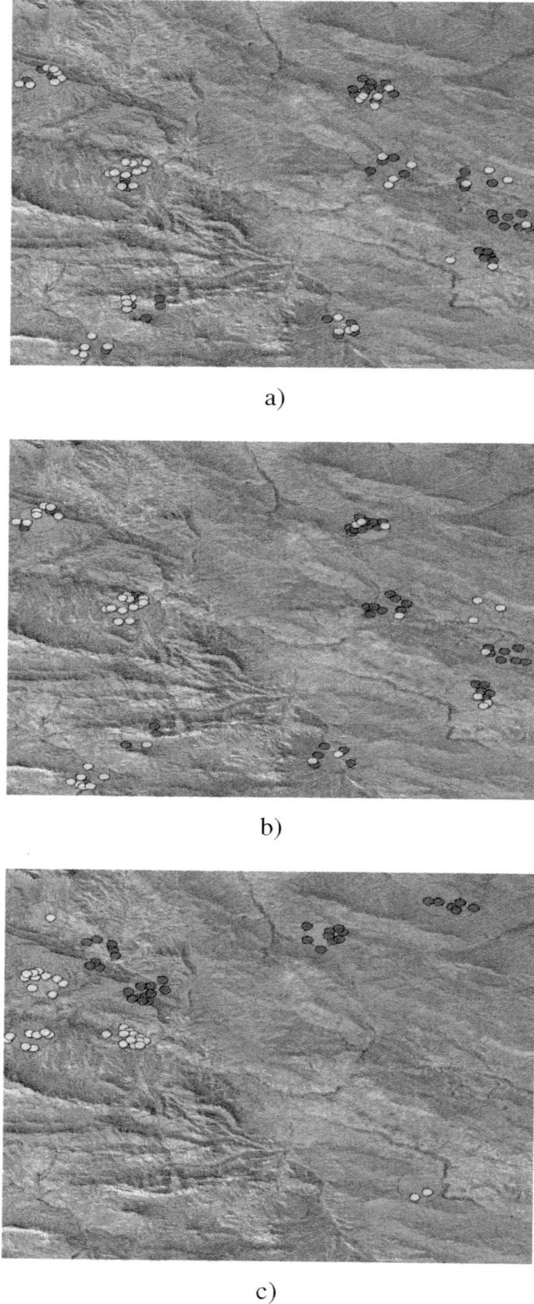

a)

b)

c)

Fig. 3. Distribution of individuals in several simulation steps. In red, Species *A*, in yellow Species *B*. a) at step 1 b) at step 3, c) at step 20.

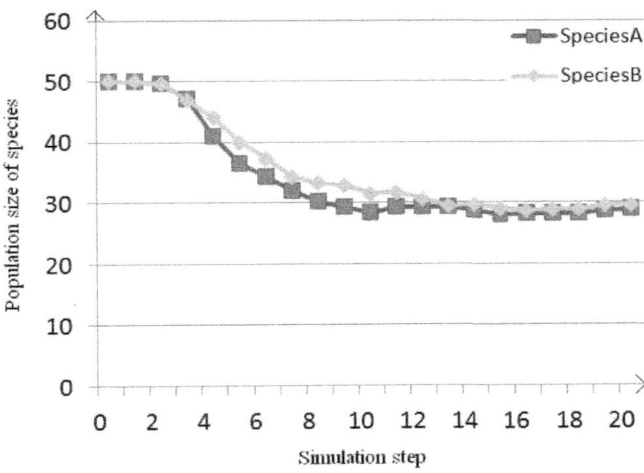

Fig. 4. Evolution of the number of individuals of each species (mean of 30 simulations)

4 Methodology

EBMs are compartment models which operate on global laws generally, defined by the equations that apply to all members of the compartments. In such models, the individuals are assumed to be homogenous and well mixed: they are all treated as identical. Moreover, EBMs do not have "real" environment which allows individuals eat, move, reproduce and interact with others individuals. Therefore, our methodology basically is to abstract/simplify local parameters and to translate them into equations of compartments.

4.1 First Step: Simplification and Abstraction Environment and Translate It into Equations

The first step of our methodology is to simplify the environment, i.e. to get rid of many local properties of the environment such as its topology, its dynamics, its nature and so on. Several questions are raised in this step:

- the homogeneity of the environment
- its discretization, i.e. patchy environment
- the perception it can offer to species (for instance, are there any refuge for species?) and so on

4.2 Second Step: Analysis and Abstract Local Behaviors of Agents and Translate Them into Equations

The second step is to analyze, one by one, the local behaviors of the agents. We then abstract and translate them into global parameters in equations. Each of these "abstractions" is tested and validated with respect to the results obtained with the simulations of the IBM.

Each step consists in:

- Building several models related to the global parameters we choose
- Exploring their dynamics and "validate" each of them with respect to the IBM simulation results
- Choosing the most relevant value of the parameters

5 Instantiation on the Case Study

In this section, we show how global parameters can be extracted from the local parameters of the IBM. An EBM consists of compartments which are usually chosen as population densities in ecology systems. We, therefore, consider compartments in our EBM as population densities. Others factors and parameters have effects on these parameters. These effects, of course, are represented by parameters in an evolution function of the compartment-population densities. We now investigate, by using the methodology presented above, how to represent these factors and parameters and such an evolution function in our EBM.

5.1 Simplification and Abstraction Environment and Translate It into Equations

The first factor is environment. The environment in the IBM is very complex. It, however, should be simple in our EBM. According to the above remarks, we consider the environment in our EBM as a simplest case of patchy environment, i.e. two patches environment. This leads to the fact that there are four compartments of the two species in two patches: species 1 (species 2, respectively) on patch 1, species 1 (species 2, respectively) on patch 2.

5.2 Analysis and Abstraction Local Behaviors of Individuals and Translate Them into Equations

Reproduction probability. This factor represents the probability that an individual reproduces after a certain number of simulation steps. It means that the population densities increase when values of this factor increases. The corresponding global parameter is growth rate which has positive effect on evolution of population densities.

Competition parameters. In the IBM, there are two kinds of competition: the intra-competition which represents the competition among individuals of the same species, and the extra-competition which represents the competition among individuals of different species. To represent this factor in EBM, the classic Lotka-Volterra competition model \cite{M89} seems to be a good candidate. We note that, in the IBM,, individuals compete with others for food. The competition, therefore, takes place on the patches.

Following this analysis, we propose therefore to use the classic Lotka-Volterra competition model to represent the evolution of population densities on both patches.

Movement/migration. Another important factor is the movement of individuals. In the IBM, SC individuals move randomly in the environment to search for food patches. It is, therefore, assumed that SC always stay on some food patches. IC individuals have two kinds of movement: the first one is a random move and the second one is a SC density dependent move, i.e. the IC individuals are more likely to move to patches where there are few SC individuals. These tactics of movement, on the fast time scale, lead to the distribution of IC on the patches ([2], [4]). Being in mind that we do not have a real environment in our EBM. Therefore, we represent the number of immigrations and emigrations on each patch by using a function of density, i.e. a migration function. This function must increase when the other species population density increase. To simplify, we choose a homogenous linear function of population density, i.e. a straight line.

Time scales. The important point is that in the IBM, all the agent behaviors are not triggered every simulation step. Indeed, while the agents move at each step, they reproduce and interact only at specific simulation steps. Local dynamics (reproduction, interaction), therefore, seems to act on slow time scale than movement process. We represent the two time scale, in our EBM, by using small parameter ε which is the ratio between two time scales.

In the next section, we use these global parameters to build our EBM. We also analysis the EBM and compare its results with the results of the ABM.

6 Equation-Based Model

6.1 Complete Model

We consider two competing species in two patch environment. Based on the above remarks, we further assume that two time scales are involved in the dynamics: a fast one corresponds to dispersal between patches and a slow for local population dynamics. According to these assumptions, the complete model reads as follows:

$$\begin{cases}
\frac{dn_{11}}{d\tau} = \left(-(\alpha_1 n_{21})n_{11} + (\alpha_2 n_{22})n_{12}\right) \\
\qquad + \varepsilon r_{11} n_{11}\left(1 - \frac{n_{11}}{K_{11}} - a_{121}\frac{n_{21}}{K_{11}}\right) \\
\frac{dn_{12}}{d\tau} = \left((\alpha_1 n_{21})n_{11} - (\alpha_2 n_{22})n_{12}\right) \\
\qquad + \varepsilon r_{12} n_{12}\left(1 - \frac{n_{12}}{K_{12}} - a_{122}\frac{n_{22}}{K_{12}}\right) \\
\frac{dn_{21}}{d\tau} = \left(-(\beta_1 n_{11})n_{21} + (\beta_2 n_{12})n_{22}\right) \\
\qquad + \varepsilon r_{21} n_{21}\left(1 - \frac{n_{21}}{K_{21}} - a_{211}\frac{n_{11}}{K_{21}}\right) \\
\frac{dn_{22}}{d\tau} = \left(-(\beta_1 n_{11})n_{21} + (\beta_2 n_{12})n_{22}\right) \\
\qquad + \varepsilon r_{22} n_{22}\left(1 - \frac{n_{22}}{K_{22}} - a_{212}\frac{n_{12}}{K_{22}}\right)
\end{cases} \tag{1}$$

where n_{1j} is the density of species *A* living on patch j , n_{2j} is the density of species *B* living on patch j $j=1,2.$. $r's$ and $K's$ represent the growth rates and carrying capacities of species. Parameters a_{12j} and a_{21j} represent the competition coefficients showing the negative effect of species *A* on species *B* and species *B* on species *A* on patch $j, j=1,2$, respectively. α_j is the dispersal rate of the species *A* leaving patch $j, j=1,2$, and β_j is the dispersal rate of the species *B* leaving patch $j, j=1,2$. ε is the ratio between two time scales. The term with ε corresponds to the slow time scale-birth death and competition processes; and the term without ε corresponds to the fast time scale-migration process. In this model, individuals of a given species use the other species density-dependent migration in the sense that if there are many individuals of a given species on a given patch then individuals of the other species are more likely to leave that patch rapidly. We note that we are interested in pre-emptive competition locally on each patch and the conditions ensure for this case are given by

$$a_{12j}K_{2j} / K_{1j} > 1, a_{21j}K_{1j} / K_{2j} > 1, \qquad j=1,2. \tag{2}$$

We are going to use aggregation of variables methods in order to derive a reduced model [4]. The first step is to look for the existence of a stable and fast equilibrium.

6.2 Fast Equilibrium

Fast equilibrium is the solution of the following system:

$$\alpha_1 n_{11} n_{21} = \alpha_2 (n_1 - n_{11})(n_2 - n_{21}), \qquad \beta_1 n_{11} n_{21} = \beta_2 (n_1 - n_{11})(n_2 - n_{21}),$$
$$n_1 = n_{11} + n_{12}, n_2 = n_{21} + n_{22} \tag{3}$$

It is easy to obtain that there are two stable and fast equilibria as follows:

$$n_{11}^* = n_1, n_{12}^* = 0; n_{21}^* = 0, n_{22}^* = n_2$$
$$\text{and} \quad n_{11}^* = 0, n_{12}^* = n_1; n_{21}^* = n_2, n_{22}^* = 0 \tag{4}$$

6.3 Aggregated Model

Substitution of the fast equilibria into the complete model (1) leads to two reduced models as follows:

Model 1 is the model which corresponds to the equilibrium $n_{11}^* = n_1, n_{12}^* = 0; n_{21}^* = 0, n_{22}^* = n_2$.

$$\begin{cases} \dfrac{dn_1}{dt} = r_{11} n_1 \left(1 - \dfrac{n_1}{K_{11}}\right) \\ \dfrac{dn_2}{dt} = r_{22} n_2 \left(1 - \dfrac{n_2}{K_{22}}\right) \end{cases} \tag{5}$$

Model 2 is the model which corresponds to the equilibrium $n_{11}^* = 0, n_{12}^* = n_1; n_{21}^* = n_2, n_{22}^* = 0$.

$$\begin{cases} \dfrac{dn_1}{dt} = r_{12} n_1 \left(1 - \dfrac{n_1}{K_{12}}\right) \\ \dfrac{dn_2}{dt} = r_{21} n_2 \left(1 - \dfrac{n_2}{K_{21}}\right) \end{cases} \tag{6}$$

The two aggregated models are two logistic models for two species on two patches. Model 1 corresponds to the case when all individuals of species *A* are located on patch 1 while all individuals of species *B* are located on patch 2 and Model 2 corresponds vice versa. This means that two species coexist globally in the patchy environment and each species has its own living patch. One can see that this result is exactly the same as the result in the ABM. Fig. 5 shows the case of model 2 when all individuals of species *B* are located on patch 1 while all individuals of species *A* are located on patch 2.

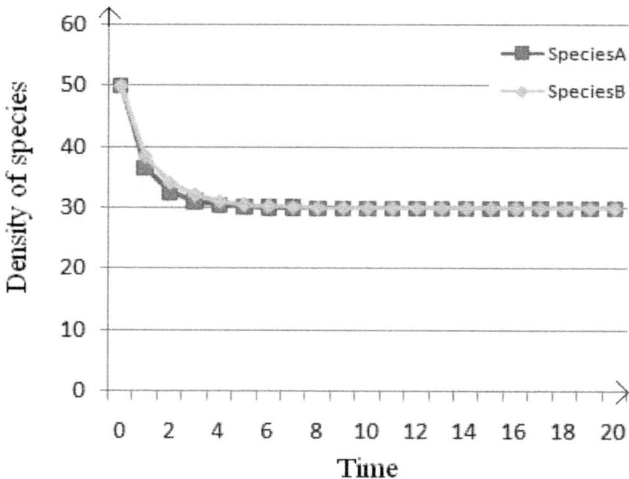

Fig. 5. Two species coexist on two patches in model 2

7 Conclusion and Perspectives

In this paper, we proposed a methodology to infer an EBM from a given ABM. This methodology was illustrated through a case study concerning the competition of two species. Our idea is to consider as a virtual laboratory to test and to see effects of parameters and then to choose parameters to build the EBM. We also showed that the coexistence result of the obtained EBM is the same as that of the ABM. We conclude that these two techniques do not compete with each other: they instead tend to be ideally complementary with respect to the set of questions a modeler would want a model to answer. In this paper, we consider a simple case study of only two competing species. It would be interesting to consider more complex case studies of more than two competing species. It would be also interesting to couple these two types of model in modeling others ecological complex systems such as prey-predator systems, host-parasitoid systems and especially in epidemiology systems where it is impossible for one to test in order to get empirical observations and thus it is useful to use ABMs as a virtual laboratory. We would like to present these contributions in the near future.

References

1. Fahse, L., Wissel, C., Grimm, V.: Reconciling classical and individual-based aprroahes in theoretical population ecology: a protocol for extracting population parameters from individual-based models. American Naturalist 152, 838–852 (1998)
2. Nguyen, N.D., Drogoul, A., Auger, P.: Methodological Steps and Issues When Deriving Individual Based-Models from Equation-Based Models: A Case Study in Population Dynamics. In: Bui, T.D., Ho, T.V., Ha, Q.T. (eds.) PRIMA 2008. LNCS (LNAI), vol. 5357, pp. 295–306. Springer, Heidelberg (2008)

3. Murray, J.D.: Mathematical Biology. Springer, Heidelberg (1989)
4. Auger, P., Bravo de la Parra, R., Poggiale, J.C., Sánchez, E., Nguyen Huu, T.: Aggregation of variables and applications to population dynamics. In: Magal, P., Ruan, S. (eds.) Structured Population Models in Biology and Epidemiology, Springer, Heidelberg (2008)
5. Grimm, V., Railsback, S.F.: Individual-based Modeling and Ecology. Princeton University Press (2005)
6. Laubenbacher, R., Jarrah, A.S., Mortveit, H., Ravi, S.S.: A mathematical formalism for agent-based modeling, arXiv:08.01.0249v1 [cs. MA] (2007); Fahse, L., Wissel, C., Grimm, V.: Reconciling classical and individual-based aprroahes in theoretical population ecology: a protocol for extracting population parameters from individual-based models. American Naturalist 152, 838–852 (1998)
7. Law, R., Dieckmann, U.: Moment approximations of individual-based models (1999), `http://www.iiasa.ac.at/Admin/PUB/Documents/IR-99-043.pdf`
8. Grimm, V., Berger, U., Bastiansen, F., Eliassen, S., Ginot, V., Giske, J., Goss-Custard, J., Grand, T., Heinz, S.K., Huse, G., Huth, A., Jepsen, J.U., Jørgensen, C., Mooij, W.M., Müller, B., Pe'er, G., Piou, C., Railsback, S.F., Robbins, A.M., Robbins, M.M., Rossmanith, E., Rüger, N., Strand, E., Souissi, S., Stillman, R.A., Vabo, R., Visser, U., DeAngelis, D.L.: A standard protocol for describing individual-based and agent-based models. Ecological Modelling 198(1-2), 115–126 (2006)
9. Amouroux, E., Chu, T.-Q., Boucher, A., Drogoul, A.: GAMA: An Environment for Implementing and Running Spatially Explicit Multi-Agent Simulations. In: Ghose, A., Governatori, G., Sadananda, R. (eds.) PRIMA 2007. LNCS, vol. 5044, pp. 359–371. Springer, Heidelberg (2009)
10. Luke, S., Cioffi-Revilla, C., Panait, L., Sullivan, K., Balan, G.: MASON: a multiagent simulation environment. Simulation 81, 517–527 (2005)
11. North, M.J., Collier, N.T., Vos, J.R.: Experiences Creating Three Implementations of the Repast Agent Modeling Toolkit. ACM Transactions on Modeling and Computer Simulation 16(1), 1–25 (2006)
12. Tisue, S., Wilensky. U.: NetLogo: A Simple Environment for Modeling Complexity. In: ICCS (2004)

Towards a Methodology for the Participatory Design of Agent-Based Models

Thanh-Quang Chu[1,2], Alexis Drogoul[1,2], Alain Boucher[1], and Jean-Daniel Zucker[1,2]

[1] IFI, Equipe MSI; IRD, UMI 209 UMMISCO
Institut de la Francophonie pour l'Informatique, 42 Ta Quang Buu, Hanoi, Vietnam
Vietnam National University, Hanoi, Vietnam
[2] IRD, UMI 209 UMMISCO
Institut de Recherche pour le Developpement, 32, av Henri Varagnat,
93143, Bondy Cedex, France
{thanh.quang,alexis.drogoul,alainboucher12,jdzucker}@gmail.com

Abstract. Developing models that effectively model human behavior and activities in social phenomena requires a tight collaboration between designers, experts and end-users. This paper presents an approach based on participatory design to find the most effective ways to succeed in this endeavor. Building up from a case study in emergency management, we identify three key design activities that have proven essential to be articulated so that users knowledge is elicited with ease and efficiency. The first is the design of the user-interface, the second the design of scenarios and the third the design of the experimental protocol. These activities pave the way for a first step towards a complete methodology.

Keywords: Participatory design, Agent-based simulation, Role-playing games, Emergency management.

1 Introduction

The participatory design (known before as Cooperative Design) attempts to actively involve all stakeholders (e.g. designers, developers, experts, end-users, etc.) in the design process to help ensure that the product designed meets their needs and is usable. The methodological solution, called Cooperative Prototyping, proposed by Grønbæk [9,10,11,12], aims at involving users in design and evaluation of early prototypes of information systems. This approach proposes solutions to two problems: on one hand, how to motivate the users to "play the game" of being in a work situation with a preliminary prototype of a future computer application; on the other hand, the necessity to make users understand that the prototype they are playing with is changeable and far from being a complete application, which means they can make proposals [9].

By applying participatory design for social simulations, which aim at modeling and understanding social phenomena or resolution of society for a given problem, we have the participatory social simulations (PSSs). The stakeholders are involved in

N. Desai, A. Liu, and M. Winikoff (Eds.): PRIMA 2010, LNAI 7057, pp. 428–442, 2012.

designing PSSs from the earliest stage [21] to validate and improve the modeled behavior in order to these systems are more realistic in simulating the resolution of society for that problem [2,3,7,8].

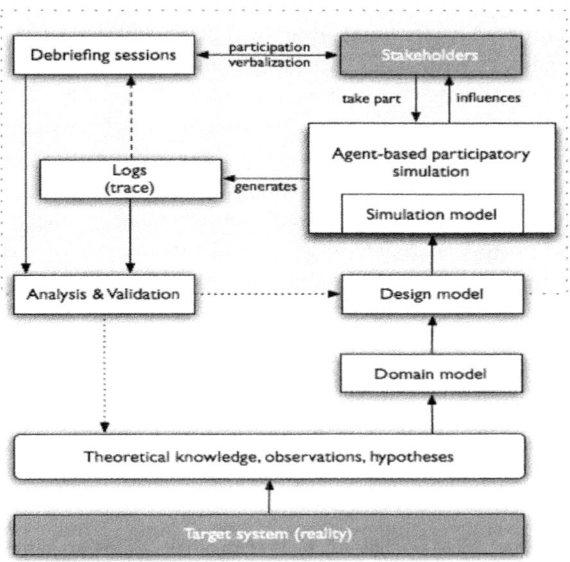

Fig. 1. The interactive diagram of the design process for PSSs: this process consists in designing the simulation, conducting the experiments, organizing debriefing sessions and analyzing the result [2]

Our research presents the participatory design process of a complete PSS. In fact, the users are involved to play the role of agents in a simulation (based on a prototype model) and help these agents in making decisions in given situations. The sequence of work situations will allow the participants to navigate from one situation to another in order that they participate actively in games. Because, the PSSs make participants understand better the model and can take part in solving problem, so the modelers (i.e. designers) can build more realistic model and improve the efficiency of model in solving the problem base on the elicited individual/collective behavior of participants.

This paper mainly addresses the question of the necessary components for effectively involving the users into agent-based simulations and eliciting their knowledge. We claim that at least three tasks need to be carefully undertaken: (a) The design of a flexible and ergonomic user-interface that would allow for real-time interactions between the participants and agents in the simulator; (b) The design of well-thought scenarios based on realistic conditions and corresponding to specific tasks and objectives; and (c) The design of an experimental protocol composed of sessions organized around a set of support scenarios, and ways to evaluate the quality of the user's participation.

In fact, the use of an ergonomic user-interface (a), with simple scenarios (b), for demonstration sessions (c) can help users to better understand the decision-making process of agents as well as the objective of the agents in the scenarios. Thus, the users can learn how to play the role of the agents and how to control them in games to reach their objectives. Afterward, the design of an interactive user-interface (a) has the duty to help users in easily controlling the agents and that of realistic scenarios (b) to help them to be at ease when applying their own real-life experience into the games. The training sessions (c) aim at improving the quality of the users' decision-making in playing games. Furthermore, the diversity, richness and interestingness of challenges supported by various scenarios (b) are conditions to stimulate the curiosity, motivate the problem solving and maintain the concentration of users during the games. Consequently, the three components above (interface design, scenarios design and experimental protocol) are necessary to make the users' trace richer (because it is collected in as many situations as possible), more reliable (because the players understand the decision-making processes of agents and use their experience in solving problems that appear similar to "real" problems and furthermore can maintain their motivation and concentration when playing games), and ready to be analyzed in the process of elicitation. To illustrate this claim, we apply and analyze these different components in a specific context of emergency management, which is presented in the following section.

2 Case-Study: A Model of Emergency Management

Urban emergency management is the organization of resources and responsibilities for dealing with many aspects of emergencies occurring in cities (e.g. search and rescue of injured persons, extinguish of fires, allow traffic through, etc). A large-scale emergency (like after an earthquake) is usually divided into different decision levels (e.g. city level, district level and ward level), in order to manage resources more effectively. In the model we will be using in this paper [17], each decision level is undertaken by a specific species of agents (i.e. a set of agents sharing the same objectives and decision models).

The *center* takes care of all the aspects of emergency at the city level; his task is to allocate the rescue agencies (e.g. *police offices, hospitals and fire stations*) to districts known as damaged. In turn, each of these agents undertakes a specific responsibility (e.g. *hospitals* take care of injured persons, *police offices* look after blocked road, *fire stations* take care of fires) at the district level; the goal of these agents is to distribute their rescue agents (e.g. *ambulances, polices, firefighters*) to smaller areas (i.e. wards) in that district. And, finally, the rescue agents undertake their specific mission at this level, by choosing an appropriate action or target at a given moment. To coordinate all these types of agents, an important part of the model deals with the description of their collective behavior: interaction and communication protocols between agents are especially detailed, as they allow them to avoid conflicts or increase their efficiency in achieving a common goal. This interaction is realized by the exchange of messages via simulated communication channels.

Our goal in using participatory design for this model has been to improve the realism of the behaviors by allowing users (often experts of emergency management) to play a role in the simulation, change the decision-making or communication of agents, and designing the agents in such a way that they can "learn" from the user's decision and change their individual or collective behavior accordingly (in the previous work [17], we addressed this issue by proposing an interactive learning algorithm, which gradually refines the weights of criteria from user's decision and combines them into an additive utility function for agents). The following sections will both report on our achievements so far and on the lessons we can draw from them from only a methodological point of view.

3 Designing User-Interface

For facilitating the observation and control of players in games, the interface should adapt, as much as possible, to the rhythm and needs of the users: providing them with the possibility to change the speed of the simulation, to zoom in and out on the situations, to change the colors and shapes of the information displayed, to focus on specific entities, to hide or reveal any pieces of information, to come back in time, etc. appears to be a cognitive (and not simply cosmetic) necessity for them to get familiarized with the tools and to grab all the information needed to take appropriate decisions. In the case of our application, responding to all the requirements above has consisted in defining six main views:

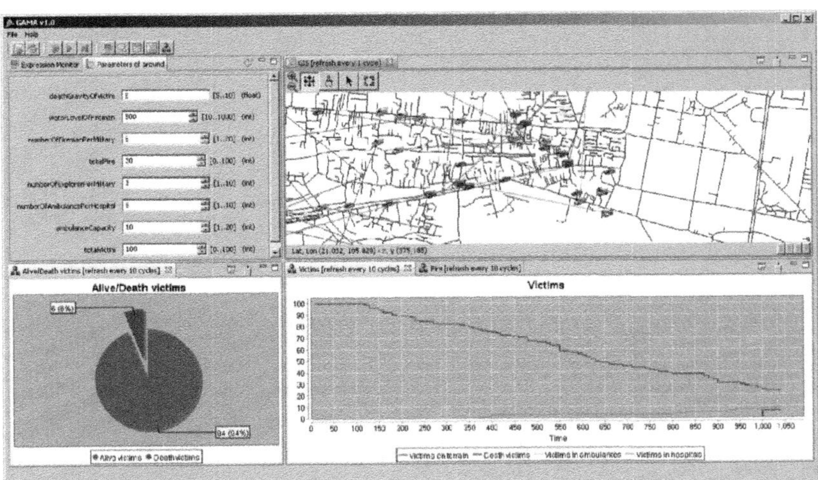

Fig. 2. Different views in user-interface of emergency simulation

The *parameter view* allows users to try different scenarios by changing the value of various input parameters.

The *chart view* shows the result of the simulations and provides an evaluation of the choices made by the users in terms of their "efficiency" (e.g. number of victims dead, number of victims saved, total time to finish extinguishing all fires, etc.).

The *display view* visualizes the simulation, in a GIS environment, at any scale. This view allows the users to zoom in to obtain detailed information, zoom out to have a more general context, as well as focus on the context of the users' agent by highlighting its location on the map, coloring its current route, direction and target. In this view, users are also able to control the agents.

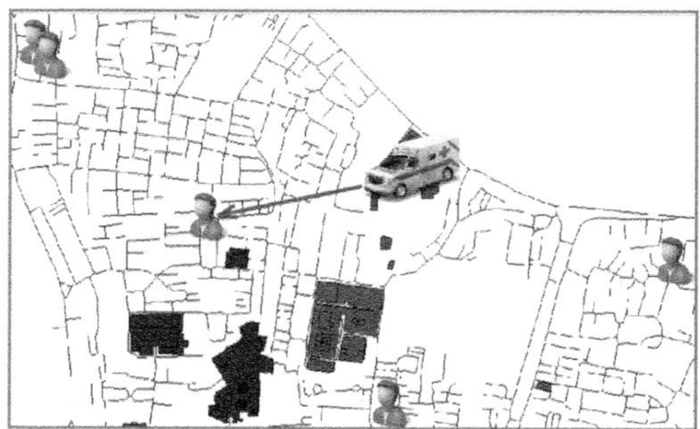

Fig. 3. Display view allows user to observe and control agents

The *dialog view* allows the user to enter in a dialog with an agent, and to emit a suggestion regarding these alternatives. This view displays the decision and reasoning of the agent and allows the user to express and explain its decisions.

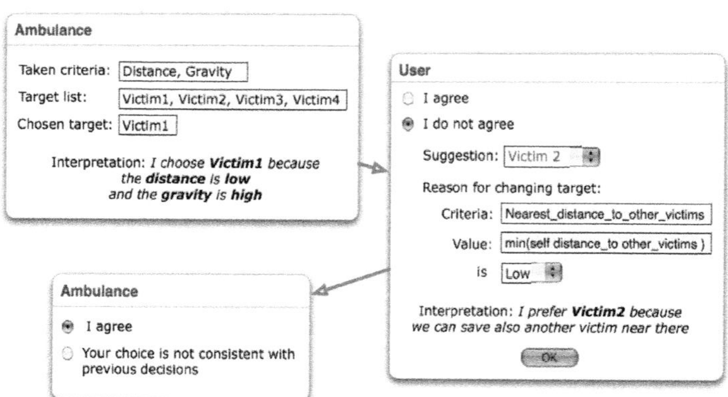

Fig. 4. View of dialog between an ambulance and user

The *agent view* shows the detail of the agents context such as the list of their attributes, messages received from other agents, the alternatives available (in terms, actions, targets and decisions), and the messages sent to other agents.

Finally, the *interaction view* shows the coordination occurring between the agents, and allows the users to add or modify the messages they are exchanging.

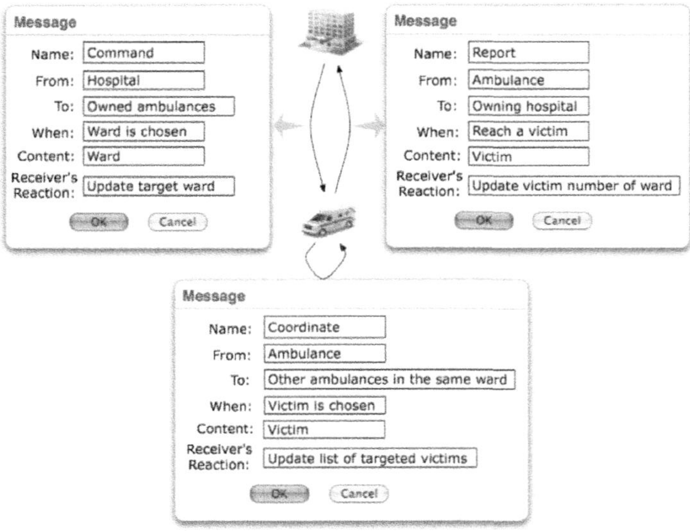

Fig. 5. Interaction view of emergency model

We can see that users have to input reasons for their intervention in *dialog view* (or formulate the attributes of messages in *interaction view*). The reasons could be simples or very complex, it depends on the situation. So, how users input their reasons in order that agents can understand these arguments? We use the modeling language of GAMA [20] (the agent-based modeling and simulation platform that we use to build our emergency model), called GAML to train users before the experiments. For example in figure 4, the string "*min(self distance_to other_victims)*" is the representation of criteria "*nearest distance from this victim to other victims*" that user want to enter for explaining his change. Although users are familiar with GAML, they cannot express easily their arguments in many cases, thus, the interface design must allow users an open way to describe these arguments in natural language or ignore this work. The more information provided by users makes easier the elicitation of user's behavior. But, the users' motivation will be loosen if they must do usually hard works.

This interface design provides users with a good condition to play in a simulation, and therefore, provides modelers with good conditions to realize experiments. However, a well-designed interface is not enough to effectively involve users. As we will see in the following section, on also has to pay attention to the design of the experimental protocol, to the organization of the sessions, to the design of scenarios and the evaluation of the users' participation.

4 Experimental Protocol

4.1 Organization Sessions

The experiments need to take place in real-time. Since we cannot, of course, ask a user or expert to play his/her role during 12 or 24 hours (like in reality), the playing sessions are cut into time-bounded, incremental episodes with their own goal and tasks. Each of these "episode" is structured in the following way: the task to be fulfilled by the agents and the timeframe within which they can accomplish its (for instance, save a maximum of victims in the minimum of time, save the most critical victims and communicate about the others, etc.) is communicated to the user and we make sure it is perfectly understood. Some episodes will of course share the same task.

For each task, a sequence of scenarios is then chosen, ranging from simple ones to more complex ones. Each scenario serves as a support for an "episode" of the session, and its results (in terms of agent's behavior after elicitation) reused for the next episode in the sequence. The behaviors susceptible to be learnt during an episode depend on the complexity provided by the scenario. For instance, in basic scenarios, agents may simply learn how to improve their moves with respect to the location of victims, fires, etc., while, in more advanced ones, they might take communication skills into account (for instance, improve their coordination with the others).

4.2 Designing Scenarios

There are many ways into which short-term focused scenarios could have been designed. We needed a method that would allow for the playing sessions to act as different "layers" of increasing complexity, each of them focusing on the learning of its own set of behaviors and using the previous ones as starting points.

As the behaviors use criteria, which represent bits of information perceived, collected or received by the agents, we chose to base the progression of the scenarios on that of the "informational context" that the agents (and therefore, the user) are facing. For instance, for a task like "locating and carrying a maximum of victims", in a situation where only one ambulance and one hospital are being simulated (see Fig. 6), the decision of the agent will be based on a subset of the criteria used in a situation where several ambulances (or hospitals, or both) are present. And the criteria used in the latter situation will be themselves a subset of those necessary to take into account if all these agents are communicating or coordinating themselves.

Of course, the scenarios space can grow as needed to account for other agents (firemen, civilians, victims themselves, etc.) or criteria (communication of orders, change in priorities, etc.). But we have to keep in mind that (1) not all of them are realistic; (2) no expert will be able to play them all.

The path they follow, in their session, from one episode to the other, is different from one expert to the other, and decided after each run through an interview with the modelers and an evaluation of their interactions with the agents.

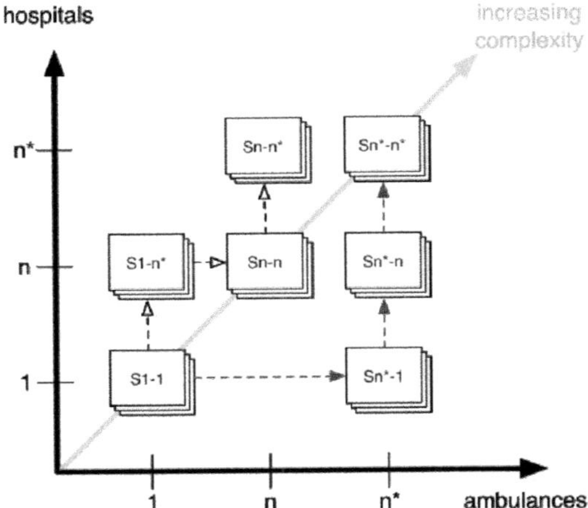

Fig. 6. The description of multiple scenarios as informational contexts of increasing complexity: In the bottom-left corner, the context only implies one ambulance and one hospital; in the top-right corner, n* indicates n agents able to communicate, which represents the most complex situation agents can face if we only take hospitals and ambulances into account

4.3 Designing Questionnaires and Evaluation

The results of participatory design depend on both the quality of the interactions between users and agents, and the effectiveness of the automated elicitation process. A complete evaluation then requires that we firstly evaluate the methodology (which produces what we can call "users' traces") and secondly the elicitation process (which aims at extracting knowledge from these traces to improve the model).

The first evaluation is based on a formalized dialog between modelers and users. Like in [1] and [16], modelers use the answer of participants to a predefined questionnaire that is designed to validate the quality of the interface (e.g. understandability, adaptation to context, etc.) as well as the quality of the scenario design (e.g. understandability, link to reality, progression, etc.). The two questionnaires we have used in our work are presented below:

1. Questionnaire to validate user-interface

- Do you understand the aim of the different views?
- Do you understand the game for the first time of playing?
- Do you understand the reasoning of the agents when they make a decision?
- Can you find easily the necessary information to understand the decision-making of agent?
- Is the information organized in a logic way, and does it facilitate your understanding?

- Is the information updated in real-time?
- Do you find that it easy to control an agent and to change its decision?
- Is it easy to find the reason why an agent does not accept your change?
- Can you easily input your arguments or explanations in order for an agent to accept your change?

2. Questionnaire to validate scenarios

- Have you understood the scenario before playing in the simulation (which agent is controlled, its objective, the evaluation measure, the context, the alternatives, the criteria, the messages)?
- Do you feel that the proposed problems are similar with the problems in real-life?
- Are the concepts in rules and guideline of games familiar with your experience?
- Do you think that the scenario proposed is similar to problems you might encounter in your profession?
- Can you find something unrealistic, illogical and incoherent in the scenario?
- Do you think that most of situations that you meet in the real-life are already proposed in the games?
- Can you propose another scenario in order for the agents to use other criteria to improve their behaviors?
- Do you understand the link between the scenarios in the sequence?
- Do you think that the sequence of scenarios is rich and diverse enough to build a reliable behavior (and therefore, a reliable emergency model)?
- Do you think that the progression of scenarios is understandable and logic?

While this evaluation is mainly qualitative, the evaluation of the elicitation process can be done quantitatively. We can in fact measure any improvement by comparing the differences of the simulation outputs before and after the modification of a model. These outputs represent the efficiency of the model in solving the emergency problem (e.g. time to take all victims to the hospitals, time to extinguish all fires). If the latter output is better than the previous one, then the emergency model is said to have improved (i.e. the user's is considered as positive); in the reverse case, the user's participation is viewed as negative.

Each modification of a model can improve its efficiency in some scenarios but decrease it in others. A good modification is one that improves it in as many scenarios as possible. To evaluate the participants, we use a measure called *achievement*, which is the average of the improvements he/she has made possible in the different scenarios he/she has played in. The *achievement* is a kind of "competition factor" between users: a high achievement means that the user played many scenarios and improved the model. To increase his achievement, a user has to concentrate and use all his experience in the simulation, thus improving the confidence in the quality of the behavior extracted from his participation.

5 Experiments

The first experiment involved master students of the IFI, (promotion 15), who played the role of non-expert users. The objective of this experiment was mainly to test the interface, eliminate its bugs, verify if the scenarios were understandable and logic. This experiment took a half-day in the classroom; each student had a laptop to run separately the simulation. All the students followed the same progression of scenarios. We conducted several experimental sessions (5 or 8 sessions in the half-day). Between two consecutive sessions, the participants and the modelers held a general discussion during 5 minutes on the interface and manipulation of the simulator. Finally, a debriefing session of 30 minutes was done at the end of the half-day to gather the feedbacks and ideas of the students.

The second experiment involved researchers and PhD students of the MSI research team, more aware of simulations and emergency management, and then more keen to play the role of "experts". The objective of this experiment was not only to test the user-interface and the realism of the scenarios but also to modify the model according to the analysis of the "traces" and to measure the improvements provided by the users. Each researcher used a separate computer to run the simulation but they all followed the same progression in scenarios. Each of them was asked to do from 9 to 12 sessions. After each session, they were asked to answer to the questionnaires while their trace was being analyzed and used to modify the model. Each time the model was modified, the same simulation was run again to quantify the improvement provided by the user.

In these two experiments, we only used a subset of scenarios in which the objective of the users is to improve the individual behavior (i.e. the human rescue mission) of ambulances in the simulation (see table 1). Thus, the "number of casualties" was the main measure to evaluate the efficiency of ambulances (and therefore, the users).

Table 1. Parameters of experimented scenarios

Scenario	Parameters			
	Hospital number	**Ambulance number**	**Victim number**	**Ambulance capacity**
1	1	1	6	1
2	1	1	8	2
3	1	1	18	3
4	2	2	33	3

Because it can be difficult for a user to formulate a new criterion to use in the decision-making of ambulances, we fixed a number of behaviors for the ambulance agents (for instance, they automatically chose the type of their target -- hospital or victim by a decision tree like in figure 7). For the set of criteria that ambulance must take into account to make a choice between different potential targets of the same type (for instance, different victims), we defined and explained in details to the users a set of five criteria before the experiment (see table 2). The task of the users during an experiment consisted, then, in choosing a victim as a "good" target for an agent, and in explaining his/her choice by picking up the criteria that seemed the most appropriate to the context.

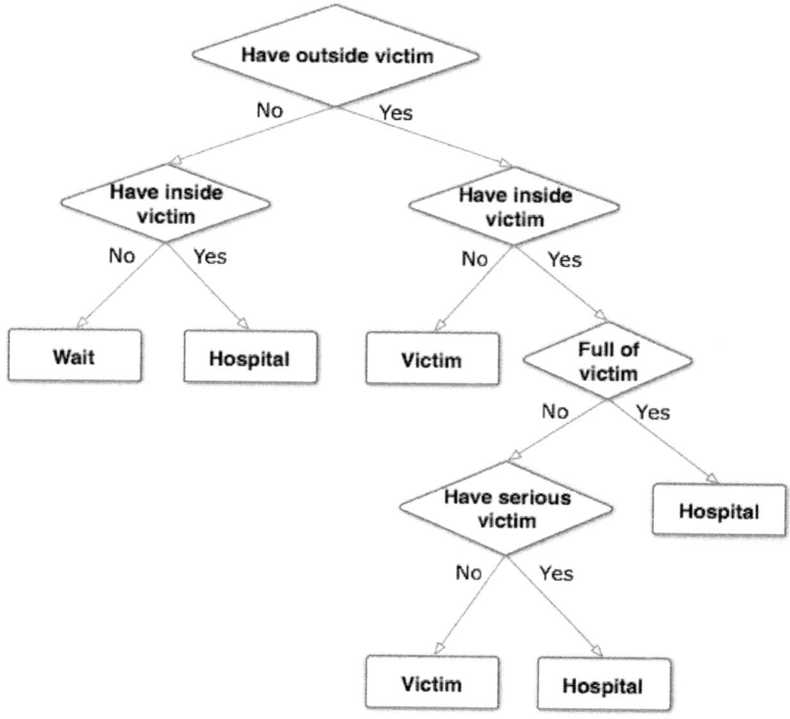

Fig. 7. Decision tree allows ambulances to choose automatically their target types (hospital or victim)

Table 2. Criteria used by ambulances for choosing victims

Criteria	Description
Distance	Distance from the ambulance to this victim
Gravity	Gravity of this victim
Distance to nearest victim	Distance from this victim to the nearest other victims
Near victim number	Number of other victims which are near this victim
Distance to nearest ambulance	Distance from this victim to the nearest other ambulance

The improvement made by users in a rescue scenario was measured by the reduction of the "number of casualties". His/her achievement was the total of his improvements in the four scenarios. Given that the scenarios are deterministic and known in advance to the modeler, the table 3 presents the highest achievement that a user could attain during the sessions.

Table 3. Parameters of experimented scenarios

Scenario		Original Model	Modified Model	Improvement
1	Criteria	Distance	Distance, Gravity	Gravity
	Dead	2	0	2
2	Criteria	Distance, Gravity	Distance, Gravity, Distance to nearest victim	Distance to nearest victim
	Dead	2	1	1
3	Criteria	Distance, Gravity, Distance to nearest victim	Distance, Gravity, Distance to nearest victim, Near victim number	Near victim number
	Dead	7	4	3
4	Criteria	Distance, Gravity, Distance to nearest victim, Near victim number	Distance, Gravity, Distance to nearest victim, Near victim number, Distance to nearest ambulance	Distance to nearest ambulance
	Dead	2	0	2
		Total Improvement		**8**

6 Results

The two experiments involved 27 participants; 16 participants showed no improvement at all, meaning that they did not understand or did not fully participate. We call them "uninterested" participants. Among the remaining 11, all reached the maximal improvement in the first scenario. But, no participant reached the optimal result for all four scenarios (see Table 4).

Table 4. Improvement of 27 participants for 4 scenarios

Improvement	Number of users
0	16/27
2	4/27
3	1/27
4	2/27
5	2/27
6	1/27
7	1/27
8	0/27

Of course, these quantitative-only results are not really significant when it comes to evaluate the methodology. So we also conducted a qualitative analysis of the users' answers to the questionnaires, and we found some arguments to explain these results. In most cases, users did not find the display of information to be clear (e.g. the choices of ambulances were neither highlighted nor grouped, the real-time update of the agents states was not displayed in all views, the situation of agents was described as too complex to analyze when it had a lot of choices and each choice a lot of variables), and so had difficulties to follow the reasoning of the agents; moreover, the control of the agent was not smooth enough and required many steps from the user. These reasons were all cited by the part (16/27) of participants who did not reach any achievement, which probably means that, in participatory design, the design of a good and ergonomic user experience is a necessary task.

The answers provided by the "concerned" participants, however, showed that the scenarios are understandable and realistic, that the concepts used in scenarios are familiar to almost all of them, and that the progression between scenarios was perceived as logic and continuous. Most of them could understand the decision-making of the agents and the goal of the scenarios without difficulty. But, the scenarios themselves were far from the reality and not enough rich and diver (i.e. too few and simple) to build a confident behavior of ambulance.

7 Conclusions and Perspectives

We have presented a methodology for participatory design of agent-based models, which is based on tree main points: the user-interface design, the scenario design and the experimental protocol. By analyzing the results obtained from experiments with participants, we have shown the importance of these tree points: (1) if the user-interface is not well designed, the participants are not interested in playing simulation. So, the user-interface is necessarily enough ergonomic and interactive to make users participate actively into simulation; (2) The scenarios must be understandable, realistic, rich, diver and continuous in order users interest in playing games and do not loose by following up the objective of scenarios; and (3) the experimental protocol makes users be responsible in improving the simulation model by answering to the questionnaires and increasing the efficiency of models. To continue towards a complete methodology for participatory design of agent-based models, we give out following propositions:

For involving more effectively users into participatory experiments, we have to build up really a simulation like *computer and video games*. Because, the *computer and video games* are fun, engaging to provoke the reactions and the concentration of users in playing games thanks to: the high level of reality in simulating virtual world; the high level of interaction between users and simulation; the interesting storyline in accompanying players around challenges, which are organized in a logical way.

Therefore, the user-interface of simulation should be designed like computer and video games to put users into situations and allow them doing as in real-life. Besides, the sequence of scenarios should be enchained like a storyline of video games to accompany users from easy challenges to complex ones. These things allow to users maintaining their motivation in solving the missions in games, and makes users overcome the difficulties with all their effort, competence and experience. So, the decision of users in playing simulation becomes more confident.

Moreover, we should provide users with free feeling in participatory experiments like playing video games by a flexible schedule to play simulation as well as flexible choice to answer the questionnaire (e.g. the users can save their results to continue in other time). The questions of interview have to focus on the details such as a button of interface, a specific agent of simulation, that will allow users answer easily and quickly the questions. In addition, these questions could be yes/no or open discussion but give to users the ideas less or more concrete in evaluating the simulator, expressing easily their ideas and suggestions to improve as much as possible the simulator.

References

1. Nguyen-Duc, M., Drogoul, A.: Using computational agents to design participatory social simulations. Journal of Artificial Societies and Social Simulation 10(4), 5 (2007), http://jasss.soc.surrey.ac.uk/10/4/5.html
2. Guyot, P., Honiden, S.: Agent-based participatory simulations: Merging multi-agent systems and role-playing games. Journal of Artificial Societies and Social Simulation 9(4) (2006), http://jasss.soc.surrey.ac.uk/9/4/8.html
3. Guyot, P., Drogoul, A., Lemaitre, C.: Using emergence in participatory simulations to design multi-agent systems. In: Proceedings of the Fourth International Joint Conference on Autonomous Agents and Multiagent Systems (AAMAS-2005), New York, USA, pp. 199–203 (2005)
4. Ishida, T.: Society-Centered Design for Socially Embedded Multiagent Systems. In: Klusch, M., Ossowski, S., Kashyap, V., Unland, R. (eds.) CIA 2004. LNCS (LNAI), vol. 3191, pp. 16–29. Springer, Heidelberg (2004)
5. Ishida, T., Nakajima, Y., Murakami, Y., Nakanishi, H.: Augmented experiment: Participatory design empowered by multiagent simulation. In: IJCAI-2007 (2007)
6. Murakami, Y., Ishida, T., Kawasoe, T., Hishiyama, R.: Scenario description for multi-agent simulation. In: AAMAS-2003, Melbourne, Australia (2003)
7. Guyot, P., Drogoul, A.: Multi-Agent Based Participatory Simulations on Various Scales. In: Ishida, T., Gasser, L., Nakashima, H. (eds.) MMAS 2005. LNCS (LNAI), vol. 3446, pp. 149–160. Springer, Heidelberg (2005)
8. Guyot, P., Drogoul, A., Honiden, S.: Power and vegotiation: lessons from agent-based participatory simulations. In: AAMAS-2006, pp. 27–33 (2006)
9. Bødker, S., Grønbæk, K.: Cooperative prototyping studies - users and designers envision a dental case record system. In: Studies in Computer Supported Cooperative Work: Theory, Practice and Design. Elsevier Science Publishers/North Holland, Amsterdam (1991)
10. Bødker, S., Grønbæk, K.: Cooperative prototyping: users and designers in mutual activity. International Journal of Man-Machine Studies (1991)
11. Bødker, S., Grønbæk, K., Kying, M.: Cooperative design: techniques and experiences from the scandinavian scene. In: Participatory Design: Principles and Practices. Lawrence Erlbaum Associates, Hillsdale (1993)
12. Grønbæk, K.: Prototyping and active user involvement in system development: Towards a cooperative prototyping approach. Ph.D. thesis, Aarhus University (1991)
13. Fiedrich, F.: An HLA-based multiagent system for optimized resource allocation after strong earthquakes. In: Proceedings of the 2006 Winter Simulation Conference, Washington, USA (2006)
14. Takahashi, T.: Agent-based disaster simulation evaluation and its probability model interpretation. In: Proceedings of ISCRAM 2007, Delft, The Netherlands (2007)

15. Nguyen, H.-P.: Decision support systems applied to earthquake and tsunami risk assessment and loss mitigation. In: Proceedings of IHOCE 2005, Kuala Lumpur, Malaysia (2005)
16. Sempé, F., Nguyen-Duc, M., Boissau, S., Boucher, A., Drogoul, A.: An Artificial Maieutic Approach for Eliciting Experts' Knowledge in Multi-Agent Simulations. In: Sichman, J.S., Antunes, L. (eds.) MABS 2005. LNCS (LNAI), vol. 3891, pp. 75–87. Springer, Heidelberg (2006)
17. Chu, T.-Q., Boucher, A., Drogoul, A., Vo, D.-A., Nguyen, H.-P., Zucker, J.-D.: Interactive Learning of Expert Criteria for Rescue Simulations. In: Bui, T.D., Ho, T.V., Ha, Q.T. (eds.) PRIMA 2008. LNCS (LNAI), vol. 5357, pp. 127–138. Springer, Heidelberg (2008)
18. Suárez, S., López, B., De La Rosa, L.-J.: Co-operation strategies for strengthening civil agents' lives in the RoboCup-Rescue simulator scenario. In: Proceedings of First International Workshop on Synthetic Simulation and Robotics to Mitigate Earthquake Disaster, Padova (2003)
19. Farinelli, A., Grisetti, G., Iocchi, L., Lo Cascio, S., Nardi, D.: Using the RoboCup-Rescue Simulator in an Italian Earthquake Scenario. In: The Program Agenzia 2000 of the Italian Consiglio Nazionale delle Ricerche (2000)
20. Amouroux, E., Chu, T.-Q., Boucher, A., Drogoul, A.: GAMA: An Environment for Implementing and Running Spatially Explicit Multi-Agent Simulations. In: Ghose, A., Governatori, G., Sadananda, R. (eds.) PRIMA 2007. LNCS, vol. 5044, pp. 359–371. Springer, Heidelberg (2009)
21. Gilbert, N., Maltby, S., Asakawa, T.: Participatory simulations for developing scenarios in environmental resource management. In: Urban, C. (ed.) 3rd Workshop on Agent-Based Simulation, pp. 67–72. SCS-Europe, Passau (2002)

A Framework for Validating Task Assignment in Multiagent Systems Using Requirements Importance

Hiroyuki Nakagawa[1], Nobukazu Yoshioka[2], Akihiko Ohsuga[1], and Shinichi Honiden[2,3]

[1] The University of Electro-Communications, 1-5-1 Chofugaoka, Chofu-shi, Tokyo, Japan
[2] National Institute of Informatics, 2-1-2 Hitotsubashi,Chiyoda-ku, Tokyo, Japan
[3] The University of Tokyo,7-3-1 Hongo, Bunkyo-ku, Tokyo, Japan
{nakagawa,ohsuga}@is.uec.ac.jp,
{nobukazu,honiden}@nii.ac.jp

Abstract. Multi-agent systems (MASs) are one of the effective approaches for dealing with the recent increase in software complexity and their autonomy. In the MAS research community, there has recently been increasing interest in the adoption of requirements engineering techniques to bridge the gap between the system requirements and the system design. One of the most important tasks based on the requirements description in the MAS design activity is the extraction of roles, which are the fundamental components of multi-agent systems, from it. It is also important to comprehend the relative degree of responsibility of the individual roles. The comprehension helps the developer decide the system architecture and discuss the performance and stability of the system. We introduce the concept of importance as a quantitative metric and an evaluation framework for the extraction of a suitable role set for the system and the task assignment to these roles. The importance is propagated from the requirements to the roles through their assigned tasks. We demonstrate the effectiveness of our framework through a case study and show that our metric and evaluation framework help not only to identify the importance of each role, but also to determine the system architecture.

1 Introduction

Agent technology offers a solution for producing complex software systems characterized by autonomous behavior, a high degree of distribution, and mobility support. A considerable number of studies have been conducted on methodologies for multi-agent system (MAS) development [1]. The MAS development process [2],[3] is structurally similar to the standard development process: it contains the requirements analysis, architectural design, detailed design, implementation, test, and maintenance phases. However, since MAS consists of multiple agents, the MAS design process is more complicated than that of generic software systems. In particular, the lack of evaluation techniques for the architecture model makes it difficult to close the gap between the requirements analysis phase and the architectural design phase of the MAS development. As a result, it is still difficult to construct a design model for MAS.

We focused on the role extraction and the task assignment using the requirements description in order to reduce the gap between these phases. By roles, we mean the

N. Desai, A. Liu, and M. Winikoff (Eds.): PRIMA 2010, LNAI 7057, pp. 443–458, 2012.

responsibilities to satisfy the requirements and that are assigned to the agents in MAS. Since role extraction and task assignment not only has an impact on the design activities, e.g., designing interactions and determining the system architecture, but also influencing the system performance, these are the most important activities in the architectural design phase.

This paper introduces the concept of importance as a quantitative metric for validating the constructed architecture model. The requirements importance is propagated from the requirements description to the architecture model and thus the MAS developer can validate a constructed architecture model based on the requirements engineer's intention. In particular, we use KAOS [4],[5] as a goal-oriented requirements description [6] to propagate the importance value. We have previously introduced a model transformation technique from a KAOS description to a MAS architecture model [7]. This previous study, in particular, used KAOS as a requirements description language for designing MAS, and the technique transforms it into a general MAS architecture model. KAOS provides a number of model descriptors for connecting the requirements description to the design model. Our approach builds upon the transformation techniques.

The primary contributions of this paper are as follows:

1. The paper introduces a quantitative metric for validating the role extraction and task assignment for MAS. The proposed framework calculates the metric by using a constructed KAOS model with goal prioritization.
2. It gives guidelines for refining the MAS architecture model and requirements description on the basis of the metric.
3. It reports the results from the application of the importance measurement on an implemented system and discusses the improvement in the architecture model using real-world development data.

The rest of this paper is organized as follows: Section 2 gives the background on the architectural design activity for multi-agent systems and identifies the requirements of the metric for evaluating the architecture models. Section 3 introduces the "importance" metric and how it is calculated in our evaluation framework. Section 4 reports on our evaluation through a case study on the architectural design of a tracking system. Section 5 discusses the possibility of automating our method and its limitations. Section 6 discusses the related work, and Section 7 concludes the paper with an outline of our future work.

2 Background

2.1 MAS Architectural Design

MAS architecture usually consists of the following elements: *roles*, *interactions*, *environmental resources*, and *organizations* [8]. The roles are responsible for accomplishing the requirements and they are assigned to the agents in MAS. Once the set of roles are determined with a suitable set of responsibilities for monitoring and controlling the environmental resources in the architectural design phase, we can discuss the communication methods needed between the roles, which are interactions, and define the system architecture, which is called the organization, on the basis of them. Therefore, the most important and fundamental element of the MAS architecture model is the roles, and a number of MAS methodologies have focused on the roles and their extraction [8], [9], [10], [11], [12].

However, current methodologies lack the guidelines for assigning requirements to roles, and therefore, role identification and the assignment of requirements to roles requires us with knowledge of the domain properties and that have design experience. It is also difficult to validate the results of the role identification because of the non-existence of a metric for checking whether the identified role set satisfies the system requirements.

Moreover, just like in human society, roles have a great impact on the organizations in MAS. For example, if a great deal of communication is required between two important roles, introducing a mediating role between these two roles may advance the system performance. It follows that we have to not only extract roles that satisfy the system requirements but also discuss whether the information processing roles should be introduced by taking into account the communications methods and the system architecture. Therefore, in this paper, we define the following items for evaluating the MAS architecture model:

1. **Validity of role set:** We can evaluate whether the extracted role set is suitable for satisfying the system requirements.
2. **Roles responsibility quantity:** We can measure the quantity of the responsibility of individual roles and evaluate the assigned loads of each role.
3. **Adequacy of system architecture:** We can evaluate the system architecture in terms of the stability and the communication efficiency.

2.2 MAS Architecture Model Construction Based on KAOS

We have successfully applied a goal-oriented requirements description in the construction of the MAS architectural design [7]. In particular, we adopted KAOS [4], [5] as our goal-oriented requirements description to generate a general MAS architecture model.

In KAOS, the system goals are refined (decomposed) into requirements and expectations in the goal model. The requirements are the goals that the target system should achieve, and the expectations are tasks of environmental actors. After refinement, the requirements and expectations are assigned to the agents[1] as their responsibilities in the responsibility model, where the agents in KAOS represent the actors, which are the target system and environmental actors, and then the operations that satisfy them are derived. Finally, all the behaviors expressed in the operations and relevant events are described. KAOS provides not only the requirements descriptors, e.g., goals, requirements, and agents, but also the system design descriptors, e.g., operations and events, which can be used for model transformation into the design model for the systems. We used the relationships between two such kinds of descriptors in the KAOS model for model transformation.

[1] Agents in KAOS represent the actors, which are the target system and environmental actors, e.g., users, devices, and relevant systems.

Table 1. Mapping from KAOS into MAS architecture model

KAOS	MAS
Agents	– Roles – Environmental actors (e.g., users, devices, and relevant systems)
Operations	– Activities
Events	– Messages constituting interactions – External events
Entities	– Environmental resources

Table 1 gives the mapping from the KAOS model into the MAS architecture model. Our transformation method puts restrictions on the requirements description. In particular, the requirements on the KAOS model have to be sufficiently decomposed to assign them to roles, and this allows role extraction from the requirements description. As for the further transformation, the operations that satisfy the requirements in the KAOS model are transformed into activities, which are the tasks that the roles can complete by themselves, and the events between the agents representing roles are transformed into messages that constitute interactions. The transformation technique maps these KAOS descriptors into the generic MAS design descriptors in order to reduce the gap between the requirements description and the MAS architecture model.

3 RE-IMPULSE

This section presents *RE-IMPULSE*, our evaluation framework for the MAS architecture model. RE-IMPULSE calculates each role's importance by using the importance of the software requirements. The framework uses the KAOS description as a requirements description for MAS and the framework calculates each role's importance by propagating and aggregating the importance value assigned to the requirements described in the KAOS model. We can not only validate an extracted role set, but can also evaluate the system architecture by using the calculated value.

3.1 Importance Metrics and Evaluation Process

RE-IMPULSE focuses on the importance of the role activities and the structural complexity of interactions. It represents these aspects as a metric, which is called the *role importance*. This single metric reduces the cost for the assignment values and simplifies the evaluation process.

As for the components of the evaluation, the role activities are the tasks that the roles can complete by themselves. These activities should be evaluated in terms of the importance of the provided functions, and therefore, importance should be assigned to the functions described in the requirements description. On the other hand, the structural complexity can be evaluated from the MAS architecture model that represents the flow of interactions. Therefore, our framework propagates the importance values from the requirements descriptors into the design descriptors, and then calculates these values on the MAS architecture model.

The evaluation process based on our framework, which is shown in Figure 1, consists of three activities.

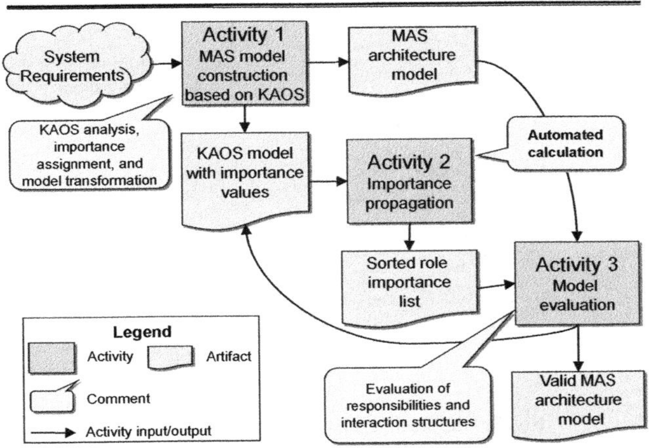

Fig. 1. Evaluation process based on RE-IMPULSE

1. **KAOS model construction:** Our framework begins by analyzing the requirements for MAS, by using the KAOS modeling described in [7]. After describing the KAOS model, requirements engineers put the importance values into the requirements in the model that can propagate to roles.
2. **Importance propagation:** After constructing the KAOS model, a calculation tool automatically propagates the importance of the requirements to the extracted roles through the KAOS elements. This tool outputs the total importance values for individual roles in descending order.
3. **Model refinement:** The developers evaluate the responsibility of the roles using the acquired importance value, and discuss whether the extracted role set and the interaction structure that forms the system architecture is sufficient. The developers review the role set or changes in the interaction structure, if needed, and reevaluate the updated model using the updated importance values.

The following sections explain each activity of our evaluation framework.

3.2 MAS Model Construction Based on KAOS

RE-IMPULSE uses the KAOS model as a requirements description for MAS. The importance propagation of RE-IMPULSE is based on the model transformation technique of our previous work described in Section 2.2, and the framework calculates each role's importance by inheriting and aggregating the importance value assigned to the requirements described in the KAOS model. As described in Section 3.1, importance should be evaluated for the functions in the requirements description. In RE-IMPULSE, the requirements engineers assign importance values to the goals in the KAOS goal model.

3.3 Importance Propagation

Next, an importance calculation tool automatically propagates the importance values assigned to the requirements through the KAOS model, assigning an aggregated

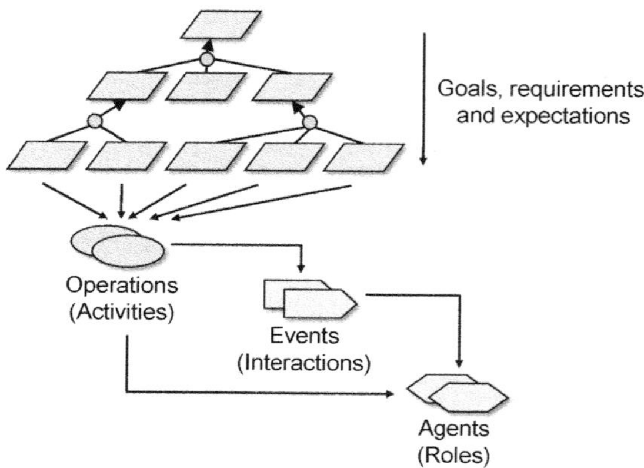

Fig. 2. Importance propagation in KAOS model

importance to each individual role. Figure 2 illustrates the flow of importance propagation between the KAOS descriptors. First, the importance values assigned to the goals are propagated to all of the nodes in the goal tree, i.e., all of the goals, requirements, and expectations. Next, the importance values assigned to the requirements and expectations are inherited in the operations that satisfy them. The values assigned to the operations are also propagated to the events, some of which are extracted as the interactions, and finally the values assigned to the operations and interactions are aggregated by each role and the role importance is then decided. This section explains the method of propagation.

As described in Section 2.2, importance should be estimated for the system requirements that derive functions, that is the goals or requirements in the KAOS model. Our framework allows for the assignment of their importance; any existing children inherit these values. Figure 3 shows a propagation example in a goal model. In our framework, the requirements engineer defines the importance by setting the ratio to the sub-goals for representing a relative value among all of their sibling goal nodes. The reason why we chose a ratio setting is that the determination of the relative importance using a comparison between the sibling goals is easier than that of the absolute importance values of the goals. If the requirements engineer does not set the ratio to the subgoals, e.g., node N and O in Figure 3, these goals inherit the equally divided importance value.

$$\text{Importance}_{child} = \text{Importance}_{parent} \cdot \text{ratio} \tag{1}$$

Note that, in general, deeper goals are assigned small values. For example, if the requirements engineer sets the importance of the root node 100 on the goal model in Figure 3, the importance of the node D is 20, on the other hand, the importance of node L is only 1.8 by using (1). In many cases, the depth of the leaf nodes differs from the other parts of the same goal model. Moreover, a deeper and more intensive analysis creates deeper goals. Therefore, the difference in importance caused by the difference in depth should be reduced, and thus, we introduce the following bias ratio.

$$\text{Importance}_{child} = \text{Importance}_{parent} \cdot \textit{bias ratio} \tag{2}$$

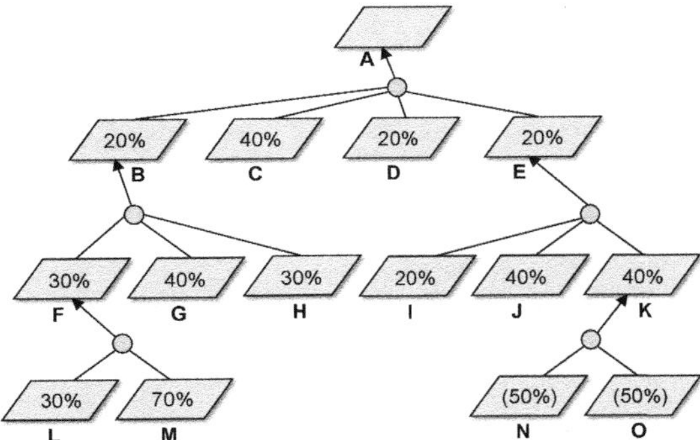

Fig. 3. Importance propagation in goal model. Values in parentheses were not explicitly set by a requirements engineer.

We will now discuss the bias. First of all, the bias should diminish reductions in the importance value. Therefore, the bias ratio should be greater than the ratio assigned to each subgoal. However, the importance value of the subgoal should not exceed that of parent goal. The bias also should reflect the order and values of the given ratio among subgoals. Taking this into account, we introduce the following bias ratio.

$$biasratio : b(r_i) = \frac{r_i}{\max(r_1, ..., r_m)} \qquad (1 \le i \le m) \tag{3}$$

where m represents the number of subgoals, and r_i represents the ratio of subgoal i. Obviously, $r_i < \frac{r_i}{\max(r_1,...,r_m)} \le 1$ $(0 < r_i)$ is always satisfied; therefore, this function provides greater value than r_i, and calculated importance does not exceed the value of parent node, which are suitable for use as the bias function. It also reflects the order and values of the given ratio among subgoals. For example, in the previous example, the importance of nodes D and L are 50 and 16.07, respectively – the difference between two nodes shrinks from 11 times to approximately 3 times.

After propagating in the goal model, the importance value is inherited by the other elements. First, for each requirement, the relevant operations inherit the corresponding importance values. The importance value of an operation is the sum of the values of the assigned requirements. In our framework, operations are the activities of the roles and environmental actors, which are the tasks that they can complete by themselves. Next, the importance values of the operations propagate to the events, some of which are the interactions between roles. Interactions are a type of communication method for the roles, which consist of messages among them. Our framework, on the basis of the transformation process in [7], identifies the events that connect operations assigned to roles as interactions. Figure 4 shows the flow for deciding the meeting time schedule described in the KAOS model. Since roles that involve interactions send and receive messages, we focus on individual message passing and assign the interaction importance to the role that sends the message. In particular, the framework calculates the interaction importance by multiplying the importance value assigned to the operation that sends the message by using the interaction weight w_{Int}, as illustrated in Figure 4.

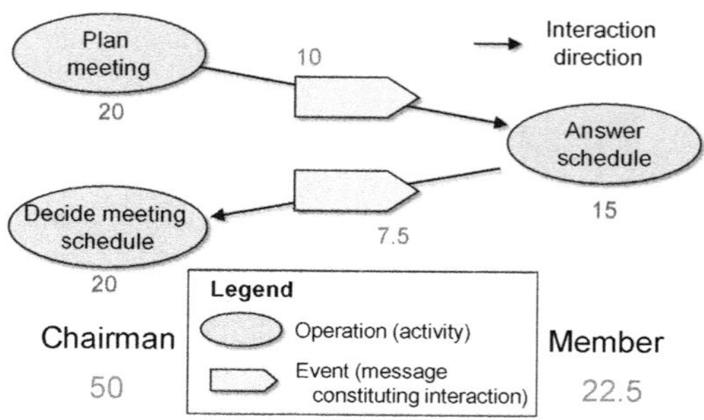

Fig. 4. KAOS operation model for deciding meeting time schedule, where $w_{Int} = 0.5$

Finally, the role importance is determined by aggregating the activity and interaction importance of the role. The importance of role R1, expressed as IR_{R1}, can be calculated from the importance of activity IA and that of interaction $II(= w_{Int} \cdot IA)$ in the following way:

$$IR_{R1} = \Sigma_{R1} IA + \Sigma_{R1} II \tag{4}$$

In Figure 4, as an example, the message from the chairman to the member is assigned the importance values 10, where the importance of the "Plan meeting" operation is 20 and $w_{Int} = 0.5$. By repeating the calculation for the other message and summing up these importance values, we can acquire the role importance, $IR_{chairman} = 50$ and $IR_{member} = 22.5$.

We developed a tool to automatically calculate role importance from a KAOS model as an Eclipse Plug-in. This tool recognizes the structure of the KAOS goal model and the relationships between model descriptors, e.g. goals, operations, and events, by parsing the corresponding XML file. We used Objectiver [13] as a KAOS modeling tool; it can output KAOS models in XML.

3.4 Model Refinement

By taking the calculation process into consideration, our metric *importance* can represent the individual roles' contributions to the system and the burden of their interactions. MAS developers can evaluate the responsibilities of individual roles and the adequateness of the system architecture by using this metric. As for the system performance and stability, it is desirable to prevent the emergence of standout roles with extreme importance values. RE-IMPULSE provides the following sequential guidelines for reducing the importance gap between roles.

1. **Review system interface:** RE-IMPULSE can evaluate not only the importance of the roles but also that of the environmental actors by applying the same calculation process. When comparing the importance values of the environmental actors with those of the roles, the developers can consider whether a new interface to reduce the environmental actors' importance should be introduced.

2. **Reassign requirements:** If particular roles have high importance values, this may show that these roles have more responsibilities. If the developers identify that the assigned responsibilities exceed the roles' capabilities, the developers should consider whether some of requirements assigned to these roles should be shifted to other roles or brand-new roles. When the importance values of particular requirements are especially high, the development process goes back to the requirements analysis phase and these requirements should be divided into smaller parts.
3. **Alter system organizational structure:** If the roles with high importance values are assigned a number of interactions, the developer reviews the interactions that form the system architecture and introduces new communication roles if they are required.
4. **Discuss suitable implementation style:** If roles with high importance values still remain, the design and implementation of these roles need more attention paid to them than the other roles. If the importance value for interactions is high, various ways of reducing the communication burden, such as the expansion of the communication interval and simplifying the message data structures, are effective.

For example, the importance of the chairman role in Figure 4 is more than twice that of the member role. In this case, if we identify that the responsibility of the chairman role exceeds its capability, we can apply "*3. Alter system organizational structure*" and add a new role *department representative* as illustrated in Figure 5, which can undertake the responsibility for collecting the member's schedules and extracting the candidate dates, to reduce the importance of the chairman role.

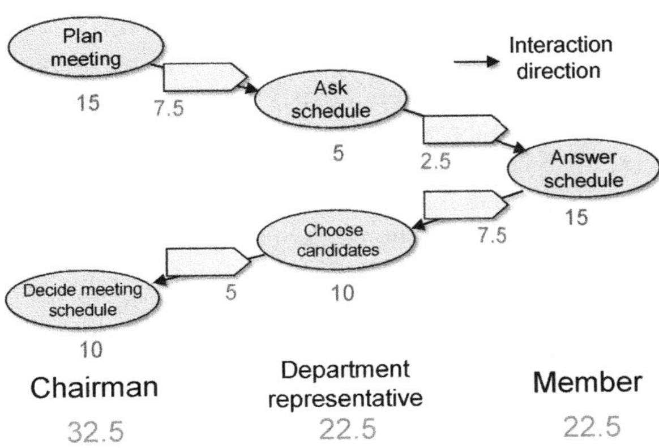

Fig. 5. Improvement by introducing intermediate role

4 Evaluation

To assess the accuracy of our metric and the effectiveness of our evaluation framework, we applied RE-IMPULSE to a MAS development project. This experiment consisted of three parts. First, we evaluated a suitable value for w_{Int} by applying our framework to a constructed MAS model with various w_{Int} values **(Exp1)**. w_{Int} is the parameter that determines the component ratio of the importance of the activities and interactions.

Next, to evaluate the adequacy of the importance as a metric, we applied our framework to the MAS model and compared the role order acquired by the importance calculation with the order that the requirements engineer had assumed **(Exp2)**. We also compared the difference between the importance values calculated in Exp2 and the values after removing some of the roles from the MAS model in order to evaluate our metric with respect to the interaction structure that forms the system architecture **(Exp3)**. Throughout this experiment, we used a tracking system, which had been implemented as a prototype system and whose KAOS model had been constructed and the architecture model had been generated by our model transformation tool.

4.1 Tracking System

The tracking system chases targets using the sensing data and a reasoning mechanism. This system consists of the six following agents derived from six roles.

- *Sensor:* This role detects the object entrance and exit on the sensing area. It also has the responsibility of notifying these events to the zone manager of its respective zone.
- *Zone manager:* This role aggregates events from the sensors and reports to the other roles.
- *User interface (UI):* This role receives tracking requests from the users and requests trackers to track the target objects. It is also responsible for displaying the tracking results.
- *Estimator:* This role infers where a target is located by using the accumulated sensing log data and its schedule data if it exists.
- *Tracker:* This role chases the target by moving to the zone managing server, which is located in the zone where the target is or is expected to arrive.
- *Monitor:* This role manages the migration histories of individual target objects. It is responsible for storing the migration logs of individual objects by using the sensing data reported from the zone manager.

This tracking system had already been implemented by constructing a KAOS model and generating an architecture model using our model transformation tool.

4.2 Exp1: Interaction Weight

First of all, in order to find the appropriate w_{Int} value, we counted the number of conducted test items with separating items for the activities and those for the interactions and the number of activities and interactions (messages) in the constructed KAOS model. Table 2 lists the numbers of them and the appropriate W_{Int} values, calculated by the ratio of test items per an activity or an interaction in the KAOS model. From Table 2, we determined the approximate average of these values, 0.8, as w_{Int} in our subsequent experiments, Exp2 and Exp3.

Table 2. Determination of w_{Int} from number of test items and described elements, where $w_{Int} = \frac{(2)/(4)}{(1)/(3)}$

Role	# test items		# elements		w_{Int}
	Act (1)	Int (2)	Act (3)	Int (4)	(Int/Act)
Sensor	15	11	2	2	**0.73**
Tracker	19	16	4	4	**0.84**
Zone manager	25	26	4	5	**0.83**
UI	10	5	2	1	**1**
Estimator	12	8	2	2	**0.66**
Monitor	11	9	3	3	**0.82**

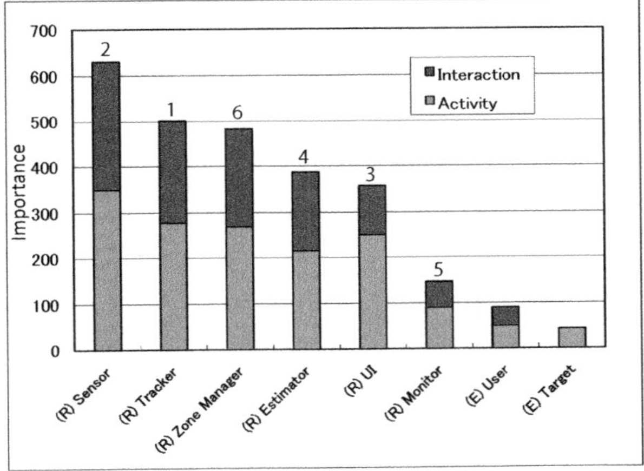

Fig. 6. Role importance in tracking system, where "(R)" denotes roles, and "(E)" denotes environmental actors. Numbers above the bars indicate the requirements engineer supplied ordering.

4.3 Exp2: Importance Analysis

Next, we evaluated the validity of the acquired role importance. The graph described in Figure 6 shows the importance of all the roles in a tracking system, where $w_{Int} = 0.8$. This graph shows the constituents of the role importance – activity importance and interaction importance. In this experiment, we also interviewed the requirements engineer of the tracking system concerning the order of the roles in the system in terms of the contribution to the system, and we acquired the following order: *tracker, sensor, user interface, estimator, monitor,* and *zone manager*.

When comparing the results shown in Figure 6, which illustrates the order, sensor, tracker, zone manager, estimator, user interface (UI), monitor, the two orderings are roughly close except for the zone manager. The considerable difference between the requirements engineer estimated order and the calculated order is a consequence of the interaction structure. The requirements engineer only paid attention to the explicit activity of the zone manager, and concluded that the aggregation of the sensing data was less important than the responsibilities of the other roles. On the other hand, our metric also evaluates the system architecture based on the interaction loads aspect, and as a result, the zone manager that communicated with multiple roles was ranked higher than the UI, estimator, and monitor roles. Therefore, the result shows that the importance metric reflects the requirements engineer's intention as well as the influence of the system interaction structure.

4.4 Exp3: Role Identification

We also observed the changes in the importance value when changing the roles' responsibilities. In this experiment, we took into account two situations where the zone manager or the monitor were not extracted as roles, respectively, and the requirements assigned to these roles were reassigned to other roles, and then, recalculated the role importance values. Figures 7 and 8 show the recalculated importance values for these two cases, respectively.

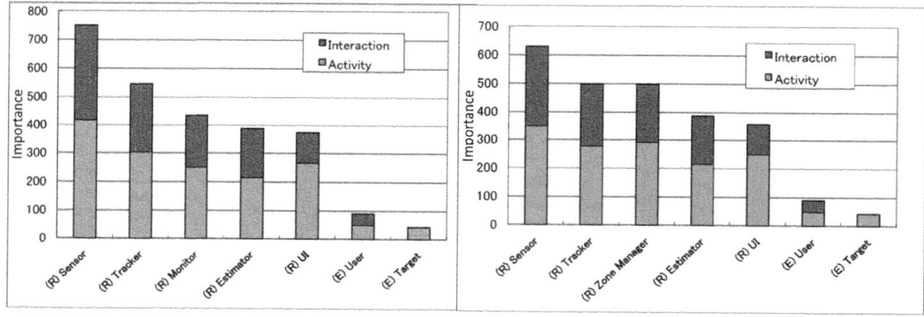

Fig. 7. Role importance when excluding *zone manager*

Fig. 8. Role importance when excluding *monitor*

First, the exclusion of the zone manager illustrated in Figure 7 caused an increase in the sensor role's importance of 120 (about 19%). The sensor already had the highest importance in Exp2, and since the zone manager was excluded, it got further load addition, and we could find that the zone manager had an essential role in the tracking system.

On the other hand, when the monitor was excluded, which is illustrated in Figure 8, there was an increase in the importance of the zone manager and UI roles, but the highest ranked role sensor did not acquire additional importance, and therefore, we found that the monitor did not have an essential role in the tracking system.

5 Discussion

We will now evaluate our framework based on the experimental results in terms of the evaluation items for the MAS architecture model described in Section 2.1, and then discuss its limitations and scope of applicability.

Validity of role set: RE-IMPULSE allows developers to validate whether the extracted roles are adequate for constructing a system or not by excluding the particular roles and recalculation of the role importance as shown in Exp3. Since the role importance originates in the requirements importance, the developers can use them as representing the requirements engineer's intention to validate the role set. This means that the activities of the requirements analysis and system design can be separated and the requirements engineers and system developers experience a reduced communication burden. RE-IMPULSE also evaluates the roles that have the responsibilities for aggregating information, such as the zone manager in our experiment.

Roles responsibility quantity: Exp2 shows that RE-IMPULSE acquired the importance order of the extracted roles close to the order that the requirements engineer had expected. The role importance value is calculated from the assigned activities and interactions; however, for the preparation of the calculation, RE-IMPULSE requires the requirements engineers to put only the importance ratio in the goal node. This means that RE-IMPULSE allows MAS developers to rank the roles by following the importance of the assigned responsibilities, even if the developers do not have any domain knowledge, and to evaluate whether the constructed MAS model is adequate for the system.

We have introduced the interaction weight w_{Int} to determine the interaction importance. In our experiment, we determined the value of w_{Int} based on Exp1, which calculated w_{Int} from the number of test cases; however, the value of w_{Int} should be adjusted according to the interaction design of the system. If the interaction is considered as more important, e.g. the MAS requires frequent communications among roles, messages are complex, or the size of messages is large, the value of w_{Int} should be adjusted upward; on the other hand, if considered as less important, the value should be adjusted downward.

Adequacy of system architecture: Since the metric consists of not only the activity importance but also the interaction importance, the metric allows the developers to evaluate the system architecture in terms of the responsibilities for forming the interaction structure. As shown in Exp3, excluding the zone manager role made the sensor role overloaded. If the role has a considerable amount of responsibility for the communications between roles in the system, the role should be introduced as the composition element of the system. Our evaluation framework provide a method for validating the system architecture from the perspective of the validity of the interaction structure.

Applicable scope and limitations: Finally, we discuss the applicable scope and limitations of our framework. As for the design process, the developers have to construct the MAS architecture model from the KAOS model as an artifact of the requirements analysis. The important MAS elements, which are the roles, interactions, and activities, must have clear relationships with the elements described in the requirements description. We use the KAOS model as a requirements description for calculating the importance value in this paper. One reason why we chose KAOS is that it provides the goal structure for propagating the importance from among the goals and requirements. The other reason is that it also provides the description elements necessary for the system design, such as the operation and event, and the relationship between them. The tool support for outputting a structured text data file, i.e., an XML file in this case, is another reason we chose KAOS, which leads to an automatic calculation. We can use other goal-oriented requirements descriptions in our framework if these descriptions have such features.

We use the importance metric for the MAS design, although we are confident that the metric can be used for designing the load balance between sub-systems in enterprise business applications. These systems have a considerable number of roles, such as managing personnel information, accounting operations, business management, and each sub-system provides each service sometimes independently and sometimes depending on other sub-systems.

6 Related Work

In the area of requirements engineering, several metrics have been proposed for requirements analysis and its evaluation. Karlsson and Ryan [14], [15] provided a methodology for assigning priorities to requirements and developing strategies for selecting an optimal set of requirements for implementation. They introduced two techniques, a pair-wise comparison technique and a numeral assignment technique to gain accurate software requirements prioritization in [14]. In [15], they also developed a methodology that ranks candidate requirements in two dimensions: according to their value and their estimated cost of implementation. Requirements prioritization is also used in the Next Release Problem [16], in which a set of customers with varying requirements are targeted for the next release of an existing software system. Several studies for its formulation and optimization [17], [18], [19] have been conducted for these problems, and Finkelstein [20] recently introduced a technique for analyzing the trade-offs between different customers fairness.

Requirements prioritization is also used for the requirements tracing. Egyed and Heindl et. al [21], [22], [23] considered the cost-quality aspects in the trace analysis. A value-based perspective helps save the unnecessary effort of tracing. Our framework does not trace the requirements in the design model; however, we can verify the influence of the requirements assignment changes in the design model by observing the changes in importance values.

Feather [24] proposed an integrated approach for the risk management with a quantitative evaluation in the requirements engineering called DDP (Defect Detection and Prevention). In DDP, the requirements engineers assess the severity of the consequences and the effectiveness of the countermeasures quantitatively. After making matrices, the requirements engineers explore the optimal combinations of countermeasures with respect to the cost constraints. The techniques for selecting the optimal way of realizing the requirements, such as on the risk management, often use two different metrics – one for the criticality of the requirements and the other for the cost of the realization countermeasures. Our current framework does not explicitly use a metric for the cost of realization. This is because it is not for the selection of the best countermeasure; however, the framework can still consider the complexity of a system architecture consisting of the role activities and interactions.

As for the MAS development, Giorgini [25] proposed an evaluation technique for a MAS requirements model described in i* [26]. This technique defines *criticality* and *complexity* as metrics. MAS developers add these two values for all the dependencies between the goals to be achieved and the roles, and then these two values are independently aggregated by the role. This technique can evaluate the goal assignment in terms of the two aspects; however, the developers have to use two different values for all the dependencies. This technique does not provide a mechanism for validating the system architecture and guidelines for design improvement.

7 Conclusions

This paper presented a new evaluation framework called RE-IMPULSE, which was designed to focus on measuring the task assignment using the requirements descriptions. We defined importance as a metric, and RE-IMPULSE enables the measure of the role importance, which expresses the quantity of the contribution for realizing the system functions by their activities and interactions, from the goal importance assessed by the requirements engineers and the relationships between the descriptors in the KAOS model. We also evaluated the accuracy of the metric and the effectiveness of the framework by applying RE-IMPULSE to a tracking system. We observed that RE-IMPULSE measured the role importance close to the requirements engineers' intention and it also considered the loads of the interactions, which influenced the system architecture. RE-IMPULSE provides developers with guidelines for validating the role extraction, task assignment, and the system architecture.

In future work, we plan to extend our framework by developing an improvement recommendation mechanism based on the acquired importance values. Our metric can be used to detect issues in the architecture model, and the mechanism will look for and recommend strategies that improve the model.

References

1. Wooldridge, M.: An Introduction to Multiagent Systems, 2nd edn. John Wiley & Sons (2009)
2. Luck, M., Ashri, R., D'Inverno, M.: Agent-Based Software Development. Artech House (2004)
3. Bernon, C., Cossentino, M., Pavón, J.: Agent-oriented software engineering. The Knowledge Engineering Review 20(2), 99–116 (2005)
4. Dardenne, A., van Lamsweerde, A., Fickas, S.: Goal-directed requirements acquisition. Science of Computer Programming 20(1-2), 3–50 (1993)
5. Letier, E.: Reasoning about Agents in Goal-Oriented Requirements Engineering. PhD thesis, Universite Catholique de Louvain (2001)
6. van Lamsweerde, A.: Goal-oriented requirements engineering: A guided tour. In: Fifth IEEE International Symposium on Requirements Engineering (RE 2001), Toronto, Canada, pp. 249–262 (2001)
7. Nakagawa, H., Karube, T., Honiden, S.: Analysis of multi-agent systems based on KAOS modeling. In: Proc. of the 28th International Conference on Software Engineering (ICSE 2006), pp. 926–929. ACM, Shanghai (2006)
8. Zambonelli, F., Jennings, N.R., Wooldridge, M.: Developing multiagent systems: The Gaia methodology. ACM Transactions on Software Engineering and Methodology 12(3), 317–370 (2003)

9. Bresciani, P., Perini, A., Giorgini, P., Giunchiglia, F., Mylopoulos, J.: Tropos: An agent-oriented software development methodology. Autonomous Agents and Multi-Agent Systems 8(3), 203–236 (2004)
10. Juan, T., Sterling, L.: The ROADMAP Meta-Model for Intelligent Adaptive Multi-Agent Systems in Open Environments. In: Giorgini, P., Müller, J.P., Odell, J.J. (eds.) AOSE 2003. LNCS, vol. 2935, pp. 53–68. Springer, Heidelberg (2004)
11. Padgham, L., Winikoff, M.: Prometheus: A Methodology for Developing Intelligent Agents. In: Giunchiglia, F., Odell, J.J., Weiss, G. (eds.) AOSE 2002. LNCS, vol. 2585, pp. 174–185. Springer, Heidelberg (2003)
12. Cossentino, M., Gaglio, S., Sabatucci, L., Seidita, V.: The PASSI and Agile PASSI MAS Meta-Models Compared with a Unifying Proposal. In: Pěchouček, M., Petta, P., Varga, L.Z. (eds.) CEEMAS 2005. LNCS (LNAI), vol. 3690, pp. 183–192. Springer, Heidelberg (2005)
13. CEDITI: Objectiver, `http://www.objectiver.com/`
14. Karlsson, J.: Software requirements prioritizing. In: Proc. of the 2nd International Conference on Requirements Engineering (ICRE 1996), p. 110. IEEE CS (1996)
15. Karlsson, J., Ryan, K.: A cost-value approach for prioritizing requirements. IEEE Software 14(5), 67–74 (1997)
16. Bagnall, A.J., Rayward-Smith, V.J., Whittley, I.M.: The next release problem. Information and Software Technology 43(14), 883–890 (2001)
17. Zhang, Y., Harman, M., Mansouri, S.A.: The multi-objective next release problem. In: Proc. of the 9th Annual Conference on Genetic and Evolutionary Computation (GECCO 2007), pp. 1129–1137. ACM (2007)
18. Greer, D., Ruhe, G.: Software release planning: an evolutionary and iterative approach. Information and Software Technology 46(4), 243–253 (2004)
19. van den Akker, M., Brinkkemper, S., Diepen, G., Versendaal, J.: Software product release planning through optimization and what-if analysis. Information and Software Technology 50(1-2), 101–111 (2008)
20. Finkelstein, A., Harman, M., Mansouri, S.A., Ren, J., Zhang, Y.: A search based approach to fairness analysis in requirement assignments to aid negotiation, mediation and decision making, vol. 14, pp. 231–245. Springer, Heidelberg (2009)
21. Heindl, M., Biffl, S.: A case study on value-based requirements tracing. In: Proc. of ESEC/FSE-13, pp. 60–69. ACM (2005)
22. Egyed, A., Biffl, S., Heindl, M., Grünbacher, P.: Determining the cost-quality trade-off for automated software traceability. In: Proc. of the 20th IEEE/ACM International Conference on Automated Software Engineering (ASE 2005), pp. 360–363. ACM (2005)
23. Egyed, A., Biffl, S., Heindl, M., Grünbacher, P.: A value-based approach for understanding cost-benefit trade-offs during automated software traceability. In: Proc. of the 3rd International Workshop on Traceability in Emerging forms of Software Engineering (TEFSE 2005), pp. 2–7. ACM (2005)
24. Feather, M.S., Cornford, S.L.: Quantitative risk-based requirements reasoning. Requirements Engineering 8(4), 248–265 (2003)
25. Bresciani, P., Giorgini, P., Mouratidis, H., Manson, G.: Multi-Agent Systems and Security Requirements Analysis. In: Lucena, C., Garcia, A., Romanovsky, A., Castro, J., Alencar, P.S.C. (eds.) SELMAS 2003. LNCS, vol. 2940, pp. 35–48. Springer, Heidelberg (2004)
26. Yu, E.S.K.: Modeling organizations for information systems requirements engineering. In: Proc. of the First IEEE International Symposium on Requirements Engineering, pp. 34–41 (1993)

Task Knowledge Patterns Reuse in Multi-Agent Systems Development

WaiShiang Cheah[1], Leon Sterling[2], and Kuldar Taveter[3]

[1] Faculty of Computer Science & IT, UNIMAS 94300 Kota Samarahan Sarawak, Malaysia
c.waishiang@gmail.com
[2] Faculty of ICT, Swinburne University of Technology, Australia
lsterling@swin.edu.au
[3] Department of Informatics, Faculty of IT, Tallinn University of Technology
kuldar.taveter@ttu.ee

Abstract. Template-based knowledge models can be viewed as design patterns for specifying a task [12]. The models can serve as reusable artifacts during the development of a multi agent system using the MAS-CommonKADS methodology. However, based on our observation of existing patterns, we note limitations of reusing those patterns in agent development. This paper presents *task knowledge patterns* that are described through our improved agent oriented template structure. The improved template structure presented in this paper provides an alternative approach to defining task knowledge patterns by incorporating a two dimensional view of agent oriented models. The task knowledge patterns introduced in this paper describe task knowledge in an agent context, while explicitly providing a description designed to encourage use and reuse in agent oriented software development. A demonstration of the reuse of task knowledge patterns in agent oriented modelling is presented in this paper. Specifically we show how a particular task knowledge pattern, selection of relevant source materials, can be used to rapidly prototype an adviser finder multi-agent system.

Keywords: agent-oriented modeling, task knowledge patterns, advisor finder.

1 Introduction

Agent technology has been used in building various domain specific applications. However, agent technology has not been widely adopted by the software community. Factors in the lack of adoption is the lack of an agreed standard among the diversity of agent oriented software engineering methodologies, and the lack of maturity in some of the methodologies [5].

The agent methodologies have been proposed to aid the agent developer with the introduction of techniques, terminology, notation and guidelines during the development of the agent system. To date, about 30 agent oriented methodologies have been designed [10]. It has been reported that some agent methodologies lack generality and are focused on specific systems and agent architectures [21]. In addition, some of the methodologies do not contain sufficient detail to be of real use.

N. Desai, A. Liu, and M. Winikoff (Eds.): PRIMA 2010, LNAI 7057, pp. 459–474, 2012.

Alternatively, one idea to help people start agent development pragmatically [3,8] is through patterns. Patterns are a means for sharing development experience to allow a developer to reuse development experience repeatedly. Patterns can allow novices to adapt expert knowledge and help develop software in a systematic and structured way. Patterns are targeted at shared recurring problems, and solution patterns can prevent the developer from reinventing the wheel during application development. The use of patterns in agent development can reduce development cost and time, promote reuse and reduce complexity [11].

The notion of reuse has played an important role during the agent development process in MAS-CommonKADS [2], Skwyrl [3] and PASSI [4]. In the MAS-commonKADS methodology, knowledge patterns are used as a reusable artefact during the development of a multi-agent system. The knowledge patterns contain predefined knowledge that represent how experts solve a specific problem; an expert's problem solving capabilities [6]; and the knowledge people have of the task they perform [7].

Expertise models of CommonKADS or knowledge patterns are reused during the analysis phase of MAS-CommonKADS. For example, the task of coordinating a meeting has been described in a template task model [13]. Instead of working iteratively to detail the template task model, an assessment template knowledge model is selected to further detail it. In other words, the assessment template knowledge model is used to guide the task modelling.

Based on our observations, current knowledge patterns are found to be lacking in terms of standardization, expressiveness and characterization capabilities. We can summarize our observations as follows:

- The template knowledge model or task knowledge pattern does not feature the concept of agent technology. It has been reported that since the patterns realize their potential in the development of an agent system, it is required to develop the pattern that is tailored to the development of agent system and use agent oriented concepts.
- Task knowledge patterns lack explicitness in expressing certain knowledge elements like control structure.
- The issue of generalization and universality of the CommonKADS template knowledge model. The template knowledge models have been used in MAS-CommonKADS for agent oriented software development. However, it is difficult to enforce the use of a particular term to mean the same thing in all domains and situations.

From the observations, we introduce several task knowledge patterns together with an improved agent oriented template structure for describing task knowledge. It has been clamed that explicitness and comprehensiveness of patterns are two of the important design properties for agent oriented pattern templates [18]. The pattern template acts as a communication medium among developers. If the pattern description is explicitly described, it will improve the communication and comprehension of the patterns for software practitioners [18]. Indirectly, this will improve the representation and delivery of the potential of patterns for agent development.

This paper introduces an improved template structure for task knowledge patterns. The improved template structure that is presented in this paper provides an alternative design for task knowledge patterns with the introduction a two dimensional view of agent oriented models. The task knowledge patterns introduced in this paper describe the task knowledge in an agent context and explicitly describe the useful description for use and reuse in agent oriented software development. Furthermore, the task knowledge patterns support the expressiveness of task knowledge among non-technical people and support rapid prototyping in agent systems.

Section two presents the brief description of knowledge pattern that is used for agent oriented software development. Section three presents an example of the task knowledge patterns that we have described in our improved template structure. In this section, the task knowledge pattern of 'selection of relevant source materials' is described. Section four presents a case study to develop an adviser finder multi agent system with patterns. Section five presents our observations based on feedback from two masters students in adopting task knowledge patterns for reuse in multi agent system development.

2 Knowledge Patterns for Agent Oriented Software Development

"What is knowledge? How is knowledge represented?" The notion of knowledge is defined and modelled in CommonKADS [12], a knowledge engineering methodology. In CommonKADS, template knowledge models are introduced and are viewed as design patterns or knowledge patterns for tasks [12]. The template knowledge model is also known as an expertise model. It contains predefined knowledge that is represented in the form of reusable model sets for developers. Several template knowledge models are included by CommonKADS. They are classification, assessment, diagnosis, monitoring, prediction, configuration design, modelling, planning, scheduling, and assignment. Each of the template knowledge models consists of the following pattern elements:

- **General characteristics:** Description of the features of a task like goals, typical examples, terminology (e.g., description of the object used for the task), input and output.
- **Default method:** Description of the task knowledge by modelling the actions and control structures for the task type through inference structure and task specification, respectively.
- **Method variation:** Description of the variation of the default method when dealing with a real application. For example, adding a new method or a new object when using the method in a certain application domain.
- **Typical domain schema:** Description of domain entities that will be used for a particular task type. For example, norm, decision and case are domain entities that will be used for assessment task type.

The knowledge has been represented at the knowledge level which has been abstracted away from the symbolic level [9]. The knowledge level was proposed by Newell. Newell introduced another system level that led to a simple and satisfactory view of knowledge and representation [9]. The representation at the knowledge level has a simple structure that provides neither any notion of how the knowledge is represented nor any specification of its processing mechanisms. CommonKADS has utilized the notion of knowledge level to model the problem solving method.

In CommonKADS, the problem solving method is modelled from three different viewpoints (task layer, inference layer, and domain layer) of expertise knowledge.

The task layer models the controlling of problem solving behaviour. Accordingly, it consists of the realization of goals for a task type with control elements like sequential control, conditional branching, iteration, recursion, and so on [6]. It deals with a dynamic view of knowledge. For example, the knowledge of 'assessment' consists of the control flow to obtain an abstract case first. This will be followed by specifying the criteria for selection, repeating the actions to take one element of the criteria and comparing it with the abstract case until producing the final decision through matching the evaluation results.

The inference layer presents the inference structure for inference actions. The inference structure represents the actions for a task type and the coupling of action with knowledge roles. The coupling determines the domain information that is required for an inference action. The domain layer represents specific terms that are needed to perform an action. Also, it is known as static knowledge, like having the constraints and preferences for the inference step of assignment [12]. Another example such as a planning task requires domain information for planning such as planning activities, physical resources available for the planning process, and planning constraints like the possible states of the resources. The domain information consists of key elements like concepts, properties of concepts, and relations between the concepts which are represented as a Unified Modelling Language (UML) class diagram. The concepts consist of domain information or terms and the relations indicate semantic relations between terms. In the paper, the terminology of task knowledge pattern and knowledge pattern is used interchangeably.

3 Task Knowledge Pattern

Task knowledge patterns are reusable artifacts that are introduced for agent oriented software development. Three desired properties are described by Oluyomi [18] in designing an agent oriented template structure. The desired properties present the overall requirements that need to be considered by a pattern designer when designing an agent oriented template structure.

We describe two of the properties within the context of this research. They are 'completeness' and 'eliminating ambiguity'. We adopt these desired properties and elaborate them in designing the template structure for the task knowledge pattern in the following description.

`Completeness` Our template structure for task knowledge is complete as it captures the levels of different 'viewpoints' of expertise knowledge. However, we introduce the level of different 'viewpoints' that is related to the aspect dimension of the behaviour category, interaction category and information category at the conceptual domain modelling level. These viewpoints are taken from the text 'The Art of Agent-Oriented Modelling' [1]. The knowledge that is modelled in our 'viewpoints' involves

- The goals that are required to be achieved for solving a problem;
- The arrangement of responsibilities in fulfilling the goals given, and
- The knowledge items that are used by goals and responsibilities.

The knowledge that is modelled at such categories and levels describes the knowledge at a higher level of abstraction. It is sensible to claim that it corresponds to the knowledge level modelling of expertise knowledge as practiced in knowledge engineering [9]. Modelling the knowledge at a high level of abstraction has advantages as follows:

- It serves to communicate knowledge to a non-technical person. Apart from the agent designer and implementer, the task knowledge pattern will support a non-technical person like a novice user. The task knowledge pattern has been shown to be useful among non-agent practitioners as discussed in section 5.
- People are not restricted by details of design such as looping, attributes of terms, detailed pre-condition and post-condition, detailed information flow or implementation constraints that will influence the generality of the task knowledge.

`Eliminate Ambiguity` The template structure must cater for explicit values and unified representation to ease the ambiguity [20, 21] of the pattern description. Explicitness of the template structure through explicit values is a common practice for designing agent patterns. The explicit value outlines a particular agent development life cycle and agent development task will create a consistent viewpoint when people intend to adopt the pattern for the task at hand [18]. It is important for having those explicit values to allow communication of the pattern with terminology that seems common in agent development.

Next, we provide the description of an example task knowledge pattern.

3.1 Example Description of Task Knowledge Patterns

The pattern elements for the task knowledge patterns are described below.

Pattern name: Represents the name of the task type or problem solving method. It indicates the name of the pattern to be modelled. The name is normally related to the problem at hand.

Intent: The purpose(s) in having this pattern. It consists of the description to elaborate on the motivation for having this pattern.

Use when/ Applicability: Descriptive of situations that lead to the usage of the pattern.

Problem: The problem that needs to be solved by this pattern.

Force: Requirement of the problem, *solution properties* in which the pattern is situated.

Solution: The knowledge level of the problem solving method in solving the problem given. It contains the description that explicitly models the knowledge in solving the task.

Dynamic: The dynamic element provides a typical scenario in describing the runtime behaviour of the pattern. In other words, it details the arrangement of the solution according to a particular situation.

An example of task knowledge pattern is as follows:

Pattern Name: Selection of Relevant Source Material

Intent:

The purpose of this pattern is to develop an agent that is able to perform a search and provide relevant results based on particular criteria. In other words, the agent will locate certain information that is supplied by the information provider from a set of keywords and then produce a relevance result.

Also known as:

Melisa [14], Amathaea [15], Sourcer [16]

Context / Applicability:
Use this pattern when
- -you want to explore within a collection of information or repository regardless of the scale of the repository.
- -you want to obtain relevant documents from your search.

Problem: Deals with the finding of a set of documents in response to a user request.

Forces: Describes the solution properties in which the pattern is situated or based in the context of the problem.

Goal: The user is able to provide his/her preferences from the solution provided. Meanwhile, the returned documents may be arranged accordingly.
Quality goal: Achieving user satisfaction is needed. The solution must be able to provide a collection of relevant results which are closer to the user keyword. When performing a query, the solution may be required to provide the returned information in an efficient manner. In this case, time to search for relevant documents must be taken into consideration when designing the solution.
Role: Three roles are involved when conducting a search. They are the role played to manage the finding like handling a query, conduct search, ranking or combined result, the role played to keep the sources for finding purpose and the role played to send the search request.
Resource: The domain entities of query, criteria, relevant content, information resource and domain are basic entities that are required in conducting the task type of 'selection of relevant source materials'.

Solution:

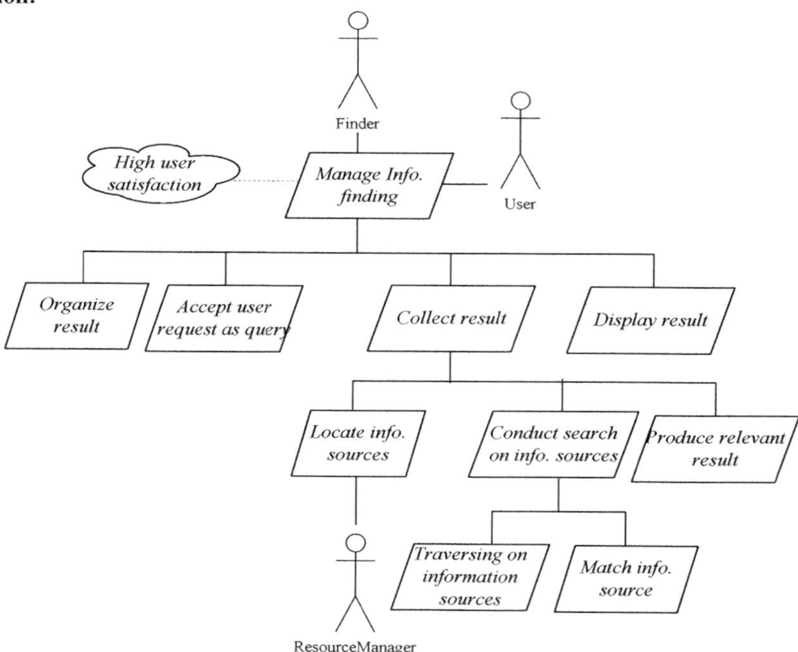

< **Goal Model**>. Goal model for selection of relevant sources

- **Organize result** Ranking and/or combination of searched results. There is a mechanism to send the user query to multiple search engines. Each search engine will be involved in information finding and the returned documents will be combined into a final result presentation.

- **Accept user request as query** The purpose of this goal is awaiting the user query.
- **Collect results** The goal of 'organize result' is the core activity in the information finding. It involves activity to obtain references by checking the query against a page hyperlink description or meta-information; performs searched on the referenced entity (e.g. documents like web page) and performs matching or evaluates on a searched item.
- **Display result** The purpose of this goal is to present the finding returned like downloaded document references, name list and so on in an appropriate manner

<Role model>. Role model for selection of relevant sources

Role name	Information finder
Description	Manage information finding
Responsibilities	Receive incoming query for information finding Obtain relevant sources. -obtaining relevant references or indexing. -Traverse given documents. -Search through the content by giving the references. -Perform matching based on user request. -Create relevant sources. -Organize relevant sources -Perform ranking and combination of searched results. Display the relevant sources.
Constraints	Query must first assign prior selection. All the search may be provided with any return.

Role name	ResourceManager
Description	Manage information finding
Responsibilities	Keeping the sources for finding purpose.
Constraints	-interact with incoming request for finding the relevant. -provide information spaces for search.

Role name	User
Description	Request for search
Responsibilities	-send request for search. -receive relevant sources material.
Constraints	-

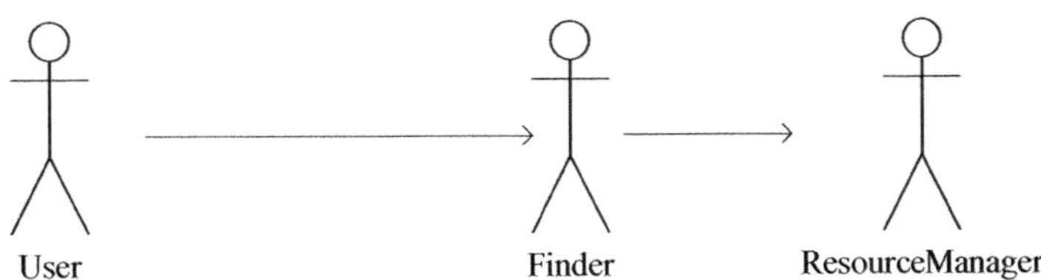

<Organizational model>. Organizational model for selection of relevant sources

Organization Structure. The members involved in dealing with information finding task type are User, Finder and ResourceManager. The Finder realizes the request from the User. The ResourceManager provides information spaces for the search by the Finder.

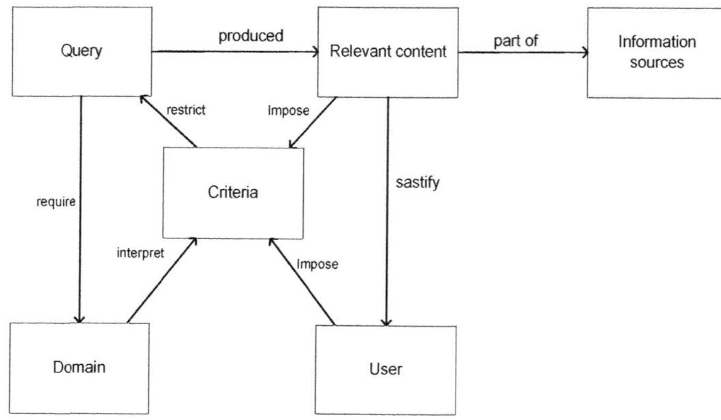

The resources that will be consumed by this task are listed in the domain model. Accordingly, further elaboration of the resources is described below.

- **Query** The domain entity that will be used in conducting a search. It is a form of user request or query term.
- **Relevant content** The domain entity that represents the response from the search, which is derived from a collection of information sources.
- **Criteria** The criteria consist of user preferences that are imposed by the user as searching criteria. For example, search modifier, special filter like search through year from, year to, abstract, maximum retrieval time per page, credit status, capability available.
- **Domain** The domain consists of a topic of discussion which describes the element of criteria and is required as part of the query's domain entity. It may contain a vector of keyword for keyword search.
- **User** The domain entity of requester. The user (e.g. software agent or human agent) that will impose a query for a finding.
- **Information sources** The domain entity that represents the sources of information like documents, semi-structural data like web, images, video, medical catalog, text file, pdf file and so on.

Consequences

The key consequence of the task knowledge pattern is to help to reduce the effort to search within the information space and produce a relevant return to the user.

Related Pattern

The 'assessment' template knowledge model in the CommonKADS is related to achieving the goal of 'collect result'. On the other hand, the task knowledge pattern of 'relaxing the search term' is related to this pattern to increase the accuracy of the search. The pattern deals with the query expansion to produce a set of queries from the user request. In other words, the early user request is expanded to enable the search in a more precise manner.

We have presented an example of a task knowledge pattern. In summary, ten task knowledge patterns are proposed [8]. In the following section, we present the use of task knowledge pattern in developing an adviser finder multi agent system within the ROADMAP and AOR methodologies.

4 Case Study

Task knowledge patterns introduced reusable models sets to prevent the developer from reinventing the wheel in solving a problem at hand. In this section, we demonstrate the reusability of the model sets (e.g. goal model, role model, organization model and domain model) in the early development stages to rapidly prototyping an adviser finder multi agent system.

The background problem of the adviser finder multi agent system is described as follow. Students receive Government scholarships to study for a PhD overseas if they are able to find an adviser within a reputable university. To find an adviser, a substantial amount of knowledge is needed which includes an "advisor domain" like research areas, research experience, professional activities and so on. These are usually described differently among the academics at different institutions. To sustain the search, it is always believed that a student will browse from one page to another, collect information from several institutions, interpret and understand the information collected and short list the candidates for potential supervisors. To facilitate the adviser finder, we propose an agent oriented adviser finder multi agent system to automate the adviser finder application. The adviser finder multi agent system accepts the user request, conducts search across semi-structured data such as academics' web pages and returns a list of potential advisers based on the user request.

4.1 Task Knowledge Patterns Reuse in Developing Adviser Finder MAS

As shown in Figure 1, a combined modelling process has been introduced by Sterling and Taveter [1] to engineer a multi agent system in a more unified way to support the rapidly prototype of agent oriented system [1]. We refine the combined modelling process for ROADMAP and AOR that places the knowledge reuse within the modelling process, as shown in Figure 1.

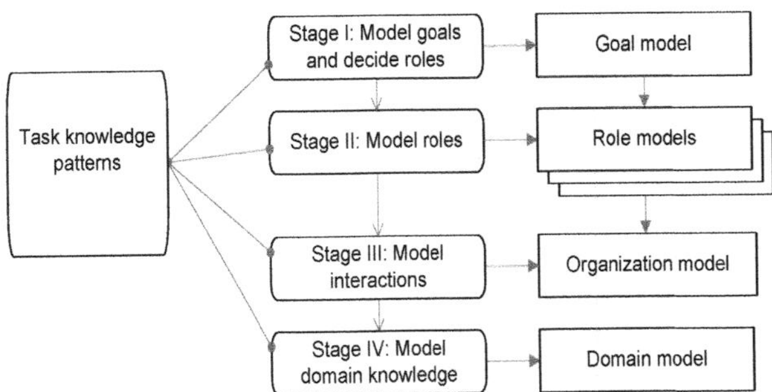

Fig. 1. Agent oriented modelling processes

Figure 1 shows how to relate the task knowledge patterns for early agent development in the combined modelling process of ROADMAP and AOR methodologies In the following description, we describe how the task knowledge patterns can be integrated in the modelling processes to rapidly prototype an adviser finder multi agent system. We present the reuse of the model sets presented in the task knowledge patterns of early stages of agent development. We demonstrate a task to manage adviser finding (e.g. a task to match information) through pattern.

It is sensible to claim that the predefined knowledge that is presented in the task knowledge patterns can provide the answer during the requirement elicitation phase for an agent system. For example, for the adviser finding problem, we can hire a position like adviserFinder to search the potential adviser which the job description can be derived from the role model and knowledge for the position will be derived from the domain model within the task knowledge pattern of 'selection of relevant source materials'. However, instead of showing how to reuse the task knowledge patterns during the requirement elicitation, we present the reuse of models set that are presented in the task knowledge patterns in modelling the goal model, role model, organization model, domain model at the early stages of agent development as shown in Figure 1.

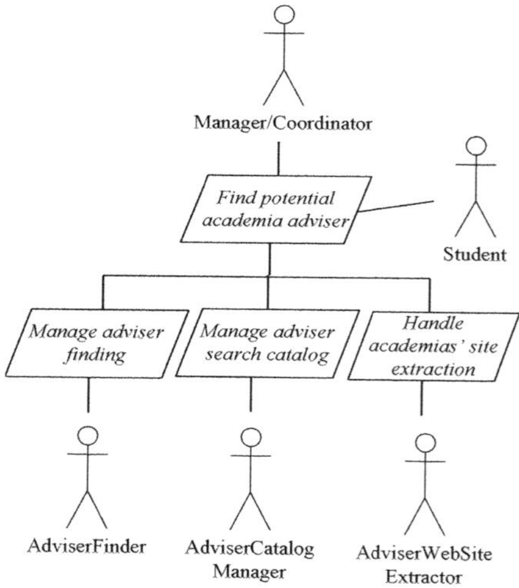

Fig. 2. Overview of goal model for the adviser finding problem

Stage I Model the goal: The early stage in agent modelling involves modelling goals and decides roles. Figure 2 shows the overview goal model for the adviser finder multi agent system. The goals and roles that have been played are derived based on the study on related kind of system [17]. We can model the requirements through an overview goal model as shown in Figure 2, the goal of 'find potential academic adviser' consists of sub-goals like 'manage adviser finding', 'manage adviser search catalogs', 'handle academic's site extraction'. We can interpret that those goals rely upon the people that played the role like adviserFinder, adviserCatalogManager, adviserWebExtractor, Student and manager for fulfilling the goals.

We can further detail the goal model of 'manage adviser finding' according to practice below. Instead of working from scratch, we can adopt the model sets that were introduced in the task knowledge patterns for solving our problem at hand. In working into this process, we presented guideline1 to integrate the task knowledge patterns in early development stages (e.g. Stage I, Stage II, Stage III and Stage IV). Assume the developer has accepted all the forces from the pattern description. The procedures of guideline1 are described below.

1. For each subgoal of a goal model, we can reuse task knowledge patterns for its further elaboration. Each of the subgoals may be further elaborated with subgoals from a goal model included by task knowledge patterns.
2. In deciding on roles, we can reuse the roles that are included by task knowledge patterns. The details of a role model can also be derived from task knowledge patterns. However, effort is needed to relate a derived role model to the application context. The roles involved in an organization can be further refined when creating the organization model.
3. We can reuse the organization model included by task knowledge patterns. The organization model can be further elaborated thereafter. For example, we can add a new role to control the processes involved or some roles can be combined or can enter into association or aggregation relationships with the other role(s) depending on the application context. The organization model provides a foundation for modelling the interactions between the agents playing the roles of the organization.
4. When creating the domain model, we can reuse domain entities and relationships between them from task knowledge patterns. A domain model thereafter needs to be refined according to the application context.

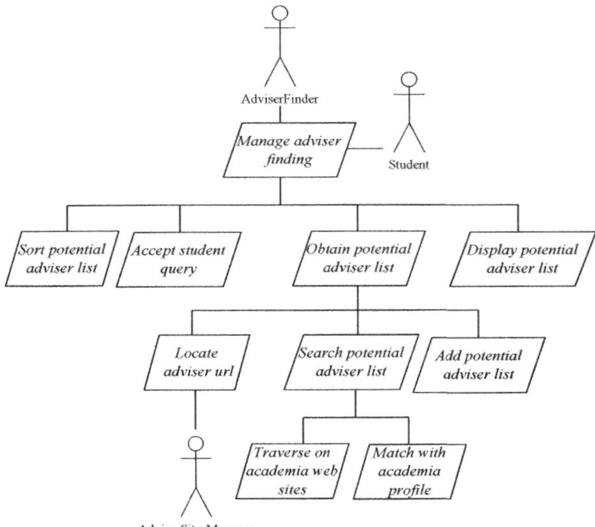

Fig. 3. Goal model for selection of potential academia adviser

The task knowledge patterns of 'selection of relevant source material' record the experience for solving the finding problem. As a result, we can reuse the goal model that is described in the task knowledge pattern to further detail the goal of 'manage adviser finding' as shown in Figure 3. We adopt the goal model that described in Section 3.1 by relating it to our context. In other words, we relate the role of user with student, the role of finder with adviserFinder, the goal of 'accept user request' with 'accept student query' and so on to further detail the goals as shown in Figure 2.

Stage II - Model the role model: We relate the role name, responsibilities and constraints of the role schema that are presented in the task knowledge pattern as described in the Section 3.1 into our application context as shown in Table 1. For example, we relate the role of 'Information Finder' with the role name of the 'AdviserFinder'; the job description of the role (e.g. responsibilities) like query with student query, traversing with academic profile and so on.

Table 1. Role model of AdviserFinder

Role name	AdviserFinder
Description	Manage potential adviser finding
Responsibilities	Receive incoming student query for adviser finding Obtain potential adviser listing -obtaining academia urls or indexing. -Traversing on academia profile. -Searching through the academia profile by giving the url -Perform matching based on student request. -Create potential adviser list -Organize potential adviser listing -Perform ranking and combination of candidate adviser. =Display the potential adviser listing
Constraints	Student query must first assign prior selection. All the search may be provided with any return.

Stage III- Model organization: The organization model models the arrangement of the roles involved for task accomplishment. The organization model for the adviser finding problem is modelled in Figure 4. The organization model is derived from the selected task knowledge patterns together with the roles that have been modelled from the overall goal model as shown in Figure 2. For example, within the task type of 'selection of relevant source material', the AdviserFinder relies on the request from the user. The ResourceManager provides information spaces for search by the AdviserFinder.

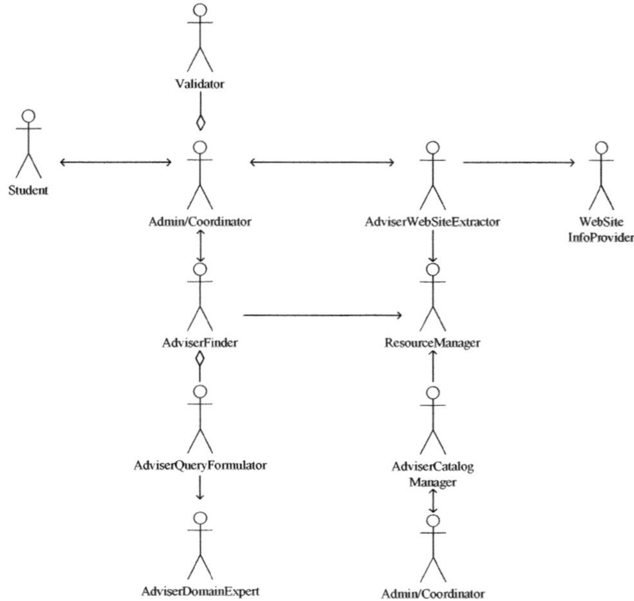

Fig. 4. Organizational model for the adviser finding MAS

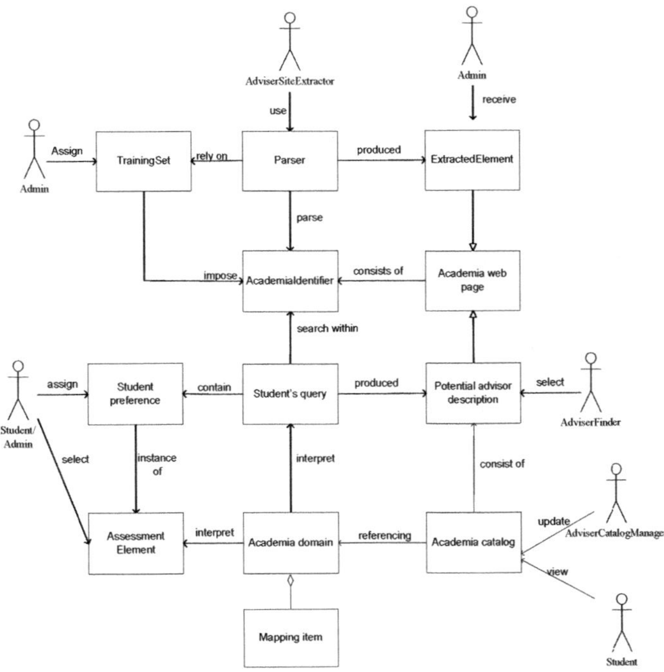

Fig. 5. Domain model for the adviser finding MAS

Stage IV- Model domain knowledge: Modelling the domain knowledge involves identifying the domain entities and the relation among the domain entities for the problem at hand. To model the domain model for the agent system, we can reuse the domain models presented in the selected task knowledge patterns during this modelling process. Figure 5 presents the domain model for adviser finding problem. We can adopt the domain models according to our application context. In this case, we can describe the domain entity of Query as StudentQuery, Domain as AcademiaDomain, Criteria as StudentPreference and AssessmentElement, RelevantContent as PontentialAdviserDescription, InformationSources as AcademiaWebPage. The domain model that presents in Figure 5 is the integration among the domain models among the text extraction pattern and categorization pattern.

We presented the modelling of goal models, role model, organization model and domain model at the early stages of multi agent system development (e.g. stage I to stage IV). We introduce the reuse of the model sets that are provided in the selected task knowledge patterns when modelling the goal models, role model, organization model and domain model. It is interesting to show that the task knowledge patterns have shared the recurring problem and solution and prevent us from reinventing the wheel for developing the adviser finder MAS. Consequently, we can put much effort to continue the modelling process for the adviser finder multi agent system at Stage V: decide agent types; Stage VI: model the knowledge of agents; Stage VII: model interactions between agents and Stage VIII: model agent behaviours as described in [8].

The screenshot for the adviser finder multi agent system is shown in Figure 7. A student posts the query through a normal search or advance search from the search by '..' menu. Figure 7 presents the screenshot of a typical search. The student can key in any search items (e.g. supervisor name, publication, research area and so on). Then the system returns with a candidate adviser list.

5 Conclusion and Discussion

Task knowledge patterns are typically reusable at the early development stages of a multiagent system and reusing them supports rapid prototyping of a multiagent system. We have proposed an improved template structure in describing the task knowledge and demonstrated how the pattern is reusable in rapidly prototype the adviser finder multi agent system. In addition to the results reported in this paper, we have conducted an evaluation of the usefulness of task knowledge patterns for agent development. Several questionnaires were prepared for conducting the evaluation. The questionnaires were designed to assess the pattern content and the learnability and usefulness of the patterns. A survey was conducted with two Masters students at Tallinn University of Technology, Estonia, with novice experience in agent-oriented software development. These students were respectively required to develop an agent-oriented recommendation system and an agent-oriented interoperability system for their Masters Thesis projects. At the beginning of their study, the students explored the ROADMAP and AOR methodologies. After that, the students were presented with task knowledge patterns for agent-oriented development. They were required to study the patterns before they started to design an agent-based system. The students had approximately two months for designing a multiagent system facilitated by task knowledge patters. Upon completion of the project, the students were provided with questionnaires to evaluate the task knowledge patterns adopted by them.

In general, novice users (e.g., students) seem to be satisfied with the usage of task knowledge patterns that have been expressed by means agent-oriented models. Both of the students surveyed agreed that the task knowledge patterns were useful when developing multi-agent systems and were easy to learn. According to the surveys, agent-oriented models were easily able to communicate ideas and concepts behind task knowledge patterns and both students preferred to adopt the patterns also for future multi-agent system development. In other words, task knowledge patterns facilitated solving the problem at hand for both students. On the other hand, the reviews also addressed the problem that the content of some patterns lack sufficient information. We have seriously considered this feedback and as a result have further refined task knowledge patterns by introducing expected runtime behaviours into the patterns. In addition, generality of patterns has been increased. For example, we removed the goal 'Content selection' from the profiling pattern because the content selection really belongs to the pattern of information finding. We also remark here that conducting a survey with just two students is naturally not sufficient for obtaining a real picture but has nevertheless provided us with useful insight and feedback about the application of task knowledge patterns. In our future research work, we plan to conduct similar surveys with more participants.

References

1. Sterling, L., Taveter, K.: The Art of Agent Oriented Modelling. MIT Press, Cambridge (2009)
2. Do, T.T., Kolp, M., Pirotte, A.: Social patterns for designing multi-agent systems. In: Proceedings of the 15th International Conference on Software Engineering and Knowledge Engineering. Citeseer (2003)
3. Cossentino, M., Sabatucci, L., Chella, A.: Patterns Reuse in the PASSI Methodology. In: Omicini, A., Petta, P., Pitt, J. (eds.) ESAW 2003. LNCS (LNAI), vol. 3071, pp. 294–310. Springer, Heidelberg (2004)
4. Luck, M., McBurney, P., et al.: Agent technology: Enabling next generation computing. In: Agent Link Community, pp. 74–75 (2003)
5. Chandrasekaran, B., Josephson, J.R., et al.: The ontology of tasks and methods. In: Proceedings of the Eleventh Workshop on Knowledge Acquisition, Modelling and Management (KAW 1998), pp. 18–23 (1997)
6. Annamalai, M.: Modelling knowledge for scientific collaboration on the semantic web, The Melbourne University. PhD (2006)
7. WaiShiang, C.: Patterns for Agent oriented software development, The Melbourne University. PhD (2010)
8. Newell, A.: The knowledge level. In: AI Magazine, Department of Computer Science, Carnegie-Mellon University (1981)
9. Koutsabasis, P., Darzentas, J.: Methodologies for agent systems development: underlying assumptions and implications for design. AI & Society 23(3), 379–407 (2009)

10. Lima, E.F.A., Machado, P.D.L., et al.: An approach to modelling and applying mobile agent design patterns. ACM SIGSOFT Software Engineering Notes 29(3), 1–8 (2004)
11. Schreiber, G.: Knowledge engineering and management: the Common KADS methodology. MIT Press (2000)
12. Henderson-Sellers, B., Giorgini, P.: Agent-oriented methodologies. Idea Group Pub. (2005)
13. Abasolo, J.M., Gómez, M.: MELISA: An ontology-based agent for information retrieval in medicine. In: Proceedings of the First International Workshop on the Semantic Web, vol. 3, pp. 73–82 (2000)
14. Tang, C., Xu, L.D., Feng, S.: An agent-based geographical information system. Knowledge-Based Systems 14, 233–242 (2001)
15. Loewus-Deitch, D., Herdrick, B.: The Sourcerer: An Expert Human Resource Agent; Nick, A., Koenemann, J., et al.: ELFI: information brokering for the domain of research funding. Computer Networks and ISDN Systems 30(16-18), 1491–1500 (1998)
16. Oluyomi, A., Karunasekera, S., et al.: Description templates for agent-oriented patterns. The Journal of Systems & Software 81(1), 20–36 (2008)
17. Yoshioka, N., Washizaki, H., et al.: A survey on security patterns. Progress in Informatics 5, 35–47 (2008)
18. Zdun, U., Avgeriou, P.: A catalog of architectural primitives for modeling architectural patterns. Information and Software Technology 50, 1003–1034 (2007)
19. Zambonelli, F., Jennings, N.R., et al.: Organisational rules as an abstraction for the analysis and design of multi-agent systems. International Journal of Software Engineering and Knowledge Engineering 11(3), 303–328 (2001)

Energy-Aware Agents for Detecting Nonessential Appliances*

Shih-chiang Lee, Gu-yuan Lin, Wan-rong Jih, Chi-Chia Huang, and Jane Yung-jen Hsu

Department of Computer Science and Information Engineering
National Taiwan University Taipei, Taiwan
{r97026,r97131,wrjih,r95046,yjhsu}@csie.ntu.edu.tw

Abstract. In the past decades, the amount of electricity used by appliances has grown dramatically. As we are demanding more electricity, we should lower the damage to our environment by using energy efficiently. Conservation of energy by looking at one's habits and notifying them to turn off unnecessary appliances can help out a lot. This research develop a framework, which is able to recognize the operating state of every electrical appliance in a house and figure current user activity. By analyzing the behavior of using appliances, the correlation between activity and appliance can help to detect the *nonessential appliance*, which is the appliance does not participate in any user activity. The real user experimental results show 96.43% in recognizing the operating state of appliances and 72.66% in detecting nonessential appliances.

Keywords: activity recognition, appliance monitoring, energy conservation.

1 Introduction

With the progress of the times, life is more convenient than ever before. However, since electricity is the main energy source of most common equipments in daily life, every country around the world is now facing the same problem: the increasing demand of electricity[1]. From 2005 U.S. Residential Energy Consumption Survey[2], the American families consumed 41% of national electricity ouput[3]. Energy problem is closely related to every one. In addition, according

* This work was partially supported by grants from the National Science Council, Taiwan (NSC 96-2628-E-002-173-MY3, NSC 99-2221-E-002-139-MY3, and NSC 099-2811-E-002-020).

[1] Global Energy Issues, World Energy Council, 2006:
http://www.worldenergy.org/documents/p001022.doc

[2] Residential Energy Consumption Survey (RECS):
http://www.eia.doe.gov/emeu/recs/

[3] Energy Use in Homes:
http://www.eia.doe.gov/energyexplained/index.cfm?page=us_energy_homes

N. Desai, A. Liu, and M. Winikoff (Eds.): PRIMA 2010, LNAI 7057, pp. 475–486, 2012.

to the statistics of Energy Information Administration[4], total consumption of electricity in 2010 is estimated to increase 5% over last year. People have to pay more attention to energy related issue to avoid energy shortage. The first and easiest way is "Do not waste electricity".

Darby's research [2] raised a conclusion that the more aware of the detailed energy consumption can provide more incentives to improve energy efficiency. There are 5-15% energy saving was reached in their experiments. Traditional electric meter measures power consumption of subscribers. It provides data about current, impedance, power factor, watt, apparent power, etc. Most people read this kind of data senselessly, and pay the electricity bill. Our idea is to use a scientific method to analyze the raw data from a center power meter, and then determine whether users are wasting energy. It then shows the suggestions to users in an easily understanding way. For example, to suggest a user to turn off the light in the kitchen when the user is watching TV in the living room.

The first step is to acquire the state of every electrical appliance in the environment. In general, people always plug in and run multiple appliances on the same circuit, which makes the detection of appliance states a great challenge. Furthermore, user's activity is inferred from the acquired appliance states. However, the individual use varies from house to house and the appliance usage may vary according to living habits, this also make the problem more complicated. Finally, with appliance states and user activity, the system filters out the appliances which are wasting energy.

This paper proposes an agent-based framework to detect energy-wasting appliances. An appliance is wasting energy if it is not necessary in user's current activity. We named such appliances *Nonessential Appliances*. The framework collect electrical power signal from electric distribution boards to monitor operating states of appliances in real time. The operating states is used to recognize user's activities. In addition, we propose an activity-appliance model. This model builds the connection between activities and appliance usages from commonsense knowledge. With this model and previous results, the framework filters out nonessential appliances. As the result, this framework urges people to reduce power consumption by reminding them to turn off nonessential appliances.

2 Related Work

The most intuitive approach to recognize an appliance in an environment is to mount sensors on every appliance [5]. With this manner, the unique characteristic of each appliance is captured. Ito *et al.* [3] and Saitoh *et al.* [8] extract features in power waveform, which includes average power consumption, peak power usage, crest factor, form factor, etc. Kato *et al.* [4] apply Linear Discriminant Analysis (LDA) to extract features. Researchers then analyze the features of appliances to predict their operating states. Serra *et al.* [9] utilized clustering techniques to detect operating states of appliances. Kato *et al.* [4] applied Support Vector

[4] U.S. Total Electricity Consumption Chart, Short-term Energy Outlook, October 2010: `http://www.eia.doe.gov/steo/gifs/Fig22.gif`

Machine (SVM) to classify appliances. However, it costs too much to mount a sensor on every appliance. Furthermore, the deployment and maintenance are troublesome. These make the approach impractical in real life.

The distribution board is the electricity gateway of an electricity subscriber. It usually divides an electrical power feed into subsidiary circuits. A non-intrusive approach to recognize appliance's operating state is to identify the power usage from the distribution board. When an appliance is switched between operating states, it usually generates some electrical noise. Patel *et al.* [7] took advantage of these noises to recognize the change of operating states of appliances. Their approach is impressive, but it disregards energy consumption, which contains essential information for energy management.

Appliance recognition is getting mature, but its application in energy saving is just started. MicroSoft Hohm[5] provides a Web-based service that can estimate household energy usage and deliver energy saving recommendations to users. Google PowerMeter[6] provides a simple analysis of the electrical consumption and users can access information from the iGoogle page. Both Hohm and PowerMeter provide home energy consumption data that helps users to make better energy efficient decisions. However, these two services only provide an overview of energy consumption, and they cannot provide more detailed information like "how many appliances are running in a house?" Therefore, we present this work to make this research field more active and bring more possibility.

3 Nonessential Appliance Detection

The *Nonessential Appliance Detection* problem is to find out electrical devices that are currently turned on but are not involved in any user's activity. These devices are wasting electric power; hence, identifying them can help people reduce their energy consumption. In addition, we call this kind of devices *Nonessential Appliances.*

3.1 Problem Formulation

Let $A = \{a_1, a_2, \ldots, a_m\}$ be a set of m activities that performed by users in the house, and $P = \{p_1, p_2, \ldots, p_n\}$ be a set of n electrical appliances. A function $f_{use}(a_i, p_j)$ denotes the relationship between activity $a_i \in A$ and appliance $p_j \in P$, such that

$$f_{use}(a_i, p_j) = \begin{cases} true & \text{if the activity } a_i \text{ uses the appliance } p_j \\ flase & \text{otherwise} \end{cases} \tag{1}$$

Given an activity $a_i \in A$, let $P_{a_i} \subseteq P$ be the set of required appliances to accomplish activity a_i. We named P_{a_i} as the *essential appliance* set of the activity a_i. Formal definition of P_{a_i} is

$$P_{a_i} = \{p_j : f_{use}(a_i, p_j) = true\}$$

[5] MicroSoft Hohm Center (`http://www.microsoft-hohm.com/Home/Default.aspx`)

[6] Google PowerMeter (`http://www.google.com/powermeter/about/`)

where $a_i \in A$ and $p_j \in P$.

Suppose that $A_c \subseteq A$ is a set of the user's current active activities. The essential appliances of the active activities A_c is formulated as

$$P_{A_c} = \bigcup_{a_i \in A_c} P_{a_i}. \quad (2)$$

Therefore, given a set of currently running appliances $P_c \subseteq P$, the *nonessential appliance* set $\widetilde{P_c} \subseteq P_c$ is defined to be

$$\widetilde{P_c} = P_c \setminus P_{A_c}, \quad (3)$$

which is the difference set of P_c and P_{A_c}. Our goal is to find all the nonessential appliance $p_j \in \widetilde{P_c}$.

4 Activity-Appliance Model

The most intuitive approach of detecting nonessential appliances $\widetilde{P_c}$ is aware of the user's behaviors when they are using electrical appliances. However, most technologies of activities recognition are intrusive, disruptive, and violated on the privacy of users. We need a non-intrusive approach to detect the nonessential appliances. Therefore, we collecting the electrical power signal from distribution boards and predicting the operating state of appliances. By giving these currently running appliances, we have to detect the active activities. As people usually perform a series of activities and use electrical appliances to facilitate their tasks, we propose the Activity-Appliance Model to make connections of activities and appliances.

4.1 Model Formulation

Ideally, according to the Boolean function $f_{use}(a_i, p_j)$ in Equation (1), the Activity-Appliance Model constructs relationships between activity a_i and appliance p_j, where $a_i \in A$ and $p_j \in P$. We recall the notations of Section 3.1, the P and A respectively represent the set of appliances and activities. However, in real life, different users have different appliance usage habits. For example, in the meal preparation, some people prefer stove to microwave, but almost anyone can find some use for a microwave. Therefore, in order to define a general relationship between activities and appliances, we have to relax the definition of function $f_{use}(a_i, p_j)$ and change its return value from the Boolean to a value of score weighting.

For the purpose of defining a general function $f_{use}(a_i, p_j)$, we have to measure what are the people's common understandings in activities and appliances. We utilized the human computation technique to collect the knowledge of daily activities and electrical appliances, especially the relationships between them [6]. This human computation game asked players questions, such as "what electrical appliances would be used for cooking?" and "What kind of activity does a microwave use for?", etc. Players answer these fill-in-the-blank questions and contribute their understandings to the activity-appliance model. We also designed yes-no questions for players to validate the others' answers. Accordingly, a function $f_{count}(a_i, p_j)$ returns how many players agree with the activity a_i will use the appliance p_j to accomplish its task. Detailed definition shows as follows:

$$f_{count}(a_i, p_j) = \begin{cases} l & \text{there are } l \text{ people answer that when they are doing the activity } a_i\text{, they use the appliance } p_j \\ 0 & \text{otherwise; no one agree to that doing the activity } a_i \text{ will use the appliance } p_j. \end{cases}$$

For example, if eleven people answer that "people use microwave for cooking", the function $f_{count}(cooking, microwave)$ returns 11, where the activity $cooking \in A$ and the appliance $microwave \in P$.

However, for the large combinations of activities and appliances, the resulting number of occurrence cannot provide much information due to the huge data. Accordingly, it is essential to rank these combinations and find the proper match of activities and appliances. To do this, for giving an activity a_i and an appliance p_j, we need a function returns the score of the relationship between the activity a_i and the appliance p_j. A relaxed function $f'_{use}(a_i, p_j)$ of the function $f_{use}(a_i, p_j)$ can be defined as

$$f'_{use}(a_i, p_j) = \Psi_{tf}(a_i, p_j) \times \Psi_{idf}(p_j)$$

where $a_i \in A$ and $p_j \in P$. The $\Psi_{tf}(a_i, p_j)$ and $\Psi_{idf}(p_j)$ are inspired by the TF-IDF weight of information retrieval, such that

$$\Psi_{tf}(a_i, p_j) = \frac{f_{count}(a_i, p_j)}{\sum_{a_k \in A} f_{count}(a_k, p_j)}$$

$$\Psi_{idf}(p_j) = \log \frac{|A|}{|\{a_r : f_{count}(a_r, p_j) > 0, a_r \in A\}|}.$$

Function $\Psi_{tf}(a_i, p_j)$ denotes the frequency of that people use the appliance p_j to perform the activity a_i. The $\Psi_{idf}(p_j)$ plays the role of measuring the general importance of the appliance p_j. The $|A|$ in $\Psi_{idf}(p_j)$ is the cardinality of activity set A; recall the definition in Section 3.1, $|A|$ is equal to m. For each activity a_r in the set $\{a_r : f_{count}(a_r, p_j) > 0, a_r \in A\}$, has the connection with the appliance p_j; that is, the value of function $f_{count}(a_r, p_j)$ must greater than zero.

4.2 Active Activity Scoring

Given the currently running appliances $P_c \subseteq P$, let $\overrightarrow{P_c}$ be the corresponding vector of P_c, such that

$$\overrightarrow{P_c} = [f_{on}(p_1), f_{on}(p_2), \cdots, f_{on}(p_n)].$$

The function $f_{on}(p_j)$ denotes the operation state of the appliance $p_j \in P$ and defines as follows:

$$f_{on}(p_j) = \begin{cases} 1 & \text{if } p_j \in P_c \text{; the appliance } p_j \text{ is running currently} \\ 0 & \text{otherwise, } i.e.\ p_j \notin P_c \text{; the appliance } p_j \text{ is suspended} \\ & \text{or power off.} \end{cases}$$

Recall the essential appliances set of activity $P_{a_i} \in P$ in Section 3.1, we relax the definition of the *essential appliance* vector as

$$\overrightarrow{P_{a_i}} = [f'_{use}(a_i, p_1), f'_{use}(a_i, p_2), \cdots, f'_{use}(a_i, p_n)], \tag{4}$$

where $p_1, p_2, \cdots$, and $p_n \in P$.

The Euclidean inner product of $\overrightarrow{P_c}$ and $\overrightarrow{P_{a_i}}$ is used for predicting the active activities A_c. For each activity $a_i \in A$, we compute the score of the activity a_i to be

$$\begin{aligned} f_{score}(a_i) &= \overrightarrow{P_c} \bullet \overrightarrow{P_{a_i}} \\ &= \sum_{p_j \in P} f_{on}(p_j) \times f'_{use}(a_i, p_j). \end{aligned} \tag{5}$$

Consequently, the active activity set $A_c \subseteq A$ contains the element $a_i \in A$ that has higher score and the formulation is

$$A_c = \{a_i : f_{score}(a_i) \geq \theta\}, \tag{6}$$

where θ is the threshold of the score value. As a result, given the currently running appliances P_c, the activity-appliance model can predict the active activities A_c.

4.3 Goal Finding

In this paper, finding nonessential appliances $\widetilde{P_c} \subseteq P_c$ is our goal. Thus far, we have the currently running appliance P_c and the active activities A_c, whereas we need to compute the difference set of P_c and P_{A_c}. Fortunately, we can use the Equation (2) to construct the essential appliances P_{A_c}, and then achieve the goal $\widetilde{P_c}$ from the Equation (3).

5 Energy-Aware Agents

Fig. 1 depicts our deployment of an agent-based framework to detect nonessential appliances $\widetilde{P_c}$. The input of this framework is the electrical power signal collected from distribution boards. Equation (3) provides the solution to find out the nonessential appliances $\widetilde{P_c}$. In other words, by solving the currently running appliances P_c and active activities A_c, we can obtain nonessential appliances $\widetilde{P_c}$.

Accordingly, the **Appliance Monitoring Agent** monitors electrical power from power distribution boards, and identifies the currently running appliances P_c

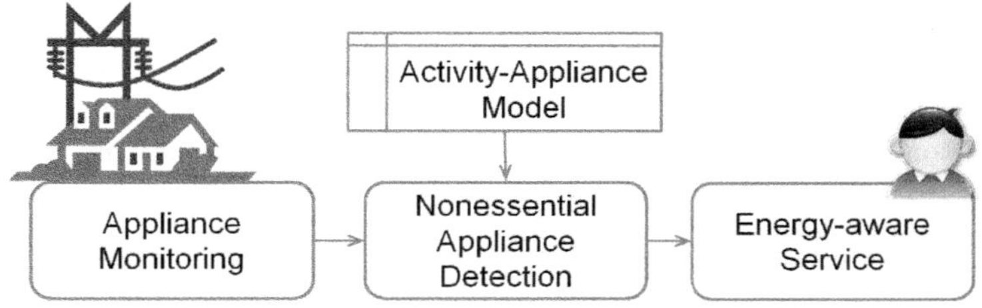

Fig. 1. Energy-aware agents

that are currently consuming electrical energy. In the **Nonessential Appliance Detection Agent**, we utilize the relationships between activities and appliances to build an **Activity-Appliance Model**, so that we can infer the user's active activities A_c, and then compute the essential appliances P_{A_c}. As a result, we can obtain the nonessential appliances $\widetilde{P_c}$, and the **Energy-aware Service Agent** will deliver energy conservation tips to the user.

5.1 Appliance Monitoring Agent

We use a non-intrusive power meter that mounted on each of the power circuit for measuring the electrical consumption. The Appliance Monitoring Agent collects the raw sensing data as its belief and predicts the corresponding appliance operating states as its desire. The reason that we predict the operating state of appliances is to find out which appliance is currently running. However, people usually plug in and run multiple appliances on the same circuit. It is hard to detect the operating state of every appliance from a circuit.

According to the waveforms of real power and reactive power, we extract 18 features from the input power signal, including the mean, variance, root mean square, maximum, minimum, difference, crest factor, form factor, and the value of maximum divided by the mean. These features are also the belief of the Appliance Monitoring Agent that uses to predict the operating state of appliances.

The Appliance Monitoring Agent uses Factorial Conditional Random Fields (FCRFs) [10] to detect and learn from using appliances. For recognizing appliances, the features of input power represent the observed variables, whereas the operating states of appliances represent the hidden variables. We use the L-BFGS[7] as the algorithm of learning process. The Loopy Belief Propagation (LBP) algorithm [11] is used to perform the message passing. A maximum a priori (MAP) estimation technique is applied to both of the inference and decoding processes. In the inference process, MAP simply propagates the maximum possibility value of the operating state to update hidden variables. As a result, MAP uses the most possible sequences of hidden variables to decode the appliance's

[7] L-BFGS is an algorithm for quasi-Newton optimization. The term L-BFGS stands for "limited memory BFGS (Broyden-Fletcher-Goldfarb-Shanno)".

operating state. An iteration limit Γ is assigned to guarantee the LBP termination and convergence [12]. After the LBP max-product algorithm converges and the MAP probability of each hidden variable is estimated, we can label every hidden variable by choosing the most likely value according to the MAP probability. Consequently, output of the Appliance Monitoring Agent is a set of currently running appliances P_c.

5.2 Nonessential Appliance Detection Agent

From the Appliance Monitoring Agent, the Nonessential Appliance Detection Agent receives the currently running appliance P_c as its belief. In addition, we utilize human-based computation to construct the Activity-Appliance Model, which is also the belief of this agent. Desires of this agent are to predict the active activities A_c and detect the nonessential appliances $\widetilde{P_c}$.

The intention of the Nonessential Appliance Detection Agent follows the description of Section 4. Accordingly, this agent performs a sequence of actions: building the activity-appliance model, scoring every activity a_i, finding the active activities A_c, and predicting the goal $\widetilde{P_c}$.

5.3 Energy-Aware Service Agent

The beliefs of the Energy-aware Service Agent include the nonessential appliances $\widetilde{P_c}$, active activities A_c, and currently running appliance P_c. In order to send the energy conservation tips to the user, the knowledge base of these tips is also the belief of this agent. Without doubt the desire is to deliver the energy-conservation tips to the user.

Currently, our Energy-aware Service Agent simply reminds the user to turn off the nonessential appliances $\widetilde{P_c}$ and shows the conservation tips to the user. When contain of active activities A_c or the currently running appliance P_c is changed, the corresponding notification shows on a LCD display.

6 Experimental Results

In this experiment, a smart power meter is mounted on a distribution board of a single dormitory room. The distribution board divides electrical power feed into five circuits. Three circuits are separately allocated to an electric water heater, an air conditioner, and three ceiling lights. As regards the other two circuits, one is for the electric oven and a dehumidifier; the other is for small appliances, such as the hair dryer, battery charger, laptop, lamp, and electric fan.

Our experimental participant is living in this en-suite room. The smart power meter continuously records electricity usage of the user for two weeks. During the experimental period, the user can perform any activity without restriction, that is, this experiment will not disturb the user's normal daily life. The following experimental results are use this data set to evaluate performances of appliance monitoring and nonessential appliance detection.

6.1 Appliance Monitoring

In this experiment, there are 4,671 valid data with 24 different activities. We deploy several machine learning methods to predict the operating state of appliances. Each method is run 5-fold cross-validation on the same experimental data with 64-second half-overlapped sliding window. The evaluation criteria for the Appliance Monitoring agent include accuracy, precision, recall, and F-score.

A comparison of appliance monitoring methods shows in Table 1, which presents the average prediction results of the appliance. In addition to the Factorial Conditional Random Fields (FCRFs), we implement three other methods for the comparison, including Parallel Conditional Random Fields (PCRFs), Hidden Markov Model (HMM), and Hidden Markov Support Vector Machine[8][1] (SVM^{hmm}). Results show that PCRFs and FCRFs significantly outperform the other two methods in the comparison of accuracy, precision, and F-score. Both FCRFs and PCRFs are CRF-like methods, except that the PCRFs only consider the target appliance's operating states without refer to the others' states.

Table 1. A comparison of appliance monitoring

Result(%)	Accuracy	Precision	Recall	F-score
SVM^{hmm}	88.81	51.62	43.36	46.22
HMM	94.69	78.55	84.13	80.58
PCRFs	96.14	92.70	76.74	83.45
FCRFs	96.43	93.01	79.32	85.06

6.2 Nonessential Appliance Detection

In this experiment, we choose six activities, including taking a shower, going to the toilet, sleeping, using a computer, reading, and blow drying. These six activities involve ten appliances that we have monitored, they are electric water heater, air conditioner, dehumidifier, electric fan, ceiling lights, hair dryer, battery charger, laptop, and desk lamp. The activity-appliance model calculates the relationship between these six activities and ten appliances. There are 256 data in our experiments. For the active activities prediction, according to Equation (6), the activity have the highest score will be picked as the active activity.

In order to verify the Equation (5) can obtain better results, we modified the scoring function of Equation (5) and replace the function $f'_{use}(a_i, p_j)$ by $\Psi_{tf}(a_i, p_j)$, that is, the modified score will be

$$\sum_{p_j \in P} f_{on}(p_j) \times \Psi_{tf}(a_i, p_j),$$

where activity $a_i \in A$ and appliance $p_j \in P$.

[8] SVM^{hmm}: Sequence Tagging with Structural Support Vector Machines, `http://www.cs.cornell.edu/People/tj/svm%5Flight/svm_hmm.html`

Table 2. Confusion matrix of predicting active activities – Ψ_{tf}

		Actual activity						recall
		A1	A2	A3	A4	A5	A6	(%)
Predicted activity	A1: Sleeping	13	0	3	0	0	0	81.25
	A2: Reading	0	0	0	0	0	0	N/A
	A3: Using a computer	0	1	36	0	7	0	81.82
	A4: Taking a shower	0	0	0	0	0	0	N/A
	A5: Going to the toilet	0	5	113	60	3	3	1.63
	A6: Blow drying	0	0	0	0	0	12	100.00
	Precision(%)	100.00	0.00	23.68	0.00	30.00	80.00	

Average precision(%): 38.95
Average recall(%): 66.17
F-score(%): 49.03
Accuracy(%): 25.00

Table 2 presents the results that calculates the score of activity a_i by using the modified score. Each row of Table 2 represents the number of count in a predicted activity, while each column represents the count of actual activity. Accordingly, the diagonal element is the number of correct prediction. The symbol A1 represents the sleeping activity, A2 is for the reading, and so on. For example, the value 13 in the row A1 and column A1, means the score function can correctly predict the sleeping activity for 13 times. In this experiments, there are 13 test cases for sleeping activity, therefore, the precision of predicting the sleeping activity is 100%. In addition, the row A1 and column A3 shows that 3 cases have been mispredicted as sleeping activity, but they belong to activity A3 (using a computer).

We observe that some activities are improperly predicted as going to toilet, because of these activities will use ceiling lights and $\Psi_{tf}(going\_to\_the\_toilet, ceiling\_lights)$ has highest value than the others. For example, when we are reading we always turn on ceiling lights and desk lamp. This is the reason that the Equation (6) does not use the frequency of an appliance to predict activity.

Results using Equation (5) is shown in Table 3. In this experiment, we only collect six samples of reading activity, and the precision of predicting reading activity is 83.33%. It shows that even for the small sample size, the activity-appliance model can obtain good quality results.

We find that the ceiling lights still affect the results of activity prediction. There are two activities, using a computer and taking a shower, are still improperly predicted as going to the toilet. Compare Table 3 with Table 2, the accuracy of predicting the toileting activity is dropped 20%, because of ceiling lights is the only one electrical device that will be used while the user is going to the toilet. In addition, for the taking a shower and going to the toilet activities, these two activities take place in the same room and they use ceiling lights. This is the reason that some of the bathing activities have been mispredicted as toileting.

In Table 3, most of the activities have higher precision than that of Table 2, except the going to the toilet and blow drying. These two activities are short term

Table 3. Confusion matrix of predicting active activities – f'_{use}

		Actual activity						recall
		A1	A2	A3	A4	A5	A6	(%)
Predicted activity	A1: Sleeping	13	0	16	0	0	0	44.83
	A2: Reading	0	5	7	0	0	0	41.67
	A3: Using a computer	0	1	127	0	9	14	84.11
	A4: Taking a shower	0	0	0	39	0	0	100.00
	A5: Going to the toilet	0	0	2	21	1	0	4.17
	A6: Blow drying	0	0	0	0	0	1	100.00
	Precision(%)	100.00	83.33	83.55	65.00	10.00	6.67	

Average precision(%): 58.09
Average recall(%): 62.46
F-score(%): 60.20
Accuracy(%): 72.66

activities and may concurrently perform with other activities. That is, simply picks highest score may cause incorrect prediction due to concurrent activities.

7 Conclusion

This paper proposes a multi-agent framework that integrated technologies of machine learning, information retrieval, and human-based computation to detect the energy-wasting appliances. We apply a statistic model, the FCRF, to predict the appliance operating state, such that can detect the running appliances. In order to build a connection between activities and appliances, a human-based computational game is developed for gathering the relationships from the huge Internet users. After people contribute their common knowledge of activities and appliances, we use the TF-IDF weight technique to build an activity-appliance model. For giving the operating state of appliances and utilizing the activity-appliance model, we can easily detect the nonessential appliances.

Experiments show that the CRF-like approaches can obtain 96.43% accuracy. Results of detecting active activities are 72.66% in average. It is necessary for us to improve the results of active activities in order to precisely detect nonessential appliances. In the future, we will try to predict more active activities rather than just taking the most significant one. The TF-IDF weighting can be adjusted to satisfy the needs of our problem. In addition, we will continue gathering the activities and appliances data for generalizing the activity-appliance model.

References

1. Altun, Y., Tsochantaridis, I., Hofmann, T.: Hidden markov support vector machines. In: Proceedings of the Twentieth International Conference on Machine Learning (ICML 2003), pp. 3–10. AAAI Press, Washington, DC (2003)
2. Darby, S.: The effectiveness of feedback on energy consumption. A Review for DEFRA of the Literature on Metering, Billing and direct Displays (2006)

3. Ito, M., Uda, R., Ichimura, S., Tago, K., Hoshi, T., Matsushita, Y.: A method of appliance detection based on features of power waveform. In: Proceedings of 2004 International Symposium on Applications and the Internet, pp. 291–294 (2004)
4. Kato, T., Cho, H., Lee, D., Toyomura, T., Yamazaki, T.: Appliance Recognition from Electric Current Signals for Information-Energy Integrated Network in Home Environments. In: Mokhtari, M., Khalil, I., Bauchet, J., Zhang, D., Nugent, C. (eds.) ICOST 2009. LNCS, vol. 5597, pp. 150–157. Springer, Heidelberg (2009)
5. Kim, Y., Schmid, T., Charbiwala, Z., Srivastava, M.: ViridiScope: design and implementation of a fine grained power monitoring system for homes. In: Proceedings of the 11th International Conference on Ubiquitous Computing, pp. 245–254. ACM (2009)
6. Kuo, Y.L., Chiang, K.Y., Chan, C.W., Lee, J.C., Wang, R., Shen, E., Hsu, J.Y.J.: Community-based game design: Experiments on social games for commonsense data collection. In: KDD 2009 Workshop on Human Computation (HCOMP 2009), Paris, France (June 2009)
7. Patel, S.N., Robertson, T., Kientz, J.A., Reynolds, M.S., Abowd, G.D.: At the Flick of a Switch: Detecting and Classifying Unique Electrical Events on the Residential Power Line. In: Krumm, J., Abowd, G.D., Seneviratne, A., Strang, T. (eds.) UbiComp 2007. LNCS, vol. 4717, pp. 271–288. Springer, Heidelberg (2007)
8. Saitoh, T., Aota, Y., Osaki, T., Konishi, R., Sugahara, K.: Current Sensor based Non-intrusive Appliance Recognition for Intelligent Outlet. In: ITC-CSCC 2008 (2008)
9. Serra, H., Correia, J., Gano, A., de Campos, A., Teixeira, I.: Domestic power consumption measurement and automatic home appliance detection. In: 2007 IEEE International Workshop on Intelligent Signal Processing, pp. 128–132 (2005)
10. Sutton, C., McCallum, A., Rohanimanesh, K.: Dynamic conditional random fields: Factorized probabilistic models for labeling and segmenting sequence data. Journal of Machine Learning Research 8 (2007)
11. Yedidia, J.S., Freeman, W.T., Weiss, Y.: Understanding belief propagation and its generalizations. In: Exploring Artificial Intelligence in the New Millennium, ch. 8, pp. 239–269. Morgan Kaufmann (2002)
12. Yedidia, J.S., Freeman, W.T., Weiss, Y.: Constructing free-energy approximations and generalized belief propagation algorithms. IEEE Transactions on Information Theory 51(7), 2282–2312 (2005)

Medical Equipment Maintenance Support with Service-Oriented Multi-agent Services

Beatriz Lopez[1], Albert Pla[1], David Daroca[2], Luis Collantes[3], Sara Lozano[3], and Joaquim Meléndez[1]

[1] eXiT Research Grup, University of Girona, Spain
{beatriz.lopez,albert.pla,joaquim.melendez}@udg.edu
[2] Telefónica I+D, Spain
ddaroca@full-on-net.com
[3] INDRA, Spain
{lcollantes,slozano}@indra.es

Abstract. Service oriented architectures (SOA) have emerged as an approach to handle the complexity of enterprise interoperability. Recently, multi-agent systems have been promoted as a technique to deal with cooperation issues involved in SOA. This cooperation is particularly important in several application domains, in which different companies are involved in a concrete service deployment. Agents, among other issues, offer the possibility to decide, if more than one option is available, providing flexibility and robustness. In this paper, we describe the agent-based cooperation process we have followed to enable partner's cooperation in an equipment maintenance workflow. The use of ontologies and relationships with standards is highlighted. The approach is illustrated in an hospital scenario considered in the AIMES project.

Keywords: Service oriented architectures, multi-agent systems, ontologies, data mining.

1 Introduction

Medical equipment maintenance has been a matter of concern to hospital managers, because they dramatically impact on the patient treatment and waiting lists, particularly when equipment on maintenance is large (as magnetic resonance imaging (MRI) equipment). To support the daily activity in medical equipment maintenance, some manufacturers have provided devices with diagnosis capabilities to facilitate maintenance. Thus, a vital signal monitoring is able to provide reports on its status when turning it on, or upon a user request. Some devices can provide diagnosis as well as predictive information (prognosis) on the equipment status. In addition, large equipment manufacturers are offering remote maintenance due to several privacy constraints, so that they are bypassing the hospital maintenance information systems and connecting their particular devices to their costumer support department. Thus, information from medical equipment is generated in the device level and gathered by either users, technicians or remote systems. Finally, the maintenance department of

N. Desai, A. Liu, and M. Winikoff (Eds.): PRIMA 2010, LNAI 7057, pp. 487–498, 2012.

the hospital receives information by means of phone calls or similar personal communications, about the status or intervention on large, complex equipment.

Nowadays, IT offers a lot of possibilities to improve this way of working. Particularly, the recent convergence of service oriented architectures (SOA) with semantic web in what is known as semantic web services (WS) enables enterprise interoperability, achieving enterprises collaboration and maintaining the internal process of each company in privacy. What is more important is that web services facilitates the modeling of the complete process involved in a maintenance equipment intervention. Thus, services can be composed in different ways thanks to management tools as BPEL4WS [1].

Recently, agent technology has enhanced service oriented architectures by incorporating flexibility and versatility [1,2]. Agents, among other issues, offer the possibility to decide, when and how to deploy a service, and they are able to adapt their behavior to changing circumstances. Thus, service coordination among distributed enterprises is achieved by means of agent negotiation. On the other hand, agents also offer a way of brokering services, as proposed in [3,4]. In this line, service composition at the inter and intra enterprise levels can also be enhanced. In this context, ontologies play a crucial role to guarantee interoperability.

Our work is concerned with the incorporation of agent technology in SOA at these two levels: inter and intra enterprise. On the one hand, inter enterprise collaboration requires from an ontology – speak the same language, unify the interface with all possible manufacturers. On the other hand, intra enterprise concerns workflow monitoring at the business level, as all the medical equipment maintenance operations being carried out so that it is guaranteed they finish at their due date. We explain along this paper how is our approach to this kind of integration of agents, ontologies and SOA.

Our work is being developed inside the AIMES project [10], "Advanced Infrastructures for Medical Equipment and Services", as an attempt to provide an IT infrastructure to hospitals so that they can optimize the service workflow in a care domain by reducing equipment downtimes. This document reviews and extends the work presented in [2].

This paper is organized as follows. First we provide in Section 2 the description of the proposed system architecture in order to enable the monitoring of the maintenance operations. Next, we analyze three case studies on Section 3. We discuss some related work in Section 4 and we end the paper in Section 5 with some conclusions.

2 Architecture for Medical Equipment Maintenance

Our aim is to develop an infrastructure that can help hospital maintenance managers in their daily duties. For this purpose, we propose a service oriented architecture that models the medical equipment maintenance process and then helps the user to monitor the current activities: which of them are in due date, which of them are delayed, what resources to re-assign in case of maintenance overload, etc. Observe then, than our novelty in the medical domains relies on providing a tool for workflow monitoring (actions at the business level), and we differentiate our contribution from pure equipment monitoring (see [11] for a comparison). Monitoring the status of a medical equipment should be something already provided by large equipment (self diagnosis).

Thus, first of all we analyze the different functionalities needed for supporting medical equipment maintenance, and we define the corresponding services required to achieve them. Since the process is complex, we propose the use of agents to make service coordination more flexible. Thus, agents are used for two purposes: monitoring and negotiating. On one hand, for each maintenance process being active, there is a workflow monitoring agent as explained below. On the other hand, negotiation agents allow the synchronization of the activities of the in house technicians with the external manufacturers when required. Finally, for interoperability purposes, we propose to use an ontology based on medical standards.

2.1 Services

Up to thirteen services have been identified in a first approach to support medical equipment maintenance (see Table 1). They are conceptually depicted in Figure 1 together with the different interfaces required among them. All of the services can be classified and described according to their role in the architecture. Thus, we have services related to information sources, historical data services, equipment services, maintenance management services, and external services.

Firstly, there are four services related with information: the facility management service (FMS), the healthcare organization management service (HOMS), the hospital information service (HIS) and the equipment localization service (ELS). The FMS is in charge of dealing with static information about devices (adding a service, removing an old one, spare parts replaced, technical handbook, troubleshooting documents, etc.). The HOMS provides information about the available technical staff for doing maintenance interventions, including their expertise and training on the medical equipment. The HIS provides information about the availability of medical equipment for maintenance purposes (i.e. when they are not scheduled for patient care). Finally, the ELS is related to dynamic information of devices so that they can be localized when required. For this purpose, RFID technologies is integrated in this service.

Table 1. Summary of services

Information sources	FMS	Facility management service
	HOMS	Healthcare organization management service
	HIS	Hospital information service
	ELS	Equipment localization service
Historical data	IDS	Infrastructure data service
	EPS	Equipment predictive service
	SS	Statistics service
Equipment	CMS	Condition monitoring service
	MMS	Maintenance management service
	MSM	Medical service management
	TTS	Trouble ticketing service
Maintenance management	SCS	Service centre service
	MES	Medical equipment service

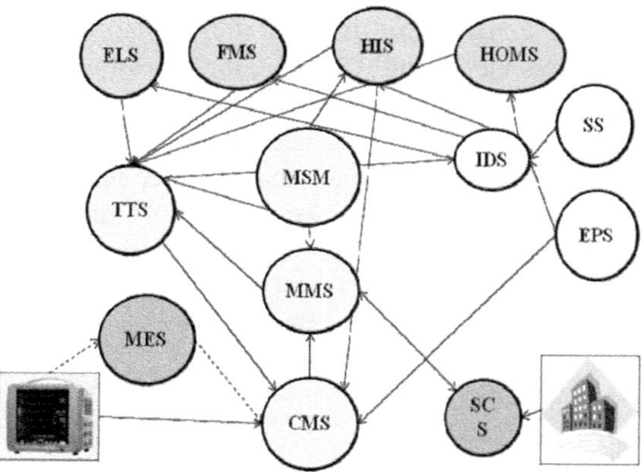

Fig. 1. Conceptual design of the different services involved in medical equipment maintenance workflow monitoring

Secondly, there are several services related to the management and treatment of historical data. They are the infrastructure data service (IDS), the equipment predictive service (EPS) and the statistics service (SS). The IDS is in charge of storing all the historical information regarding maintenance operations. The EPS uses the information kept by the IDS in order to apply different data mining tools so that different patterns can be extracted about equipment and maintenance workflow and predictions can be generated. Finally, the SS provide different statistics in order to know, for example, the real cost of an equipment in its life cycle. The statistics can help the hospital responsible when dealing with new equipment investment decisions.

Thirdly, there are a set of services related to maintenance workflows: the condition monitoring service (CMS), the maintenance management service (MMS), the medical service manager (MSM) and the trouble ticketing service (TTS). The CMS deals with the status information of medical equipment in order to determine maintenance interventions. The MMS is responsible of setting up the appropriate maintenance operations, according to the evaluations performed by the CMS, and tracing them. The MSM coordinates the equipment maintenance activities with patient scheduling, among others. The TTS generates a trouble ticket for every maintenance workflow instantiation and keeps the information about them up to date.

Fourthly, there are the external services. They represent collaborations with other enterprises or equipment. They are the service centre service (SCS) and the medical equipment service (MES). The SCS communicates with remote service providers. These services are especially helpful with large equipment, since their manufacturers provide external maintenance. On the other hand, the MES is responsible for dealing with the data acquisition of the remaining equipment of the hospital.

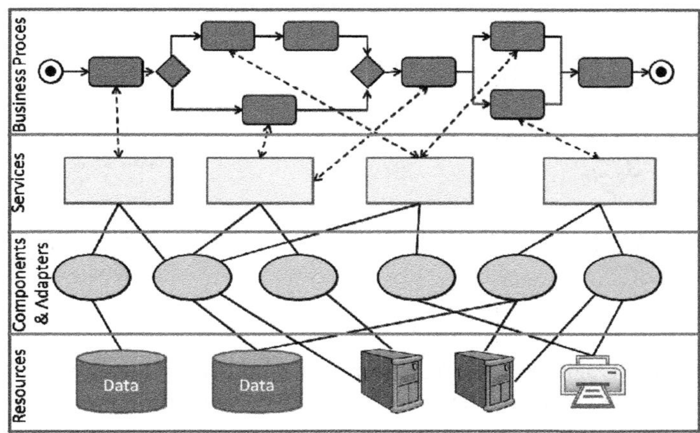

Fig. 2. Services and workflows

Services are combined into workflows which model business activities (see Figure 2), in a typical Service Oriented approach. When a business activity should be deployed, a workflow instance is created; thus, different workflow instances can run concurrently (see Figure 3).

2.2 Introducing Agents

There are two services that require special decision making features that make them suitable to be designed by using the agent paradigm. They are the MMS and the SCS.

On one hand, the MMS trace all the maintenance workflows instances being executed at a given moment inside a company (intra-company communication). To coordinate the different maintenance inventions, we can model each workflow instance as a workflow monitoring agent (WM), so that it introduces flexibility to the architecture when doing this coordination.

WM agents can be organized in a multi-agent architecture according to several criteria, as the in-house technician responsible of the maintenances and the kind of medical equipment, among other. An additional agent should also assume the role of coordinator, dealing with possible preventive and predictive issues (see Figure 4).

In principle, we prefer the agent organization based on the kind of equipment: small, medium and large, since different technicians can be assigned to the same maintenance intervention. Moreover, the experience of each technician is related also to the kind of equipment. In this sense, we distinguish different types of equipment according to their diagnosis capabilities, as follows:

- Small: devices without diagnosis capabilities and non repairable equipment.
- Medium: devices with the ability for auto-diagnosis.
- Large: devices without prerequisites for auto-diagnosis.

Thus, WM agents can be organized accordingly.

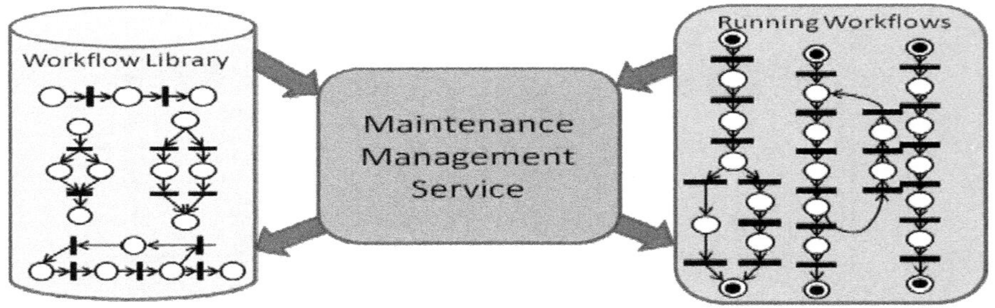

Fig. 3. Workflow instances

On the other hand, the SCS, responsible of third party interactions in maintenance, can also be implemented by means of agents. This situation is especially important in large equipment, were external technicians intervention is usually performed. That is, large equipment cannot be diagnosed by in-house technicians due to some manufacturers' constraints. Instead, medical equipment manufacturers, as Siemens or Dräguer provide remote access services that connect their equipment with the technical manufacturers own staff (outside the hospital). As a consequence, the final communication between in-house and external technicians is usually performed by informal means, as phone calls or personal communications, incurring in some maintenance delays due to some kind of lack of understanding. The SOA offers in this sense, by means of the SCS service, the possibility of connecting both business models: the hospital maintenance and the manufacturer's maintenance (inter-company communication). There should be a SCS agent per each remote provider, and they should be provided with negotiation capabilities. The simplest ones could be only aware of the maintenance contract and to assure that it is satisfied. However, the possibility of dealing with the different parts involved in the maintenance process, as arrival of spare parts, in-house download of equipment information, filling up repairing questionnaires, etc., should be also considered.

2.3 Using Ontologies

The proposed architecture highlights the heterogeneity of devices and maintenance teams commonly present in hospitals' infrastructure (different manufacturers working with different proprietary formats, different data communication levels…). In this setting, it is necessary to provide an environment where various devices, maintenance systems and technicians can easily connect and communicate to the system, in a "plug and play" way, effectively overcoming problems that arise from the heterogeneity of such devices.

A solution to reconcile different data formats and models is to build a unified domain model. Two main issues need to be studied in order to build this unified view of the domain: is there any standard that can serve to this purpose?, how can this standard be introduced in the proposed architecture? We following address these questions, by suggesting the use of ontologies as a possible solution.

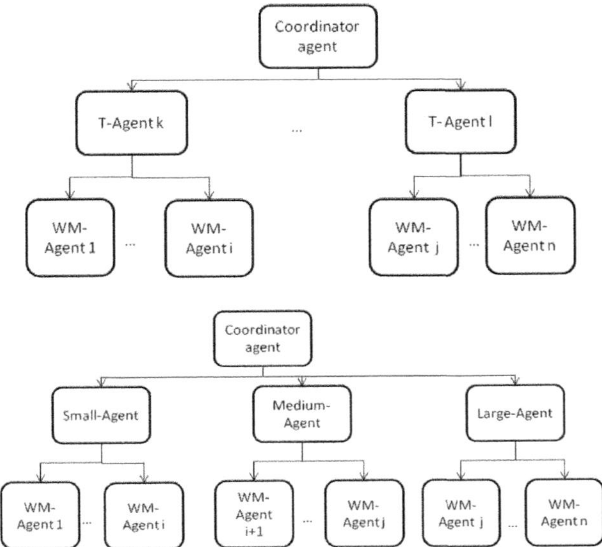

Fig. 4. Two possible workflow monitoring (WM) organizations with agents. *Top*: each workflow instance is monitored by a WM-Agent. *Bottom*: WM-Agents are grouped according to different maintenance workflow typologies.

There are some standards in the health domain that could be applied to the architecture presented in this paper. Standards like ISO 9001:2008 or ISO 13485:2004 cover part of the infrastructure needs like medical devices quality management. The choice of the ISO11073 is not arbitrary and is well founded in major vendors (Siemens Medical, Dräger, GE of Philips), health authorities (NHS National Programme for Information Technology (UK), Federal Drug Administration Center for Devices and Radiological Health (US)) and user interests support it.

In order to use the ISO11073 standard in the system, it is necessary to ensure the correct adaptation of devices' connection and communication to the standard, in the heterogeneous domain the architecture is targeted to. Different modeling techniques can be analyzed in order to conclude which of them provides more benefits for the system as a whole (in terms of integration, communication or usability). But the objective is not only to build the model that covers the standard but also to provide an added value (supplementary knowledge about devices) which supports to future incorporation of predictive maintenance tools (as explained in [12], for example). In this direction, one important aspect that should be taken into account in the election of the technique to use, would be the possibility to establish semantic relations between devices present in the hospital infrastructure in order to extract new knowledge for building predictions about devices behavior and failures (e.g. common heat sensible component in different devices and conditioning air failure in the room, the situation drives to a potential failure of these devices).

A possible solution is to use taxonomies, as a hierarchical relationship based system, represented by standardized keywords applied to the specific domain and fulfilled the ISO11073 standard. In this case a unified modeling is provided, and the hierarchical relationships between devices are provided. But the impossibility of extracting any other relation between devices apart from hierarchical (no possible to answer what are the devices that have the heat sensible components and are in the air failure room) highlights the limitation of extract conclusions with enough quality to improve system results.

Ontological modeling goes one step further than taxonomies. The use of the Web Ontology Language (OWL), for example, allows defining relations between several different concepts giving a complete description of the domain. The hierarchy of terms in the modeled universe is flexible and new instances can be easily added using the concepts defined in the basic reference pattern. Using ontologies it is possible to model the exterior appearance of the devices, the data types generated, the medical data provided, communication features such as protocols or addresses, the location of the device in the assistance facilities, etc. All this information can be considered as a whole in order to infer more knowledge e.g. from relations between concepts. Additionally, ontologies provide information consistence, an important aspect to detect failures in the devices' work. Finally, a more complete taxonomy can be (dynamically) obtained attending to multiple, heterogeneous attributes of the device.

Some open functionality enabled by ontologies could be:

- Grouping and classification of medical equipment by their use (patient devices against medical staff devices…).
- Grouping and classification by components (same PSU, monitor…) .
- Grouping by location: plan maintenance activities (devices in the same stage, same kind of devices, call a 3rd part maintenance service to examine all the devices of a particular brand…)
- Workflows of use (after use device1, always is used device2)
- Maintenance calendar: last revision, last repair, next scheduled maintenance activity…
- Communication errors: communication protocol A, period of time X between messages, last NACK message, last message X+n seconds then network failure (inference), device shut down…
- Device failure: last medical device measure, medical value threshold, sensor tolerance, then sensor failure (inference).

3 Use of the Architecture

In this section we describe three different case studies of the use of the architecture corresponding to three different maintenance interventions: starting up a workflow instance (i.e. starting a preventive maintenance operation), reactive and predictive interventions on workflow instances.

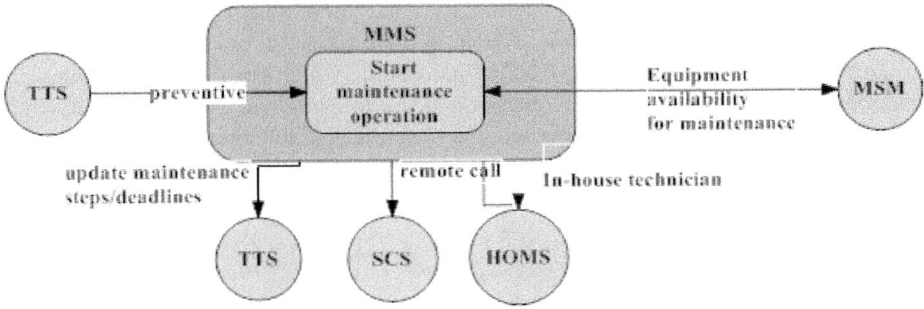

Fig. 5. Preventive maintenance intervention

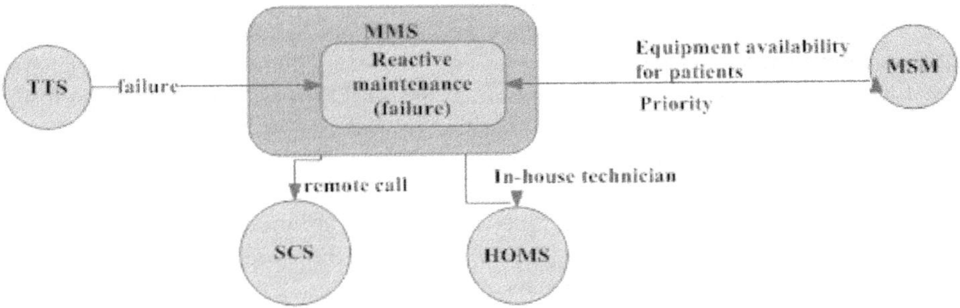

Fig. 6. Reactive maintenance intervention

3.1 Starting Up a Workflow Instance Monitoring

Preventive maintenance is a schedule of planned maintenance actions aimed at the prevention of breakdowns and failures. The primary goal of preventive maintenance is to prevent the failure of equipment before it actually occurs, according to periodically planned revisions following manufacturers' recommendation.

Long-term benefits of preventive maintenance include improved system reliability, decreased cost of replacement, decreased system downtime, and better inventory management. Long-term effects and cost comparisons usually favour preventive maintenance over performing maintenance actions only when the system fails. Finally, the final object of preventive maintenance is to improve the lifecycle of a system.

Preventive maintenance interventions are decided in the CMS and handled by a WM agent under the MMS (as shown in Figure 5). The MMS has access to the actual medical equipment schedule (by means of the MSM) in order to weight the priorities of actions to take. Otherwise, to manage the maintenance actions, they have a 'priority' number, according to their importance. Other services involved are the TTS, that keeps track of all the maintenance activities performed and their due dates, the SCS that intervenes in case of large devices, and the HOMS that informs about the available in-house technicians and scalability information, among other rules. The fixed time intervals for preventive maintenance are determined by rules of operation but with the evolvement of reliable prediction these rules can be changed.

In this scenario, WM agents in MMS help on deciding about the allocation of resources. Even if a maintenance operation takes longer than usual, it could send a warning message. Moreover, and in case that the maintenance operation involves dealing with a third-party service, agents should negotiate thanks to the ontology.

3.2 Reactive Intervention

Reactive maintenance is a response action to workflow deviation aimed to correct the problem. The main task in a reactive maintenance is to identify the subjects involved, understanding the business process, understanding the information and communication technology used in the process and identification of problems within the process. In our architecture, reactive maintenance operations are handled by the TTS: when a maintenance activity arrives to its due date without being complete, the TTS generates an alarm and starts a reactive intervention on the workflow instance, as shown in Figure 6. The main steps involved are similar that the ones of the preventive intervention, because a revision and escalation of the activities of the maintenance workflow should be considered/revised.

In this scenario, MMS as agents help on re-scheduling the maintenance operations if, the reactive, urgent one, cannot be started because there are no resources available (e.g, because an overload on maintenance activities).

3.3 Predictive Workflow Maintenance

A predictive maintenance has as target to anticipate potential problems could appear in a maintenance action or process and to ensure the QoS, the availability and the continuity which are needed in the equipment present in a hospital. The predictions are built using the historical experience (data) in order to extract patterns and conclusions and to prepare corrective plans to improve future maintenance actions. For a high quality predictive system, it is imperative to have a wide information source in order to extract the better knowledge about the infrastructure. In our architecture, there are different services involved with information sources: equipment status and location, technical/medical profile and availability, and patient scheduling among others, and such data are used to build the system knowledge by using mainly two techniques: data mining techniques and equipment ontological modeling.

The IDS compiles the information of the overall system, and manages and stores it in historical databases. It has an interface with the other services in charge to save and work with current information the system receives at the moment. The EPS applies data mining techniques to the historical databases and builds the knowledge database which, together with knowledge inferred from equipment model based on ontologies, is used by the predictions engine. Such engine defines predictions of potential problems that are use to define new or improved maintenance plans attending to potential failures in the equipment, future availability of technical staff by profile or patient scheduling requirements.

In this scenario, MMS as agents help on deciding about the opportunity of starting the predictive operation, if there are no resources available (as for example, because an overload on other, more urgent, maintenance activities). And then, the agent could postpone (if there is enough margin before the equipment predicted failure) the maintenance operation for a while.

4 Related Work

There are several previous projects related to equipment maintenance, as PROTEUS [5] or DYNAMITE [6]. The former project focus on medical equipment also, but mainly related to operations. Our work is more related to workflow improvements. On the other hand, DYNAMITE is mainly concerned with prediction issues, while in the present work all kind of action issues when tracking a maintenance workflow are considered: failures, preventions and predictions.

Another interesting work is [7], in which the authors propose a methodology for dynamically changing workflows in a controlled way. This work is complementary to our in the sense that the authors are explicitly dealing with what happens when workflow instances have to be changed due to escalation issues, for example.

Finally, the use of agents for workflow management in business has been a matter of study recently. For example, Wu et al.[8],use agents to control the authorization operations in a given framework. In [9] a mechanism based on agents is proposed to monitor workflows in order to tackle uncertainty in the business processes.

5 Conclusions

Service Oriented Architecture (SOA) is a paradigm for organizing and utilizing distributed capabilities that may be under the control of different ownership domains. Recently, the use of agents in SOA improves the coordination of the different services of a SOA at different levels (inter and intra enterprise). In this paper we propose a SOA based on multi-agent systems to deal with workflow monitoring in a medical equipment maintenance scenario.

We have described our architecture at the conceptual level. Then, we have shown how agents can be used to handle the tracing of the different maintenance workflow instances being executed, as well as to negotiate with different external technicians involved in the process. In this scenario, where interoperability plays a crucial role, the use of standards for dealing with equipment information, as the ISO 11073, can provide some advantages for future prediction tasks. All this information should be gathered in an ontological model to boost interoperability and offer a tool to infer complementary knowledge about the domain.

The architecture is the result of a work inside the AIMES consortium. It is a first approach to deal with the monitoring issues on maintenance operations, with the final goal of providing a global infrastructure for medical equipment maintenance management. The SOA and all the services proposed come after the study of maintenance management of twelve German hospitals of different size [11]. Currently there is a prototype demonstrator being tested and evaluated by the staff of a German hospital.

Acknowledgments. Thanks to the representatives of the contributing enterprises, who belong to the EU-Project "AIMES – Advanced Infrastructure for Medical Equipment and Services", for the constructive subject-specific collaboration. This project t is encouraged by the German BMBF (support code 01ISO8001E) and Spanish Avanza I+D programme (support code TSI-020400-2008-47) within the EU-programme ITEA2.

References

1. Anane, R., Li, Y., Tsai, C.-F., Chao, K.-M., Younas, M.: An Agent-Based Compositional Framework. In: Zhang, Y., Tanaka, K., Yu, J.X., Wang, S., Li, M. (eds.) APWeb 2005. LNCS, vol. 3399, pp. 579–584. Springer, Heidelberg (2005)
2. Lopez, B., Martín, A., Daroca, D., Meléndez, J., Lozano, S.: Medical equipment maintenance workflow monitoring with service-oriented multi-agent services. Presented at 7th International Conference on Service Oriented Computing (ICSOC 2009) (Industry Track), Stockholm, Sweden, November 24-27 (2009)
3. Zarour, N., Boufaida, M., Seinturier, L., Estraillier, P.: Supporting virtual enterprise systems using agent coordination. Knowledge and Information Systems 8, 330–349 (2005)
4. Huang, C.J., Trappey, A.J.C., Yao, Y.-H.: Developing an agent-based workflow management system for collaborative product design. Industrial Management & Data Systems 106(5), 680–699 (2006)
5. Bangemann, T., Rebeuf, X., Reboul, D., Schulze, A., Szymanski, J., Thomesse, J.P., Thron, M., Zerhouni, N.: PROTEUS: Creating distributed maintenance systems through an integration platform. Computers in Industry 57, 539–551 (2006)
6. Holmberg, K., Helle, A., Halme, J.: Prognostics for Industrial Machinery Availability. In: POHTO 2005 Int. Seminar on Maintenance, Condition Monitoring & Diagnostics, Oulu, Finland (2005)
7. Reichert, M., Dadam, P.: ADEPTflex—Supporting Dynamic Changes of Workflows Without Losing Control. Journal of Intelligent Information Systems 10, 93–129 (1998)
8. Wu, S., Sheth, A., Miller, J., Luo, Z.: Authorization and Access Control of Application Data in Workflow Systems. Journal of Intelligent Information Systems 18(1), 71–94 (2002)
9. Wang, M., Wang, H.: Intelligent Agent Supported Flexible Workflow Monitoring System. In: Pidduck, A.B., Mylopoulos, J., Woo, C.C., Ozsu, M.T. (eds.) CAiSE 2002. LNCS, vol. 2348, pp. 787–791. Springer, Heidelberg (2002)
10. AIMES project, `http://www.aimes-project.eu/`
11. López, B., Meléndez, J., Wissel, H., Haase, H., Laatz, K., Grosser, O.S.: Towards Medical Device Maintenance Workflow Monitoring. World Academy of Science, Engineering and Technology 54, 103–109 (2009)
12. Meléndez, J., López, B., Millán-Ruiz, D.: Probabilistic models to assist maintenance of multiple instruments. In: 14th IEEE International Conference on Emerging Technologies and Factory Automation (ETFA), Palma de Mallorca, Spain, September 22-26 (2009); CD Proceedings. Ref. 004774. Copyright: 978-1-4244-2728-4/09/$25.00 ©2009 IEEE

An Agent-Oriented Approach to Service Analysis and Design

Hoa Khanh Dam and Aditya Ghose

School of Computer Science and Software Engineering
University of Wollongong
Northfields Av, Wollongong, NSW 2522, Australia
hoa@uow.edu.au, aditya@uow.edu.au

Abstract. The agent paradigm, with its new way of thinking about software systems as a collection of autonomous, flexible and robust agents, offers a promising solution for modelling and implementing distributed complex systems. Intelligent agents and services share a substantial number of key concepts such as autonomy, reactivity, loose coupling and strong encapsulation. There has been, however, little work on leveraging such a deep connection between agents and services. In this paper, we argue that agent-oriented software engineering (AOSE) provides an important basis for service analysis and design at the business service level. In particular, we show how concepts and techniques in AOSE can be used to analyse and model business services in the context of service ecosystems.

1 Introduction

We now live in a growing services-based economy in which every product today has virtually a service component to it [1]. In this context, many services interact with one another in different ways in order to meet growing customer demands. Business domains involving large and complex collections of loosely coupled services provided by autonomous enterprises are becoming increasingly prevalent. For example, there are multiple services on offer at an international airport. Some rely on others for execution. There is a passenger transport service (taking a person from one airport to another), which relies on the baggage handling service, a security screening service, a business class lounge service and so on. Each of those services can be offered in other business contexts. For instance, the baggage handling service can be independently used for cargo air-freighting, or the security screening service can be independently offered in other high security venues. Such interactions among and between independent and autonomous services are what define a *service ecosystem* [2]. The emergence of such an ecosystem can be seen in various places such as in the form of Shared Service Centres providing central, standardised services from different agencies or departments in the public sector [3] or a Web service ecosystem on the Internet where Web services providers are interconnecting in their offerings in unforseen ways [4].

N. Desai, A. Liu, and M. Winikoff (Eds.): PRIMA 2010, LNAI 7057, pp. 499–510, 2012.

Therefore, there is an increasing demand to design and build high quality service ecosystems. However, developing such an ecosystem of services is a challenging task due to their loosely coupled nature and openness, and the autonomy of their participants. In fact, each service within an ecosystem are autonomous in which they should operate independently and make decisions without direct intervention of other business partners. Individual services should have their own thread of control and have their own objectives. In order for services within an ecosystem to fulfil both their individual and overall objectives, they need to interact with one another. However, establishing loosely coupled collaboration between autonomous services is still a critical challenge in developing a service ecosystem [5]. In this context, a key question is how to analyse, design and model services, their capabilities and their related business processes in such a way that services have autonomy over their choice of action and have ability to initiate (and respond to) interactions in a flexible manner.

Since the 1990s, intelligent agent technology has evolved rapidly along with a growing number of agent languages, architectures, and theories proposed in the literature. The emerging agent-oriented paradigm, with its potential to significantly improve the development of high-quality and complex systems, has attracted an increasing amount of interest from the research and business communities. Indeed, there have been numerous agent-based applications in a wide variety of domains such as weather alerting [6], business process management [7], holonic manufacturing [8], e-commerce, and information management [9]. A software agent is a piece of software which is situated in an environment, acts on its own and interacts with other similar entities to achieve some design goals [10]. An agent also works pro-actively to pursue certain goals while, at the same time, it responds in a timely fashion to changes that occur in its environment. Agents can interact with other agents and humans with the aim of accomplishing their goals. This agent view provides a well suited level of abstraction for modelling, an effective way of decomposing, and an appropriate method for dealing with the dependencies and interactions in complex software systems [11].

There are strong connections between between agents and services, and are to some degree recognized and addressed in the literature (e.g. [12,13]). Similarly to agents, services can be can be viewed as autonomous, reactive components in a loosely-coupled architecture. Principles such as strong encapsulation, loosely coupling are well-supported in agent-oriented methodologies. This paper will argue that agent-oriented software engineering provides an important basis for analysis and modeling of service ecosystems. We will show that decomposing the problem space of a service ecosystem in an agent-oriented way is very effective. We will also explain why it is appropriate to apply an agent-oriented philosophy to the modelling and managing relationships and interactions within service ecosystems in such a way that the dependencies and interactions in those complex ecosystems are effectively dealt with.

The paper is structured as follows. In the next section, we provide a brief overview of agent-oriented software engineering and highlight some of its key advantages. We then describe how AOSE can be adapted to service analysis and design in section 3. Finally, we conclude and outline some future directions for this research in section 4.

2 Agent-Oriented Software Engineering

Agent Oriented Software Engineering (AOSE) is a promising new approach to software engineering that uses the notion of agents as the primary method for analysing, designing and implementing software systems [11]. The effectiveness of AOSE resides in its ability to translate the distinctive features of agents into useful properties of (complex) software systems and to provide an intuitive metaphor that operates at a higher level of abstraction compared to the object oriented model.

The technical embodiment of agency can lead to reduced coupling, resulting in software systems that are more modular, decentralized and changeable. Indeed, the autonomous property of agents can be viewed as encapsulating invocation. Any publicly accessible method of an object can be invoked externally, and once the method is invoked the object performs the corresponding actions. On the other hand, when receiving a message, an agent has control over how it deals with the message. This ability to encapsulate behaviour activation (action choice) is very useful in open environments in which the system consists of organisations that have different goals [11]. Additionally, the robustness, reactiveness and pro-activeness also results in reduced coupling [14]. Once an agent acquires a goal, it commits to achieve the goal by possibly trying different alternatives in responding to changes in the environment. This means that there is no need for continuous supervision and checking since the agent solely takes responsibility for accomplishing its adopted goals. As a result, it leads to less communication and thus reduced coupling.

Loose coupling and strong encapsulation brought by agents are important, especially because they facilitate the process of evolving software by localising changes to an agent or a group of agents. For instance, the BDI architecture (discussed in the previous section) can be used to model and implement goal-directed process selection [15]. Traditionally, the calling process contains the names of the called processes (and possibly other information such as the locations, the data needs, or even the implementation), and the conditions specifying which (process) to call in which circumstance. The major disadvantage of this conventional approach is that the calling process is dependent on the called processes, and thus they are not able to be developed independently of one another. A goal-directed approach can separate the conditions of use from the calling processes and place them in the called processes. As a result, processes become loosely coupled and process selection is made dynamically at run time based on the usage context. In addition, if any chosen process fails, the call is made again (i.e. reposted) and a new matching process is invoked. This offers a better and more automatic handling of exceptions or failures. Furthermore, called processes can be created or changed without affecting the existing ones and the calling process. These benefits multiply each time the called process is reused in other calling processes.

In addition, agents can lead to the expansion of functionalities, complexities and quality of the real world applications [16]. For example, multi-agent systems with a number of autonomous agents suits the highly distributed environment where such agents are able to act and work independently to each other. In addition, the inherently robust and flexible properties of multiagent systems allow them to work in a more dynamic and/or open environment with error-prone information sources. These properties significantly increase the reliability and failure-tolerance of the system in terms of autonomously recovering from failure and adapting to changes in the environment. Therefore, issues such as improving the unforeseen reuse of software components, developing self-managed software systems can be better addressed using the ideas of multi-agents.

It has also been argued that AOSE, equipped with the rich representation capabilities of agents, is suitable (and reliable) for modelling complex organisational processes [17,9,16]. Jenning and Wooldridge in [18,11] have shown that agent-orientation facilitates complexity management in three aspects: decomposition, abstraction, and organisation. Firstly, they argue that decomposing the problem space of a complex system in an agent-oriented way is very effective. Secondly, they are able to demonstrate the ability of agents in representing high-level abstractions of active entities in a software system, and consequently reducing the gap between business users and system architects. Finally, they explain why it is appropriate to apply an agent-oriented philosophy to the modelling and managing of organisational relationships in such a way that the dependencies and interactions in those complex organisations are effectively dealt with.

As agents have been increasingly recognised as possibly the next prominent paradigm of developing software, there has been a growth of interest in agent-oriented software engineering. A significant amount of AOSE work has focussed on developing new methodologies and tools for software development using the agent concepts. In fact, as far as we are aware of, there have been nearly fifty agent-oriented methodologies proposed to date [19]. Those methodologies (e.g. Tropos [20], Gaia [21], Tropos [20], Prometheus [14], O-MaSE [22], PASSI [23] etc.), Prometheus [14]) offer notations and models, methods and techniques, processes and (for some methodologies) tool support that a software developer can use to develop an agent-based application. Recent studies (e.g. [24]) have shown that AOSE methodologies provide reasonable support for basic agent-oriented concepts such as autonomy, mental attitudes, pro-activeness, and reactiveness. In the next section, we will show how several ideas and techniques proposed in AOSE methodologies can be adapted to be used in the context of service analysis and design.

3 The Case for AOSE to Service Analysis and Design

3.1 Service Identification

A crucial task of service analysis and design is identifying service candidates. The importance of service identification is amplified when the target system is a service ecosystem which consists of a large number of services. Existing work (e.g. [25,26,27]) tend to focus on proposing techniques for describing and decomposing business services and fail to address the important issue of how such services can be identified at the first place. Since services are the fundamental entities in service-based systems, we believe that a critical requirement for an service analysis and design methodology is to assist the developers identify the services constituting the system.

A service ecosystem can be considered as an organisation of services. This view matches with AOSE methodologies. In fact, a large number of AOSE methodologies adopt an organisational view of the world and encourage a designer to think of building agent-based systems as a process of organizational design. The software system organisation is similar to a real world organisation. It has a certain number of entities playing different roles. For instance, a university organisation has several key roles such as administration, teaching, research, students, etc. These roles are played by different people in the university such as managers, lecturers, students, etc. Different roles in an organisation interact with each other to achieve their own goals and also to contribute towards the overall goals of the organisation.

Based on that motivation, a common technique used in most of AOSE methodologies to deal with agent identification is to start from identifying roles. Agents are then formed by grouping these roles into "chunks". There are different techniques and models provided by AOSE methodologies to help the designers group or map these roles into agents. For instance, Prometheus [14] provides clear techniques to deal with agent identification in terms of group functionalities into agents. This is based on considerations of both cohesion and coupling - one wants to reduce coupling and increase cohesion. Putting agents that write or read the same data together seems to reduce coupling between agents. In other words, functionalities that use and/or produce the same data tend to belong to the same agent.

Such techniques are also particulary useful in identifying services. In fact, a service ecosystem can also be viewed as a society or organisation. Hence, in order to identifying the constituting services, a natural way is to identify roles, their goals and their relationships. Roles allow for a combination of both top-down and bottom-up design. They are identified by a top-down process of goal development. At the same time, they provide a bottom-up mechanism for determining service types and their responsibility. Let us take the example of a pizza restaurant. A natural first step is to identify business goals of the pizza restaurant. Examples of such goals include making pizza, delivering pizza, managing inventory, ordering pizza and so on. The next step is to identify various roles participating in the operation of a pizza restaurant by grouping related goals. For example, there is a role responsible for making pizza, a role for managing the inventory, a role for handling delivery and so on. Figure 1 shows how different roles in a pizza restaurant are identified and represented using Prometheus, a prominent agent-oriented methodology [14]. Such roles provide a foundation for service identification in which services play multiple roles (e.g. pizza order service, pizza transportation service, and pizza cooking service). Roles can also serve as an indication for defining the capabilities which a service offer.

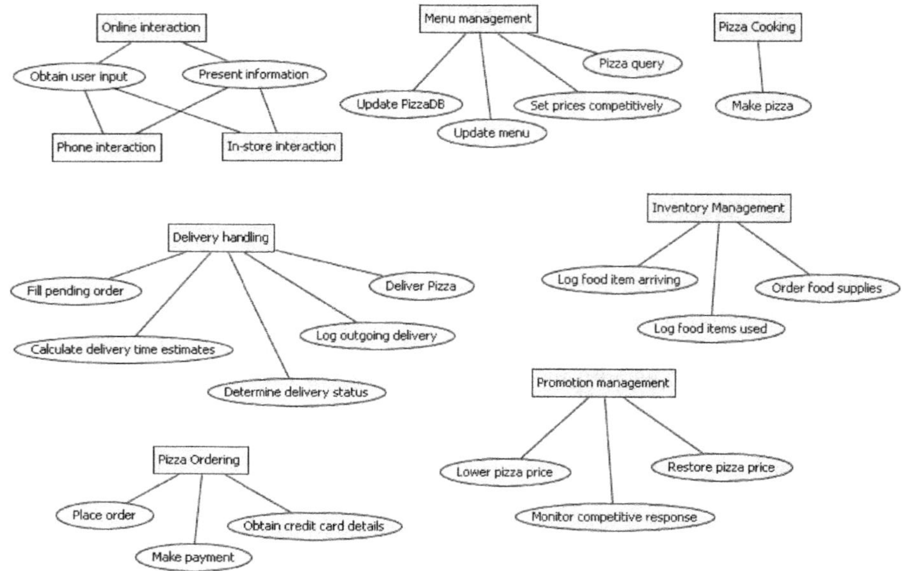

Fig. 1. Roles for the pizza restaurant

3.2 Service Interactions

The current standard approach for designing service interactions is message-centric. Specifically, the design process is driven by messages exchanged during the interaction and tends to focus on data and control flows. In addition, interactions are also defined by interaction protocols which specify the allowable sequence of messages exchanged between service providers and service consumers (e.g. the Unified Service Description Language[1]). Such a message-centric approach however poses several limitations in designing interactions for service ecosystems. Firstly, as we have earlier argued, in a service ecosystem, services should be flexible and robust in terms of pursuing their goals by attempting alternatives in spite of failures. Interaction protocols however restricts the flexibility and robustness of services. Alternative means to achieving the interaction's objectives is limited to the options the designer have defined. Although it is possible to add an unlimited number of alternatives, a large number of alternatives described using message-centric notations leads to protocols that are difficult to understand and manage. Therefore, in practice message-centric modelling results in brittle service interactions that are neither flexible or robust. Secondly, since the message-centric approaches are based on low-level abstractions, they tend to fail to conceptually capture the business intent of the interactions between services. Existing service interaction protocols tend to over-constraint the business behaviour of participant business services.

[1] `http://www.internet-of-services.com`

The above issues have been recognised in the agent community and recent work in AOSE have proposed a number of alternative approaches design the interactions which are not driven by messages. These approaches shift the focus onto a higher level of abstraction which are more suitable to support complex, dynamic, interactions. In particular, a number of approaches (e.g. [28,29]) proposes to design agent interactions using social commitments, in which agent participants progress through interactions by making and fulfilling commitments to each other. Other approaches proposes to design interactions on the basis of agent plans and goals. For instance, the Hermes methodology [30] proposes to model interactions in terms of interaction goals, available actions and constraints. Based on the constraints defined by the designer, the agents then work out the allowable message sequences to use during the interactions. In addition, this approach allows the designer to model failure recovery: if a given interaction goal fails then they may specify that accomplishing a previous interaction goal may allow the interaction to continue. For example, if booking a hotel for particular dates cannot be achieved, then rolling back and finding alternative travel dates may solve the problem.

In those alternative approaches, the designer does not need to define legal message sequences explicitly but instead they emerge from the interaction due to the agents' need to fulfil their commitments or achieve their interaction goals. This increases the flexibility and robustness of interactions in terms of providing more valid message sequences than what a designer could have explicitly defined. In addition, those approaches are able to capture the business intent (in forms of goals and commitments) of the interactions.

In our view, those AOSE methodologies can be adapted to design flexible and robust interactions in service ecosystems. Such interaction modelling facilities in AOSE can be useful for service touchpoint modelling which is a critical issue for services modelling. In fact, service interactions take place at *service touchpoints* [31]. Through touchpoints the service is experienced and perceived with all the senses. In a service ecosystem, a provider can deliver services across multiple touchpoints such as the Internet, self-service technologies or face-to-face communication. As an example, many pizza restaurants (e.g. Pizza Hut) now allow their customers to order over the phone, the Internet, or the traditional in-store service desks (refer to figure 1). Touchpoints modeling is critical for services since touchpoints have always been considered as the crucial moment where the consumer judges service quality and the service value revealed. In this context, flexibility and robustness are key to the success of a touchpoint. In addition, it is the consistency across the many touchpoints that will affect quality perception. In order to create such consistency, the design of service interactions should be driven by interaction goals or commitments to capture the business intents at a higher abstraction level than the traditional message-centric approaches. For example, the passenger can check-in at different touchpoints, i.e. using different check-in facilities, each of which is different in terms of how the actual interaction takes place. However, they all share the same goals, e.g. successful check-in a passenger, and should be the basis for design interactions.

3.3 Business Process Modelling

One of main challenges facing the service oriented computing community is to develop dynamic and adaptive processes for service composition and orchestration [32]. This requires that a business process should be able to pro-actively adapt itself quickly to respond to environmental demands and changes. We believe that such a requirement should be addressed at the modelling level. With this respect, the *Belief-Desire-Intention* (BDI) model [33], one of the most well-established and widely-used agent models, can offer a solution to model dynamic and adaptive processes. The key concepts in the BDI model are: *beliefs*, i.e. representing information about the environment, the agent itself, or other agents; *desires*, i.e. representing the objectives to be accomplished, i.e. goals; and *intentions*, i.e. representing the currently chosen courses of action to pursue a certain desire that the agent has committed to pursuing, i.e. plans. More specifically, BDI agents have a collection of pre-defined plan recipes (or types), usually referred to as a plan library [34]. Each plan consists of: (a) an invocation condition which defines the event that triggers this plan (i.e. the event that the plan is *relevant* for); (b) a context condition (usually referring to the agent's beliefs) which defines the situation in which the plan is *applicable*, i.e. it is sensible to use the plan in a particular situation; and a plan body containing a sequence of primitive actions and subgoals that are performed for plan execution to be successful. It should be noted that subgoals can trigger further plans.

A typical execution cycle that implements the decision-making of an agent can be viewed as consisting of the following steps. First, an event is received from the environment, or is generated internally by belief changes or plan execution. The agent responds to this event by selecting from its plan library a set of plans that are relevant (i.e. match the invocation condition) for handling the event (by looking at the plans' definition). The agent then determines the subset of the relevant plans that is applicable in terms of handling the particular event. The determination of a plan's applicability involves checking whether the plan's context condition holds in the current situation. The agent selects one of the applicable plans and executes it by performing its actions and sub-goals. A plan can be successfully executed, in which case the (sub-)goal is regarded to have been accomplished. Execution of a plan, however, can fail in some situations, e.g. a sub-goal may have no applicable plans, or an action can fail, or a test can be false. In these cases, if the agent is attempting to achieve a goal, a mechanism that handles failure is used. Typically, the agent tries an alternative applicable plan for responding to the triggering event of the failed plan. It is also noted that failures propagate upwards through the event-plan tree: if a plan fails its parent event is re-posted; if this fails then the parent of the event fails and so on.

BDI agents offer two important qualities: robustness and flexibility. BDI agents are robust since they are able to pursue persistent goals over time (i.e. pro-activeness). In other words, agents will keep on trying to achieve a goal despite previously failed attempts. In order to be able to recover from such failures, agents have multiple ways of dealing with a given goal and such alternatives can be used in case any of them fail. This gives agents flexibility in terms of exercising choice over their actions. Flexibility and robustness are considered as useful qualities that a software system should possess, especially if it operates in complex, dynamic, open and failure-prone environments.

Those properties of the BDI model also offer a suitable solution for the business process modelling within service design. More specifically, the BDI architecture can be used to model and implement goal-directed process selection [15]. Traditionally, the calling process contains the names of the called processes (and possibly other information such as the locations, the data needs, or even the implementation), and the conditions specifying which (process) to call in which circumstance. The major disadvantage of this conventional approach is that the calling process is dependent on the called processes, and thus they are not able to be developed independently of one another. A goal-directed approach can separate the conditions of use from the calling processes and place them in the called processes. Such conditions form different possible contexts of the process. As a result, processes become loosely coupled and process selection is made dynamically at run time based on the usage context. In addition, if any chosen process fails, the call is made again (i.e. reposted) and a new matching process is invoked. This offers a better and more automatic handling of exceptions or failures. Furthermore, called processes can be created or changed without affecting the existing ones and the calling process. These benefits multiply each time the called process is reused in other calling processes.

3.4 Value Modelling

A key component of services modelling is value modelling. It is important that we should understand how a service delivers value to its stakeholders. Ideally, value models should be stakeholder-specific - in other words, we need to be able to account for the fact that a service delivers different kinds of value to distinct stakeholders, and in different ways. A value model is critical in service design - it provides a guiding framework that ensures that a service design maximizes the value it delivers to its key stakeholders. Value models, when correlated to service design components, also support service re-design. When a service must be modified to account for changes in the operating context, for instance, a value model can help decide which components of a service design may be discarded (when there are options, we pick those components that deliver lower value) and which components might be modified. Value models can represent value on a variety of scales, both quantitative and qualitative, or via preference orderings over design elements.

A key insight that is often ignored in the literature on services science is the fact that a value model is fundamentally a requirements model. A service delivers value by providing certain functionalities, under certain non-functional or quality-of-service constraints. Goal models, which are central to most AOSE frameworks, provide an appropriate basis for modelling the functional aspects of service value. Softgoal models, also common in AOSE frameworks (e.g. [20]), enable us to model the non-functional aspects of service value.

4 Conclusions and Future Work

Together with the grow of services across different sectors in the society, service ecosystems emerge as a complex collection of services in which they interact with one another to meet customer demands. In these ecosystems, participant services are highly independent, autonomous, flexible and reactive to environment changes. Due to those complexities, designing high quality service ecosystems is a very challenging task.

However, such challenges have previously been addressed to a certain extend by the agent paradigm, another important technology which has emerged since the past decade. In this paper we have argued that agent-oriented software engineering (AOSE) methodologies provide a number of techniques that can be adopted to the analysis and design of services. More specifically, we have shown that the organisational view of a system which AOSE methodologies take is also suitable to service ecosystems. In addition, we have described a number of emerging approaches in AOSE which shift the focus of interaction design from messages to goals and commitments. Such approaches are suitable for designing service interactions in service ecosystems since they allow the designer to work at a higher level abstraction and to define flexible and robust interactions. We have also briefly described the BDI model, which is widely used by AOSE methodologies to model agent plans, and have shown that this model is suitable to model the business processes of services.

Those key ideas proposed in this paper can to a number of directions for further research. In particularly, we plan to develop a methodology for service analysis and design which systematically adopts AOSE techniques that are suitable for services as discussed in this paper. This methodology would specifically support for modelling service ecosystems in several key areas including service identification, service interactions, business processes, and value modelling. Future work is also needed to investigate how ideas and techniques proposed by AOSE methodologies to support the design of negotiation, cooperation, and teamwork can be used for modelling service ecosystems.

References

1. Paulson, L.D.: Services science: A new field for today's economy. Computer 39(8), 18–21 (2006)
2. Sawatani, Y.: Research in service ecosystems. In: Proceedings of Management of Engineering and Technology (PICMET 2007), Portland, USA, pp. 2763–2768 (2007)
3. Janssen, M., Wagenaar, R.: An analysis of a shared services centre in e-government. In: HICSS 2004: Proceedings of the 37th Annual Hawaii International Conference on System Sciences (HICSS 2004) - Track 5, p. 50124.2. IEEE Computer Society, Washington, DC (2004)
4. Barros, A.P., Dumas, M.: The rise of web service ecosystems. IT Professional 8(5), 31–37 (2006)

5. Ruokolainen, T., Kutvonen, L.: Managing interoperability knowledge in open service ecosystems. In: Proceedings of the 13th Enterprise Distributed Object Computing Conference Workshops, EDOCW, Auckland, New Zealand, pp. 203–211. IEEE (September 2009)
6. Mathieson, I., Dance, S., Padgham, L., Gorman, M., Winikoff, M.: An open meteorological alerting system: Issues and solutions. In: Estivill-Castro, V. (ed.) Proceedings of the 27th Australasian Computer Science Conference, Dunedin, New Zealand, pp. 351–358 (2004)
7. Burmeister, B., Arnold, M., Copaciu, F., Rimassa, G.: BDI-Agents for agile goal-oriented business processes. In: Padgham, Parkes, Müller, Parsons (eds.) Proceedings of the 7th International Conference on Autonomous Agents and Multiagent Systems (AAMAS 2008), Estoril, Portugal, pp. 37–44 (May 2008)
8. Monostori, L., Váncza, J., Kumara, S.: Agent based systems for manufacturing. CIRP Annals-Manufacturing Technology 55(2), 697–720 (2006)
9. Munroe, S., Miller, T., Belecheanu, R.A., Pěchouček, M., McBurney, P., Luck, M.: Crossing the agent technology chasm: Lessons, experiences and challenges in commercial applications of agents. Knowledge Engineering Review 21(4), 345–392 (2006)
10. Wooldridge, M., Jennings, N.R.: Intelligent agents: Theory and practice. The Knowledge Engineering Review 10(2), 115–152 (1995)
11. Jennings, N.R.: An agent-based approach for building complex software systems. Communications of the ACM 44(4), 35–41 (2001)
12. Ghose, A.: Industry traction for MAS technology: would a rose by any other name smell as sweet. Int. J. Agent-Oriented Softw. Eng. 3(4), 397–401 (2009)
13. Cabri, G., Leonardi, L., Puviani, M.: Service-oriented agent methodologies. In: WETICE 2007: Proceedings of the 16th IEEE International Workshops on Enabling Technologies: Infrastructure for Collaborative Enterprises, pp. 24–29. IEEE Computer Society, Washington, DC (2007)
14. Padgham, L., Winikoff, M.: Developing intelligent agent systems: A practical guide. John Wiley & Sons, Chichester (2004) ISBN 0-470-86120-7
15. Georgeff, M.: Service orchestration: The next big challenge. DM Direct Special Report (June 2006)
16. Luck, M., McBurney, P., Shehory, O., Willmott, S.: Agent Technology: Computing as Interaction (A Roadmap for Agent Based Computing). AgentLink (2005)
17. Jennings, N.R., Sycara, K., Wooldridge, M.: A roadmap of agent research and development. Journal of Autonomous Agents and Multi-Agent Systems 1(1), 7–38 (1998)
18. Jennings, N.R., Wooldridge, M.: Agent-Oriented Software Engineering. In: Garijo, F.J., Boman, M. (eds.) MAAMAW 1999. LNCS, vol. 1647, pp. 1–7. Springer, Heidelberg (1999)
19. Henderson-Sellers, B., Giorgini, P. (eds.): Agent-Oriented Methodologies. Idea Group Publishing (2005)
20. Bresciani, P., Perini, A., Giorgini, P., Giunchiglia, F., Mylopoulos, J.: Tropos: An agent-oriented software development methodology. Autonomous Agents and Multi-Agent Systems 8(3), 203–236 (2004)
21. Zambonelli, F., Jennings, N.R., Wooldridge, M.: Developing multiagent systems: The Gaia methodology. ACM Transactions on Software Engineering and Methodology 12(3), 317–370 (2003)
22. DeLoach, S.A.: Engineering Organization-Based Multiagent Systems. In: Garcia, A.F., Choren, R., de Lucena, C.J.P., Giorgini, P., Holvoet, T., Romanovsky, A.B. (eds.) SELMAS 2005. LNCS, vol. 3914, pp. 109–125. Springer, Heidelberg (2006)

23. Cossentino, M.: From requirements to code with the PASSI methodology. In: Henderson-Sellers, B., Giorgini, P. (eds.) Agent-Oriented Methodologies, pp. 79–106. Idea Group Inc. (2005)
24. Dam, K.H., Winikoff, M.: Comparing Agent-Oriented Methodologies. In: Giorgini, P., Henderson-Sellers, B., Winikoff, M. (eds.) AOIS 2003. LNCS (LNAI), vol. 3030, pp. 78–93. Springer, Heidelberg (2004)
25. Scheithauer, G., Augustin, S., Wirtz, G.: Describing services for service ecosystems, pp. 242–255 (2009)
26. Dhanesha, K.A., Hartman, A., Jain, A.N.: A model for designing generic services. In: SCC 2009: Proceedings of the 2009 IEEE International Conference on Services Computing, pp. 435–442. IEEE Computer Society, Washington, DC (2009)
27. Lê, L.-S., Ghose, A., Morrison, E.: Definition of a Description Language for Business Service Decomposition. In: Morin, J.-H., Ralyté, J., Snene, M. (eds.) IESS 2010. LNBIP, vol. 53, pp. 96–110. Springer, Heidelberg (2010)
28. Winikoff, M.: Designing commitment-based agent interactions. In: IAT 2006: Proceedings of the IEEE/WIC/ACM International Conference on Intelligent Agent Technology, pp. 363–370. IEEE Computer Society, Washington, DC (2006)
29. Yolum, P., Singh, M.P.: Flexible protocol specification and execution: applying event calculus planning using commitments. In: AAMAS 2002: Proceedings of the first International Joint Conference on Autonomous Agents and Multiagent Systems, pp. 527–534. ACM, New York (2002)
30. Cheong, C., Winikoff, M.: Hermes: a methodology for goal oriented agent interactions. In: AAMAS 2005: Proceedings of the Fourth International Joint Conference on Autonomous Agents and Multiagent Systems, pp. 1121–1122. ACM, New York (2005)
31. Bitner, M.: Evaluating service encounters: the effects of physical surroundings and employee responses. Journal of Marketing 54(2), 69–82 (1990)
32. Papazoglou, M.P., Traverso, P., Dustdar, S., Leymann, F.: Service-oriented computing: State of the art and research challenges. Computer 40(11), 38–45 (2007)
33. Bratman, M.E.: Intentions, Plans, and Practical Reason. Harvard University Press, Cambridge (1987)
34. Rao, A.S., Georgeff, M.P.: BDI-agents: from theory to practice. In: Proceedings of the First Intl. Conference on Multiagent Systems, San Francisco (1995)

Agent-Based Modelling for Risk Assessment of Routine Clinical Processes

Wayne Wobcke[1] and Adam Dunn[2]

[1] School of Computer Science and Engineering University of New South Wales
Sydney NSW 2052, Australia
wobcke@cse.unsw.edu.au

[2] Centre for Health Informatics University of New South Wales
Sydney NSW 2052, Australia
a.dunn@unsw.edu.au

Abstract. Prospective risk analysis is difficult in complex sociotechnical systems where humans interact with one other and with information systems. Traditional prospective risk analysis methods typically capture one risk at a time and rely on the specification of a chronological sequence of errors occurring in combination. The aim here is to introduce agent-based risk assessment (ABRA), which addresses these issues by simulating multiple concurrent and sequential interactions amongst autonomous agents that act according to their own goals. The methodology underlying the construction, simulation and validation of ABRA models is detailed along with practical considerations associated with implementation, for which the Brahms agent-based simulation framework is used. The challenges of implementing agent-based risk assessment models include the need for well-defined work processes and reliable observational data, and difficulties associated with behavioural validation. As an example illustrating the technique, a simple race condition hazard is implemented using an ABRA model. The work process involves a human operator and a machine interface that interact to sometimes produce the erroneous transfer of information. The correctness of the model is confirmed by comparing the simulated results against the well-defined theoretical baseline.

1 Introduction

Risk analysis is essential in any complex organization to improve the quality of service through minimizing errors and adverse consequences. Healthcare, in particular, is one area in which hazards are many, costs are high, and resource pressures are such that errors occur more frequently than desirable. Managing the risk of adverse events is therefore an important part of the management of healthcare systems. This paper introduces the use of agent-based models for the analysis and assessment of risk arising from routine clinical processes, processes which have a relatively well-defined workflow but which are also the source of potential adverse events. The aim of this paper is to describe, in a general way, the application of agent-based modelling as an aid to decision making in support of risk management in complex workflows. Healthcare is a particularly interesting domain of application due to its inherent complexity. The main advantage of agent-based modelling in comparison to alternative existing approaches is that the models enable the study of combinations of conditions and events that together

N. Desai, A. Liu, and M. Winikoff (Eds.): PRIMA 2010, LNAI 7057, pp. 511–522, 2012.

contribute to risk to be identified and compared to one another, enabling different potential interventions that aim to reduce risk to be assessed on the basis of their overall effect on the system.

Our particular work has been applied to a study of patient transfers between wards in a hospital, which is the source of adverse events such as misidentification (getting the "wrong patient") and infection control (insufficient precautions being taken to prevent the spread of infection), Dunn *et al.* [9]. Hospitals, like many large organizations, are complex sociotechnical systems, by which we mean that they can be considered a complex system involving interactions between human agents and information systems (use of the term "complex system" is not meant to imply any mathematical property). Hospitals involve a large number of people with shared objectives and overlapping information systems designed to support communication. Hospital work processes often span different locations and times, involve one or more information systems, multiple individuals, and involve activities that happen in parallel and in sequence. This complexity means that even the role of "human error" in relation to "system errors" in generating adverse events is not straightforward, as emphasized by Rasumussen *et al.* [19], Reason [20] and West [25]. Further complicating the analysis of error is that adverse events are often the result of a chain of events, Woolf *et al.* [28].

Hospitals, moreover, can be differentiated from other large organizations in a number of ways that make risk analysis more difficult and critical. First, hospitals are often dealing with life-and-death situations, so the adverse consequences of any mistakes can be more serious than in other organizations. Second, with a greater focus on human-human interactions than compared, for example, to manufacturing plants, the variety of ways of carrying out tasks is much greater, giving more scope for errors and violations of work practices to occur, and hence create the risk of adverse events. For the same reasons, analysis of the risks, how multiple events combine to both add to or ameliorate risk, is more difficult in such an environment, underlining the need for analytical tools.

Let us begin by clarifying what we mean by "risk analysis" in healthcare, following the attempt to standardize vocabulary in Runciman, Merry and Walton [22]. The basic objective of healthcare is *safety*, which can be defined as freedom from hazard, where it is assumed that the "hazards" involved are understood. Safety is inversely related to risk, where *risk* is defined as the probability of an adverse event; as in the financial sector, risk is influenced by exposure to the circumstances generating the adverse event (for example, the more one drives, the greater one's exposure to the risk of a car accident). An *adverse event* is defined as an incident that causes some harm, where "harm" is also understood. An adverse event is associated with a *severity*, allowing the consequences of different adverse events to be compared. Risk management can be considered a combination of *risk analysis* (identification of adverse events and their likelihoods), *risk assessment* (evaluation of various risks) and *risk mitigation* (reduction of these risks). Risk management typically focuses on reducing the exposure to the risk via controllable conditions, since these are conditions can be manipulated by modifications to existing work practices, in contrast to external factors. The point of view adopted here is that since work practices in sociotechnical systems are complex and intricate, risk can never be eliminated, only mitigated. Hence methods for assessing the degree of risk associated with work practices are needed to allow adequate assessment of risk.

Risk analysis and assessment is made difficult because hospitals are systems that are dynamic (subject to changing conditions, staff and work practices) and "non-linear" (which here simply means that the workflows are not linear sequences of tasks). That is, hospital workflows are characterized by a diverse range of activities and operations, with many convergent and divergent pathways. Thus there is a need to model combinations of events that together may contribute to, or ameliorate, risk. Since hospitals are sociotechnical systems consisting of humans and information systems, there is also a need to model the "human factors" associated with any work practice. As a particular instance where this makes a difference to the analysis is in the addition of redundancy to a process. Typically in any engineering process, added redundancy reduces risk. However, redundancy in a sociotechnical system does not necessarily reduce risk: instead, if multiple people are required to carry out the same (redundant) task, this can lead to a "diffusion of responsibility," West [25], where everyone assumes that someone else performs the task, leading to the potential result that no-one takes responsibility for the task and hence (on some occasions) no-one performs the task at all.

There is clearly a tradeoff between safety and efficiency in healthcare, in that there are pressures to "deliver" more healthcare (treat larger numbers of patients with fewer resources), that are at odds with the aim of providing a safe and high quality service. Let us briefly define the types of events in healthcare work practices that contribute to the increased risk of an adverse event. We distinguish errors, violations and workarounds. An *error* is a knowledge, rule or skill-based mistake (i.e. the practitioner was lacking some vital information, or did not know how to perform a procedure, resulting in an "incorrect" outcome), or merely a slip (an operation was performed inaccurately) [22]. By analogy to tennis, some errors are "unforced" and some are "forced" (inevitable given the circumstances, such as the state of the patient or the number of patients in the emergency department). Some errors arise particularly because outcomes are often subject to chance, in that some operations are not guaranteed to yield a favourable outcome even if performed "correctly" and according to best practice. A *violation*, on the other hand, is an action or procedure contrary to prescribed policy, such as omitting an action in the workflow or performing the process in a different way. Some violations may have the positive effect of optimizing work practices or improving outcomes. An example violation with such a positive effect is where a patient is admitted to emergency surgery without the proper documentation, which may save the patient's life. Finally, a *workaround*, though more difficult to define, can be regarded as a modification to standard work practice done with the aim of continuing or optimizing the process when the normal task cannot be performed or is inefficient, for example, scanning the bar code on a patient's chart instead of the wristband when the patient is inaccessible (see Koppel *et al.* [15]). Perhaps some workarounds originate as violations (done deliberately by someone knows why the violation occurs) but become entrenched as a standard practice (done unconsciously by someone who does not know why the violation occurs). Spear and Schmidhofer [24] discuss how workarounds contribute to adverse events in hospitals. The important point is that errors, violations and workarounds all occur regularly within complex work practices, and so *must* be taken into account in any analysis of the associated risk. An analysis of risk based purely on prescribed "correct" work practices will be inaccurate in relation to how that work is actually performed.

In the remainder of this paper, we provide a brief summary of existing approaches to risk management in healthcare, introduce the use of agent-based modelling for risk assessment, and give a simple example illustrating the technique. We conclude with a discussion of the advantages and limitations of agent-based risk assessment.

2 Approaches to Risk Analysis in Healthcare

Risk management techniques have been imported into healthcare from a variety of sources, having been successfully applied in the food, manufacturing, aviation and nuclear industries, amongst others. However, as discussed above, sociotechnical systems such as healthcare present new challenges when adapting existing methodologies. In this section, we summarize several approaches to risk analysis that have been applied in healthcare; as an initial general comment, we find it remarkable that, despite the importance of risk management in large organizations, there are so few published studies in the healthcare domain.

Existing methods for performing risk analysis can be divided into *retrospective* and *prospective* methods. Retrospective analysis methods aim to analyse the cause of a particular adverse event after the event has occurred. The main objectives are to understand why an event occurred, to assign blame or responsibility, and to improve work practices so that the event does not occur again. The typical approach is *root cause analysis*, Rasmussen *et al.* [19], applied in the complex setting of healthcare systems, Iedema *et al.* [13]. The basic approach is to identify a causal chain of events leading to the adverse event, identifying distinguished events (or sequences of events) leading to the outcome. A major limitation of root cause analysis is that by focusing on a single adverse event, there is no obvious way to generalize the analysis to other scenarios, in particular to quantify the risk of the event's recurrence. The main advantage of the approach is that causes that may be omitted in other models can be discovered.

Methods for prospective risk analysis tend to be more useful in risk assessment. Methods include hazard analysis and critical control points (HACCP) [1,12,4], failure mode and effects analysis (FMEA) [8,6,5,10,21,7], and probabilistic risk assessment methods such as event tree analysis (ETA) and fault tree analysis (FTA) [17,29]. To give an idea of the methods, hazard analysis and critical control points is a staged methodology that consists of identifying hazards and their risks and severities, determining critical control points in a process, specifying criteria to ensure control, monitoring control points, taking corrective action and verifying the system is working as planned. This may be used to prevent incidences of food contamination; typical applications in healthcare are to equipment decontamination [12], drug preparation [4] and reducing the risk of infection in surgery [1].

Failure mode and effects analysis is a similar methodology but where multiple process failures are analysed. The analysis also includes a method to compare different types of failures by assigning numbers to their frequency, severity and detectability, which are multiplied together to give a risk priority number. The approach has been applied in healthcare to reducing risk in blood transfusion [6], improving safety in the production of chemical solutions [5] and the safe application of chemotherapy [21], amongst other applications.

Probabilistic risk assessment methods provide an improved method for estimating the probabilities associated with adverse events, through the construction of an event tree or fault tree [17,29]. An *event tree* is a forward-branching structure defining the range of possible outcomes in a given scenario, while a *fault tree* is an AND/OR tree whose root is an adverse event and whose structure gives the causal conditions leading to the event, along with probabilities assigned to basic events that are combined using product and sum, and which are assumed independent. However, as with root cause analysis, the focus is on single events, not complex combinations of events.

Methods for prospective risk analysis rely heavily on subjective factors, which is useful where data is limited or data collection is especially difficult or time-consuming. However, the subjective nature of the techniques means that it is difficult to compare different risk mitigation strategies, and the techniques do not provide enough quantitative information to examine which combinations of specific actions or events contribute most often to adverse events. However, an important aspect of these techniques is that team members are required to discuss and agree on the steps to be taken, which has the valuable side-effect that team members better understand one another's work.

In summary, there are several weaknesses of existing approaches to risk assessment, especially as applied to healthcare. A basic deficiency of methods for retrospective analysis is that they do not show how to reduce risk, they can be used only to identify causes of adverse events after they occur – any estimate of the associated risk requires further (prospective) analysis. Concerning methods for prospective analysis, in a domain such as healthcare, it is hard to quantify the degree of risk of adverse events in such a way that reliable estimates of costs and benefits can be obtained. This makes it difficult to compare different risk mitigation strategies. Particular models are based on limited data or subjective factors, and there is a difficulty in handling unobserved or rare events, which may cause the greatest harm though having a low probability of occurrence, and so cannot be ignored.

3 Agent-Based Risk Assessment

Agent-based risk assessment (ABRA) builds on existing risk analysis methods to address the weaknesses of existing approaches mentioned above. ABRA is designed to capture ways in which real work practices deviate from prescribed work practices to determine how these deviations combine to create or pass along the risk of adverse events. In ABRA, the work process is simulated to produce trajectories that vary depending on the choices and interactions of the agents in the model. The method is used to examine risk by counting the trajectories in which the opportunity for an adverse event is present, and is therefore also able to examine how often individual actions lead to risky trajectories and explicitly model the effects of risk mitigation strategies.

The basic idea is illustrated in Figure 1. Each *trajectory* is one simulation of the process representing the work practice. The diagram shows how trajectories can both diverge and converge as complex workflows are implemented in a variety of ways, including actions some of which create risk (by introducing a deviation), some of which propagate risk (by compounding errors), and some of which reduce risk (by recovering from earlier errors). The risk is defined as the likelihood of a trajectory ending up in a "region of risk", and is estimated by repeated simulation of the process. Thus agent-based risk assessment models are similar to both event trees and fault trees, in that there is a forward-branching structure representing multiple failures (plus the potential to recover from those failures).

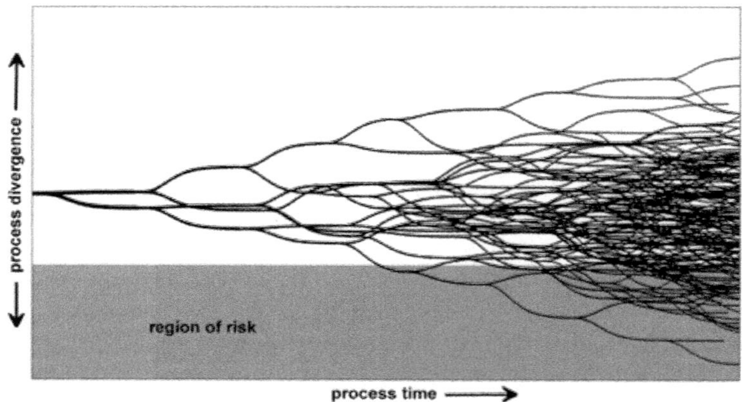

Fig. 1. Processes are represented as a series of trajectories, where each opportunity for deviation is indicated by a fork. A proportion of trajectories are indicated to diverge far enough away from the prescribed work practice to create the risk of an adverse event.

In more detail, agent-based risk assessment involves the following steps: (i) formal specification of prescribed work practices using information policies and guidelines, (these represent the activities agents perform to achieve their goals); (ii) from a formal specification of "what is supposed to happen", an agent model is derived, including probabilistic functions to represent the likelihood of each deviation from the prescribed work practice; (iii) given this model, results are produced as maps of trajectory likelihoods, generated by aggregating over repeated simulation, and validated by comparing against empirical data. We briefly discuss issues arising in the creation and validation of an agent-based risk assessment model. In the next section, this method is illustrated for a race condition hazard.

For step (i), work processes tend to be provided in qualitative formats such as policy or guideline documents, and detailed constraints and activities may require consultation with experts or detailed ethnography. Preparing a formal specification therefore requires a mapping from qualitative information about "what is supposed to happen" into a formal specification of work plans in the form of activities and choices undertaken by individuals in their respective roles.

For step (ii), we have chosen to define and implement agents using the Brahms simulation environment [23], though other frameworks could also be used. The notion of "agent" is conventional: each agent is an autonomous entity that exhibits goal-oriented behaviour, Wooldridge and Jennings [27]. Agents act in the world, but not all the agent's behaviour is the result of rational decision making. That is, there is an element of "situated" behaviour, which is what makes Brahms suitable as a modelling framework (though we do not believe that all cognition and action is situated). To model complex workflow processes, each agent is defined by a set of activities which represents their individual knowledge of the work process (a set of pre-defined plans). In such workflows, agents are autonomous (act independently), proactive (initiate new activities to achieve their goals) and interact (communicate with other agents), and hold a set of beliefs about the world (based on their limited perception of the environment).

For step (iii), to apply the model to assessment of risk in a given scenario, repeated simulations of the scenario with identical initial conditions are performed in order to "map" the potential for risk. Since the agents make decisions based on probability, repeated simulation may result in many different trajectories. The aggregation of trajectories using simple statistics forms a map of the possible pathways through which the scenario may evolve. The proportion of pathways associated with risk indicates the reliability of the process. Further, the map provides a way to understand which combinations of activities and violations create risk, and how often.

The number of simulations required for replicative validation of an ABRA model depends on the rarity of individual trajectories. To determine the number of simulations required to observe a rare trajectory, it is possible to use a binomial distribution where the success is defined by the presence of a specific trajectory. The less common the trajectory, the greater the number of simulations required to be confident (a likelihood greater than or equal to 95%) of observing that trajectory (at $P=0.05$, $n=93$; at $P=0.01$, $n=473$; at $P=0.005$, $n=947$). This also implies that it is difficult to obtain an accurate estimate of how often a rare trajectory is likely to occur given limited empirical data. More simply, there is a tradeoff between the ability of ABRA to explicitly model rare events and the ability to rigorously validate behaviour against the real world.

A major question with any type of model is validation. A relatively strict validation of an agent-based model tests the structure of the model and its ability to replicate observed behaviour as well as predict the behaviour of the system in unseen configurations, Barlas [2]. However, there are unresolved difficulties associated with empirical validation of agent-based models [26,14]. For example, when the purpose of constructing an agent-based model is to examine situations that are costly or impossible to observe in the real world, Epstein [11], the requirements of the validation are at odds with the purpose of the model. For this reason, computational models of healthcare organizations and their processes rarely conform to the requirements of validation, Bharathy and Silverman [3]. In cases where validation is performed, modellers tend to focus on structural and replicative validation.

We have previously implemented agent-based risk assessment for a case study that examines two scenarios involved in transfer of patients from one ward to another: the patient misidentification scenario, and the inadequate infection control scenario, Dunn *et al.* [9]. The model was calibrated the using data from 101 patient transfers observed in a hospital, Ong and Coiera [18], and the results were validated for the infection control scenario (it was not possible to validate the model for the misidentification scenario since there were no occurrences of misidentification in the data). Repeated simulations using the calibrated model were undertaken to create a distribution of possible process outcomes. The likelihood of end-of-chain risk is the main outcome measure, reported for each of the two scenarios. The simulations demonstrate end-of-chain risk of 8% and 24% for the misidentification and infection control scenarios, respectively. Interestingly, over 95% of the simulations in both scenarios were unique, indicating that the in-patient transfer process diverges from prescribed work practices in a variety of ways.

4 Example

As a demonstration of agent-based risk assessment in routine workflow processes, a simple artificial example is presented, inspired by the Therac-25 accidents described in Leveson and Turner [16]. The example is based on a *critical race condition* between two communicating agents, where two parallel processes compete to change the state of the system and the ordering determines the final state. In this case, a human operator enters information into an interface, realizes a mistake and attempts to modify the information already entered. The machine interface begins to interpret the information on-screen without *locking* the state of the information on-screen. Since the timing is non-deterministic, the operator may *interrupt* the machine interface before it has acted on the information (in which case the machine acts on the new information), or may modify what is displayed on-screen after that information has already been acted upon. The operator receives no feedback on which of these two cases have emerged. This process is represented in Figure 2.

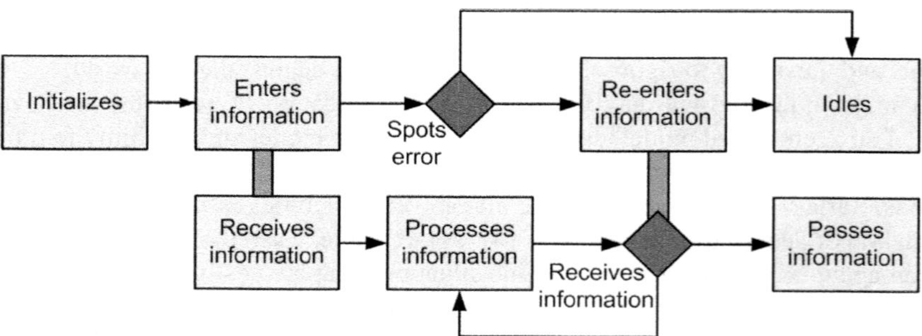

Fig. 2. An example process involving a human operator and an interface to a machine is described by a series of activities performed in sequence (left to right) by the human operator (top) and the interface to a machine (bottom). The two agents interact along vertical channels and diamonds represent choices available to the agents (see text).

The formal specification of the agents follows directly from Figure 2. The human agent is represented by four activities: the initialization of the process, the entering of information, the checking of information and a final idle state. The machine interface agent is represented by three activities: receiving information, processing information and passing information. The human agent includes one violation, the choice of checking the entered information, which is assigned a probability of 55%. The machine interface is reactive but will reprocess newly-entered information only if it has not already passed along the existing information. It is this step that defines the race condition and the associated hazard – that is, the likelihood that the interface will have passed along incorrect information and the operator believes that the information has been corrected.

Since the example process is a simple one involving a single hazard, it is possible to derive the exact likelihood of the hazard given the distribution of the times associated with the agents' activities (this will not be possible with more complex workflows). As an example, we specify the distribution of possible times as a uniform random distribution. As illustrated in Figure 3, the human operator will always take between 10 and 60 seconds to check the information (which is done 55% of the time), while the machine interface will always take between 30 and 90 seconds to process the information (which is done in 100% of the cases). The figure shows that the operator may potentially take longer than the interface when re-entering information in 55% of 40% of the instances of the process, of which half may be expected to produce an error (11%).

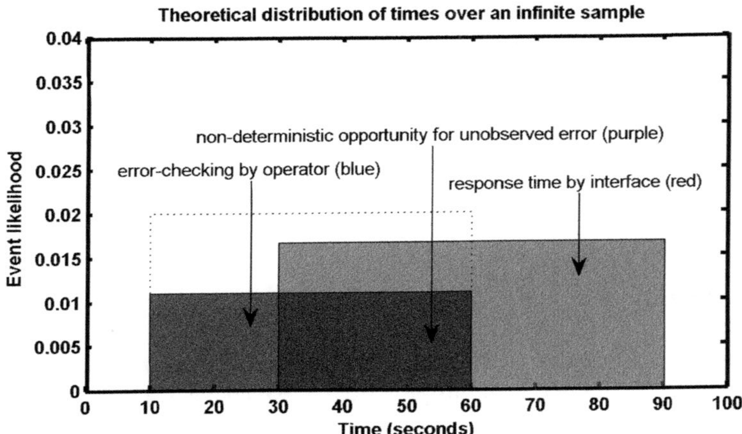

Fig. 3. Expected likelihoods (by second) for the race condition hazard, including the time taken by the human agent for error-checking (left blue rectangle), the time taken by the machine interface to process the original information (right red rectangle), and the region in which the human enters new information but the machine interface may pass along the original information without being interrupted (overlapping area in purple)

We performed 500 simulations of the process in Brahms and examined the results to count the number of simulations in which the operator chooses to check the information, and the number of times the race condition fails. The race condition fails when the machine interface passes along the information before the human finishes re-entering new information. Of those 500 simulations, the operator checks the information in 275. Of those 275, the machine fails to reprocess the new information in 69. This proportion (13.8%) defines the risk of the hazard of the race condition scenario given the specific timing chosen. Since the agent-based simulation also provides details about which activities were performed and how long they took, it is also possible to illustrate a set of trajectories for the process (Figure 4). In this diagram, the two possible trajectories taken by the operator are represented by a single "fork", and the reaction of the machine interface depends on the operator and the timing of the two agents working in parallel.

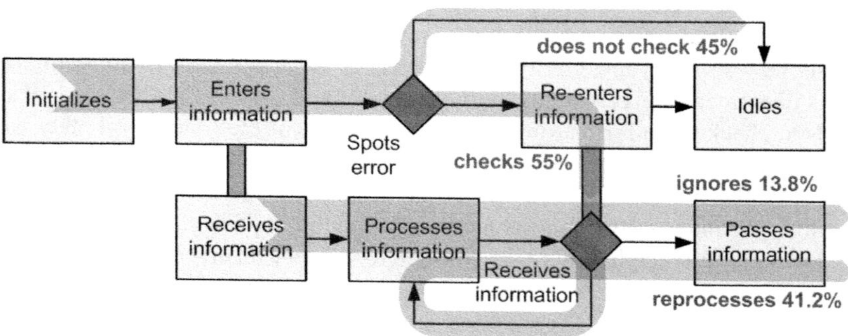

Fig. 4. The aggregated results of 500 simulation instances for the race condition hazard example. The boxes, arrows and channels are given as in Figure 3. The upper red regions represent the percentage of trajectories following each path for the human agent, and the lower purple regions represent the percentage of trajectories following each path for the subset of instances where the human has attempted to re-enter new information (55%).

5 Conclusion

Agent-based risk assessment (ABRA) uses the specific advantages of the agent-based modelling paradigm in the domain of prospective risk analysis, including the explicit modelling of individual behaviour, partial knowledge based on perception, and choice of execution based on that partial knowledge. The ABRA approach is a useful complement to existing prospective risk analysis techniques that is appropriate for complex sociotechnical environments.

The principal advantages of ABRA over existing methods of prospective risk analysis are that it allows for greater precision, the same model can account for multiple scenarios and it simulates unobserved rare events that are otherwise difficult to analyse. The approach applies to any routine clinical process, captures combinations of events, captures the timing of events and decision making of agents, and can handle the many distinct and unique trajectories that are characteristic of workflows in complex sociotechnical systems.

The limitations of the method include the greater requirements for well-defined workflows and reliable observations, and that the model can be time-consuming to construct and difficult to validate, especially for rare trajectories. As with any prospective risk assessment method, it is difficult to identify new causes that are not included in the initial model. In this respect, the analysis and assessment of risk can only ever be as good as the model of the original work practice.

Acknowledgements. This work was funded by an Australian Research Council Linkage Grant (LP0775532) and a National Health and Medical Research Council Program Grant (568612). Thanks to our collaborators, both academic and clinical, especially Mei-Sing Ong, for discussions on the in-patient transfer scenario, and to colleagues at the Decision Systems Laboratory of the University of Wollongong for comments on a seminar on this work.

References

1. Baird, D.R., Henry, M., Liddell, K.G., Mitchell, C.M., Sneddon, J.G.: Post-Operative Endophthalmitis: The Application of Hazard Analysis Critical Control Points (HACCP) to an Infection Control Problem. Journal of Hospital Infection 49, 14–22 (2001)
2. Barlas, Y.: Formal Aspects of Model Validity and Validation in System Dynamics. System Dynamics Review 12, 183–210 (1996)
3. Bharathy, G., Silverman, B.: Validating Agent Based Social Systems Models. In: Proceedings of the 2010 Winter Simulation Conference, pp. 441–453 (2010)
4. Bonan, B., Martelli, N., Berhoune, M., Maestroni, M.-L., Havard, L., Prognon, P.: The Application of Hazard Analysis and Critical Control Points and Risk Management in the Preparation of Anti-Cancer Drugs. International Journal for Quality in Health Care 21, 44–50 (2009)
5. Bonnabry, P., Cingria, L., Sadeghipour, F., Ing, H., Fonzo-Christe, C., Pfister, R.E.: Use of a Systematic Risk Analysis Method to Improve Safety in the Production of Paediatric Parenteral Nutrition Solutions. Quality and Safety in Health Care 14, 93–98 (2005)
6. Burgmeier, J.: Failure Mode and Effect Analysis: An Application in Reducing Risk in Blood Transfusion. Joint Commission Journal on Quality Improvement 28, 331–339 (2002)
7. Chiozza, M.L., Ponzetti, C.: FMEA: A Model for Reducing Medical Errors. Clinica Chimica Acta 404, 75–78 (2009)
8. Cohen, M.R., Senders, J., Davis, N.M.: Failure Mode and Effects Analysis: A Novel Approach to Avoiding Dangerous Medication Errors and Accidents. Hospital Pharmacy 29, 319–330 (1994)
9. Dunn, A.G., Ong, M.-S., Westbrook, J.I., Magrabi, F., Coiera, E., Wobcke, W.R.: A Simulation Framework for Mapping Risks in Clinical Processes: The Case of In-Patient Transfers. Journal of the American Medical Informatics Association (to appear, 2011)
10. Duwe, B., Fuchs, B.D., Hansen-Flaschen, J.: Failure Mode and Effects Analysis Application to Critical Care Medicine. Critical Care Clinics 21, 21–30 (2005)
11. Epstein, J.M.: Why Model? Journal of Artificial Societies and Social Simulation 11(4), 12 (2008)
12. Griffith, C., Obee, P., Cooper, R.: The Clinical Application of Hazard Analysis Critical Control Points (HACCP). American Journal of Infection Control 33, e39 (2005)
13. Iedema, R.A.M., Jorm, C., Long, D., Braithwaite, J., Travaglia, J., Westbrook, M.: Turning the Medical Gaze in Upon Itself: Root Cause Analysis and the Investigation of Clinical Error. Social Science & Medicine 62, 1605–1615 (2006)
14. Klügl, F.: A Validation Methodology for Agent-Based Simulations. In: Proceedings of the 2008 ACM Symposium on Applied Computing, pp. 39–43 (2008)
15. Koppel, R., Wetterneck, T., Telles, J.L., Karsh, B.-T.: Workarounds to Barcode Medication Administration Systems: Their Occurences, Causes, and Threats to Patient Safety. Journal of the American Medical Informatics Association 15, 408–423 (2008)
16. Leveson, N., Turner, C.S.: An Investigation of the Therac-25 Accidents. IEEE Computer 26(7), 18–41 (1993)

17. Marx, D.A., Slonim, A.D.: Assessing Patient Safety Risk Before the Injury Occurs: An Introduction to Sociotechnical Probabilistic Risk Modelling in Health Care. Quality and Safety in Health Care 12, ii33–ii38 (2003)
18. Ong, M.-S., Coiera, E.: Safety Through Redundancy: A Case Study of In-Hospital Patient Transfers. Quality and Safety in Health Care (2010) (to appear)
19. Rasmussen, J., Nixon, P., Warner, F.: Human Error and the Problem of Causality in Analysis of Accidents [and Discussion]. Philosophical Transactions of the Royal Society of London, Series B, Biological Sciences 327, 449–462 (1990)
20. Reason, J.: Human Error: Models and Management. British Medical Journal 320, 768–770 (2000)
21. Robinson, D.L., Heigham, M., Clark, J.: Using Failure Mode and Effects Analysis for Safe Administration of Chemotherapy to Hospitalized Children with Cancer. Joint Commission Journal on Quality and Patient Safety 32, 161–166 (2006)
22. Runciman, B., Merry, A., Walton, M.: Safety and Ethics in Healthcare, Ashgate, Aldershot (2007)
23. Sierhuis, M., Clancey, W.J., van Hoof, R.J.J.: Brahms: A Multi-Agent Modelling Environment for Simulating Work Processes and Practices. International Journal of Simulation and Process Modelling 3, 134–152 (2007)
24. Spear, S.J., Schmidhofer, M.: Ambiguity and Workarounds as Contributors to Medical Error. Annals of Internal Medicine 142, 627–630 (2005)
25. West, E.: Organisational Sources of Safety and Danger: Sociological Contributions to the Study of Adverse Events. Quality and Safety in Health Care 9, 120–126 (2000)
26. Windrum, P., Fagiolo, G., Moneta, A.: Empirical Validation of Agent-Based Models: Alternatives and Prospects. Journal of Artificial Societies and Social Simulation 10(2), 8 (2007)
27. Wooldridge, M., Jennings, N.R.: Intelligent Agents: Theory and Practice. The Knowledge Engineering Review 10, 115–152 (1995)
28. Woolf, S.H., Kuzel, A.J., Dovey, S.M., Phillips Jr., R.L.: A String of Mistakes: The Importance of Cascade Analysis in Describing, Counting, and Preventing Medical Errors. Annals of Family Medicine 2, 317–326 (2004)
29. Wreathall, J., Nemeth, C.: Assessing Risk: The Role of Probabilistic Risk Assessment (PRA) in Patient Safety Improvement. Quality and Safety in Health Care 13, 206–212 (2004)

Healthgrids, the SHARE Project, Medical Data and Agents: Retrospect and Prospect

Tony Solomonides[1,2]

[1] HealthGrid, 36, rue Charles-de-Montesquieu, F-63430 Pont-du-Château, France
[2] University of Exeter, School of Biosciences, The Queen's Drive, Exeter, Devon, EX4 4QJ, United Kingdom
tony.solomonides@gmail.com

Abstract. The application of grid computing to biomedical research domains in the early years of the century has opened up promising prospects for the extension of this philosophy to translational medicine and hence to personalized healthcare. As the business side of the healthcare 'enterprise' also moves to take advantage of the related technology of cloud computing, the management of personal healthcare data on one hand, and of medical knowledge on the other, come to the fore as the principal challenges for successful adoption. We conclude by exploring the potential role of agents to address this and related challenges.

Keywords: Healthgrids, cloud computing, electronic patient records, data protection, medical knowledge, agents.

1 Introduction

The last decade has seen the start, if not yet the full fruition, of major developments in the fields of medical and healthcare informatics. A parallel maturing of genomic sciences has led many to predict an era of 'personalized medicine' – an era when predictive analysis based on the genome would identify not only potential threats for the well person but also optimal treatment for a patient; and an era when laboratory results would be translated into treatments through more extensive and deeper use of informatics to prepare clinical trials, identify suitable 'subjects' and reduce lab time through simulation. This inevitably brings researchers' access to electronic patient records into focus and thus leads to the 'ELSE' – ethical, legal, social and economic – issues that present at least as great a challenge as the technical problems inherent in this vision.

The current climate of austerity following the international credit fiasco also disguises and accentuates at the same time another development which impacts on our proposed programme. As life prospects have improved and people live much longer, healthcare systems have struggled to keep up with the changes in the age-structure of populations. This may be more obvious in developed economies, but there is evidence that certain conditions – obesity, diabetes, cardiovascular disease – associated with a

N. Desai, A. Liu, and M. Winikoff (Eds.): PRIMA 2010, LNAI 7057, pp. 523–534, 2012.

wealthier ageing population are also affecting developing countries, such as India, whose economy is rapidly growing. As healthcare services struggle to cope, it is inevitable that governments would choose to promote a philosophy of responsibility and self-care. In any case, those with access to the internet have already demonstrated an enormous appetite for information about medical conditions, diagnoses, treatments and fellow-sufferer experiences. The increasing – and deeper – use of information technologies thus appears overdetermined.

This paper describes these developments as seen from a particular point of view, through the lens of particular projects and debates that have been of interest to the author. From a first experience of healthgrid computing in the MammoGrid project – a project that helped name the field of "healthgrids" – via other exemplars, notably Health-e-Child, the author had the good fortune to work with some of the pioneers in the field to develop the SHARE road map for healthgrids. This led him to identify specific "ELSE" challenges to address and hence to the experience reported here.

2 MammoGrid and Other First-Generation Projects

MammoGrid was among the first few projects to be funded through the European Commission's e-Health Unit, then under the direction of the visionary Jean-Claude Healy. Its implicit aim, along with other projects, was to provide a concrete example of the use of a novel computational technology in healthcare; its clearly articulated aim was to establish a platform for the collaboration of two breast-cancer units, at Addenbrookes, Cambridge, UK, and the Istituto di Radiologia, Udine, Italy. A team from CERN and UWE in Geneva provided grid infrastructure and management. A team at the University Oxford, UK, and its spin-off company, Mirada Solutions, conducted image quality analysis while the Universities of Pisa and Sassari in Italy provided image annotation services. The medical collaboration envisaged in the project aimed at, first, second opinion in diagnosis, and second, epidemiology. Both of these were accomplished, the latter rather more conspicuously than the former [1], [2]. What concerns us here more than the medical success of the project was its means of handling medical data. Although the data involved in the project was off-line and anonymized, the potential implications of disclosure were considered and considerable attention was paid to 'provenance', a full metadata record of the source and subsequent processing of any data that was incorporated in the project. We give a full description of the underlying query process, not least because it illustrates the ethical and legal dimensions involved and motivate some of our later work.

In the MammoGrid scheme, data is shared by being made available over the grid "virtual private network" – i.e. a highly secure grid layer – through a virtual database. Physically, the data is stored at its home location and can be queried by a suitably authorized and authenticated user from one of the partner locations through a highly orchestrated query service. The project in fact used more than one grid infrastructure in its duration, beginning with the *ad hoc* grid *AliEn* originally devised for the CERN experiment Alice (then under planning for the Large Hadron Collider). When it migrated to the more "designed" EGEE [3] infrastructure *gLite*, the conceptual architecture of the project had the clinically clean structure shown below in Figure 1.

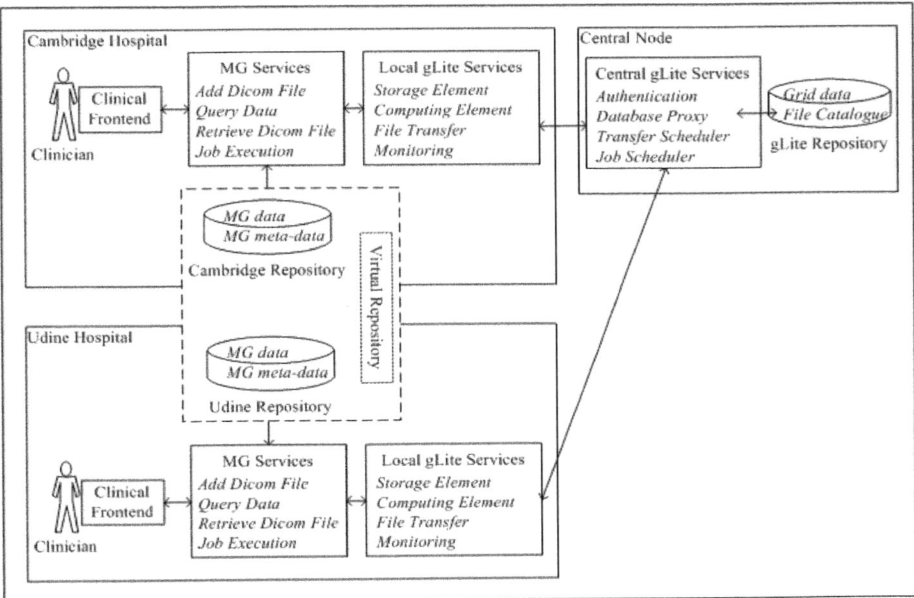

Fig. 1. The conceptual architecture of the MammoGrid database. Note the clean separation of concerns between services provided by MammoGrid, services provided by the grid infrastructure locally and those provided "centrally". (Reproduced from [4] with permission).

Clinical queries are accepted, parsed and executed as shown below in Figure 2. A metadata service supports translation of users' queries (using their own domain language) to a formal query corresponding to the structure of the database; the formal query may then be factored into a local query and a set of remote queries. The latter are distributed across the grid by a "remote query handler" which also has the responsibility of assembling the responses, so that they can be joined to the local results to obtain the complete query response.

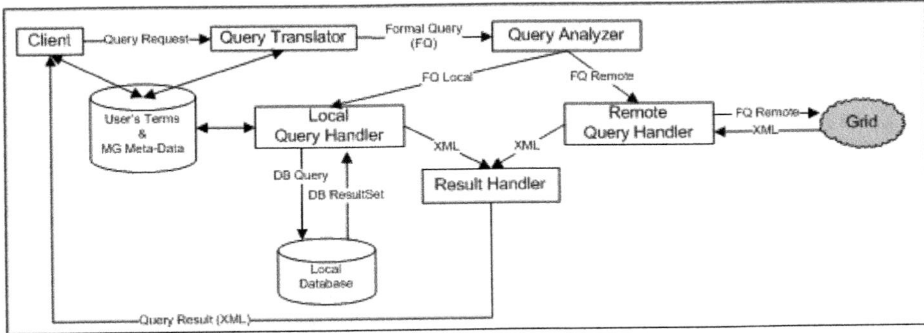

Fig. 2. Clinical query handling in MammoGrid. (Reproduced from [4] with permission).

The sensitivity of these data movements in a "real world" setting is clear. Among the considerations that cannot be ignored is the fact that the mammograms by themselves do not provide complete information either for diagnosis or for epidemiology. There is now a large literature on how much can be discovered about an individual if information from their personal health record is fused with other, often public, sources of information (e.g. the electoral register or social networks) so the naïve notion that a record has been pseudonymized, therefore it is secure, has been entirely undermined.

We have focused on MammoGrid because it is intimately familiar and provides an illustration for our later work, but it would be a mistake to give the impression that it was in any sense an isolated example. Leading up to the funding of the earliest healthgrid projects, the EU had published the results of the project Bioinfomed in the form of a white paper, *Synergy between Medical Informatics and Bioinformatics: Facilitating Genomic Medicine for Future Healthcare* [5] which painted a now-familiar picture of the field through its characterization of different levels of bio-social organization (molecule-cell-tissue-organ-organism-community) and their evident correspondence with academic and clinical disciplines and informatics practices. Its central argument was that if these were appropriately coordinated, they would begin to pave the road to an integrated discipline of "biomedicine" with deep implications for healthcare.

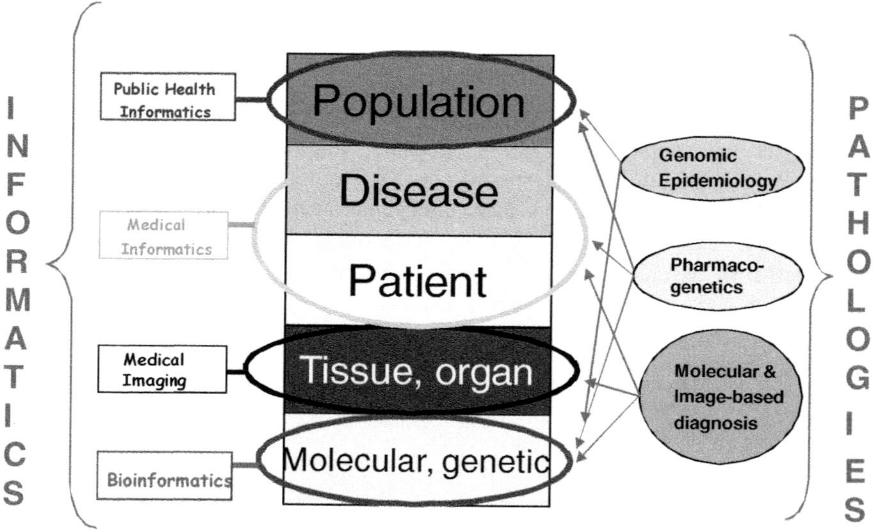

Fig. 3. Levels of bio-social organization, informatics specialisms, medical sub-disciplines and corresponding pathologies. (Adapted from a presentation by Fernando Martin-Sanchez with permission).

At about the same time, a significant number of projects had sprung up across Europe, both EU- and national government-funded, variously tackling a range of diseases and biomedical problems. One deserving special mention was Grid-Enabled

Medical Simulation Services (GEMSS) [6] which covered a wide range of conditions (from vascular surgery to maxillofacial reconstruction) which require sophisticated simulation; notably, GEMSS also devoted considerable effort to issues of privacy, confidentiality and data protection. Concurrently, two very large "cyberinfrastructure" projects, the Bio-Informatics Research Network (BIRN) [7] and the Cancer Biomedical Informatics Grid (caBIG) [8] had been launched in the United States.

All these projects identified, in different but congruent ways, similar sets of problems: technical problems of scalability, interoperability and usability; a glut of standards and terminologies that could scarcely be reconciled; economic problems of investment (once the generous government funding had ceased) and social organizational ones of acceptance and trust. Many had had bruising encounters with Ethics Committees and Institutional Review Boards, but remained defiantly optimistic. It was time to take stock and see how to harness all the goodwill and energy behind this novel approach to biomedical and healthcare computing if it were ever to become the infrastructure of choice in Europe.

3 SHARE: From Vision to Road Map

Along with the projects that had had a clear medical focus, such as those discussed above, there had also been considerable interest in grid computing from projects whose challenge was derived from related fields, such as pharmaceutical design or physiological simulation. The highly distributed nature of grids also lent itself to biosurveillance and studies of the interaction between climate and health, as well as the mapping of economically catastrophic diseases, for example in animals.

The WISDOM project set itself the initial goal of identifying suitable ligands for attacking malaria (hence its name – *Wide In-Silico Docking On Malaria*) but has in fact since broadened its scope to other docking simulation challenges, most notably H5N1, the avian influenza virus. [9] The Virtual Physiological Human "Network of Excellence" [10], an umbrella programme, promotes simulation of the human body with the goal of integrating simulations at different levels of the bio-social scale, so that, perhaps, a model of molecular mutation could be linked to a model of tumour growth at the cellular level or a model of disease development in an individual could be coupled to an epidemiological model of the disease in the community.

The SHARE project set itself the goal of establishing healthgrids as "the infrastructure of choice for biomedical research and healthcare in Europe" within the next decade or so. Its vision was of an environment, created through the sharing of resources and services, in which heterogeneous and dispersed health data at different levels, as well as knowledge and applications, can be accessed by all users as a tailored information system according to their level of authorization and without loss of quality of information or service. As envisaged in Bioinfomed, the data would potentially range across the entire bio-social spectrum: molecular data (e.g. genomics, proteomics); cellular data (e.g. pathways); tissue data (e.g. cancer types, wound healing); personal data (e.g. EHR); and population data (e.g. epidemiology).

Grid infrastructures for biomedical informatics and health care implies, among other things, the availability of grid services, most notably for data and knowledge management; the deployment of these services on infrastructures involving healthcare centres (e.g. hospitals), medical research laboratories and public health administrations; and the definition and adoption of international standards and interoperability mechanisms for medical information stored on the grid. In order to achieve this, the project had to set targets, assess the status quo, identify key gaps, barriers and opportunities, short term objectives, key developments and actors to achieve the vision. Thus, the road map had to answer the questions: *What needs to be done? How is it to be done? Who should do it?*

The then-current classification of grids (into data- and computational grids) had to be elaborated in the face of reality in the biomedical and healthcare domains. Nevertheless, it proved a useful hook on which to hang exemplars for the purpose of understanding their basic requirements.

- Computational Grids
  - Conceived as inexpensive parallel computation.
  - Use case examined: *drug discovery*.
- Data Grids
  - Conceived as a means of massive, rapid, intelligent storage.
  - Use cases: *epidemiology, an avian flu surveillance network.*
- Collaboration Grids
  - A collaborative infrastructure offering computational, data, workflow, and other services to support distributed teams.
  - Use cases: *VPH, breast cancer, paediatrics.*
- Knowledge Grids
  - Scaling up from data to information and then to knowledge; aspects of AI.
  - Use case: *use of grids in general healthcare, COPD.*

The challenges identified by SHARE inevitably were of a socio-technical nature. While some had a strong technical flavour, none was entirely free of social considerations. At the one end of the spectrum, technical challenges in the development of healthgrids would have to address issues of security, performance, and usability, if ever the ideal of distributed data integration and workflow would be realised. In order to provide solid exemplars for adoption, standards would be needed in at least three different senses: reference services and implementations, with reference sites for reassurance, some compromise in standards between healthcare and grid, and common ontologies. Broad use, i.e. grid deployment in medical research centres, would require attention to ease of installation and maintenance, adaptation of user interfaces to medical use, compromises and agreements on IT policies and the interfacing of clinical facilities to a grid.

This brings us naturally to the "ELSE" questions – ethical, legal, social and economic issues – that, as technologists, we might have hoped, or at least imagined, that, for good or ill, *someone else* would have addressed. Among the 'soft' issues which present challenges to the deployment of healthgrids in healthcare are community questions – of ownership of data (doctors, hospitals or patients?) and the relative openness of grids vs. the highly restrictive regulation of hospital data. Questions also of sufficient experience to develop and disseminate good practices in relation to (e.g.) matching healthgrids to existing IT processes in research centres and healthcare institutions, sharing data within the usual ethical, legal and regulatory constraints, governance – who should govern a European healthgrid? – and creating demand for healthgrids through awareness of success and a clear business case.

As we prepared the final road map of SHARE [11], some of us had formed the clear view that the ELSE issues, especially those of ethics and law, were the greater stumbling block and moreover, they would only be addressed if technologists chose to meet policy makers halfway. Unless those amongst us who understood the potential of the technology took it upon themselves to address ethical and legal issues, policy makers and ethicists would have no investment in changing policy (e.g. to favour research) or moving the goalposts (e.g. to recognize that the choice of technical architecture may impact on the security of the data and our ability to protect it from misuse). Far from waging a campaign against regulation, which appeared to be the route some scientists were taking, this was a move to acknowledge the legitimate concerns of both sides of the argument and to make the first conciliatory move to bring researchers and regulators together in a common cause – ultimately, to allow patients to benefit from the knowledge implicit in their own medical records.

4 Regulation and Automation of Compliance

When the motor car was introduced in the UK, it was a legal requirement that a man (usually) walk ahead of the car with a red flag to warn pedestrians and to ensure that the car did not exceed 5 mph. This was not a capricious piece of legislation, but an irrelevant one. Motorized machinery up to this time had meant large unwieldy agricultural vehicles whose 'driver' could not see sufficiently well all round to ensure the safety of pedestrians; and the 'travel' undertaken in these vehicles simply meant transfer from one farm to another. This is a good analogue for what may be happening in the world of ethical and legal data protection as the underlying information technology becomes ever more sophisticated. The next programme of research was devoted to avoiding a restriction of this (irrelevant) nature on healthgrids. The very idea behind the concept was to make sharing and exchange of data and workflows as smooth and uninterrupted as possible. We set out to show that technology could at least meet law and ethics halfway.

At this point, it is necessary to say a few words about regulatory frameworks in Europe. On some issues, often controversial, there is a European directive. (E.g. there is something called the European Working Time Directive which is said to restrict working hours to 48 per week.) European directives are not legislation: they have to be 'transposed' as national legislation separately by each member state. Consequently, there is no guarantee of consistency. It is as if all federal legislation had to be translated into state legislation, state by state, before it could have any effect. In our case, the relevant directive is "95/46/EC Data Protection Directive". The definitions of relevant terms (e.g. "personal data") and restrictions on data disclosure vary from country to country, even though all legislation is supposed to correspond to 95/46/EC. In any case, regulatory frameworks are diverse and complex, and it is known that at the national level implementation of 95/46/EC has been various and that diversity in Europe is driven by cultural, as well as by ethical and legal dimensions.

Text law is too complex to be interpreted by non legal expert users, such as biomedical researchers, clinicians and technologists. Enforcement of privacy obligations at process level depends on legal guidance from an expert or on fixed guidelines that can be looked up by a non-expert. In the next step in this project, we accepted that we would have to rely on guidelines rather than on text law. This may be considered a limitation, but in practice, it is precisely what happens in hospitals every day. Another assumption we make is that the participants are trustworthy, that they do have the autonomy to break the rules, but that this would also be recorded and therefore they will be answerable for the breach.

In her PhD at the University of the West of England, Bristol, Hanene Rahmouni analysed the problem of privacy compliance in healthgrids and concluded that it can be subdivided in some respects and it can be factored in others, in a way that makes it amenable to treatment by means of knowledge representation and reasoning technologies. A subdivision of the problem is portrayed in Figure 4 below.

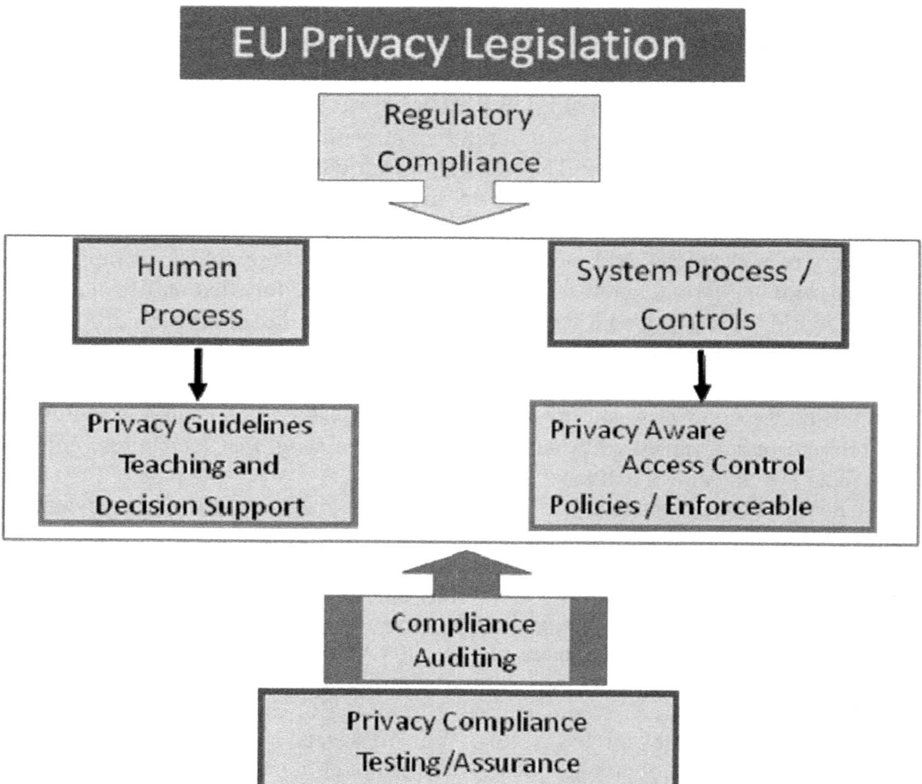

Fig. 4. An analysis of the problem of data sharing in a healthgrid collaboration. The left hand pathway is normative/permissive, while the one on the right hand is prescriptive/coercive. (Adapted from Hanene Rahmouni [12] with permission).

Whether one wishes to treat the advisory route on the left hand of Figure 4 or the operationally deterministic one on the right, an analysis of the problem reveals that there are two stages to a sharing operation: the first involves the analysis of the context (of the data, of the requester and of the purpose of the request) which leads to a view in principle whether the data is sharable or not. The second provides the obligations that must be imposed on the recipient (i.e. the requester) of the data. Thus we may think of these as pre- and post-conditions for the sharing of medical data. In the context of a healthgrid, the two stages may be identified with, first, uploading the data (i.e. information about its existence and structure, say) into the virtual database and second, someone accessing those data from the grid database. Not only will the system determine whether the requester is authorized and authenticated for such access, it will ensure that the obligations to which the recipient must be subject are inseparably attached to the data. This does not preclude abuse, of course, without additional technology, such as self-deleting data. However, all such measures are potentially subverted by a malicious or clever enough abuser of the system.

A schematic representation of the solution adopted by Rahmouni is shown below in Figure 5. The information about the context is represented in a Web Ontology Language (OWL) ontology and is captured in the antecedent of the rule. The rule itself, which is expressed in the Semantic Web Rule Language (SWRL), determines whether the specific sharing of the data can be allowed, and if so, with what obligations on the recipient.

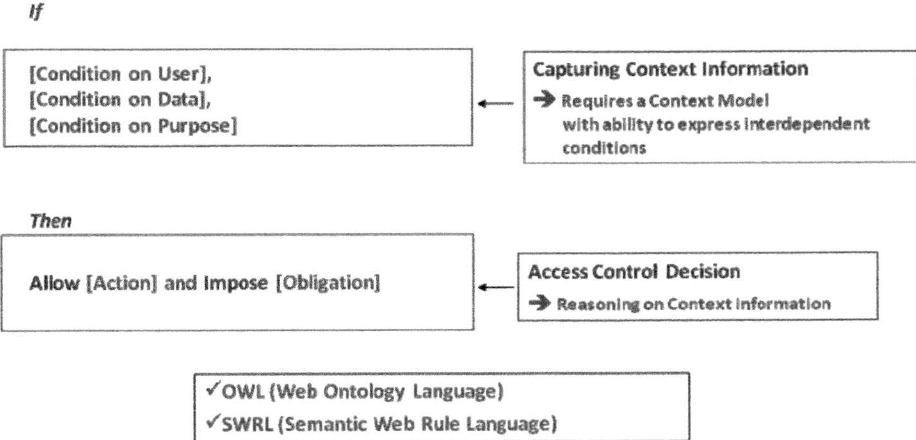

Fig. 5. Two stages in the problem of data sharing in a healthgrid collaboration. The antecedent determines the context and thus the preconditions of sharing the data and the consequent reveals the action and the post-condition obligations to be imposed on sharing the data. (Adapted from Hanene Rahmouni [12] with permission).

The OWL/SWRL knowledge base is translated into an Extensible Access Control Language (XACML) rule and then it can be said to be ready to be applied at the operational level. In a diagrammatic representation conforming to the standard XACML schema, the process is sequenced as shown below in Figure 6. The Policy Decision Point (PDP) and Policy Enforcement Point (PEP) are key. The Policy Information Point here has been implemented as the Semantic Web Knowledge Base and the Context Handler. The Policy Administration Point is simply shown as a store. The data flow then is: (1) User requests some data; (2) the PEP requests a decision from the PDP, which (3) seeks the relevant attributes from the Context Handler; (4) the Context Handler requests attributes values from the Knowledge Base, which (5) duly supplies them. (6) These are returned to the PDP, (7) which issues a decision to the PEP; finally, (8) the decision is enforced and (9) a response is sent to the user.

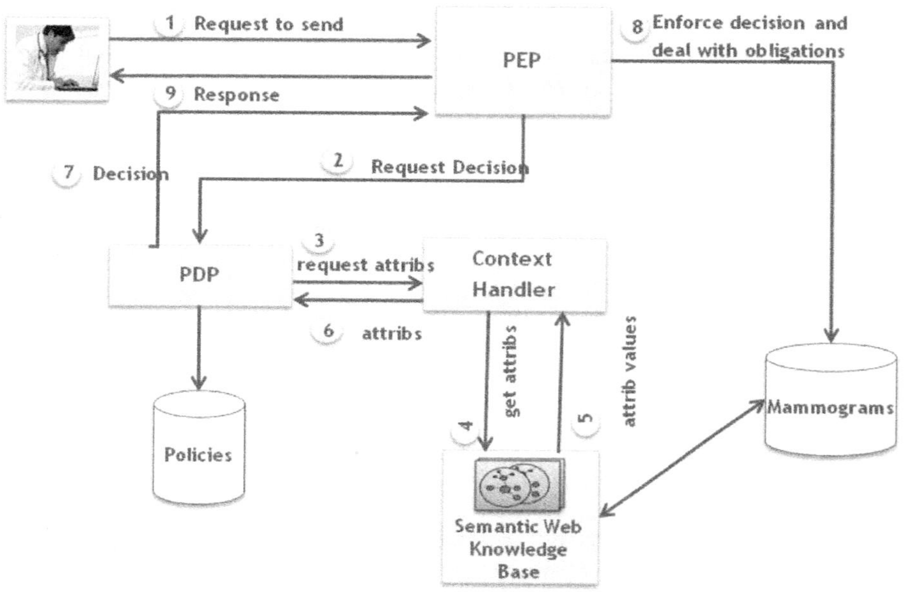

Fig. 6. The XACML machinery for data sharing in a healthgrid collaboration. (Adapted from Hanene Rahmouni [12] with permission).

It has thus been shown that we can model contexts of medical data sharing by means of ontology, reason about which privacy requirements should be assigned to them, extend the ontology to allow the specification of adequate attribute-based access control policies, and map the semantic web policies to XACML to prove enforceability. In her thesis, Rahmouni shows that the approach can be extended to determine documentation requirements for compliance audit, testing and assurance.

5 Management of Medical Records and Agents

It is our contention that the approach outlined above can be extended to manage the full richness of medical data, by which we understand "data+metadata" as an indivisible whole. A diagnosis of "manic psychosis" made by a House Officer in the Accident & Emergency clinic on a Saturday night, perhaps in the midst of other troublesome patients and their friends, is very different from the diagnosis of "manic psychosis" by a Consultant Psychiatrist in the privacy and calm of her consulting room. However, they may look exactly the same to the clerical coder in a basement room who is required to encode patient encounters for purposes of reimbursement.

However, it is inconceivable that data of such complexity and richness can be tackled without support from something like agent-based artificial intelligence. Data must be extracted and managed; consent for them to be shared – or not – must be maintained; implications for the patient in terms of visits to clinics and management of appointments; implications for the patient in terms of predictive and preventive interventions to maintain wellness; all these can be more easily conceptualized if an object in the programming framework is an agent with a particular point of view – whether this is the patient's privacy or the promptness of his treatment.

An agent-based consent framework may serve to illustrate and reinforce this point. Patients are said to be reluctant to provide consent for their data to be used for research because they do not know how it will be handled, they worry about loss of privacy, they have little idea of what benefit may be derived from research using their data, and so on. If we have a framework within which we can reason about the context of our data, and we can begin to think in terms of an automatic service that would validate consent requests (i.e. determine whether an action is compatible or not with the permissions the patient has given), would maintain a record of accesses to the data, would be able to link accesses to the data with specific research or publications, and inform the patient about these. With these actions performed by agents, it is possible to imagine negotiation about secondary use so as to permit maximal use of data within the constraints of consent, patient preferences as to what forms of information to receive back, feedback summarized in an appropriate form and only about matters that the patient cares about. A temporal element may be introduced and managed by agents, requesting consent renewal or informing the patient that consent has lapsed.

The introduction of agent-based medical data management would not be without its challenges. However, examples such as the management of privacy compliance as described in this paper, or a robust, agent-managed consent maintenance service, would give patients, carers, researchers, clinicians and managers reason to place some trust in a system that does work and allow progress to be made from there to more demanding areas where the solution is still subject to further research.

Acknowledgments. The work reported here was done in the context of a succession of EU-funded projects (MammoGrid, SHARE, Health-e-Child, EuroPGDcode, neuGRID) and in collaboration with the partners in these projects. The author is grateful to his former colleagues and students at UWE, Bristol, to HealthGrid and to the many partners whose ideas have been incorporated in this paper.

References

1. Warren, R., Solomonides, T., et al.: A Prototype Distributed Mammographic Database for Europe. Clinical Radiology 62(11), 1044–1051 (2007)
2. Warren, R., Thompson, D., et al.: A Comparison of Some Anthropometric Parameters between an Italian and a UK Population: "proof of principle" of a European project using MammoGrid. Clinical Radiology 62(11), 1052–1060 (2007)
3. EGEE – Enabling Grids for E-Science, http://www.eu-egee.org/
4. del Frate, C., Galvez, J., et al.: Final Results and Exploitation Plans for MammoGrid. In: Hernandez, V., Blanquer, I., et al. (eds.) Challenges and Opportunities of Healthgrids - Proceedings of HealthGrid 2006. Studies in Health Technology and Informatics, vol. 120, pp. 305–315 (2006)
5. Martin-Sanchez, F., Iakovidis, I., et al.: Synergy between medical informatics and bioinformatics: facilitating genomic medicine for future health care. J. Biomed. Inform. 37(1), 30–42 (2004), http://bioinfomed.isciii.es/
6. GEMSS – Grid Enabled Medical Simulation Services; information flier, ftp://ftp.cordis.europa.eu/pub/ist/docs/grids/gemms_achievement.pdf
7. Biomedical Informatics Research Network (BIRN), http://birncommunity.org/
8. Cancer Biomedical Informatics Grid (caBIG), https://cabig.nci.nih.gov/
9. WISDOM Initiative for grid-enabled drug discovery against neglected and emergent diseases, http://wisdom.eu-egee.fr/
10. VPH The Virtual Physiological Human Network of Excellence, http://www.vph-noe.eu/
11. SHARE Road Map (full and abbreviated editions), http://roadmap.healthgrid.org/
12. Boussi Rahmouni, H.: Ontology-Based Privacy Compliance for Health Data Disclosure in Europe, PhD thesis, University of the West of England, Bristol, UK (2011)

An Intelligent Approach to Surgery Scheduling

Sankalp Khanna[1,2], Abdul Sattar[2], Justin Boyle[1], David Hansen[1], and Bela Stantic[2]

[1] The Australian e-Health Research Centre, 71/918,RBWH, Herston, QLD 4029, Australia
{Sankalp.Khanna,Justin.Boyle,David.Hansen}@csiro.au

[2] Institute for Integrated and Intelligent Systems, Griffith University, QLD 4111, Australia
{A.Sattar,B.Stantic}@griffith.edu.au

Abstract. The Multiagent Systems paradigm offers expressively rich and natural fit mechanisms for modeling and negotiation for solving distributed problems. Solving complex and distributed real world problems in dynamic domains however presents a significant challenge and requires the integration of technology innovation and domain expertise to create intelligent solutions. Scheduling of patients, staff, and resources for elective surgery in an under-resourced and overburdened public health system presents an excellent example of this class of problems. In this paper, we discuss the research challenges presented by the problem and outline our efforts of applying distributed constraint optimization, intelligent decision support, and prediction based theater allocation to address these challenges. We also discuss how these technologies can be used to drive better planning and change management in the context of surgery scheduling.

Keywords: Multiagent Systems, Distributed Constraint Optimization.

1 Introduction

Scheduling has been a well studied area in Computer Science research. Incorporating knowledge from areas of Operations Research, Artificial Intelligence and Multiagent Systems (MAS), several previous efforts have focused on finding practical ways of solving scheduling problems in real world domains. The problem is made particularly difficult when scheduling needs to occur in a distributed manner across several departments. While each department is working at optimizing its own resources, optimal utilization requires several departmental schedules to be optimized horizontally. Faced with the challenge of an encumbered public health system, the Elective Surgery Scheduling Problem (ESSP) presents an excellent real-world example of this class of problems.

Despite being a relatively young research area, the Distributed Constraint Reasoning formalism has evolved rapidly to offer efficient and sophisticated algorithms to model and solve a variety of naturally distributed multiagent problems. Several notable Distributed Constraint Optimization Problem (DCOP)

N. Desai, A. Liu, and M. Winikoff (Eds.): PRIMA 2010, LNAI 7057, pp. 535–550, 2012.

approaches employing techniques from search (e.g. ADOPT and its several variants), dynamic programming (e.g. DPOP [23] and its several variants) and cooperative mediation (e.g. APO [19]) have emerged and are being successfully used to model and solve problems in many fields, including sensor networks [17][21][28], meeting scheduling [18] and coordination of unmanned aerial vehicles [29].

Current complete DCOP algorithms, however, largely fail to scale well enough to solve large complex problems, typically the class of problems we seek to address. Further, while DCOP algorithms can theoretically utilize decomposition or compilation to deal with complex sub-problems, this generally results in blowing the distributed problem size out of proportion. Local search algorithms, that trade off completeness for practical efficiency, have been proposed for dealing with DCOPs, but are generally synchronous and thus unsuitable for addressing the class of problems that interest our study. Also, while DCOP offers an excellent mapping for representing many real world problems, the general design of DCOP algorithms is static, and uses tree structures that need to be continually rebuilt in dynamic environments. In addition, given the nature of the real world domains relevant to our research, partial centralization based strategies would not be a good fit here because of obvious departmental privacy and decision control concerns.

We have proposed a multiagent architecture for modeling and solving dynamic complex distributed optimization problems, like the ESSP. In our model, intelligent agents, armed with the constraints, preferences, and priorities of the administrators, optimize schedules for their respective departments. They then negotiate in a privacy-preserving manner (i.e. without sharing more information than is essential) to resolve inter-agent constraints. The architecture of each agent incorporates an interface module to handle internal and external communication, an intelligence module to handle decision making and learning, and a DCOP engine to drive the optimization. This marriage of rational agency and distributed constraint optimization, wherein the optimization algorithm forms the core of the agent negotiation protocol and guides interaction between agents working on related but departmentally autonomous problems, is novel and necessitated by the problem domain.

In order to overcome the shortcomings of traditional DCOP algorithms, the DCOP engine employs a novel asynchronous DCOP algorithm, the Dynamic Complex Distributed Constraint Optimization Problem Algorithm (DCDCOP). DCDCOP preserves the decentralized decision control mechanisms of the problem at hand and offers a robust, flexible, and efficient mechanism for modeling and solving dynamic complex problems.

We have also developed a proof of concept implementation, the Automated Scheduler of Elective Surgery (ASES) system, that is designed to reflect and complement existing manual methods of elective surgery scheduling, while offering efficient mechanisms for negotiation and optimization. The use of predictive technologies to better manage sharing of theaters between elective and emergency surgery has also been explored.

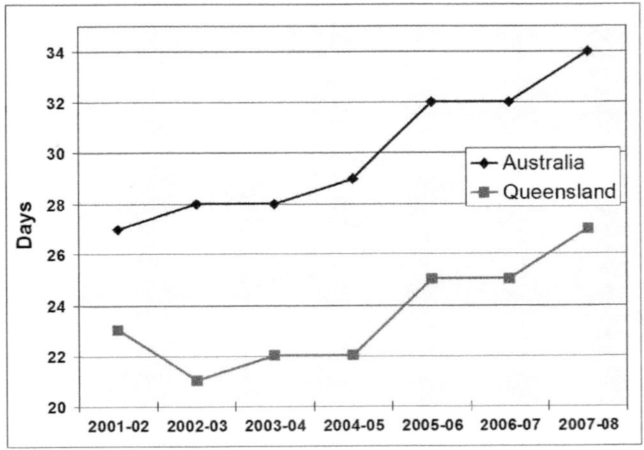

Fig. 1. Median Waiting Time for Elective Surgery

The rest of this paper is organized as follows. In Section 2, we present a case study describing the processes involved in scheduling elective surgery at a large public hospital in Queensland. This is followed by a brief introduction to multiagent systems and distributed constraint optimization, and a discussion of the state-of-the-art solutions to the scheduling in health. In Section 3, we propose our multiagent methodology for modeling and solving the ESSP. We discuss the agent architecture and various functional components, and justify our choice of DCDCOP to drive the DCOP engine. We then discuss the ASES implementation and the effect of fluctuation in resource levels on theater utilization. This is followed by an evaluation of the efficacy of prediction-driven theater allocation in Section 3.4. We conclude with a description of ongoing and future work, mapping key challenges in the journey towards deployment.

2 Background

2.1 Elective Surgery Scheduling - A Case Study

Elective surgery is a planned, non-emergency surgical procedure, which can be scheduled at the patient's and surgeon's convenience. The escalating demand for elective surgery is however compounded by a shortage of trained surgeons, anaesthetists and nurses. Recent statistics [1] show that despite repeated government intervention, elective surgery wait times continue to grow in Australia (Fig. 1). Though slightly better, Queensland statistics follow similar trends. Our research into public elective surgery wait times in Queensland,Australia, found that a significant number of patients were subjected to longer than desirable wait times. This was despite recent initiatives including increased budget allocation, treatment of long-wait patients in private hospitals, and increased clinical staffing. As of 1 April 2010, 33,620 patients were waiting for elective surgery, of

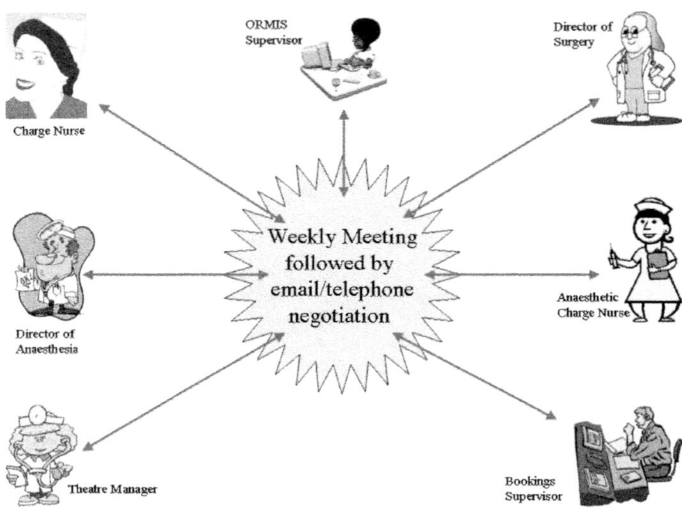

Fig. 2. Current Model for Scheduling Elective Surgery at the Princess Alexandra Hospital

whom almost 18% had waited longer than a clinically desirable time [26]. Any improvement in scheduling processes would not only result in improved staff and resource utilization, but also lead to reduced patient in-waiting and in-care times, increased patient and staff satisfaction, and increased hospital revenue.

We discuss scheduling processes at a leading public hospital in Queensland to help establish a better understanding of the intricacies involved.

21 operating theaters are available. The theater schedule is divided into 3.5 hour slots. Two slots are allocated per day, one in the morning and one in the afternoon. Elective procedures are generally rescheduled in case of emergency.

Each department connected (i.e. allocating staff or other resources) to the surgery carries out their individual scheduling activity. The bookings department assigns patients to slots in consultation with the relevant surgical teams. The bookings are recorded into the *Operating Room Management Information System* (ORMIS). The different departments can access this information by looking into ORMIS or by accessing the latest *Bookings Schedule* on the shared drive, where it is updated everyday at 3PM.

Every Thursday the managers of the different departments meet and review bookings for the week ahead (Fig. 2). Each session is discussed and existing schedule conflicts are resolved. However, events like unexpected emergencies, variation in patients' health state, and sudden perturbations in staffing, often lead to schedule changes. All changes made subsequent to the meeting are conducted on a case-by-case basis by individual departments. Coordinating these changes requires ad-hoc conventional communication. In keeping with the dynamics of the domain, the schedule needs to be updated quickly and efficiently. This is often not possible because of delays in inter-departmental communication. Changes made under such circumstances can often result in inefficient or compromised schedules. For example, if a procedure is canceled at the last minute, the bookings department may want to offer the slot to another patient. However, due to the reliance on ad-hoc inter-departmental coordination, the involved parties may be unreachable. As a consequence, the slot would then go unused.

2.2 MAS and DCOP to the Rescue

Multiagent Systems [30] are a popular paradigm for modeling distributed systems. Intelligent autonomous agents incorporate powerful capabilities such as reactivity, proactiveness, cooperation, learning and intention management. Hospitals exhibit a high level of departmental autonomy and thus multiagent technology offers expressively rich tools for modeling the hospital scheduling environment. Further, multiagent systems also offer the Distributed Constraint Optimization Problem (DCOP) formalism for modeling and solving naturally distributed optimization problems efficiently.

Formally, we can define a DCOP as consisting of:

1. A finite ordered set of Agents $A = \{A_1, A_2, ..., A_k | k \in \mathbb{N}^*\}$, where, for each Agent A there exists :
   (a) A finite ordered set of variables $V = \{V_1, V_2, ..., V_n | n \in \mathbb{N}^*\}$,
   (b) A domain set $D = \{D_1, D_2, ..., D_n\}$, containing a finite and discrete domain D_i for each V_i,
   (c) A constraint set C=$\{C_1, C_2, ..., C_m \ | m \in \mathbb{N}^*\}$, where each $C_j, \forall j \in [1, m]$, is defined as a cost function (f) on a pair of variables (i, i'). i.e. $C_j = f_{ii'} : D_i \times D_{i'} \rightarrow \mathbb{N}, \forall V_i, V_{i'} \in V$, and
   (d) An ordered solution set $S = \{v_1, v_2, ..., v_n | v_i \in D_i, \forall i \in [1, n]\}$ where each v_i is an instantiation of the variable V_i and the aggregate cost of the assignment $F(S) = \sum_{(x_i, x_{i'} \in V)} f_{ii'}(d_i, d_{i'}), x_i \leftarrow d_i, x_{i'} \leftarrow d_{i'} \in S$.
2. The solution set of the DCOP S^* is defined as the set of the solution sets of each agent.

Employing techniques from search, dynamic programming, and cooperative mediation, DCOP offers efficient and sophisticated algorithms like ADOPT [20], DPOP [23], and NCBB [5], to model and solve a variety of naturally distributed problems. Recent research efforts [16][4][10] have however identified shortcomings in DCOP algorithms when applied to dynamic and complex environments.

2.3 Current State of the Art

Over the last two decades, several research efforts have been directed at solving the scheduling problem, though most have been directed at the classical "job shop scheduling problem" [32][25][8]. Further, research in the Operations Research domain has also looked at the problem of scheduling for Operating Theaters and proposed efficient solvers [7][15][24][14] to handle the task, but most such solvers approach the problem as a centralized one.

A review and analysis of health-related scheduling systems proposed by recent research revealed that most were based on simplistic case studies and did not map the complexities of the domain they were modeling. While several systems, including *DISA* [6], *MedPage*[22], and *Policy Agents* [12], used multiagent systems to model their domains, distributed schedule optimization was largely overlooked or proposed as one of the future aims. We also found that since transient elective surgery scheduling data is not captured in any current mechanisms, there is a lack of benchmark problems in this domain.

The evaluation of state-of-the-art commercial surgery scheduling softwares like ORMIS[1], OPERA[2], and MEDITECH Operating Room Management solution[3], also found that while these provide sophisticated interfaces for users to enter scheduling decisions, and handy tools to detect conflicts and manage schedules, decision making and optimization are largely left to the operators of the system. This results in several staff hours being spent each week on cumbersomely optimizing and aligning schedules. Krempels and Panchenko [13] reveal that in the Operation Theater Scheduling domain they study, it takes one person 3-5 full working days to create a Nurse Roster. Several discussions and interviews with hospital administrators and schedulers also revealed that the most popular tools for departmental scheduling were still paper templates, excel spreadsheets and whiteboards, with software systems being used to record manually optimized schedules.

Given the need for maintaining the departmental decision control nature of the problem domain, we focus our research on distributed problem solving, specifically multiagent representations of the problem.

3 The Solution

We believe that, while all of the methods addressed in section 2.3 help to improve the state-of-the-art, what is missing is an intelligent flexible methodology that can adapt itself to the complexity of the problem, without modifying or scaling it down. Optimally solving local problems and handling changes caused by the dynamic nature of the environment in a timely manner is also a non-trivial challenge. We argue thus that incorporating optimization internally for each agent, and as an integral element of the inter-agent negotiation process, is critical to the success of any proposed system.

We have proposed an agent-oriented methodology where each department involved in the scheduling of its resources, be they patients, staff or equipment, is represented by an intelligent agent [11]. These agents are customized to the constraints, preference and priorities of the party they represent. It is the responsibility of the agents to react to messages from other agents and optimize their local schedule accordingly. As necessary, the agents then negotiate in a privacy-preserving manner to resolve inter-agent constraints (Fig. 3).

[1] `http://isoftsanidad.es/text/products/2593.asp`

[2] `http://www.chca.ca/opera.php?lang=en`

[3] `http://www.meditech.com/ProductBriefs/pages/productpageorm.htm`

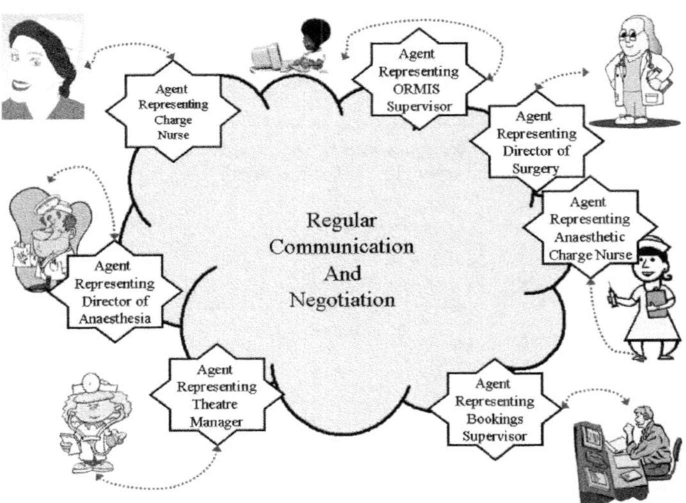

Fig. 3. Proposed Model for Scheduling Elective Surgery at the Princess Alexandra Hospital

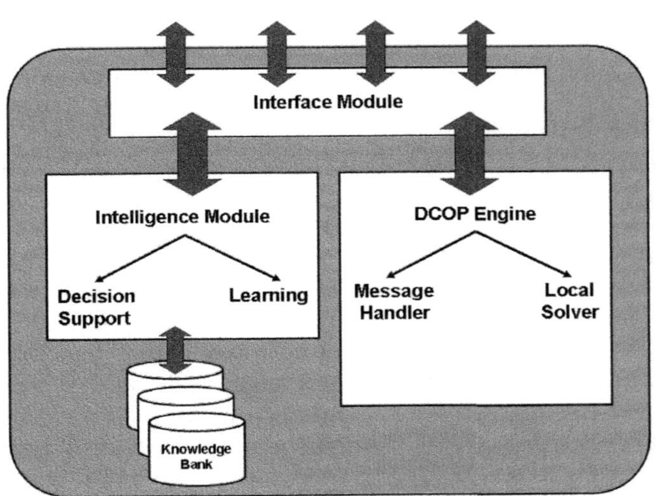

Fig. 4. Agent Architecture

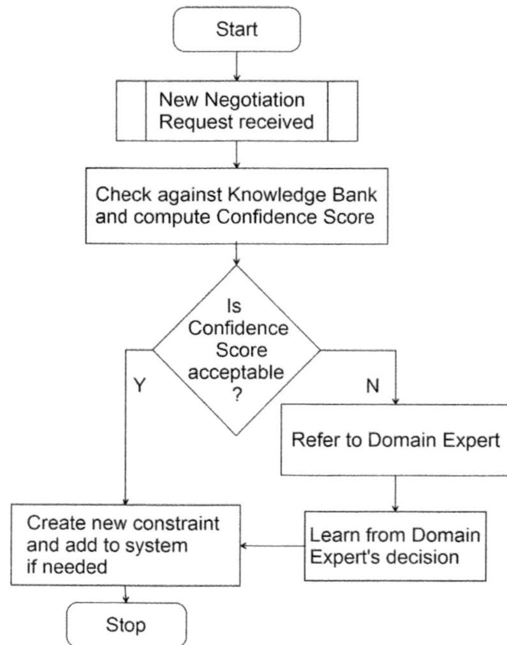

Fig. 5. Intelligent Decision Support

3.1 Proposed Architecture

The architecture of individual agents within our methodology (Fig. 4) consists of a number of modules. An interface module handles communication with other agents and users. Decision support and learning is handled by the intelligence module. Negotiation and optimization is driven by the DCOP engine.

To better understand the architecture, we consider a negotiation as it would be handled by the Intelligence module. In many scenarios, the system needs user-input to make a decision about a negotiation request received. For example, if a slot opening permits a procedure to be brought forward, the Bookings department may request such a change. However, the Nurse Unit Manager may accommodate the change at short notice only at her discretion, or after explicit discussion with the staff involved. In situations such as this, there is no alternative but to defer the decision to the user. In this instance, the Intelligence module would refer the decision to the user based on the the system suggested by Khanna et al. [11]. It is designed to mimic the behavior of the domain expert in these scenarios and to build a knowledge bank by learning from decisions taken by the domain expert. The decision flow of this module is presented in Fig. 5.

The agents thus have a number of capabilities. They can learn user preferences and domain knowledge. The environment is monitored for changes necessitating

Algorithm 1. The DCDCOP Algorithm

```
Calculate static measures
Solve_local_problem
Calculate dynamic measures
Send message (DU, CurrContext) to all neighbours
Receive messages
when received (messageDU, msgContext) do
    if msgContext and CurrContext are consistent then
        add msgContext to CurrContext
        if DU > msgDU then
            Solve_local_problem
        end
        else if DU = msgDU and higher_order then
            Solve_local_problem
        end
        Calculate dynamic measures
        Send message (DU, CurrContext) to all neighbours
    end
end

Procedure: Solve_local_problem
Branch and Bound to solve local problem
```

updates to the schedule. They use logical reasoning to identify the need for and to guide negotiation. An advanced DCOP algorithm is used to optimize local schedules while ensuring efficient alignment of the global schedule.

3.2 DCDCOP : Driving the DCOP Engine

The DCOP algorithm we utilize in our solution needs to be robust in a number of ways. It must be scalable to the variety and complexity of the involved agents' sub-problems. Negotiation resolution must be timely with respect to the environment under which the negotiation is taking place. The ability to separate the communication protocol from the details of the local solver is also essential, as this facilitates the customization of the local solver to each agent's unique problem while maintaining communication compatibility.

We have previously proposed DCDCOP [10] (see Algorithm 1), where agents solve their local sub-problem using a local solver of their choice and then employ a novel metric called Degree of Unsatisfaction (DU) to guide inter-agent negotiation and solve inter-agent constraints. DCDCOP has been shown [9] to outperform ADOPT, DPOP, and NCBB, by more than an order of magnitude. Comparison with a DSA[31]-like variant, CostDCOP, also proves the effectiveness of the DU metric in guiding the algorithm towards an optimal solution [9].

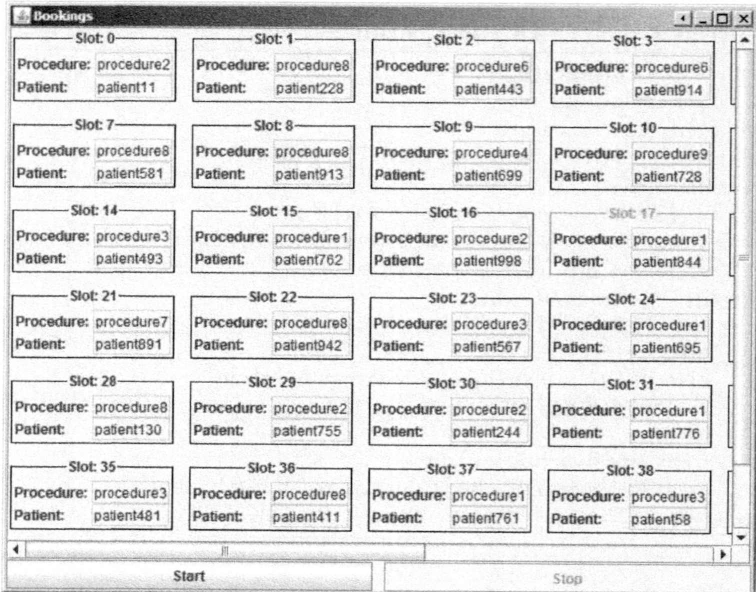

Fig. 6. Bookings Agent

Resources

Stock

Item	#
resource0	3
resource1	10
resource2	15
resource3	5
resource4	10

Costs

Resource	Cost
resourceA	9.0
resource0	21.0
resource9	67.0
resource8	83.0
resource7	47.0

Availability

Item	#
resource0	0
resource1	1
resource2	2
resource3	2
resource4	2

Descriptions

Resource	Description
resourceA	description of resource A
resource0	description of resource 0
resource9	description of resource 9
resource8	description of resource 8
resource7	description of resource 7

Requirements

Procedu...	resource0	resourc...	resource2	resourc...	resource4	resourc...	resource6	resourc...	resource8	resourc...
proced...	0	1	0	0	0	1	0	0	0	0
proced...	0	0	1	0	0	0	0	1	0	0
proced...	1	1	0	0	0	0	0	0	0	0
proced...	0	1	0	0	0	0	1	0	0	0
proced...	0	1	0	0	0	0	1	0	0	0

Allocations

Slot	Proced...	resourc...	resourc...	resourc...	resourc...	resourc...	resourc...	resourc...	resourc...	resourc...	resour...
0	proced...	1	1	0	0	0	0	0	0	0	0
2	proced...	0	0	1	0	1	0	0	0	0	0
3	proced...	0	0	1	0	1	0	0	0	0	0
5	proced...	0	0	0	0	1	0	1	0	0	0
6	proced...	1	1	0	0	0	0	0	0	0	0

Fig. 7. Resources Agent

Given its ability to preserve the distributed sub-problem structure, and its computational superiority over ADOPT, DPOP, and NCBB, we have chosen DCDCOP to drive the DCOP engine in our proposed solution.

3.3 ASES - An Automated Scheduler for Elective Surgery

In this section, we discuss ASES, a Multiagent System implementation [9] developed as a proof-of-concept demonstration of ideas discussed in previous sections. ASES has been implemented using Jason [2]. Jason is a Java implementation of Agentspeak(L) [27]. In addition to providing extended Agentspeak(L) syntax and semantics for the development of individual agents, Jason provides facilities for the specification of multiagent systems. Crucial in so doing is the provision for speech-act-based communication. This speech-act-based communication underlies our DCOP communication implementation.

ASES models the scheduling activity of 4 agents: Bookings, Nursing, Anaesthesiology, and Theater Resources. The Bookings and Resource agents are briefly discussed to present a better understanding of their activities.

The Bookings agent (Fig. 6) receives randomly generated requests to add or modify bookings. Each request includes the patient and procedure information. When a slot is allocated, the Bookings agent sends this information out to all agents concerned. If an agent is unable to provide resources, a message is returned to the Bookings agent, resulting in the allocation being cancelled and another message being sent out to all agents concerned.

The Resource agent (Fig. 7) calculates the equipment required for the procedure to schedule. If the required resources are unavailable, the Resource agent requests that the Bookings agent reschedule the procedure. Thus, equipment is allocated on a first-come first-served basis. This models the hospital's current resource allocation strategy. However, work is underway to enhance this process to utilize procedure/patient priorities required.

Simulations carried out using the ASES system allow for ASES to be used as a tool to test system bottlenecks. For example, reducing available resources by 10% (simulating equipment breakdown) significantly increases resource contention and allows the system to achieve only unto 93% theater utilization. Unlike the Resource agent, the resources available to the Nursing agent are not fixed. The Nurse Unit Manager is able to hire casual/temporary nurses when necessary. However, their use is to be minimized. This is modeled by assigning a higher cost to casual/temporary nursing staff.

3.4 Prediction Based Theater Allocation

In Queensland, as in many acute care hospitals around the world, operating theaters are shared between elective and emergency services as per a static allocation strategy, This involves blocking off one or more theaters for emergency surgery and/or handling trauma cases. However, there is a lot of fluctuation in demand for emergency services. When emergency demand increases, elective surgery procedures are generally put on hold and rescheduled to a later time.

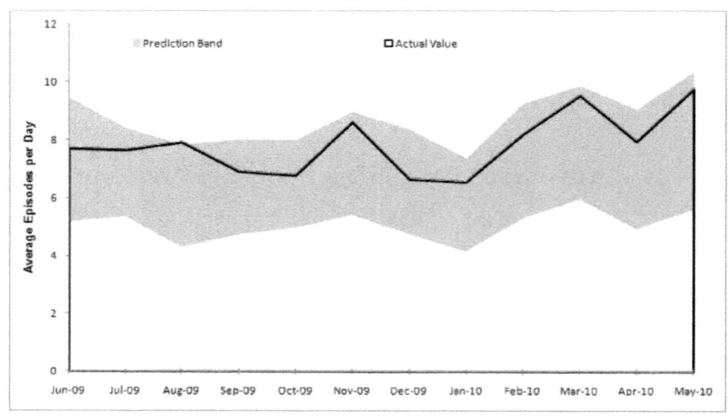

Fig. 8. Elective Surgery : Actual Vs Predicted Episodes

Quick rescheduling measures are thus required to allow departments to confirm availability of staff and resources at the earliest to ensure this process does not inconvenience patients too much and to minimize the impact of this rescheduling on the rest of the elective surgery schedule. Further, reduced demand for emergency services provides an opportunity for opening up these available beds for elective surgery if efficient scheduling mechanisms are available. Recently introduced tools like the Patient Admissions Prediction Tool (PAPT) [3] allow accurate prediction of patient load for the next hour, the rest of the day, into next week, or even on holidays.

We looked at the daily and monthly variance exhibited by these services, and evaluated the value of using predictions based on historic data to guide a dynamic resource sharing model. For this analysis, PAPT was used to predict the number of monthly episodes of elective and emergency surgery at a 750-bed urban hospital in Queensland, Australia for one year, from June 2009 to May 2010. Predictions were in the form of a monthly estimate and 95% prediction interval, and were validated using real hospital data for the same period. Figures 8 and 9 represent the variance in actual and predicted episodes for Elective and Emergency Surgery respectively.

The standard deviation of daily Elective and Emergency surgery cases across the year was 6.6 and 1.8 patients/day respectively. Monthly standard deviation for Elective and Emergency cases was 32.9 and 10.3 patients/month respectively. The Mean Absolute Percentage Error (MAPE) for monthly surgery predictions was 11.7% for Elective Surgery and 9.4% for Emergency Surgery. The observed number of Elective surgery cases were within the 95% prediction interval more often than Emergency surgery observations, likely due to the higher sample sizes. The analysis provides evidence to support our argument that prediction-guided dynamic resource sharing would work better than a static allocation model for sharing theaters between elective and emergency surgery.

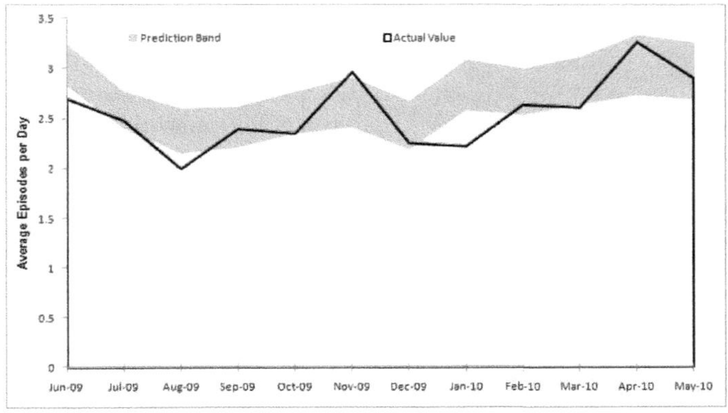

Fig. 9. Emergency Surgery : Actual Vs Predicted Episodes

4 Conclusion and Future Work

Motivated by the challenge of better managing the task of scheduling elective surgery in public hospitals, we have proposed a methodology where intelligent agents, trained with the constraints, preferences, and priorities of the administrators, optimize schedules for their respective departments and then negotiate in a privacy-preserving manner to resolve inter-agent constraints.

The architecture of each agent incorporates an interface module to handle internal and external communication, an intelligence module to handle decision making and learning, and a DCOP engine to drive the optimization. Using this methodology, the system can translate from the current practice of resolving conflicts during weekly meetings to one where ongoing negotiation ensures that the departmental schedules are largely conflict free at all times, thus making the weekly meetings redundant. The use of agents also significantly reduces delays in inter-departmental information flow and negotiation. Though delays resulting from waiting for user interaction are unavoidable, the need for such interaction will also decrease as the system learns and builds its knowledge bank for automated decision support.

The underlying DCOP engine in our approach is driven by a novel asynchronous DCOP algorithm, the Dynamic Complex Distributed Constraint Optimization Problem Algorithm (DCDCOP), that preserves the decentralized decision control mechanisms of the problem at hand and offers a robust, flexible, and efficient mechanism for modeling and solving dynamic complex problems. We have experimentally evaluated our DCDCOP algorithm against the state-of-the-art asynchronous DCOP algorithms.

We have also developed a prototype proof-of-concept application, ASES, that demonstrates the efficacy of our approach. Further, we have also investigated the efficacy of Prediction driven dynamic resource sharing for as an alternative to a static policy for sharing of theaters between elective and emergency surgery.

We are currently working on further development of the ASES prototype, specifically on incorporating intelligent decision support within the agents. We are also working on developing the DCOP engine to incorporate complex inter-agent constraints and input from the intelligence module into the DCDCOP algorithm. Implementing DCDCOP and other DCOP algorithms within ASES to evaluate them on benchmark scheduling problems is also proposed. Maheswaran el al. [18] have shown that the performance of ADOPT in solving real world problems is significantly worse than in solving similar-sized map coloring problems. Benchmarking the algorithms within ASES would thus provide better insight on their relative performances. Incorporating domain expert interaction and override functionality are also future aims for the ASES system.

We are also working towards employing various local solver algorithms within DCDCOP to produce a family of algorithms that can adapt themselves to the nature of the problem at hand. For example, agents with larger sub-problems could employ local search to perform faster, though incomplete, search within the node, while agents with smaller sub problems could benefit with using faster complete search within the node. Investigating the interaction between agents using different local solvers and the efficacy of the *DU* metric in this scenario is also to be investigated.

Translating domain rules to constraints, quantifying cost functions to represent these constraints, incorporating multi-criteria optimization, and quantifying confidence scores for intelligent decision support are also key research challenges that must be addressed before our research can actually be fully deployed in a real hospital environment. Lastly, gaining acceptance from the end-users of the system is a challenge for all new systems but we expect the time already spent working closely with these practitioners, and studying their requirements, will help bridge this gap.

Acknowledgments. The authors wish to thank Dr. Peter Moran and his colleagues at the Princess Alexandra Hospital for their ongoing support, for allowing us into their world of surgery, and for sharing their invaluable expertise.

References

1. Australian Medical Association. Public Hospital Report Card 2009 (October 2009), http://ama.com.au/node/5030
2. Bordini, R.H., Wooldridge, M., Hübner, J.F.: Programming Multi-Agent Systems in AgentSpeak using Jason. John Wiley & Sons (2007)
3. Boyle, J., Jessup, M., Crilly, J., Green, D., Lind, J., Wallis, M., Miller, P., Fitzgerald, G.: Predicting emergency department admissions. Emergency Medicine Journal (June 2011)
4. Burke, D.A.: Exploiting Problem Structure in Distributed Constraint Optimisation with Complex Local Problems. PhD thesis, Department of Computer Science, University College Cork, Ireland (2008)
5. Chechetka, A., Sycara, K.: An any-space algorithm for distributed constraint optimization. In: Proceedings of AAAI Spring Symposium on Distributed Plan and Schedule Management (March 2006)

6. Friha, L.: DISA: Distributed Interactive Scheduler using Abstractions. PhD thesis, University of Geneva, Geneva (July 1998)
7. Jebali, A., Hadj Alouane, A.B., Ladet, P.: Operating rooms scheduling. International Journal of Production Economics 99(1-2), 52–62 (2006)
8. Jones, A., Rabelo, J.: Survey of job shop scheduling techniques (1998)
9. Khanna, S.: Distributed Constraint Optimization and Scheduling in Dynamic Environments. PhD Thesis, Institute for Integrated and Intelligent Systems, Griffith University, Australia (2010)
10. Khanna, S., Sattar, A., Hansen, D., Stantic, B.: An Efficient Algorithm for Solving Dynamic Complex DCOP Problems. In: WI-IAT 2009: Proceedings of the IEEE/WIC/ACM International Joint Conference on Web Intelligence and Intelligent Agent Technology, pp. 339–346 (2009)
11. Khanna, S., Sattar, A., Maeder, A., Stantic, B.: Intelligent Scheduling in Complex Dynamic Distributed Environments. In: Medinfo 2007: Proceedings of the 12th World Congress on Health (Medical) Informatics; Building Sustainable Health Systems, Brisbane, Australia, pp. 1665–1666 (2007)
12. Krempels, K., Panchenko, A.: An Approach for Automated Surgery Scheduling. In: 6th International Conference on the Practice and Theory of Automated Timetabling, pp. 209–233 (2006)
13. Krempels, K.-H., Panchenko, A.: Dialog-based intelligent operation theatre scheduler. In: Burke, H.R.E.K. (ed.) 6th International Conference on the Practice and Theory of Automated Timetabling, pp. 524–527. Masaryk University, Brno (2006)
14. Lamiri, M., Grimaud, F., Xie, X.: Optimization methods for a stochastic surgery planning problem. International Journal of Production Economics 120(2), 400–410 (2009); Special Issue on Introduction to Design and Analysis of Production Systems
15. Lamiri, M., Xie, X., Dolgui, A., Grimaud, F.: A stochastic model for operating room planning with elective and emergency demand for surgery. European Journal of Operational Research 185(3), 1026–1037 (2008)
16. Lass, R.N., Sultanik, E.A., Regli, W.C.: Dynamic distributed constraint reasoning. In: Proceedings of the Twenty-Third AAAI Conference on Artificial Intelligence, Chicago, pp. 1466–1469 (2008)
17. Lesser, V., Ortiz, C., Tambe, M. (eds.): Distributed Sensor Networks: A Multiagent Perspective (Edited book), vol. 9. Kluwer Academic Publishers (May 2003)
18. Maheswaran, R.T., Tambe, M., Bowring, E., Pearce, J.P., Varakantham, P.: Taking DCOP to the real world: Efficient complete solutions for distributed Multi-Event scheduling. In: Proceedings of the Third International Joint Conference on Autonomous Agents and Multiagent Systems, New York, vol. 1, pp. 310–317 (2004)
19. Mailler, R., Lesser, V.: Solving Distributed Constraint Optimization Problems Using Cooperative Mediation. In: Proceedings of the Third International Joint Conference on Autonomous Agents and Multiagent Systems, New York, vol. 1, pp. 438–445 (2004)
20. Modi, P.J., Shen, W., Tambe, M., Yokoo, M.: An asynchronous complete method for distributed constraint optimization. In: Proceedings of the Second International Joint Conference on Autonomous Agents and Multiagent Systems, Melbourne, pp. 161–168 (2003)
21. Modi, P.J., Shen, W.-M., Tambe, M., Yokoo, M.: Adopt: Asynchronous distributed constraint optimization with quality guarantees. Artificial Intelligence 161(1-2), 149–180 (2005)

22. Paulussen, T., Zöller, A., Rothlauf, F., Heinzl, A., Braubach, L., Pokahr, A., Lamersdorf, W.: Agent-based Patient Scheduling in Hospitals. In: Multiagent Engineering - Theory and Applications in Enterprises, pp. 255–275. Springer, Heidelberg (2006)
23. Petcu, A., Faltings, B.: A scalable method for multiagent constraint optimization. In: Proceedings of the Nineteenth International Joint Conference on Artificial Intelligence, Edinburgh, Scotland, pp. 266–271 (August 2005)
24. Pham, D.-N., Klinkert, A.: Surgical case scheduling as a generalized job shop scheduling problem. European Journal of Operational Research 185(3), 1011–1025 (2008)
25. Prosser, P., Buchanan, I.: Intelligent scheduling: Past, present and future. Intelligent Systems Engineering 3(2), 67–78 (1994)
26. Queensland Health. Quarterly Public Hospitals Performance Report March Quarter (2010), http://www.health.qld.gov.au/surgical_access
27. Rao, A.S.: AgentSpeak(L): BDI Agents Speak Out in a Logical Computable Language. In: Perram, J., Van de Velde, W. (eds.) MAAMAW 1996. LNCS, vol. 1038, pp. 42–55. Springer, Heidelberg (1996)
28. Scerri, P., Modi, J., Shen, W.-M., Tambe, M.: Are multiagent algorithms relevant for real hardware?: a case study of distributed constraint algorithms. In: SAC 2003: Proceedings of the 2003 ACM Symposium on Applied Computing, pp. 38–44. ACM, New York (2003)
29. Schurr, N., Okamoto, S., Maheswaran, R.T., Scerri, P., Tambe, M.: Evolution of a teamwork model. In: Cognition and Multi-Agent Interaction: From Cognitive Modeling to Social Simulation, pp. 307–327 (2005)
30. Woolridge, M.: Introduction to Multiagent Systems, 2nd edn. John Wiley & Sons, Inc. (2009)
31. Zhang, W., Xing, Z., Wang, G., Wittenburg, L.: An analysis and application of distributed constraint satisfaction and optimization algorithms in sensor networks. In: AAMAS 2003: Proceedings of the Second International Joint Conference on Autonomous Agents and Multiagent Systems, pp. 185–192. ACM, New York (2003)
32. Zweben, M., Fox, M.: Intelligent scheduling. Morgan Kaufmann Publishers Inc., San Francisco (1994)

Using Distributed Agents for Patient Scheduling

Graham Billiau[1], Chee Fon Chang[1], Aditya Ghose[1], and Alexis Andrew Miller[2]

[1] Decision Systems lab, Center for Oncology Informatics,
Illawarra Medical & Health Research Institute
University of Wollongong, NSW, Australia
{gdb339,c03,aditya}@uow.edu.au
[2] Illawarra Cancer Care Centre
Wollongong Hospital, Wollongong, NSW, Australia
amiller@uow.edu.au

Abstract. Ensuring optimum use of scarce resources is one of the largest challenges facing health providers today. However it is not easy to generate an optimised schedule, as the health system is unusually and highly dynamic. Scheduling systems must be extremely flexible while still producing an efficient, acceptable schedule. Furthermore the scheduling system should be able to cross health boundaries inside and outside hospitals to perform load sharing.

To solve this problem we propose an encoding of the patient scheduling problem as a dynamic distributed constraint optimisation problem and show how it can be solved using Support Based Distributed Optimisation. The resulting system will be able to generate good schedules and update them in real time. It is also able to maintain privacy across hospital boundaries to enable load balancing.

1 Introduction

There are many sources of inefficiency in the health system, including staff forced to use several different software systems that are not properly integrated. Duplicating work on multiple systems often with laborious hand copying wastes time [1].

Inefficiencies due to a poor schedule have been identified as problematic. A good schedule will not only reduce the amount of time wasted on waiting for patients to arrive and travelling, but will also improve patient satisfaction by providing care at times that suit them with reasonable waiting times [2].

Research has focused on optimising the utilisation of operating rooms, and shown that reducing organisational barriers and applying sophisticated optimisation techniques can improve the utilisation of operating rooms in an already efficient hospital by 4.5% [3]. This shows that significant gains in efficiency can be made within the health system. In fact, the QE Foundation estimates "that 100 billion dollars over ten years can be saved in Medicare, Medicaid and VA spending alone by using [their] methodologies." [4].

Constraint Optimisation Problems (COP) are a proven method of modelling and solving scheduling and optimisation problems, and so are an ideal tool to

N. Desai, A. Liu, and M. Winikoff (Eds.): PRIMA 2010, LNAI 7057, pp. 551–560, 2012.

solve patient scheduling problems. A COP consists of a set of variables, each of which has an associated domain, a set of constraints and a set of objectives. The variables typically represent the state of an object, but can also represent decisions, preferences and many other concepts. The domain of each variable is the values that the variable is allowed to take on. This normally must be a finite set. Constraints are used to represent the interactions between variables, e.g. patients cannot be treated while the equipment used is broken. Finally the objectives can define the solution type you prefer, e.g. maximise patient satisfaction or maximise efficiency [5]. A COP solver takes a problem modelled as a COP and attempts to find a legal value for all the variables in the problem while doing its best to satisfy the objectives. There are two general classes of solving algorithms. Local search algorithms only consider a small part of the problem at a time, so are able to find a solution quickly, but it is rarely the best solution. Complete algorithms consider the entire search space, so take a long time, but will always find the best solution [5].

Distributed Constraint Optimisation Problems (DCOPs) are the same as COPs except that the problem is distributed across many agents. In this model, each agent has its own local COP which is considered to be a variable in the larger DCOP. In addition the concept of privacy is introduced, since any variable in the local COPs that is referenced by a constraint or an objective in the DCOP must be public, while all other variables are private [6].

A Dynamic Distributed Constraint Optimisation Problem (DynDCOP) extends the DCOP with explicit modelling of how the problem changes over time. This change can take the form of adding or removing any of the aspects of the problem, whether a variable, a constraint or even an entire agent. By doing so it becomes much easier to cope with the changes. In the previous versions of COPs, if the problem changes the solver has to be terminated. The problem is then updated to reflect the change and the solver is restarted. All previous work done by the solver is lost at this point, and in extreme cases can prevent it ever finding a solution. DynDCOP solvers are able to cope with such changes. They only throw out the previous work that is now invalid, so they are able to find and maintain a solution even when the problem changes quickly [7].

Local search solvers are ideally suited for DynDCOPs as they keep less of an internal state. As less of their work is invalidated when the problem changes, they can recover faster. Complete solvers have more work to redo before they can find a new solution. Recently, some algorithms, such as R-DPOP [8], Dynamic Constraint Optimisation Ant Algorithm (DynCOAA) [9] and Support Based Distributed Optimisation (SBDO) [10,11] have been developed to solve DynDCOPs.

R-DPOP is a complete algorithm and an extension of the DPOP algorithm, which is built on the dynamic programming paradigm. A Depth First Search (DFS) tree construction algorithm constantly runs in the background to create and maintain the hierarchy between agents. Meanwhile each agent calculates the optimal assignment to itself for each possible value of its parents and pseudoparents, taking into account the utility of its children and communicates that to its parent. These utility hypercubes must constantly be repaired as the problem changes. This algorithm is capable of finding the optimal solution if the problem remains static for long enough. It also requires very few messages, but they can be large messages, which in turn means that each agent has high memory requirements to store the messages.

DynCOAA is built using ant colony optimisation technology, and therefore is a local search algorithm. New ants can be spawned anywhere within the agent network and visit (assign a value to) every variable within one agent before moving onto the next agent. Global communication between agents is required to update the pheromone trails as well as to communicate the best solution found. This does allow the algorithm to ensure that the global solution quality is monotonically non-decreasing. When the problem changes all of the ants that are currently travelling become invalid and so further communication is required to destroy those ants and spawn new ones.

Neither of those algorithms take into consideration the possibility of agents failing for any reason, such as hardware failure or malicious attack. It is particularly important to be able to continue solving even when agents fail in dynamic solvers, as they are often expected to run continuously for a long duration. SBDO uses a unique communication strategy based on argumentation which allows it to overcome this problem. The argumentation strategy means that any agent can send a message to any of its neighbours at any time, and makes it a local search algorithm allowing the algorithm to react very quickly to changes in the problem and then propagating modifications to the solution only as far as is required. As there is no global communication, not even indirectly, the algorithm can scale to very large numbers of agents. To compute a solution each agent chooses one of its neighbours as its support. It then takes the assignments it received from that agent as the premises for its own assignment, then sends that to all its neighbours as an argument.

2 Encoding

Each of the actors in the scheduling system for a Radiation Oncology department are represented by agents. Only the core actors, patients, Linear Accelerators (linacs) and simulators are considered in this paper. Other actors such as nurses, consultation rooms and oncologists will be added to the final system to be able to find the best solution. There is one agent in the DynDCOP for each actor that must participate in the scheduling process. This agent has all the relevant knowledge of the actor and is responsible for getting the best outcome for its actor. The agents in the system can be loosely grouped into two categories, person agents and resource agents.

Informally a person agent has as part of its private knowledge a set of preferences ("I would like treatment between 8am and 8:45am"), a set of constraints ("I'm not available on Thursday") and other private knowledge (treatment urgency, treatment details, pay rate, etc.) The agent's public knowledge consists of a set of variables which represent the patients current schedule, a set of constraints ("Each subsequent fraction of radiotherapy must be delivered at least

6 hours after the previous fraction") and a set of objectives ("Once committed, an appointment should not move by more than 15 minutes").

Person agents only communicate with resource agents. This is to reduce the links between agents and so minimise the exchange of messages as well as to have tighter control over the information flow. The typical messages sent between person agents and resource agents are "I would gain X utility from this time slot" and "you can't have this time slot". Only person agents know the specific services that a person must take part in and the order in which they occur, and the person agent is solely responsible for ensuring their schedule is correct. The schedule will be defined by private constraints.

Similarly resource agents also have public and private knowledge. The agents' public knowledge consists of the time slots are currently occupied. The occupant of any given time slot is technically public information but it can be concealed. It also contains the times when the resource is unavailable, as well as constraints such as "only one patient can occupy a given time slot". In its private knowledge, there are other constraints such as "a nurse must also be present".

Resource agents communicate with both person agents and other resource agents. The resource agents will normally be another resource that this one depends on. In general, resource agents do not communicate across hospital boundaries, preventing the information flow that may violate hospital privacy. The Resource agents have no knowledge of the rest of the schedule of each person agent, or even other resource agents. They are solely responsible for ensuring that the resource they represent is optimally utilised.

Formally the COP representing a person agent is:

$$COP_p = \langle \mathcal{X}_p, \mathcal{D}_p, \mathcal{C}_p, \mathcal{R}_p, \mathcal{K}_p \rangle$$

- $\mathcal{X}_p$ is all the variables this agent has. $\mathcal{X}_p = \{T_0, \ldots, T_n\}$
  - T is a single time slot, typically an entry in a calendar. $T = \langle s, e, d, r, c \rangle$
    - s is the start time for this time slot.
    - e is the end time for this time slot.
    - d is the date of this time slot.
    - r is the resource that is used/supported during this time slot.
    - c is whether this time slot has been confirmed.
- $\mathcal{D}_p$ is the domain for each of the variables. $\mathcal{D}_p = \{D_{pm}, D_{ps}, D_{pe}, D_{pd}, D_{pc}\}$
  - D_{pr} is the set of all resources.
  - $D_{ps} = D_{pe}$ are the set of all minutes in a day, 0000 – 2359.
  - D_{pd} is the set of dates in the Gregorian calender.
  - $D_{pc} = \{\text{True}, \text{False}\}$
- $\mathcal{C}_p$ is the set of all constraints that are local to this agent. This is almost entirely dependant on what person this agent represents.
  - No pair of appointments can overlap.
- $\mathcal{R}_p$ is the set of objective functions local to this agent. This is also entirely dependant on what person this agent represents.
- $\mathcal{K}_p$ is the agents knowledge. This is all private information that is defined by what person this agent represents.

The extra elements required for a patient agent are:

- $\mathcal{C}_p$ is the set of all constraints that are local to this agent. Covered formally later.
  - Each fraction must be at least 6 hours after the previous fraction.
  - The first fraction must be on or after the patients ready for care date.
  - The patient must receive 9 or 10 fractions per fortnight.
  - The end time must be exactly duration minutes after the start time.
  - The radiotherapy schedule must be synchronised with their chemotherapy schedule.
  - Two fractions can't have the same number.
  - All fractions must be delivered by the same linac.
  - The scheduling appointment must be before all the treatment appointments.
- $\mathcal{R}_p$ is the set of objective functions local to this agent. Covered formally later.
  - Once committed an appointment should not move by more than 15 minutes.
  - Minimise the date of the last fraction.
  - Respect the patients preferences.
- $\mathcal{K}_p$ is the agents knowledge. $\mathcal{K}_p = \langle r, d, n, p, c \rangle$
  - r is the patients ready for care date.
  - d is the number of minutes required to deliver one fraction.
  - n is the number of fractions required.
  - p is the patients preferences.

The COP for representing a resource agent is:

- $\mathcal{X}_p$ is all the variables this agent has. $\mathcal{X}_p = \{T_0, \ldots, T_n\}$
  - T is a single time slot, typically an entry in a calendar. $T = \langle s, e, d, r, c \rangle$
    * s is the start time for this time slot.
    * e is the end time for this time slot.
    * d is the date of this time slot.
    * R is the set of resources that are used/supported during this time slot.
    * P is the set of people that are required to operate this resource.
    * c is whether this time slot has been confirmed.
- $\mathcal{D}_p$ is the domain for each of the variables. $\mathcal{D}_p = \{D_{pm}, D_{ps}, D_{pe}, D_{pd}, D_{pc}\}$
  - D_{rr} is the power set of all resources.
  - D_{rp} is the power set of all people.
  - $D_{rs} = D_{pe}$ are the set of all minutes in a day, 0000 – 2359.
  - D_{rd} is the set of dates in the Gregorian calender.
  - $D_{pc} = \{\text{True}, \text{False}\}$
- $\mathcal{C}_p$ is the set of all constraints that are local to this agent. This is almost entirely dependant on what resource this agent represents.
  - No pair of appointments can overlap.

- $\mathcal{R}_p$ is the set of objective functions local to this agent. This is also entirely dependant on what resource this agent represents.
- $\mathcal{K}_p$ is the agents knowledge. This is both public and private information and is largely dependant on what resource this agent represents.
  - l is the resources physical location.
  - c is the cost of operating this resource.

The extra elements required for a linac agent are:

- $\mathcal{C}_p$ is the set of all constraints that are local to this agent. Covered formally later.
  - A nurse, a patient and two physicists are required to operate the linac.
  - No appointments between 0000 and 0800.
  - No appointments between 1800 and 2359.
  - No appointments on weekends.
  - No appointments between 1200 and 2359 when day of week is Friday and week of year is even.
- $\mathcal{R}_p$ is the set of objective functions local to this agent.
  - minimise the amount of time each day when this resource is free.

The extra elements required for a simulator agent are:

- $\mathcal{C}_p$ is the set of all constraints that are local to this agent. Covered formally later.
  - A patient and a physicist and an oncologist are required to operate the simulator.
  - No appointments between 0000 and 0800.
  - No appointments between 1800 and 2359.
  - No appointments on weekends.
- $\mathcal{R}_p$ is the set of objective functions local to this agent.
  - minimise the amount of time each day when this resource is free.

This encoding intentionally does not include the concept of hospital boundaries. The intention is to allow easy communication between hospitals, and explicitly encoding them would restrict that. However they do still exist and must be taken into account, both for privacy and to identify nearby resources. It is flexible enough that the basic types of agents can be extended to model most things in the health system. There are some resources, such as waiting rooms, that can not be easily modelled using the classes of agents presented here. However it is easy enough to create a new class of agent to represent them.

We shall illustrate how the agents interact using a simple example. Consider a radiotherapy treatment centre with 2 simulators, 2 Linear Accelerators (linac) and 20 patients, where each patient must undergo a simulation in a simulator before being treated on a linac. Each patient will be assigned to one of the two simulators and one of the two linacs, resulting in a neighbour graph that is similar to the one in figure 2 Initially they will be assigned randomly, so that each patient is then a neighbour of exactly one linac and one simulator. They will then start negotiating for their preferred time slot. Those who think they can get a better time slot on the other resource will change their resource assignment. Removing the first linac or simulator from their list of neighbours and adding the other one. In this way the patients will rearrange themselves, both on resources and time slots to get a solution that optimises the objectives.

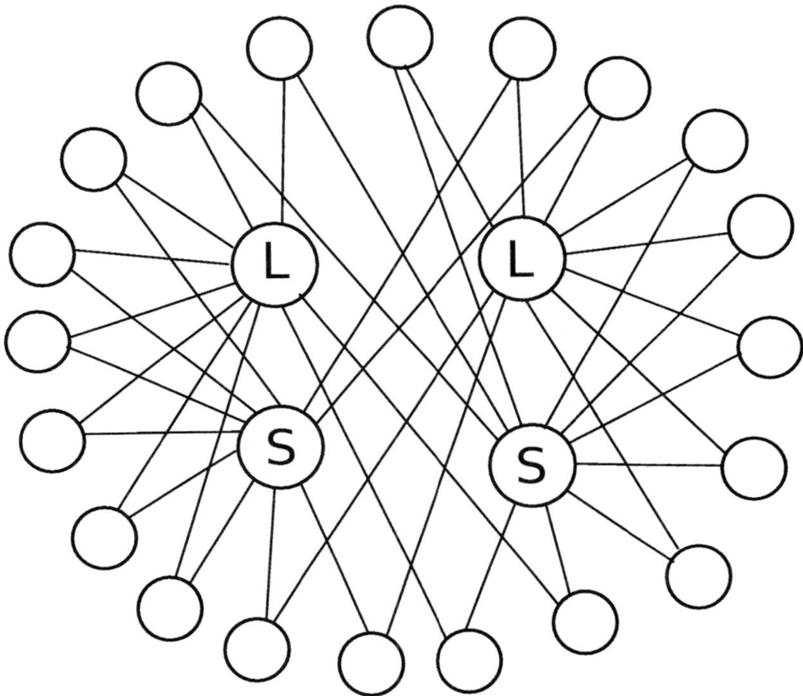

Fig. 1. The connections between agents in this model

3 Solving

The Support Based Distributed Optimisation algorithm was designed to solve problems of the sort where there are large numbers of distributed agents that must communicate to improve some optimisation objectives [10,11].

To achieve this, a novel augmentation strategy is used as the basis for inter-agent communication. Each agent chooses one agent (possibly itself) to be its support, and only what the agent's support claims in its latest argument is what the agent believes to be true about the world. Only this 'true' information is used by the agent when assigning values to its own variables.

When choosing which agent to use as its support, the agent always chooses the strongest argument. This is decided (in decreasing order) by the utility claimed in the argument, the number of agents contributing to the argument and randomly.

By doing so the assignments that lead to the highest utility are adopted by more agents and so are more likely to appear in the final solution.

The arguments from other agents are not completely ignored. They must be checked to see if they are consistent with the hard constraints. Each time a new argument is received it must be checked against all the constraints that the agent knows. Though the agent still does not consider other arguments, it only considers the assignments within this argument. If the combination of assignments is inconsistent then the agent must send a rebuttal. In this way it guarantees that all the constraints will be satisfied.

This problem formulation leads to a star shaped communication network, with resource agents as the hubs and person agents as the leaves. There will be significantly higher density of links within the bounds of each hospital than there is going between hospitals. The links between hospitals correspond to patients that are using resources from both hospitals or resources in one hospital that requires the support of another hospital. The structure of the communication network shows that there is only a small amount of data transferred between hospitals, Which minimises the potential for violating privacy.

Unfortunately SBDO is not well suited to solving problems with this structure. This is because the algorithm relies on agents forming coalitions in order to influence the value of more powerful agents. However in star shaped networks the weak (person) agents can not communicate with each other to form a coalition and influence the powerful (resource) agents. Because of this the resource agent will only take notice of one of the (potentially hundreds of) neighbouring person agents. In order to overcome this the way that resource agents operate must be modified.

Because of this, resource agents must be SBDO wrappers around a centralised optimisation algorithm. The centralised algorithm uses the partial knowledge of each person agents preferences to attempt to schedule treatments. When there is a conflict between two agents, A and B, it must elicit more preferences from the agents. To do so it constructs an argument using A as support to send to B, and an argument using B as support to send to A. If more than two agents conflict, the algorithm chooses to support the set of assignments that leads to the best utility. The agents response (or lack thereof) indicates their preferences. While the resource agent retains the person agent as a neighbour it caches the latest utilities received from the person agent.

In the standard SBDO algorithm when an agent is removed from the set of neighbours, all the knowledge related to that agent is also removed, which poses problems in this setting. Because when a patient agent changes the resource it plans to use, it adds the new resource agent to its neighbours and removes the old one. However it must remember the utility gained from using the previous resource, both to ensure that the change leads to a better solution, and to ensure that it doesn't change back if the new solution is also sub-optimal. These saved utility values do not have to be kept up to date, they simply serve to inform the agent's later choices. Only person agents need to retain this information.

For every resource agent that a person agent contacts, the person agent must record the most recent local utility gain from the schedule offered by that agent. That is, the value of the objective functions that depend, either directly or indirectly, on a variable controlled by that agent. The agent can then periodically compare the estimated utility gain from other resource agents, either a best guess or the stored value, to decide if it is worthwhile changing. To influence how often person agents change between resources, objective functions can be defined that emulate stability constraints in other algorithms. These serve to provide an estimate of both the cost associated with changing to a different resource, and the probable utility gain.

4 Example

A patient begins to interact with the oncology system in a hospital as soon as they are referred with a diagnosis of cancer. One of the practical constraints within a radiotherapy department is that a patient should receive all their treatment on the same linac, thereby limiting the opportunities for load balancing. As a result, load balancing must occur when the patient is first given a referral.

When a patient is diagnosed with cancer, they firstly need to meet their doctor for a consultation to discuss their options for treatment. At this point an agent containing all of the patient's current relevant information/preferences is created by the referring doctor to represent the patient. The patient agent will then consider all of the possible places that the patient could receive treatment, and eventually determine the "optimal" place for the patient to receive treatment. The "optimal" place is determined by the minimum time for daily sequential radiotherapy treatments to commence on the linac, having been seen by the oncologist and having undergone simulation and planning. On determining this optimal solution, the agent will reserve a consultation appointment with the oncologist, reserve a time for simulation and reserve treatment slots on the linac. A summary of this solution, the consultation date and treatment start date, will be presented to the real patient for approval. If accepted the reserved consultation, simulation and first treatment appointments are confirmed. Subsequent treatment appointments cannot be confirmed as they are determined by the oncologist at consultation or, less commonly, at simulation. The referring doctor can then provide the referral to the oncologist and confirm the appointment time with the patient.

During the consultation with the oncologist, the details of the patient's treatment are agreed and the simulation time is confirmed. The agent can now confirm the provisional treatment times. The resource agent representing the linac can confirm individual treatment times some time before they are scheduled.

5 Conclusion

Significant gains in the efficiency of the public health systems can be achieved by good scheduling. Support Based Distributed Optimisation is ideally suited to this task as it is dynamic, distributed, fault tolerant and guarantees that the constraints will be satisfied.

We have shown how radiotherapy treatments can be modelled as a dynamic distributed constraint optimisation problem. In demonstrating the weaknesses of support based distributed optimisation, we have provided a process that can solve this problem efficiently. Finally we have described the interactions between the actors and the scheduling system for a typical scenario.

References

1. Cohen, S.: The pursuit of efficiency: Automation in health care. Hospital and Healthcare Management
2. Cascardo, D.C.: Smart scheduling: The key to practice efficiency. Medscape Today (2000)
3. Van Houdenhoven, M., van Oostrum, J.M., Hans, E.W., Wullink, G., Kazemier, G.: Improving operating room efficiency by applying bin-packing and portfolio techniques to surgical case scheduling. In: Anesthesia & Analgesia (2007)
4. Foundation, Q., `http://www.qefoundation.org` (accessed August 20, 2010)
5. Schiex, T., Fargier, H., Verfaillie, G.: Valued constraint satisfaction problems: Hard and easy problems. In: Proceedings of the 15th International Joint Conference on Artificial Intelligence, Montreal, Canada (1995)
6. Yokoo, M., Durfee, E.H., Ishida, T., Kuwabara, K.: The distributed constraint satisfaction problem - formalization and algorithms. IEEE Transactions on Knowledge and Data Engineering 10(5), 673–685 (1998)
7. Verfaillie, G., Jussien, N.: Constraint solving in uncertain and dynamic environments: A survey. Constraints 10(3), 253–281 (2005)
8. Petcu, A., Faltings, B.: R-dpop: Optimal solution stability in continuous-time optimization. In: IAT 2007 (November 2007)
9. Mertens, K.: An Ant-Based Approach for Solving Dynamic Constraint Optimization Problems. PhD thesis, Katholieke Universiteit Leuven (December 2006)
10. Billiau, G., Ghose, A.: Sbdo: A new robust approach to dynamic distributed constraint optimisation. In: Yang, J.-J., Yokoo, M., Ito, T., Jin, Z., Scerri, P. (eds.) PRIMA 2009. LNCS, vol. 5925, pp. 641–648. Springer, Heidelberg (2009)
11. Billiau, G., Chang, C.F., Ghose, A.: Sbdo: A New Robust Approach to Dynamic Distributed Constraint Optimisation. In: Desai, N., Liu, A., Winikoff, M. (eds.) PRIMA 2010. LNCS(LNAI), vol. 7057, pp. 11–26. Springer, Heidelberg (2011)

Software Agents in Clinical Workflow, Clinical Guidelines and Clinical Trial Medicine

Alexis Andrew Miller[1,2] and Fiona Hegi-Johnson[3]

[1] Illawarra Cancer Care Centre, Wollongong Hospital, Wollongong NSW 2500 Australia
[2] Centre for Oncology Informatics, Illawarra Health & Medical Research Institute, University of Wollongong, Gwynneville NSW 2500 Australia
[3] Department of Radiation Oncology, Royal North Shore Hospital, St Leonards NSW 2056 Australia

Abstract. Software agents can be used to assist with or even automate many parts of a business process or workflow. In this paper we describe what needs to be done to use software agents to assist the oncology trial workflow.

The most pressing problem is simply getting the existing data in a machine readable format. To this end we propose the Clinical Knowledge Markup Language for representing all this information.

Agents can then be used for a multitude of tasks such as identifying patients that are eligible for a given trial, suggesting treatment based on past trials and automating data collection.

1 Introduction

Software agents are a pervasive informatics technology, with usefulness in processes of information and workflow management. A software agent can be designed to embody and fulfil almost any process with rules and requirements.

Medical practice can be viewed as having components in common with a business process. However there are substantial differences between a business processes such as manufacturing an automobile and achieving a cure in a patient with cancer.

For most of its history, oncology has been driven by data. Initially data was largely anecdotal, then larger cumulative reports of practices that showed promise, and subsequently into the modern era where the usefulness of a treatment is determined by clinical trial rather than expert opinion or populism. Pragmatically, if something is thought to work, it can be shown to work irrespective known mechanism. As a result, modern oncological practice heavily reflects what has been discovered in clinical trials – as it should. These reports of what works are reflected in published Clinical Guidelines, of which there are now a plethora. But before Clinical Guidelines are produced, clinical trials will have already penetrated into routine clinical practise. The trials will also have lead to new and more specific trial questions.

It should be stressed that the clinical work which is undertaken within a trial and the clinical work which is undertaken outside a clinical trial do not differ in type. Like the Clinical Guideline specification, the clinical trial work is, in fact, normal clinical activity.

N. Desai, A. Liu, and M. Winikoff (Eds.): PRIMA 2010, LNAI 7057, pp. 561–574, 2012.

From a business perspective, both the clinical guideline and the oncology trial are processes of workflow and information flow that have a rigid form of manual process management imposed. Being within a specific domain, these guideline and trial processes could be negotiated by a series of software agents.

2 Structure of a Clinical Trial

Within the clinical trial there are several people and many temporal events that occur before a patient can be entered into a trial and then finally be said to have successfully negotiated the trial process.

The initial process of protocol development and site accreditation is not dealt with here.

The trial infrastructure imposes two organisational facets on to the normal clinical workflow:

There is the organisational structure which selects the eligible patient and excludes the ineligible patient, thereby constraining the heterogeneity introduced in indiscriminate patient selection.

There is the organisational structure of specific and restrictive business rules defining the nature of the clinical workflow, thereby constraining it to match the workflow described in the protocol.

This constrained clinical workflow mandates the collection of specified data (Clinical Report Forms – CRF) from parts of the clinical workflow which are then submitted to the trial apparatus as the recorded data. In all cases the primary data resides within the clinical workflow. Quality assurance of the trial consists of verifying that data collection is complete and that data collected and presented to the trial agency is indeed identical to the data in the clinical record. Several well publicised cases have made trial organisations highly particular about the veracity of trial data [1][2]. Given that billions of dollars of trade hinge on successful, unimpeachable trials, commercial groups pay large sums of money to ensure veracity of trial results, even though the incremental costs are modest [3].

The trial process in medicine is well established with costs associated with data collection, quality assurance and storage. The current paradigm for trial conduct involves the employment of trial staff who spend their time chasing clinicians to complete data forms and to sign documents. Each new trial process requires a trial coordinator to shepherd the normal clinical workflow to meet the trial specifications. Each new trial coordinator has to be housed and paid. The data collected must then be checked by external auditors.

While the clinical trial business model has been refined and now has high levels of governance, the nature of the clinical trial business has not changed since the inception of the randomised clinical trial. The steps of the clinical trial can be divided into clinical and non-clinical components. (Figure 1)

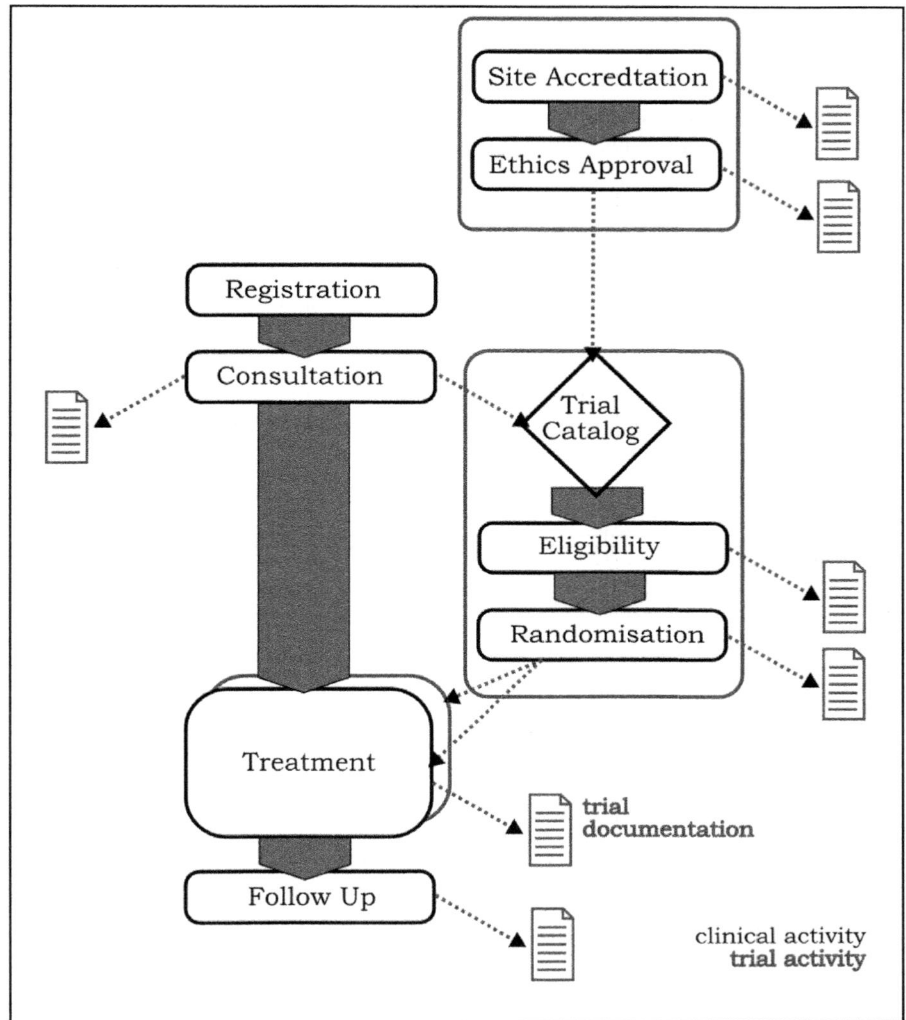

Fig. 1. Clinical workflow V Trial workflow

The non-clinical component consists of three components. The first occurs before the clinical phase of the trial begins and includes protocol development leading to protocol documentation, establishment of quality assurance procedures, data collection protocols and forms, and training of interested staff. Within local institutions, this phase includes seeking local Ethics Committee approval for the experimental protocol and the employment and training of Trial Coordinators.

The second phase begins when the protocol is open to patients who enter the trial through the clinical phase. This phase includes the screening of patients to find suitable candidates who must meet inclusion and not meet exclusion criteria (Figure 2). Once a patient has the required profile, has been offered inclusion on the trial and consents to be involved, the process of randomisation to a specific treatment is undertaken. That specific treatment is then delivered to the patient over a treatment course, following which the patient enters a follow up period. This trial phase is characterised by the production, recording, storage and transfer of data relating to the patient's treatment and response to treatment. Typically these data are recorded in standardised nomenclature which is increasingly becoming internationally standardised [4].

The final stage notionally commences after the clinical phase has ended, but is increasing seen during the clinical phase as the requirements for data governance are increased. Data from a patient who has completed therapy is submitted and reviewed for quality. Where complex idiosyncratically variable treatments, such as surgery or radiotherapy, are used, data relating to the quality of the therapy might be required before the patient can proceed on the protocol. The outcomes of treatment are recorded in the clinical notes and also reported according to trial protocol.

ELIGIBILITY: *(See Section 3.0 for details)*

Histologically confirmed localized adenocarcinoma of the prostate with an elevated PSA. *(Section 3.1.1)*
- Estimated risk of lymph node involvement > 15% *(see the risk equation in Section 1.4.3)*
- No involved common iliac or para-aortic nodes or distant mets.
- Pathological lymph-node-positive patients are ineligible.
- No prior cryosurgery for prostate cancer.
- Karnofsky performance status ≥ 70.
- No prior or concurrent hormonal therapy *(except allowed by Section 3.1.6)*, radiation or chemotherapy.
- PSA is mandatory; *(PSA must be ≤ 100)*
- Liver function tests ≤ 1.2 x upper limits of normal.
- Must be ineligible for RTOG 94-08
- Treatment must begin within 6 weeks after randomization and within 60 days of surgical staging.
- Must sign a study-specific consent form prior to randomization.
- Previous or concurrent cancers other than superficial basal or squamous cell skin carcinoma unless disease free for at least five years.

Fig. 2. Inclusion and Exclusion criteria for the RTOG 94-13 trial

Clinical and trial data are not identical. A portion of the clinical data is included in the trial data, but there is additional data submitted to the trial organisation which is not part of the clinical record. The trial data is more stringent in requiring a positive or negative response to certain questions which might be obtained in the normal clinical setting but not recorded, or not required because of questionable clinical relevance. Trial data is increasingly wide reaching in an attempt to get more standardised data on the chance that it might prove to be relevant [5] or prove useful in establishing a rationale for use in the event of primary end points being negative. Formal Quality of Life (QOL) estimates during clinical trials of treatment efficacy are such an extension - if an intervention shows no improvement in cure but has a better QOL, the new intervention can be justified. In both cases, the increasing data requirements impose a hefty workload increase which results in substantial costs [5]. Patient-derived assessments might be more truthful and easier to obtain than physician-derived assessments.

So while the business processes of the clinical trial are well established, there has been little abstraction of the process so that all trials can be mapped to a single relevant model. Given that trial data and clinical data overlap, and that trial data is extracted during the clinical workflow, and that trial treatment is delivered as if it were clinical treatment, the business model for trials can be expected to substantially overlap with the business model for routine clinical workflow.

This overlap can clearly be seen in treatment recommendations for patients outside of trial protocols and eligible for trial protocols. Routine clinical workflow is not a random assignment of therapy to any patient, there are clinical recommendations based on previous trial results that determine what will be offered to the next patient. In fact, after a trial has produced a finding of a significant benefit, future patients eligibility for this treatment is determined by matching the same inclusion and exclusion criteria as were used in recruiting patients onto the trial that resulted in a positive outcome. This is the nature of the advancement of medicine in the modern scientific era which is based on experimentation. These changes have seen the promotion of the notion of 'personalised medicine' – treatment fitted more closely to your profile, whether a demographic or a DNA profile. However, the nirvana of 'personalised medicine' cannot be achieved unless the clinical record includes all of the patient's data points before making a decision. As current trial data includes non-clinical information (such as DNA profiles), this data will need to become part of the clinical record to achieve personalised treatment. Such changes have happened in the past as seen with Estrogen Receptor levels in breast cancer and PSA levels in prostate cancer.

The nature of the business process described however argues that any software built to service the clinical portion of a trial must, ipso facto, be able to be used for routine clinical management. Sadly this is not the case. Business process models for normal clinical workflow or information flow do not exist except as single departmental instances (Ford, Johns Hopkins). Trial software is tailored towards the data requirements of trial organisations and clinical software is rarely capable of being used to support trials (although there are exceptions - Miller HIMJ 2006). Unfortunately, business process model and clinical trial development occur in different professional groups who know little about the others' requirements, a pattern also existing between business people and requirement engineers. (Armanas 2007) Finding a language that can specify a software model as well as a clinical business rule would assist in bridging this divide.

These semantic questions about the use and re-use of clinical data whether derived from a patient to inform treatment choice, or from a clinical trial protocol to inform eligibility, or from a clinical trial result to direct therapy offered, are not new (Miller).

3 The Clinical Guideline

The clinical guideline is based on the results of the clinical trial and seeks to curtail variability in the management of similar and standard patients. The guideline does not mandate adherence, rather it advises what the current 'gold standard' is.

Like the clinical trial, it is applicable to a specific subset of patients who meet certain diagnosis, stage and eligibility criteria.

4 Software Agents in Trial Medicine

The major obstacles for trials are the identification of eligible patients [6], and the organisation of data collection. These obstacles increase the duration time of trials and also increase the costs of trials as people are used to ensure that the data collection is timely and successful. Agents have a role in both of these processes.

Agents can be designed to identify patients eligible for a particular trial by real time assessment of data entered into Oncology Information Systems (OIS). The rational use of the OIS with respect to timely identification of data deficits and analysis has already been described [7].

The second requirement in trials is a mechanism for coordinating all of the events, assessments and data submissions required by the trial. Agents are also adept at managing recurring events based upon schedules, and instituting QA routines to ensure that data is provided and consistent. Agents can automate the booking of patients for assessment by oncologists and present the required assessments to the clinician without prompting the required data collection.

5 Software agents in Clinical Medicine

Where patient accrual into a trial has been managed by a software agent, the same agent can be used to also recognise similar patients if the trial eventually proves to establish a new standard of treatment. The use of these agents in clinical practice can standardise the management of cancer according to published data. It is said that we could improve cancer cure and care just by applying what we already know [8].

The use of software agents capable of scheduled contact with patients through email or SMS will permit the accumulation of a vast quantity of patient derived assessments that do not require any input from clinical staff.

6 Obstacles to the Use of Software Agents in Trial and Clinical Medicine

There are several obstacles to the implementation of agents into trial and clinical medicine which relate to software, users and markup language.

6.1 Problems with Software

Clinical departments predominantly utilise proprietary software for their needs. This software is designed for clinical workflow management. While this proprietary software may be capable of managing trial patients, developing these capabilities has a low priority in software development. In fact, the requirement of trials for a proscribed workflow including mandatory assessments is almost the antithesis of the proprietary software development paradigm which is constantly adding "functionality" to increase choice in the way that clinical work is undertaken. Generally non-trial departments do not take kindly to having their clinical workflow constrained.

This approach is short-sighted. While all patients are not the same, they are also not infinitely variable. If patients were infinitely variable, trials would not be possible. The variation that does occur is catered for within the eligibility criteria of the trial process. If a trial affects clinical practice, then the same eligibility criteria apply in routine management. However, in clinical practice the repeated description of routine treatment by clinicians is not supported by the commercial software.

6.2 Problems with Software Use

The use of software agents requires a software system populated with data, on which to watch and act. A less recognised requirement is that the data be entered into the software system at a time when the software agents have the desired impact.

Software agents cannot act on paper. Software agents cannot act on a software system lacking data. Software agents cannot efficiently inform about eligibility for trials when the data is entered at the end of the patient's treatment.

In short, the rational, efficient use of software agents requires that a software system already be in place, that it is in routine use, and that the nature of its use serves the purpose of the agent [9]. Thus an agent designed to find patients for trial inclusion as they present to a clinical department must have the patient's data entered into the information system before or when they arrive in the department [10]. Developing this system of operation is a major undertaking [11].

While there is trial-based software, it is not used in the clinical scenario to manage patients and so cannot be used to identify eligible patients within normal work flow.

6.3 Lack of a Communication Protocol between the Clinical and Trial Scenarios

If the previous assertions are correct, a protocol for the specification of a clinical trial will also include the specification of routine clinical workflow, and a specification for the reporting of clinical trials that makes abstracts obsolete. Such a protocol would reflect the underlying knowledge structure, knowledge acquisition and clinical work flow, in short the ontology of the expert domain. This ontology would aid the design and implementation of software agents. Any agent designed to match a patient's characteristics with eligibility criteria (inclusion and exclusion) in a trial would utilise this function.

7 Clinical Knowledge Markup Language

The development of a clinical knowledge markup language could come from several sources, but must include the domain expert who is being assisted by the technology, and the published literature on which patient treatment is based. Unfortunately automated methods are error prone and immature.

I shall use a single trial as an example of the clinical trial and published literature interaction. The Radiation Therapy Oncology Group of the USA undertook a 2x2 randomised phase III trial in 1994 investigating radiotherapy fields (prostate V prostate + pelvic lymph nodes) and hormone therapy (neoadjuvant and concurrent for 4 months V adjuvant for 4 months). Known a "RTOG 94-13", the trial was specified in a protocol [12], reported in the literature [13]and is used within clinical guidelines [14], and in clinical practice [15].

The protocol includes a specification of the treatment arms and the treatment to be applied in each arm, the eligibility criteria, and outcomes to be measured.

The literature report includes a specification of the treatment arms and the treatment applied in each arm, truncated eligibility criteria, and outcomes achieved highlighting which arm is superior.

The clinical guideline includes a specification of the selected superior treatment arm and eligibility criteria.

In clinical practice, a patient receives treatment which may or may not be that of the superior treatment arm. This may be due to patient or physician preference.

The relationship between the trial protocol and literature report is demonstrated below where excerpts of the relevant documents are displayed. Each portion has been coded into a handcrafted XML format. It is plain from this coding that there is a consistent structure but this has not been specified in a formal ontology to date.

Table 1. RTOG 00394-13 trial publications

Summary of the Trial Protocol	
Radiation :	Patients on Arms 1 and 3 will receive whole pelvic irradiation to 50.4 Gy *(1.8 Gy/day five times a week x 28 fractions)* followed by a 19.8 Gy boost *(1.8 Gy/day,five times a week x 11 fractions)* to a total dose of 70.2 Gy to the prostate. **Total: 39 fractions in 8 weeks** Patients on Arms 2 and 4 will receive RT to prostate only *(1.8 Gy/day five days a week x 39 fractions)* to a total dose of 70.2 Gy. **Total: 39 fractions in 8 weeks**
Total Androgen Suppression (TAS):	Patients on Arms 1 and 2 will receive Flutamide *(two 125 mg capsules t.i.d., p.o.)* and Zoladex *(3.6 mg s.c. monthly x four months)* or Lupron, beginning 2 months before RT and continuing until RT is completed. Patients on Arms 3 and 4 will receive Flutamide and Zoladex *(or Lupron)* for four months beginning at completion of RT.
Summary of the Literature Report.	

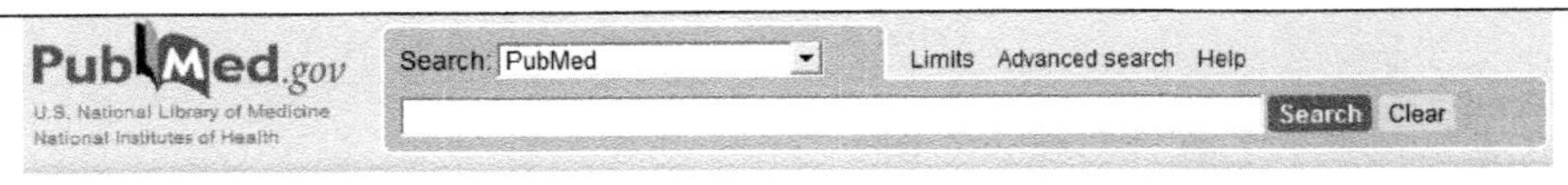

Display Settings: Abstract

Send to:

J Clin Oncol. 2003 May 15;21(10):1904-11.

Phase III trial comparing whole-pelvic versus prostate-only radiotherapy and neoadjuvant versus adjuvant combined androgen suppression: Radiation Therapy Oncology Group 9413.

Roach M 3rd, DeSilvio M, Lawton C, Uhl V, Machtay M, Seider MJ, Rotman M, Jones C, Asbell SO, Valicenti RK, Han S, Thomas CR Jr, Shipley WS; Radiation Therapy Oncology Group 9413.

University of California San Francisco, 1600 Divisadero St, Suite H1031, San Francisco, CA 94143-1708, USA. roach@radonc17.ucsf.edu

Comment in:

J Clin Oncol. 2003 May 15;21(10):1899-901.
J Clin Oncol. 2004 Jun 1;22(11):2254-5; author reply 2255-7.

Abstract

PURPOSE: This trial tested the hypothesis that combined androgen suppression (CAS) and whole-pelvic (WP) radiotherapy (RT) followed by a boost to the prostate improves progression-free survival (PFS) by 10% compared with CAS and prostate-only (PO) RT. This trial also tested the hypothesis that neoadjuvant and concurrent hormonal therapy (NCHT) improves PFS compared with adjuvant hormonal therapy (AHT) by 10%.

MATERIALS AND METHODS: Eligibility included localized prostate cancer with an elevated prostate-specific antigen (PSA) < or = 100 ng/mL and an estimated risk of lymph node (LN) involvement of 15%. Between April 1, 1995, and June 1, 1999, 1,323 patients were accrued. Patients were randomly assigned to WP + NCHT, PO + NCHT, WP + AHT, or PO + AHT. Failure for PFS was defined as the first occurrence of local, regional, or distant disease; PSA failure; or death for any cause.

RESULTS: With a median follow-up of 59.5 months, WP RT was associated with a 4-year PFS of 54% compared with 47% in patients treated with PO RT (P =.022). Patients treated with NCHT experienced a 4-year PFS of 52% versus 49% for AHT (P =.56). When comparing all four arms, there was a progression-free difference among WP RT + NCHT, PO RT + NCHT, WP RT + AHT, and PO RT + AHT (60% v 44% v 49% v 50%, respectively; P =.008). No survival advantage has yet been seen.

CONCLUSION: WP RT + NCHT improves PFS compared with PO RT and NCHT or PO RT and AHT, and compared with WP RT + AHT in patients with a risk of LN involvement of 15%.

Guideline advice for similar patients to those included in RTOG 94-13

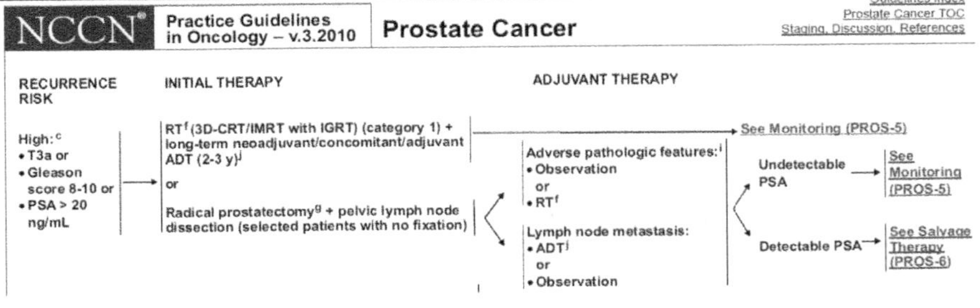

Guidelines Index
Prostate Cancer TOC
Staging, Discussion, References

Practice Guidelines in Oncology – v.3.2010 **Prostate Cancer**

PRINCIPLES OF RADIATION THERAPY

External Beam Radiotherapy:

- 3D conformal and IMRT (intensity modulated radiation therapy) techniques should be employed. Image guided radiation therapy (IGRT) is required if dose ≥ 78 Gy.
- Doses of 75.6-79 Gy in conventional 36-41 fractions to the prostate (± seminal vesicles for part of the therapy) are appropriate for patients with low-risk cancers. For patients with intermediate- or high-risk disease, doses between 78-80+ Gy provide improved PSA-assessed disease control.
- Patients with high-risk cancers are candidates for pelvic lymph node irradiation and the addition of neoadjuvant/concomitant/adjuvant ADT for a total of 2-3 y (category 1).
- Patients with intermediate risk cancer may be considered for pelvic lymph node irradiation and 4-6 mo-neoadjuvant/concomitant/adjuvant ADT.
- Patients with low risk cancer should not receive pelvic lymph node irradiation or ADT.

Table 2. XML example

Trial Protocol

```xml
<Protocol>
  <Intent>Curative</Intent>
  <Arm>
    <Arm_Title>1. P&WP + NCHT </Arm_Title>
    <Modality>
      <Radiotherapy>
        <Phase1>
          <Target>
            <Anatomy>Prostate</Anatomy>
            <Anatomy>Pelviclymph nodes<Anatomy>
          </Target>
          <Dose>50.4Gy</Dose>
          <Fractions>28</Fractions>
          <FractionsperWeek>5</FractionsperWeek>
        </Phase1>
        <Phase2>
          <Target><Anatomy>Prostate</Anatomy></Target>
          <Dose>19.8Gy</Dose>
          <Fractions>11</Fractions>
          <FractionsperWeek>5</FractionsperWeek>
        </Phase2>
      </Radiotherapy>
      <HormoneTherapy>
        <Duration>4 months</Duration>
        <StartDate>2 months before start of radiotherapy</StartDate>
        <Drug>
          <DrugName>Flutamide</DrugName>
          <Dose>250mg</Dose>
          <Frequency>three times a day</Frequency>
          <Route>oral</Route>
        </Drug>
        <Drug>
          <DrugClass>GnRH</DrugClass>
          <Option1>
            <DrugName>Zoladex (goserelin acetate)</DrugName>
            <Dose>3.6mg</Dose>
            <Frequency>monthly</Frequency>
            <Route>subcutaneous</Route>
          </Option1>
          <Option2>
            <DrugName>Lucrin (leuprorelin acetate)</DrugName>
            <Dose>7.5mg</Dose>
            <Frequency>monthly</Frequency>
            <Route>intramuscular</Route>
          </Option2>
        </Drug>
      </HormoneTherapy>
  </Arm>
  <Arm>
    <Arm_Title>2. P + NCHT </Arm_Title>
      <Modality>
        <Radiotherapy>
          <Phase1>
            <Target><Anatomy>Prostate</Anatomy></Target>
```

	<Dose>50.4Gy</Dose> <Fractions>28</Fractions> <FractionsperWeek>5</FractionsperWeek> </Phase1> <Phase2> <Target><Anatomy>Prostate</Anatomy></Target> <Dose>19.8Gy</Dose> <Fractions>11</Fractions> <FractionsperWeek>5</FractionsperWeek> </Phase2> <Phase3> <Target><Anatomy>Prostate</Anatomy></Target> <Dose>70.2Gy</Dose> <Fractions>39</Fractions> <FractionsperWeek>5</FractionsperWeek> </Phase3> </Radiotherapy> <HormoneTherapy> <Duration>4 months</Duration> <StartDate>2 months before start of radiotherapy</StartDate> <StartDate>end of radiotherapy</StartDate> <Drug> <DrugName>Flutamide</DrugName> <Dose>250mg</Dose> <Frequency>three times a day</Frequency> <Route>oral</Route> </Drug> <Drug> <DrugClass>GnRH</DrugClass> <Option1> <DrugName>Zoladex (goserelin acetate)</DrugName> <Dose>3.6mg</Dose> <Frequency>monthly</Frequency> <Route>subcutaneous</Route> </Option1> <Option2> <DrugName>Lucrin (leuprorelin acetate)</DrugName> <Dose>7.5mg</Dose> <Frequency>monthly</Frequency> <Route>intramuscular</Route> </Option2> </Drug> </HormoneTherapy> </Modality> </Arm> <Arm> ... </Arm> <Arm> ... </Arm> </Protocol>
Literature Report	<CKML> <date_start> April 1, 1995</date_start> <date_end> June 1, 1999</date_end>

```
<patients_accrued>1323 </patients_accrued>
<inclusion_criteria>
  <ICD10topography>prostate</ICD10topography>
  <stage>
    <StageGrouping_Classification>TNM
      <StageGrouping>I</StageGrouping>
      <StageGrouping>II</StageGrouping>
      <StageGrouping>III</StageGrouping>
    </StageGrouping_Classification>
    <PSA>=<100 ng/mL</PSA>
    <LN_risk_estimate>=>15%</ LN_risk_estimate>
  </stage>
</inclusion_criteria>
<Protocol_Randomized>yes</Protocol_Randomized>
<intent>curative</intent>
<median_followup>59.5 months</median_followup>
<Arm>
  <arm_name>WP + NCHT</arm_name>
    <modality>
      <Radiotherapy>
        <Radiotherapy_Timing>primary</Chemotherapy_Timing>
        <Target><Anatomy>prostate + whole pelvis</Anatomy></Target>
      </Radiotherapy>
      <Hormonetherapy>
        <Hormonetherapy_Timing>
          neoadjuvant & concurrent
        </Hormonetherapy_Timing>
      </Hormonetherapy >
    </modality>
    <outcome>
      <progression_free_survival>60%</progression_free_survival>
      <significance>P =.008</significance>
    </outcome>
  </arm>
  <arm>
  <arm_name> PO + NCHT</arm_name>
    <modality>
      <Radiotherapy>
        <Radiotherapy_Timing>primary</Chemotherapy_Timing>
        <Target><Anatomy>prostate</Anatomy></Target>
      </Radiotherapy>
      <Hormonetherapy>
        <Hormonetherapy_Timing>
          neoadjuvant & concurrent
        </Hormonetherapy_Timing>
      </Hormonetherapy >
```

```
      </modality>
      <outcome>
        <progression_free_survival>44%</progression_free_survival>
        <significance>P =.008</significance>
      </outcome>
    </arm>
    <arm>
      ...
    </arm>
    <arm>
      ...
    </arm>
    <Outcome_definition>
      <local_recurrence>yes</local_recurrence >
      <regional_ recurrence >yes</regional_recurrence>
      <distant_ recurrence >yes<distant_recurrence >
      <PSA_failure>yes</PSA_failure>
      <death>yes</death>
    </Outcome_definition>
  </Protocol_randomised>
</CKML>
```


8 Conclusion

Software agents permit standardisation of business process, even in the practice of medicine. However these agents must be employed in clinical scenarios that relate to a particular patient's particular predicaments. As such software agents must negotiate according to the knowledge of the expert domain.

Guidelines, trial protocols, literature reports and clinical work flow are interconnected forms of knowledge representation. The trial protocol with discovered clinical knowledge is published in a literature report that influences clinical workflow. When that influence is pervasive, the knowledge is expressed within a clinical guideline.

The knowledge representation of guidelines cannot be undertaken in isolation from the other related forms of representation. Software agents that deal with selection of patients for clinical trials will be re-used for selection of patients for routine clinical work flow and for the application of guidelines.

References

[1] Bezwoda, W., Seymour, L., Dansey, R.: High-dose chemotherapy with hematopoietic rescue as primary treatment for metastatic breast cancer: a randomized trial. Journal of Clinical Oncology 13, 2483 (1995)

[2] NCI Issues Information on Falsified Data in NSABP Trials. JNCI Journal of the National Cancer Institute 86, 487–489 (1994)
[3] Goldman, D.P., Berry, S.H., McCabe, M.S., Kilgore, M.L., Potosky, A.L., Schoenbaum, M.L., Schonlau, M., Weeks, J.C., Kaplan, R., Escarce, J.J.: Incremental treatment costs in national cancer institute-sponsored clinical trials. JAMA: The Journal of the American Medical Association 289, 2970–2977 (2003)
[4] CDISC (2010), http://www.cdisc.org/
[5] Scott, J., Hinder, V.: Quality or Quantity? Data Collection in Clinical Trials. Cancer Trials New Zealand, University of Auckland
[6] Lara, P.N., Higdon, R., Lim, N., Kwan, K., Tanaka, M., Lau, D.H., Wun, T., Welborn, J., Meyers, F.J., Christensen, S., O'Donnell, R., Richman, C., Scudder, S.A., Tuscano, J., Gandara, D.R., Lam, K.S.: Prospective evaluation of cancer clinical trial accrual patterns: identifying potential barriers to enrollment. Journal of Clinical Oncology: Official Journal of the American Society of Clinical Oncology 19, 1728–1733 (2001)
[7] Miller, A.A.: New informatics-based work flow paradigms in radiation oncology: the potential impact on epidemiological cancer research. Health Information Management Journal 34, 84–87 (2006)
[8] Peters, L.J., O'Sullivan, B., Giralt, J., Fitzgerald, T.J., Trotti, A., Bernier, J., Bourhis, J., Yuen, K., Fisher, R., Rischin, D.: Critical impact of radiotherapy protocol compliance and quality in the treatment of advanced head and neck cancer: results from TROG 02.02. Journal of Clinical Oncology 28, 2996–3001 (2010)
[9] Miller, A.A.: New informatics-based work flow paradigms in radiation oncology: the potential impact on epidemiological cancer research. Health Information Management Journal 34, 84–87 (2006)
[10] Miller, A.A., Phillips, A.K.: A contemporary case study illustrating the integration of health information technologies into the organisation and clinical practice of radiation oncology. Health Information Management Journal 34, 136–145 (2006)
[11] Yu, P., Gandhidasan, S., Miller, A.A.: Different usage of the same oncology information system in two hospitals in Sydney–lessons go beyond the initial introduction. International Journal of Medical Informatics 79, 422–429 (2010)
[12] Roach III, M., Lawton, C.A., Donnelly, B., Grignon, D.: RTOG 94-13: A Phase III Trial Comparing Definitive Whole Pelvic Irradiation Followed by a Conedown Boost to Boost Irradiation Only and Comparing Neoadjuvant to Adjuvant Total Androgen Suppression (TAS), Fairmont, VA (1994)
[13] Roach, M., DeSilvio, M., Lawton, C., Uhl, V., Machtay, M., Seider, M.J., Rotman, M., Jones, C., Asbell, S.O., Valicenti, R.K., Han, S., Thomas, C.R., Shipley, W.S.: Phase III trial comparing whole-pelvic versus prostate-only radiotherapy and neoadjuvant versus adjuvant combined androgen suppression: Radiation Therapy Oncology Group 9413. Journal of Clinical Oncology: Official Journal of the American Society of Clinical Oncology 21, 1904–1911 (2003)
[14] National Comprehensive Cancer Network, NCCN Clinical Practice Guidelines in Oncology (NCCN Guidelines™) - Prostate Cancer (2010)
[15] Zelefsky, M.J., Moughan, J., Owen, J., Zietman, A.L., Roach, M., Hanks, G.E.: Changing trends in national practice for external beam radiotherapy for clinically localized prostate cancer: 1999 Patterns of Care survey for prostate cancer. International Journal of Radiation Oncology, Biology, Physics 59, 1053–1061 (2004)

Using Belief Theory to Formalize the Agent Behavior: Application to the Simulation of Avian Flu Propagation

Patrick Taillandier[1,2], Edouard Amouroux[1,2], Duc An Vo[1,2], and Ana-Maria Olteanu-Raimond[3]

[1] IRD, UMI UMMISCO 209,
32 avenue Henri Varagnat, 93143 Bondy, France
[2] IFI, MSI, UMI 209,
ngo 42 Ta Quang Buu, Hanoi, Vietnam
[3] France Telecom, SENSE Laboratory
38-40, rue du Général Leclerc, 92794 Issy les Moulineaux, France
patrick.taillandier@gmail.com, edouard.amouroux@ird.fr, voducanvn@yahoo.com, anamaria.raimond@yahoo.fr

Abstract. Multi-agent simulations are powerful tools to study complex systems. However, a major difficulty raised by these simulations concerns the design of the agent behavior. Indeed, when the agent behavior is lead by many conflicting criteria (needs and desires), its definition is very complex. In order to address this issue, we propose to use the belief theory to formalize the agent behavior. This formal theory allows to manage the criteria incompleteness, uncertainty and imprecision. The formalism proposed divides the decision making process in three steps: the first one consists in computing the basic belief masses of each criterion; the second one in merging these belief masses; and the last one in making a decision from the merged belief masses. An application of the approach is proposed in the context of a model dedicated to the study of the avian flu propagation.

Keywords: multi-agent simulation, agent behavior formalization, belief theory, avian flu propagation.

1 Introduction

Agent-based simulations are now widely used to study complex systems. However, the problem of the agent design is still an open issue. Indeed, designing realistic agents is a complex task, in particular when their behavior is lead by many conflicting needs and desires. A reason of this complexity comes from the lack of practicable formalisms to define the agent decision-making process. In consequence, most of modern models still use ad hoc formalisms to represent the agent behaviors.

In this paper, we propose a new approach to formalize the behavior of agents: this one is based on the belief theory. This theory allows to formalize the reasoning. It can be used to make a decision between several alternatives according to a set of criteria. An advantage of this theory is that it allows to make decision even with incompleteness, uncertainly and imprecision, which is particularly interesting in the simulation context.

N. Desai, A. Liu, and M. Winikoff (Eds.): PRIMA 2010, LNAI 7057, pp. 575–587, 2012.

The paper is organized as follows. In Section 2, the general context of our work is introduced, in particular the problem of the agent behavior formalization. Section 3 is devoted to the presentation of the belief theory and its application for agent behavior design. Section 4 describes an application of our formalism to define the behavior of poultry flocks in the context of a study of the avian flu propagation. Finally, Section 5 concludes and presents the perspectives of this work.

2 Context

2.1 Formalisms to Represent the Agent Behavior

In this paper, we are interested in the formalisms used to represent the agent behavior. If many formalisms were defined in the multi-agent community (final state machine, BDI [1], motivational [2], etc.), these ones are not of much use for agent-based simulations. A reason is their inadequacy to the simulation context: a formalism, to be used in simulation, has to allow thousands of agents to make a decision from many criteria in a short amount of time. Thus, the formalisms, such as BDI, that are designed for cognitive agents, rather than reactive ones, are usually not usable for multi-agent simulation. Formalisms such as final state machine can be used for simple agents, but its representation capability is fairly limited.

2.2 Agent Behavior as a Multi-criteria Decision Making Problem

We propose to formulate the behavior of the agents as a multi-criteria decision making problem: at each step of the simulation, the agent has to make a decision: which action to apply? The action choice will be guided by the needs and desires of the agent. We propose to formulate these needs and desires as a set of criteria. Thus, the agent behavior consists in choosing, according to a set of criteria, the most pertinent action.

In the literature, several approaches were proposed to solve this type of multi-criteria decision-making problems.

A first family of approaches, called *partial aggregation* approaches, consists in comparing the different possible decisions per pair by the mean of outranking relations [3, 4].

Another family of approaches, called *complete aggregation* approaches, consists in aggregating all criteria in a single criterion (utility function), which is then used to make the decision [5, 6].

A last family of approaches, which is highly interactive, consists in devising a preliminary solution and comparing it with other possible solutions to determine the best one [7, 8].

Partial aggregation approaches allow to address the problem of criterion incompatibility but lack of clarity compare to *complete aggregation* approaches [9].

The approach we are interested in belongs to the *complete aggregation* approaches. It inherits from the signal detection theory [10] and is built on the belief theory. In the next section, we describe this approach and its application for the agent behavior design.

3 Use of the Belief Theory to Design the Agent Behavior

3.1 Multi-criteria Decision Making Using the Belief Theory

Generality

The belief theory, also called Dempster-Shafer theory, was proposed by Shafer in 1976 [11]. It is based on the Theory of Evidence introduced by Dempster [12], which concerns the lower and upper probability distributions. It allows to manage incompleteness, uncertainty and imprecision of data. It has been used with success for many applications (e.g. [13, 14, 15]).

The belief theory first defines a *frame of discernment*, noted Θ. It is composed of a finite set of hypotheses corresponding to the potential solutions of the considered problem.

$$\Theta=\{H_1, H_2, \ldots, H_N\}$$

From this frame of discernment, let us define the set of all possible assumptions, noted 2^{Θ}:

$$2^{\Theta} = \{\emptyset, \{H_1\}, \{H_2\}, \ldots, \{H_1, H_2\}, \ldots, \Theta\}$$

Each set $\{H_i, \ldots, H_j\}$ represents the proposition that the solution of the problem is one of the hypotheses of this set.

The belief theory is based on the basic belief assignment, i.e. a function that assigns to a proposition P, with $P \in 2^{\Theta}$, a value named the basic belief mass (*bbm)*, noted $m_j(P)$. It represents how much a criterion j -called source of information- supports the proposition P. The *bbm* is ranged between 0 and 1 and is defined as follows:

$$\sum_{P \in 2^{\Theta}} m_j(P) = 1$$

Decision Making Approach

In our agent behavior context, each hypothesis represents the fact that an action of the set of actions *A* is the best one. For example: "$\{H_1\}$: the best action of *A* is a_1", "$\{H_2\}$: the best action of *A* is a_2", "$\{H_1, H_2\}$: the best action of *A* can be either a_1 or a_2", etc.

The decision making approach is composed of four steps.

Step 1

This first step consists in initializing the basic belief masses. For this step, we propose to use the works of Appriou [16]. He proposed to "specialize" the criteria for one hypothesis of the discernment frame. Thus, the criteria give one's opinion only in favor of a hypothesis, in disfavor of it or do not give their opinion. For each hypothesis H_i of Θ, a subset S^i of 2^Θ is defined:

$$Si = \{\{Hi\}, \{\neg Hi\}, \Theta\}$$

- $\{H_i\}$: this proposition means that the hypothesis H_i is true.
- $\{\neg H_i\} = \Theta - \{H_i\}$: this proposition means that the hypothesis H_i is false.
- Θ: this proposition means the ignorance (i.e. every hypotheses can be true).

Thus, the initialization of the basic belief masses consists in computing, for each criterion j and for each hypothesis H_i of Θ, the basic belief masses $m_j^{H_i}(\{H_i\})$,

$$m_j^{H_i}(\{\neg H_i\}) \text{ and } m_j^{H_i}(\Theta).$$

To compute all the *bbm*, belief functions have to be defined. A belief function is a function that returns a float value between 0 and 1 according to the value of a considered criterion for a given hypothesis. Let *bf* be a belief functions, j a criterion and H_i a decision of Θ. We note $V_j^{H_i}$ the value of the criterion j for the hypothesis H_i.

$$bf(V_j^{H_i}) : \Re \to [0,1]$$

Examples of belief functions are given Sections 4.2.

Step 2

This step consists in combining criteria with each other. We propose to use the conjunctive operator introduced in [17] to provide a combined *bbm* synthesizing the knowledge from the different criteria. Let us consider two criteria C_1 and C_2. The conjunctive operator is defined as follows:

$$\forall H_i \in \Theta, \forall P \in \{\{H_i\}, \{\neg H_i\}, \Theta\}, m_{C_1C_2}^{H_i}(P) = \sum_{P' \cap P'' = P} m_{C_1}^{H_i}(P') \times m_{C_2}^{H_i}(P'')$$

The fusion of criteria can introduce a conflict, e.g. when one criterion assigns a *bbm* not null for the proposition $\{H_i\}$ and another criterion assigns a *bbm* not null for the proposition $\{\neg H_i\}$ (i.e. when $P' \cap P'' = \phi$). This conflict will be taken into account in the decision.

For example, let $\{C_1, C_2\}$ be a set of criteria, and H_1 an hypothesis of Θ. Let the *bbm* be defined as follows:

$$m_{C_1}^{H_1}(\{d_1\}) = 0.5,\ m_{C_1}^{H_1}(\{\neg d_1\}) = 0.3,\ m_{C_1}^{H_1}(\Theta) = 0.2$$
$$m_{C_2}^{H_1}(\{d_1\}) = 0.8,\ m_{C_2}^{H_1}(\{\neg d_1\}) = 0,\ m_{C_2}^{H_1}(\Theta) = 0.2$$

The belief masses resulting after the fusion of C_1 and C_2 are equal to:

$$m^{H_1}_{C_1C_2}(\{H_1\}) = m^{H_1}_{C_1}(\{H_1\}) \times m^{H_1}_{C_2}(\{H_1\}) + m^{H_1}_{C_1}(\{H_1\}) \times m^{H_1}_{C_2}(\Theta) + m^{H_1}_{C_1}(\Theta) \times m^{H_1}_{C_2}(\{H_1\}) = 0.66$$
$$m^{H_1}_{C_1C_2}(\{\neg H_1\}) = m^{H_1}_{C_1}(\{\neg H_1\}) \times m^{H_1}_{C_2}(\{\neg H_1\}) + m^{H_1}_{C_1}(\{\neg H_1\}) \times m^{H_1}_{C_2}(\Theta) + m^{H_1}_{C_1}(\Theta) \times m^{H_1}_{C_2}(\{\neg H_1\}) = 0.06$$
$$m^{H_1}_{C_1C_2}(\Theta) = m^{H_1}_{C_1}(\Theta) \times m^{H_1}_{C_2}(\Theta) = 0.04$$
$$m^{H_1}_{C_1C_2}(\phi) = m^{H_1}_{C_1}(\{H_1\}) \times m^{H_1}_{C_2}(\{\neg H_1\}) + m^{H_1}_{C_1}(\{\neg H_1\}) \times m^{H_1}_{C_2}(\{H_1\}) = 0.24$$

This conjunctive operator is commutative and associative. Thus, it is possible to combine the result of a previous fusion with the belief masses of another criterion.

Let C be the criterion set. At the end of this step, for each decision H_i of Θ, we obtain the combined belief masses $m^{H_i}_{C}(\{H_i\})$, $m^{H_i}_{C}(\{\neg H_i\})$, $m^{H_i}_{C}(\Theta)$ and $m^{H_i}_{C}(\phi)$.

Step 3

This step consists in combining hypotheses with each other. This combination is interesting because it allows to take into account in the final ranking, the fact that some criteria reject some hypothesis ($\neg H_i$).

We propose to use the Dempster operator [12] to compute the belief masses resulting from the combination of two hypotheses H_i and H_j:

$$\forall P \in 2^{\Theta}, m^{H_i,H_j}_{C}(P) = \frac{1}{1 - m^{H_i,H_j}_{C}(\phi)} \sum_{P' \cap P'' = P} m^{H_i,H_j}_{C}(P') \times m^{H_i,H_j}_{C}(P'')$$

The coefficient $\frac{1}{1 - m^{H_i,H_j}_{C}(\phi)}$ is used to normalize the belief masses obtained. In the case of a total conflict ($m^{H_i,H_j}_{C}(\phi) = 1$), no decision can be made.

For example, let Θ be composed of two hypotheses, H_1 and H_2 ($\Theta = \{H_1, H_2\}$, $\{\neg H_1\} = \{H_2\}$, $\{\neg H_2\} = \{H_1\}$). Let the belief masses be defined as follows:

$$m^{H_1}_{C}(\{H_1\}) = 0.66, m^{H_1}_{C}(\{\neg H_1\}) = 0.06, m^{H_1}_{C}(\Theta) = 0.04, m^{H_1}_{C}(\phi) = 0.24$$
$$m^{H_2}_{C}(\{H_2\}) = 0, m^{H_2}_{C}(\{\neg H_2\}) = 0.5, m^{H_2}_{C}(\Theta) = 0.5, m^{H_2}_{C}(\phi) = 0$$

The belief masses resulting from the fusion of C_1 and C_2 are equal to:

$$\begin{aligned} m^{\Theta}_{C}(\phi) = {} & m^{H_1}_{C}(\{H_1\}) \times m^{H_2}_{C}(\{H_2\}) + m^{H_1}_{C}(\{H_1\}) \times m^{H_2}_{C}(\{\phi\}) + m^{H_1}_{C}(\{\neg H_1\}) \times m^{H_2}_{C}(\{\neg H_2\}) \\ & + m^{H_1}_{C}(\{\neg H_1\}) \times m^{H_2}_{C}(\{\phi\}) + m^{H_1}_{C}(\Theta) \times m^{H_2}_{C}(\{\phi\}) + m^{H_1}_{C}(\{\phi\}) \times m^{H_2}_{C}(\{H_2\}) \\ & + m^{H_1}_{C}(\{\phi\}) \times m^{H_2}_{C}(\{\neg H_2\}) + m^{H_1}_{C}(\{\phi\}) \times m^{H_2}_{C}(\{\Theta\}) + m^{H_1}_{C}(\{\phi\}) \times m^{H_2}_{C}(\{\phi\}) = 0.27 \end{aligned}$$

$$\begin{aligned} m^{\Theta}_{C}(\{H_1\}) = {} & \frac{1}{1 - m^{\Theta}_{C}(\phi)} \times [m^{H_1}_{C}(\{H_1\}) \times m^{H_2}_{C}(\{\neg H_2\}) + m^{H_1}_{C}(\{H_1\}) \times m^{H_2}_{C}(\Theta) \\ & + m^{H_1}_{C}(\Theta) \times m^{H_2}_{C}(\{\neg H_2\})] = 0.93 \end{aligned}$$

$$\begin{aligned} m^{\Theta}_{C}(\{H_2\}) = {} & \frac{1}{1 - m^{\Theta}_{C}(\phi)} \times [m^{H_1}_{C}(\{\neg H_1\}) \times m^{H_2}_{C}(\{H_2\}) + m^{H_1}_{C}(\{\neg H_1\}) \times m^{H_2}_{C}(\Theta) \\ & + m^{H_1}_{C}(\Theta) \times m^{H_2}_{C}(\{H_2\})] = 0.04 \end{aligned}$$

$$m^{\Theta}_{C}(\Theta) = \frac{1}{1 - m^{\Theta}_{C}(\phi)} \times [m^{H_1}_{C}(\Theta) \times m^{H_2}_{C}(\Theta)] = 0.03$$

At the end of this step, a belief mass for each proposition $m_C^\Theta(\{H_1\}), m_C^\Theta(\{H_2\})$, ..., $m_C^\Theta(\{H_1, H_2\})$, ... , $m_C^\Theta(\Theta)$ is obtained.

Step 4

The last step consists in making the decision. We are only interested in the propositions that concern a unique hypothesis (one action) and not a set of hypotheses. Thus, to evaluate each proposition we propose to use the *pignistic* probability [18].

The *pignistic* probability of a proposition A is computed by the following formulae:

$$P(A) = \sum_{A \subseteq B} m(B) \frac{|A|}{|B|}$$

More a proposition maximizes this probability, more the corresponding hypothesis is true. Thus, the decision making will be based on this probability.

For example, let Θ be composed of two hypotheses, H_1 and H_2 and the belief masses of all the propositions be defined as follows:

$m_C^\Theta(\{H_1\}) = 0.93$, $m_C^\Theta(\{H_2\}) = 0.04$, $m_C^\Theta(\Theta) = 0.03$

The resulting *pignistic* probabilities are:

$P(\{H_1\}) = m_C^\Theta(\{H_1\}) \times \frac{1}{1} + m_C^\Theta(\Theta) \times \frac{1}{2} = 0.945$ $\quad P(\{H_2\}) = m_C^\Theta(\{H_2\}) \times \frac{1}{1} + m_C^\Theta(\Theta) \times \frac{1}{2} = 0.055$

Thus, H_1 has more chance to be true than H_2.

3.2 Application of the Belief Theory to Define the Agent Behavior

As presented in the previous section, the belief theory allows to make a decision from a set of possible actions according to a set of criteria.

In order to use the belief theory to formalize the behavior of an agent, the modeler has to define several elements:

- A set of criteria that allow to evaluate the different possible actions.
- For each criterion: a belief function for the hypotheses "this action is the best one", "this action is not the best one", "ignorance".

Remark that it is possible to decrease the complexity of the decision making computation by filtering the possible actions: only actions that are pareto-optimal are kept .

For some agents, it will also be possible (and mandatory) to divide the decision making process into several sub-processes. This division can be use to decrease the complexity of the decision process or to use different sets of criteria that will correspond to different steps of reasoning. Indeed, for example, it is possible to divide the decision making process into two steps: the first one consisting of choosing a general objective for the agent (e.g. eating, drinking) and a second consisting in choosing the best place to carry out this objective. Another example is given in Section 4.2.

4 Application: Model Dedicated to the Avian Flu Propagation

In order to illustrate our agent behavior formalism, we present an application of it for a real model about the H5N1 endemic in North Vietnam. After a brief presentation of a context, we focus on the agent behavior design. A description of the complete model is available in [19].

4.1 Application Context

H5N1 is still a major threat for both economy and health. It has spread over Asia, Europe and some parts of Africa. Nowadays, the endemic appears to be circumscribed to South East Asia mainly. Nevertheless, the eradication of the virus is far from being achieved. In the North Vietnam context, epidemiologists need to study the mechanisms of its local spread and persistence in the context of semi-industrialized and traditional poultry sectors, in order to limit the impact of the virus. To do so agent-based modeling has been selected for its capabilities of detailed representation, especially concerning the environment, and its flexibility.

Consequently, the purpose of the proposed models is to investigate and evaluate the importance of various factors, including poultry production, environments (especially aquatic ones), topography, etc, on the persistence and spread of H5N1 within a village or a commune in the Red River delta. Specifically, the model is about investigating the relationships between environments (as virus reservoirs) and the traditional or semi-commercial poultry production systems.

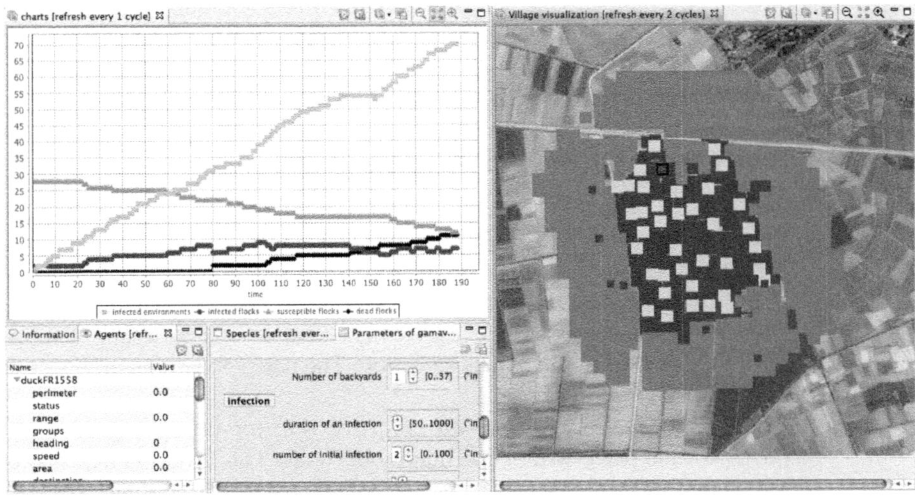

Fig. 1. Model implemented with the GAMA platform [20, 21]

The real system modeled here is the H5N1 endemics in the traditional and semi-industrial poultry production sector in the Red River Delta (North Vietnam). We limit the represented system to a village (several prototypes were determined using principle component analysis). Within this system, we focus on farms and poultry flocks. Here, poultry flocks can be duck or chicken. These flocks have various behaviors depending on the types of production. As implied by this description several natural environments are represented: building, inner-village ground, road, rice-field (flooded or dry) and pond. Figure 1 shows a snapshot of the model implemented with the GAMA platform [20, 21].

In the next section, we focus on the design of the Flock agent behavior. In particular, we illustrate how the formalism presented in Section 3 is used to design this behavior.

4.2 Flock Behavior Design

In this model, we chose to divide the agent behavior in two steps: first, the agent analyses the best places to eat, to drink and to rest, second, the agent chooses an objective. This one can be to "eat", to "drink", to "go home", "to rest" or "no objective". If no objective is defined, the agent wanders.

The division of the behavior in two steps allows to use different sets of criteria for each step. Moreover, it decreases the computational resources required to make the decision. Indeed, as we are in the context of multi-agent based simulation, the computation complexity of the process is an important factor. The choice to compute first the best places for each activity is mandatory as it impacts the choice of the objective. This allows us to represent the opportunist behavior of a flock, for example: a flock seeing a good place to eat (very close, with a lot of foods and no other flock in the neighborhood) can be tempted to eat at this place even if it is not hungry.

4.2.1 Place Selection

We defined several criteria to assess the quality of each type of places (eating places, drinking places and resting places), each type of places has the same pool types of criterions. Here the list of criterion along its "belief functions":

- *Distance to the place*: this criterion allows to assess the distance between the flock and the candidate places. The belief functions of this criterion are illustrated in Figure 2.
- *Quantity of resources*: this criterion allows to assess the quantity of food contains in the candidate places. Remark that this criterion is not use in the context of the resting place selection. The belief functions of this criterion are presented in Figure 3.
- *Quality of the place regarding an objective* (i.e. for eating objective, the quality of the place will be the quality of food). This criterion depends on the nature of places: water (W), rice-field (RF), dry-culture (DC) or ground (G). For instance, a flock usually prefers to eat in a rice-field, but it can also eat in a dry-culture field, or at worse directly on the ground or in water. Figures 4, 5 and 6 respectively present the belief functions for the *eating*, *drinking* and *resting* objective.

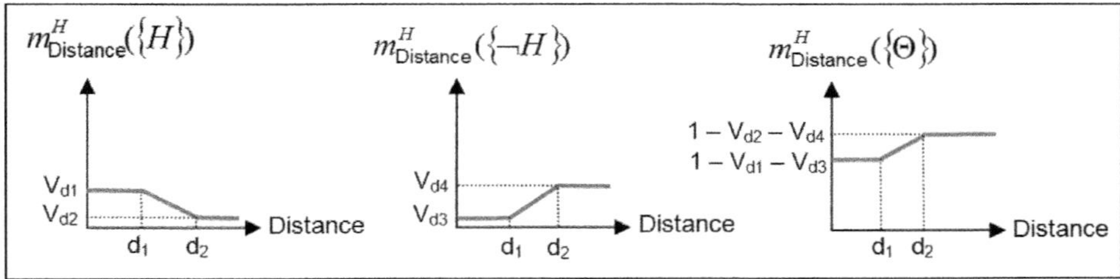

Fig. 2. Belief functions for the *distance* criterion

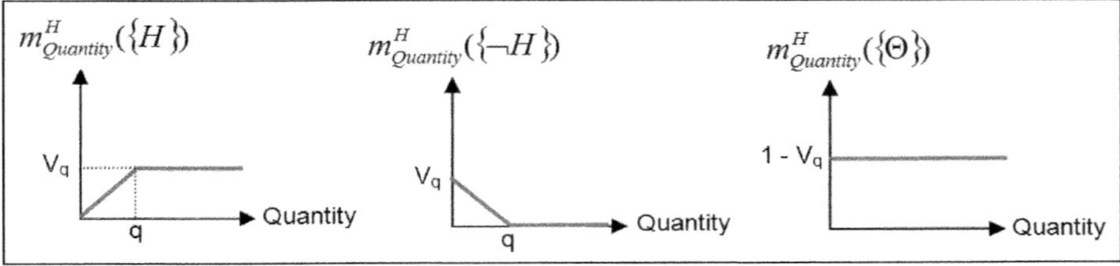

Fig. 3. Belief functions for the *quantity of resources* criterion

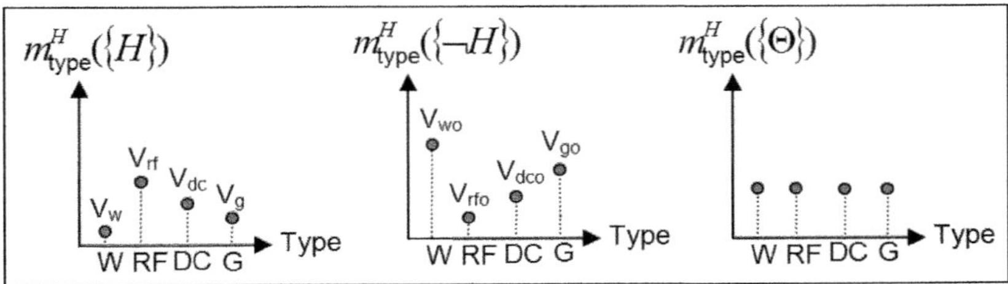

Fig. 4. Belief functions for the quality of the place for eating criterion

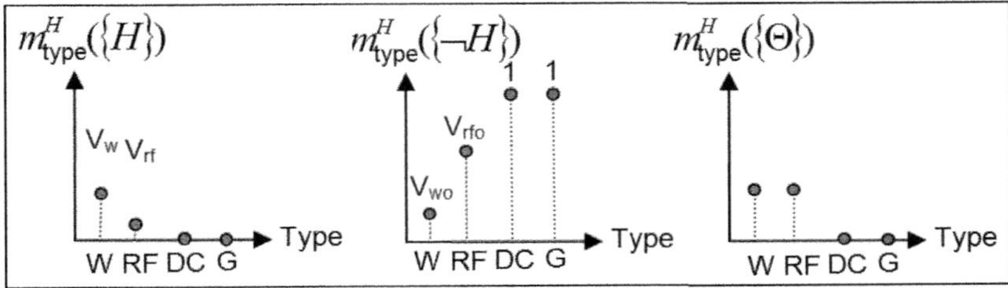

Fig. 5. Belief functions for the quality of the place for drinking criterion

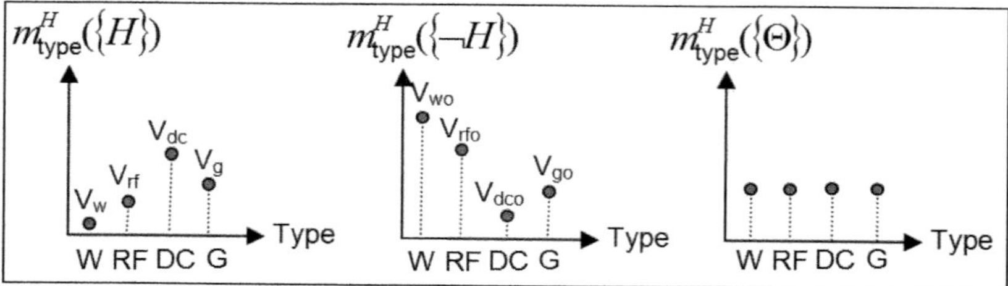

Fig. 6. Belief functions for the quality of the place for resting criterion

- *"Agoraphobia"*: usually, flocks try to avoid to go to place too near of other flocks. Thus, this criterion allows to assess this "agoraphobia". The belief functions of this criterion are illustrated in Figure 7. These functions take as input the number flocks located at distance inferior to 200m to the considered flock.

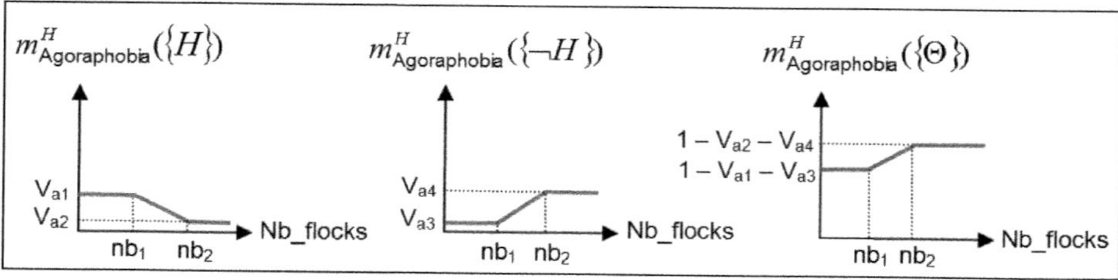

Fig. 7. Belief functions for the *agoraphobia* criterion

Once the value of each criterion has been computed, the agent filters the possible candidates in order to keep only the ones belonging to the Pareto-optimal front. Then, the decision making process presented in Section 3 is used to select the most relevant ones (one for each objective: *eating*, *drinking* and *resting*).

4.2.2 Objective Selection

The second step consists in computing the best objective among the five defined: "eating", "drinking", "resting", "go home" and "no objective". The evaluation of these objectives is based on the internal state of the agents and the time of the day (the environment influence is taken into account during the places selection). The internal state variables related to the objective selection are hunger, thirst, tiredness and "homesickness" levels. They are continuously updated according to the agent's action, for example: if a flock is resting, it will decrease its tiredness and slowly increase the hunger and thirsts levels.

The objective choice is based on several criteria that are described hereafter:

- *Time of the day*: this criterion allows to specify time intervals for each objective. Indeed, some activities are more likely to be done at specific hours (e.g. going back home at sunset). Figure 9 presents the belief functions of this criterion. These functions take as input the difference between the current time of the day and the time intervals defined for each objective.

- *Eating objective*: [7am-9am] ∪ [2pm-4pm]
- *Drinking objective*: [8am-9am] ∪ [2pm-5pm]
- *Resting objective*: [9am-2pm]
- *Going home objective*: [5pm-7pm]

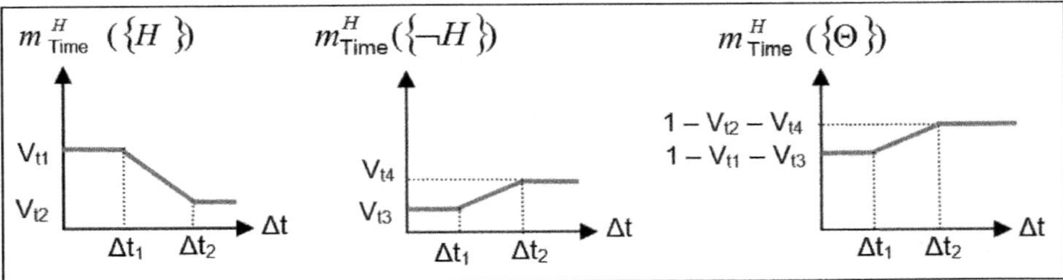

Fig. 8. Belief functions for the *time* criterion

- *Adequacy to the flock needs*: this criterion assesses the adequacy between the agent need (internal state) and the different objectives. Figure 9 presents the belief functions of this criterion. These functions take as input:
  - *Eating objective*: Hunger = max_food_level – current_ food_level
  - *Drinking objective*: Thirst =max_water_level – current_ water_level
  - *Resting objective*: Tiredness = time_since_last_rest
  - *Going home*: "Home-sickness" = time_since_last_going_home

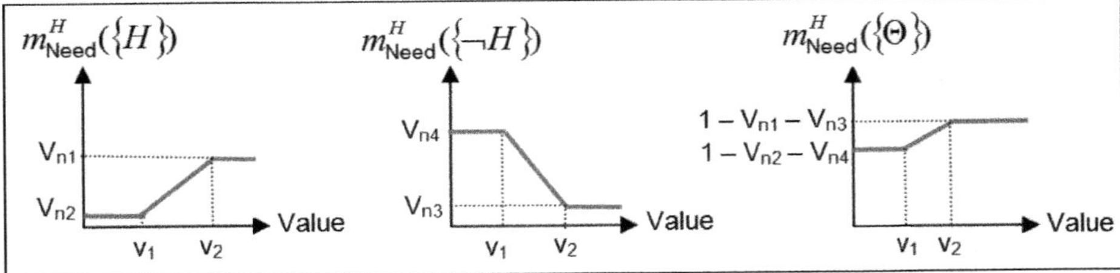

Fig. 9. Belief functions for the *need* criterion

- *Quality of the best selected place*: this criterion assesses the quality of the best selected places (the ones selected in Section 4.2.1). The belief functions of this criterion are presented in Figure 10. These functions take as input the value computed at the end of the first step. Concerning the "going home" objective, the value is constant. Indeed, only one place can be chosen for this objective (the flock farm),

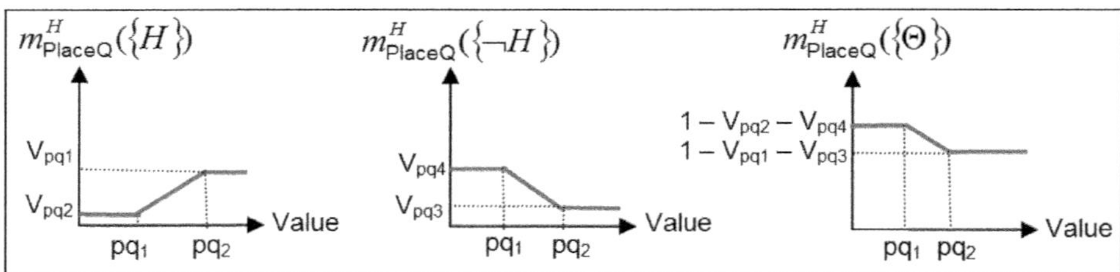

Fig. 10. Belief functions for the *place quality* criterion

Once the value of each criterion has been computed, the agent uses the decision making process presented in Section 3 to select the most relevant objective (among "eating", "drinking", "resting" and "going home"). If the pignistic probability computed for this objective is lower than a predefined threshold (defined by thematician through interaction with the simulation), no objective is selected and the agent wanders; otherwise, the agent carried out its selected objective.

5 Conclusion

In this paper, we proposed to use the belief theory to formalize the agent behavior. We present an application of this formalism for a model dedicated to study H5N1 propagation in North Vietnam. It allowed us to have a precise and realistic representation of flock's behavior while being tunable by field specialist.

In terms of perspective, we want to apply our approach to other models, in particular social model integrating numerous decision criteria. We think that it would be of even more interest to represent more elaborated behavior such has human ones.

A key issue in the use of our formalism concerns the definition of the belief functions. In this context, we propose to develop methods to learn directly through a participatory approach. This approach could be based on the one that we proposed in [22, 23].

References

1. Rao, A.S., Georgeff, M.P.: Modeling Rational Agents within a BDI-Architecture. In: Proceedings of the Second International Conference on Principles of Knowledge Representation and Reasoning, pp. 473–484 (1991)
2. Robert, G., Guillot, A.: A motivational architecture of action selection for non-player characters in dynamic environments. International Journal of Intelligent Games & Simulation 4, 1–12 (2005)
3. Figueira, J., Mousseau, V., Roy, B.: ELECTRE Methods. In: Figueira, J., Greco, S., Ehrgott, M. (eds.) Multiple Criteria Decision Analysis: State of the Art Surveys, pp. 133–162. Springer, New York (2005)
4. Behzadian, M., Kazemzadeh, R., Albadvi, A., Aghdasi, M.: PROMETHEE: A comprehensive literature review on methodologies and applications. European Journal of Operational Research (2009)

5. Geoffrion, A., Dyer, J., Feinberg, A.: An interactive approach for multicriterion optimisation with an application to the operation of an academic department. Manage. Sci. 19(4), 357–368 (1972)
6. Jacquet-Lagreze, E., Siskos, J.: Assessing a set of additive utility functions for multicriteria decision making, the UTA method. European Journal of Operational Research 10(2), 151–164 (1982)
7. Benayoun, R., Laritchev, O., de Mongolfier, J., Tegny, J.: Linear programming with multiple objective functions: Step method (stem). Math. Program. 1(3), 366–375 (1971)
8. Ignizio, J.: A review of goal programming: a tool for multi objective analysis. J. Oper. Res. Soc. 29(11), 1109–1119 (1978)
9. Ben Mena, S.: Introduction aux méthodes multicritères d'aide à la décision. Biotechnol. Agro. Soc. Environ. 4(2), 83–93 (2000)
10. Marcum, J.: A statistical theory of target detection by pulsed radar. IEEE Trans. Info. Thry. (1960)
11. Shafer, G.: A mathematical theory of evidence. Princeton University Press (1976)
12. Dempster, A.: Upper and lower probabilities induced by multivalued mapping. Annals of Mathematical Statistics 38, 325–339 (1967)
13. Omrani, H., Ion-Boussier, L., Trigano, P.: A new approach for impacts assessment of urban mobility. WSEAS Transaction on Information Science and Applications 4(3), 439–444 (2007)
14. Olteanu-Raimond, A.M., Mustière, S.: Data matching - a matter of belief. In: 13th International Symposium on Spatial Data Handling (SDH 2008), Montpellier, France (2008)
15. Taillandier, P., Duchêne, C., Drogoul, A.: Using Belief Theory to Diagnose Control Knowledge Quality. Application to cartographic generalization. In: IEEE-RIVF, Danang City, Vietnam (2009)
16. Appriou, A.: Probabilité et incertitude en fusion de données multi-senseurs. Revue Scientifique et Technique de la Défense 1, 27–40 (1991)
17. Smets, P., Kennes, R.: The transferable belief model. Artificial Intelligence 66(2), 191–234 (1994)
18. Smets, P.: Constructing the pignistic probability function in a context of uncertainty. Uncertainty in Artificial Intelligence 5, 29–39 (1990)
19. Amouroux, E., Gaudou, B., Desvaux, S., Drogoul, A.: O.D.D.: a Promising but Incomplete Formalism For Individual-Based Model Specification. Paper to appear in 'IEEE International Conference on Computing and Telecommunication Technologies' (2010)
20. Amouroux, E., Chu, T.-Q., Boucher, A., Drogoul, A.: GAMA: An Environment for Implementing and Running Spatially Explicit Multi-Agent Simulations. In: Ghose, A., Governatori, G., Sadananda, R. (eds.) PRIMA 2007. LNCS, vol. 5044, pp. 359–371. Springer, Heidelberg (2007)
21. Taillandier, P., Drogoul, A., Vo, D.A., Amouroux, A.: GAMA: A Simulation Platform that Integrates Geographical Information Data, Agent-Based Modeling and Multi-Scale Control. In: Desai, N., Liu, A., Winikoff, M. (eds.) PRIMA 2010. LNCS(LNAI), vol. 7057, pp. 244–260. Springer, Heidelberg (2011)
22. Taillandier, P., Buard, E.: Designing Agent Behaviour in Agent-Based Simulation through Participatory Method. In: Yang, J.-J., Yokoo, M., Ito, T., Jin, Z., Scerri, P. (eds.) PRIMA 2009. LNCS, vol. 5925, pp. 571–578. Springer, Heidelberg (2009)
23. Taillandier, P., Chu, T.Q.: Using Participatory Paradigm to Learn Human Behaviour. In: International Conference on Knowledge and Systems Engineering, Hanoi, Vietnam, pp. 55–60 (2009)

A Cluster-Based Approach for Disturbed, Spatialized, Distributed Information Gathering Systems

Quang-Anh Nguyen Vu[1], Benoit Gaudou[2], Richard Canal[1], Salima Hassas[3], and Frédéric Armetta[3]

[1] UMI 209 UMMISCO, Institut de la Francophonie pour l'Informatique (IFI), Hanoi, Vietnam
nguyenvu.quanganh@yahoo.com, richard.canal@auf.org
[2] UMR CNRS 5505, Institut de Recherche en Informatique de Toulouse, université Paul Sabatier Toulouse 3, France
benoit.gaudou@univ-tlse1.fr
[3] Laboratoire LIESP, université Claude Bernard Lyon 1, France
{hassas,farmetta}@bat710.univ-lyon1.fr

Abstract. In a distributed spatialized information collecting system managed by a swarm of agents, where some are supposed disturbed, the maintenance of the system coherence and cooperation between reliable elements is a challenge. This paper tackles the problem of finding an efficient mechanism to ensure the coherence of the system and to optimize system performance. The main contribution of this paper consists of two major steps: *(i) use trust-based mechanism to ensure the coherence and the robustness of the system; (ii) allow reliable elements to create dynamic clusters based on trust.* We propose two different organizations in order to manage these issues and show how they must interact: a social one in which each agent maintains a TrustSet to estimate trust on others; a spacial one in which reliable elements are grouped in an "ad hoc type" network to improve cooperation between themselves.

1 Introduction

Let consider the example of a swarm of potentially defectuous mobile robots that have to collaboratively map a zone affected by dangers. Robots can collect information from the ground and exchange their data with other agents. Perception and communication are supposed range limited. The system could be represented as a multi-agents system (MAS) in which each agent (representing a robot) aims at obtaining the most precise representation of its environment by collecting information directly (*e.g.* via sensors) and indirectly (*e.g.* via communication with other agents). Assuming that some agents disturb the system by transmitting false or inaccurate information about the environment because of their flawed perception *(e.g.* their sensors are awry or inoperative), we study ways to improve the coherence of the system (*i.e.* the adequation between the agents' environment representation and the real environment) and its robustness

N. Desai, A. Liu, and M. Winikoff (Eds.): PRIMA 2010, LNAI 7057, pp. 588–603, 2012.

(*i.e.* the agents' capability to adopt strategies allowing to maintain this coherence despite the disturbed communication system) [1,2]. To limit the influence of unreliable agents, we intend to give agents the capacity to dynamically build a two layers self-organization:

(i) a social organization: each agent builds a personal data structure called 'TrustSet' in which it computes its own trust evaluation toward other agents in the system. The TrustSet is mainly composed of a TrustGraph and a TrustTable. Both structures are updated by using direct and indirect interactions between agents. While interacting, the model of trustworthiness is refined and used to appreciate the reliability of other agents in order to reject undesirable communication. Trust is also used to evaluate the reliability of gathered information.

(ii) a spatial organization: in a second step, agents that are spatially close and recognized as reliable organize themselves into physical clusters (*e.g.* ad hoc networks). This organization allows a better coordination between agents. Optimization of the system performance (in terms of exploration time, energy saving) is achieved by avoiding situations such as the overlapping of exploration areas (*e.g.* multiple agents exploring the same target) and by enhancing communication exchanges between agents belonging to the cluster.

The management of the group communication based on the concept of cluster appears to be a promising way due to benefits it brings to the system:

- A better cooperation between agents: a cluster can improve the moving strategy of agents by sharing tasks to complete their work faster.
- A minimization of data redundancies induced by agents collaborating instead of competing.
- Exchanged information moves quickly and securely in a stable cluster where perturbation is minimum.

After the introduction, this paper is organized as follows: Section 2 presents both spatial and social organizations. The notion of cluster is introduced in Section 3 before examining its dynamics. The interaction between the spatial organization and the social organization introduced as "Cluster TrustGraph" is analyzed in Section 4. Section 5 deals with dynamics in cluster topology before presenting general properties of clusters in Section 6. Finally Section 7 presents the conclusion and future research.

2 Social / Spatial organization - Logical / Physical layer

As presented above, the main contribution of this article is to propose a mechanism for agents to build coalitions [3,4] that we name "*clusters*". A cluster can be viewed as a kind of emerging ad hoc network where nodes decide to join together on the basis of different criteria. Literature defines mobile ad hoc network as mobile groups of wireless nodes which cooperatively form a network independent of any fixed infrastructure or centralized administration [5,6]. Agents are free to move randomly and to organize themselves arbitrarily. The network topology may change rapidly and unpredictably [7].

We are therefore interested in the question of the self-organization (without human intervention) of agents in a kind of meta-agent structure inside which they can maintain connectivity to ensure the existence of a reliable communication channel between its members throughout the mission. Our goal is to build the topology of a distributed information collecting system on two different layers in order to better manage communication inside groups of agents:

- the *"logical layer"* built from the social organization which is elaborated from the computation by each agent of a TrustSet based on communication with other agents,
- the *"physical layer"* built from the spatial organization which is constituted by groups of neighboring agents trusting themselves, the "clusters", in which the connectivity must be maintained as in an ad hoc network.

In the sequel, we use the following notations: V denotes the set of the agents, $E(V) = \{\overline{XY} \mid X, Y \in V, X \neq Y\}$ the set of the links between the agents of V and $E'(V) = \left\{\overrightarrow{XY} \mid X, Y \in V, X \neq Y\right\}$ the set of the directed links between agents of V.

2.1 Social Organization

As far as social organization is concerned, each agent builds a data structure called TrustSet in which it can compute its own trust evaluation toward other agents in the system. By associating a reliability to information and a trust to members of the community, each agent improves its perception of the world. As the TrustSet is presented in details in [2], we present here only the main data structures composing it: the TrustGraph and the TrustTable. The public part, the TrustGraph, is a directed valued graph which contains both direct trust values and indirect trust values. The private part, the TrustTable, is a simple table in which the agent stores the intrinsic trust values: trust values, used in the agent's decision-making process, that are computed from direct and indirect trust values by using particular algorithms that can differ from one agent to another one.

Definition 1. (TrustGraph). *A TrustGraph is a weighted digraph (directed graph) with an origin. If* $A \in V$ *is the origin of the digraph, let* $TG_A = (V_A, E'_A, w_A)$ *the TrustGraph of the agent* A *where* $V_A \subseteq V$ *is a set of vertexes,* E'_A *a set of directed edges* $E'_A \subseteq E'(V_A)$ *and* $w_A : E'_A \to [0, 1]$ *a weight function.*

A TrustGraph is a directed graph without loops (*i.e.* paths joining a node to itself) associated to an agent A representing the set of agents connected to A (either agents it has met, or agents it has heard about when communicating). When two vertexes are connected by an edge, it means that the agents represented by the vertexes have met each other. For instance, if B meets C and then meets A, two directed edges are added to the TrustGraph of agent A: $\overrightarrow{AB}$ and $\overrightarrow{BC}$. Moreover edges carry information about agents' trust estimation. The

TrustGraph is built thanks to collected or transmitted information. It will be communicated to other agents at each meeting.

Definition 2. (Direct Trust). *The confidence value $w_A(\overrightarrow{AX})$ is assigned to an edge connecting the origin A to a node X in TG_A represents the direct trust DT_{AX} of A in agent X .*

Direct Trust is computed by comparing information collected by the agent itself with information collected by the agent it meets.

Definition 3. (Indirect Trust). *The confidence value $w_A(\overrightarrow{XY})$ is assigned to an edge connecting a node X different from the origin to a node Y ($Y \neq X$) in TG_A represents the indirect trust IT_{XY} of agent X in agent Y.*

Indirect Trust is computed from trust values obtained via communication.

Definition 4. (Intrinsic Trust). *The intrinsic trust T_{AX} represents the trust the origin agent A computes about any other agent X taking into account its own DT_{AX} and all the trusts along the various paths linking A to X in TG_A.*

Example 1. In [2], we proposed the following formula to compute the intrinsic trust of A in any agent X of its TrustGraph:

$$T_{AX} = \frac{T_{AA} * DT_{AX} + \sum_{Y \in V_A} (T_{AY} * IT_{YX})}{T_{AA} + \sum_{Y \in V_A} T_{AY}}$$

The computation of the intrinsic trust of A in X accommodates the propagation of trusts along a path and the combination of trusts from different paths. We note that $T_{AX} = DT_{AX}$ when only one edge connects A to X and T_{AA} is set to 1 (the trust of the origin agent in itself is initialized to 1 if we consider that it has no reason to have doubts about its own reliability).

Definition 5. (TrustTable). *The set of intrinsic trusts of agent A denoted by $\{T_{AX} \mid X \in V_A\}$ is stored in a table called TrustTable denoted by TT_A.*

The TrustTable is computed thanks to algorithms that can be specific to a particular agent and it will not be communicated to other agents. The intrinsic trusts must be recalculated after the update of trusts in the TrustGraph if one of the basic elements has changed or if a new element enters into its calculation.

Definition 6. (TrustSet). *Let $TS_A = (TG_A, TT_A)$ be the TrustSet of agent A which is a pair of a public part, the TrustGraph, and a private part, the TrustTable.*

Each agent stores its own TrustSet. When an agent X wants to cooperate with another agent Y, based on its TrustSet, X can estimate trust toward Y directly or indirectly. Interested readers can refer to [2] for a detailed representation of the TrustSet and of the algorithms built to update the TrustGraph and the TrustTable, which change over time and to compute information reliability.

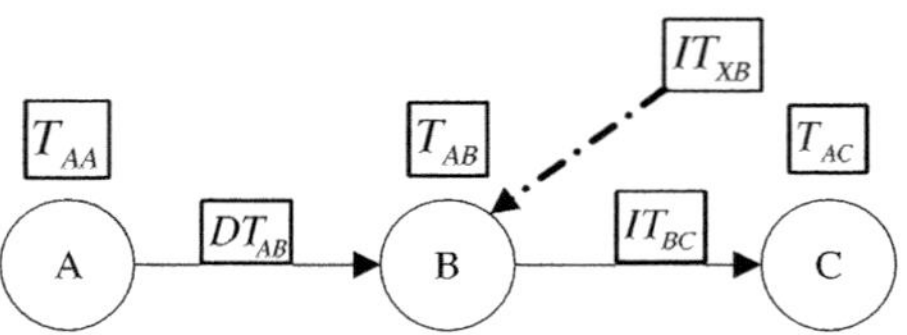

Fig. 1. Example of TrustSet

Example 2. An example of TrustSet built by A is proposed in Figure 1: it includes a TrustGraph formally represented by $TG_A = (\{A, B, C\}, \{\overrightarrow{AB}, \overrightarrow{BC}\}, w_A)$ with $w_A(\overrightarrow{AB}) = DT_{AB}$ and $w_A(\overrightarrow{BC}) = IT_{BC}$ and a TrustTable represented by $TT_A = \{T_{AA}, T_{AB}, T_{AC}\}$. DT_{AB} is the direct trust of A in B, IT_{BC} the trust of B in C communicated to A by B. T_{AA} is the intrinsic trust of A in itself, T_{AB} the intrinsic trust of A in B (calculated from the direct trust DT_{AB} and from all the possible indirect trusts IT_{XB} associated to edges leading to B).

The TrustSet is stored in a decentralized way in each agent. This choice induces several advantages. It avoids the failure of a single point in a centralized system: the system can run normally although there are failures in some agents of the system. It can also save network resources such as power, bandwidth and computation power in a mobile wireless environment.

N.B.: We deliberately omitted the time notations to simplify the expressions. Each agent keeps its TrustSet up to date at each step of the simulation. So the TrustSet values are computed at each moment t from the trust values available at this same moment.

2.2 Spatial Organization

Due to the mobility of the agents in the distributed information collecting system we study, the topology of the pysical network composed by the agents has a significant impact on the communication system. At first, meetings between agents will induce a particular social organization between agents associated to TrustSets. Once well-grounded, this social organization will induce a particular kind of spatial organization that we call "cluster": agents that fully trust each other will stay connected in order to collaborate more efficiently. After its formation, a cluster can be regarded as an ad hoc like network that automatically "emerges" from the social organization. With trust established as a criterion of cluster creation and maintenance, dissonant agents will be automatically excluded from clusters.

Let $\delta(X, Y)$ denote the spatial distance between two agents X and Y.

Let $VN = \{X \mid X \in V, \exists Y \in V, X \neq Y, \delta(X, Y) \leq r\}$ be the set of all spatially neighboring agents, where r denotes the agents communication range.

Let $EN(V) = \{\overline{XY} \mid X, Y \in VN \textit{ and } \delta(X, Y) \leq r\}$ be the set of all links between spatially neighboring agents.

Definition 7. (Neighbor Agents). *In V, two agents A and B are said neighbors iff $(A, B) \in VN$, $A, B \in V$.*

Definition 8. (CLUSTER). *A cluster on a set of agents V, denoted by $Cl = (V_{Cl}, E_{Cl})$, is a graph which satisfies at one moment t the constraints below:*
(1) $V_{Cl} \neq \emptyset$
(2) $E_{Cl} \neq \emptyset$
(3) $V_{Cl} \subseteq VN$
(4) $E_{Cl} \subseteq EN(V)$
(5) $\forall \overline{XY} \in E_{Cl}$, $X \in V_{Cl}$, $Y \in V_{Cl}$, $T_{XY} \geq Upp$ *and* $T_{YX} \geq Upp$, *where* Upp *(*$Upp \in [0,1]$*) is the trust level above which an agent is considered as reliable.*

Theorem 1. $(V_{Cl}, E_{Cl}) \subseteq (V, E(V))$

Proof. *As* $V_{Cl} \subseteq VN$, $E_{Cl} \subseteq EN(V)$ *and* $VN \subseteq V$, $EN(V) \subseteq E(V)$ *so* $(V_{Cl}, E_{Cl}) \subseteq (V, E(V))$.

- In the sequel, Cl_X with $X \in V$ will denote the cluster in which X is an element (*i.e.* $X \in V_{Cl_X}$). We can show thanks to the constraint (4) that, in the case where there is one agent in the cluster, there is always at least one other agent Y in that cluster: $\exists Y \in V_{Cl_X} | \overline{XY} \in E_{Cl_X}$.
- For any group of agents $T \subset V$, Cl_T will denote the cluster in which $V_{Cl_T} = T$.
- Cl_{XY} with $X, Y \in V$ will represent the cluster composed by the two agents X and Y. $V_{Cl_{XY}} = \{X, Y\}$, $E_{Cl_{XY}} = \{\overline{XY}\}$.

3 Cluster Dynamics

3.1 Creation of the Cluster

In this section, we study how an agent can build a cluster with another agent. A cluster is initialized by two agents who satisfy two conditions: they trust each other and they are neighbors.

The clustering at the physical layer will happen once agents trust each other, so this process will take time because trust values change over time from an initial value set to 0.5. The *Algorithm 1* presents how two neighbors that trust each other build a cluster.

Note that as $Cl_{XY} = Cl_{YX}$ by definition of a cluster. The roles of agents are not significant: the same cluster is produced if it is created by X or by Y.

3.2 Merging Clusters

After a certain time, necessary for agents to get a good evaluation of trust in other agents, agents begin to create clusters according to *Algorithm 1*. This algorithm can be used in cases where agents do not belong to any cluster. However when at least one of both agents belongs to a cluster, they must apply another algorithm presented in *Algorithm 2*. This algorithm describes how a single agent ia integrated into a cluster and how two clusters can merge.

Algorithm 1. Creating cluster with two neighbors

Input : Two neighbor agents X and Y who do not belong to any cluster.
Output : A new cluster Cl_{XY} with two agents is created in case of success. Do nothing otherwise.

Begin
  If $T_{XY} \geq Upp$ **Then**
    An initiator X sends a cluster formation request to the agent Y
    if $T_{YX} \geq Upp$ **then**
      Y sends its acceptation to X
      X creates a new cluster Cl_{XY} and informs Y of the creation of the cluster
    end
  End
End

Definition 9. (AGENT/CLUSTER MERGING). *An agent Y is said to be integrated into cluster Cl_X if and only if for every agent $Z \in Cl_X$, there exists a trust value $T_{ZY} \geq Upp$.*

Definition 10. (CLUSTERS MERGING). *A cluster Cl_X is said to be integrated into cluster Cl_Y if and only if for any agent $X, Y \in Cl_X \cup Cl_Y$, there exists a trust value $T_{XY} \geq Upp$.*

Definition 11. (MERGING OPERATOR $\oplus$). *Let $Cl_X = (V_{Cl_X}, E_{Cl_X})$ and $Cl_Y = (V_{Cl_Y}, E_{Cl_Y})$ two different clusters. We define $Cl_Z = Cl_X \oplus Cl_Y$ as $Cl_Z = (V_{Cl_Z}, E_{Cl_Z})$ with $V_{Cl_Z} = V_{Cl_X} \cup V_{Cl_Y}$ and $E_{Cl_Z} = E_{Cl_X} \cup E_{Cl_Y} \cup \{\overline{XY}\}$.*

Theorem 2. *If agent X belongs to both Cl_X, Cl'_X then $Cl_X = Cl'_X$.*

Proof. If $\exists Cl_X \mid X \in Cl_X$ and $\exists Cl'_X \mid X \in Cl'_X$ then by applying the merging operation on both clusters we get: $Cl_X = Cl_X \oplus Cl'_X$, $Cl'_X = Cl_X \oplus Cl'_X$ so $Cl_X = Cl'_X$.

3.3 Exclusion of an Element from a Cluster

Definition 12. (AGENT/CLUSTER EXCLUDING). *An agent Y must be excluded from a cluster Cl_X if and only if there exists $Y \in Cl_X$ that trust value T_{YX} becomes less than Upp.*

Definition 13. (EXCLUDING OPERATOR $\ominus$). *Let $Cl_X = (V_{Cl_X}, E_{Cl_X})$ be a cluster and $Y \in V_{Cl_X}$ an agent. We define $Cl_Z = Cl_X \ominus Y$ as $Cl_Z = (V_{Cl_Z}, E_{Cl_Z})$ with $V_{Cl_Z} = V_{Cl_X} \setminus \{Y\}$ and $E_{Cl_Z} = E_{Cl_X} \setminus \{\overline{KY} \mid \forall K \in V_{Cl_X}\} \cup \{\overline{YL} \mid \forall L \in V_{Cl_X}\}$.*

Algorithm 2. Merging clusters

Input : Two neighbor agents X, Y with agent X belonging to Cl_X
Output : The cluster Cl_X updated.

Begin
  If $T_{ZY} \geq Upp \mid \forall Z \in Cl_X$ **then**
    if $T_{YX} \geq Upp$ **then**
      if $\nexists Cl_Y, Y \in Cl_Y$ **then**
        $Cl_X = Cl_X \oplus (Y, \{\overline{XY}\})$
        X sends cluster formation request to its neighbor agent Y
        end
      if $\exists Cl_Y, Y \in Cl_Y$ and $T_{XY} \geq Upp \mid \forall X, Y \in Cl_X \cup Cl_Y$ **then**
      $Cl_X = Cl_X \oplus Cl_Y$
      X sends cluster formation request to its neighbor agent Y
      end
    end
  End
End

4 Cluster TrustGraph

After the previous static description of TrustGraph in social organization, we address in this section the issue of links between TrustGraphs which are stored in each agent in a social organization and high level clusters emerging in a spatial organization, *i.e.* how TrustGraphs of a cluster agents are exchanged and how they can be merged together.

We aim to build a shared TrustGraph which is stored in each individual and can be shared with others in a cluster (*i.e.* all agents in a cluster could have the same TrustGraph). This way, reliable information is exchanged locally through individual interactions in order to avoid many drawbacks, such as single point failure, requirement of infrastructure, problem of performance bottleneck, etc.

The shared TrustGraph of a cluster must be designed in a distributed way suited to a group dynamics that uses frequent topology and membership changes. At each communication with an agent Y, the agent X will eventually communicate to Y its data (information items collected directly by the agent) but also some of its metadata (all information about trust). In particular, it will share its TrustGraph, which contains all public metadata, but will not share its TrustTable because it is built by a personal computation and thus contains private information. After receiving a TrustGraph, an agent integrates it in its own one. Then it uses the obtained TrustGraph to update its TrustTable. The TrustGraph of agent X is updated when it receives the TrustGraph of agent Y following 3 stages[1] as follows:

[1] Interested readers can refer to [2] for the detailed stages in section "Merging TrustGraphs".

- X calculates its trust T_{XY} in Y or updates the existing value by comparing its own data with received ones. In case of a new cluster Cl_{XY} is created, a direct trust link $\overrightarrow{XY}$ on its TrustGraph is replaced by a bidirectional link $\overleftrightarrow{XY}$.
- X connects the TrustGraph of Y to its own TrustGraph;
- X corrects all inconsistencies in the shared paths.

The TrustGraph sent by an agent must contain its building information (*e.g.* ids of agents whose TrustSets are merged, the time of mergings, etc.).

When agents meet new neighbors (or when a new agent enters the cluster), they will exchange and update their TrustGraphs using the Merging TrustGraphs algorithms.

When an agent meets old neighbors, after checking the TrustGraph building information, an agent decides or not to update its own TrustGraph (*i.e.* when the agent detects that one of the basic components of its TrustGraph has changed, it will update its TrustGraph).

From its shared TrustGraph, an agent A can compute its private TrustTable to estimate the trust value allocated by its cluster to another agent Y (Y does not belong to A's cluster) using the formula: $T_Y^{Cl} = \frac{\sum_{X \in V_{Cl}} T_{XY}^A}{Card(V_{Cl})}$, where T_Y^{Cl} denotes the trust of the cluster Cl on the agent Y and T_{XY}^A the intrinsic trust of agent X ($X \in V_{Cl}$) on agent Y in the TrustTable of A.

5 Dealing with the Dynamics in Cluster Topology

This section describes three different topologies of the same cluster corresponding to levels built in preceding sections: spatial organization, social organization and intrinsic trust organization. Two of these topologies are virtual (social and intrinsic trust), one is real. They influence each other, *i.e.* any change at the intrinsic trust level will produce immediate changes in social and spatial organizations.

5.1 Spatial Organization (Cluster Spatial Organization):

On the spatial organization, the one and only physical organization, node mobility creates a dynamics in cluster topology. This dynamics depends on the movement of each agent in the cluster and on the necessary cluster reconfigurations (induced by the various merging and excluding operations). The chosen topology for clusters plays a significant role in the communication strategy between agents and therefore in the system performance. For instance, a dense topology will induce high exploration domains overlapping and so good data reliability but poor time performance, while a sparse topology will be vulnerable to link failures and network partitioning.

Further, the objective of the spatial organization viewed as a meta agent is to spread out as large as possible in the ground to collect as many new data as possible. On the other hand, the agents involved in this spatial organization

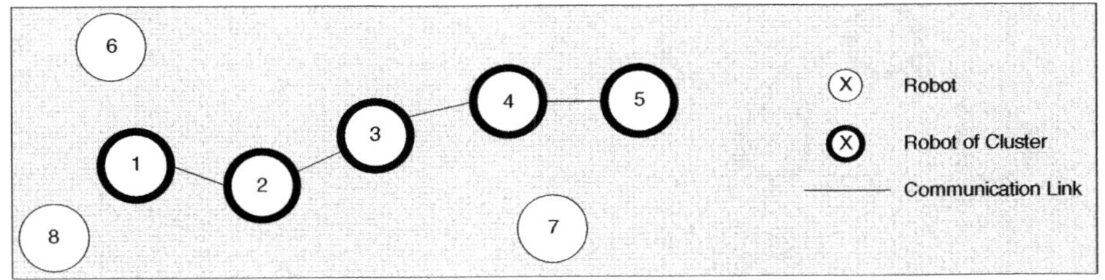

Fig. 2. Cluster spatial organization

must keep in touch with each other to assure a reliable communication channel throughout the mission.

We will refer to an existing algorithm for maintaining connectivity between agents belonging to the same cluster in Section 6.1.

An example of a *Cluster spatial organization* is illustrated in the Figure 2 which represents an **undirected graph** $G_{spa} = (V_{spa}, E_{spa})$ where $V_{spa} = \{1, 2, 3, 4, 5\}$ is the set of robots in the cluster and $E_{spa} = \{\overline{12}, \overline{23}, \overline{34}, \overline{45}\}$ connections between them. The introduction or exclusion of agents in or from a cluster can cause important changes in its topology. For instance, if robot 3 is excluded from the cluster, robot 2 and robot 4 would aim to come closer so that the connectivity between the cluster agents is maintained.

5.2 Social Organization (Cluster TrustGraph):

Social organization is related to both agents in cluster and agents on which agents of the cluster have computed a trust. We can associate to this virtual organization a "*Cluster TrustGraph*" which contains both **reliable trust links** materializing connections between agents inside the cluster and simple trust links materializing connections between agents in which at least one of them does not belong to the cluster. A Cluster TrustGraph differs from an agent TrustGraph in that it has as many origins as the cluster has members. An agent TrustGraph has only one origin, the agent itself. A Cluster TrustGraph can be seen as the transitive closing of the TrustGraphs of its members.

Definition 14. (Reliable trust Link). *A double link* $\left(\overrightarrow{AB}, \overleftarrow{AB}\right) \in E'(V)^2$ *denoted by* $\overleftrightarrow{AB}$ *is called a reliable trust link if and only if* $T_{AB} \geq Upp$ *and* $T_{BA} \geq Upp$.

Figure 3 illustrates one of the *Cluster TrustGraphs* which can be associated to the *Cluster spatial organization* built in Figure 2. The *Cluster TrustGraph* is represented by a **graph** $G_{soc} = (V_{soc}, E_{soc})$ where $V_{soc} = \{1, 2, 3, 4, 5, 6, 7, 8\}$ and $E_{soc} = \left\{\overleftrightarrow{12}, \overleftrightarrow{23}, \overleftrightarrow{34}, \overleftrightarrow{45}, \overrightarrow{38}, \overrightarrow{36}, \overrightarrow{63}, \overrightarrow{56}, \overrightarrow{67}\right\}$. In E_{soc}, we find reliable trust links and simple trust links. $\overleftrightarrow{12}$ is a reliable link which means that robot 1 and robot 2 have mutually a direct trust on each other, $T_{12} \geq Upp$ and $T_{21} \geq Upp$. $\overrightarrow{36}, \overrightarrow{63}$

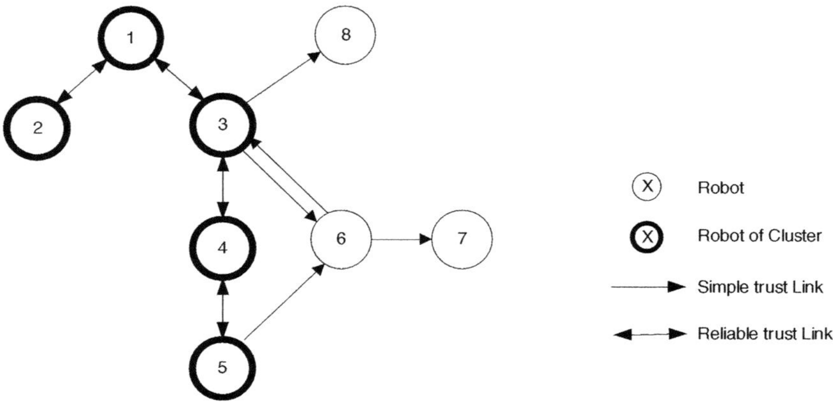

Fig. 3. Cluster TrustGraph

is a also a bidirectional trust link but at least the robot 3 or the robot 6 has a trust on its partner less than *Upp*. Otherwise the robot 6 would be included in the cluster.

5.3 Intrinsic Trust Level (Cluster Intrinsic TrustGraph):

This second virtual level takes for basis the intrinsic trust values each agent computes on other agents. So there must be a reliable link between all the reliable nodes of the cluster. It means that any cluster agent has an intrinsic trust$\geq Upp$ on all agents in the cluster. It is the condition for which each agent has been accepted in the cluster and remains in the cluster. If one of these links is no more reliable, one of the agents must leave the cluster.

Let's note that these links are not physical links. This representation simply describes the quality of the trust links associating the members of the cluster. It also includes the intrinsic simple connections to agents outside the cluster. This level is rather related to the agents TrustTables from which the concept of cluster is derived.

An example of *Cluster intrinsic TrustGraph* is shown in Figure 4. The cluster is represented by a **bidirected complete graph** $G_{iTG} = (V_{iTG}, E_{iTG})$ where $V_{iTG} = \{1, 2, 3, 4, 5\}$ and $E_{iTG} = \left\{\overleftrightarrow{XY} \mid X, Y \in V_{iTG}; X \neq Y\right\}$.

6 Cluster General Properties

In this section we address the problem of maintaining the connectivity between cluster agents with, in the same time, the necessity to provide a reliable communication system and a role-based cooperation. A well-organized cluster will bring many benefits of performance to the system such as a better agents

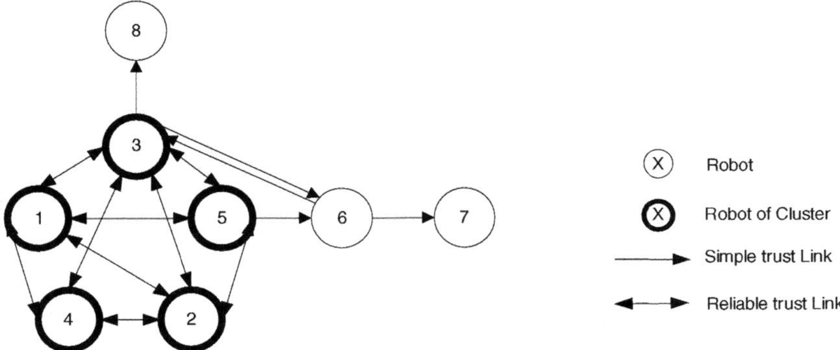

Fig. 4. Cluster Intrinsic TrustGraph

cooperation, a minimization of data redundancies and an improvement on the quality of exchanged information.

6.1 Maintaining Connectivity

One of the main properties of clusters is the capacity of maintaining connectivity between its elements to ensure a communication channel between reliable agents. The problem of connectivity maintenance is to ensure the existence of a reliable communication channel throughout the mission. The difficulty in the chosen example of mapping mobile robots is that any robot can potentially break down and cause the disjunction of any robot from the rest of the team. Hence the reliable communication channel we are promoting will be broken and we cannot presuppose the availability of another communication infrastructure which will be operational and compatible with our agents. In our context, we use an existing algorithm to maintain connectivity between cluster agents using the mechanisms of sensitivity proposed by Le *et al.* [8] in which is introduced the "*sensitivity connectivity*" - an original concept in MANETs - to build a distributed representation and local connectivity.

To maintain the network connectivity for elements in the network, we use a "*reference robot*" as the axis of the cluster. Generally, the robot with the greatest number of connexions with trusted robots is chosen. While moving to perform its task, each robot must remain in contact with at least one neighboring robot from which a channel of communication with the reference robot can be established. If the robots maintain this strategy, then the connectivity of the whole system will be ensured. A connectivity-awareness for a given robot is materialized by a connectivity table containing a set of access paths which represent a partial view of the network connectivity[2].

[2] Interested readers can refer to [8] for detailed distributed algorithm that includes mobile robots into a multi-robot system aware of network connectivity. The authors also proved that their proposal can be used to check biconnectivity more efficiently.

6.2 Reliable Communication

In a distributed information gathering system, robots need to communicate to cooperate effectively. Many studies have concluded that even the exchange of a small amount of information improves MAS performance for some tasks [9,10]. To achieve a high degree of flexibility and autonomy, communication between robots should be based on wireless communication technologies. In addition, the used communication technology must allow robots to self-organize to be operational without any centralized administration, and must be able to adapt to the mobility of robots during their mission. A network with such characteristics is known as a mobile ad hoc network: a MANET. These characteristics make MANETs very flexible and easy to deploy. For this reason, the use of MANETs for communication between robots belonging to the same cluster, in places where we cannot reasonably suppose the existence of a robust communication infrastructure, is extremely adequate.

A robot belonging to a cluster is not only an "ordinary" networked node but also a router that relays messages for its neighbors. Communication between robots which are not neighbors can thus take place through consecutive intermediate relaying nodes. Communication in clusters can be interpreted as follows in terms of ad hoc networks: when neighboring and reliable robots have constituted a cluster, they are considered as an ad hoc type network. Thus they can communicate and rely on MANET routing protocol for message transmission so that in a finite period of time, a message sent by a robot is received correctly by all the elements of its cluster. As each agent implicated in the information transmission (the agents of the cluster) is supposed reliable, the received information can be accepted by the agents without defiance.

6.3 Role-Based Cooperation

Moreover we aim to create a role-based cooperation for cluster agents. We define a role as a clearly identified behavior description. Several roles are generally required to perform a given task. We propose to use roles to describe clusters needed to perform the various tasks necessary to carry off a given mission.

The basic idea of our approach is to consider each cluster as a group. The master of the cluster (*e.g.* the "reference agent") plays the role of a group manager. The second step is to build a description of the system and to provide it to the cluster agents so that they can take it into account in their decision-making process. Thus, agents independently choose the roles which they think most appropriate for themselves. The reference agent can help cluster agents in case of conflict between agents (*e.g.* many agents want to execute the same task or the same role). To resolve conflicts, a protocol of roles allocation based on auction is usually used. At first, each agent sends to the reference agent its offer about the price it asks to finish the task (price takes the form in our application of an energy level, a time period...). Then the reference agent selects the agent proposing the lowest task price. The choice of the reference node depends on the goal of the application and might involve multiple criteria such as energy level, number of neighbors, hardware requirements, etc. It doesn't differ much from a Contract Net protocol.

In this approach, we define a role as the description of a well-defined behavior. Several roles are generally required to perform a given task. We propose to use roles to describe groups necessary to achieve the possible tasks in a given mission. The task sharing between robots in a group will help to improve the time to finish the mission and accelerate the system convergence (*i.e.* performance of system).

The protocol of roles allocation we need for a cluster must allow dynamical changes in the overall organization. So the protocol we use is inspired by the algorithm DMAC (Distributed and Mobility-Adaptive Clustering) proposed by Basagni [11] to partition a mobile ad hoc network (MANET) in clusters.

In the project of mapping mobile robots [12], we have for instance distinguished two roles. The first one is a "*reliability role*" with the objective of maintaining the physical reality of the cluster which represents a reliable "*nucleus*" of agents. The second one is an "*exploration role*" with the objective of collecting a maximum of data for the benefice of the cluster. This choice comes from the idea that the constraint to remain physically connected to a cluster can be viewed as a limit to the exploration capabilities of the set of its agents. So, some agents (the number is linked to the real cluster size) remain in the nucleus of the cluster and the other ones can leave the cluster nucleus as "explorers", some appointments with the cluster preset and stored in their memory. When they come back to the cluster, the explorers share their knowledge with the nucleus (not only new reliable collected data from the ground but also new metadata about robots unknown from the cluster) and so improve the exploration field of the cluster.

7 Conclusion and Future Works

In this paper, we have proposed a mechanism to improve cooperation between reliable agents in a disturbed, spatialized data gathering system where information collection and transmission can be altered by unreliable agents. In our approach, each agent computes a trust value assigned to other agents in order to build (from local to global) a highest level structure designed as a cluster on which we can apply improvements on communication, data gathering and role-sharing derived from ad hoc networks algorithms. Clusters must be seen as emerging ad hoc networks with a special dynamics based on a social value that is trust. Then we showed how social and spatial (virtual and real) organizations can be linked in order to achieve interesting emerging associations of agents intended to reach the objective set to the system in better ways. We characterized the link between the logical and the physical levels by a Cluster TrustGraph built from the agent TrustGraphs. This graph which is the exclusive result of the social and physical emerging organization interplay is stored in each agent of the cluster. To get a better view of the associated interactions, we introduced three different topologies of the same cluster corresponding to the following three levels: spatial organization, social organization and intrinsic trust level organization. Finally, some suggestions were given about the main characteristics of a cluster and how we can use them to improve the performance of the system.

The advantage of our approach is that each cluster agent cooperates better with all the agents of its cluster by minimizing the data redundancy caused by overlapping agents and by limiting the information latency inside the cluster. Such a cooperation induces at the same time better coherence and better robustness of the system. Aiming to justify our propositions and investigate the benefits of clusters in terms of performance, extensive simulation studies using GAMA platform [13] are currently being carried out.

The future work will focus on the community self-organization about communication management, on the structuring of sub communities according to their reliability and on the limits of perturbation a disturbed system can support by using a complex system approach [14].

References

1. Nguyen Vu, Q.A., Gaudou, B., Canal, R., Hassas, S., Armetta, F.: Stratégie de communication dans un systéme de collecte d'information á base d'agents perturbés. In: Journées Francophones des Systémes Multi-Agents (JFSMA), France, pp. 207–217 (2009)
2. Nguyen Vu, Q.A., Gaudou, B., Canal, R., Hassas, S., Armetta, F.: TrustSets - Using trust to detect deceitful agents in a distributed information collecting system. In: 2010 IEEE-RIVF International Conference on Computing and Communication Technologies (2010)
3. Horling, B., Lesser, V.: A survey of multi-agent organizational paradigms. The Knowledge Engineering Review 19(4), 281–316 (2004)
4. Parker, L.E., Reardon, C.M., Choxi, H., Bolden, C.: Using critical junctures and environmentally-dependent information for management of tightly-coupled cooperation in heterogeneous robot teams. In: ICRA 2009: Proceedings of the, IEEE International Conference on Robotics and Automation, pp. 2872–2879. IEEE Press, Piscataway (2009)
5. Drira, K., Kheddouci, H., Tabbane, N.: Virtual dynamic topology for routing in mobile ad hoc networks. In: Proceedings of the International Conference on Late Advances in Networks ICLAN 2006, France, pp. 129–134 (2006)
6. Perkins, C.E.: Ad Hoc Networking. Addison-Wesley Professional (2008)
7. Haddad, M., Kheddouci, H.: A survey on graph based service discovery approaches for ad hoc networks. International Transactions on Systems Science and Applications (2007)
8. Le, V.T., Bouraqadi, N., Stinckwich, S., Moraru, V., Doniec, A.: Making networked robots connectivity-aware. In: ICRA 2009: Proceedings of the 2009 IEEE International Conference on Robotics and Automation, pp. 1835–1840. IEEE Press, Piscataway (2009)
9. Maclennan, B.: Synthetic ethology: An approach to the study of communication, pp. 631–658. Addison-Wesley (1991)
10. Balch, T., Ronald, Arkin, C.: Communication in reactive multiagent robotic systems. Autonomous Robots 1, 27–52 (1994)

11. Basagni, S.: Distributed clustering for ad hoc networks. In: ISPAN 1999: Proceedings of the 1999 International Symposium on Parallel Architectures, Algorithms and Networks, p. 310. IEEE Computer Society, Washington, DC, USA (1999)
12. Nguyen Vu, Q.A., Gaudou, B., Canal, R., Hassas, S., Armetta, F., Stinckwich, S.: Using trust and cluster organisation to improve robot swarm mapping. In: ROSIN 2010: Workshop on Robots and Sensors integration in Future Rescue INformation System (2010) (to appear)
13. Amouroux, E., Quang, C., Boucher, A., Drogoul, A.: GAMA: an Environment for Implementing and Running Spatially Explicit Multi-Agent Simulations. In: Ghose, A., Governatori, G., Sadananda, R. (eds.) PRIMA 2007. LNCS, vol. 5044, pp. 359–371. Springer, Heidelberg (2007)
14. Hassas, S.: Systèmes complexes à base de multi-agents situès. Universitè Claude Bernard-Lyon 1, Mèmoire d'habilitation à diriger les recherches (2003)

Simulation of the Emotion Dynamics in a Group of Agents in an Evacuation Situation

Le Van Minh[1,2], Carole Adam[3], Richard Canal[1,4], Benoit Gaudou[5,6], Ho Tuong Vinh[1,4], and Patrick Taillandier[6]

[1] Institut de la Francophonie pour l'Informatique (IFI), Hanoi, Vietnam
[2] Danang University (UDN), Danang, Vietnam
[3] RMIT University, Melbourne, Australia
[4] UMI 209 UMMISCO, Institut de Recherche pour le Développement (IRD), Bondy, France
[5] Université de Toulouse, Toulouse, France
[6] Institut de Recherche en Informatique de Toulouse (IRIT), UMR CNRS 5505, Toulouse, France

{minh.levan246,carole.adam.rmit,benoit.gaudou,ho.tuong.vinh, patrick.taillandier}@gmail.com, richard.canal@auf.org

Abstract. Nowadays, more and more emergency evacuation simulations are used to evaluate the safety level of a building during an emergency evacuation after an accident. The heart of this kind of simulations is the simulation of human behavior because simulation results depend for a big part on how this behavior is simulated. However, human behaviors in a real emergency situation are determined by a lot of cognitive mechanisms. In order to make the simulation more realistic, plenty of factors (*e.g.* innate characteristics, perception of the environment, internal rules, personality and even emotions) that affect human behaviors must be taken into account. This paper focuses on the influence of emotions, and more precisely on the influence of their dynamics and propagation from an agent to another. The main contribution of this work is the development of a model of emotions taking into account their dynamics and their propagation and its integration in an evacuation simulation. The first results of the simulation show the benefits of considering emotion propagation.

Keywords: emotion, emotional agent, emotion propagation, emergency evacuation.

1 Introduction

Nowadays, the computing power available on any personal computer allows one to create simulations including thousands of agents, as for example in simulations of the traffic in a city, or simulations of the emergency evacuation from a building... In order to make the simulation as realistic as possible, each agent in the simulation is designed to operate autonomously (which means that the

N. Desai, A. Liu, and M. Winikoff (Eds.): PRIMA 2010, LNAI 7057, pp. 604–619, 2012.

agent is not controlled by any central agent and he makes his decisions using his own cognitive resources) and to interact with other agents.

Many researches show that adding emotions (*e.g.* joy, fear, anger, hope...) into these agents provides huge benefits because emotions improve the quality of agents' behaviors and then the quality of the whole simulation [13]. Indeed emotions play a very important role in human beings' life by influencing their decision-making and reasoning processes and their interactions with others [6,8]. Therefore, we should not ignore emotions when creating a virtual human simulation.

The recent studies in the domain of artificial agents allow one to give each agent ways to express pertinent emotions [7] and to reason about not only his own emotions but also about others agents' ones [1]. Critical issues remain concerning the "transmission" of emotions among agents in the simulation, the emergence of a common emotion in a group of agents and the effect of this emotion on each individual.

We thus propose in this paper a model of emotions taking into account both the emotion dynamics (when emotions appear and how their intensity level evolves over time) and the emotion propagation (how they are "sent" and "received" and how a received emotion influences the receiver). In this paper we focus on fear (with various intensity levels) and test our model by implementing it into agents used in a simulation of emergency evacuation in a burning shopping center.

This paper is organized as follows. Section 2 presents a brief state of the art on emotions. In Section 3, we present our model of emotions, emotion dynamics and propagation. Furthermore, in Section 4, we present the implementation of our model and discuss in Section 5 the first results of our simulation.

2 State of the Art

2.1 Simulation of Pedestrian Evacuation

Plenty of simulations of emergency evacuation have been developed [18,20,19]. Most of them concentrate on human behaviors, and more particularly on their movement, in an emergency situation. The typical model of this kind of simulations is the pedestrian evacuation model developed by Crooks on the RepastJ platform [14][1]. In this simulation, agents representing human beings leave their office when the fire appears. This simulation is focused on the human movement and on the role of obstacles on the passage to the door: *e.g.* the wall of the room, the table...

Since the human behaviors in the real world are much more complex than those of the agents in the simulation (*e.g.* planned tasks of a person are often updated in case of a stressful situation), many researchers have proposed to introduce additional factors to make the agents' behavior more human-like.

[1] Interested readers can download the model on the website `http://www.casa.ucl.ac.uk/andrew/repastmodels/fire/fire.zip`.

In particular, Musse and Thalmann described a hierarchical model of virtual crowds for real-time simulations [12]. In their simulation, the human behaviors executed by simulated agents are classified in three types: innate or scripted behaviors, behaviors defined by rules and behaviors controlled by external factors. Furthermore, Hollmann *et al.* [9] improved the human behaviors model in urgent situations by adding the two following attributes: *available time* and *estimated required time*. When these two variables reach a particular threshold, the agent changes his behavior (*e.g.* he accelerates in order to get to the goal location, changes the goal location or even ignores some of the planned tasks to concentrate on the ultimate goal).

As mentioned previously, emotions play an important role in human behaviors in particular in emergency situations. We choose to integrate emotions in evacuation simulations. Therefore the first question is how to define and describe emotions.

2.2 Theories of Emotions

In the 19th century, James and Lange proposed a physiological theory of emotion [10]. Their theory indicates that the human autonomous nervous system creates physiological events like heart rate and respiration in response to various human experiences. The emotions are the sentiments that appear as results of this physiological change. According to this theory, humans can express their emotions via their physiological states and can guess the emotions of others based on this kind of expression.

While this physiological theory advocates that emotions result from physiological factors, many scientists defend the idea that cognitive factors are very important in the process of emotion triggering. They propose various so called cognitive theories. In the domain of cognitive theories of emotions, Arnold [3] and Lazarus [11] argue that human beings always evaluate what they perceive and the emotion triggered by this perception is thus the result of an appraisal process. They proposed the cognitive appraisal theory. Following these purely psychological researches, Ortony, Clore and Collins [15] define a typology of emotions (known as the OCC typology) depending on the type of stimulus appraised and various appraisal variables. They distinguish three kinds of stimuli: events, actions of agents, aspects of objects. The 20 emotions defined are deeply related to mental attitudes, this eases their integration into artificial agents.

In [5], Cabanac proposed a four-dimension model of consciousness. In this model, every state of consciousness is described in 4 dimensions: the qualitative dimension, the intensive dimension, the hedonic dimension and the time dimension. He then proposed a definition of emotions based on his model of consciousness: "Emotion is any mental experience with high intensity and high hedonicity" [5].

In [4], Bosse *et al.* proposed a model of emotion contagion. In their model, the propagation of emotions depends on six factors: the current level of the sender's emotion, the current level of the receiver's emotion, the extent to which the sender expresses the emotion, the receiver's openness or sensitivity for emotions, the strength of the channel from the sender to the receiver and the tendency to adapt emotions upward or downward [4].

2.3 Existing Models of Emotional Agent

In [16], Parunak *et al.* propose a model of emotions for situated agents called DETT. "DETT (Disposition, Emotion, Trigger, Tendency) is an environmentally mediated model of emotion that captures the essential features of the widely-used OCC (Ortony, Clore, Collins) model of emotion" [16]. Contrarily to most agents architectures using the OCC typology, in DETT emotions are triggered by the perception module (rather than being the result of an internal reasoning).

In [22], Zoumpoulaki *et al.* propose a multi-agent framework for emergency evacuation. The multi-agent model presented in the paper is a combination of the BDI (Belief, Desire and Intention) architecture [17] for the agent's reasoning process, the OCEAN (Openness, Conscientiousness, Extraversion, Agreeableness and Neuroticism) for the model of personality and the OCC model for emotions. This kind of framework can be used to simulate emotions in controllable situations, but in the case of an extremely serious emergency, when the situation becomes truly chaotic, we argue that people do not have enough time to make reasoned decisions but rather make decisions based on simple heuristics such as emotions. In the sequel we consider situations of extreme emergency; that is why we have only simple agents feeling extreme emotions (like fear). Their behavior is mainly directed by the emotion they are feeling and the emotions received from other agents.

3 Proposed Model of Emotional Agent

3.1 A Two-Dimensional Model of Emotion for Emergency Evacuation Simulations

As described in the previous section, we consider an emotion as a particular mental state which is triggered by the individual appraisal of various stimuli. Stimuli in our case will be either events of the environment or behaviors of other agents, both being perceived by the agent. The subject appraises these stimuli according to his knowledge and his current emotions.

From the psychological four-dimensional model proposed by Cabanac [5] and the multi-agent framework integrating personality and emotion proposed by Zoumpoulaki *et al.* [22], it appears that the more emotions are simulated, the more realistic the simulation becomes but the more complicated relevant results will be extracted from the simulation, which leads to difficulties in the evaluation phase when we evaluate the role of emotions and of their propagation in emergency situations. In order to emphasize the effect of emotions and of their transmission, we propose a simple model of emotion – a two-dimension model of emotions – which allows us to have simulation results that remain simple to analyze. Our model is the reduction of Cabanac's four-dimensional model [5] by

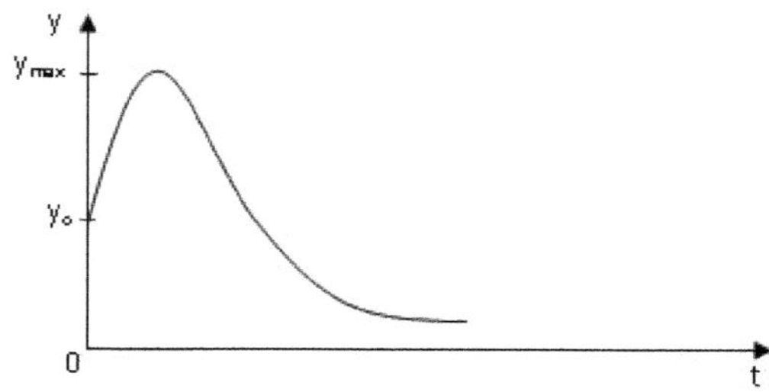

Fig. 1. Decay of the emotion

ignoring the qualitative dimension (Axis x) and the hedonic dimension (Axis z). We consider that the emotion triggered in every emergency evacuation is the fear. We concentrate on this emotion and the two remaining dimensions represent its intensity and the duration of the emotion. Thus, the emotional model proposed is a two-dimensional model with 2 axes: the emotion intensity (Axis y) and the emotion duration (Axis t).

"Axis y" represents the intensity of the emotion. In our proposition, the value of $y(t)$ is continuous and always positive. If $y(t) < \epsilon$ (a very small threshold), the emotion disappears. The initial value of $y(t)$ (*i.e.* when the emotion is triggered) is calculated by the appraising process. We suppose that an agent has the capability to calm down over time and thus reduce the intensity of his emotion. Then the value of $y(t)$ decreases gradually following the formula $y(t) = y(t-1)/\alpha, (\alpha > 1)$ (1) (with α is the decay coefficient).

"Axis t" represents the duration of the emotion. Due to the decay equation (1), the intensity of the emotion will follow the evolution presented in Figure 1, in the ideal case where there is no other stimulus.

3.2 Architecture of the Emotional Agent

We present in Figure 2 the architecture of our emotional agent.

Simplifications. In the sequel, we consider the three following simplifications. They allow us to simplify conceptually and computationally our model and thus improve the simulation performance and make the simulation more effective.

Simplification 1. The current emotion of the agent does not have any influence on the process of perception. The current emotion is taken into account only in the process of evaluation of the perception outputs (emotional appraisal) that triggers emotion.

Simplification 2. There is only one emotion in the agent at one moment. This also means that only one emotion can be taken into account in the appraisal process and that this process can create only one emotion.

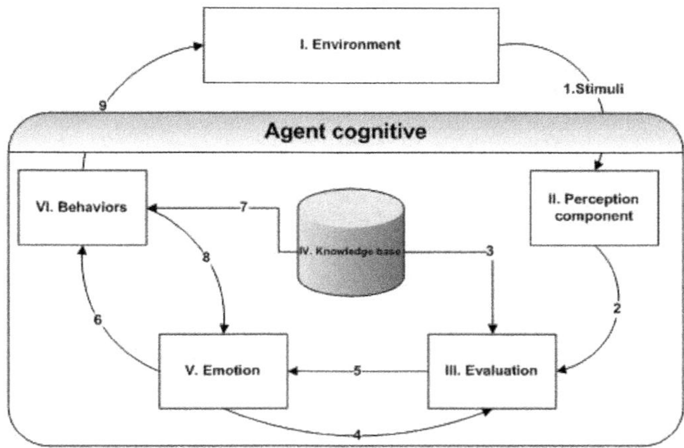

Fig. 2. Model of the emotional agent

Simplification 3. The agent acts immediately once the emotion appears. The agent does not update his knowledge base before performing an action.

Description of the architecture. We describe here the main process of the agent architecture.

1. **Perception of the stimuli** (*Perception component* in the Figure 2): first, the agent perceives the stimulus (coming from Arrow 1). In this work, the type of emotion simulated is the fear. Therefore, only the stimuli which contribute to fear are perceived, the rest is ignored. According to the source of the stimuli, the agent classifies the stimulus into 1 of 2 possible types.

a. Indirect stimulus: This type of stimulus is caused by the environment. They do not trigger directly an emotion. They can only affect the intensity of existing emotions. For example: a child who is alone in the middle of the graveyard, under the heavy rain; if this child is scared, any additional noise will increase the level of his fear.

b. Direct stimulus: This type of stimulus is caused by events of the environment or by the behavior of other agents. Each stimulus provokes one type of emotion with a specific intensity.

2. **Appraisal of the stimuli** (*Evaluation* component in Figure 2): The results of the perception (Arrow 2) are appraised according to the knowledge of the agent (Arrow 3) and his current emotion (Arrow 4). There are 2 types of stimulus so there are also 2 types of evaluation. In the end of this process, the agent creates an emotion.

a. Evaluation of indirect stimuli: the agent searches in his knowledge base for rules relating to the indirect stimuli perceived. If some rules are found, the agent acquires the global variable (γ_i). As the stimulus can have either a positive effect or a negative effect on the agent, this global variable (γ_i) can have a positive value or a negative value. With one stimulus, γ_i can be different from an agent to

```
If (γ < 0) then Δy = Δy * (1 + |γ|) ;
/*The negative effect of environment increases the
intensity of the fear */
Else Δy = Δy / (1 + |γ|) ;
/* The positive effect of environment reduces the
intensity of the fear */
Δy = Δy * β ;
/* β : Coefficient of sensitivity of agent */
y = min(y + Δ, ymax)
```

Fig. 3. Algorithm to calculate the intensity of the fear

another one according to his knowledge base: an agent can give a positive value to γ_i, whereas another agent can give it a negative value. For example, consider a child in a dark room; the darkness is the indirect stimulus; if this child can normally see, this stimulus is negative; if this child is blind, darkness does not scare him; so this stimulus will not be perceived or will have a neutral value. After having evaluated all the indirect stimuli, the agent has a set of γ_i that he aggregates with: $\gamma = \sum_{i>0} \gamma_i$.

b. Evaluation of direct stimuli: the agent finds in his knowledge base the rules matching with the direct stimuli perceived. According to rules found, the agent acquires an additional intensity value (Δy).

c. Computation of the intensity: the intensity of the temporary emotion is computed by the algorithm presented in the Figure 3.

In the algorithm, "y" represents the intensity of the fear. When "y" reaches a determined threshold, the agent will change his behavior. The maximal value of "y" is "y_{max}" which is defined as an input parameter of the simulation that limits an overgrowing emotion intensity. In our model, we consider that agents perceive other agents' emotions depending on their sensitivity factor α. This sensitivity coefficient is a positive constant and varies from an agent to another one. According to this coefficient, an agent can perceive emotion more easily than others.

3. **Computation of behaviors** (*Behaviors* component in Figure 2): once the new emotion has been created, the agent reacts immediately to the stimulus from the environment. Initially, the agent finds in his knowledge base the rules related to the emotion and then executes the corresponding behavior. The agent executes two kinds of action in one step: he reduces the intensity according to the formula (1) and reacts to the stimulus. When the agent reacts to the stimulus, his behavior affects not only the environment but also the other agents. The other agents perceive thus these behaviors and interpret them as stimuli.

3.3 Model of Emotion Propagation

According to the agent model proposed, an agent appraises the stimuli caused by the actions of other agents in the process of evaluation. When an agent reacts

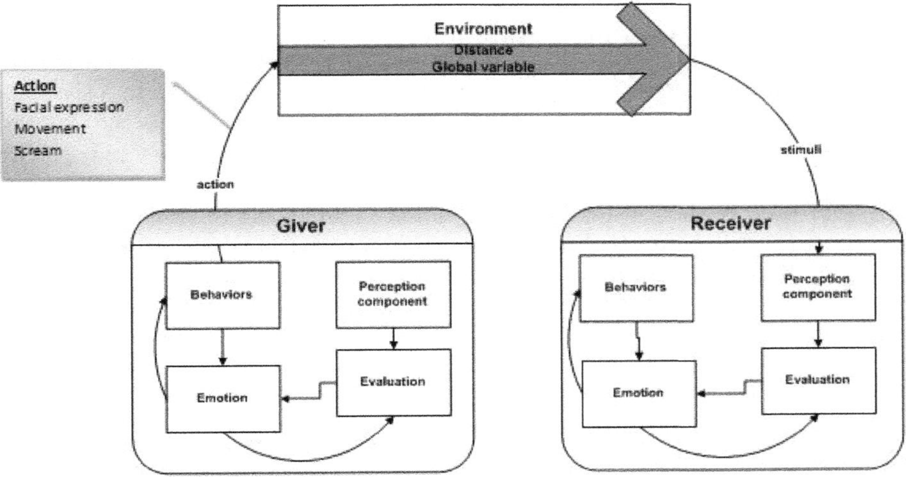

Fig. 4. Emotional propagation model

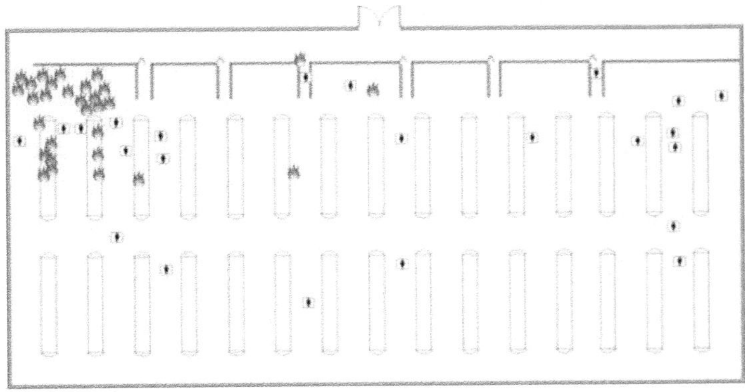

Fig. 5. Overview of the simulation

to the environment, he expresses his emotion via his behavior. Then, an agent can recognize the emotion of the other ones according to the behaviors that he perceives. The emotion of an agent can thus spread over a group of agents. Figure 4 describes the way an agent gives his emotion to others via his behaviors.

4 Implementation of the Emotional Agent

In this section we present the situation that we want to simulate, the details of the agents involved in this simulation and how we can improve their behavior by introducing emotions. The model is implemented on the GAMA platform [2,21].

4.1 Description of the Application Case: Pedestrian Evacuation in a Burning Shopping Center

The simulation aims at representing the scenario described below. In a shopping center, while people are shopping, the fire appears. Figure 5 presents the overview of the simulation. The people who see the fire may be scared. They may scream or change their movement speed. Other agents who perceive these actions may feel their fear. With this simulation we aim at highlighting the important role of emotions (in this case, the fear) in an emergency evacuation, and in particular the fact that the casualty rate can highly be increased, in the case of a panicked crowd.

4.2 Description of the Agents

In our simulation, we use two kinds of agent: agents representing human beings and agents representing fire. In the sequel we describe in details the implementation of both kinds of agent.

Human Agent

Attributes	Methods
Size: agent size **Perception_range**: radius within which an agent can perceive a stimulus **Propagation_range**: radius within which an agent can propagate information to others **Emotion_type**: type of emotion (in this model, emotion_type is "fear") **Emotion_intensity**: intensity of the emotion **Sensitivity_ability** (α): the sensitivity of an agent. The greater this attribute is, the more sensible the agent is **Decay_ability**: the capability to reduce the intensity of emotion. The greater this coefficient is, the faster the emotion disappears **Global_variable**: the global effect of environment on each agent. This coefficient is set randomly at the beginning of the simulation	**Wander(speed:float)**: the agent moves randomly **GoToTarget(speed:float)**: the agent goes to his target **AvoidObstacle()**: The agent avoids the obstacles and the other agents **PerceiveStimuli()**: the agent perceives stimuli within his range of perception **PropagateInformation()**: the agent propagates information within his range of propagation **Reflex()**: the agent evaluates the stimulus in order to choose his behavior **ChangeColor(color:Color)**: the agent changes his color

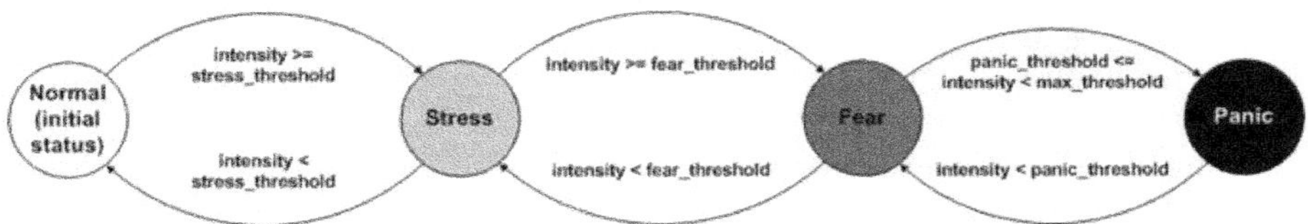

Fig. 6. Levels of the fear

No	Behaviors	Normal	Stress	Fear	Panic
1	Display in color				
2	Avoid obstacle	yes	yes	yes	yes
3	Perceive stimuli	yes	yes	yes	yes
4	Wander with normal speed	yes	no	no	no
5	Quit the shopping center with normal speed	no	yes	no	no
6	Quit the shopping center with great speed	no	no	yes	no
7	Wander with great speed	no	no	no	yes
8	Propagate information to others	no	yes	yes	yes

Fig. 7. List of behaviors

Fire agent

Attributes	Methods
Size: size of one piece of fire **Duration**: duration of the fire **Propagation_range**: range within which the fire can spread at each step	**Propagate()**: the agent propagates himself within the range of propagation

4.3 Description of the Emotion (The Fear)

As mentioned above, the emotion that influences the most the behavior of agents in an emergency situation is the fear. We choose thus to limit the emotions involved in the simulation to the fear. In our simulation, we distinguish four levels of fear (depending on the intensity level of the emotion): normal, stress, fear and panic. Figure 6 presents these levels.

At each level of fear, the agent may execute different behaviors or a behavior with different manners (*e.g.* wander with a normal speed when the agent is in the state normal or wander with a high speed when he is panicked). In our model we proposed seven behaviors described in Figure 7.

1. Display in color: the agent uses this behavior to show graphically his current fear level. At each level of fear the agent uses the method *Change-Color(color:Color)* to show a particular color (white, light blue, blue, dark blue).

2. Avoid obstacle: this is a fundamental behavior. At every step an agent moves, he invokes the method *AvoidObstacle()* to avoid collisions with obstacles (wall, other agents...)

3. Perceive the stimuli: this is also a fundamental behavior: this method is invoked at each step. The agent can perceive the fire or get emotional information from the behavior of other agents.

4. Wander with normal speed: this behavior shows that the agent is in a non-stressful state. The agent wanders with a normal speed if he is not scared. In this case, the agent invokes the method *Wander(speed : float)* with the normal value of speed.

5. Quit the shopping center with normal speed: this behavior shows that the agent is aware of a fire. The agent who is scared with the average intensity keeps his reasoning capabilities: he can thus find a way to escape. The agent invokes the method *GoToTarget(speed : float)* with the normal value of speed.

6. Quit the shopping center with great speed: this behavior is similar to the behavior 5 but in this case, the agent is truly afraid: the value of the speed is thus higher.

7. Wander with great speed: similar to the behavior 4 but in this case the speed is higher. This behavior illustrates the case when the fear is so intense that the agent becomes panicked, loses awareness and thus cannot control himself.

8. Propagate the information: As soon as the agent feels any kind of fear (stress, fear or panic), he invokes the method *PropagateInformation()* to spread this emotional information to other agents.

5 Experimentation

In this section, we present the tests led on the emergency evacuation model. In order to evaluate the role of the emotional factor in the emergency evacuation, we propose two measures that we use to monitor our model: **Emotional Rate** (ER) is the percentage of people who are in a fear state in a unit of time; **Survivor Rate** (SR) is the percentage of people who succeed to escape the building. Our experimentation is separated into three models: a model without emotion, a model with emotion but without propagation and a model with emotion and propagation. In each test case, the parameters of the emotional factors are set with the average value so that the simulation is closer to actual situations.

5.1 Model without Emotion

In this test case, we set the values of the *propagation_range* and of the *perception_range* to zero, which means that the human agent cannot perceive the emotion of other agents. In this case, the human agents are not aware of the danger. And when the fire propagates in a wide area, these agents do not change their behavior to survive. In consequence, the survivor rate (SR) is very low.

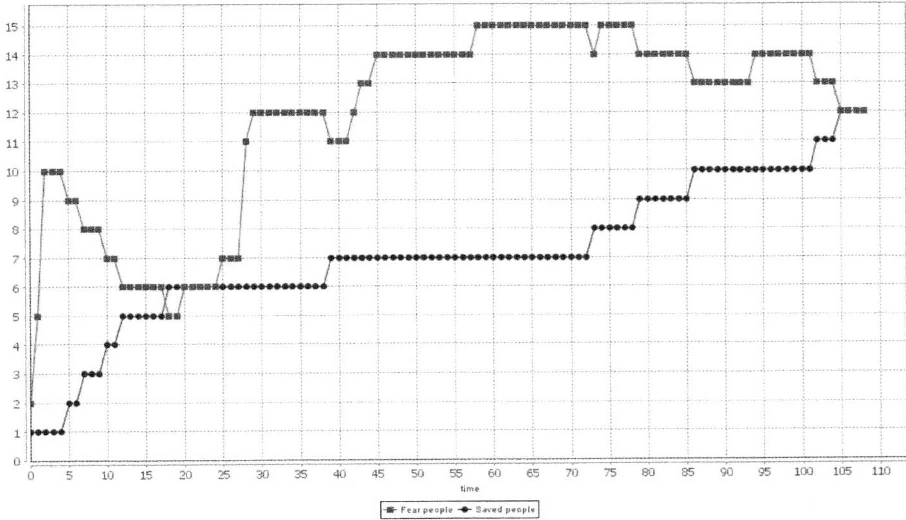

Fig. 8. Evolution of the emotion rate and of the number of survivors

5.2 Model with Emotions but without Propagation

In this test case, the value of the *propagation_range* is zero and the *perception_range* is set randomly in its definition interval. In this case, the human agents can themselves perceive the fire which can trigger fear but cannot propagate their emotion to others. Only the people who see the fire may become afraid and then flee the danger to save their life. The others who do not see the fire are not scared. This is why the emotional rate (ER) is higher than in the first test case but still low. With the people who are not aware of the danger, it may be too late to survive because the fire spreads quickly and blocks the exit. Thus, in this test case, the survivor rate (SR) is still low. The chart in Figure 8 shows the progress of the two indicators during the simulation.

5.3 Model with Emotions and Propagation

In this test case, the value of the *propagation_range* and of the *perception_range* are set randomly in their definition interval, which means that the people can feel the fear by perceiving the stimuli from the environment and can inform the others about their fear. They can perceive not only the fire but also the behaviors of others. In the chart in the Figure 9, at step 40, the emotional propagation happens, the emotional rate (ER) jumps thus significantly and then the survivor rate (SR) increases quickly. That is why the survivor rate is higher.

5.4 Discussion

After having executed the simulation 100 times and making statistics on the data obtained, we find that the benefits of the emotional factors in the simulation of

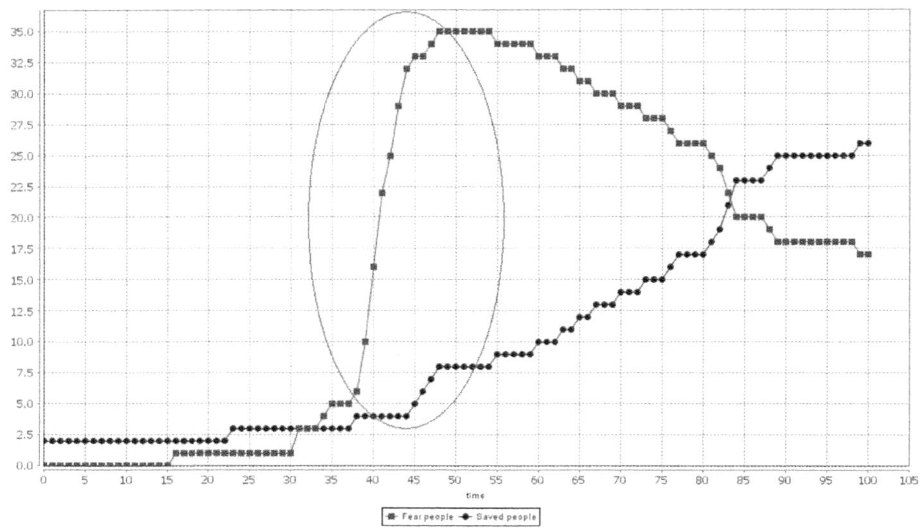

Fig. 9. Evolutions of the emotion rate and the number of survivors

the emergency evacuation is very important. In the chart of the Figure 10, in the case of emotions with propagation, the percentage of survivors is the highest (45.03 %).

We can summarize our model by responding to following questions.

How an emotion appears? The agent perceives stimuli; he evaluates them according to his knowledge and his current emotion; then, a new emotion appears.

Which may influence the appraisal process of the stimuli? The stimuli, the empathy of the agent and effects of the environment influence the evaluation of emotion. The intensity of emotion of each agent is different to each other, although they perceive the same stimuli at the same time. When the agents perceive the fire, some may be scared, others may not. This is all because of the empathy.

How can an agent show his emotion? Through his behaviors, an agent shows his current emotion. In our simulation, these behaviors are: appearance change (like the human facial expression), the movement speed or other ways to inform other agents (scream, cry...).

How can the propagation of emotions happen? An agent perceives the others' behaviors, evaluates them like any environmental stimuli. Then, an emotion appears. Thus, the emotion spreads over agents.

In our research, we found that there is an amplification of the emotional intensity in the mob. We name it the emotional circle effect. It means that, when the

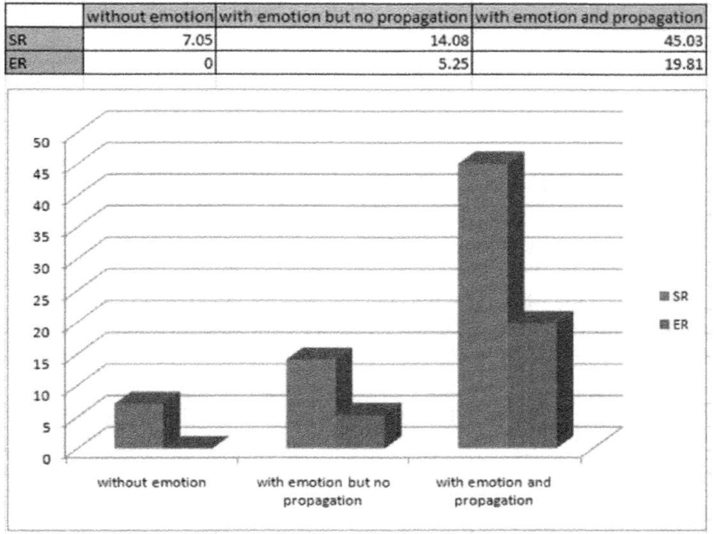

	without emotion	with emotion but no propagation	with emotion and propagation
SR	7.05	14.08	45.03
ER	0	5.25	19.81

Fig. 10. Evolutions of the emotion rate and the number of survivors

first agent perceives the fire, he is scared and executes a behavior revealing his fear; the other agents perceive these behaviors; they are scared in turn and react to this emotion; the first agent mentioned perceives these behaviors and then the intensity of his own fear is increased. This type of process is repeated and the intensity of the fear in the mod jumps significantly. In a real situation, this kind of phenomenon happens frequently and is not limited to the fear inducing panic but also for example to the joy: the joy of the spectators in the stadium is much more intensive than that of the man who watches the match on his television at home.

6 Conclusion

Theoretically we proposed a model of emotion based on cognitive theories of emotion and then a architecture of emotional agent. According to the theory proposed, we can improve the emergency evacuation by adding emotional factors.

Practically we described the model of the simulation of the emergency evacuation in a burning shopping center. In addition, according to our simulation, we succeeded to prove the important role of emotions in the emergency evacuation.

In our research, we simulate only one emotion. The behaviors of agent are also affected by only one emotion. Simulating a multi-emotion model is thus the principal perspective of our research. In the multi-emotion model, each stimulus can trigger more than one emotion and, because many current emotions influence not only the appraisal process but also the behaviors; the simulation will thus become more and more complex.

Acknowledgment. This work was funded by the project EPIS, a French IRD SPIRALES research program that is developed by research teamwork MSI-IRD UMMISCO.

References

1. Adam, C., Gaudou, B., Login, D., Lorini, E.: Logical modeling of emotions for ambient intelligence. In: Mastrogiovanni, F., Chong, N.Y. (eds.) Handbook of Research on Ambient Intelligence: Trends and Perspectives. IGI Global Publisher (2009) (to appear in 2010)
2. Amouroux, E., Chu, T., Boucher, A., Drogoul, A.: Gama: an environment for implementing and running spatially explicit multi-agent simulations. In: Pacific Rim International Workshop on Multi-Agents, Bangkoku, Thailand, pp. 359–371 (2007)
3. Arnold, M.B.: Emotion and personality. Columbia University Press, New York (1960)
4. Bosse, T., Duell, R., Memon, Z.A., Treur, J., van der Wal, C.N.: A Multi-Agent Model for Emotion Contagion Spirals Integrated Within a Supporting Ambient Agent Model. In: Yang, J.-J., Yokoo, M., Ito, T., Jin, Z., Scerri, P. (eds.) PRIMA 2009. LNCS (LNAI), vol. 5925, pp. 48–67. Springer, Heidelberg (2009)
5. Cabanac, M.: What is emotion? Behavioural Processes 60, 69–83 (2002)
6. Damasio, A.R.: Descartes' Error: Emotion, Reason, and the Human Brain. Putnam Pub. Group (1994)
7. De Rosis, F., Pelachaud, C., Poggi, I., Carofiglio, V., De Carolis, B.: From greta's mind to her face: Modelling the dynamics of affective states in a conversational embodied agent. International Journal of Human-Computer Studies 59, 81–118 (2003)
8. Forgas, J.: Mood and judgment: The affect infusion model (aim). Psychological Bulletin 117, 39–66 (1995)
9. Hollmann, C., Lawrence, P.J., Galea, E.R.: Introducing emotion modelling to agent-based pedestrian circulation simulation. In: PED 2010. NIST, Maryland (2010)
10. Lange, C., James, W.: The emotions. Hafner, New York (1967)
11. Lazarus, R.S.: Emotion and Adaptation. Oxford University Press (1991)
12. Musse, S.R., Thalmann, D.: Hierarchical model for real time simulation of virtual human crowds. IEEE Transactions on Visualization and Computer Graphics 7(2), 152–164 (2001)
13. Nair, R., Tambe, M., Marsella, S.: The role of emotions in multiagent team work. In: Fellous, J.M., Arbib, M. (eds.) Who Needs Emotions: the Brain Meets the Robot. Oxford University Press (2005)
14. North, M., Collier, N., Vos, J.: Experiences creating three implementations of the repast agent modeling toolkit. ACM Transactions on Modeling and Computer Simulation 16(1), 1–25 (2006)
15. Ortony, A., Clore, G., Collins, A.: The cognitive structure of emotions. Cambridge University Press, United Kingdom (1988)
16. Parunak, H.V.D., Bisson, R., Brueckner, S., Matthews, R., Sauter, J.: A model of emotions for situated agents. In: Proceedings of the Fifth International Joint Conference on Autonomous Agents and Multiagent Systems, AAMAS 2006, Hakodate, Hokkaido, Japan, pp. 993–995 (2006)

17. Rao, A.S., Georgeff, M.P.: Modeling rational agents within a bdi-architecture. In: Allen, J.A., Fikes, R., Sandewall, E. (eds.) Proc. Second Int. Conf. on Principles of Knowledge Representation and Reasoning (KR 1991), pp. 473–484. Morgan Kaufmann Publishers (1991)
18. Ren, A., Chen, C., Luo, Y.: Simulation of Emergency Evacuation in Virtual Reality. Tsinghua Science Technology 13(5), 674–680 (2008)
19. Shendarkar, A., Vasudevan, K., Lee, S., Son, Y.J.: Crowd simulation for emergency response using BDI agents based on immersive virtual reality. Simulation Modelling Practice and Theory 16(9), 1415–1429 (2008)
20. Stroehle, J.: How do pedestrian crowds react when they are in an emergency situation - models and software Pedestrian behavior (2008)
21. Taillandier, P., Drogoul, A., Vo, D., Amouroux, E.: Gama: A Simulation Platform That Integrates Geographical Information Data, Agent-Based Modeling and Multi-Scale Control. In: Desai, N., Liu, A., Winikoff, M. (eds.) PRIMA 2010. LNCS(LNAI), vol. 7057, pp. 244–260. Springer, Heidelberg (2011)
22. Zoumpoulaki, A., Avradinis, N., Vosinakis, S.: A Multi-Agent Simulation Frame Work for Emergency Evacuations Incorporating Personality and Emotions. In: Konstantopoulos, S., Perantonis, S., Karkaletsis, V., Spyropoulos, C.D., Vouros, G. (eds.) SETN 2010. LNCS (LNAI), vol. 6040, pp. 423–428. Springer, Heidelberg (2010)

From Biological to Urban Cells: Lessons from Three Multilevel Agent-Based Models

Javier Gil-Quijano[1], Thomas Louail[2,3], and Guillaume Hutzler[2]

[1] CEA, LIST, LIMA, 91191 Gif-sur-Yvette CEDEX, France
[2] IBISC Laboratory, Evry-Val d'Essonne University, Evry, France
[3] Geographie-Cités Laboratory, CNRS, Paris 1-Paris 7 Universities, Paris, France

Abstract. Modeling complex systems often implies to consider entities at several levels of organization and levels of scales. Taking into account these levels, their mutual interactions, and the organizational dynamics at the interface between levels, is a difficult problem, for which the proposed solutions are often related to a specific disciplinary field or a particular case study. In order to develop a broader methodology for designing multilevel models, we propose an analytical framework of existing approaches, drawn in particular from the study of three examples in biology and geography.

1 Introduction

Natural and social complex systems are often characterized by many different entities, heterogeneous in nature and dimensions, at various levels of organization. The interaction between these entities are intricated, and act at very different time and spatial scales. Addressing questions about these systems requires to consider simultaneously multiple levels of organization. Paradoxically, in this context, most of the "multiscale" or "multilevel" models implement a solution where the description of the thematic knowledge occur at one level only. The choice of this level of description determines the selection of the entities of the real system that are reified as agents in the model. The simulated system can then be analyzed at two organizational levels: at the agents' level on the one hand, through the analysis of their trajectories; at the system's level on the other hand, through a set of measures used to characterize the structures produced during the simulation. It should be noted that such systems can also be measured at intermediary levels that appear to be relevant to the modeler. These levels can for example correspond to *groups* of agents that share common characteristics. In practice, however, this refinement is rarely implemented.

In that case, it seems problematic to talk about truly multilevel modeling since only the "lower" level is present in the model and specified as such by the modeler. The "higher" levels are in this case the ones that can be observed by the experimenter who "looks at" and analyzes the simulations, but these levels are not reified in the model. This *emergentist* approach, which is single-level regarding the design of the model, and bi-level regarding the analysis of

N. Desai, A. Liu, and M. Winikoff (Eds.): PRIMA 2010, LNAI 7057, pp. 620–635, 2012.

results, is by far the most commonly used in agent-based simulation. However, this approach can not always be satisfactorily applied when modeling real systems. Indeed, a number of complex systems dynamics can not be understood without integrating multiple levels of organization, and multiple processes that can not be reduced to a purely emergentist approach. In particular, social systems inherently include a structuring role of higher levels on lower levels. Thus, the corresponding domain theories are rarely single-level, either because there is a lack of knowledge at a given level or because the domain's ontologies mix entities and actors of different levels of organization. It is for example difficult to imagine modeling the evolution of a whole city over several years, on the basis of the sole specification of the behavior of its inhabitants. Moreover, it would be too expensive from a computational point of view to simulate a large system as a whole at the most detailed level. For example, simulating a cell consisting in more than 4.10^{13} molecules (e.g. a cell of a rat's liver) at the atomic level, or even at the molecular level, is indeed completely unrealistic.

In the end, the question that is addressed by the model requires considering entities at different levels (for example the molecular and cellular levels, or the individual, neighborhood and city levels) which, as Servat et al. recall in [16], is part of the scientist's "intellectual gymnastics": to make different points of views and different descriptions of the same system co-exist, and to coherently articulate them. And indeed, we perceive the world at several scale levels. They also underline two additional reasons that justify the integration of multiple levels. The first reason is computational, the collective behavior of many distributed systems changing remarkably when the number of their components reaches a critically large value. It is thus important to enable the simulation of such large numbers of components, which makes it impossible to model systems at the smallest possible scale. To circumvent this difficulty, we can imagine dynamically replacing some groups of agents by "super-agents". These would embed behavioral rules that would be equivalent to the measured result of the accumulated actions of the individual agents. That would allow to enhance the performance, and the modeler could then take advantage of the saved computational power to "zoom in" other parts of the system that he/she would like to model in more details. The second reason is "thematical". If an agent is able to realize that it belongs to (or is categorized as belonging to) a group of higher organizational level, like a social class, it might conscientiously affect his behavior in order to reinforce (or oppositely to diverge) his belonging to this group. In a general manner, integrating entities and rules of multiple levels of organization is an important issue. It should allow to tackle original questions, as compared to the possibilities offered by classical bi-level, micro-macro modeling.

Additionally, rather than representing all components and their relations, the key point should be to consider *simultaneously* the level of the system's components and the level of their emergent properties, as Lesne expressed in [9]. It implies that our efforts should worth be made in accurately describing how the different levels articulate and influence each other, rather than solely juxtaposing many levels in a single model. Articulating levels implies to explicitly represent each of them into the model, and explicitly define how they are coupled. In agent-based modeling, this means that the model should incorporate some rules that specify how the agents associated to a given level would impact and modify agents at other levels. This is presently a central question in the agent-based modeling community and several projects focus on developing simulation platforms that allow to take into account simultaneously several levels within a single model (as for example the 3WORLDS project [6] in ecology, or more generally in the GAMA platform [17]).

Before illustrating these different aspects by the presentation of three recent applications of multilevel simulation in section 3, we start in section 2 by a work of definition necessary to clarify the manipulated concepts. In the examples section, we concentrate on isolating the different organizational levels represented in each model and the mechanisms that support their coupling. In section 4, we generalize their underlying multi-agent organizations and we throw light upon their similarities and differences. From that discussion we propose a classification of multilevel agent-based architectures, based upon the criteria identified in this comparison. Finally, we conclude by discussing the research perspectives opened by this comparative study.

2 Multiscale or Multilevel ?

Scale or level, multiscale or multilevel ? The concepts of scale and level are frequently used to model complex systems and to characterize the manipulated abstractions, their granularity and their position in a hierarchy that structures and organizes the system. These two terms are often used interchangeably, moreover they are used in diverse manners depending on the disciplines, which is potentially very confusing.

The concept of *scale* is frequently characterized by an adjective that relates it to space or time: spatial scale, temporal scale. The term *level* is often associated with terms such as *micro*, *macro* or *meso* that situate the described system or phenomenon in respect to its size, its characteristic evolution time or an inclusion relation with other systems or subsystems. At first sight, we consider that the concept of *scale* refers to a dimension of analysis on which the phenomenon of interest can be measured. This dimension can be spatial or temporal, but also quantitative. The spatial and temporal dimensions refer respectively to the size of the entities involved in the phenomenon (typically from nanometers to thousands of miles throughout all the intermediate sizes), and the characteristic time associated with the behaviors of these entities and their interactions (from nanoseconds to centuries). The quantitative dimension refers to the number of entities involved in the phenomenon (typically from 2 to some billions).

Compared to that definition of scale, the concept of *level* is used to situate the studied phenomenon and/or the entities that compose it, along the considered dimension of analysis. A level usually corresponds to all the entities whose size and/or characteristic evolution time have the same or comparable orders of magnitude. If one sticks to this use of the scale and level concepts and being strict, one should not use the "multiscale " term to describe models. Indeed, most of the times "multiscale" means that the model considers entities at different levels along the spatial scale. Later in this article we will not use the *multiscale* adjective anymore to characterize models, prefering the use of the *multilevel* adjective instead.

It should be immediately noted that the concept of level is both *relative* and bounded to a modeling choice. With *relative*, we mean that an entity, which is considered in a given phenomenon, can not be totally described as belonging to a given level. For example, from the perspective of molecular biology, molecules are related to the micro level while the cell is associated to the macro level; from the standpoint of physiology, the cells are associated to the micro level and the macro level corresponds to the tissue. Moreover, the association of an entity with a given level is not exclusively related to the entity's characteristics along a given scale but it is the result of the analysis and modeling choices. Indeed, the decision of combining diverse entities within a given level often involves the fact that the entities belong to a structure or a relevant organization in terms of the system's description. It is indeed common to speak of "level of organization" or "level of abstraction".

Let us finally present two additional concepts that are useful in our analysis: *hierarchy* and *structure*. The concept of hierarchy, because systems are often described as a hierarchical interlocking of levels (molecules, cells, tissues, organs, individuals, group, society). The concept of structure, as it is often the recognition of a structuring set of entities at one level that allows the definition of entities at a higher level. In [5] the concept of *hierarchy* is defined as "A conceptually or causally linked system of grouping objects or processes along an analytical scale", and three types of hierarchies are distinguished: exclusive, inclusive and constitutive. An *exclusive hierarchy* is a hierarchy in which there is no inclusion relationship between entities in a level and higher level entities. For example, this is the case of military ranking systems or food chains in which individuals of a certain trophic level feed on lower-level individuals. Conversely, in inclusive or constitutive hierarchies the entities of a given level are included in a top-level entity. The objects in an *inclusive hierarchies* exhibit a categorical relationship similar to that present in hierarchies of classes in a object-oriented programming language or in taxonomical hierarchies (domain, kingdom, phylum, class, order, family, genus, species). In the case of *constitutive hierarchies*, entities of one level are grouped into new entities of the next level, the latter being characterized by new organizations, functions and emergent properties (molecules, cells, tissues, organs, individuals). To determine the levels where entities must be placed, more than their sizes, the important point is to consider the group they form, that is, how the entities organize within their group.

3 The Models

Now that the context has been clarified, we will focus on three proposed agent-based simulation models in which multilevel modeling issues have been addressed explicitly. The first example deals with the growth of a cancerous tumor, addressed at the molecular and cellular levels. The second deals with housing choices of households in Bogota, treated individually at the level of households and housings but also at the level of *groups* of housings and households. Finally, the third presents a model of urban morphogenesis, considered at inter- and intra-urban levels.

The objective is not to make an in-depth presentation either of the models or of their results, but rather to focus on how they implement the concept of multilevel modeling. To do this, and to facilitate the comparison between these different models, we will answer the following questions:

1. *Specification of the levels*: what are the different identified levels, what are the types of objects and/or agents defined at these levels, and how are these types defined (are they specified beforehand or are they dynamically discovered)?
2. *Instanciation of the objects*: how is the instanciation of the objects and/or agents done (is it done statically by explicitly defining the agents of the model or are they created dynamically in the simulation depending on the context)?
3. *Coupling between the levels*: how are the different levels coupled with one another (what is the nature of the interactions between agents of different levels)?

3.1 Cancer Cells Migration

Context and objective. When speaking about cancer, one of the major factors of bad prognosis is associated with the appearance of secondary tumors, called metastases. These secondary tumors can develop when a cell of the primary tumor switches from a proliferating to a migrating state, thus escaping towards other organs elsewhere in the body. When the micro-environmental conditions permit, the cell stops its migration and returns to a proliferating state, which leads to the development of a secondary tumor. We are interested in the micro-environmental conditions around the tumor which could lead to the metastatic escape of a cell. We study more precisely the role of a protein, which is suspected to have a role both in triggering the morphologic transformations of the cells and in providing loose adhesion contacts that enable the escape [11].

The model. We developed a first agent-based model in which both cells and proteins are modeled as individual entities. The growth of the tumor is modeled by implementing a cellular division behavior, which depends mainly, for the cell, on its capacity to feed itself from surrounding nutrients. This proliferating behavior is coupled to an inter-cellular repulsion behavior. The model also takes into account the dynamics of production and internalization of proteins by the cells. The differential access to nutrients leads to three distinct states for the cells inside the tumor: a cell that has a satisfactory access to nutrients (external layer) is active and has both the proliferating and the protein production/internalization behaviors; a cell that receives too few nutrients dies (core);

cells in-between receive enough nutrients to produce and internalize the proteins but too few to proliferate, thus becoming quiescent (intermediate region).

The main trouble is that when tumors reach a size of several thousands of cells, the number of proteins reaches several hundreds of thousands. We get therefore quickly limited by the size of the tumors that can reasonably be simulated. The proposed solution consists in abstracting some details of the model in regions where they are not necessary, thus allowing to simulate bigger tumors or to add details in the most interesting regions. Given that the main interesting area is at the interface between the external layer of the tumor and the environment, we proposed to replace the internal region of the tumor by an aggregated model, abstracting the set of cells and proteins in the core region as a global model of ingoing and outgoing flows. From a spatial point of view, this model is delimited by the entire set of necrosed and quiescent cells, and all the proteins in the so-defined area. Since these cells are static, or have a very limited mobility, this permits to neglect the repulsive movements of the cells (mainly due to the cellular-division behavior of the cells in the external proliferating layer). It is then a matter of calculating the interactions between the aggregated model and the external cells or proteins. It is straightforward to determine the cells or proteins that have to be integrated in the aggregated model: these are the quiescent cells, and the proteins in the corresponding area or the ones that, during their random diffusion movement, collide with the aggregated model. Symmetrically, in order to determine how many proteins will be released by this model, it is necessary to evaluate the relative proportion of necrosed and quiescent cells, so as to evaluate the number of cells that produce and internalize these proteins (the quiescent ones). It is then possible to update the concentration of proteins inside the aggregated model. By assimilating the proteins diffusing inside the model to a perfect gas, we can then calculate the "pressure" inside the model, thus determining the statistical quantity of proteins that leave the aggregated model. These proteins are finally stochastically distributed around the aggregated model, at the immediate vicinity of the frontier.

Agents and levels. In this model, objects of very different sizes (cells and proteins) coexist. The levels correspond to two types of objects both types being defined beforehand. The instantiation is done by creating an initial cell, which itself creates other cells by successive division steps. The cellular and molecular levels are coupled thanks to the activity of the cells: the latter produce and internalize proteins. By simulating these agents together, a cluster of cells is produced. That cluster is observed and identified as the tumor. Up to this point, there is no scale crossing, but only the interaction, in a common environment, of objects of different levels in the spatial scale. The tumor's level is only observed and does not perform any active role in simulation.

On the contrary, when the aggregated model is introduced (see figure 1), we identify at run time an intermediate level (between the cellular and tumor levels) entity, which is reified during the simulation. This corresponds to the introduction of the additional modeling level of a multicellular tissue at the heart of the tumor. This kind of object is specified beforehand: we know for

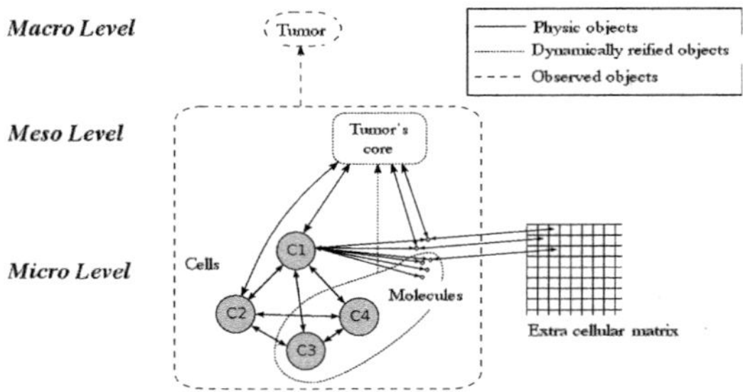

Fig. 1. Introduction of an aggregated model to account for the core of the tumour

sure that the simulation will lead to the development of a tumor and we can therefore anticipate the appearance of this object. However, its instantiation will depend on the time at which such an object is observed in the simulation. The coupling of this structure with the other objects (cells and proteins) depends on if they are inside or outside the aggregated model. The coupling with the internal objects is implemented thanks to a set of very simple differential equations, which describe the evolution of the relative quantities of necrosed and quiescent cells, the evolution of the concentration of proteins inside the model and the amount of externalized proteins. The coupling with the external objects is implemented by describing both the conditions that lead the external objects to be integrated into the aggregated model and the rules defining the externalization of proteins. The dynamics of the aggregated object can then be seen as the numerical integration of very simple differential equations.

The multilevel character of this model can be seen in two complementary ways. The first one consists in noticing that the model, which is composed of both cells and proteins, integrates objects of very different sizes. The second one consists in proposing that objects corresponding to abstractions of higher levels of organization be introduced dynamically in the simulation.

3.2 SimulBogota : Households and Housings in Bogota City

Context and objective. The objective of the SimulBogota model [7] is to reproduce the evolution of the spatial distribution of the population of the city of Bogota throughout several decades. This evolution depends on both the internal and external migrations as well as on the evolution of the population and of the housing-stock. The evolution of the population of households is the result of individual events (marriage, divorce, emancipation, death, etc.) that produce socio-economical changes as well as the creation and destruction of households. The evolution of the housing-stock depends mainly on both the housing-renewal and the aging-of-buildings processes. In the case of Bogota, these processes are the result of very complex dynamics that not only involve the construction controlled by planning policies, but also informal mechanisms such as self-construction and illegal occupation of housing estates.

The model. To implement our model, the only available data were the socio-economical descriptions of households and housings as well as their spatial distribution for the years 1973 and 1993. In the absence of sufficient data, a model centered on the explicit representation of the decision and evolution mechanisms at the individual's level is inadequate or even impossible. Under these conditions, we proposed to consider *groups of households* and *groups of housings* as main modeling entities. This reduces the complexity of simulations by taking an aggregate level into account, in which the decision process that leads households to move is placed. However, it is necessary to consider the populations of households and housings in order to model the evolution of groups.

In this model we explicitly consider two levels of modeling, *the microscopic level* that contains data that describe the populations of households and housings and *the mesoscopic level* that contains the groups of households and the groups of housings. The model is mainly composed of three mechanisms executed in sequence at each step of simulation:

1. Formation of groups: this allows to go from the microscopic level (households and housings) to the mesoscopic level (groups of households and groups of housings). It is an automated clustering mechanism [7] performed on the data that represent households and housings.
2. Interaction between groups: this allows to rehouse the households in the city. It is an auction-based mechanism that is used to exchange housing-units between groups of households. These interactions are governed both by a set of lists of housing-preferences, which are built dynamically[1] and a static matrix of costs of moving between urban areas. In this mechanism, we assume that households seek to move closer to households of their social group and to occupy the same group of housings. It is therefore a self-reinforced mechanism of spatial segregation.
3. Evolution of the population: this is a mechanism based on the execution of global rules of evolution of the populations of households and housings. These rules allow the creation or deletion of entities at the microscopic level (households or housings). Each rule associates an entity profile with a number of entities to be treated. These rules do not represent individual events (which are very difficult to be considered and very data-consuming) but global trends of evolution.

In order to trace the evolution of groups, a last mechanism is implemented, which allows to relate the groups found in two successive steps of simulation.

Agents and levels. In this model, in order to reduce the complexity of simulations and the amount of data required to represent the dynamics of intra-urban migrations, we introduced an intermediate level composed of *"artificial"* structures: groups composed of similar microscopic entities. These structures have no "physical" equivalent and they are the result of the analysis of households data

[1] Preferences evolve according to the changes in the spatial distribution of the groups.

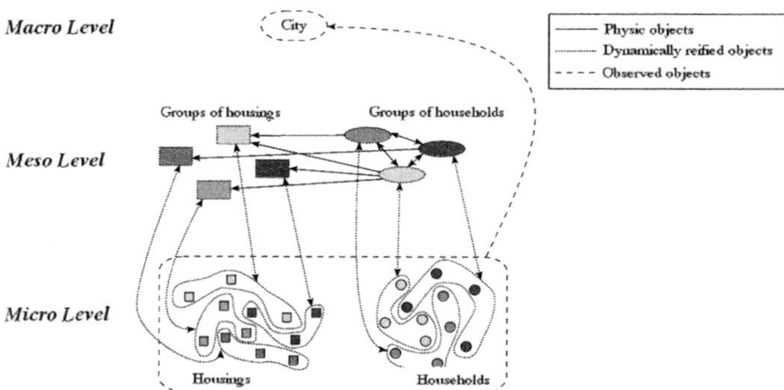

Fig. 2. Diagram of interactions between levels in the simulation of the evolution of the spatial distribution of population in SIMULBOGOTA

and housings data (microscopic level). Thus, physical objects, at the microscopic level, coexist with artificial objects, at the mesoscopic level, that are dynamically reified by clustering the objects of the microscopic level into homogeneous groups (see figure 2). Compared to models of physical phenomena, an additional question arises: it is necessary to define the number of groups to be considered, knowing that a small number can produce an oversimplification of the model, while a high number may get groups extremely closer to the microscopic level and cause a loss of the model's synthesis ability. Even if the *level of groups has been specified beforehand*, the number of considered groups is determined at run time and *the groups are dynamically instantiated* from the results of clustering the data of households and housings at every simulation's step.

From the evolution's perspective, general rules were constructed from descriptive data of households and housings. The core of the evolution mechanism is therefore located at the microscopic level and its effects are propagated to the level of groups by the clustering mechanism (bottom-up coupling). However, there is no direct interaction between microscopic entities. The microscopic level is used as an *anchor with reality* while the level of groups provides *a synthetic vision of reality*, which facilitates the formulation and the assessment of hypotheses about the behavior of the system, thus leading to a better understanding of the modeled phenomenon.

The "artificiality" of groups conditions the design of both the inter-groups interaction mechanisms and the interlevel interaction mechanisms. When simulating groups of micro-entities, one has to deal with abstract entities, that have no "physical" counterpart. Since the modeler can not rely on well established rules (or that can be easily deduced) that describe the behavior of the groups, he is therefore *free* in defining the interaction mechanisms. Since we know very little about the functioning of groups, the mechanism chosen to represent the interaction between groups is as artificial as the groups themselves. The proposed mechanism, based on auctions of housings, has no physical ground, it is simply an artifact that allows the dynamic multi-criteria matching between groups of households and groups of housings. The design of this mechanism has therefore more to do with modelers' intuition than with inspiration from "real" mechanisms. This mechanism, which is used to rehouse households, establishes the top-down coupling between the level of groups and the microscopic level.

3.3 Simpop3 : Exploring Urban Dynamics at Three Geographical Scales Simultaneously

Context and objective. The SIMPOP models are agent-based models dedicated to the understanding and reproduction of urban growth over periods of several centuries. Those models are used to study the different geographical parameters that lead to the differences that exist at different geographical levels (city, region, nation, continent) between the systems of cities in Europe and in United States. The first of these models, SIMPOP1 [2] has been one of the very first applications of MAS systems in geography. In this section, we briefly present two independent models, SIMPOP2 and SIMPOPNANO. We then discuss their coupling, which results in a new multilevel model, SIMPOP3. The latter allows to tackle new geographical questions, regarding the multilevel processes that take part in the growth of urban systems.

The SIMPOP2 model is based on the urban evolutionary theory [14] and focus on the modeling of systems of cities considered as self-organized complex systems. In that model, some generic and universal properties of the systems of cities are identified and separated from specific processes related to the history of each system. Thanks to that dissociation, SIMPOP2 allows to reproduce the differences that exist between global properties (for example hierarchical distribution of cities' sizes) of different systems of cities. SIMPOPNANO [10] is an attempt to reproduce the emergence of typical patterns of organization *inside the city* and their long-time evolution (200 years), under the dependence of both the topology of the street networks, and the performance of the transports networks. The objective is twofold: to compare the morphogenesis of cities in Europe and United States and to isolate the minimal set of factors that allow to reproduce the observed differences between the cities of the two continents in terms of densities, prices and activities repartitions [1].

The Simpop2 model. *Cities* are the model's main agents. They interact through the exchange of goods associated to the *urban functions* that they own. An *urban function* characterizes a role played by the city that owns that function (heavy industry, car industry, regional capital, etc.) in the system of cities. Each function has a specific period during which it is active. The spatial interactions between cities are of several types. They depend on the *urban function* that mediates the "communication": spatial proximity, administrative frontier or specialized large scale network. In parallel to these exchanges, cities compete for the acquisition of new innovations, which are represented by the dynamic arrival of new urban functions in the system during the simulation. At run time, the interaction network generate progressive specialization of the cities and differentiation between them. At the global level, the consequence is the emergence of a system of cities, whose properties can be determined by measuring key indicators as the total population, primacy indexes, etc.

The SimpopNano model. In this model, agents are of two types: *neighborhood* agents, which represent autonomous portions of the city space, and *urban functions* agents (the same as in SIMPOP2), which represent the main families of socio-economical activities owned by the city. *Functions* have employees to localize. They also have a budget to do so. *Neighborhoods* are linked to a dynamical network and differ by their accessibility and their functional composition. The combination of these two indicators make them more or less attractive for functions, and equally more or less expensive. *Functions* differentiate by their economic power and by their localization strategies. At each time step the model simulates the competition for space of these urban functions inside the neighborhoods. As a consequence of that competition one can observe at run time the structuration of the *emerging city*. Several measures are used to characterize the structures dynamically produced: densities and prices gradients, activities repartition maps, or functional specialization indexes of the neighborhood, etc.

The Simpop3 model. SIMPOP3 includes agents at two levels: at the *micro* level, the urban functions and neighborhoods agents of SIMPOPNANO are considered. At the intermediate (*meso*) level, the urban functions and the cities agents of SIMPOP2 are considered. The link between levels is performed by the exchange of *urban functions*.

SIMPOP3's execution relies on the alternate execution of a SIMPOP2 iteration followed by a SIMPOPNANO iteration:

– at each time step SIMPOP2 computes the cities spatial interactions and the next state of each of them, i.e. the new functions they acquire, and the number of employees and budget of each of their functions;
– the SIMPOP2's outputs are used as input data of SIMPOPNANO, which ventilates these functions staff among the city's neighborhood. Urban functions pay their implantations with the money they have generated at the city level by the sell of goods produced by the function to other cities. SIMPOPNANO outputs an indicator of the spatial "performance" of the functions, which qualify the quality of the functions' repartition inside the city.
– This indicator is considered by the newly arriving urban functions agents to decide in which cities of the system of cities they will implant.

Agents and levels. In SIMPOP2, the spatial specification level, i.e. the level at which the thematic knowledge on the system is formalized as agents and interaction rules, is the level of cities. The cities are primary (micro level) entities, these are the agents of the model. The system of cities is then the emergent level (macro level). SIMPOPNANO "works" at a more nested level: the spatial specification level is the level of neighborhoods, in which the urban functions (the same that are acquired by the city in SIMPOP2) must localize their employees. In this case, the city level is the emergent level. The "city" emerging from SIMPOPNANO is not the same as the one that is specified as an agent in SIMPOP2. The city of SIMPOPNANO is an entity that only exists at runtime, through a combination of

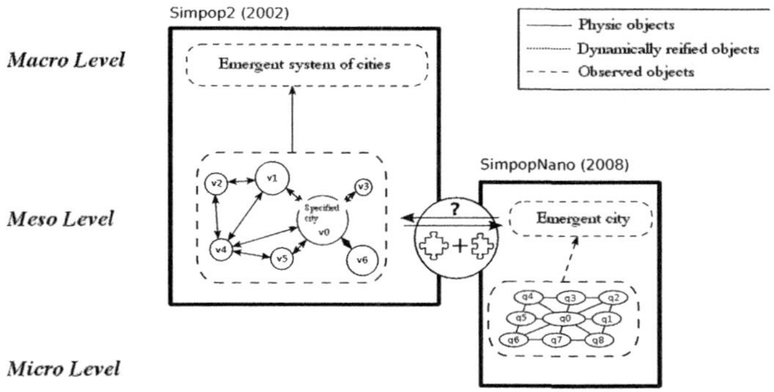

Fig. 3. SIMPOP3: a multilevel MAS to test urban theories at the crossing of scales

measures that let the geographer decide whether the spatial structure emerging of the model "looks like" a real city or not. For SIMPOP3, we have faced the need to build a bridge between these two representations of the same city: the agent specified in SIMPOP2, and the structure emerging from SIMPOPNANO. This is summarized by figure 3.

To implement this articulation between the two models, we have choosen to identify an entity that would be common to the two levels. This entity should represent the mutual influence between an individual city and the system of cities. The concept of *urban function* has been instantiated in the model as a somewhat "multilevel" agent. Urban function is an abstract concept defined by geographers to qualify the role played by a city in the system of cities it belongs to. This concept is relevant at the inter-urban scale. To implement the coupling, the concept has been generalized, and we have made the hypothesis that this concept could be used to qualify the various kinds of socio-economical activities that interact inside the city, and whose behavior shapes its spatial organization. In fact, this is the transfer of this inter-urban concept to the intra-urban level that allowed us to design a bridge that links these three spatial levels all together. The urban function agent is like a buffer: it encapsulates variables that are affected by the dynamics at each level.

4 Towards Multilevel Multi-agent Organizations

Elaborating from the three preceding examples, and from other models taken from the literature, one can try to categorize multilevel models around three aspects:

1. *Multimodels*: we consider here models originally independent, placed at different levels, interacting with each other. The outputs of the upper level models are used to define global parameters of the lower level models; the outputs of the lower level models are considered as ingoing flows in upper level models. We can distinguish between two sub-categories:

(a) the different models are executed alternatively (it is the case for example in SIMPOP3). In that case, the coupling between the models is generally weak but difficulties may appear if the different models share objects that each of them may modify (the "urban function" entity in SIMPOP3).
(b) a multi-agent model is encapsulated inside a higher-level agent. In the model of tumor growth, this would correspond to the fact that we model the internal dynamics of cells, rather than considering a fixed rate production of proteins. This would allow to take into account the genetic regulation networks controlling the production of these proteins. One has to be careful, in that case, to the scheduling of the agents of the different levels, which doesn't necessarily occur at the same time scale.

2. *Models with multilevel specification*: we consider here models where there exist interactions between entities placed at different levels along the spatial, temporal or quantitative scales. One can achieve this through two distinct approaches:
   (a) through the static specification of the simulated entities (e.g. cells interacting with proteins in the tumor growth model; SIMPOP3). Again, problems arise with the scheduling of agents. In the specific case of cells and proteins, the characteristic timescales are indeed very different. This imposes to focus on discrete-events simulation approaches, or to handle several schedulers in parallel for the different types of simulated objects.
   (b) through the dynamic specification of the simulated entities: implementation of mechanisms such as a "dynamic magnifier" that allow to focus on critical areas by raising the spatial resolution and the level of details (e.g. the fractal model of the environment proposed by [12]). The main difficulty in that case lies in the continuous adaptation that is required to retain the higher possible level of details on the areas of interest, for example the ones where agents are situated.
3. *Multilevel models with dynamic reification*: we deal here with models that produce higher-level agents by automatic "observation" of the simulation, characterization of higher-level structures and reification of the structures as objects. We can again distinguish between two distinct cases:
   (a) the agents of the two levels do not directly interact with one another (e.g. simulBogota) because the entities of the two levels are not in the same modeling space. In some way, this case reminds the (1a) case, because we also have an alternating execution of models of the micro and macro levels: indeed, the simulator repeatedly computes the evolution of the model at the micro level, then dynamically reifies the macro level, and computes the evolution of the model at this macro level.
   (b) the agents of the two levels can interact with one another and with the agents of the other level: the entities of the two levels are in the same modeling space (e.g. tumor growth model with the aggregated model, RIVAGE [16], or [4] that develops hierarchical holonic approaches). This approach however induces a greater complexity since it requires to be able to detect the emergence of a structure and to characterize its dynamics and its interactions with the other agents, so as to be able to reify

it. Moreover, it is necessary to control that the conditions required for the structure to be maintained hold, and if it is not the case, to dissolve the structure as such and to transform it back into individual agents.

In the examples that we have presented, only constitutive hierarchies are modeled. In these cases, levels can be either pre-specified beforehand or automatically discovered. When modeling exclusive hierarchies however, the entities and levels are usually specified beforehand. The modeling of exclusive hierarchies can be addressed by the methodologies dealing with the design of organizations. In that case, the modeling process focuses on the specification of roles, norms, functions that define the agents' behaviors and their interactions. Several methodologies have been developed to address organizations modeling, among which are MOISE [8] or AGR [3]. As the effort is done on specification of the entities and their interactions, we consider that these types of models can be included into the second category.

With respect to the modeling of constitutive hierarchies, in our knowledge no general methodology exists. However there exists methodologies that can be used to tackle the design of models of some of the described categories. The categories 1 and 2 can be addressed by multimodeling methodologies. Some of these methodologies are based on the DEVS approach [18]. The Virtual Laboratory Environment (VLE) proposed by [15] implements that approach. VLE provides modules for developing Petri nets, differential equations and spatialized agent based models among others. It also provides the capability to integrate existing models. The modular (every model is considered as an atomic and independent module) approach of VLE and the light coupling between models (based on the input/output events triggering) gives to VLE the flexibility needed to adapt to a large number of multilevel problems where levels can be specified beforehand as independent models. The design of constitutive hierarchies has also been tackled by simulation platforms such as SWARM[2] that proposes the possibility of designing hierarchies as recursive groups of agents.

Nevertheless, these approaches are not well fitted to the case of automatic discovery and analysis of levels (category 3). A significant effort in that direction is currently being done in the development of the GAMA platform (related to the 3WORLDS project [6]), which includes the use of statistical tools for the automatic discovering and tracking of emergent structures in simulations of ecological systems.

5 Conclusion

We have presented three agent-based models that can all, one way or another, be qualified as "multilevel". These models are but very different with one another, by their application domains, the scales of the modeled entities, or the approaches implemented to handle the complexity associated to the coexistence of different levels of organization. We proposed an analytical framework, which still needs to

[2] http://www.swarm.org

be completed and refined by integrating other works from the community, but which already enables the classification of multilevel models, and against which we positioned our models.

By so doing, we do not pretend proposing a step-by-step methodology for the design of new multilevel models. Instead, our aim is on the one hand to show that different modeling problematics can lead to very different solutions, and on the other hand to help the modeler identify the difficulties peculiar to each of the approaches. The identification of these difficulties also leads us to propose some directions for the implementation of agent-based inter-level coupling. We illustrated the pertinence of such couplings on the three presented examples, as well as on other examples drawn from the literature.

When existing models have demonstrated their "quality", it is both useful and important to reuse them, which implies to be able to couple models at different scales or based on heterogeneous formalisms (discrete/continuous for example). To this end, on the one hand microscopic models can be encapsulated as higher-level agents, on the other hand continuous models (e.g. differential equations) can be used in the definition of global variables and dynamics that can feed lower-level models.

Because lots of complex systems have a dynamical structure, it is also important that the reification of entities of the system as agents could itself evolve dynamically. To achieve this, it is necessary to enable the automatic detection [13] and reification of emergent properties. Reciprocally, it is necessary to enable the splitting of agents into underlying organizations, interactively. By adapting the levels of description upon the system, the aim is not so much to gain in terms of computational efficiency, as to gain in terms of expressiveness and intelligibility. By selecting the most pertinent levels of organization and description, the aim is indeed to gain the deeper possible understanding of the mechanisms at work in the modeled system.

References

1. Bertaud, A.: The spatial organization of cities: deliberate outcome or unforeseen consequence (2004), `http://alain-bertaud.com/images/AB_The_spatial_organization_of_cities_Version_3.pdf`
2. Bura, S., Guerin-Pace, F., Mathian, H., Pumain, D., Sanders, L.: Multi-agents system and the dynamics of a settlement system. Geog. Anal. 28(2), 161–178 (1996)
3. Ferber, J., Gutknecht, O., Michel, F.: From Agents to Organizations: an Organizational View of Multiagent Systems. In: Giorgini, P., Müller, J.P., Odell, J. (eds.) AOSE 2003. LNCS, vol. 2935, pp. 214–230. Springer, Heidelberg (2004)
4. Gaud, N., Galland, S., Gechter, F., Hilaire, V., Koukam, A.: Holonic multilevel simulation of complex systems: Application to real-time pedestrians simulation in virtual urban environment. Sim. Model. Pract. and Th. 16(10), 1659–1676 (2008)
5. Gibson, C.C., Ostrom, E., Ahn, T.K.: The concept of scale and the human dimensions of global change: a survey. Ecological Economics 32(2), 217–239 (2000)
6. Gignoux, J., Davies, I., Hill, D.: 3worlds: a new platform for simulating ecological systems. In: 1st Open Inter. Conf. on Modelling and Simulation, Clermont-Ferrand, pp. 49–64 (2005)

7. Gil-Quijano, J., Piron, M., Drogoul, A.: Mechanisms of automated formation and evolution of social-groups: A multi-agent system to model the intra-urban mobilities of Bogotá city. In: Social Simulation: Technologies, Advances and New Discoveries, ch. 12, pp. 151–168. Idea Group Inc. (2007)
8. Hubner, J.F., Sichman, J.S., Boissier, O.: Developing organised multiagent systems using the moise model: programming issues at the system and agent levels. International Journal of Agent-Oriented Software Engineering 1(3), 370–395 (2007)
9. Lesne, A.: Multi-scale approaches. Encyc. of Math. Phys. 3, 465–482 (2006)
10. Louail, T.: Can geometry explain socio-economical differences between US and european cities. In: AB2S Workshop, Paris, ISC-PIF (November 2008)
11. Maquerlot, F., Galiacy, S., Malo, M., Guignabert, C., Lawrence, D.A., d'Ortho, M.-P., Barlovatz-Meimon, G.: Dual role for plasminogen activator inhibitor type 1 as soluble and as matricellular regulator of epithelial alveolar cell wound healing. Am. J. Pathol. 169, 1624–1632 (2006)
12. Marilleau, N., Cambier, C., Drogoul, A., Perrier, E., Chotte, J.L., Blanchart, E.: Multiscale mas modelling to simulate the soil environment: Application to soil ecology. Simulation Modelling Practice and Theory 16, 736–745 (2008)
13. Moncion, T., Hutzler, G., Amar, P.: Detection of emergent phenomena in multi-agent systems. In: Proceedings of the Evry Spring School on Modelling Complex Biological Systems in the Context of Genomics, pp. 45–49. EDP Sciences (2007)
14. Pumain, D.: Pour une théorie évolutive des villes. L'Espace Géographique 2, 119–134 (1997)
15. Quesnel, G., Duboz, R., Ramat, E.: The Virtual Laboratory Environment An operational framework for multi-modelling, simulation and analysis of complex dynamical systems. Sim. Model. Pract. and Th. 17(4), 641–653 (2009)
16. Servat, D., Perrier, E., Treuil, J.-P., Drogoul, A.: When Agents Emerge From Agents: Introducing Multi-Scale Viewpoints In Multi-agent simulations. In: Sichman, J.S., Conte, R., Gilbert, N. (eds.) MABS 1998. LNCS (LNAI), vol. 1534, pp. 183–198. Springer, Heidelberg (1998)
17. Vo, D.-A., Drogoul, A., Zucker, J.-D.: A Modelling Language to Represent and Specify Emerging Structures in Agent-Based Model. In: Desai, N., Liu, A., Winikoff, M. (eds.) PRIMA 2010. LNCS(LNAI), vol. 7057, pp. 212–227. Springer, Heidelberg (2012)
18. Zeigler, B.P., Kim, T.G., Praehofer, H.: Theory of Modeling and Simulation: Integrating Discrete Event and Continuous Complex Dynamic Systems, vol. 1. Academic Press (2000)

Multi-agent Based Simulation of Traffic in Vietnam

The Duy Bui, Duc Hai Ngo, and Cong Tran

College of Technology
Vietnam National University, Hanoi
{duybt}@vnu.edu.vn

Abstract. There is always need for a good simulation for traffic in Vietnam in order to help transportation planners to improve the current traffic system. Over recent days, there has been severe traffic congestion in many streets of big cities in Vietnam such as Hanoi and HoChiMinh city. There is an urgent need for measures to deal with increasing congestions. The simulation of traffic in Vietnam is a hard problem due to two main reasons including: (1) the traffic participants in Vietnam do not give way according to the rule; (2) the participants do not consider that when waiting for the vehicles in front, stopping in the intersection is obstructing the traffic flow. In this paper, we propose a multi-agent based simulation system for traffic in Vietnam to help transportation planners to find treatments to the problem of congestion of the traffic system in Vietnam as well as to test new designs before committing resources to actually building the transportation infrastructure. By allowing a user to design different road systems as well as to create different simulation scenarios with different agent profiles, our system can simulate the dynamic of traffic in Vietnam in different situations.

Keywords: Traffic simulation, Multi-agent based simulation.

1 Introduction

For all countries, transportation is one major part of infrastructure, which has a direct impact on the economic and social development of the country. However, building a good transportation system is always a difficult problem for every country in the world. In developed countries, the development of transportation system always requires huge expenses. In addition, transportation planners always have to have a strategic vision, which can identify a clear plan to develop the transport system.

In Vietnam, transport infrastructure does not keep up with the social and economic development, thus obstructing the modernisation and industrialisation of the country. Currently in Vietnam, traffic is a sore issue for policy makers. In cities such as Hanoi, the transport system is chaotic, due to narrow road, increasing number of vehicles, and lack of consciousness to follow the traffic rules from participants. The result is an increase in congestion, accidents and

N. Desai, A. Liu, and M. Winikoff (Eds.): PRIMA 2010, LNAI 7057, pp. 636–648, 2012.

environmental pollution. So the search for solutions to develop transport systems in Vietnam is still a challenging question.

In many countries, the traffic simulation system on a computer has long been studied for finding and evaluating solutions to develop transport systems [1, 2, 4, 7, 8, 9, 10, 11]. Before blocking a road, opening a new route or timing the green light and red light in the real world, the developers can test the system in the simulation system. Either for the purpose of modeling short-term traffic dynamic on a single road section or for transportation planning describing behavioral pattern in a network on a larger time scale, existing simulation systems often assume that the behaviour of drivers involves accelerating, braking, and changing lanes. This results in a range of methods from mathematical models, macroscopic models to nanoscopic models [5].

The traffic in Vietnam, however, is difficult to model due to the more complicated behaviour of drivers. As the drivers do not follow the lanes, the traffic simulation becomes closer to the crowd simulation. Therefore, mathematical models or macroscopic models are difficult to obtain in this case. Instead, microscopic models are more suitable. In this paper, we propose a microscopic approach of using multi-agent based simulation for the traffic in Vietnam. The driving behaviour of an agent in our system is characterized by different parameters such as planning time, maximum speed, and acceleration rate. By allowing a user to design different road systems as well as to create different simulation scenarios with different agent profiles, our system can simulate the dynamic of traffic in Vietnam in different situations. The system can be used to find treatments to the problem of congestion of the traffic system in Vietnam as well as to test new designs before committing resources to actually build the transportation infrastructure.

The rest of the paper is organized as follows. We provide background on traffic simulation in Section 2. Section 3 describes the traffic in Vietnam and explains why the simulation of traffic in Vietnam is a difficult problem. In Section 4, we describe our simulation system for the traffic in Vietnam. Some experiments and results are presented in Section 5.

2 Traffic Simulation

Traffic simulation can be used to: find treatments for a problem of a traffic system; test new designs of transportation facilities before the commitment of resources to construction; analyze safety of a system; or train traffic management personnel [6].

A traffic simulation system takes a "scenario", e.g. a road system or a highway network configuration, and produces the simulation results in two formats: statistical and graphical. Quantitative descriptions of what is likely to happen can be provided by the statistical results while the graphical and animated results can provide the user with insights to understand why the system is behaving this way.

Time is a basic independent variable in almost all traffic simulation models. Continuous simulation models describe how the elements of a system change state continuously over time in response to continuous stimuli. Discrete simulation models represent real-world systems by asserting that their states change abruptly at points in time. There are generally two types of discrete models: discrete time (e.g. [9, 1]) and discrete event (e.g. [8]). With discrete time models, activities which change the states of the system elements are computed within each time interval. The discrete event models only perform the calculation based on the happening of events.

Simulation models of traffic can also be categorized by level of detail: macroscopic [4, 8], microscopic [1, 9, 10, 11], mesoscopic [2, 7], and nanoscopic [3]. A macroscopic model describes entities and their activities and interactions at a low level of detail. For example, the traffic stream may be represented in some aggregate manner such as a statistical histogram or by scalar values of flow rate, density and speed. A microscopic model describes both the system entities and their interactions at a high level of detail. A mesoscopic model generally represents most entities at a high level of detail but describes their activities and interactions at a much lower level of detail than would a microscopic model. With nanoscopic models, nanosimulation attempts to model drivers' steering behaviour and more detailed components of perception-reaction time in order to depict the the human performance.

As a powerful tool of microscopic simulation, multi-agent based simulation has been used for traffic domain, e.g. [10, 11]. Giving each vehicle three subsystems, including Controller, Sensors and Driver model, Sukthankar et al. [10] have simulated every detailed movement of vehicles. By calculating the movement of each agent based on finite state machine, Wan and Tang [11] have simulated a traffic flow which comprises of autonomous agents/vehicles. Both systems use 3D graphics to display the simulation.

3 The Traffic in Vietnam

There is always need for a good simulation for traffic in Vietnam in order to help transportation planners to improve the current traffic system. Nevertheless, the simulation of traffic in Vietnam is a hard problem. There are several reasons for this. The first reason, and we think the major one, is that in general, the traffic participants in Vietnam do not give way according to the rule. For example, the rule is that when entering the roundabout, a vehicle must give way to all vehicles coming from its left side (in Vietnam, they drive on the right). Another rule is that when a vehicle steers to the left or to the right, it must check and give way for all the vehicles coming straight. However, almost no one would follow this rule. This results in very dynamic behavior of each traffic participant. Dependent on each situation, the driver can make different decisions such as reduce speed, stop, increase speed, steer to the left, or steer to the right.

The second reason is that the participants do not consider that when waiting for the vehicles in front, stopping in the intersection is obstructing the traffic flow. Therefore, the traffic participants will always try to fill in any space in front of them, or even to the left or the right if there is obstruction in front. This also makes the behavior of each traffic participant more dynamic.

The third reason is that the behaviour of traffic participants varies very much from person to person. Depending on whether the participant is young, middle-aged, or old, and whether it is a male or a female, the reaction to a certain traffic situation will be very much different. For example, when there is another vehicle in front, an old person may slow down or even stop his/her vehicle while a male young person might steer his vehicle to the left or to the right for another itinerary.

For those reasons, the simulation of traffic in Vietnam becomes a problem with many different parameters. Therefore, finding a mathematic model for this problem is very difficult. In this case, agent based simulation seems to be a better solution.

4 Simulation of Traffic in Vietnam

In this section, we describe our agent based simulation system for the traffic in Vietnam. The system comprises of two main components:

- the road system and permitted travel directions in the road system,
- the agents representing the drivers of motorbikes and cars together with their vehicles in the road system.

Probably, the most important part of the system is how agents create and execute their plan to travel in the system. This will be discussed in details together with how different profiles of agents will affect how a plan is created.

4.1 The Road System

The road system is built up from multiple road areas.

Area

Roads systems are built from the arrangement of basic components, which are called Area. Each Area has entries and exits which are called Gates. Each Gate is simply described by two points. There is a road line between an entry and an exit. This road line may be a road segment (Road) or a sequence of road segments. Figure 1 describes the structure of an area. In each Area, a road segment contains information about pavements, and permitted travel directions, which an agent will use to calculate its plan.

Connecting areas together to build a road system

Multiple areas can be connected together to form a road system. Two areas can be connected together if there is one entry of an area which fits (in position and size) an exit of the other. Figure 2 shows the connection of such two areas. In this figure, the exit of Area1 is connected to the entry of Area2. Area1 has one entry and one exit, Area2 has one entry and two exits. Thus, there are total one entry, two exits and two road lines in this road system.

With the structure of road areas, we can create various kinds of road systems with arbitrary shape. Moreover, dividing a road system into areas also helps to increase the performance of the calculation for the plan of agents.

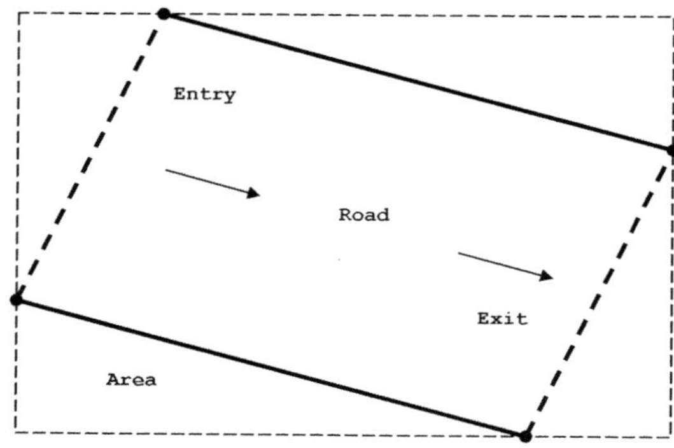

Fig. 1. Road Area

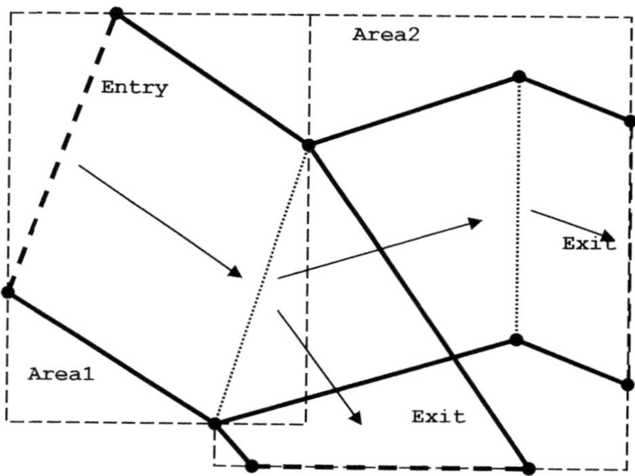

Fig. 2. Connection road areas

4.2 Agents Representing Traffic Participants

In a simulation system using an agent-based model, one of the important components needing to identify is agents. In our system, the traffic vehicles contain car and motorbikes, so each agent represents a car driver or a motorbike driver.

An agent's behaviour
Each agent representing a traffic participant needs to perform some actions to control his/her vehicle's movement. The actions of the agent must be both proactive and reactive, which means the actions will bring the agent to the target while trying to avoid obstructions (e.g. other agents and pavements). In our simulation system, we consider two types of actions:

- speed adjustment (including accelerating and braking),
- steering, which involves not only changing lanes but moving to any adjacent available space .

Agent profile
Each agent makes a decision for a certain move upon the current situation. However, different agents may make different decisions in a similar situation. In our simulation system, the behaviour of agent is affected by several attributes, which are:

- Maximum speed,
- Safe speed,
- Acceleration rate,
- Plan time,
- Maximum steering angle.

These attributes are used to calculate the plan for agents upon a certain traffic situation, which will be described later.

We group agents into several groups which we assume that the attributes of agents in the same group are similar. The groups are formed based on age and render. For each group, a group profile contains the values of attributes for that group.

4.3 Agent's Planning

In this section, we will describe an agent's planning algorithm to find travelling route in a certain traffic situation. We also describe how an agent's attributes affect the way the agent moves from a position to the target in a road system.

The control cycle for agents in our system is as follows:

```
while the agent has not reached the target
    calculating a plan for a given amount of time ahead
    while the plan is still feasible and the plan is not over
        perform the next action in the plan.
```

The calculation of a plan for an agent contains three steps:

(1) Determining optimal route,
(2) Detecting possible collisions on optimal route,
(3) If there are collisions, determining alternative route to avoid collisions.

Determining the optimal route
Optimal route is the route that the agent should follow to reach the target in as fast as possible providing that there is not any obstruction on the route. In our simulation system, a route is sampled by a sequence of points. From a certain position, the optimal route of the agent to reach its target is determined by a greedy algorithm as follows.

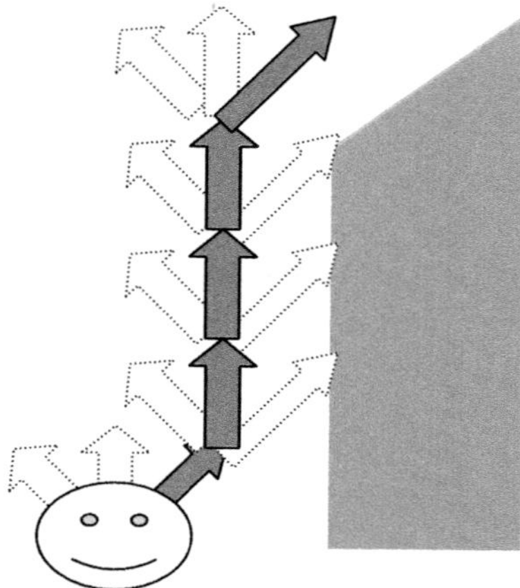

Fig. 3. Determining optimal route

Denoting Δl the distance between two sampling continuous points, v the current speed of an agent. The duration that the agent move from one sampling point to the next sampling point is:

$$\Delta t = \Delta l \div v$$

Because an agent can only plan for a certain amount of time ahead, the number of sampling points on the planned ideal route is:

$$\begin{aligned} n &= \text{plan\_time} \div \Delta t \\ &= \text{plan\_time} * \Delta l \div v \end{aligned}$$

From the starting point, supposing that the agent has three choices: go ahead, steer to the left and steer to the right, which results in three points to select for the optimal route (see Figure 3). The point to be selected is the one that is nearest to the target.

Detecting possible collisions on the optimal route
After determining the optimal route, the agent needs to check whether there might be collisions when following the optimal route. Supposing that the agent can observe and get information about position, moving direction and current speed of all other agents within a certain range, this information can be used to calculate if there might be collisions on the optimal route. Figure 4 illustrates this collision detecting process. In this figure, an agent A can find that at the first and the second position on optimal route, there will not be any collision happening. However, at the fourth position, agent A will be too close to agent B and it is considered that a collision will happen at this position. In this situation, agent A has two choices: to reduce speed or to steer to avoid collision. If agent A's

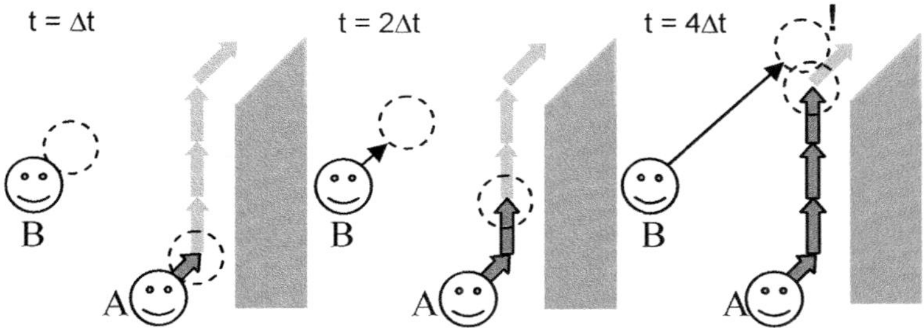

Fig. 4. Detecting possible collisions

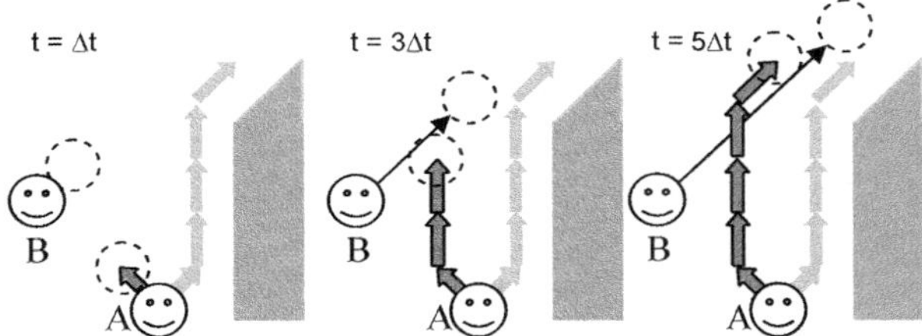

Fig. 5. Determining alternative route to avoid collisions

current speed is higher than its safe speed limit, it will reduce speed. Otherwise, it will decide to steer.

Determining alternative route to avoid collisions
When there might be collisions in the planned route, an alternative route is calculated so that the alternative route is in parallel with the optimal route. Figure 5 illustrates an example of determining an alternative route. In this figure, if agent A uses the optimal route, it might collide with agent B at the fifth sampling point. Alternatively, a route to avoid the collision while being close to the optimal as much as possible is the one that the agent steers left on the first sampling point.

5 Experiments and Result

We have built our own agent based simulation system from the design mentioned above (see Figure 6). The system runs in two modes: design mode and simulation mode. In design mode, the user may design various road systems from some road templates as well as setup experiments by varying attributes of different agent profiles and number of agents for each agent profile. In the simulation mode, the system provides both visual and statistical information for a simulation scenario.

We have performed two experiments to illustrate our simulation system. In the first experiment, the road system is set up similarly with a real roundabout

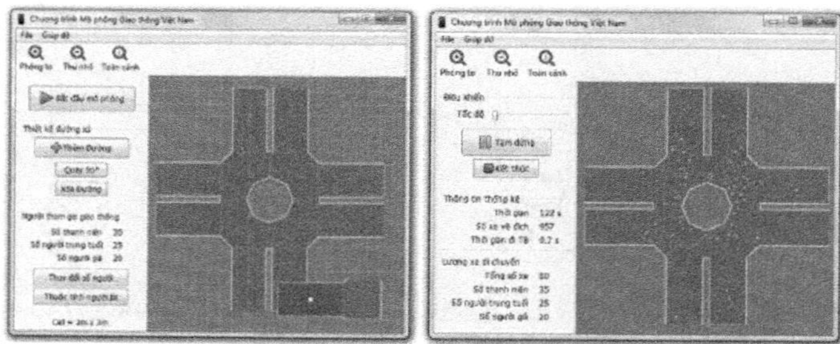

Fig. 6. A look at our simulation system

Table 1. A sample of the value of different attributes of different group profiles

	Young	Middle-aged	Old
Male			
Maximum speed	50 km/h	45 km/h	40 km/h
Safe speed	35 km/h	31 km/h	25 km/h
Acceleration	18 km/h/s	16km/h/s	13 km/h/s
Plan time	650 ms	800 ms	800 ms
Female			
Maximum speed	45 km/h	43 km/h	37 km/h
Safe speed	32 km/h	28 km/h	22 km/h
Acceleration	15 km/h/s	13 km/h/s	10 km/h/s
Plan time	650 ms	800 ms	800 ms

in Hanoi (the roundabout among Tran Duy Hung and, Pham Hung, Khuat Duy Tien, and Lang-Hoa Lac road), which can be seen in Figure 7. We have six different agent profiles (Young male, Young female, Middle-aged male, Middle-aged female, Old male, Old female) in this experiment with the value of attributes for each profile described in Table 1. With the number of motorbikes of 180 and number of cars of 30 equally divided to six profiles, the simulation shows that all vehicles can go through the roundabout quick and conveniently (see Figure 8). The average time to pass the roundabout is about 19 seconds, which is quite similar to what we observed from real situation. If we modify so that there are more young people than old people, the average time to pass the roundabout is shorter, which is reasonable. When we increase the number of motorbikes to 300 and the number of cars to 120, congestion happens after some time, which is shown in Figure 9. This is what happens everyday in Vietnam. Without policemen, the congestion might last for several hours.

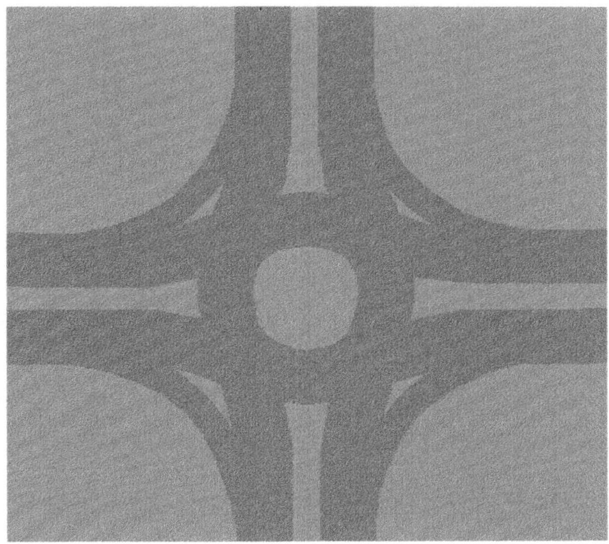

Fig. 7. A road system setup for experiment

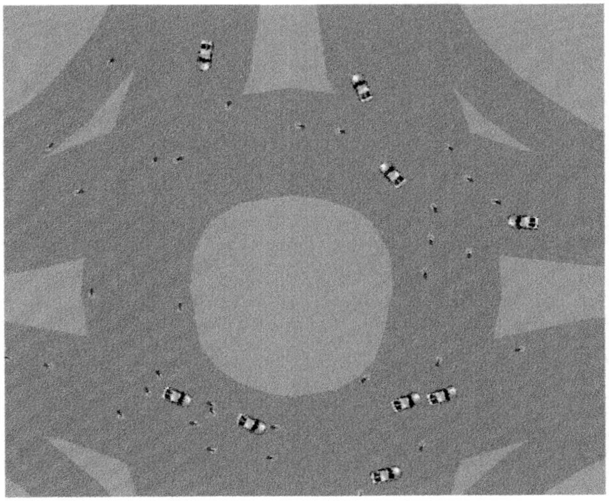

Fig. 8. A situation where vehicles can go through the roundabout quick and conveniently

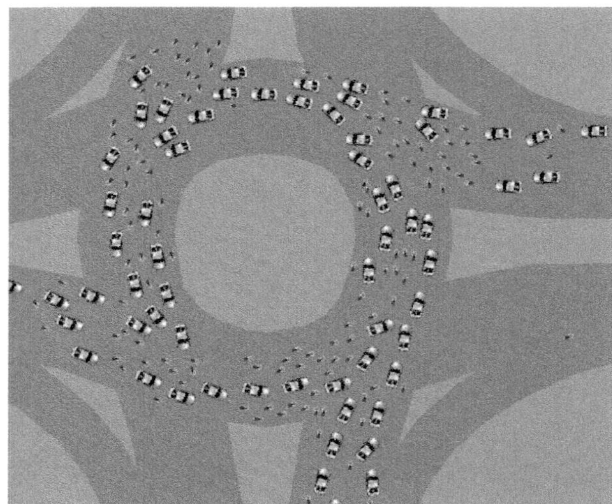

Fig. 9. A situation where traffic congestion happens

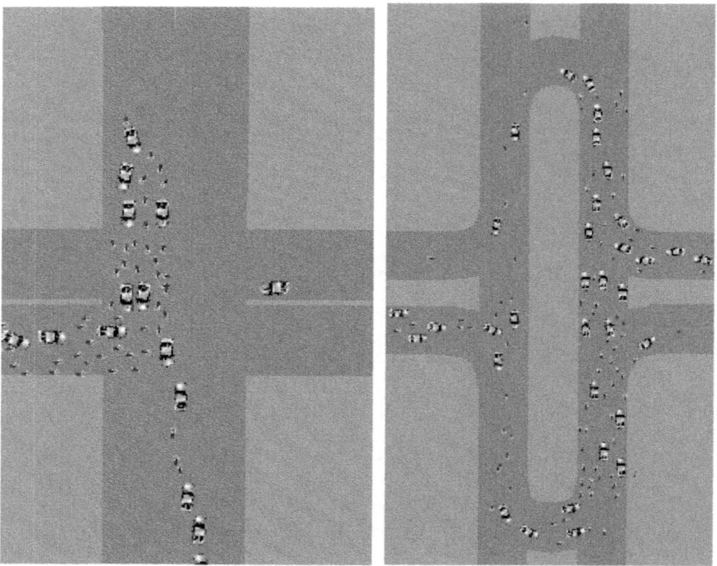

Fig. 10. With the same intersection, experiments show that the solutions of blocking one direction to make detour (the right figure) is effective in solving traffic congestion in Vietnam

We have also performed an experiment to check how effective the solution of blocking one direction to make detour for intersection in Vietnam is. Figure 10 shows the original intersection on the left, and the modified one on the right. With the original one, congestion might happen already when the number of motorbikes is 60 and the number of cars is 30. With the modified one, with 120 motorbikes and 60 cars, vehicles can still go through the intersection although a little bit slow. This shows that blocking one direction in intersection, which they have done recently in Vietnam, is an effective solution.

6 Conclusion

A traffic simulation system can help transportation planners to find treatments to many traffic problems such as congestions as well as to save money to test new designs before actually build the transportation infrastructure. The multi-agent based simulation system we proposed in this paper is dedicated to the chaotic traffic in Vietnam which has many different characteristics to the traffic in other countries. Our system can simulate the dynamic of traffic in Vietnam in different situations. With our system, the user can carry out different experiments with different self-designed road systems as well as with different numbers of agents of different profiles. Nevertheless, like other simulation systems, the simulation cannot capture all the dynamic characteristics of the real traffic system, especially the traffic system in Vietnam. In the future, we intend to perform intensive real data collection in order to verify and validate our simulation model.

References

1. Barcelo, J., Ferrer, J.L.: A simulation study for an area of dublin using the aimsun2 traffic simulator. Technical report, Department of Statistics and Operation Research, Universitat Politecnica de Catalunya, Spain (1995)
2. de Palma, A., Marchal, F., Nesterov, Y.: Metropolis: A modular system for dynamic traffic simulation (1996), `http://www.ceic.com/metro/`
3. Gettman, D., Head, L.: Surrogate safety measures from traffic simulation models. In: The 82nd TRB Annual Meeting, TRB, National Research Council, Washington (2003)
4. Haj-Salem, H., Elloumi, N., Mammar, S., Chrisoulakis, M.P.J., Middelham, F.: Metacor: A macroscopic modelling tool for urban corridor. In: Proceedings of the First World Congress on Applications of Transport Telematics and Intelligent Transportation Systems (1994)
5. Kesting, A., Treiber, M., Helbing, D.: Agents for traffic simulation. In: Uhrmacher, A., Weyns, D. (eds.) Multi-Agent Systems: Simulation and Applications. CRC (2009)
6. Lieberman, E., Rathi, A.K.: Traffic simulation. In: Gartner, H., Messer, C.J., Rathi, A.K. (eds.) Revised Monograph on Traffic Flow Theory: A State-of-the-Art Report. Turner-Fairbank Highway Research Center, Federal Highway Administration, U.S. Dept. of Transportation (2005)

7. Mahmassani, H.S., Peeta, S.: Network performace under system optimal and user equilibrium dynamic assignments: Implications for advances traffic information systems. Transportation Research Record 1408, 93 (1995)
8. Payne, H.J.: Freflo: A macroscopic simulation model of freeway traffic: Version 1 - user's guide. Technical report, ESSOR Report (1978)
9. Sibley, S.W.: Netsim for microcomputers - simulates microscopic traffic flow on urban streets. Public Roads 49 (1985)
10. Sukthankar, R., Pomerleau, D., Thorpe, C.: Shiva: Simulated highways for intelligent vehicle algorithms. In: Proceedings of Intelligent Vehicles 1995 (1995)
11. Wan, T., Tang, W.: An intelligent vehicle model for 3d visual traffic simulation. In: International Conference on Visual Information Engineering, VIE 2003 (2003)

Author Index

GPSR Compliance

The European Union's (EU) General Product Safety Regulation (GPSR) is a set of rules that requires consumer products to be safe and our obligations to ensure this.

If you have any concerns about our products, you can contact us on ProductSafety@springernature.com

In case Publisher is established outside the EU, the EU authorized representative is:

Springer Nature Customer Service Center GmbH
Europaplatz 3
69115 Heidelberg, Germany

Batch number: 09490866

Printed by Printforce, the Netherlands